Financing Residential Real Estate

20th Edition

Megan Dorsey
David Rockwell

Rockwell Publishing Company

Table of Contents

Chapter 1
Finance and Investment

Borrowing Money to Buy a Home

Investments and Returns

Types of Investments
- Ownership investments
- Debt investments
- Securities

Investment Risk
- Safety, liquidity, and yield
- Diversification
- Lending risks
  - Risk of default
  - Risk of loss
  - Interest rate risk
  - Prepayment risk
- Misjudging risk

Market Interest Rates

Introduction

Financing—lending and borrowing money—is fundamental to the real estate business. If mortgage financing weren't available, buyers would have to pay cash for their homes, something most people can't afford to do.

This book has a practical focus; it explains the basic process of obtaining a loan to purchase a home and discusses the financing options available to home buyers. The opening chapters present background information about the U.S. financial system and mortgage industry, including how government fiscal and monetary policy affects mortgage lending, the relationship between the primary and secondary mortgage markets, the different types of mortgage lenders, and the various sources of loan funds. All of these factors directly or indirectly affect whether home buyers can get the financing they need and, if so, on what terms.

From an economic perspective, mortgage loans are a type of investment, one of many types that compete for a share of the available investment funds. This chapter provides an overview of investing and explains some of the underlying investment considerations that determine what kinds of loans mortgage lenders are (and are not) willing to make.

Borrowing Money to Buy a Home

In the United States, owning a home has long been considered an essential part of a middle-class lifestyle. It's seen as a mark of achievement, and also as part of the groundwork for future prosperity and security. It is debatable exactly how beneficial home ownership actually is—especially after the 2007–2008 financial crisis, when home values fell significantly in many parts of the country (see Chapter 4). Nonetheless, most Americans will buy a home if they can afford to do so.

Whether an individual or a family can afford a home depends on many factors, including housing prices, income level, tax considerations, and so on. Among the most important factors is the availability of mortgage financing. A home is the most expensive purchase most people ever make, and they usually need to borrow a large amount of money to do it.

In a typical mortgage loan transaction, the lender loans the home buyer a large portion of the purchase price and requires him to provide

Factors that affect whether someone can afford to buy a home:
- Housing prices
- Income
- Tax considerations
- Availability of financing

the rest out of his own resources, as a downpayment. In return for the loan, the buyer must execute a mortgage or a deed of trust in the lender's favor. This creates a **lien**, giving the lender a security interest in the property being purchased, so that the property serves as **collateral** for the loan.

Typical mortgage financing:
- Loan covers much of price
- Downpayment is from buyer's own resources
- Purchased property serves as collateral

The buyer agrees to pay back the **principal** (the amount borrowed) by means of monthly payments over a specified period (the repayment period or **loan term**). In addition, as long as part of the debt is outstanding, the buyer must pay the lender a specified percentage of the remaining principal balance as **interest**. From the buyer's point of view, the interest is the cost of borrowing money; it's the amount the lender charges him for the temporary use of the principal.

Principal: the original amount borrowed, or the part of the loan that remains to be repaid

Interest: the cost of borrowing money

When the full amount borrowed and all of the interest owed have been repaid, the lender releases the property from the lien. This might not happen until the end of the loan term, when all of the scheduled monthly payments have been made. Or the loan could be paid off earlier—for example, out of the sale proceeds if the home is sold.

On the other hand, if the loan isn't repaid as agreed, the lien created by the mortgage or deed of trust gives the lender the right to foreclose. In a **foreclosure**, property is sold against the owner's will, so that a debt can be repaid from the proceeds of the forced sale.

Foreclosure: forced sale of property to pay off a debt secured by a lien

Home buyers need loans, and lenders generally want to make loans—after all, that's the business they're in. But from a lender's point of view, a loan is an investment. The interest paid by the borrower will be the lender's primary **return** (profit) on its investment. When evaluating a prospective borrower's loan application, a lender considers whether the proposed loan is likely to be a profitable investment under current (and foreseeable) economic conditions. If not, the lender won't make the loan.

Loan is an investment; lender is an investor

Interest is lender's return on the loan/investment

Because loans are investments, the availability of affordable mortgage financing fluctuates with general economic conditions. To understand mortgage lending, it's necessary to look at it in the broader context of investing and the economy as a whole.

Investments and Returns

The national economy—the system of businesses, industries, and trade that provides us with jobs, income, places to live, and goods and services—is driven in part by **investment capital**. Investment capital

Investment capital: accumulated wealth (savings) made available to fund enterprises

is simply money (accumulated wealth, or savings) that's used to fund business enterprises and other ventures, projects, and transactions.

An investor supplies capital for an enterprise or a project in the expectation (or the hope) that it will generate additional wealth for the investor—a return on the investment. Depending on the type of investment, the investor's return may take various forms, including interest, appreciation, rents, or dividends.

Return of investment: recapture of amount originally invested

Return on investment: investor's profit

A return *on* an investment is distinguished from a return *of* the investment. A return of the investment, also called **recapture**, refers to getting back the full amount originally invested. A return on the investment, by contrast, is a profit over and above the amount originally invested.

Sometimes an investor only breaks even, receiving a return of the investment without a return on the investment. And sometimes an investor may lose part or even all of the money originally invested. In other words, if an investment turns out badly, the investor might not even receive a return of the investment, much less a return on the investment.

Types of Investments

There are two general categories of investments: ownership investments and debt investments.

Ownership Investments

Ownership investment: investor purchases an asset or a property interest in an asset

When an investor uses her investment funds to purchase an asset or an interest in an asset, it's an ownership investment. If the asset is income-producing, the net income it generates during the investor's period of ownership is a return on the investment.

Return on ownership investment may be:
 • Net income, and/or
 • Appreciation

The investor will also get a return in the form of **appreciation** if the asset increases in value (appreciates) over time. An asset may appreciate because of **inflation** (a general increase in prices due to economic forces), or because the demand for that type of asset increases, or as a result of both inflation and increased demand. A return that takes the form of appreciation ordinarily isn't **realized**—actually received by the investor—until the asset is sold.

Real Estate Investment. The purchase of real estate is an example of an ownership investment. If the real estate is an income-producing property such as an apartment building, the net income from the property (rents paid by the tenants, minus the operating expenses) provides a return for the investor/owner.

Whether or not the property is income-producing, the investor may receive a higher price than she paid for it when the property is sold. The appreciation—the difference between the price paid (the amount invested) and the price received—is a return on the investment. On the other hand, if the property has lost value (depreciated) since it was purchased, when it's sold the investor won't even receive a return of the full amount originally invested.

Corporate Stock. The purchase of shares of corporate stock is another example of an ownership investment. The shares represent an ownership interest in the corporation. The corporation uses the funds invested by the stockholders to help its business grow and generate profits. If the corporation pays **dividends** (a share of its profits) to the stockholders, the dividends are one type of return they receive on their investment. They can also receive a return in the form of appreciation: if the corporation is successful, the value of the corporation's stock goes up, and stockholders can sell their shares at a profit.

Ownership investment examples:
- Real estate purchases
- Stock purchases

Debt Investments

With a debt investment, the investor lends money to an individual or a company. In exchange for the temporary use of the funds, the investor/lender charges the borrower **interest**, a specified percentage of the amount owed, until the debt is repaid. The investor acquires no ownership interest in whatever the borrower is using the money for. The investor is involved only as a creditor, and the investor's main return is the interest the borrower pays.

Debt investment: investor provides money to an entity that will eventually repay it

Loans. Any form of loan that will earn interest for the lender is a debt investment, including the residential mortgage loans that we're concerned with in this book. When a bank loans a couple money so that they can buy a home, the loan represents a debt investment for the bank. The borrowers agree to repay the bank's invested capital in monthly installments over a period of years, and also to pay interest on the capital.

Note that at the same time the bank is making a debt investment, the home buyers are making an ownership investment. They're investing their own savings (the downpayment) plus the money they're borrowing, in order to purchase an asset (the home). Their primary reason for buying the home may be to have a place to live, but if the home appreciates while they own it, they'll get a return on their investment when they sell it.

Bonds. Another example of a debt investment is the purchase of bonds. A **bond** is a certificate of indebtedness issued by a governmental body or business entity. An investor who buys bonds (a bondholder) is essentially loaning the price paid for the bonds to the entity that issued them.

With most bonds, the issuer makes periodic payments of interest to the bondholder. The rate at which interest accrues on the bond is called the coupon rate. On the bond's maturity date, the issuer pays the bondholder a lump sum called the face amount (or face value) of the bond, which is usually the same as the original purchase price.

> **Example:** If you purchased a ten-year bond for $50,000 with a coupon rate of 5%, you'd receive interest payments amounting to $2,500 each year (5% of $50,000) for ten years. At the end of that period, on the maturity date, the issuer would pay you the face amount, $50,000.

Debt investment examples:
- Loans
- Bonds
- Savings accounts

Savings Accounts. An ordinary savings account is also a debt investment. A depositor puts his money into a savings account for safekeeping and so that it will earn interest. The financial institution uses its depositors' funds to make loans to home buyers and other borrowers. In effect, the depositors are loaning their money to the financial institution (and receiving interest as a return on their investment) to enable the financial institution to make debt investments of its own (loans to customers). To make a profit, the financial institution must charge a higher interest rate on the loans it makes than the rate it pays on its savings accounts.

A debt investment similar to a savings account is the **certificate of deposit**, or CD. With a CD, in return for interest payments the investor/depositor agrees to keep funds on deposit (and available for use by the financial institution) during a specified period, such as 6, 12, or 24 months. If the depositor withdraws the funds before the end of the commitment period, the financial institution charges a penalty. As a general rule, CDs with longer commitment periods have higher interest rates than shorter-term CDs.

Fig. 1.1 Types of investments

Ownership Investments
- Investment capital used to purchase an asset or a property interest in an asset or company
- Stocks, real estate, mutual funds
- Possible returns: appreciation, rental income, and/or dividends

Debt Investments
- Investment capital provided temporarily, subject to withdrawal or eventual repayment
- Loans, bonds, savings accounts, CDs
- Returns take the form of interest

Securities
- Investment instruments
- Ownership interest or right to repayment, without direct managerial control
- Traded in established financial markets
- Stocks and bonds

Securities

Certain types of investments are categorized as **securities**. A security is an investment instrument (such as a share certificate) that grants the holder an interest or a right to payment, without giving the holder direct managerial control over the enterprise in question. Securities may be either ownership investments or debt investments; stocks and bonds are the most prominent examples.

A key characteristic of securities is that they can be bought or sold easily in financial markets established for that purpose. Stocks may be traded on a stock exchange, bonds may be traded in the bond market, and so on. Thus, securities are **liquid assets**—assets that can quickly be converted into cash.

Mutual Funds. A simple way for individuals to invest in securities is through a **mutual fund**. A mutual fund is a company that buys and sells stocks and bonds on behalf of its investors. An investor purchases shares in the company, which then uses the investor/owner's capital to invest in securities. The fund managers, who are investment

Securities are investment instruments that:
- Give the holder an interest or right to payment
- Do not give the holder direct managerial control

Securities are liquid assets that can be sold easily in established financial markets

professionals, choose which securities to buy and when to sell them. This makes it much simpler for an individual with limited knowledge of the financial markets to invest in a variety of securities and benefit from diversification (discussed later in this chapter).

Securities Regulation. To protect investors, both the issuance and the trading of securities are regulated by the federal Securities and Exchange Commission (SEC). The SEC requires companies to disclose certain financial information to the public, in order to help prospective investors judge which securities are likely to be good investments. The SEC also enforces the rules against insider trading. It's illegal for "insiders" such as company executives and stockbrokers to reap profits or avoid losses in the securities markets by taking advantage of information that isn't yet available to the public.

Securities and the Mortgage Industry. Securities trading affects mortgage lending in two main ways. First, it has an impact on mortgage interest rates and the availability of funds for home loans, since mortgage lending competes with other types of investments. Second, mortgages themselves can be pooled together and "securitized" for sale to investors. These mortgage-backed securities have played a crucial role in the mortgage industry. We'll look at mortgage-backed securities in Chapter 3, when we discuss the secondary market.

SEC regulates securities trading to protect investors
• Financial disclosures required
• No insider trading

Investment Risk

The pool of funds available for investment is large but not unlimited, and all of the different investment opportunities in the economy are in competition for those funds. When deciding where to put their money, investors have to weigh the benefits of particular investments against the risks they entail.

Investment opportunities compete for available investment funds

Key Investment Characteristics

Investors consider any investment opportunity in terms of three potential advantages: safety, liquidity, and yield.

Safety. An investment is considered safe if there's little risk that the investor will actually lose money on it. Even if the investment doesn't generate the profit hoped for, the investor will at least be able to recover the money originally invested. In other words, the investor

Safety: low risk of losing amount originally invested

can probably count on a return *of* the investment, if not a return *on* the investment.

Liquidity. An investment is liquid if it can be converted into cash (liquidated) quickly. Liquidity is important in case the investor suddenly needs cash for unexpected expenses, or perhaps for better investment opportunities. With an investment that's **illiquid** (not liquid), the investor's funds are effectively "locked up" and unavailable for other purposes.

> **Example:** Two investors each have $20,000 to invest. Investor A uses his $20,000 to buy stock, a liquid asset. Investor B uses her $20,000 to buy real estate, an illiquid asset.
>
> Six months later, both investors decide they want to use the funds they've invested for some other purpose. Investor A can sell his stock—cash in his investment—without delay. It will be much more complicated and time-consuming for Investor B to sell her real estate. Depending on B's situation, the delay may merely be an inconvenience, or it could result in financial difficulties or a missed opportunity.

While real estate and other illiquid assets can be excellent investments, their lack of liquidity has consequences that prospective investors should take into account.

Yield. An investment's yield is its rate of return. Investments that are both safe and liquid typically offer the lowest yields.

Yield: investor's rate of return

> **Example:** Patterson deposits $5,000 in an ordinary savings account. This investment is very safe, because the deposited funds are federally insured against loss. It's also very liquid, because the funds can be withdrawn at any time without penalty. However, the investment's yield (the annual interest rate that the bank pays to Patterson) is only 0.02%.

In a sense, investors "pay" for safety and liquidity with low yields. For a high yield, an investor must be willing to take the risk of losing some (or possibly even all) of the original capital if the investment turns out badly. It may also be necessary to sacrifice liquidity, allowing the capital to be tied up for a while.

Safe, liquid investments offer comparatively low yields

As a general rule, the greater the risk, the higher the potential yield needs to be; otherwise, investors won't be willing to make the investment. The higher yield compensates the investors for the additional risk. Investors generally also expect higher yields for long-term investments, those that will take longer to achieve the desired yield.

Investors expect higher yields for greater risks

Yield isn't necessarily fixed
when an investment is made

Of course, the yield from a particular investment isn't necessarily fixed at the time the investment is made. The yield may change with market conditions, such as a rise or fall in interest rates. In the case of ownership investments, the enterprise or property invested in may turn out to be either more or less successful or valuable than anticipated, making the actual yield higher or lower than the projected yield. In the case of debt investments, a bond default or loan default may result in a sharply reduced yield.

Diversification

Portfolio: investor's mix of
investments plus cash reserves

Diversification: putting money
into a variety of different
investments to reduce the risk
of loss

An investor's mix of investments, plus any cash reserves, is referred to as a **portfolio**. To reduce risk, investors are advised to **diversify** their portfolios, putting their money into a variety of different types of investments. A diversified investment portfolio is more likely to match the growth of the economy overall, instead of being subject to fluctuations in one particular sector of the economy. Thus, an investor with a diversified portfolio is less likely to face a serious net loss; if one investment does poorly, there's a fair chance that the other investments will offset that loss with good returns.

Lending Risks

The particular risks involved in mortgage lending, from the lender/investor's point of view, include the risk of default, the risk of foreclosure loss, interest rate risk, and prepayment risk.

Risk of Default. The degree of risk associated with a particular loan depends largely on how likely it is that the borrower will default. A **default** occurs when the borrower fails to make the payments as scheduled.

When deciding whether to approve a loan application, a lender evaluates the risk of default. Through the underwriting process (see Chapter 8), the loan applicants are screened to determine whether they are likely to pay off the proposed loan on schedule. If a prospective borrower looks like a good risk—that is, if the risk of default is low—the lender will probably agree to make the loan. If the risk of default is somewhat higher, the lender might make the loan but charge a higher interest rate to compensate for the extra risk. If the risk of default is too great, the lender will decline to make the loan.

Risk of Loss. In addition to screening prospective borrowers to evaluate the risk of default, lenders take steps to limit the risk of loss in the event that a borrower eventually does default. These steps include appraising the property to make sure that it's worth enough to serve as collateral for the loan in case foreclosure becomes necessary. In some cases, the lender will also require mortgage insurance on the loan. (Appraisal is covered in Chapter 9; mortgage insurance in Chapter 10.)

Borrowers are also required to keep the collateral property adequately insured against fire and other natural hazards, in order to protect lenders from losses that might otherwise result from the impairment of the collateral.

Lenders face:
- Risk of default (borrower)
- Risk of loss (collateral)
- Interest rate risk
- Prepayment risk

Interest Rate Risk. Another type of risk that a lender may face in connection with a loan is interest rate risk. This is the risk that after the lender has loaned money to a borrower at a certain interest rate, market interest rates will rise.

> **Example:** A lender makes a $400,000 mortgage loan to a home buyer. Based on market interest rates, the lender agrees to make the loan at a fixed interest rate of 4%. That interest rate represents the lender's return on its $400,000 investment.
>
> Shortly after the loan closes, market interest rates begin a steep climb. A year later, they've reached 6.25%. The lender would prefer to reinvest its $400,000 now, to get a 6.25% return instead of a 4% return. But the loan agreement allows the borrower to repay the lender over a 30-year term. The lender's money is tied up and can't be reinvested until it's repaid.

Interest rate risk increases with the length of the loan term. The longer the loan term, the longer the lender's funds could be tied up. This makes interest rate risk a particular concern for mortgage lenders, because home purchase mortgages have very long repayment periods compared to other types of loans. (In the U.S., 30-year repayment periods are common for mortgages. See Chapter 6.)

Mortgage lenders have devised a number of ways of dealing with interest rate risk, including adjustable-rate mortgages (see Chapter 6) and selling loans on the secondary market (see Chapter 3).

Prepayment Risk. It isn't only rising interest rates that can cause trouble for a mortgage lender. When market interest rates fall, a lender often has to worry about borrowers **prepaying** their loans—paying back all or part of the principal balance sooner than expected. This might not sound like a problem for the lender, but it can be one.

Prepayment: paying back all or part of the principal before it's due

Example: The Henrys financed the purchase of their home when market interest rates were relatively high. They got a 30-year mortgage from Acme Savings at 7% interest.

Now it's four years later, and the outstanding balance on the mortgage is $192,400. Market interest rates have dropped to 4.5% since the Henrys bought their house, so they decide to refinance. They borrow $193,000 from Widget Bank at 4.5% interest and use the new loan to pay off their old 7% loan.

When the Henrys prepay the old mortgage, Acme Savings has to reinvest the $192,400 they've paid back. It's unlikely that loaning that money to other borrowers will provide Acme with a 7% return, like the Henrys' mortgage did. When the mortgage was prepaid, that effectively reduced Acme's yield on the investment.

As in the example, a significant decline in interest rates typically leads to a great deal of refinancing and loan prepayment.

Because prepayment can work to a lender's disadvantage, some loan agreements allow the lender to charge the borrower a penalty if the loan is prepaid. The penalty helps the lender recoup some of the interest lost when the loan is paid off early (and may even discourage prepayment altogether). Prepayment penalties are discussed in more detail in Chapter 5.

Misjudging Risk

Unfortunately, whatever steps an investor takes to evaluate how risky an investment is, she may turn out to be wrong—perhaps very wrong. Various factors contribute to poor investment decisions.

Naturally, poor decisions often involve a failure to correctly predict future events.

Example: Home prices have been going up rapidly and steadily for many years. Jan Dillon wants to buy a rental house, and Acme Savings agrees to loan her the money she needs for the purchase. Both the buyer and the lender are making investment decisions, and both are basing their decisions partly on the assumption that home prices will continue to rise for a long time to come. They're also both assuming that Dillon, who has been earning a good salary at her job for a long time, will continue to have that steady income.

If those predictions turned out to be correct, both investments might be very profitable. Instead, not long after the lender makes the loan and Dillon buys the rental house, economic forces cause home prices to start dropping suddenly, and a general economic downturn ensues. Dillon loses her job. She defaults on the loan, and Acme forecloses. The property doesn't sell for nearly enough to cover the amount Dillon owes Acme. Dillon loses all the money she invested in the house, and Acme takes a substantial loss on the loan.

Predicting future events is never easy, but it can be made much more difficult by inaccurate information. Sometimes a person who stands to benefit will deliberately provide an investor with false or misleading information. For example, a loan applicant might lie to the lender about his financial situation, or a lender might conceal unfair loan terms or charges from a prospective home buyer. Of course, investment decisions based on false information often turn out badly for the investor.

On the other hand, in many cases an investor has no one to blame for a loss but herself. Poor investment decisions were certainly among the factors that led to the subprime mortgage crisis, which we'll discuss in Chapter 4. Incorrect predictions, inaccurate information, deception, and recklessness all played a role, along with bad luck.

Market Interest Rates

We've referred more than once to "market interest rates," a concept that will come up repeatedly throughout the book. Market interest rates are the typical rates that lenders are currently charging borrowers for particular types of loans. The going rate for a residential mortgage may depend on the size of the loan, whether it has a fixed or adjustable interest rate, how long the loan term is, and certain other factors. A prospective borrower's credit score also affects the rate lenders are willing to offer. A borrower with a mediocre credit score can generally expect to pay a considerably higher interest rate than one with a good score. (Credit scoring is covered in Chapter 8.)

Market interest rate: typical rate charged for a certain type of loan in the current market

To attract business, some lenders offer borrowers an interest rate below the going market rate. But in most cases lenders with dramatically lower rates make up for it by charging higher loan fees (see Chapter 7). On the other hand, lenders won't charge much more than the market rate, to avoid losing customers to competing lenders.

At one time, market interest rates for mortgages varied significantly from one area of the country to another. That's no longer true; now the regional variations tend to be relatively slight. This is largely a result of the growth of the secondary market (see Chapter 3).

Mortgage rates affect real estate activity:
- High rates cause a slowdown
- Low rates spur the market

Mortgage "prices" (interest rates) respond to changes in supply and demand

Of course, market interest rates for mortgage loans have a considerable impact on real estate activity. If mortgage rates rise extremely high, as they did in the 1980s, that can bring real estate activity to a standstill. On the other hand, low rates can stimulate home sales (and also spur lots of refinancing).

The forces that cause market interest rates to rise and fall are very complex. But basically, like other kinds of prices, market interest rates for mortgage loans are affected by supply and demand: if supply exceeds demand, prices (rates) go down; if demand exceeds supply, prices (rates) go up. We'll discuss some of the factors that affect the supply of and demand for mortgage funds in Chapters 2 and 3.

Outline: Finance and Investment

I. Borrowing Money to Buy a Home
   A. Average buyer's ability to afford a home depends in part on the availability of mortgage financing.
   B. From lender's point of view, a loan is an investment.
      1. Interest is lender's primary return on the investment.
      2. Lender will make a loan only if it appears to be a profitable investment under prevailing economic conditions.

II. Investments and Returns
   A. Investment capital: accumulated wealth (savings) made available to fund enterprises, projects, and transactions.
   B. Investor supplies capital in the expectation that it will generate additional wealth for the investor.
   C. Returns
      1. Return *on* investment: a profit over and above the amount originally invested.
      2. Return *of* investment: recapturing the amount originally invested (breaking even).

III. Types of Investments
   A. Ownership investments: investor buys a property interest in an asset.
      1. Ownership investments may generate net income, pay dividends, and/or appreciate.
      2. Examples: purchase of real estate, purchase of corporate stock.
   B. Debt investments: investor provides money that is to be paid back.
      1. Debt investments generate interest income.
      2. Examples: loans, bonds, savings accounts, certificates of deposit.
   C. Securities: may be either ownership investments or debt investments.
      1. Examples: stocks, bonds, mortgage-backed securities.
      2. Designed to be liquid investments, easily bought and sold in established markets.
      3. Mutual funds: investor purchases shares in a mutual fund company; fund managers use the capital to buy and sell securities.
      4. Federal Securities and Exchange Commission (SEC) regulates issuance and trading of securities to protect investors.

IV. Investment Risk
   A. Key investment characteristics
      1. Safety: low risk of losing part or all of original investment amount.
      2. Liquidity
         a. Liquid asset can be converted into cash (sold) quickly.
         b. Liquidity tends to increase safety (reduce risk of loss).
      3. Yield: rate of return.
         a. Investor usually pays for safety and liquidity with lower yield.
         b. Generally, the greater the risk, the higher the yield investors will demand.
         c. Investment's yield is not necessarily fixed at outset; may change with economy, success or failure of enterprise, etc.
   B. Diversified investment portfolio reduces overall risk of loss.
   C. Lending risks
      1. Risk of default: borrower might not repay loan.
      2. Risk of loss: property might depreciate; foreclosure proceeds might not cover loan balance.
      3. Interest rate risk: market rates may rise while loan funds are tied up at low rate.
      4. Prepayment risk: loan may be paid off sooner than expected if market rates decline.

V. Misjudging Risk
   A. Investment decisions involve predicting future events, and the predictions may prove to be incorrect.
   B. If investment decision was based on mistaken or deceptive information, investor often loses money.

VI. Market Interest Rates
   A. Market rates are typical rates paid for a particular type of loan in the current market.
   B. Factors that may affect market rates for mortgages include size of loan, fixed or adjustable rate, length of loan term, region of country, and/or borrower's credit score.
   C. Real estate activity usually increases with low rates, and decreases with high rates.
   D. Market interest rates go up when demand for mortgage funds exceeds supply, and go down when supply exceeds demand.

Key Terms

Mortgage loan: A loan secured by a mortgage or deed of trust that creates a lien against real property; especially, a loan used to purchase real property when that same property serves as security for the loan.

Lien: A nonpossessory interest in real property, giving the lienholder the right to foreclose if the owner does not pay a debt owed to the lienholder.

Collateral: Property (personal or real) accepted by a lender as security for a loan. The lender has the right to keep or sell the collateral if the borrower fails to repay the loan as agreed.

Principal: The original amount of a loan, or the remainder of that amount after part of it has been repaid.

Interest: A periodic charge that a lender requires a borrower to pay in exchange for the temporary use of the borrowed funds, usually expressed as an annual percentage of the remaining principal balance. Sometimes referred to as the cost of borrowing money.

Investment: When someone (an investor) makes a sum of money (investment capital) available for use by another person or entity, in the expectation that this will generate a return (a profit) for the investor.

Investment capital: Accumulated wealth (savings) made available to fund business enterprises or other ventures, projects, or transactions.

Return on investment: A profit that an investment generates for an investor, over and above the amount of money that he originally invested in it.

Return of investment: When an investment generates enough money for an investor to replace the amount of money she originally invested in it. Also called recapture.

Ownership investment: An investment in which the investor's funds are used to purchase an asset or a property interest in an asset.

Debt investment: An investment in which temporary use of the investor's funds is exchanged for interest payments, pursuant to an agreement that requires repayment of the funds or allows withdrawal of the funds.

Appreciation: An increase in the value of an asset over time; the opposite of depreciation.

Dividend: A share of a company's profits paid to a stockholder as a return on the investment.

Certificate of deposit (CD): A savings arrangement in which a depositor agrees to leave money on deposit for the use of the financial institution for a specified period, or pay a penalty for earlier withdrawal.

Securities: Investment instruments that confer an interest or a right to payment, without allowing direct managerial control over the enterprise invested in.

Stock: A share of a corporation's stock represents a fractional ownership interest in the corporation; a shareholder may receive a return on the investment in the form of dividends and/or appreciation of the share's value.

Bond: A certificate of indebtedness issued by a governmental body or a business entity; it will generate a return for the bondholder in the form of periodic payments of interest until the principal is repaid in a lump sum.

Mutual fund: A company that invests its capital in a diversified portfolio of securities on behalf of its investors, who own shares in the fund.

Liquid asset: An investment that can be quickly and easily converted into cash.

Yield: The rate of return that an investor receives on an investment, usually stated as an annual percentage of the amount invested.

Portfolio: The mix of investments and cash reserves held by an investor.

Diversification: The practice of investing in a variety of different ways and/or in a variety of different sectors of the economy, to make a portfolio safer.

Interest rate risk: The risk that, after a loan is made for a specified term at a fixed interest rate, market interest rates will rise and the lender will miss the opportunity to invest the loaned funds at a higher rate.

Prepayment risk: The risk that a loan will be paid off sooner than expected (often because market interest rates have dropped), reducing the lender's anticipated yield.

Market interest rates: The rates that, under current economic conditions, are typically paid on particular types of investments or charged for particular types of loans.

Chapter Quiz

1. In connection with a loan, the term "principal" refers to the:
   a. amount borrowed
   b. lender
   c. property purchased
   d. repayment period

2. Stocks and bonds are the primary examples of:
   a. ownership investments
   b. securities
   c. collateral
   d. All of the above

3. All of the following are debt investments, except:
   a. savings account
   b. government bond
   c. certificate of deposit
   d. purchase of real estate

4. A company that invests in a diversified portfolio of stocks and bonds on behalf of its investors/owners is called a/an:
   a. mutual fund
   b. security fund
   c. insider trading firm
   d. liquidity firm

5. Stevenson borrowed money from Acme Savings to buy a rental house. He paid 15% down. Which of the following is true?
   a. Acme has made a debt investment
   b. Stevenson has made an ownership investment
   c. Both of the above
   d. Neither of the above

6. The return that a mortgage lender receives on its typical investments takes the form of:
   a. appreciation
   b. dividends
   c. rental income
   d. interest

7. The phrase "return on an investment" refers to:
   a. recapture of the amount originally invested
   b. an annual yield of at least 10%
   c. an investor's profit over and above the amount originally invested
   d. net income after deducting dividends

8. As a general rule, the safer the investment:
   a. the less liquid the yield
   b. the less certain the yield
   c. the lower the yield
   d. the higher the yield

9. When market interest rates are rising, a lender making a 30-year loan at a fixed interest rate will probably be most concerned about:
   a. prepayment risk
   b. liquidity risk
   c. mutual fund risk
   d. interest rate risk

10. An investor who might need to cash in investments to cover unexpected expenses is likely to be especially concerned about:
    a. bond yields
    b. liquidity
    c. prepayment risk
    d. insider trading

Answer Key

1. a. A loan's principal is the money that was borrowed—the amount originally borrowed, and once repayment has begun, the amount that remains to be paid—as opposed to the interest that accrues on the principal.

2. b. Stocks and bonds are examples of securities, investment instruments that are traded in established financial markets. (Stocks are ownership investments, but bonds are debt investments.)

3. d. The purchase of real estate is an ownership investment, not a debt investment.

4. a. A mutual fund invests the capital provided by its shareholders in a diversified portfolio of securities; the fund managers who make the decisions are investment professionals.

5. c. Acme's loan to Stevenson was a debt investment, and Stevenson's real estate purchase was an ownership investment.

6. d. A mortgage lender's typical investments (mortgage loans) provide a return in the form of interest payments.

7. c. A return *on* an investment is a profit for the investor. (A return *of* the investment is the recapture of the amount originally invested.)

8. c. The safer the investment, the lower the yield. High-yield investments tend to be high-risk investments.

9. d. The lender will be most concerned about interest rate risk, the risk that market rates will rise significantly while the lender's funds are tied up in long-term loans at lower rates.

10. b. If an investor might need to cash in an investment on short notice, it's better if the investment is a liquid one—one that's easily converted into cash.

Chapter 2
Federal Fiscal and Monetary Policy

Fiscal Policy
- Spending and debt financing
- Taxation
  - Deduction of mortgage interest
  - Exclusion of gain on the sale of a home
  - Depreciation deductions for investors

Monetary Policy
- Federal Reserve System
- Economic growth and inflation
- Tools for implementing monetary policy
  - Reserve requirements
  - Interest rates
  - Open market operations
- Changes in monetary policy

Introduction

The federal government has many ways of influencing the economy as a whole, and real estate finance in particular. For instance, the government oversees the secondary mortgage market (see Chapter 3) and regulates lending institutions (see Chapter 4). It also influences the cost of borrowing money through fiscal and monetary policy, which is the subject of this chapter.

As you might expect, the factor that has the biggest impact on the cost of borrowing money is the interest rate charged by the lender. As we discussed in Chapter 1, market interest rates represent the current cost of money: the price that a borrower will have to pay to get a loan today. The cost of money, like the cost of other things in our society, is controlled primarily by the law of supply and demand. If the supply of money is large—if there is a large amount of money in circulation—interest rates tend to fall. Lower interest rates encourage more people to borrow money for both business and personal purposes, including borrowing to finance the purchase of homes. Then, as the money supply tightens, interest rates tend to rise, and fewer people can afford to borrow.

Government influences interest rates through:
- *Fiscal policy*
- *Monetary policy*

The cost of borrowing money is influenced by the federal government in two ways:

1. with its **fiscal policy**, and
2. with its **monetary policy**.

Fiscal policy refers to the government's actions in raising revenue (mainly through taxation), spending money, and managing its debt. These activities can indirectly affect the nation's money supply, and therefore the cost of money. Monetary policy refers to the government's direct efforts to control the money supply and the cost of money.

Fiscal Policy

Fiscal policy:
- *Raising revenue (taxation)*
- *Government spending*
- *Debt financing*

Fiscal policy is determined by the government's executive branch (the president and the administration) and legislative branch (Congress). The two branches establish the federal tax laws (which generate the government's largest source of income) and the federal budget (which determines how the money will be spent). The U.S. Treasury Department carries out the fiscal policy; it is responsible for managing the federal government's finances, including the national debt.

Spending and Debt Financing

When the federal government spends more money than it takes in (through taxation and other income sources), a shortfall known as the **federal deficit** results. A deficit has occurred in most years since the Great Depression of the 1930s.

When there is a deficit, the Treasury obtains funds to cover the shortfall by issuing interest-bearing securities for sale to investors. Depending on their term, these securities are referred to as Treasury bills (one year or less), Treasury notes (two to ten years), Treasury inflation-protected securities (five, ten, or thirty years), or Treasury bonds (more than ten years). In issuing these securities, the federal government is actually borrowing money from the private sector. And when the government borrows to cover the deficit, less money is available for private borrowers.

Federal deficit absorbs investment funds from private sector

Some economists believe the federal deficit has little, if any, effect on interest rates. Others believe large-scale federal borrowing pushes interest rates upward, because private borrowers are forced to compete for the limited funds remaining.

Taxation

The other element of fiscal policy is taxation. When taxes are low, taxpayers have more money to lend and invest. When taxes are high, taxpayers not only have less money to lend or invest, they are also more likely to invest what money they do have in tax-exempt securities instead of taxable investments. Since real estate and mortgage-backed securities are taxable investments, this has a significant impact on residential finance.

When taxes are high, taxpayers:
- Have less money to lend or invest
- Tend to prefer tax-free investments

Taxation also affects mortgage financing and the real estate industry in other ways. While the primary purpose of taxation is to raise revenue, some provisions of the income tax laws are used to implement the federal government's social policy of encouraging homeownership. This is accomplished through tax exemptions, deductions, and exclusions. We'll take a brief look at some provisions in the federal tax code that affect the demand for real estate, and therefore have an indirect impact on the cost of mortgage funds.

Deduction of Mortgage Interest. Taxpayers who own their home may deduct the interest they pay on their mortgage from their taxable income, which reduces the amount of taxes they have to pay. (Interest on other forms of consumer debt is not deductible.) Owners of rental property may also deduct interest paid on any loans used to purchase the property as a business expense.

Limits. There are limits on the deductibility of home mortgage interest. A taxpayer generally can deduct all of the interest paid on loans for buying, building, or substantially improving first and second residences, as long as the loan amounts don't add up to more than a specified limit. (If the loan amounts exceed the limit, the interest paid on the excess is not deductible.) For many years the limit has been $1,000,000, but for homes purchased after mid-December 2017, the limit is reduced to $750,000.

Home equity loans. Beginning in 2018, the interest on a home equity loan is deductible (subject to the limits just explained) only if the loan funds are used for substantial home improvements, such as an addition or a new roof. If a home equity loan is used to pay for expenses unrelated to improving the home, such as credit card debt or college expenses, the interest is not deductible. (Previously, a taxpayer could deduct interest on home equity loans totaling up to $100,000, even if the loans were used to pay for expenses unrelated to the home.) Note that these rules also apply to home equity lines of credit.

Tax benefits for homeowners:
- Mortgage interest deduction
- Exclusion of gain on sale of principal residence

Exclusion of Gain on the Sale of a Home. Another tax code provision that benefits homeowners allows a gain or profit on the sale of a principal residence to be excluded from taxation. A taxpayer who sells her principal residence may exclude a gain of up to $250,000, or up to $500,000 for married couples filing a joint return. If the gain on the sale exceeds the $250,000 or $500,000 limit, the excess is taxed at the capital gains rate. (The maximum capital gains tax rate is lower than the maximum tax rate on ordinary income.)

Note that if a taxpayer converts a home to his principal residence (previously holding it as a vacation residence or a rental, for example), the amount of excludable gain may be lower. However, if the taxpayer lives in the residence for a long enough period of time, the full exclusion will become available.

Eligibility. To qualify for the exclusion, the taxpayer must have both owned and used the property as a principal residence for at least two years during the five-year period before its sale. Because of this rule, the exclusion is available only once every two years.

If the sellers are married and filing a joint return, only one spouse has to meet the ownership test, but both spouses must meet the use test. If only one spouse meets both the ownership test and the use test, the maximum exclusion the married couple can claim is $250,000, even if they file a joint return.

In special circumstances, taxpayers who owned and used a principal residence for less than two years may be able to claim a reduced exclusion. A reduced exclusion would be allowed if a home was sold after only a year because of a change in the taxpayer's health or place of employment, or because of some other unforeseen circumstances.

The deductibility of mortgage interest and the exclusion of gain on the sale of a principal residence both make it significantly less expensive to own a home. Together, these provisions are quite effective in helping to fulfill the government's policy of encouraging homeownership.

Depreciation Deductions for Investors. Many other provisions in the federal tax code also have an impact on real estate investment. To take one example, owners of income property, such as apartment buildings and rental homes, are allowed to take depreciation deductions (also called cost recovery deductions). In other words, they can deduct some of the cost of buildings and other property improvements that eventually will wear out and have to be replaced. The cost is spread out over a number of years (for residential rental properties, usually 27½ years), rather than deducted all at once. When the government changes the rules for these depreciation deductions—for example, by requiring them to be stretched out over a greater number of years—it can affect the profitability of investing in real estate.

Thus, how the federal government raises revenue—how much it taxes income, how it taxes different kinds of income, and what tax

Depreciation deductions affect real estate investment

deductions and exclusions it allows—can stimulate or dampen the demand for real estate and increase or decrease the availability of mortgage funds.

Monetary Policy

The federal government exercises considerable control over the nation's money supply (how much money is in circulation). Monetary policy refers to the government's efforts to control the money supply to keep the national economy running smoothly. Monetary policy is set and implemented by the Federal Reserve System, commonly called "the Fed."

The Federal Reserve System

The Federal Reserve System regulates commercial banks, and its responsibility for monetary policy grew out of that function.

The Fed:
- Regulates commercial banks
- Sets and implements monetary policy

Historical Background. In the early nineteenth century, there was very little government regulation of depository institutions in the United States. The security of bank deposits depended primarily on the integrity of bank managers. Not surprisingly, serious problems sometimes developed. For example, a bank might loan out nearly all of its deposits and keep almost no funds in reserve. When a depositor tried to make a withdrawal, the bank might not have enough cash on hand to fulfill the request. To protect the public against this kind of mismanagement, in 1863 Congress passed the National Bank Act, which established basic banking regulations and procedures for supervising commercial banks.

In spite of the 1863 law, certain problems persisted, and the public lacked confidence in the banking industry. Economic downturns periodically led to financial panics involving "a run on the bank," in which most of a bank's depositors would suddenly doubt the security of their money and withdraw it all at once. This could cause even a financially sound bank to fail, and the depositors who had not withdrawn their money would be left empty-handed.

Federal Reserve was established to strengthen the financial system and improve public confidence

To strengthen the financial system and improve public confidence, support grew for the creation of a central bank for the U.S., similar to the central banks of other countries. The American public had long resisted the idea of a central bank; average citizens tended to be

Fig. 2.1 *The organization of the Federal Reserve System*

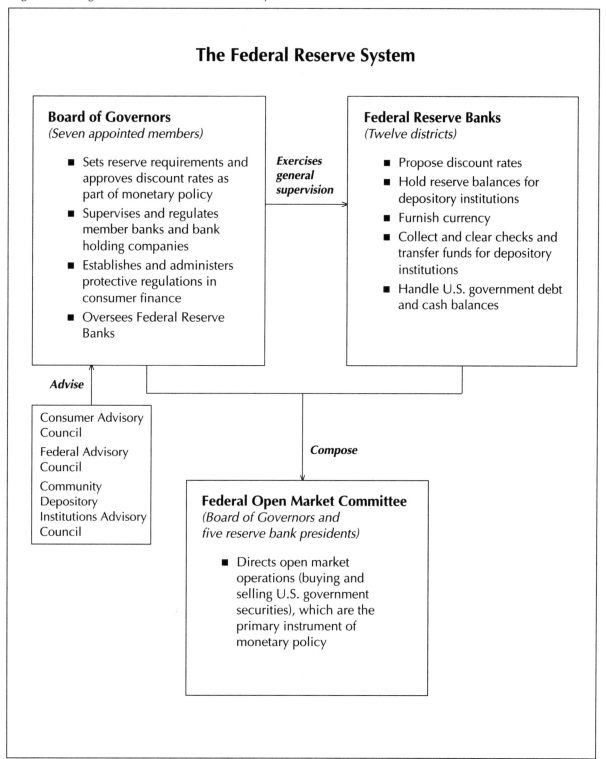

Source: The Federal Reserve

hostile toward banks, Wall Street interests, and centralized authority in general. However, huge losses suffered by depositors in a series of bank panics in 1907 finally overcame public resistance.

In the Federal Reserve Acts of 1913 and 1916, Congress created the Federal Reserve System and established the modern banking system. The Fed would regulate commercial banks, perform periodic bank examinations, and impose **reserve requirements**, specifying what proportion of a bank's deposits had to be held in reserve, available for immediate withdrawal on demand by depositors. In addition, the Federal Reserve would serve as a "lender of last resort," providing short-term backup loans to banks that ran low on funds.

The creation of the Federal Reserve improved the financial system in many ways, but it did not entirely solve the problem of financial panics and bank runs. A more direct solution, federal deposit insurance, was developed during the Depression of the 1930s. The Federal Deposit Insurance Corporation and the Federal Savings and Loan Insurance Corporation were created as part of the New Deal.

Organization. To prevent the centralization of too much power, Congress included checks and balances in the Federal Reserve System. Its structure was designed to spread power three different ways: 1) geographically; 2) between the private and government sectors; and 3) among bankers, businesses, and the public. The Federal Reserve System includes:

- twelve regional Federal Reserve Banks in twelve Federal Reserve Districts,
- the Federal Reserve Board,
- the Federal Open Market Committee,
- several advisory councils, and
- over 3,000 member banks.

The system is controlled by the seven-member Board of Governors, known as the **Federal Reserve Board** (see Figure 2.1). The governors are appointed by the U.S. president and confirmed by the Senate for 14-year terms. To prevent one area of the country from having disproportionate power on the board, the governors must be chosen from different Federal Reserve Districts. The board's chairman is chosen from among the governors for a four-year term, and may be reappointed repeatedly. Some Fed chairmen have served under several presidents.

The Board of Governors controls the Fed's monetary policy. All seven governors are on the Federal Open Market Committee, which we'll discuss shortly. The governors set reserve requirements for commercial banks and, through the process of review and approval, effectively control the discount rate set by the Federal Reserve Banks. (We'll discuss the discount rate shortly, too.) The governors also have substantial control over regulations affecting the activities of commercial banks and bank holding companies.

Fed chairman and Federal Reserve Board make decisions concerning monetary policy

Each of the twelve Federal Reserve Districts has one main Federal Reserve Bank, and some districts have branch banks as well. Each reserve bank has a nine-member board of directors. These nine directors appoint the president of their reserve bank, subject to the approval of the Board of Governors.

12 regional Federal Reserve Banks:
- *Owned by member banks*
- *Make discount loans*
- *Set discount rates (with Board approval)*
- *Appoint bankers to Federal Advisory Council*

All of the Federal Reserve Banks are involved to some degree in monetary policy. Each reserve bank has a staff that conducts research on economic conditions in its district, and each reserve bank selects one banker to be a member of the Federal Advisory Council. The Advisory Council meets and consults with the Board of Governors regarding monetary policy.

Economic Growth and Inflation

The Federal Reserve's ultimate goal in setting and implementing monetary policy is a healthy U.S. economy. The economy is considered healthy when there is sustainable economic growth with low unemployment, stable prices, and reasonable interest rates.

Sustainable economic growth is neither too weak nor too strong, and neither too slow nor too fast. If growth is too strong and too fast, it's usually accompanied by **inflation**, a trend of general price increases throughout the economy. Uncontrolled inflation eventually chokes economic growth. The ideal is for the economy to grow steadily, but at a moderate pace that won't trigger severe inflation.

Inflation: prices increasing throughout the economy

When the economy is stagnating, the Fed takes action to stimulate growth. But if the economy starts booming and inflation threatens to gain momentum, the Fed takes action to slow down growth and keep inflation in check.

Goal is sustainable growth with inflation in check

Tools for Implementing Monetary Policy

The Fed relies on three main tools to implement its monetary policy and influence the economy:

Fed's tools for monetary
policy:
• Reserve requirements
• Discount rate and federal
  funds rate target
• Open market operations

- reserve requirements,
- interest rates (the discount rate and federal funds rate), and
- open market operations.

Reserve Requirements. A commercial bank's reserve requirement is the percentage of its deposits the bank is required to maintain on reserve, either in its own vaults or on deposit at the Federal Reserve Bank in its district. The requirements are set by the Federal Reserve Board and may reach 10%, depending on the amount of deposits at the institution. It used to be that only member banks were required to keep reserves at the reserve banks. But the Depository Institutions Deregulation and Monetary Control Act of 1980 subjected all commercial banks to the same reserve requirements, regardless of whether they were members of the Federal Reserve, and also imposed reserve requirements on savings banks, savings and loans, and credit unions. The same act also gave all commercial banks access to some Federal Reserve benefits such as check clearing and discount loans. As a result, there are now fewer differences between member and nonmember banks.

As explained earlier, the original purpose of reserve requirements was to help avert financial panics by giving depositors confidence that their deposits were safe and accessible. The requirements protect depositors by helping to ensure that their bank will have enough funds available to meet unusual customer demand.

At the same time, reserve requirements also enable the Fed to exercise some control over the growth of credit. By increasing reserve requirements, the Fed reduces the amount of money that banks have available to lend, which usually causes interest rates to rise and puts a brake on growth. On the other hand, a reduction in reserve requirements frees more money for lending by banks, leading to lower interest rates and stimulating growth.

When reserve requirements:
• Increase: decreases funds
  available for lending
  and increases interest rates
• Decrease: increases
  supply of funds and
  decreases interest rates

Interest Rates. The Fed has more direct control over two key interest rates: the federal discount rate and the federal funds rate.

The **discount rate** is the interest rate charged when a bank borrows money from one of the Federal Reserve Banks to cover a shortfall in

Federal discount rate:
interest rate charged banks
that borrow from the Fed

funds. The discount rate is set by the Federal Reserve Banks with the approval of the Fed's Board of Governors.

The **federal funds rate** is the interest rate banks charge each other for overnight loans. A bank that doesn't have enough funds to meet its reserve requirements may borrow the money needed from a bank that has excess reserves. Unlike the discount rate, the federal funds rate is not set directly by the Fed; the banks themselves can determine how much they'll charge each other for overnight loans. However, when the Federal Open Market Committee meets, it sets a target for the federal funds rate. It also issues a directive indicating what open market operations will be conducted in an effort to achieve the target rate.

Federal funds rate: interest rate banks charge each other for overnight loans

When the Federal Reserve raises or lowers the discount rate or the target for the federal funds rate, it's regarded as an indication of the Fed's overall view of the economy. For example, if either or both of these interest rates are lowered, that's seen as a signal that the Fed feels the economy needs a boost, since lower interest rates usually stimulate economic activity.

Lower interest rates stimulate economic activity

Lenders often respond to a change in the funds rate or the discount rate by making a corresponding change in the interest rates they charge on loans to their customers. For example, if the federal funds rate drops a quarter of a percentage point, market interest rates are likely to follow suit. However, this relationship is complicated by anticipation; sometimes lenders increase or decrease their rates in anticipation of an interest rate change by the Fed. In that case, the actual change in the federal funds rate or discount rate may have little impact.

Keep in mind that the market interest rates most affected by changes in the discount rate and federal funds rate are short-term interest rates. The Fed's interest rate adjustments don't have such a direct influence on long-term interest rates, which include the market interest rates for home purchase mortgages. Mortgage rates are, of course, affected by changes in the economy, but they generally don't change in response to an increase or decrease in the discount rate or federal funds rate. When you hear that the Fed has raised or lowered interest rates, consider it an indication of the strength or weakness of the economy, but don't expect a corresponding change in mortgage interest rates, at least not immediately. At times, long-term interest rates actually move counter to short-term rates.

Long-term interest rates (like mortgage rates) don't respond directly to Fed's interest rate adjustments

Open market operations:
the Fed buys and sells
government securities

Open Market Operations. The Fed also buys and sells government securities. These transactions are called open market operations. They are conducted by the Securities Department of the Federal Reserve Bank of New York (often referred to as "the Trading Desk," or just "the Desk"), following directives from the **Federal Open Market Committee** (FOMC). Open market operations are the most important tool for controlling the money supply, so the FOMC is the most important policymaking organization in the Fed.

The FOMC has eight regularly scheduled meetings per year. It consists of twelve members: the seven members of the Federal Reserve Board, the president of the New York Federal Reserve Bank, and four other Reserve Bank presidents.

Open market operations are the Fed's primary method of controlling the money supply (which in turn affects inflation and interest rates). Only money in circulation is considered part of the money supply, so actions by the Fed that put money into circulation increase the money supply, and actions that take money out of circulation decrease the money supply.

Money supply:
• Increases when Fed buys
government securities
• Decreases when Fed sells
government securities

When the Fed buys government securities, it increases the money supply. The Fed may pay for the securities in cash, by check, or if purchasing from a bank, simply by crediting the bank's reserves with the Fed. Any of these actions puts more money into circulation. On the other hand, when the Fed sells government securities, the money the buyer uses to pay for the securities is taken out of circulation, decreasing the money supply.

Other things being equal, an increase in the money supply is supposed to lead to lower interest rates. But other things are seldom equal, and several factors may apply upward pressure to interest rates at the same time that an increase in the money supply is exerting downward pressure. For example, lenders might increase interest rates simply in anticipation of possible inflation. The Fed uses open market operations and its other tools to balance these complicated forces. It tries to manage the money supply to adequately serve the growth of the economy at reasonable interest rates, without fueling inflation or fears of inflation that could lead to higher interest rates.

Changes in Monetary Policy

In the years since its creation, the Fed has frequently modified its monetary policy, changing the objectives and also the tools employed to reach those objectives. Since the Fed really has no direct control over inflation or market interest rates, it works toward its goals by tracking certain economic indicators and by taking action to influence those indicators. At various times, the Fed has focused on the discount rate, reserve requirements, general money market conditions, the federal funds rate, and changes in one or more of its measures of the money supply. Its actions are more or less experimental, and when a particular experiment does not seem to be working, the Fed may try a different one.

Monetary policy is experimental, and Fed changes strategies from time to time

We can illustrate this by looking at shifts in monetary policy over the last 50 years or so. During the 1970s, the Fed's practice was to moderate interest rates by increasing the money supply whenever interest rates started to rise. Although this succeeded in keeping interest rates down, inflation worsened as money was pumped into the economy to satisfy the demands of borrowers. Concerned about inflation, the Fed then adopted a different approach. It stopped its efforts to control interest rates by increasing the money supply, and instead tried to control inflation by restricting the growth of the money supply. In the months that followed, interest rates soared. (The high rates caused problems for savings and loans, which led to their deregulation. See Chapter 4.)

In the early 1980s, the Fed again shifted course. Inflation had fallen sharply, but interest rates remained high and volatile. The Fed put emphasis on preventing the large fluctuations in interest rates. The result was positive. Over the next couple of decades, the inflation rate remained relatively moderate and interest rates fell to a reasonable level.

In the early years of the new century, however, the economy began slowing. The Fed tried to spur growth by gradually lowering the key interest rates to levels that hadn't been seen since the early 1960s. (The federal funds rate target was down to 1% in 2003.) When the economy began improving, inflation once again became a concern. This led to a steady series of increases in the key interest rates. By mid-2006, the Fed had increased the funds rate target to 5.25%.

Monetary policy and the financial crisis. Fairly quickly, though, credit began to tighten and general economic growth faltered. In 2007, the Fed began lowering rates again, hoping to encourage the flow of credit to businesses. Nonetheless, the "credit crunch" continued. As the U.S. economy slid into the worst financial crisis since the Great Depression (see Chapter 4), the Fed reacted sharply, dropping

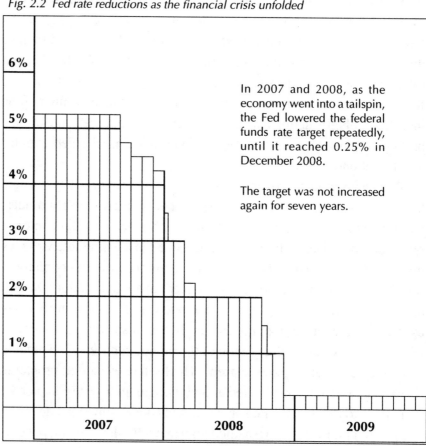

Fig. 2.2 Fed rate reductions as the financial crisis unfolded

In 2007 and 2008, as the economy went into a tailspin, the Fed lowered the federal funds rate target repeatedly, until it reached 0.25% in December 2008.

The target was not increased again for seven years.

the federal funds rate target to just 0.25% by the end of 2008. (See Figure 2.2.)

It took seven years before the Fed felt enough confidence in the economy to begin slowly raising interest rates again. A series of 0.25% increases starting at the end of 2015 brought the federal funds rate target back up to 2.0% by the middle of 2018.

Another change in monetary policy the Fed made in response to the financial crisis was a temporary program of "quantitative easing." This involved using trillions of dollars in federal money to buy financial assets from banks, substantially increasing the money supply and making credit more available. The program lasted from 2008 to 2014 and was considered important in helping the economy recover from the crisis.

Outline: Federal Fiscal and Monetary Policy

I. Government Influences on Finance
   A. The federal government influences real estate finance by influencing the cost of mortgage funds.
   B. Market interest rates represent the cost of borrowing money, which is subject to the rules of supply and demand.
   C. The federal government affects the cost of borrowing through fiscal policy and monetary policy.

II. Fiscal Policy
   A. Fiscal policy includes government spending, debt financing, and raising revenue through taxation.
   B. Federal fiscal policy is determined by both the legislative and executive branches, and is carried out by the U.S. Treasury Department.
   C. If the federal government spends more money than it receives in a year, a deficit occurs.
   D. To finance the shortfall, the government sells interest-bearing securities to investors.
   E. When private investors lend money to the government to cover a deficit, less money is available to private borrowers.
      1. Some economists believe federal deficits have little effect on interest rates.
      2. Other economists believe deficit spending pushes interest rates up because government borrowing takes funds out of the money market and increases demand for funds.

III. Taxation
   A. Taxation affects mortgage rates by affecting how much money taxpayers have available to lend or invest.
   B. Taxation also affects mortgage rates through tax exemptions, deductions, and exclusions, which may affect demand for mortgages.
   C. Taxpayers can deduct interest paid on home mortgage loans from their taxable income, which reduces the amount of taxes they pay.
      1. Interest on loans for buying, building, or improving a home is deductible; however, there is a cap on loan size after which interest paid on the excess is not deductible.
   D. Taxpayers may exclude from taxation the gain received from selling a principal residence.
      1. A gain of up to $250,000 for an individual or $500,000 for a married couple filing jointly may be excluded.

2. To qualify for this exclusion, the taxpayers must have owned the property and used it as a principal residence for at least two of the previous five years.

E. Taxpayers may take deductions for the depreciation of investment property.

IV. Monetary Policy

A. Federal government monetary policy refers to the government's control over the money supply, which is implemented by the Federal Reserve System (or "Fed").

B. Historical background

1. Banks were first regulated in 1863 through the National Bank Act, which created basic procedures for supervising banks.

2. The Federal Reserve Acts of 1913 and 1916 created the modern banking system.

3. The Federal Reserve System imposes reserve requirements, specifying what amount of a bank's deposits must be kept in reserve to be available for withdrawal.

4. The Federal Reserve acts as a lender of last resort, providing short-term loans to banks running low on funds.

5. The stability of the banking industry was bolstered in the 1930s with the creation of the Federal Deposit Insurance Corporation.

C. Organization of the Federal Reserve

1. The Federal Reserve System is decentralized into 12 regional Federal Reserve Banks.

2. The system is controlled by the seven-member Board of Governors, each chosen for 14-year terms from different Federal Reserve Districts.

D. Economic growth and inflation

1. If economic growth occurs too quickly, inflation results, causing price increases that hamper further growth.

2. If inflation appears to be a possibility, the Fed will take action to slow growth and limit inflation.

V. Tools for Implementing Monetary Policy

A. Reserve requirements: a percentage of deposits that each bank must maintain either in its own vaults or on deposit with the Federal Reserve Bank.

1. Reserve requirements were originally intended to avert financial panic by making sure that depositors were always able to withdraw deposits.

2. Reserve requirements also allow the Fed to control the money supply.

3. An increase in reserve requirements reduces the amount of money banks have available to lend and therefore increases interest rates.

    B. Interest rates: the Fed controls two key interest rates, the federal discount rate and federal funds rate.

        1. The discount rate is the rate charged to member banks when they borrow money from the Fed to cover a shortfall in funds.

        2. The federal funds rate is the rate banks charge each other for loans to cover shortfalls.

        3. Lenders' market interest rates will usually rise or fall in response to changes in the federal rates, although long-term rates (such as mortgages) are not immediately affected.

    C. Open market operations: the Fed controls the money supply by buying and selling government securities.

        1. If the Fed buys government securities, it puts more money into the money supply, which by itself will decrease interest rates.

        2. If the Fed sells government securities, it takes money from investors out of the money supply, which will increase interest rates.

VI. Changes in Monetary Policy

    A. The Fed modifies its monetary policy in response to changing economic indicators.

    B. These policy changes are experimental attempts to control complex economic forces.

Key Terms

Fiscal policy: Government actions in raising revenue through taxation, spending money, and financing budget deficits.

Monetary policy: Government action in controlling the money supply and therefore the cost of borrowing money.

Federal deficit: A shortfall in funds that occurs when the federal government spends more money than it collects in a particular year.

Home mortgage interest deduction: Interest paid on mortgage loans secured by the taxpayer's home or homes is deductible, up to certain limits.

Exclusion of gain on sale of home: A taxpayer may exclude from taxation any gain on the sale of a principal residence, up to a limit of $250,000 (or $500,000 if married and filing jointly).

Depreciation deductions: Owners of income property can deduct the cost of assets that will wear out and eventually have to be replaced. Also called cost recovery deductions.

Federal Reserve System: The Federal Reserve System regulates commercial banks and implements the nation's monetary policy. Often referred to as "the Fed."

Reserve requirements: The Fed requires commercial banks to hold a certain portion of their deposits on reserve for immediate withdrawal by depositors.

Federal Reserve Bank: There are 12 Federal Reserve Banks, one for each Federal Reserve District, owned by the commercial banks within that district.

Federal Reserve Board: The Federal Reserve System is controlled by a seven-member Board of Governors, known as the Federal Reserve Board. Each of the seven members is appointed from a different district to a 14-year term.

Inflation: A trend of general price increases throughout the economy.

Discount rate: The interest rate that a Federal Reserve Bank charges on short-term loans to member banks; the Fed sets this rate directly.

Federal funds rate: The interest rate that banks charge one another for overnight loans; the Fed sets a target for this rate.

Open market operations: The Fed adjusts the money supply by engaging in open market operations; as it buys and sells government securities, it changes the amount of money available in circulation.

Federal Open Market Committee: The Federal Open Market Committee is a board that makes decisions regarding open market operations by the Fed.

Chapter Quiz

1. The government controls the money supply and cost of money through:
   a. fiscal policy
   b. monetary policy
   c. budgetary policy
   d. fiduciary policy

2. In a given year, the federal government spends more money than it receives as revenue. The result is a federal:
   a. deficit
   b. debt
   c. surplus
   d. default

3. Which item may be excluded from taxation, rather than simply taken as a deduction?
   a. Home mortgage interest
   b. Home equity loan interest
   c. Gain on the sale of a principal residence
   d. Depreciation of investment property

4. The gain from the sale of which of the following properties would be excluded from taxation?
   a. Residential rental owned for the last ten years
   b. Residential property used as a primary residence from ten years ago until five years ago
   c. Vacation home owned for the last five years
   d. Residential property used as a primary residence from four years ago until one year ago

5. Which of the following is the best definition of reserve requirements?
   a. Buying and selling government securities on the open market
   b. Setting interest rates for loans to banks facing cash shortfalls
   c. Requiring banks to make a certain percentage of deposits available for immediate withdrawal
   d. Controlling inflation by raising interest rates (to slow growth)

6. How many Federal Reserve Districts and Federal Reserve Banks are there?
   a. 7
   b. 9
   c. 12
   d. 14

7. Inflation occurs when:
   a. rapid economic growth causes prices to increase
   b. the Fed raises interest rates
   c. the Fed decreases the pool of available funds by selling government securities
   d. economic stagnation causes higher unemployment

8. The interest rate charged by the Federal Reserve when a member bank borrows money to cover a shortfall in funds is the:
   a. federal funds rate
   b. federal discount rate
   c. federal key rate
   d. market interest rate

9. The Federal Reserve decides to decrease the supply of money available. To do so, it will:
   a. buy government securities and increase reserve requirements
   b. buy government securities and decrease reserve requirements
   c. sell government securities and increase reserve requirements
   d. sell government securities and decrease reserve requirements

10. In the early 1980s, the Fed tried to control inflation by restricting growth of the money supply. What happened?
    a. Interest rates shot up
    b. Interest rates plunged
    c. Inflation got worse
    d. The government bought back most of its government securities

Answer Key

1. b. Monetary policy refers to the government's efforts to control the money supply and thus the cost of borrowing money.

2. a. A federal deficit results if, in a particular year, the government spends more than it takes in.

3. c. Gain on the sale of a principal residence of up to $250,000 (or $500,000 for a married couple filing jointly) may be excluded from taxation.

4. d. To qualify for exclusion of gain, the taxpayer must have owned and used the property as a principal residence for at least two years during the five-year period before its sale.

5. c. Reserve requirements specify what percentage of a bank's deposits must be kept in reserve, available for immediate withdrawal by depositors.

6. c. There are 12 Federal Reserve Districts, each of which has its own Federal Reserve Bank.

7. a. Inflation occurs when economic growth is too rapid and prices throughout the economy shoot up. The Fed may take action to limit inflation—by raising interest rates, for example.

8. b. The federal discount rate is the interest rate charged by the Fed when a bank borrows funds to cover a shortfall in funds on deposit.

9. c. Both selling government securities on the open market and increasing reserve requirements remove money from the money supply that would otherwise be available to lend. A reduced money supply will increase the demand for funds and increase the cost of borrowing money.

10. a. The result of the Fed's efforts to decrease the money supply in the early 1980s was a decline in inflation, but also a sharp increase in interest rates.

Chapter 3
The Primary and Secondary Markets

The Two Mortgage Markets
- Primary market and funds for mortgage lending
  - Local financing
  - Real estate cycles
  - National forces affect local cycles
  - Addressing the problem of cycles
- Secondary market
  - Buying and selling loans
  - Mortgage-backed securities
  - Functions of the secondary market

Fannie Mae and Freddie Mac
- Creation of the entities
- GSE status
- MBS programs
- Standardized documents and underwriting
- Impact of the GSEs
- The GSEs and the subprime crisis
  - Conservatorship
  - Federal guaranty

Introduction

The residential mortgage industry is made up of the financial institutions, private companies, agencies, and other investors that make investment funds available to people who want to finance (or refinance) the purchase or construction of a home. The industry is divided into two "markets" that supply the funds for mortgage loans: the primary market and the secondary market.

In this chapter, we'll explain the two markets and the relationship between them. We'll also discuss two secondary market enterprises, Fannie Mae and Freddie Mac, and the mortgage-backed securities that are traded in the secondary market. (The different types of lenders in the primary market and other aspects of the mortgage industry will be covered in Chapter 4.)

Both the primary market and the secondary market have undergone fundamental changes as part of the fallout from the subprime mortgage crisis and subsequent recession. At the end of this chapter we'll discuss some of those changes; the crisis itself is covered in Chapter 4.

The Two Mortgage Markets

Primary market: where lenders make loans to home buyers

Secondary market: where lenders sell loans to investors

Home buyers borrow the money they need from banks and other mortgage lenders. Those loan transactions take place in the financial arena known in the mortgage industry as the **primary mortgage market**. To obtain money to make more loans, lenders often sell their loans to investors. These transactions take place in another arena, the **secondary mortgage market**. As you'll see, the secondary market has come to play an extremely important role in making financing available to home buyers in the primary market.

The Primary Market and Funds for Mortgage Lending

Loan origination:
• Processing application
• Approval decision
• Funding the loan

In the primary mortgage market, home buyers apply for mortgage loans and residential mortgage lenders **originate** them. Loan origination includes processing the application, deciding to approve the loan, and then funding the loan. Where do lenders get the funds they use to make mortgage loans? The answer to that question changed significantly over the course of the twentieth century.

Local Financing. At one time, the primary market was purely a local market, consisting of the various financial institutions in a community—local banks, savings and loan associations, and so on. Although the primary market is considerably more complicated than that today (as a result of interstate banking, online lenders, and other developments), it will be easier to explain the relationship between the primary market and the secondary market if we start with a simple example along traditional lines.

> **Example:** The Browns live in a small city called Seacliff. When the Browns want to borrow money so that they can buy a house, they apply for a loan from one of the local financial institutions, Vault Savings Bank. Vault is a mortgage lender in the primary market.
>
> Vault Savings Bank's main source of funds for making mortgage loans is the savings of its depositors, who are individuals and businesses in the Seacliff area. Vault uses the savings deposits to make loans to residents of that same community. It pays depositors 2% interest for the use of their savings, and it charges borrowers 6% interest on their mortgage loans. The difference between the interest rate charged to borrowers and the rate paid to depositors (less the bank's operational costs) is Vault's profit.

In the past, the basic model of mortgage financing presented in the example worked well: local lenders had an adequate supply of mortgage funds to meet the community's demand, enabling most people who wanted to finance the purchase of a home to do so. The residential real estate market was essentially local, and mortgage financing was originally a local matter, too.

Real Estate Cycles. Unfortunately, a local mortgage financing system doesn't always function smoothly; supply and demand aren't always in balance. Local real estate markets go through active periods followed by slumps. These periodic changes are called **real estate cycles**. They may be dramatic or moderate, short-term or long-term. They may be affected by economic, political, or social factors, such as changes in employment levels, in tax policy, or in lifestyles.

Real estate cycles can create problems for local financial institutions and for potential home buyers.

> **Example:** A new industry recently started up in Seacliff, and the local economy is booming. As a result of this new prosperity, the residents are saving somewhat more, but they're also spending more, and many people want to buy or build homes in the area.

Primary market was originally a local market, made up of local lending institutions

Availability of local funds for lending may be disrupted by local real estate cycles

Vault Savings Bank and the other local financial institutions don't have enough funds on deposit to meet the increased demand for mortgage loans. This might prevent some members of the community who want to finance the purchase of a home from doing so. It might also prevent local lenders from doing as much business as they otherwise could.

On the other hand, sometimes a community's demand for mortgage funds is weak. If the local economy goes into a slump, many people who might otherwise buy homes can't afford to. Local banks may have funds available for mortgage loans, but fewer borrowers meet the lenders' requirements. This reduces the banks' main source of income (interest on loans), so that the institution also suffers from the local economic woes.

National Forces Affect Local Cycles. Local conditions are not the only factor that affects a community's supply of and demand for mortgage funds. National economic and political forces and social trends may also have an impact on local real estate cycles.

Disintermediation: when depository institutions lose funds to higher-yielding investments

For example, a phenomenon known as **disintermediation** can reduce the supply of funds that local financial institutions have available for mortgage lending. Disintermediation occurs when depositors withdraw their funds from savings accounts and put them into competing investments that offer higher returns, such as stocks and bonds. The changes in interest rates and investment yields that lead to disintermediation take place on a national level.

Disintermediation can affect the local supply of mortgage funds; other national factors can also affect local demand. For example, if Congress changes the federal tax code in a way that favors homeownership, that encourages more people nationwide to purchase homes. The demand for mortgage financing in a local real estate market such as Seacliff's is likely to increase as a result.

Addressing the Problem of Cycles. At one time, there wasn't very much that local financial institutions—lenders in the primary market—could do about real estate cycles in their community. If the demand for mortgage funds exceeded the supply, some of the demand would go unmet; potential home buyers would have to wait, and the banks would miss out on opportunities to make money. If supply exceeded demand, the banks would have to make relatively unprofitable investments until demand picked up again, or they might even have to let funds on deposit sit uninvested.

What local financial institutions needed was a source of additional funds to lend when demand exceeded supply, and a place to invest their surplus funds when supply exceeded demand. The creation of a secondary mortgage market helped meet both of these needs.

The Secondary Market

The primary mortgage market is where lenders make mortgage loans; the secondary mortgage market is where lenders sell those loans to investors. The secondary market is a national market in which mortgages secured by residential real estate all over the country can be bought and sold.

Buying and Selling Loans. The idea of buying or selling a loan may be unfamiliar. But a loan is an investment and, like other investments (stocks, bonds, and so on), mortgage loans can be bought and sold.

Secondary market activities:
- Buying and selling loans
- Issuing mortgage-backed securities

Valuing loans. The purchaser of a loan pays the lender the present value of the lender's right to receive payments from the borrower over the life of the loan. The present value is determined by comparing the rate of return on the loan to the rate of return available on other investments.

> **Example:** A bank makes a home loan of $190,500 at 5.5% interest. One year later, approximately $187,900 of principal remains to be paid on the loan. But if market interest rates have gone up to 7% for investments of similar quality, then the present value of the loan is less than $187,900. The present value is the amount of money it would take to generate the same amount of income at a 7% rate of return. A 5.5% return on $187,900 would be $10,335 per year. This same return could be achieved by investing $147,640 at 7% interest. So (all other factors being equal) the present value of the loan is $147,640 rather than its face value of $187,900. If the bank decided to sell the loan at this point, the buyer would pay only $147,640.

Many factors affect the value of a loan; the degree of risk associated with it is especially important. In the example, the loan was being compared to "investments of similar quality," which means investments involving approximately the same degree of risk as the loan. Of course, investors may overestimate or underestimate the riskiness of a loan or other investment, and therefore under- or overvalue it. A severe underestimation (or disregard) of risk played a central role in creating the subprime mortgage crisis. (See Chapter 4.)

Fig. 3.1 The two mortgage markets

Primary Market	Secondary Market
• Mortgage lenders such as banks and mortgage companies make loans to home buyers	• Lenders from all over the country sell loans to Fannie Mae, Freddie Mac, and other investors

Who buys loans? A lender that decides to sell some of its mortgage loans may sell them directly to another lender in a different part of the country. For example, a bank in Arizona might get cash to make more loans by selling some of its loans to a bank in New York.

More often, lenders sell their mortgage loans to:

- the Federal National Mortgage Association, known as **Fannie Mae,** or
- the Federal Home Loan Mortgage Corporation, known as **Freddie Mac.**

Fannie Mae and Freddie Mac are **government-sponsored enterprises,** or GSEs. As we'll discuss later, this means they are private companies chartered and supervised by the government.

The federal government created Fannie Mae and Freddie Mac in order to establish a strong secondary market for residential mortgage loans. They are the major purchasers of residential loans on the secondary market. (A third entity, the Government National Mortgage Association, known as Ginnie Mae, also plays a role in the secondary market. Unlike Fannie and Freddie, however, Ginnie Mae doesn't buy loans from lenders.)

A lender can "package" a group of similar loans together for sale to Fannie Mae or Freddie Mac. To be accepted for purchase, the packaged loans must meet standards of quality set by the GSE that's going to buy them. We'll discuss these standards in more detail later in the chapter.

After loans have been sold to Fannie Mae or Freddie Mac, they may be serviced by the lender that originated them, or by another entity acting as a servicer. **Loan servicing** includes tasks such as processing borrowers' payments, dealing with collection problems, and working with borrowers to prevent default.

Loans are purchased on the secondary market by the GSEs and other investors

Loan servicing:
- Processing payments
- Collections
- Preventing default

Mortgage-backed Securities. In addition to buying mortgages from lenders around the country, Fannie Mae and Freddie Mac also issue mortgage-backed securities. A **mortgage-backed security** (MBS) is an investment instrument that has mortgages as collateral; it's a type of bond. The GSEs create mortgage-backed securities by buying a large number of mortgage loans, "pooling" them together, and pledging the pool as collateral for the securities. This is called **securitizing** loans.

Mortgage-backed securities: investment instruments with pools of mortgage loans as collateral

Investors who buy mortgage-backed securities receive a return on their investment in the form of monthly payments of principal and interest from the GSE that issued the securities (Fannie Mae or Freddie Mac). As the mortgage loans in the pool are repaid by the borrowers, the GSE passes the payments of principal and interest on to the MBS investors.

For investors, buying mortgage-backed securities is much more convenient than buying the actual mortgage loans. The securities are more liquid than the mortgages, and they can be purchased in relatively small denominations.

Although most mortgage-backed securities are issued by Fannie Mae or Freddie Mac, private firms can also buy and pool mortgage loans and issue securities based on the pools. These are referred to as "private-label" mortgage-backed securities.

Functions of the Secondary Market. The development of the secondary market transformed the mortgage industry in the U.S. The secondary market gave primary market lenders a way to address an imbalance in a community's supply of and demand for mortgage funds. This moderated the adverse effects of local real estate cycles and provided a measure of stability in local markets.

Secondary market functions:
- Promotes homeownership and investment
- Provides funds
- Stabilizes primary market

> **Example:** Acme Savings & Loan has a long list of prospective borrowers who need funds for the purchase of homes. Acme's problem is that all of its savings deposits are already tied up in mortgage loans. But by selling its existing mortgage loans on the secondary market, Acme can get the funds it needs to make new loans and satisfy its customers. The effects of a tight money market in Acme's local community are moderated because Acme can get funds in the national secondary market.
>
> If Acme Savings & Loan had a surplus of deposits instead of a shortfall, it might have a difficult time finding enough local investments to absorb its funds. In this case, Acme could buy mortgages or mortgage-backed securities on the secondary market—in essence, investing in real estate located all over the country, without ever seeing the properties it is helping to finance or meeting the borrowers who are buying them.

51

Fig. 3.2 *Mortgage funds flow from the secondary market, to lenders, to borrowers*

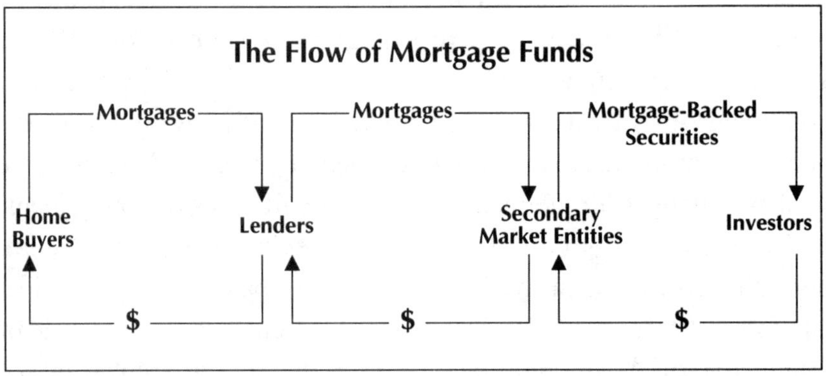

The Flow of Mortgage Funds

Mortgages → Mortgages → Mortgage-Backed Securities

Home Buyers → Lenders → Secondary Market Entities → Investors

$ — $ — $

The secondary market also draws investment funds into the mortgage industry and into real estate, substantially increasing the availability of mortgage funds nationwide and promoting home-ownership.

Availability of funds in primary market depends on secondary market

The availability of funds in the primary market now depends to a great extent on the secondary market. Figure 3.2 shows how mortgage funds flow between the primary and secondary markets. First, a home buyer receives mortgage funds from a lending institution in the primary market. Next, the lender sells the mortgage on the secondary market, most often to one of the government-sponsored enterprises (Fannie Mae or Freddie Mac). The GSE places the mortgage in a pool with many other loans and issues mortgage-backed securities based on the pool. As the GSE sells these securities to investors, more funds become available to the entity for the purchase of new mortgages from the primary market. When the GSE purchases more mortgages, more funds become available for primary market lenders to make loans to borrowers.

If a lender does not sell a loan on the secondary market (either by choice or because no one wants to buy it), the lender keeps the loan **in portfolio**—that is, it holds onto the loan and receives the principal and interest payments from the borrower. But the secondary market is such an important source of funds that most residential lenders sell

Most lenders sell most of their residential mortgage loans

the majority of their mortgage loans. In 2017, for example, lenders kept around 29% of their new home loans in portfolio, which means that approximately 71% were sold on the secondary market. (Loans kept in portfolio are sometimes referred to as **portfolio loans**.)

Fannie Mae and Freddie Mac

Now that we've provided an overview of the secondary market, let's take a closer look at the government-sponsored enterprises that help keep that market working: Fannie Mae and Freddie Mac.

Creation of the Entities

The federal government created Fannie Mae and Freddie Mac at separate points during the course of the twentieth century.

Fannie Mae. The Federal National Mortgage Association was created in 1938. It eventually became better known by the nickname Fannie Mae (based on its acronym, FNMA).

Fannie Mae was part of the federal government's efforts to fix unprecedented credit problems during the Great Depression (see Chapter 4). The government had earlier established the Federal Housing Administration and the FHA-insured loan program to help make home financing affordable again, and Fannie Mae's original purpose was to provide a secondary market for FHA-insured loans.

By 1948, Fannie Mae was purchasing FHA-insured loans on a large scale. That same year, Congress authorized Fannie Mae to start buying loans from the new VA-guaranteed loan program, which had been established in the wake of World War II.

Two decades later, Congress took steps to increase the size and scope of the secondary market, hoping to moderate the disruptive economic effects of local and regional real estate cycles. In 1968, Fannie Mae was reorganized as a government-sponsored enterprise. That meant it became a private corporation owned by stockholders, although it was still chartered by Congress and supervised by the Department of Housing and Urban Development (HUD).

At the same time that it turned Fannie Mae into a private corporation, Congress created a new wholly owned government corporation, the Government National Mortgage Association, or Ginnie Mae, as an agency within HUD. Today, Ginnie Mae guarantees securities backed by FHA and VA loans, but it does not purchase loans or sell securities on the secondary market like Fannie Mae and Freddie Mac.

Freddie Mac. The Federal Home Loan Mortgage Corporation, nicknamed Freddie Mac, was created in 1970 by the Emergency Home

Fannie Mae: Federal National Mortgage Association (FNMA)

Government-sponsored enterprise (GSE):
- Created and supervised by the federal government
- But owned by private stockholders

Freddie Mac: Federal Home Loan Mortgage Corporation (FHLMC)

Finance Act. From the outset, Freddie Mac was a government-sponsored enterprise—a private corporation owned by its stockholders but chartered by Congress and supervised by HUD. So now there were two GSEs, Fannie Mae and Freddie Mac, involved in the secondary mortgage market.

Freddie Mac's original purpose was to assist savings and loan associations, which were hit particularly hard by a recession in 1969 and 1970. Savings and loans (S&Ls) mostly made **conventional loans**—loans that aren't insured or guaranteed by the government—and there wasn't a dependable secondary market for conventional loans at that time. As a result, S&Ls had kept most of their loans in portfolio. By purchasing their conventional loans, Freddie Mac enabled S&Ls to acquire additional funds for lending. The Emergency Home Finance Act also permitted Fannie Mae to start buying conventional loans.

Conventional loans make up a substantial portion of the residential mortgage market in the United States. Because Fannie Mae and Freddie Mac buy conventional loans, they have a great impact on the mortgage industry.

GSE Status

As government-sponsored enterprises, Fannie Mae and Freddie Mac were given certain advantages over ordinary private corporations. For example, by the terms of their congressional charters, the GSEs were exempted from certain types of taxes and from some of the registration and disclosure requirements of the Securities and Exchange Commission.

On the other hand, GSE status also imposed certain restrictions and responsibilities on Fannie Mae and Freddie Mac. They were restricted

---

Fig. 3.3 Fannie Mae and Freddie Mac buy loans on the secondary market

Fannie Mae and Freddie Mac

- Government-sponsored enterprises (GSEs)
- Buy conventional, FHA, and VA loans from all types of residential lenders
- Issue mortgage-backed securities based on pools of conventional, FHA, or VA loans

by charter to investment in residential mortgage assets (essentially, mortgage loans and mortgage-backed securities). They also had to meet affordable housing goals set annually by the federal government. This requirement led the GSEs to develop and promote programs to provide affordable home financing and rental housing for low- and middle-income families and in areas historically underserved by lenders, such as inner-city neighborhoods.

GSEs required to meet affordable housing goals

MBS Programs

The first mortgage-backed securities program was actually started by Ginnie Mae in 1970. At that time, it offered investors securities backed by pools of FHA and VA loans. Both Fannie Mae and Freddie Mac eventually followed in Ginnie Mae's footsteps. They established MBS programs of their own, issuing securities backed primarily by pools of conventional mortgages.

In the 1980s, Congress changed how mortgage-backed securities were taxed and removed certain statutory restrictions to make the securities more competitive with corporate bonds. Mortgage-backed securities became steadily more popular, fueling the expansion of the secondary market.

Mortgage-backed securities could be purchased directly from Fannie Mae and Freddie Mac. These direct purchases were typically made by large institutional investors, such as life insurance companies, pension funds, and charitable endowments. Smaller companies and individual investors tended to buy and sell the securities on Wall Street, through securities dealers.

One feature of mortgage-backed securities that investors found particularly attractive was that the securities were guaranteed by the GSE that issued them. Under the terms of the guaranty, investors receive full payment from the GSE each month even if borrowers default on some of the mortgages in the pool backing the securities. (Guaranty fees and servicing fees are subtracted before payments are passed along to investors.)

Standardized Documents and Underwriting

Among the key factors that have enabled the secondary market to function successfully are standardized loan documents and underwriting rules.

Quality Control. For conventional loans, Fannie Mae and Freddie Mac publish uniform loan application forms, appraisal forms, and mortgage documents, and they also issue their own underwriting guidelines. Underwriting guidelines are the rules lenders apply when they're qualifying loan applicants and deciding whether or not to make particular loans (see Chapter 8). Conventional loans sold to Fannie Mae or Freddie Mac must comply with the entity's underwriting rules, not just the lender's own rules.

Underwriting guidelines: rules lenders apply when deciding whether to approve a loan

If a lender makes a conventional loan that doesn't conform to a GSE's underwriting guidelines or fails to use the uniform documents, the entity generally won't buy the loan from the lender. Not only that, if an entity buys a loan and later discovers that the lender violated the guidelines, the lender can be required to buy the loan back. (Of course, lenders planning to keep conventional loans in portfolio or sell them to entities other than Fannie and Freddie may apply underwriting standards that are either looser or stricter than the GSE guidelines. Even lenders planning to sell their loans to Fannie or Freddie sometimes choose to apply stricter standards; this provides a margin for error, protecting the lenders against being required to repurchase the loans later on.)

The standardized documents and underwriting guidelines are intended to ensure that loans purchased by the GSEs are of at least a certain minimum quality. Quality control is important for the GSEs and for MBS investors who are, in effect, investing in real estate sight unseen. They depend on primary market lenders to adequately evaluate borrowers and properties and make sound lending decisions.

Influencing Lending Practices. The underwriting guidelines set by Fannie Mae and Freddie Mac have strongly influenced lending practices in the primary market. For example, once the GSEs began accepting adjustable-rate mortgages (ARMs) and 15-year fixed-rate mortgages, those types of financing became readily available in the primary market. Lenders were much more willing to make those types of loans after they were assured the loans could be sold on the secondary market.

The GSEs and Subprime Loans. Loans made to borrowers with the highest credit rating (an A rating) are called **prime loans**; loans made to less creditworthy buyers are **subprime loans** (see Chapter 4). At one time, Fannie Mae and Freddie Mac bought only prime loans, at

Subprime loans: loans made to less creditworthy buyers

least as a general rule. Subprime loans generally weren't eligible for purchase because they didn't meet Fannie Mae and Freddie Mac's underwriting standards. In a sense, Fannie Mae and Freddie Mac's underwriting standards came to define the boundary between prime and subprime lending.

But that boundary began to blur around 2005, when Fannie Mae and Freddie Mac started buying significant numbers of subprime and less than prime loans (for example, "no doc" loans, where the borrowers may or may not be subprime). HUD encouraged them to do this to help meet their affordable housing goals, since many of the people affordable housing programs are intended to help can't qualify for prime loans. The GSEs loosened their underwriting guidelines and started purchasing the very top layer of subprime loans, referred to as A-minus loans. This step was controversial at the time, and it eventually had undesirable consequences.

Impact of the GSEs

The federal government gave Fannie Mae and Freddie Mac the mission of increasing the overall availability of home mortgage funds throughout the country and limiting the adverse effects of local economic conditions on real estate markets. For decades, the GSEs were considered very successful in fulfilling that mission. In addition, they were credited with helping to dramatically increase homeownership rates, reduce mortgage interest rates, make underwriting practices in the mortgage industry sounder and fairer, and provide mortgage lenders access to global capital markets as a source of funds.

Of course, Fannie Mae and Freddie Mac were also subject to criticism. Some critics contended that claims about how much the GSEs benefited the public were exaggerated. Many argued that they had grown too large and wielded too much power in the mortgage industry, limiting opportunities for other investors and enterprises. (For example, when the GSEs began gradually expanding into the subprime market, some businesses already involved in the market saw it as an unfair encroachment on their territory.) There was also criticism of how the GSEs were being run. In 2003 and 2004, the companies' reputations were seriously tarnished by massive accounting scandals, which eventually led to the resignation of top executives and the payment of huge fines ($125 million for Freddie Mac and $400 million for Fannie Mae).

The GSEs and the Subprime Crisis

In spite of these accounting scandals, Fannie Mae and Freddie Mac continued to play a major role in the mortgage industry. But only a few years later, as the subprime mortgage crisis began to unfold—with home prices plunging and mortgage default rates soaring—the two GSEs stumbled badly. While the GSEs originally had only a comparatively small share of their assets invested in the subprime market, by 2007 almost one-third of their new purchases and guarantees were of low-doc, interest-only, and other relatively risky loans. This left the GSEs badly exposed when these risky loans went into default in mounting numbers. Investors took note of the GSEs' crumbling portfolios, and the prices of Fannie Mae and Freddie Mac stocks plunged, further undermining their financial stability.

Federal Conservatorship. By 2008, foreclosures and other effects of the crisis were taking such a toll on Fannie Mae and Freddie Mac that insolvency loomed. This was an alarming prospect; if the GSEs failed, many economists thought it would have a devastating impact on the U.S. economy as a whole. In response, Congress passed the Housing and Economic Recovery Act of 2008 (HERA). In addition to measures addressing other aspects of the subprime mortgage crisis that we'll discuss in Chapter 4, HERA included provisions concerning Fannie Mae and Freddie Mac.

The Federal Housing Finance Agency (FHFA) regulates Fannie Mae and Freddie Mac

HERA created a new regulator for the two GSEs, the **Federal Housing Finance Agency** (FHFA). The previous regulator, the Office of Federal Housing Enterprise Oversight, was part of HUD, but the FHFA is an independent agency.

The statute also authorized the FHFA to take control of both Fannie Mae and Freddie Mac if that step appeared necessary, and in September 2008 the FHFA placed both entities into conservatorship. The conservatorship had no termination date and was to continue until the entities' solvency was restored.

The FHFA immediately replaced top management at Fannie Mae and Freddie Mac and withdrew voting power from their shareholders and directors. However, the most important steps taken were financial. The FHFA announced that the government would buy mortgage-backed securities from Fannie Mae and Freddie Mac as needed to achieve and maintain solvency, and that it would also directly infuse billions of dollars of capital into the two companies (by making stock purchases).

Despite this plan to restore the GSEs' financial health by buying their stock and mortgage-backed securities, the FHFA indicated that its longer-term goal was to reduce the size and economic power of Fannie Mae and Freddie Mac. Although Fannie and Freddie have now returned to profitability, the conservatorship continues and their ultimate fate is uncertain.

Federal Guaranty. As mentioned earlier, Fannie Mae and Freddie Mac guarantee their mortgage-backed securities. The GSEs promise to pay the MBS purchasers even if borrowers default on the underlying mortgages. However, a guaranty usually becomes worthless if the guarantor goes bankrupt. Before the conservatorship, the U.S. government had no legal obligation to stand behind Fannie Mae or Freddie Mac's securities if either GSE failed. Even so, it was widely believed that Fannie Mae and Freddie Mac's securities carried an implicit federal guaranty, based on the assumption that the government would almost certainly come to the rescue of MBS investors in the event that Fannie Mae or Freddie Mac became insolvent.

When the Federal Housing Finance Agency assumed control of the GSEs in 2008, the government removed any doubt about a federal guaranty. The risk seemed too great that a GSE's default on payments owed to MBS investors would devastate the entire economy. The FHFA, under its conservancy power, announced that the government would now guarantee all of the mortgage-backed securities sold by both Fannie Mae and Freddie Mac. This guaranty put the U.S. Treasury firmly behind trillions of dollars of GSE debt. It was a drastic and potentially expensive step, but now that the housing market has recovered, taxpayers have essentially received a full return of their investment. Even so, the GSEs still retain guaranty liability for some potentially bad loans.

Outline: The Primary and Secondary Markets

I. The Two Mortgage Markets

    A. Primary market: financial arena in which home buyers apply for loans and lenders originate them.

        1. Traditionally a local market, made up of local lending institutions.

        2. Problem: local market is subject to real estate cycles.

            a. When business is booming, local community's demand for mortgage funds may exceed local lenders' supply.

            b. In an economic slump, local lenders' supply of mortgage funds may exceed local demand.

            c. Secondary market helps cure problem of real estate cycles.

    B. Secondary market: national market in which mortgage loans are bought and sold.

        1. Mortgage loans can be sold like other types of investments.

            a. Present value of loan based on yield currently available on investments of similar quality (same degree of risk).

            b. Lender may sell loans to other lenders or investors in another part of the country, or to one of two government-sponsored enterprises (GSEs): Fannie Mae or Freddie Mac.

        2. Mortgage-backed securities

            a. Fannie Mae and Freddie Mac securitize the loans they buy.

            b. Each GSE buys many mortgages and pools them together; pooled loans are pledged as collateral for the securities issued by the GSE.

            c. Investors who buy mortgage-backed securities receive monthly payments of principal and interest from the GSE as pooled loans are repaid.

        3. Functions of the secondary market

            a. Moderates adverse effects of local real estate cycles.

            b. Makes funds available for mortgage loans nationwide.

            c. Promotes homeownership and real estate investment.

            d. Flow of mortgage funds: GSEs use funds from sale of securities to buy more mortgage loans from primary market, and primary market lenders use funds from sale of loans to make more loans to borrowers.

II. Fannie Mae and Freddie Mac
  A. Creation
    1. Fannie Mae (Federal National Mortgage Association)
      a. U.S. government created Fannie Mae in 1938.
      b. Original purpose: buying FHA-insured loans from lenders.
      c. Reorganized as a private corporation in 1968, but remains a government-sponsored enterprise (GSE) supervised by FHFA.
    2. Freddie Mac (Federal Home Loan Mortgage Corporation): GSE created in 1970 to help savings and loans by buying conventional loans.
  B. GSE status
    1. Fannie Mae and Freddie Mac limited to residential mortgages and mortgage-backed securities.
    2. Required to meet annual affordable housing goals.
  C. MBS programs
    1. First mortgage-backed securities program started by Ginnie Mae in 1970, backed by pools of FHA and VA loans.
    2. Fannie Mae and Freddie Mac soon followed, issuing MBSs backed by pools of conventional mortgages.
    3. Attractive to investors because MBSs were guaranteed by GSE that issued them.
  D. Standardized documents and underwriting
    1. Loans sold to GSE must meet GSE's underwriting guidelines, which are standardized across the country.
    2. GSE's rules give MBS investors confidence in loan quality.
    3. Lenders are more willing to make specific types of loans once Fannie Mae and Freddie Mac have decided to purchase them.
    4. GSEs and subprime loans
      a. GSEs originally purchased only prime loans.
      b. HUD encouraged looser underwriting standards and the purchase of A-minus subprime loans to meet affordable housing goals.
  E. Impact of the GSEs
    1. Fannie Mae and Freddie Mac credited with increased homeownership rates, reduced loan processing times, sounder and fairer underwriting, and reduced mortgage interest rates.
    2. But their reputations were tarnished first by accounting scandals and then by their role in the subprime mortgage crisis.

F. The GSEs and the Subprime Crisis

1. As crisis unfolded and many borrowers defaulted on subprime loans, the two GSEs stumbled badly.

2. Federal conservatorship

    a. In 2008, Congress put GSEs under regulation of Federal Housing Finance Agency (FHFA) as part of plan to address fallout of crisis.

    b. Later that year, FHFA took control of both GSEs and put them into federal conservatorship until both could become financially stable again.

    c. To help Fannie Mae and Freddie Mac achieve solvency again, FHFA purchased mortgage-backed securities from both GSEs and invested billions in their stock.

3. Federal guaranty

    a. Previously, Fannie Mae and Freddie Mac guaranteed their MBSs, but federal government had no legal obligation to back up those guaranties.

    b. Under conservancy power, federal government now guarantees all mortgage-backed securities sold by Fannie Mae and Freddie Mac.

Key Terms

Primary mortgage market: The financial arena in which mortgage loans are originated, where lenders make loans to home buyers.

Secondary mortgage market: The financial arena in which investors buy mortgage loans from lenders throughout the country.

Loan origination: Processing a loan application, deciding whether to approve or reject the application, and funding the loan.

Real estate cycles: Ups and downs in the level of activity in a local real estate market, where a boom may be followed by a slump, or vice versa.

Law of supply and demand: A basic rule of economics which holds that prices (or interest rates) tend to rise when supply decreases or demand increases, and tend to fall when supply increases or demand decreases.

Disintermediation: When depositors withdraw their savings from financial institutions and put the money into other types of investments that have higher yields.

Fannie Mae and Freddie Mac: Two government-sponsored enterprises that play a major role in the secondary market; they buy loans that conform to their underwriting standards and (using the loans as collateral) issue and guarantee mortgage-backed securities.

Government-sponsored enterprise (GSE): An entity that is privately owned but created, chartered, and supervised by the government. A GSE functions as a private corporation but must fulfill special legal responsibilities imposed by the government.

Mortgage-backed security (MBS): An investment instrument that has a pool of mortgage loans as collateral; usually issued by Fannie Mae or Freddie Mac, but may be a private label MBS instead.

MBS guaranty: A guaranty offered by an issuer of mortgage-backed securities, which provides that the MBS investors will receive the expected payments of principal and interest from the issuer, even if borrowers fail to make their payments on some of the pooled mortgage loans.

Loan servicing: Processing loan payments, keeping payment records, and handling collection problems and defaults. The entity that services a loan is not necessarily the lender that originated it.

Securitization: When Fannie Mae, Freddie Mac, or other secondary market participants create mortgage-backed securities by buying a large number of mortgage loans, "pooling" them together, and pledging the pool as collateral for the securities.

Portfolio loan: A mortgage loan that the lender keeps in its own investment portfolio until the loan is repaid (instead of selling the loan on the secondary market).

Conventional loan: A loan that is not insured or guaranteed by a government agency.

Subprime loan: A loan that is riskier for the lender than a standard (prime) loan, often made to a borrower who would not be able to qualify for standard financing, and typically involving a higher interest rate and fees to make up for the extra risk of default.

Chapter Quiz

1. The Cantors just borrowed money from Seacliff Savings to finance the purchase of a home. This transaction took place in the:
   a. subprimary market
   b. primary market
   c. secondary market
   d. None of the above

2. The federal government created Fannie Mae and Freddie Mac in order to:
   a. originate residential mortgage loans nationwide
   b. help moderate the adverse effects of real estate cycles
   c. bring inflation under control at the local level
   d. stimulate disintermediation

3. A lending institution with more mortgage loan applicants than available loan funds would be likely to:
   a. buy mortgage-backed securities from another lender
   b. issue mortgage-backed securities in the primary market
   c. buy mortgages on the secondary market
   d. sell mortgages to Fannie Mae or Freddie Mac

4. A lender cannot sell a mortgage loan to Fannie Mae unless:
   a. it followed Fannie Mae's underwriting guidelines
   b. it is a federally certified primary market entity
   c. it is a federally insured savings and loan association
   d. the loan is either FHA-insured or VA-guaranteed

5. A mortgage-backed security is a type of:
   a. mortgage loan
   b. corporate debt certificate
   c. investment instrument
   d. guaranty

6. Taking a home buyer's loan application is a step in the:
   a. loan servicing process
   b. loan origination process
   c. loan guaranty process
   d. MBS process

7. Investors prefer to buy mortgage-backed securities instead of mortgages because the securities are:
   a. less liquid, and therefore safer
   b. serviced by the federal government
   c. guaranteed
   d. None of the above

8. Most residential mortgage loans are:
   a. kept in portfolio
   b. sold on the secondary market
   c. sold on the primary market
   d. None of the above

9. An investor's return on mortgage-backed securities usually takes the form of:
   a. monthly servicing fees
   b. annual dividends from the mortgage pool
   c. monthly payments of principal and interest
   d. annual installment bonds

10. As government-sponsored enterprises, Fannie Mae and Freddie Mac are:
    a. private corporations owned by stockholders
    b. government agencies financed with taxpayer dollars
    c. regulated by the Federal Housing Finance Agency (FHFA)
    d. Both a) and c)

Answer Key

1. b. Loan transactions take place in the primary market.

2. b. Moderating the negative effects of local real estate cycles and stabilizing the primary market were among the government's goals in creating Fannie Mae and Freddie Mac.

3. d. A mortgage lender with more loan applicants than funds could raise the money to make more loans by selling some of its existing loans to Fannie Mae or Freddie Mac, or to some other secondary market investor.

4. a. A loan that's going to be sold to one of the GSEs must comply with that entity's underwriting guidelines (not just the lender's own guidelines).

5. c. A mortgage-backed security is a type of investment instrument.

6. b. Loan origination refers to processing the loan application, making the decision to approve the loan, and funding the loan.

7. c. Mortgage-backed securities are usually guaranteed by the entity that issues them. Under a 2008 conservatorship, MBSs issued by Fannie Mae and Freddie Mac are also guaranteed by the federal government.

8. b. Nowadays, mortgage lenders tend to sell most of their loans on the secondary market.

9. c. MBS investors usually receive monthly payments of principal and interest from the entity that issued the securities.

10. d. The government-sponsored enterprises are private corporations owned by their stockholders, but supervised by the Federal Housing Finance Agency, an independent agency.

Chapter 4
The Mortgage Industry

Description of the Mortgage Industry

- Basic steps in the mortgage process
- Loan origination
- Types of loan originators
- Government regulation of loan originators

Mortgage Lenders

- Types of lenders
- Government regulation of mortgage lenders
- Alternative sources of financing

Government Intervention in Mortgage Lending

- Great Depression
- Savings and loan crisis
- Mortgage market and financial crisis

Introduction

The previous chapter explained the relationship between the primary market and the secondary market. These two markets give the mortgage industry its basic structure. In this chapter, we'll take a closer look at how the mortgage industry works, with an emphasis on the primary market. We'll also explain how actions and activities in one market can have a significant impact on the other market.

We'll start the chapter with an overview of the different types of entities that play a role in the primary market. As you will see, those entities may be involved in some or all of the steps in the mortgage lending process. The second half of the chapter describes how major economic crises have periodically led the federal government to intervene in the mortgage industry. In addition to the Great Depression in the 1930s and the savings and loan crisis in the 1970s, we'll discuss the crisis that unfolded in the residential mortgage market in 2007–2008 and spread to the rest of the economy.

Description of the Mortgage Industry

We'll begin our examination of the mortgage industry with a basic overview of residential mortgage transactions. We'll touch on the basic steps in the mortgage process, define "loan originator," and explain retail versus wholesale lending.

Basic Steps in the Mortgage Process

In its most basic form, the residential mortgage process will involve:

- a home buyer who needs a mortgage loan;
- a loan originator, who works with the buyer to complete the loan application and gather supporting documentation and other material to get the loan application approved; and
- a mortgage lender, who reviews the completed application and funds the loan (if the application meets the lender's underwriting standards).

Once the loan has been made, there is still more to be done. During the repayment period, a mortgage loan requires servicing: ongoing administration that includes payment processing, loan modification (if necessary), and related duties. A lender may choose to keep loan servicing in-house or it can transfer these duties to a separate entity, called a **loan servicer**.

Also, as we discussed in Chapter 3, the mortgage lender may decide to sell the loan to an investor on the secondary market. This transfer of loan ownership could have an impact on the borrower later on if she has trouble making payments or has some other problem with the loan.

Loan servicing involves processing payments and dealing with the borrower during the repayment period

Loan Origination

Loan origination refers to the processing of a loan application, including collecting all the necessary information about the borrowers and submitting the required documentation to the lender for review. In the past, nearly all mortgage loans were originated in basically the same way. Each stage of the process was handled by a lender who was sought out by the prospective home buyers. An employee of the lender (typically called a loan officer) would help the buyers decide what type of financing they wanted and help them prepare their application. The application would be submitted to the lender's in-house underwriting department, where the buyers' financial situation and the value of the property serving as collateral would be reviewed. If the loan application was approved, the lender would fund the loan.

Transactions like this are sometimes referred to as **retail loans** or **direct lending**. Retail transactions are still common, but they are no longer the only type of mortgage transaction. Many loan originations are much more complicated now, because of the growth of the secondary market, the emergence of national financial institutions, the rise of mortgage companies, and the presence of online lenders.

Retail lending: the lender deals directly with the borrower

Today, the person who helps buyers apply for a loan—the **loan originator**—may or may not be the lender's employee, and the lender may or may not be the ultimate owner of the loan. If asked, many buyers may not be able to identify exactly who is providing the money they're using to purchase their house. To understand how the role of a loan originator has evolved, we need to take a moment to discuss some historical developments in the financing industry.

Wholesale Lending. In the 1990s, federal regulations were loosened to allow interstate bank mergers, which led to the development of very large lenders doing business nationwide. These large lenders came to

Wholesale lending: the borrower deals with a loan correspondent, who represents the lender

dominate the mortgage industry. In 2017, about half of U.S. mortgage loans came from ten lenders. Large lenders are often **wholesale lenders**: lenders that have vast quantities of money available for lending, but use outside entities to find their borrowers.

As we have already noted, a retail lender works directly with customers (home buyers) and usually handles the entire origination process from the application through closing. In contrast to the retail lender, the wholesale lender is much more removed from the buyer, working through an intermediary to handle the loan application process. Intermediaries in a wholesale lending transaction may be referred to as **loan correspondents** or **mortgage brokers**.

Mortgage brokers and loan correspondents find borrowers for wholesale lenders

Using loan correspondents or mortgage brokers to handle loan origination reduces the lender's overhead. For example, a wholesale lender can save on the cost of local office space and employees. On the other hand, if mistakes occur during the loan application process, a wholesale lender is less likely to know about it or have the ability to prevent similar mistakes from being made in the future.

In any case, it's important to keep in mind that several different entities can play a role in the mortgage process: one entity may underwrite the loan, another may fund the loan, yet another may service the loan, and still another may end up owning the loan.

Types of Loan Originators

Now let's take a look at the two main types of loan originators: loan officers and mortgage brokers.

Loan Officers. As was explained earlier, if a home buyer is applying directly to the lender for a mortgage loan, the loan originator for that kind of transaction will be the lender's loan officer. The loan officer will help the buyer complete the loan application and make sure all the necessary financial documents and supporting information have been submitted and verified. The loan officer will then pass the completed application on to the lender's underwriting department, for further review and a funding decision. While you may encounter some confusion or disagreement surrounding the term "loan officer," it generally refers to a loan originator who is processing loan applications for a specific mortgage lender.

Loan officer: a loan originator working for a particular lender

Mortgage Brokers. In contrast to a loan officer who works for a single lender, a mortgage broker is usually an independent contractor who works with multiple lenders. A mortgage broker is an intermediary, a go-between who brings borrowers together with lenders in exchange for a commission. Home buyers go to a mortgage broker for help in finding a loan; the broker informs the buyers about various financing options that are offered by different lenders.

Mortgage broker: a loan originator who usually works with multiple lenders

After the buyers have decided which type of loan they want to apply for, the mortgage broker helps them complete a loan application. Although the mortgage broker has access to the underwriting standards for each lender he represents, a mortgage broker can give the buyers only a preliminary loan approval. The actual underwriting decision and formal loan approval must be issued by the lender.

Table-funded loans. As we've said, mortgage brokers are intermediaries for mortgage lenders, and usually don't use any of their own assets to fund the loan. However, certain kinds of transactions—table-funded loans—may create the impression that the mortgage broker is acting as both the loan originator and the lender, when in fact the true lender is another entity.

In a **table-funded loan**, a mortgage broker stays involved in the lending process all the way to closing, even naming itself as the originating lender in the loan documents. However, the broker assigns the rights to that loan to the true mortgage lender during the closing process. Federal regulators have ruled that table-funded loans are never really "funded" by the mortgage broker, as the actual loan funds are carefully timed to be delivered at closing by the true lender. In this type of transaction, it's easy to understand how a borrower might think the mortgage broker is acting as the initial mortgage lender.

Government Regulation of Loan Originators

Recognizing both the important role loan originators play in the mortgage industry and the potential for predatory practices, Congress passed the **Secure and Fair Enforcement for Mortgage Licensing Act**. This law is often called the SAFE Mortgage Licensing Act. SAFE is designed to prevent abusive practices during loan origination by:

- requiring all residential mortgage loan originators to be state-licensed or federally registered;

- requiring all states to comply with standard reporting requirements and use uniform license application forms for state-licensed loan originators;
- increasing the tracking and reporting of loan originator information (background checks and fingerprinting, employment history, and disciplinary actions) across state lines;
- imposing fiduciary duties on all loan originators; and
- enhancing consumer protection and anti-fraud measures.

SAFE requires residential loan originators to be registered or licensed

Loan originators who are employed by a depository institution (or a subsidiary) generally must be federally registered, but do not have to be state-licensed. All other loan originators generally must be state-licensed. Both federally registered and state-licensed originators are listed in the Nationwide Mortgage Licensing System and Registry. Annual renewal of this registration is required.

Real estate agents who receive compensation for arranging loans must be licensed loan originators

Although real estate agents are usually exempt from the requirements of this law, an agent is considered a loan originator (and thus must be licensed) if she is compensated by a lender or a mortgage broker for helping to arrange a loan.

Mortgage Lenders

Once a loan originator has helped a home buyer complete a loan application, the next step is submitting that application to a mortgage lender for evaluation and, hopefully, approval. For a loan officer, this means submitting the application to the underwriting department of the lender she works for. For a mortgage broker, it means submitting the application to the lender chosen by the buyer with the broker's advice.

Types of Lenders

The majority of home buyers obtain financing from one of these four types of lenders in the primary market:

- commercial banks,
- thrift institutions,
- credit unions, and
- mortgage companies.

Commercial Banks. As their name suggests, commercial banks originally developed to serve commercial enterprises: merchants and other businesses. At first, banks just provided a secure place for keeping money. Later they began paying interest on deposits and using those deposited funds to make loans. They also began offering what are now called checking accounts to facilitate commercial transactions.

Commercial banks accept deposits and make loans

Commercial banks have always emphasized commercial lending, supplying capital for business ventures and construction activities. Originally, residential mortgages weren't a significant part of their lending business. Various developments in the twentieth century, including regulatory changes and the expansion of the secondary market, helped make residential mortgage lending more attractive to commercial banks.

Traditionally, commercial banks didn't make many home mortgage loans

In the U.S., commercial banks are either national banks (chartered by the federal government) or state banks (chartered by a state government).

Commercial banks should be distinguished from **investment banks**. Investment banks are securities firms, commonly known as stock brokerages. They raise capital for corporations, arrange for the issuance of government and corporate bonds, manage corporate finances, and handle mergers and acquisitions. They also provide investment advice to clients and manage their investments. Investment banks don't accept deposits from individuals or make loans to individuals, and they aren't regulated in the same way that commercial banks and other depository institutions are.

Investment banks: securities firms involved in corporate finance

In the past, banks were required to choose between commercial banking services and investment banking services; a bank was prohibited from offering a combination of these services. With the passage of the Financial Services Modernization Act (also called the Gramm-Leach-Bliley Act), it became legal for a holding company to have a bank, a securities firm, and an insurance company as subsidiaries. (A holding company is basically a corporate entity created for the purpose of owning other companies.)

Thrift Institutions. Savings banks and savings and loan associations are generally grouped together and referred to as thrift institutions, or simply as **thrifts**. Like commercial banks, thrifts are governed by either a federal or a state charter.

Thrifts: savings and loans and savings banks

Savings banks started out in the early nineteenth century by offering financial services to small depositors, especially immigrants and members of the new industrial working class. They are sometimes called mutual savings banks, because many were originally organized as mutual companies, owned by and operated for the benefit of their depositors rather than stockholders.

Savings and loan associations (S&Ls) also developed in the nineteenth century. Originally called building and loan associations, S&Ls were formed in local communities to finance the construction of homes. An association was designed to serve only its members, who would pool their assets and then take turns using the money to build houses for themselves. After all the members had satisfied their financing needs, the association would be dissolved. Over the years, however, savings and loan associations began to make some loans to nonmembers, and they eventually became permanent institutions.

The institutions' traditional emphasis on home mortgages and savings accounts was the basis for the name "thrifts," and for much of their history they were restricted by law to providing only a limited range of services. Regulatory changes in the 1970s and early 1980s allowed thrifts to become more like commercial banks. For example, they began offering checking accounts as well as savings accounts, and they got involved in other types of lending besides home mortgages. Deregulation in this arena was one of the factors that led to the savings and loan crisis, discussed later in this chapter.

Thrifts make mortgage loans and other consumer loans

Today, thrifts offer essentially the same consumer services as commercial banks: checking accounts, savings accounts, credit cards, and so on. In addition to home mortgage loans, thrifts make consumer loans, providing financing for the purchase of furniture, appliances, and cars. They also offer financial services to businesses, but typically on a much smaller scale than commercial banks.

Credit union: a nonprofit depository institution that serves the members of a particular group

Credit Unions. Credit unions got their start in the U.S. in the early twentieth century. They are nonprofit cooperative organizations designed to serve the members of a particular group, such as a labor union or a professional association, or the employees of a large company. Like other depository institutions, credit unions may be organized under either a federal or state charter.

Originally, credit unions didn't make mortgage loans. They specialized instead in small, personal loans that were often unsecured. (In other words, no collateral was required.) This type of loan generally wasn't available from banks or savings and loans at that time, and small borrowers had previously turned to pawn shops and loan sharks. Credit unions provided an alternative.

Later on, many credit unions emphasized home equity loans. A home equity loan is a mortgage on the borrower's equity in the home she already owns (see Chapter 5). These are generally short-term loans. The legislation deregulating financial institutions in the early 1980s allowed credit unions to begin offering their members long-term home purchase loans as well.

As nonprofit organizations, credit unions are generally exempt from taxation. That advantage, along with certain others, enables credit unions to loan money to their members at interest rates that are slightly below market rates. They can also offer interest rates on deposits that are slightly higher than market rates. Credit unions have been significantly increasing their involvement in mortgage lending in recent years.

Mortgage Companies. The types of mortgage lenders we've looked at so far—banks, thrifts, and credit unions—are depository institutions: government-regulated entities that hold customers' deposits and provide a wide range of financial services in addition to offering mortgage loans. In contrast, **mortgage companies** are not depository institutions, and their business is focused exclusively on mortgage lending and affiliated services.

Mortgage companies (aka mortgage bankers) are not depository institutions

Mortgage companies are also called mortgage banking companies or mortgage bankers. The first ones in the U.S. were established in the 1930s. Today, some mortgage companies are direct subsidiaries or affiliates of large banks or thrifts, but there are still many that aren't. Mortgage companies that aren't associated with a bank or a thrift are called independent mortgage companies.

Note that some mortgage companies engage in mortgage brokerage activities (helping buyers find financing) as well as mortgage banking (making loans). A business called "Acme Mortgage" might be strictly a mortgage banker, strictly a mortgage broker, or a combination of the two, making loans to some borrowers and providing mortgage brokerage services to others. In addition, many mortgage companies are involved in loan servicing activities.

Since mortgage companies aren't depository institutions, they can't use customers' deposits to fund loans. They have to raise the

Fig. 4.1 Mortgage companies may be mortgage bankers, mortgage brokers, or both

Mortgage Banker	Mortgage Broker
• A type of lender	• An intermediary, not a lender
• Takes buyer's application, makes underwriting decision, and funds loan	• Helps buyer choose and apply for a loan

necessary capital in other ways. For example, a mortgage company may have a line of credit with a financial institution, draw on its line of credit for funds to make mortgage loans, and then sell the mortgages to secondary market investors. The mortgage company then uses the proceeds of those sales to repay its own creditor and to make more loans. Alternatively, a mortgage company may simply act as a loan correspondent, making loans on behalf of large investors such as pension funds or insurance companies. (Banks and thrifts may also act as loan correspondents, but mortgage companies specialized in that role early on.)

Government Regulation of Mortgage Lenders

Depository institutions are subject to a complicated system of regulation. There are state regulators for state-chartered institutions and federal regulators for federally chartered institutions. Not only that, different types of institutions are regulated by different state or federal agencies. On the federal level, the regulatory agencies include the Federal Reserve System, the Federal Deposit Insurance Corporation, the National Credit Union Administration, the Office of the Comptroller of the Currency, and the Consumer Financial Protection Bureau (discussed below).

Regulators periodically examine depository institutions

Depository institutions undergo periodic examinations by government regulators to ensure that their operations comply with the law. The Federal Financial Institutions Examination Council is an interagency body that prescribes examination procedures for federal regulators. In addition to enforcing financial regulations concerning capital requirements, reserve requirements, accounting procedures, and so on, regulators enforce federal consumer protection laws and fair lending laws, such as the Truth in Lending Act, the Real Estate

Settlement Procedures Act, and the Equal Credit Opportunity Act. (These laws are covered in Chapter 14.)

Among the various types of mortgage lenders, independent mortgage companies have historically been subject to the least regulation. In 2010, however, the Consumer Financial Protection Act was passed as part of the larger Dodd-Frank Act (discussed later in this chapter). Among other things, this law established a new independent regulatory agency within the Federal Reserve, the **Consumer Financial Protection Bureau** (CFPB), which is responsible for supervising "non-bank" entities that originate, broker, or service residential mortgage loans or offer foreclosure relief services. The CFPB has formulated rules intended specifically for these independent, non-bank mortgage companies.

In addition, the CFPB was given primary rulemaking and enforcement authority for the federal consumer protection laws and fair lending laws covered in Chapter 14. In this capacity, the CFPB has authority over depository institutions as well as non-bank entities.

Alternative Sources of Financing

Most home buyers obtain financing from one of the four types of lenders we've discussed so far—from a bank, a thrift, a credit union, or a mortgage company. But there are other sources of financing.

Sometimes an individual with capital to invest will make mortgage loans to home buyers on a small scale. This type of private lending business is legal in some places and not in others, depending on state licensing laws and various other restrictions. **Usury laws** (limits on interest rates for certain types of loans), disclosure laws, and predatory lending laws also may apply to this type of transaction.

Private investment groups such as real estate limited partnerships and real estate investment trusts put a great deal of money into real estate. They generally don't offer loans directly to buyers, however.

Probably the most important alternative for buyers is seller financing. Home builders and residential developers frequently offer financing to buyers who purchase homes or lots from them. And ordinary home sellers sometimes provide part or even all of the financing necessary for the purchase of their property. Home sellers are an especially important source of financing in periods when institutional loans are hard to come by or market interest rates are high. Seller financing is covered in Chapter 13.

Sellers are an important source of financing when institutional loans are expensive

Government Intervention in Mortgage Lending

In addition to regulating mortgage lenders, from time to time the federal government has intervened in the mortgage industry more directly. The creation of Fannie Mae and Freddie Mac, discussed in Chapter 3, is an example of this type of intervention. There are some other government interventions that you should be aware of, because of their long-term effects on the industry. These have occurred in response to the Great Depression in the 1930s, the savings and loan crisis in the 1980s, and the mortgage market and financial crisis in 2007–2008.

The Great Depression and the Mortgage Industry

The nineteenth century was a period of rapid growth in the United States, as the country expanded westward. Money poured into investments that promised high returns, including real estate. In addition to depository institutions, many private investors got involved in mortgage lending. The mortgage business remained prosperous through the first decades of the twentieth century, up until the Depression.

The economic collapse of the 1930s had a severe impact on housing and mortgage lending in the U.S. As unemployment rose to staggering levels, hundreds of thousands of homeowners throughout the country defaulted on their mortgages. At the worst point, about half the outstanding home mortgage debt was in default. Foreclosures became commonplace; government officials estimated that in 1933 nearly one thousand homes were foreclosed on every day. Some states declared a moratorium on foreclosures, allowing defaulting borrowers to stay in their homes. Many financial institutions failed, and mortgage lending and home construction came to a standstill. As part of the New Deal, a broad plan to pull the nation out of the economic crisis, the federal government stepped in to try to revive the mortgage industry.

Several of the agencies and programs that were instituted at this point long outlasted the Depression. These include the Federal Housing Administration (FHA), which encouraged residential lending by offering mortgage insurance to protect against foreclosure losses; the Federal Home Loan Bank Board (FHLBB), which assisted savings and loans; and, as we discussed in Chapter 3, the Federal National Mortgage Association (Fannie Mae), which provided a secondary market for FHA-insured loans.

Mortgage lending and home construction virtually ceased during the Depression

One important reaction to the Depression foreclosures was the introduction of long-term, fixed-rate, amortized home purchase loans. The mortgages offered through the FHA-insured loan program could be paid off over a 20- or 30-year term at an unchanging rate of interest. They were also fully amortized: each monthly payment included a share of the principal as well as interest, and the regular monthly payments were sufficient to pay off the principal in full by the end of the term. (Amortization is covered in Chapter 6.)

These features of FHA-insured mortgages made it much easier for home buyers to avoid default and foreclosure. Once that advantage was well-established, lenders began to offer long-term, fixed-rate, fully amortized loans outside of the FHA program. By the early 1940s, these longer-term loans had become standard. They became even more common after World War II, when many returning veterans bought homes with financing obtained through the Veterans Administration's new guaranteed loan program.

In the late 1990s and the early years of this century, many home buyers were attracted to adjustable-rate mortgages with low teaser rates, loans with interest-only payments, or partially amortized loans that had lower monthly payments but required a large balloon payment after only five or seven years. As we'll discuss later in this chapter, that shift to "nontraditional" mortgage loan products, combined with lax underwriting standards, contributed significantly to the 2008 financial crisis. One response to the crisis was a shift back to the standard 30-year, fixed-rate loan. (The pendulum continues to swing, however; adjustable-rate mortgages and some other types of nontraditional loans have gradually regained favor since the crisis, although the riskiest types have not.)

Depression foreclosures led to the introduction of long-term, fixed-rate, amortized mortgage loans

---

Fig. 4.2 Mortgage loans changed dramatically after the Great Depression

Standard Loan, circa 1930	**Standard Loan, circa 1940**
• Renewable at lender's discretion every five years, and interest rate could go up	• Thirty-year term
	• Fixed interest rate
• Interest-only payments; full principal amount still owed at end of term	• Amortized so that regular payments pay off all principal and interest by end of term

The Savings and Loan Crisis

From the 1950s until the 1980s, savings and loans were the largest source of mortgage financing

Another chapter in the history of mortgage lending that had far-reaching effects was the savings and loan crisis in the 1980s. Savings and loans dominated the U.S. residential mortgage industry in the 1950s, yet 30 years later many S&Ls faced insolvency.

Market interest rates skyrocketed in the late 1970s and early 1980s

Market interest rates soared to unprecedented heights in the late 1970s and early 1980s. As a result, lending institutions—especially savings and loan associations—began experiencing financial difficulties. Regulations imposed a decade earlier limited how much interest savings and loans could pay their depositors, so S&Ls now found themselves unable to offer attractive returns. They ended up losing a large portion of their deposits to competing investments such as money market funds and government bonds. (See the discussion of disintermediation in Chapter 3.) Making matters much worse, the S&Ls had most of their funds tied up in long-term mortgages at what were now considered very low interest rates.

Congress passed several bills that loosened regulatory restrictions on savings and loan associations, hoping that more people would make deposits with them. However, things just got worse as some S&Ls tried new, riskier investments in order to get back into black ink. The result was a sharp increase in the failure rate of savings and loans. Hundreds of federally insured S&Ls became insolvent, and eventually the Federal Savings and Loan Insurance Corporation could not meet all of the liabilities. Finally, to protect S&L depositors, the federal government stepped in. Congress passed the **Financial Institutions Reform, Recovery, and Enforcement Act** (FIRREA) in 1989, which imposed new rules on savings and loans to prevent high-risk transactions. FIRREA also eliminated the Federal Savings and Loan Insurance Corporation, reorganizing the Federal Deposit Insurance Corporation (FDIC) to cover S&L deposits as well as bank deposits. The bailout of the savings and loan industry ultimately cost taxpayers about $124 billion.

Hundreds of S&Ls became insolvent, leading to a government bailout of the industry

Although the savings and loan industry gradually recovered from its crisis, there were far fewer savings and loan associations now than there were in the 1970s. The composition of the primary mortgage market changed. Where S&Ls had once dominated, mortgage companies came to the forefront. (More recently, very large banks have come to play as important a role as mortgage companies.)

The Mortgage Market and Financial Crisis

The final event that we'll discuss in our history of the mortgage industry is the financial crisis that began with the collapse of the housing bubble in 2006–2007 and came to a head in 2008. An epidemic of subprime mortgage foreclosures had far-reaching consequences and ended up crippling the entire U.S. economy (which in turn affected the global economy). We'll describe the events leading up to the crisis and how the government responded.

Housing bubble: an artificial increase in property values

In the half-dozen years prior to 2006, easy-to-obtain home loans and high profits for real estate investors became the norm. With property values climbing steadily, many buyers came to view their homes not merely as a place to live but as an investment opportunity. To make the most of their investment, they wanted mortgage loans that required only a minimal downpayment and permitted them to make very low monthly payments in the early years of the loan term. They expected ever-increasing home prices would allow them to sell or refinance their homes before the monthly payments increased or a balloon payment became due.

Many lenders promoted nontraditional mortgage products tailored to this new type of customer. For example, borrowers could buy homes using piggyback loans: primary and secondary loans from the same lender that equaled the total purchase price of the home—meaning no downpayment was required. (Piggyback loans are also discussed in Chapter 10.) The features that made nontraditional mortgages more flexible for borrowers also made the risk of default much greater. In addition, many of these loans with high-risk features were subprime loans, made to borrowers with low credit scores or other financial problems. (Subprime lending made up less than 5% of home mortgage originations in the early 1990s, but it accounted for about 20% of originations in 2006.) On top of that, some lenders were asking borrowers for little or no documentation of their ability to repay the loans. Reckless and/or predatory lending practices were helping borrowers buy houses they couldn't actually afford, adding fuel to the hot housing market.

The risky subprime market grew rapidly between 1994 and 2006

Then the bubble burst. Home prices had been artificially inflated by the investment climate and other forces; now, obeying the law of supply and demand, prices started falling, and kept falling. (In some parts of the country, houses lost a third or even half of their value in the course of just a couple of years.) At the same time, many homeowners suddenly had to make much higher mortgage payments, as interest rates rose on adjustable-rate loans, or introductory low-payment periods ended, or both. Because they'd made very small downpayments, overextended borrowers had little or no equity in their homes, so refinancing wasn't an option. And due to the poor market, selling the property wouldn't generate enough funds to cover the mortgage debt. Loan defaults surged.

As the housing market crumbled, financial losses spilled into other areas of the economy. The U.S. economy entered a **recession**—an extended period of negative economic growth—in December 2007, although the recession wasn't formally declared until a year later.

People were losing their jobs at an alarming rate, which caused the foreclosure epidemic to spread from subprime borrowers to homeowners in general. Financial institutions that held large portfolios of mortgage-backed securities took heavy hits and in some cases went bankrupt. Fannie Mae and Freddie Mac faced staggering losses.

When the severity and extent of the downturn started becoming clear, the federal government took action. Over the course of 2007–2008 the Fed cut key interest rates nearly to zero, trying to stimulate economic activity (see Chapter 2). In July 2008 Congress passed the Housing and Economic Recovery Act (HERA), which was designed to shore up the housing market in various ways; one HERA program offered refinancing options for struggling homeowners, for example. At the beginning of September, the government placed Fannie Mae and Freddie Mac into conservatorship (see Chapter 3).

HERA: federal law passed to strengthen the housing market

However, the housing market and general economic conditions continued to worsen. Home prices had fallen so far that millions of homeowners found themselves "underwater," owing more on their mortgage than their property was worth. In other words, they had negative equity in their homes. For investors as well as consumers, alarm was turning into panic. The stock market dropped sharply, inflicting further damage. (It lost over half its value during the crisis.)

In October 2008 Congress passed an emergency bailout bill known as the Troubled Asset Relief Program, or TARP. As authorized by the TARP bill, the Treasury Department bought huge amounts of the stock and assets of the country's largest banks and other financial institutions deemed "too big to fail" (because of the disastrous impact

TARP: $700 billion bailout law

their bankruptcy would have on the economy). The TARP purchases protected the financial institutions' solvency and also made more funds available for lending.

More legislation followed. Most notably, in 2010 Congress passed the **Dodd-Frank Wall Street Reform and Consumer Protection Act**, significantly toughening the government's financial regulatory scheme and addressing problematic lending and appraisal practices that contributed to the crisis. (We discuss specific provisions of the Dodd-Frank Act in other chapters.)

Dodd-Frank Act brought about sweeping changes to the financial regulatory scheme and mortgage industry practices

The recession officially lasted from December 2007 through June 2009 in the U.S., but the mortgage industry and many other segments of the economy took several years more to fully recover. The crisis was the worst economic downturn since the Great Depression, over 70 years earlier.

Outline: The Mortgage Industry

I. Basic Steps in the Mortgage Process
   A. Residential mortgage process involves:
      1. a home buyer,
      2. a loan originator (who takes the loan application), and
      3. a mortgage lender (who makes the loan).
   B. Loan originator and lender may or may not be the same entity.
   C. Often lender arranges for another entity (a loan servicer) to service the loan, processing payments and so on.

II. Loan Origination
   A. Retail vs. wholesale lenders
      1. Retail lenders deal directly with borrowers; borrower doesn't apply for the loan through a mortgage broker or other intermediary.
      2. With wholesale lenders, borrower applies for the loan through an intermediary—a mortgage broker or loan correspondent (not an employee of the lender).
   B. Types of loan originators
      1. Loan officers work for a retail lender; they help borrowers complete loan applications and submit them to the lender's underwriting department.
      2. Mortgage brokers are usually independent contractors who work with multiple lenders; they are intermediaries who bring borrower and lender together in exchange for a commission.
   C. Government regulation of loan originators
      1. Secure and Fair Enforcement for Mortgage Licensing Act (SAFE Act) requires residential mortgage loan originators to be either state-licensed or federally registered.
      2. Real estate agents who receive commissions for helping arrange loans must be licensed.

III. Mortgage Lenders
   A. Four main types of residential lenders: commercial banks, thrift institutions, credit unions, and mortgage companies.
   B. Commercial banks
      1. Commercial banks were originally oriented toward commercial lending for activities like business ventures and construction; residential mortgages were a small part of their business.
      2. Regulatory changes made residential lending more attractive to commercial banks.

3. Commercial banks are chartered either by the federal government or the state government.

4. Commercial banks are not the same thing as investment banks.

    a. Investment banks focus on selling securities and underwriting offerings of stocks and bonds. They don't provide ordinary banking services or make loans to individuals.

C. Thrift institutions

1. Savings banks: traditionally oriented toward small depositors, offering savings accounts and making mortgage and consumer loans; today, savings banks offer the same services as commercial banks.

2. Savings and loan associations: originally created to finance home construction with services only available to members; later they began issuing loans to nonmembers and taking deposits from small depositors. Deregulation in the 1970s allowed S&Ls to become more like banks.

D. Credit unions

1. Credit unions are nonprofit cooperatives that serve members of a particular group, such as a labor union or employees of a large company.

2. Credit unions originally specialized in small, unsecured loans, but expanded into home equity loans and eventually home purchase loans.

E. Mortgage companies

1. Mortgage companies, also known as mortgage bankers, are not depository institutions. They focus entirely on mortgage loans.

2. Mortgage companies may borrow money, use it to originate mortgages, and sell the mortgages to secondary market investors.

3. Mortgage companies may also act as loan correspondents, originating loans on behalf of a large investor and servicing the loans in exchange for servicing fees.

4. Some mortgage companies are strictly mortgage bankers and some are strictly mortgage brokers, while others engage in both activities.

    a. Mortgage banker: originates loans.

    b. Mortgage broker: merely brings borrower and lender together.

F. Government regulation of mortgage lenders

1. Regulators of federally chartered depository institutions include the Federal Reserve System, Federal Deposit Insurance Corporation, National Credit Union Administration, Office of the Comptroller of the Currency, and Consumer Financial Protection Bureau.

2. Federal Financial Institutions Examination Council prescribes examination procedures for regular inspection of federally chartered depository institutions.

      3.   Independent mortgage companies (nonbank entities) are regulated and supervised by the Consumer Financial Protection Bureau.

      4.   CFPB also has primary rulemaking and enforcement authority for federal consumer protection and fair lending laws, for depository institutions as well as nonbank entities.

  G. Alternative sources of financing

      1.   Real estate investment trusts and real estate limited partnerships are one alternative source for financing; generally only for builders, not individual home buyers.

      2.   Most important source of alternative financing for home buyers is home sellers, who may provide primary or secondary financing.

IV. Government Intervention in Mortgage Lending

  A. Great Depression (1930s)

      1.   The most severe economic downturn in U.S. history led to a huge wave of home mortgage defaults and foreclosures.

      2.   Federal government enacted a number of reforms to fix the mortgage industry, including creation of the Federal Housing Administration (FHA) and Fannie Mae.

      3.   FHA provided insurance that protected lenders against default, so that lenders could be more confident about issuing long-term (20- or 30-year) fully amortized loans with fixed interest rates.

      4.   This type of loan became the industry standard after the Depression.

  B. Savings and loan crisis (1980s)

      1.   Savings and loans came to dominate the residential lending market in post-World War II years.

      2.   Deregulation in early 1980s allowed S&Ls to engage in new investments, many of which were risky and didn't pay off, causing many S&Ls to fail.

      3.   Congress reformed the S&L industry through the Financial Institutions Reform, Recovery, and Enforcement Act (FIRREA), but fewer S&Ls remained, and mortgage companies wound up with a much larger share of the residential lending market.

  C. Mortgage market and financial crisis (2007–2008)

      1.   Housing bubble: artificially high run-up in house prices that peaked in 2006.

      2.   Residential lenders helped create the bubble by:

          a.   lending aggressively to subprime borrowers,

          b.   allowing underwriting standards to deteriorate, and

          c.   making loans with dangerous features, such as little or no down-payment and an introductory period with a very low interest rate.

3. Many borrowers mistakenly believed that rising home prices would make it possible to sell the property or refinance the mortgage before the interest rate increased and they started having to make higher payments.

4. When housing bubble burst and prices started falling, homeowners who had made small downpayments had little or no equity; they ended up underwater, owing more to their lender than their property was worth.

5. In 2008, the federal government responded with various measures, including:

   a. cutting interest rates,

   b. the Housing and Economic Recovery Act (HERA),

   c. placing Fannie Mae and Freddie Mac into conservatorship, and

   d. a bailout bill for financial institutions, the Troubled Asset Relief Program (TARP).

6. Dodd-Frank Act (2010) made sweeping changes to the financial regulatory scheme and addressed lending and appraisal practices implicated in the crisis.

Key Terms

Loan origination: The processing of a loan application from the initial submission of information to the funding of the loan.

Commercial bank: A type of financial institution that traditionally has emphasized commercial lending, but which also makes many residential mortgage loans.

Investment bank: A firm that handles corporate finances, arranges for the issuance of government and corporate bonds, and provides investment advice to clients. Also called a securities firm or stock brokerage.

Savings bank: A type of financial institution that has traditionally emphasized consumer loans and accounts for small depositors, and which also makes mortgage loans. Also called a mutual savings bank or thrift.

Savings and loan association: A type of financial institution that has traditionally specialized in home mortgage loans; also called a savings association or a thrift.

Thrift institution: A savings bank or a savings and loan association.

Credit union: A type of financial institution that serves the members of a particular group, such as a professional organization or labor union. Credit unions have traditionally emphasized consumer loans, and now also make residential mortgage loans.

Mortgage banker: A type of real estate lender that originates loans on behalf of investors or with its own line of credit; may service loans as well. Also called a mortgage company.

Mortgage broker: An intermediary who brings real estate lenders and borrowers together and negotiates loan arrangements between them.

Loan correspondent: An intermediary who originates or arranges loans on behalf of a wholesale lender or a large investor, and may also service the loans.

SAFE Mortgage Licensing Act: A federal law that created a national system of licensing and registration for residential mortgage loan originators.

Federal Housing Administration (FHA): An agency within the Department of Housing and Urban Development that provides mortgage insurance to encourage lenders to make more affordable home loans.

Financial Institutions Reform, Recovery and Enforcement Act (FIRREA): A federal law enacted in 1989 in response to the savings and loan crisis; it reorganized the federal agencies that oversee financial institutions.

Wholesale lending: Loans made by large lenders or investors through loan correspondents or mortgage brokers.

Retail lending: Loan transactions in which the borrower applies directly to the lender, rather than to a loan correspondent or mortgage broker.

Subprime lending: Making riskier loans to borrowers who might otherwise be unable to qualify for a loan, often requiring higher interest rates and fees to make up for the increased risk of default.

Dodd-Frank Wall Street Reform and Consumer Protection Act: A comprehensive law passed in 2010, which instituted broad changes to the federal government's regulatory scheme concerning all consumer finance products.

Chapter Quiz

1. The 30-year, fixed-rate, fully amortized loan is generally regarded as the "standard" type of mortgage loan. This came about largely as a result of the:
   a. Financial Institutions Reform, Recovery, and Enforcement Act (FIRREA)
   b. Garn–St. Germain Act
   c. large numbers of foreclosures that took place during the Depression
   d. deregulation of financial institutions

2. As a general rule, mortgage companies do not:
   a. keep any loans in portfolio
   b. sell their loans on the secondary market
   c. service loans
   d. act as loan correspondents

3. FIRREA:
   a. deregulated financial institutions
   b. established the secondary market
   c. abolished the Federal Reserve System
   d. was enacted in response to the S&L crisis

4. A depository institution that is oriented toward serving members of a particular group, such as employees of a large company, is a:
   a. commercial bank
   b. credit union
   c. savings and loan association
   d. savings bank

5. An intermediary that brings together lenders and borrowers and arranges loans for a commission is a:
   a. mortgage banker
   b. mortgage broker
   c. loan servicer
   d. subprime lender

6. In a table-funded loan, the mortgage broker:
   a. stays involved in the transaction all the way to closing
   b. typically names itself as the lender in the loan documents
   c. assigns the loan to the true lender during closing
   d. All of the above

7. A wholesale lender:
   a. originates and services loans on behalf of a retail lender
   b. makes loans to high-risk borrowers
   c. provides short-term lines of credit to home buyers
   d. makes loans through loan correspondents

8. Which of these federal statutes was passed in 2010 in response to the mortgage crisis, created the Consumer Financial Protection Bureau, and made sweeping changes in the financial regulatory system?
    a. Financial Institutions Reform, Recovery, and Enforcement Act
    b. Dodd-Frank Wall Street Reform and Consumer Protection Act
    c. Housing and Economic Recovery Act
    d. Troubled Asset Relief Program

9. Mortgage companies:
    a. don't actually lend funds, but simply broker loans
    b. typically make auto and small business loans as well as home purchase loans
    c. are not banks and don't offer savings or checking accounts
    d. use their depositors' funds to make loans

10. The SAFE Act:
    a. requires loan originators to be federally registered or state-licensed
    b. requires lenders to use loan correspondents or other intermediaries
    c. bailed out the financial industry after the mortgage crisis
    d. was repealed by the Dodd-Frank Act

Answer Key

1. c. The FHA-insured loan program was created during the Depression in response to the foreclosure crisis. The program introduced long-term, fixed-rate, fully amortized mortgage loans as an alternative to the short-term mortgages that had been common before the Depression. These safer long-term loans eventually became standard for residential lenders.

2. a. Mortgage companies typically do not keep loans in portfolio, but sell them on the secondary market.

3. d. FIRREA is a federal law passed in 1989 in response to the savings and loan crisis. It imposed reforms on the thrift industry, to provide greater oversight and prevent high-risk transactions.

4. b. A credit union is a depository institution with membership oriented to members of a particular group, such as a labor union or professional organization.

5. b. A mortgage broker is an intermediary who helps lenders and borrowers find each other, in exchange for a commission. By contrast, a mortgage banker originates loans with its own line of credit, usually for the benefit of investors.

6. d. In a table-funded loan, the loan funds are "brought to the table" during closing by the actual lender.

7. d. A wholesale lender is a large investor that makes loans through many loan correspondents, who specialize in local real estate markets and originate loans on the investor's behalf.

8. b. The 2010 Dodd-Frank Act created the Consumer Financial Protection Bureau and restructured the financial regulatory system in the wake of the mortgage crisis.

9. c. Mortgage companies lend money for mortgages only. Their funds come from various sources, but they are not banks and they don't have depositors.

10. a. The SAFE Act established a nationwide registration system for mortgage loan originators. It also requires them to be state-licensed, unless they're employed by a depository institution or a subsidiary.

Chapter 5
Finance Instruments

Promissory Notes

- Basic provisions
- Negotiability
- Types of notes

Security Instruments

- Purpose
- Historical background
- Mortgages
- Deeds of trust
- Foreclosure
- Alternatives to foreclosure

Finance Instrument Provisions

- Subordination clauses
- Late charge provisions
- Prepayment provisions
- Partial release clauses
- Acceleration clauses
- Alienation clauses and assumptions

Types of Real Estate Loans

Introduction

The "instruments" discussed in this chapter are the legal documents used in real estate finance transactions: promissory notes, mortgages, and deeds of trust. We'll give an overview of how these instruments work, and also explain the provisions commonly found in them.

This chapter is only an introduction to finance instruments, to give you a basic understanding of their purpose and the differences between them. The information presented here should not be used as the basis for personal action or to advise clients or customers. The laws governing creditor-debtor relations vary substantially from one state to another, and they are also subject to change by judicial or legislative action. As a result, it is important to consult an attorney for current, state-specific advice concerning real estate loans and the effect of finance instruments.

Finance instruments:
- Promissory notes
- Mortgages
- Deeds of trust

Promissory Notes

A promissory note is a written promise to pay money. The one who makes the promise (the debtor) is called the **maker** or **issuer** of the note; the one to whom the promise is made (the creditor) is called the **payee**. In a typical real estate loan transaction, the maker is the buyer, who is borrowing money to finance the purchase of property, and the payee is the lender. (Or if the seller is extending credit to the buyer, the payee is the seller.) The promissory note is the basic evidence of the debt; it shows who owes how much money to whom.

Promissory note:
- Maker is borrower
- Payee is lender
- Note is evidence of debt and promise to repay

Basic Provisions of a Note

A promissory note can be a very brief and simple document, as you can see from the example in Figure 5.1. The note states the names of the parties, the date, the amount of the debt (the principal), the interest rate, and how and when the money is to be repaid. It may also specify the maturity date, which is the date by which the loan should be repaid in full. The term "promissory note" should be used in the document.

In addition, the note may include provisions dealing with other rights held by the parties. For example, the note might address the maker's right to prepay the loan, or the payee's remedies if the money is not repaid according to the terms of the agreement. Real estate lend-

Fig. 5.1 Simple promissory note

PROMISSORY NOTE

FOR VALUE RECEIVED, Maker promises to pay to the order of _____ , or to Bearer,

THE SUM OF $_____

PAID AS FOLLOWS: $_____ OR MORE per month starting _____ , including interest at _____% per annum.

ACCELERATION: In the event of default, Payee or Bearer can declare all sums due and payable at once.

Maker/Borrower_____

Date _____

---

ers often protect themselves with late charges, acceleration clauses, and similar provisions, which we'll discuss later in this chapter. Other provisions of the financing agreement between the borrower and lender are found in the mortgage or deed of trust instead of the note.

A promissory note must be signed by the maker, but the payee's signature isn't required. A legal description of the property also isn't required, because the note concerns only the debt, not the property. The legal description appears instead in the mortgage or deed of trust.

Negotiability

Promissory notes used in real estate financing are usually **negotiable instruments**. The Uniform Commercial Code (UCC), which every state has enacted into law in some form, sets forth the requirements for negotiable instruments. Under the UCC, a negotiable instrument is a written, unconditional promise to pay a certain sum of money, on demand or on a certain date; it must be payable "to the order of" a specified person or to the bearer, and it must be signed by the maker. An ordinary check is the most familiar example.

A negotiable instrument is freely transferable. That means the payee can transfer the instrument—and the right to payment that it represents—to a third party. For example, if the payee on a check

A negotiable instrument is freely transferable

endorses the check and gives it to someone else, the right to cash the check is transferred to that person. Real estate lenders use negotiable promissory notes so that they have the option of selling their notes (and their loans) on the secondary market to obtain immediate cash. (See Chapter 3.)

Without Recourse. If a promissory note or other negotiable instrument is endorsed "without recourse," it means that the issue of future payments is strictly between the maker and the third party the instrument is being endorsed to. The original payee will not be liable if the maker fails to pay as agreed.

Holder in Due Course. If a third party buys a negotiable promissory note from the payee for value, in good faith, and without notice of defenses against it, the third party purchaser is referred to as a holder in due course. The maker of a note is required to pay a holder in due course the amount owed even if there are certain defenses that the maker might have been able to raise against the original payee.

Types of Notes

Types of notes:
- Straight note
- Installment note

Promissory notes are sometimes classified according to the way in which the principal and interest are to be paid off. With a **straight note**, the required periodic payments are interest only, and the full amount of the principal is due in a lump sum on the maturity date. With an **installment note**, the periodic payments include part of the principal as well as the interest that has accrued. If an installment note is fully amortized, the periodic payments are enough to pay off all of the principal and interest by the maturity date. Amortization is explained in Chapter 6.

Whether the payments required by the promissory note are interest-only or amortized, the interest paid on a real estate loan is virtually always simple interest. This means that the interest is computed only on the remaining principal balance. (By contrast, compound interest is computed on the principal amount plus any accrued interest.)

Security Instruments

Note is accompanied by security instrument

In a real estate loan transaction, the promissory note is accompanied by a security instrument: either a mortgage or a deed of trust.

The Purpose of Security Instruments

While the note establishes the borrower's obligation to repay the loan, the security instrument makes the property the collateral (the security) for the loan. The security instrument gives the lender a **security interest** in the property, enabling the lender to foreclose on the property if the borrower doesn't repay the loan as agreed, or fails to fulfill another obligation contained in the security instrument. In a foreclosure, the lender forces the sale of the property and collects the debt out of the sale proceeds.

Security instrument (mortgage or deed of trust) gives lender the right to foreclose

A lender can enforce a promissory note even if it is unsecured (meaning the borrower has not executed a security instrument in the lender's favor). In that situation, if the borrower doesn't repay the loan as agreed in the note, the lender can file a lawsuit and obtain a judgment against the borrower. But without a security instrument and without collateral, the lender (now the judgment creditor) may have no way of collecting the judgment. The borrower might have already sold her property and spent the proceeds, leaving little or nothing for the lender.

A secured lender is in a much better position than an unsecured lender. Since a real estate loan involves a large amount of money, real estate lenders always require borrowers to sign a security instrument to back up the promissory note.

Historical Background

To understand how security instruments work, it may be helpful to know how they developed.

In the oldest and simplest form of secured lending, a borrower would give a lender a valuable item of property to hold as collateral. The lender would keep possession of the collateral until the loan was repaid, then return it to the borrower. If the loan was not repaid, the lender would keep the collateral. This type of secured lending still exists; pawnshops are the most obvious example.

Transferring possession of small items of personal property (such as jewelry) to a lender was a straightforward matter. But when land was used as collateral, a transfer of possession to the lender could be complicated and inconvenient. It was also unnecessary, since the borrower could not move the land or conceal it from the lender. As a result, it became a standard arrangement for a borrower to remain in possession of his land and merely transfer the title to the lender.

Once the loan had been repaid, the lender was required to transfer title back to the borrower.

When title to property is transferred only as collateral, unaccompanied by possessory rights, the lender's interest in the property is referred to as **legal title**, or sometimes as naked title or bare title. The property rights the borrower retains (without legal title) are referred to as equitable rights or **equitable title**. The original function of mortgages and deeds of trust was to transfer legal title to land from borrower to lender.

Eventually, in many jurisdictions, a transfer of legal title was no longer considered necessary for the lender's protection. Instead, it became established that a mortgage or deed of trust simply created a **lien** against the borrower's property in favor of the lender. A lien is a financial encumbrance on a property owner's title that allows the lienholder to foreclose on the property to collect a debt. (When property is made the collateral for a loan without relinquishing possession and without transferring title to the lender, it's called **hypothecation**.)

In some states, referred to as "title theory" states, a security instrument is still considered to transfer legal title to the property to the lender until the loan is paid off. Other states are "lien theory" states, where a security instrument creates a lien and doesn't transfer title. Nowadays this distinction is not particularly useful; either way, the security instrument enables the lender to foreclose.

The rights of the lender and the borrower under the terms of a security instrument vary according to the type of instrument used and according to the laws of the state where the property is located. In some states, mortgages are used in all transactions, and they're foreclosed through a judicial process. In other states, deeds of trust and nonjudicial foreclosure are used instead. There are also states where both types of security instruments are in use and both judicial and nonjudicial foreclosure are allowed. We'll explain the difference between a mortgage and a deed of trust, and then discuss foreclosure procedures.

Mortgages

Mortgage:
- Mortgagor is borrower
- Mortgagee is lender
- Foreclosure by judicial process

A mortgage is a two-party security instrument in which the borrower (called the **mortgagor**) mortgages his property to the lender (the **mortgagee**). The document must include the names of the parties and an accurate legal description of the mortgaged property, and it must identify the promissory note that it secures.

Covenants. In the mortgage, the mortgagor promises to pay the property taxes, keep the property insured against fire and other hazards, and maintain any structures in good repair. These promises are intended to protect the property, so that the mortgagee's security does not lose its value. The mortgagee is allowed to inspect the property periodically to make sure that the mortgagor is maintaining it.

If the mortgagor fails to fulfill these or any other obligations imposed by the mortgage, or fails to pay as agreed in the promissory note, he is in default, and the mortgagee can foreclose.

Recording. After a mortgage is executed, the mortgagee has the document recorded to establish the priority of the mortgagee's security interest in the property. As we'll discuss, the priority of the mortgagee's security interest will be very important in the event of a foreclosure.

Satisfaction. When a mortgage has been paid off, the mortgagee is required to give the mortgagor a document that releases the property from the mortgage lien. This document is called a satisfaction of mortgage, or sometimes a "satisfaction piece." The mortgagor has the satisfaction document recorded to provide public notice that the property is no longer encumbered by the mortgage.

Deeds of Trust

The deed of trust (sometimes called a trust deed) is used for the same purpose as a mortgage: to secure the debtor's obligations under a loan agreement. The deed of trust involves three parties rather than two. The borrower is called the **grantor** or **trustor**; the lender is called the **beneficiary**; and there is an independent third party called the **trustee**. The trustee's role is to arrange for the property to be released from the deed of trust when the loan is paid off, or to arrange for foreclosure if necessary.

Deed of trust:
- Grantor is borrower
- Beneficiary is lender
- Trustee is independent third party with power of sale
- Nonjudicial foreclosure

A deed of trust usually includes all of the same basic provisions that are found in a mortgage: the parties, the property, and the promissory note are identified; the grantor promises to pay the taxes and to insure and maintain the property; and the beneficiary has the right to inspect the property. Like a mortgage, a deed of trust should be recorded immediately to establish the priority of the lender's security interest.

When a deed of trust loan has been paid off, the trustee executes a **deed of reconveyance**, releasing the property from the lien. Like a satisfaction of mortgage, the deed of reconveyance is recorded to provide public notice that the property is no longer encumbered by the deed of trust. Either a satisfaction of mortgage or a deed of reconveyance may be more generally referred to as a **lien release**.

Note that the terminology connected with a deed of trust—the fact that the instrument is called a deed, and that the trustee "reconveys" the property to the grantor—reflects its roots in title theory.

Foreclosure

The key difference between mortgages and deeds of trust concerns the procedures the lender must follow in order to foreclose. Since foreclosure procedures vary considerably from state to state, this section will provide only a very general overview.

As you know, lenders frequently sell their loans to other lenders, investors, or secondary market entities. By the time a borrower goes into foreclosure, the party holding the mortgage or deed of trust may not be the original lender. However, in our discussion of foreclosure, we'll simply refer to the foreclosing party as the "lender."

Traditionally, to foreclose on a mortgage, the lender had to file a lawsuit against the borrower. If the lender proved the borrower was in default, a court-ordered auction of the property (a **sheriff's sale**) was held. The property was sold to the highest bidder at the auction, and the lender was entitled to the proceeds of the sale. This type of foreclosure process is called **judicial foreclosure**, and it is still used today.

Eventually, in many jurisdictions, an alternative to judicial foreclosure was developed. **Nonjudicial foreclosure** is generally associated with deeds of trust rather than mortgages. When the borrower defaults, the lender is not required to file a lawsuit and obtain a court order to foreclose. Instead, the trustee appointed in the deed of trust arranges for the property to be sold at a **trustee's sale**. Like a sheriff's sale, a trustee's sale is a public auction. The trustee sells the property to the highest bidder on the lender's behalf.

Power of Sale. Because court supervision is not required, nonjudicial foreclosure is generally less expensive and faster than judicial foreclosure. But nonjudicial foreclosure proceedings are permitted only if the security agreement contains a **power of sale** clause. This provision, which is standard in a deed of trust, authorizes the trustee to sell the property if the borrower defaults. In some states, a power of sale clause may also be included in a mortgage, enabling the mortgagee to foreclose nonjudicially.

A typical power of sale clause might read as follows:

> Upon default by Grantor in the payment of any indebtedness secured hereby or in the performance of any agreement contained herein, and upon written request of Beneficiary, Trustee shall sell the trust property, in accordance with the Deed of Trust Act of this state, at public auction to the highest bidder.

In many states deeds of trust are now more widely used than mortgages. In other states mortgages remain the standard real estate security instrument; in some of those states, state law does not permit nonjudicial foreclosure.

In states that do allow nonjudicial foreclosure, a lender may have the option of foreclosing a deed of trust or mortgage judicially even though the instrument contains a power of sale clause. We'll explain why a lender might prefer judicial foreclosure under certain circumstances after we've discussed the procedures in more detail.

Judicial Foreclosure Procedures. In this section, for simplicity's sake, we'll describe the foreclosure of a mortgage. However, if state law allows lenders to foreclose a deed of trust judicially, the same procedures would usually be followed in that situation.

Judicial foreclosure:
- Acceleration of debt
- Foreclosure lawsuit
- Equitable right of redemption
- Order of execution
- Public notice of sale
- Sheriff's sale
- Statutory right of redemption

Acceleration. When a mortgagor defaults—either by failing to repay the loan or by breaching covenants in the mortgage—the mortgagee notifies the mortgagor that the entire outstanding loan balance (not merely any delinquent payments) must be paid off at once, or

Fig. 5.2 Security instruments and foreclosure procedures

Mortgage without power of sale clause
Judicial foreclosure only

Mortgage with power of sale clause
May be foreclosed either judicially or nonjudicially

Deed of trust
Always includes power of sale clause
May be foreclosed either judicially or nonjudicially

the mortgagee will foreclose. This is called **accelerating** the loan; in effect, the due date of the debt is moved up to the present, speeding up repayment. A provision in the mortgage known as an acceleration clause gives the mortgagee the right to demand immediate payment in full in the event of default.

Lawsuit. Not surprisingly, the defaulting mortgagor is usually unable to pay off the entire debt as demanded. (This payoff is especially unlikely if home prices have fallen, since refinancing or selling will net less than the amount owed.) The mortgagee's next step is to initiate a lawsuit, called a foreclosure action, in the county where the property is located. The purpose of this legal proceeding is to ask a judge to order the county sheriff to seize and sell the property. The defendants in the lawsuit are the mortgagor and any junior lienholders—other creditors who have liens against the property that have lower priority than the foreclosing lender's mortgage. The junior lienholders are included in the lawsuit because their security interests are likely to be affected by the foreclosure.

At the same time that the lawsuit is started, the mortgagee has a document called a **lis pendens** recorded. A lis pendens states that the property is subject to a foreclosure action. By recording the lis pendens, the mortgagee provides constructive notice to anyone who might consider buying the property from the mortgagor (or acquiring some other interest in it) that the title may be affected by the pending lawsuit.

Reinstatement vs. equitable redemption. In some states, the mortgagor has a right to "cure" the default and **reinstate** the loan during the period when the lawsuit is pending. (This period typically lasts three or four months, though legal filings and scheduling delays can lengthen the time to a year or more in some places.) If the default was a failure to make payments on the loan, the mortgagor can cure it by paying the delinquent amounts, plus interest and whatever costs have been incurred because of the foreclosure (such as court costs and attorneys' fees). If the mortgagor cures the default, the foreclosure is terminated and the loan is reinstated; the parties are back to where they were before the default.

In other states, however, a defaulting mortgagor doesn't have a right to cure and reinstate the loan. But the mortgagor does have an **equitable right of redemption**. This is the right to **redeem** the property—retain ownership of it—by paying off the entire outstanding loan balance (not just the delinquent payments), plus costs incurred as a result of the foreclosure. Redemption stops the foreclosure,

Some states allow mortgagor to cure the default and reinstate the loan

Equitable right of redemption: mortgagor can redeem the property before sheriff's sale satisfies the debt, and terminates the lender's security interest in the property. (This is in contrast to a reinstatement, in which the lender and borrower continue their financial relationship.)

Court order and notice of sale. Unless the mortgagor redeems the property (or in those states that allow it, cures and reinstates the loan), the scheduled court hearing in the foreclosure action is held. In most cases, after reviewing the note and mortgage and the facts concerning the default, the judge issues a court order directing the sheriff to seize the property and sell it. This type of court order is often called a **writ of execution**.

Acting under the court order, the sheriff notifies the public of the place and date of the sale. This usually requires posting notices at the property and the courthouse and running an advertisement of the sale in a newspaper circulated in the county. The number of times the ad must be published depends on state law, but the process generally takes several weeks.

In those states where the mortgagor has the right to cure the default and reinstate the loan, that right typically ends as soon as the judge orders the property sold. But the equitable right of redemption lasts until the sheriff's sale is held. The mortgagor can still prevent the sale and redeem the property by paying off the debt, plus costs.

Sheriff's sale. The sheriff's sale (sometimes called an execution sale) is a public auction. It is usually held at the county courthouse, and anyone who wants to bid on the property can attend. The property is sold to the highest bidder, who is given a **certificate of sale**.

The proceeds of the sale are first applied to pay for the costs of the sale, and then to pay off the mortgage and any other liens against the property. The mortgage and other liens are paid in order of their priority, which is usually established by their recording dates: the lien that was recorded first has the highest priority, and it is paid off first. The lien with the second highest priority is paid off only if there are sufficient funds left over—and so on, down the list. The proceeds are not prorated among the various lienholders. (This is why lien priority is so important to a lender: the difference between first and second lien position can be the difference between payment in full and no payment at all.) If the sale proceeds are enough to pay off all the liens, any surplus goes to the debtor.

If the foreclosure sale proceeds are not enough to fully pay off the mortgage (usually because the property's value has declined since the loan was made), the shortfall—the difference between the

Sheriff's sale:
- Public auction
- Foreclosed property sold to highest bidder
- Purchaser gets certificate of sale

Fig. 5.3 Steps in a judicial foreclosure

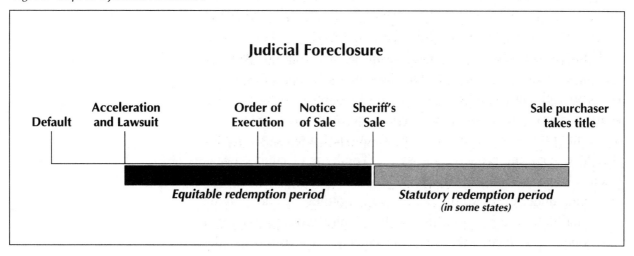

If sheriff's sale proceeds do not cover the debt, lender may be entitled to deficiency judgment

sale proceeds and the amount owed to the lender—is referred to as a deficiency. The court may award the lender a personal judgment against the debtor for the amount of the deficiency. This is called a **deficiency judgment**.

Some states place restrictions on a lender's right to obtain a deficiency judgment. The most common restrictions apply to purchase money mortgages secured by the borrower's homestead or principal residence. For those loans, some states prohibit a deficiency judgment altogether. Other states limit the deficiency judgment to the difference between the amount owed and the home's fair market value (which may be much greater than the foreclosure sale proceeds).

Post-sale redemption. Following the sale, the debtor (the former mortgagor) may have an additional period of time to redeem the property. To redeem it at this stage, the debtor usually must pay the sale purchaser the amount paid for the property at the sheriff's sale, plus accrued interest from the time of the sale. This right to redeem the property following the sheriff's sale is called the **statutory right of redemption**. It's called a statutory right because it was established by the state legislature in a statute. By contrast, the pre-sale right of redemption is referred to as an equitable right because it was originally created by the courts as a matter of equity (fairness).

Statutory right of redemption: mortgagor can redeem the property after the sheriff's sale

Many states don't allow post-sale redemption. In those that do, the length of the statutory redemption period varies; it may be six months or even as long as two years. The amount of time allowed may depend on factors such as whether the property is agricultural land, or whether the mortgagee is willing to waive the right to a deficiency judgment.

Rights of purchaser. The purchaser at the sheriff's sale may be entitled either to take possession of the property or to collect rent from the debtor during the statutory redemption period. However, if the property is homestead property, some states permit the debtor to remain on the property without paying rent. At the end of the statutory redemption period, if the property has not been redeemed, the sheriff's sale purchaser receives a **sheriff's deed** to the property.

Depending on state law concerning notice requirements and redemption, and also on factors such as the number of legal motions filed by the debtor, court congestion, and the availability of the sheriff for foreclosures, judicial foreclosure of a mortgage may take anywhere from a few months to a few years from the time of default until a sheriff's deed is delivered to the purchaser, finally divesting the debtor of title.

Nonjudicial Foreclosure. In this section we'll describe the foreclosure of a deed of trust. But essentially the same procedures would apply to a mortgage with a power of sale clause, if the mortgagee chose nonjudicial foreclosure.

To foreclose a deed of trust nonjudicially, the trustee must follow steps similar to those taken by the sheriff in a judicial foreclosure. The trustee must give notice of the default to the grantor (and in some states must also record the notice of default), and then give notice of the impending sale to the public. As with judicial foreclosure, most states require that this notice of sale be posted at the property and published in a newspaper circulated in the county, so that the greatest number of potential buyers will have an opportunity to attend and bid at the trustee's sale.

Nonjudicial foreclosure:
- Notice of default
- Public notice of sale
- Cure & reinstatement
- Trustee's sale
- No post-sale redemption

After giving the grantor notice of default, the trustee must allow at least a certain length of time to expire before issuing the notice of sale (in most states, the minimum period is between three and six months). There is also a minimum period between the time the notice of sale is issued and the date of the sale (for example, one month). The grantor is allowed to cure the default and reinstate the loan by paying only the delinquent amounts plus costs. The right to cure and reinstate ends shortly before the trustee's sale is held (for example, five days before the sale).

The statutory right of redemption that may follow the sheriff's sale in a judicial foreclosure does not apply to a trustee's sale in most states. When the property is sold at the trustee's sale, a **trustee's deed** is given to the successful bidder. The debtor is immediately divested

Fig. 5.4 Steps in a nonjudicial foreclosure

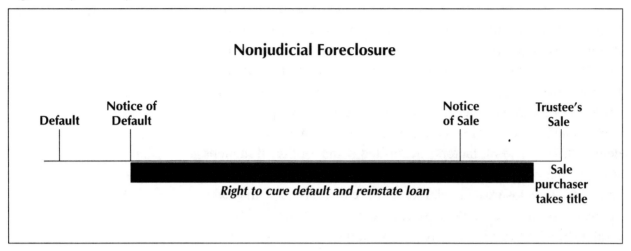

Nonjudicial Foreclosure

Default | Notice of Default | Notice of Sale | Trustee's Sale

Right to cure default and reinstate loan

Sale purchaser takes title

of title and may have only a short period of time (perhaps 20 or 30 days) to vacate the property. As in a sheriff's sale, the trustee's sale proceeds are first applied to the sale costs, then to the debt and other liens in order of priority; any surplus is given to the debtor.

The entire nonjudicial foreclosure process can usually be accomplished in well under a year (often in six or seven months) and without many of the expenses involved in court proceedings. Naturally, there are expenses connected with a trustee's sale, but they tend to be substantially less than those connected with a court-ordered sheriff's sale. However, the debtor may be entitled to challenge the nonjudicial foreclosure in court, just as with a judicial foreclosure.

Restrictions. Even in states that allow it, a variety of restrictions may be placed on the use of nonjudicial foreclosure; for example, a post-sale redemption period might be required for agricultural property. In several states the beneficiary is not allowed to obtain a deficiency judgment after a trustee's sale, even if the sale proceeds were far less than the amount of the debt. However, if the beneficiary chooses to foreclose the deed of trust judicially (just like a mortgage), then all of the procedures and rights relating to judicial foreclosure apply. The beneficiary might decide that the possibility of a deficiency judgment outweighs the delay and costs associated with judicial foreclosure.

No deficiency judgment after nonjudicial foreclosure in some states

Comparing Judicial and Nonjudicial Foreclosure. As we said, if a security instrument includes a power of sale clause—as a deed of trust always does—the lender may be allowed to choose between foreclosing judicially or nonjudicially. From a lender's point of view, judicial foreclosure can have two main advantages over nonjudicial foreclosure, depending on state law. The first advantage concerns the difference between the equitable right of redemption and the right to cure and reinstate. In a nonjudicial foreclosure, the borrower generally has the right to cure the default and reinstate the loan even after the lender has accelerated it. But in a judicial foreclosure, some states do not give the borrower the right to cure and reinstate; the borrower can stop the foreclosure only by exercising the equitable right of redemption and paying off the entire debt. The lender is not required to continue its relationship with a borrower who has proved unreliable.

The second possible advantage of judicial foreclosure for a lender is the right to obtain a deficiency judgment against the borrower if the property does not bring enough at the sheriff's sale to satisfy the debt. In states where deficiency judgments are prohibited after nonjudicial foreclosure, a lender is likely to protect itself by choosing judicial foreclosure if the property has lost value since the loan was made.

The main advantage of nonjudicial foreclosure for the lender is that it's fairly quick and inexpensive compared to judicial foreclosure. It is because of this advantage that deeds of trust have almost completely replaced mortgages in many states. And in some states where mortgages are still the dominant real estate security instrument, it's now common or even standard for a mortgage to have a power of sale clause.

The advantages and disadvantages of the two forms of foreclosure for the borrower correspond to those for the lender, but in reverse. From the borrower's point of view, the right to cure the default and reinstate the loan is an important advantage of nonjudicial foreclosure. Without that right, a borrower who misses just a couple of payments might lose the home, since most delinquent borrowers can't afford to pay off the debt completely in order to stop the foreclosure and redeem the property. On the other hand, in a judicial foreclosure the borrower usually has a long time to get the money together to pay off the debt, because of slow court proceedings and the statutory redemption period.

Alternatives to Foreclosure

A homeowner who can no longer make the payments on her mortgage may have alternatives to foreclosure, even if the property is worth less than the amount owed (making it impossible to sell the property for enough to pay off the mortgage). There are three basic alternatives to foreclosure: loan workouts, deeds in lieu of foreclosure, and short sales. A lender or loan servicer may agree to forego

Lender's point of view:
- Advantages of judicial foreclosure:
  - Borrower may not be able to reinstate loan
  - Right to deficiency judgment
- Advantages of nonjudicial foreclosure:
  - Quick and inexpensive

Borrower's point of view:
- Advantages of judicial foreclosure:
  - Slow process
  - Post-sale redemption
- Advantage of nonjudicial foreclosure:
  - Right to cure & reinstate

Alternatives to foreclosure:
- Loan workout
- Deed in lieu
- Short sale

foreclosure and take one of these other paths in order to save on attorney fees and court costs, as well as to put an end to a money-losing situation with relative speed.

Loan Workouts. A borrower hoping to avoid foreclosure typically begins by requesting a loan workout from the lender or loan servicer. Some workouts involve a repayment plan, such as a simple adjustment in the timing of payments. The borrower gets extra time to make up a missed payment or is allowed to skip a few payments, with the skipped payments added on to the repayment period. This is all the relief that some borrowers need.

Loan workout:
• Repayment plan, or
• Modification of terms

Homeowners in more severe financial distress should seek a loan modification, an actual change in the terms of their loan. Examples of possible modifications include changing an adjustable-rate mortgage into a fixed-rate mortgage, reducing the interest rate, and/or reducing the amount of principal owed. The aim is to permanently lower the borrower's monthly payment amount to an affordable level.

To be eligible for a loan workout, the borrower usually must demonstrate financial hardship—that is, a genuine inability to make the mortgage payments. The borrower is typically required to complete an application and provide copies of pay stubs, bank statements, bills, and so on. Note that some lenders and servicers won't consider a loan workout until the borrower is at least 90 days behind on the payments.

As part of its response to the 2007–2008 mortgage crisis (see Chapter 4), the federal government took steps to encourage and in some cases require lenders and servicers to negotiate modification agreements. For example, for many loans sold to Fannie Mae or Freddie Mac, a borrower who is 90 days delinquent must be offered a trial modification. If the borrower successfully makes the reduced payments on time during the trial period and meets other eligibility requirements, the modified loan terms become permanent. There are also modification programs for FHA-insured and VA-guaranteed loans.

Deed in lieu: borrower deeds property to lender to satisfy debt

Deed in Lieu of Foreclosure. If a borrower can't negotiate a satisfactory loan workout and must give up the property, he can offer the lender a deed in lieu of foreclosure (often simply called "a deed in lieu"). With a deed in lieu, the borrower deeds the property to the lender and this satisfies the debt.

Giving the lender a deed in lieu is a simpler and less public process than foreclosure. However, the borrower's credit rating will suffer nearly as much as with a foreclosure (this is also true of a short sale, discussed below). Typically, the borrower's credit record bears a notation such as "Settlement of Debt for Less than Full Amount" (as opposed to "Paid in Full").

Since the lender is usually receiving title to a property that is worth less than the outstanding balance on the loan, the lender may want the borrower to sign a promissory note to cover any shortfall that results when the lender later sells the property. Obviously, the borrower will want to negotiate a solution with the lender that avoids this.

A lender who accepts a deed in lieu of foreclosure takes title subject to any junior liens against the property (such as a second mortgage). Thus, lenders almost never agree to accept a deed in lieu if there are junior liens. A lender would usually prefer to proceed with foreclosure, a process that extinguishes junior liens, rather than risk having to pay off the junior lienholders.

Short Sales. As an alternative to a deed in lieu, an owner facing foreclosure may seek the lender's consent to a short sale. In a short sale, the owner sells the house for whatever it will bring (something "short" of the amount owed, because the home's value has decreased). The lender receives the sale proceeds and, in return, releases the borrower from the debt. As when arranging a deed in lieu, the borrower will want to make sure that the lender doesn't have the right to sue for a deficiency following the sale.

Short sale: lender agrees to accept proceeds of sale to satisfy debt, even if proceeds are less than amount owed

The existence of junior liens won't necessarily prevent a lender from approving a short sale. This is because—unlike with a deed in lieu—the lender isn't taking responsibility for the property or its liens. However, the presence of multiple liens will complicate matters, since all of the lienholders must consent to the sale. The junior lienholders aren't likely to get much, if anything, from a short sale and may not be willing to approve the transaction. In this situation, a foreclosure may be inevitable.

Let's look at the process of obtaining consent from a lender for one of these alternatives to foreclosure.

Obtaining Lender Consent. Homeowners seeking a loan workout, deed in lieu of foreclosure, or short sale will usually negotiate with their loan servicer, if there is one; otherwise, they will seek approval directly from the lender. Either way, the process can be challenging.

Financial institutions often have various departments that must each give independent approval to a foreclosure alternative. If there is more than one lender, the situation becomes even more complex.

Borrowers who want help with this potentially long and frustrating process can contact nonprofit housing counseling services. Alternatively, borrowers can hire a professional mortgage negotiator; this type of service is often provided by real estate licensees.

Note that many states have passed legislation regulating distressed property consultants, entities that offer services to property owners who are on the brink of foreclosure. Additionally, the Federal Trade Commission has issued rules specifically aimed at the practices of for-profit companies offering these services.

Unfortunately, sometimes a lender cannot agree to one of these foreclosure alternatives, even though it makes financial sense to do so. As we mentioned in Chapter 3, many mortgages have been securitized (that is, grouped together in a pool, with interests or shares in the pool sold off to investors). Many of the contracts governing the sale of these mortgage-backed securities to investors include guarantees promising that few (if any) of the pooled loans can be modified without investor consent. (Accepting a deed in lieu or a short sale constitutes modifying the terms of a loan.) Obtaining consent from all the investors for changes to each individual loan just isn't practical. Thus, the holder of a securitized mortgage that goes into default may have no legal choice but to foreclose.

Income Tax Implications. Loan modifications, deeds in lieu, and short sales all may result in borrowers owing less money than they originally agreed to pay their lender. This reduction of debt is referred to as **debt relief**, or sometimes as debt forgiveness. Generally, the Internal Revenue Service treats debt relief as taxable income. In other words, the taxpayer will have to pay income tax on the amount of debt that was forgiven. This IRS treatment of debt relief may seem a little surprising, but keep in mind that the borrower had the use of the debt to buy or improve a house, and also got to deduct the interest paid on the debt from his income.

Note that the IRS does not treat mortgage debt relief as income for certain homeowners who received the debt relief on their principal residence between 2007 and 2017. This also applies to debt discharged in 2018, provided there was a written agreement in 2017.

Debt relief: a reduction of debt, as in a successful short sale; usually taxable as income

Also, no matter when the debt relief was received, some or all of it won't count as income if the borrower was insolvent at the time of the forgiveness. A person is insolvent if his liabilities exceed his assets. If a borrower was suffering financial distress severe enough to justify debt forgiveness, demonstrating insolvency may not be difficult.

Finance Instrument Provisions

This section of the chapter covers a variety of important provisions that may appear in real estate finance instruments. Some of them are used only in certain types of transactions; others are virtually always used. Depending on the transaction, the rights and responsibilities of the borrower and the lender may be affected by:

- a subordination clause,
- a late charge provision,
- a prepayment provision,
- a partial release clause,
- an acceleration clause, and/or
- an alienation clause.

Clauses often found in finance instruments:
- Subordination
- Late charge
- Prepayment
- Partial release
- Acceleration
- Alienation

Subordination Clauses

Ordinarily, the priority among mortgages and deeds of trust is determined by the date of recording: the first one recorded has first lien position, the highest priority. In some situations, however, the parties may want to give an instrument that was recorded later priority over one that was recorded earlier.

This is particularly common in construction financing. In many cases a developer who applies for a construction loan has already borrowed money to purchase the land that's going to be built on, so a mortgage or deed of trust against the property has already been recorded. But because construction loans involve some extra risk, lenders usually refuse to make a construction loan unless they can be assured of first lien position. In order for the later construction loan mortgage or deed of trust to take priority over the earlier instrument, the earlier instrument must contain a subordination clause.

A **subordination clause** states that the security instrument in which it appears will be subordinate (junior) to another security instrument that is to be recorded later.

Subordination clause gives mortgage recorded earlier lower priority than another mortgage that will be recorded later

> Lender agrees that this instrument shall be subordinate to a lien to be given by Borrower to secure funds for the construction of improvements on the Property, provided said lien is duly recorded and the amount secured by said lien does not exceed $125,000.

Inclusion of a subordination clause must be negotiated at the time of the earlier transaction (in our example, when the developer bought the land and the earlier security instrument was signed). If a subordination clause was not included in the earlier security instrument, the earlier lender might be willing to sign a separate subordination agreement later on. A prudent developer wouldn't count on that, however.

Subordination profoundly affects the strength of both lenders' security interests, so any subordination provision should be drafted or reviewed by a real estate lawyer.

Late Charge Provisions

In real estate loan transactions, the promissory note usually provides for late charges if the borrower doesn't make the payments on time. A lender typically allows for a grace period after the payment's actual due date, but if the payment hasn't reached the lender by the time the grace period expires, a late fee will be added to the amount overdue.

State laws protecting borrowers from excessive late charges and unfair collection practices may override provision in note

Many states have laws that protect borrowers by limiting excessive late charges and prohibiting unfair collection practices. For example, lenders generally aren't permitted to charge more than one late fee on a single overdue payment, even if the payment remains overdue for more than one month.

Prepayment Provisions

Prepayment charge imposed if loan repaid early, to compensate lender for lost interest

Some promissory notes have a provision that imposes a penalty on the borrower if she repays some or all of the principal before it is due. This is called **prepaying** the loan. Prepayment deprives the lender of some of the interest it expected to receive on its investment over the loan term. In effect, a prepayment penalty compensates the lender for the lost interest.

As an example, the following provision imposes a penalty if the borrower prepays more than 20% of the original loan amount in one of the first three years of the loan term. If the borrower's prepayment exceeds that limit, the borrower is required to pay the lender 0.5% of the original loan amount as a penalty.

> If, within three years from the date of this note, Borrower makes any prepayments of principal in excess of twenty percent of the original principal amount in any twelve-month period beginning with the date of this note or anniversary dates thereof ("loan year"), Borrower shall pay the Note Holder one half of one percent of the original principal amount.

Most residential loan agreements do not have a prepayment penalty provision. Prepayment penalties are prohibited in loans that will be sold to Fannie Mae or Freddie Mac, and also in FHA-insured and VA-guaranteed loans. They are more likely to be found in subprime loans.

Partial Release Clauses

A partial release clause in a mortgage is often called a partial satisfaction clause; in a deed of trust, it's often called a partial reconveyance clause. This provision obligates the lender to release part of the property from the lien when part of the debt has been paid.

Example: The Harveys borrowed money to purchase five acres of land. Their mortgage includes a partial satisfaction clause. The clause states that when the borrowers have repaid 25% of the loan amount, the lender will release one acre of their land from the mortgage lien.

A partial release clause is typically included in a mortgage or deed of trust covering a subdivision that is in the process of being developed and sold (this type of loan is sometimes called a blanket loan). When the developers find a buyer for a lot, they pay the lender a specified portion of the loan amount to have that lot released from the lien. A partial release clause like the one below permits them to acquire clear title to that lot and convey it to the buyer, without having to pay off the whole loan.

Partial release: part of the property is released from lien when part of debt is paid

> Upon payment of all sums due with respect to any lot subject to this lien, Lender shall release said lot from the lien at no cost to Borrower.

Acceleration Clauses

Almost all promissory notes, mortgages, and deeds of trust contain an acceleration clause. As we explained earlier, this provision allows the lender to accelerate the debt: that is, to declare the entire outstanding balance immediately due and payable if the borrower defaults.

This means that a borrower who misses even one payment might discover the next month that he owes not just two payments, but rather the entire remaining balance. In practice, though, most lenders wait until payments are at least a couple of months delinquent before accelerating a loan. In an effort to aid distressed homeowners, several states have enacted laws requiring lenders to wait for various periods of time before accelerating a loan or taking other foreclosure steps.

Here is a typical acceleration clause:

> In case the Mortgagor [or Trustor] fails to pay any installment of principal or interest secured hereby when due or to keep or perform any covenant or agreement aforesaid, then the whole indebtedness hereby secured shall become due and payable, at the election of the Mortgagee [or Beneficiary].

Keep in mind that a lender's right to accelerate a loan is effectively limited when state law gives the borrower the right to cure the default and reinstate the loan.

Alienation Clauses and Assumptions

In the real estate context, **alienation** refers to transfer of ownership. An alienation clause (often called a **due-on-sale** clause) in a security instrument is designed to limit the borrower's right to transfer title to the property without the lender's permission, unless the loan is paid off first.

Acceleration: upon default, lender may declare entire debt due immediately

To understand the purpose of an alienation clause, let's look first at what happens if a borrower transfers the security property without paying off the loan. There are essentially three possibilities:

- the new owner may simply take title subject to the loan;
- there may be an assumption of the loan by the new owner without a release of the original borrower; or
- there may be an assumption and release.

Whenever ownership of real property is transferred, the new owner takes title **subject to** any existing liens, including an existing mortgage or deed of trust. The buyer is not personally liable to the lender, but the lender still has the power to foreclose on the property, in spite of the transfer of ownership.

The new owner may or may not agree to **assume** the loan. In an assumption, the new owner (the assumptor) takes on legal responsibility for repaying the loan. But unless the lender agrees to a release, the original borrower (the former owner) remains secondarily liable to the lender even after an assumption. If there is a foreclosure and the lender obtains a deficiency judgment, the original borrower can be forced to pay it if the assumptor does not.

Buyer who assumes loan takes on primary liability, but unreleased seller remains secondarily liable

Even though the original borrower is still liable to the lender after selling the property, the transfer of ownership may increase the lender's risk. The new owner could be a much worse credit risk than the original borrower, or might allow the security property to deteriorate. So the lender wants some control over transfer of the property, to ensure that any new owner is no more likely to default than the original borrower.

An alienation clause gives the lender that control. Most alienation clauses are triggered not only by a complete transfer of ownership, but also by the transfer of any significant interest in the property (including a long-term lease or any lease with an option to purchase). In the event of a transfer, the clause usually gives the lender the right to declare the entire loan balance due immediately—hence the name "due-on-sale" clause. This is acceleration of the loan triggered by transfer, instead of by default.

Alienation clause allows lender to call in the loan if borrower transfers an interest in the property

> If all or any part of the Property or an interest therein is sold or transferred by Borrower without Lender's prior written consent, Lender may, at Lender's option, declare all the sums secured by this instrument to be immediately due and payable.

If the lender is not satisfied with the person the borrower intends to sell the property to, the lender cannot forbid the sale; but it can require the borrower to pay off the loan rather than allowing the new owner to assume it.

If the proposed buyer is a good credit risk, the lender is likely to approve the assumption. The lender may reset the loan's interest rate, charging the buyer a rate between the loan's original rate and the current market rate. This is sometimes called a "blended rate." The lender will also charge an **assumption fee**, which may be as substantial as a loan origination fee—for example, 1.5% of the loan balance.

Alienation clauses are now standard in residential security instruments. They appear in the security instruments used by Fannie Mae and Freddie Mac for conventional loans, and also in the security instruments used in FHA and VA loan transactions. However, some recent loans and many older loans do not have alienation clauses. To find out whether a seller's loan can be assumed without the lender's approval or whether it contains an alienation clause, contact the lender.

When the lender's consent to a sale is required, it should be obtained in the form of a **certificate of reduction** (sometimes called an estoppel letter). A certificate of reduction acknowledges the transfer of ownership and waives the lender's right to accelerate the loan on account of the transfer. By providing the certificate, the lender is estopped (legally prevented) from later trying to enforce the alienation clause based on this sale.

A certificate of reduction is often requested even in a transaction where the security instrument for the seller's existing loan does not contain an alienation clause. The lender is asked to state in the reduction certificate the amount of the outstanding principal balance, and also to acknowledge that the loan is not in default. The buyer then has written confirmation of the amount and the status of the obligation she is planning to assume or take title subject to.

Sidebar notes:

Lender that allows assumption may raise interest rate

Certificate of reduction:
- Acknowledges transfer and waives due-on-sale clause, or
- States balance and status of loan without any change in the existing loan's terms

When taking a listing, a real estate agent should ask the seller about the existing financing and consider whether offering assumption might be a good marketing tool. If the seller would like to offer assumption, the lender should be asked for a certificate of reduction. (Note that many lenders charge a fee to prepare the certificate.) If an assumption of the seller's loan is eventually arranged, both parties—the seller and the buyer—should obtain legal advice, and the agreement should be drawn up by a lawyer.

Types of Real Estate Loans

Real estate finance terminology includes many terms for various types of mortgage loans—terms that describe the status, purpose, or function of different loans. We'll end this chapter with a review of some of the most common of these terms.

In accordance with general usage, we often use "mortgage" or "mortgage loan" to refer to any loan secured by real property, whether the security instrument actually used is a mortgage or a deed of trust. Keep in mind that in many states a deed of trust could be (and perhaps usually would be) used instead of a mortgage to make any of these types of loans.

Junior or Senior Mortgage. A **junior mortgage** is one that has lower lien priority than another mortgage (or deed of trust) against the same property. In relation to the junior mortgage, the mortgage with higher lien priority may be called a **senior mortgage**. A senior mortgage with first lien position is called a **first mortgage**; a junior mortgage may be referred to as a second mortgage or third mortgage, depending on its relative lien priority. And sometimes you'll hear a junior mortgage called a subordinate mortgage.

Senior mortgage has higher lien priority than junior mortgage

A property may become encumbered with two mortgages (or maybe even more than two) in a number of different situations. When property is purchased, a junior mortgage loan may provide secondary financing to supplement the primary loan that's secured by the first mortgage. (Secondary financing is discussed in Chapters 6 and 13.) A land purchase mortgage that has been subordinated to a construction mortgage is another example of a junior mortgage. And many junior mortgages secure home equity loans (see below).

As we discussed earlier, foreclosure of a mortgage affects any junior liens against the property. If a property has a senior mortgage and a junior mortgage against it and the senior lender forecloses, the foreclosure extinguishes the lien of the junior mortgage. The junior lender will be paid only after the senior lender has been paid in full. If the foreclosure sale proceeds aren't sufficient to pay off the senior lender and the other lienholders with higher priority, the junior lender receives no share of the proceeds. The junior lender could still sue the debtor, but the junior loan is now an unsecured loan.

If a junior mortgage is foreclosed on, the foreclosure sale purchaser takes title to the property subject to the lien of the senior mortgage. Foreclosure on the junior mortgage does not extinguish the senior mortgage.

Purchase Money Mortgage. A mortgage given by the buyer to the seller in a seller-financed transaction is often referred to as a **purchase money mortgage**. Instead of paying the full price in cash at closing, the buyer gives the seller a mortgage on the property and pays the price off in installments.

Purchase money mortgage: a mortgage given by the buyer to the seller in a seller-financed transaction

> **Example:** The sales price for the home is $180,000. The buyer gives the seller a $20,000 downpayment and signs a promissory note and purchase money mortgage in favor of the seller for the remaining $160,000. The buyer will make monthly installment payments to the seller at 7% interest over the next 15 years, until the full price has been paid.

You may also see the term "purchase money mortgage" used more broadly, to refer to any mortgage loan used to finance the purchase of the property that is serving as the collateral for the loan. In this book, though, we use "purchase loan" for that broader meaning instead. Purchase money mortgages used for seller financing are covered in Chapter 13.

Home Equity Loan. A property owner can obtain a mortgage loan using her equity in property that she already owns as collateral. This is called an **equity loan**; when the property is the borrower's residence, it's called a **home equity loan**.

Home equity loan: a loan secured by a mortgage against the borrower's equity in a home he already owns

A property owner's equity is the difference between the property's current market value and the liens against it. In other words, it's the portion of the property's value that the owner owns free and clear—the portion that is available to serve as collateral for another loan. With an equity loan, the lender agrees to loan a sum of money to the property owner in exchange for a second mortgage against the property.

> **Example:** The Hutchinsons bought their house six years ago for $260,000, making a $20,000 downpayment and borrowing $240,000 for the purchase. Naturally, the loan is secured with a mortgage against the house. Their equity at the time of purchase is the amount of their downpayment, $20,000.
>
> The Hutchinsons' house has appreciated since they bought it, and it's worth about $280,000 in the current market. The balance due on the mortgage is now $223,000. So the Hutchinsons' equity is $57,000 ($280,000 – $223,000 = $57,000).
>
> When the Hutchinsons have some unexpected medical expenses, they apply to a lender for a $15,000 home equity loan. To provide security for the loan, they sign a deed of trust that gives the lender a junior lien against their property.

Home equity loans are often used to finance remodeling or other improvements to the property. They're also frequently used for expenses unrelated to the property, such as unexpected bills, as in the example above. Until recently, the interest on home equity loans was tax-deductible no matter what the loan was used for, but as of 2018 it is deductible only if the loan is used to make substantial improvements to the home (see Chapter 2).

The interest rates charged on home equity loans are higher than the rates on home purchase loans. Since a home equity loan is a second mortgage, it represents a greater risk to the lender (see the discussion of junior mortgages, above). The higher interest rate compensates the lender for the additional risk.

Instead of having to apply for a home equity loan, some homeowners have a **home equity line of credit** (or **HELOC**) that they can draw on when the need arises. This works in much the same way as a credit card—with a credit limit and minimum monthly payments based on the amount borrowed—except that the debt is automatically secured by the borrower's home. The line of credit is a revolving credit account, in contrast to the home equity loan, which is an installment loan with regular payments made over a certain term.

Refinancing: a new loan that's used to pay off an existing mortgage against the same property

Refinance Mortgage. Borrowers who refinance their mortgage loan are actually obtaining an entirely new loan to replace the existing one. Funds from the refinance loan are used to pay off the existing loan. Depending on the situation, refinancing may be arranged with the same lender that made the existing loan, or with a different lender.

Borrowers often choose to refinance when market interest rates drop; refinancing at a lower interest rate can result in substantial savings over the long run. However, they must take into account the loan fee, appraisal fee, and other expenses connected with the refinancing; these can add up to thousands of dollars. Refinancing to take advantage of lower interest rates may not make financial sense if the borrower expects to sell the property, or to refinance again in the following two or three years; there might not be enough time to recover the cost of the refinancing through savings on interest.

Another situation in which a borrower is likely to refinance is when the payoff date of the existing mortgage is approaching and a large balloon payment will be required. (See the discussion of partial amortization in Chapter 6.) Funds from the refinance loan will be used to make that balloon payment.

While a basic refinance loan is for no more than the amount needed to pay off the existing mortgage and cover the refinancing costs, borrowers who have a significant amount of equity when they refinance may have the option of a "cash-out" refinance loan. With cash-out refinancing, the loan amount is more than the amount of the existing mortgage balance plus the refinancing costs, so that the borrowers also receive some cash from the refinance lender. This is another way for homeowners to tap into their equity. As with a home equity loan, the cash from the refinancing may be used for remodeling or other improvements, or for expenses unrelated to the property.

Bridge loan provides cash for purchase of a new home pending sale of the old home

Bridge Loan. It often happens that buyers are ready to purchase a new home before they've succeeded in selling their current home. They need funds for their downpayment and closing costs right away, without waiting for the proceeds from the eventual sale of the current home. In this situation, the buyers may be able to obtain a **bridge loan**. A bridge loan is secured by equity in the property that is for sale, and it will be paid off when that sale closes. In most cases, a bridge loan calls for interest-only payments (see Chapter 6), and the principal is due when the loan is paid off. A bridge loan may also be called a **swing loan** or a **gap loan**.

Budget Mortgage. The monthly payment on a budget mortgage includes not just principal and interest on the loan, but also impounds: one-twelfth of the year's real estate taxes and insurance premiums. The lender deposits this portion of each payment in an **impound account** (also called a reserve account or escrow account) and pays the taxes and other expenses out of the account when they come due. Most residential loans are secured by budget mortgages. This is the safest and most practical way for lenders to make sure the property expenses are paid on time.

Budget mortgage: monthly payments include property taxes and hazard insurance

Package Mortgage. When personal property and real property are financed with a single mortgage loan, it's called a package mortgage.

Package mortgage is secured by personal property as well as real property

> **Example:** A restaurant building on a city lot is being sold. The buyer also wants to purchase the restaurant equipment (ovens, freezers, and so on) that's in the building. The equipment is considered to be personal property, not fixtures. The buyer's purchase of this personal property along with the real property could be financed with a package mortgage.

Alternatively, a buyer may finance personal property separately from the real property, obtaining a separate loan either from the same lender or from a different lender. In that situation, in addition to executing a mortgage that creates a security interest in the real property, the buyer executes a **security agreement** that creates a security interest in the personal property. Under the Uniform Commercial Code, a lender with a security interest in personal property provides public notice and establishes the priority of that interest by filing a **financing statement** in the office of the Secretary of State in the state where the transaction takes place. The financing statement serves the same purpose in regard to personal property that a recorded mortgage or deed of trust serves for real property.

A key advantage of using a package mortgage, instead of financing the personal property separately, is that the mortgage term is usually much longer than the term of an ordinary loan for personal property. So the package mortgage allows the borrower to pay for the personal property over a longer period. In addition, the interest rate on the mortgage may be lower than the rate for a personal property loan, and the interest paid will be tax-deductible. (Normally, interest on a personal property loan is only deductible if the property is used in a trade or business or for investment.)

Fig. 5.5 Comparison of biweekly loan payments to ordinary monthly payments

Example: $400,000 loan, 5% fixed rate, 30-year amortization			
Schedule	Payments	No. of Payments	Total Paid
Monthly	$2,147.29	360	$773,024
Biweekly	$1,073.65	656	$704,340
The biweekly loan would be paid off in a little over 25 years, with total interest payments of approximately $68,684 less than the loan with monthly payments.			

Biweekly Mortgage. The **biweekly mortgage** allows the borrower to repay a conventional loan in a shorter period than the loan's stated term. With a biweekly mortgage, both the interest rate and the payment amount are fixed, but payments are made every two weeks instead of every month. Each payment is equal to half of what the monthly payment would be for a fully amortized, 30-year, fixed-rate loan of the same amount at the same interest rate.

The attraction of the biweekly loan is the amount of interest the borrower can save. For example, a $400,000 loan at 5% interest paid on a biweekly basis saves almost $69,000 in interest compared to the monthly payment plan (see Figure 5.5). By paying every two weeks (26 payments per year), the borrower makes the equivalent of 13 monthly payments a year. As a result, biweekly loans are usually paid off in around 25 years, instead of 30 years.

Most lenders require biweekly borrowers to authorize automatic transfers from their checking accounts to reduce the extra processing cost in handling 26 payments instead of the 12 required for a standard mortgage. The borrower may also be required to buy overdraft protection. Since many people get paid on a biweekly basis, setting up the mortgage payment on the same basis can make sense. However, the borrower must make sure the funds are available for payment every two weeks.

Blanket Mortgage. Sometimes a borrower mortgages two or more pieces of property as security for one loan. For example, a ten-acre parcel subdivided into twenty lots might be used to secure one loan made to the subdivider. Blanket mortgages usually have a partial release clause (also called a partial satisfaction clause or, in a deed of trust, a partial reconveyance clause). As we discussed earlier, this provision requires the lender to release some of the security property

Biweekly mortgage:
- 26 half payments per year, equivalent to 13 monthly payments
- Loan paid off in 25 years

Blanket mortgage:
- Secured by more than one parcel of land
- Partial release clause

from the blanket lien when a specified portion of the overall debt has been paid off.

> **Example:** A ten-acre parcel subdivided into twenty lots secures a $500,000 loan. After selling one lot for $50,000, the subdivider pays the lender $45,000 and receives a release for the lot that is being sold. The blanket mortgage is no longer a lien against that lot, so the subdivider can convey clear title to the lot buyer.

The properties covered by a blanket mortgage do not have to be contiguous or neighboring parcels. A borrower who owns pieces of land in two different counties could offer both pieces of land as collateral for a single blanket mortgage loan. (To fully protect the lender's security interest, the blanket mortgage document would have to be recorded in both counties.)

Construction Loan. A construction loan (sometimes called an **interim loan**) is a short-term loan used to finance the construction of improvements on land already owned by the borrower. The mortgage for this type of loan creates a lien against both the land and the improvements under construction.

Construction loans can be very profitable, but they are considered risky. Accordingly, lenders charge high interest rates and loan fees on construction loans, and they supervise the progress of the construction. There is always a danger that the borrower will overspend on the construction project and exhaust the loan proceeds before construction is completed. If the borrower cannot afford to finish, the lender is left with a security interest in a partially completed project.

Lenders have devised a number of plans for disbursement of construction loan proceeds that guard against overspending by the borrower. Perhaps the most common is the **fixed disbursement plan**. This calls for a series of predetermined disbursements, called **obligatory advances**, at various stages of construction. Interest begins to accrue with the first disbursement.

> **Example:** The construction loan agreement stipulates that the lender will release 10% of the proceeds when the project is 20% complete, and thereafter 20% draws will be available whenever construction has progressed another 20% toward completion.

The lender will often hold back 10% or more of the loan proceeds until the period for claiming construction liens (mechanic's or materialmen's liens) has expired, to protect against unpaid liens that

Construction loan: temporary financing that provides funds for construction until project is completed could affect the marketability of the property. The construction loan agreement usually states that if a valid construction lien is recorded, the lender may use the undisbursed portion of the loan to pay it off.

When the construction is completed, the construction loan is replaced by permanent financing that is called a **take-out loan**. The borrower then repays the amount borrowed, plus interest, over a specified term, as with an ordinary mortgage.

Nonrecourse mortgage:
- Lender can't sue borrower
- Foreclosure is lender's only remedy

Nonrecourse Mortgage. A nonrecourse mortgage is one that gives the lender no recourse against the borrower. That means the lender's only remedy in the event of default is foreclosure on the collateral property; the borrower is not personally liable for repayment of the loan.

A loan may be a nonrecourse mortgage for one of two reasons. The loan contract itself may provide that the lender will have no recourse against the borrower in the event of default. Or, as we discussed earlier in this chapter, state law may prevent the lender from obtaining a deficiency judgment against the borrower. In either case, the loan may be considered a nonrecourse mortgage.

Participation mortgage entitles lender to a share of the property's earnings

Participation Mortgage. A participation mortgage allows the lender to participate in the earnings generated by the mortgaged property, usually in addition to collecting interest payments on the principal. In some cases the lender participates by becoming a part-owner of the property. Participation loans are most common on large commercial projects where the lender is an insurance company or other large investor.

Shared appreciation mortgage entitles lender to a share of increases in property's value

Shared Appreciation Mortgage. Real property usually appreciates (increases in value), given sufficient time. Appreciation normally benefits only the property owner, by adding to her equity. With a shared appreciation mortgage, however, the lender is entitled to a specified share of the increase in the property's value. This type of mortgage is rare, especially during times when home prices are flat or falling. Nonetheless, some suggest that shared appreciation mortgages could play a role in helping to correct a housing market downturn. Analysts note that if the government provides direct financial aid to troubled homeowners, a shared appreciation arrangement might eventually provide a return to taxpayers in exchange for the tax dollars spent.

Wraparound Mortgage. A wraparound mortgage is a new mortgage that includes, or "wraps around," an existing first mortgage on the

Fig. 5.6 Types of mortgage loans

- **Junior or Senior**
  Refers to lien priority

- **Purchase Money**
  Used for seller financing

- **Home Equity**
  Secured by equity in property already owned

- **Refinance**
  New loan used to pay off old

- **Bridge**
  Provides cash for purchase of new home pending sale of old

- **Budget**
  Payments include share of taxes and insurance

- **Package**
  Secured by both personal and real property

- **Biweekly**
  Payments made every two weeks

- **Blanket**
  Secured by multiple parcels

- **Construction**
  Temporary loan funds project until completed

- **Nonrecourse**
  Foreclosure is lender's only remedy

- **Participation**
  Lender receives share of property's earnings

- **Shared Appreciation**
  Lender receives share of equity

- **Wraparound**
  Underlying loan is still being paid off

- **Reverse**
  Elderly owner receives payments from lender

property. Wraparounds are used almost exclusively in seller-financed transactions, and we will discuss them in detail in Chapter 13.

Reverse Mortgage. A reverse mortgage is sometimes called a reverse equity mortgage, a reverse annuity mortgage, or (in the FHA loan program) a home equity conversion mortgage. It is designed to provide income to older homeowners. With this type of loan, a homeowner borrows against the home's equity in order to receive a lump sum payment, a line of credit, or monthly payments from the lender. This can make it possible for an elderly person who might otherwise have to sell his home (and invest the proceeds to obtain a source of income) to keep the home.

Typically, a reverse mortgage borrower is required to be over a certain age (generally 62) and must own the home with little or no outstanding mortgage balance. The amount of the payment from the lender depends on the appraised value of the home, the age of the homeowner, the interest charged, and the terms of repayment. The home usually must be sold when the last owner dies in order to pay back the mortgage.

Wraparound mortgage is a form of seller financing

Reverse mortgage provides elderly homeowners with a source of income, without requiring them to sell their home

Outline: Finance Instruments

I. Promissory Notes

    A. A promissory note is basic evidence of a borrower's legal obligation to pay a debt.

        1. The debtor (usually a buyer) is the maker of the note; the creditor (the lender) is the payee.

        2. The note will specify the names of the parties, the date, the amount of debt, the interest rate, and how and when the money will be repaid.

    B. Promissory notes used for real estate loans are negotiable, to facilitate resale of the loans on the secondary market.

        1. A negotiable instrument is freely transferable by the payee to a third party.

        2. If a promissory note is endorsed "without recourse," the original payee will not be liable if the maker fails to make payments to the third party.

        3. A third party purchaser who buys a promissory note from a payee in good faith is known as a holder in due course.

    C. Types of notes

        1. Straight note: required payments are interest-only, with a balloon payment at the end of the term.

        2. Installment note: payments include part of the principal as well as interest.

II. Security Instruments

    A. A security instrument makes the borrower's property collateral for the loan and gives the lender the right to foreclose in the event of default.

    B. Types of security instruments

        1. Mortgage: a security instrument in which a borrower (the mortgagor) mortgages his property to the lender (the mortgagee).

        2. Deed of trust: a security instrument that includes a power of sale clause, so that a trustee can foreclose nonjudicially in the event of default; the borrower is called the grantor (or trustor) and the lender is the beneficiary.

III. Foreclosure

    A. Types of foreclosure

        1. Judicial foreclosure: a mortgagee files a lawsuit against a defaulting borrower, asking the court to order the property to be sold to the highest bidder at a sheriff's sale.

    2.   Nonjudicial foreclosure: with a deed of trust, the lender does not need to file a lawsuit in the event of default; the property is sold to the highest bidder at the trustee's sale.

B. Judicial foreclosure process

    1.   In a judicial foreclosure, the borrower is sometimes allowed to repay the delinquent amount and reinstate the loan at any point before the court hearing occurs.

    2.   In other states, the borrower can't reinstate the loan, but may stop the foreclosure and redeem the property by paying off the entire loan balance before the sheriff's sale; this is known as the equitable right of redemption.

    3.   If the foreclosure action goes to trial, in most cases the judge will issue a court order called a writ of execution, ordering the sheriff to seize and sell the property.

    4.   Proceeds from the sheriff's sale will be used to pay off the mortgage and other liens, with any surplus going to the debtor.

    5.   If the proceeds do not pay off the mortgage and other liens, the lender may have the right to obtain a deficiency judgment against the borrower for the amount of the shortfall.

    6.   The debtor may have an additional period of time after the sheriff's sale to redeem the property, known as the statutory redemption period.

    7.   At the end of the statutory redemption period, the purchaser at the sheriff's sale receives a sheriff's deed to the property.

C. Nonjudicial foreclosure process

    1.   The trustee will provide notice of default to the borrower and then give notice of a trustee's sale.

    2.   In the period before the sale, the borrower may reinstate the loan by paying the delinquent amount plus costs.

    3.   The winning bidder at a trustee's sale usually receives a trustee's deed without delay; a deed of trust borrower generally does not have a post-sale right of redemption.

    4.   In some states, the lender does not have a right to a deficiency judgment after a nonjudicial foreclosure.

D. Alternatives to foreclosure

    1.   Loan workouts

        a.   The borrower may be able to convince the lender to arrange a repayment plan to pay off past due amounts.

       b.   Alternatively, the lender may agree to modify the terms of the loan to reduce the monthly payment amount; if the borrower makes the payments on time during a trial period and meets other criteria, the new loan terms become permanent.

  2. Deed in lieu of foreclosure: the borrower can deed the property to the lender to satisfy the debt; if the property is worth considerably less than the amount owed, the borrower may be required to sign a promissory note for the difference.

  3. Short sale: the borrower may obtain the lender's consent to sell the home for less than the full amount owed; the lender accepts the sale proceeds and releases the borrower from the debt.

  4. To obtain lender consent for some of these alternatives, the borrower may have to be at least 90 days behind on payments and prove financial hardship by filling out an application and providing copies of pay stubs, bank statements, bills, etc.

  5. Borrowers receiving a reduction of debt may be liable to the IRS for income taxes on this debt relief.

IV. Finance Instrument Provisions

  A. Subordination clause: allows an instrument recorded later to take priority over an earlier recorded instrument.

  B. Late charge provision: adds a late fee to overdue payments.

  C. Prepayment provision: may impose a penalty if the borrower repays some or all of the principal before it is due, to compensate the lender for lost interest.

  D. Partial release clause: in a security instrument covering multiple parcels, provides for the release of part of the security property when part of the debt has been paid.

  E. Acceleration clause: allows the lender to declare the entire loan balance immediately due in the event of a default.

  F. Alienation clause: limits the borrower's right to transfer the property without the lender's permission unless the loan is paid off first.

    1. If the loan isn't paid off, the new owner takes title subject to existing liens, so the lender retains the power to foreclose on the property.

    2. Alternatively, the new owner may assume the loan, taking on responsibility for repayment.

       a.   In an assumption, the former owner (the original borrower) retains secondary liability unless released by the lender.

       b.   If the lender approves the assumption, an assumption fee will be charged, and the lender could also increase the interest rate.

V. Types of Real Estate Loans

A. Junior or senior mortgage: a senior mortgage has first lien position, while a junior mortgage has lower lien priority.

B. Purchase money mortgage: any mortgage loan used to buy the property that serves as security for the loan; or (in its narrower sense) a mortgage that a buyer gives to a seller in a seller-financed transaction.

C. Home equity loan: a loan using property that the borrower already owns as collateral.

D. Refinance mortgage: a new mortgage used to replace an existing mortgage on the same property, often used by borrowers when interest rates drop.

E. Bridge loan: a temporary loan used by buyers to purchase a new home before the sale of their old home closes.

F. Budget mortgage: a mortgage where payments include not just principal and interest, but also property taxes and hazard insurance.

G. Biweekly mortgage: requires a payment every two weeks, so that the loan is paid off on an accelerated schedule.

H. Package mortgage: a mortgage that covers the purchase of both real property and personal property (such as fixtures or equipment).

I. Blanket mortgage: a mortgage that uses multiple properties as collateral and contains a partial release clause.

J. Construction loan: a short-term loan used to finance construction of improvements on land already owned by the borrower.

K. Nonrecourse mortgage: a mortgage that does not allow for a deficiency judgment against the borrower; the lender's only remedy is foreclosure.

L. Participation mortgage: a mortgage where the lender receives a percentage of earnings generated by the property as well as interest payments.

M. Shared appreciation mortgage: a mortgage where a lender is entitled to a portion of any increase in the property's value.

N. Reverse mortgage: a mortgage where a lender gives a lump sum payment, a line of credit, or monthly payments to a homeowner who meets certain age and equity requirements; the home will typically be sold when the last owner dies, in order to pay back the mortgage.

Key Terms

Promissory note: A written, legally binding promise to repay a debt, which may or may not be a negotiable instrument.

Maker: In a promissory note, the party who promises to pay; the debtor or borrower.

Payee: In a promissory note, the party who is entitled to be paid; the creditor or lender.

Negotiable instrument: An instrument (such as a promissory note or check) establishing a right to payment, which is freely transferable from one person to another.

Holder in due course: A third party purchaser of a promissory note who purchased the note for value and in good faith.

Straight note: A promissory note that calls for regular payments of interest only.

Installment note: A promissory note that calls for regular payments of principal and interest until the debt is paid off, as used in an amortized loan.

Security instrument: A document that creates a voluntary lien against real property to secure repayment of a loan.

Hypothecation: Making property security for a loan without surrendering possession or transferring title to the lender.

Legal title: Title held as security, without the right to possess the property.

Equitable title: The property rights that a borrower retains while a lender or vendor holds legal title.

Lien: A nonpossessory interest in property giving the lienholder the right to foreclose if the owner does not pay a debt owed to the lienholder.

Mortgage: A security instrument that creates a voluntary lien on a property to secure repayment of a debt; the parties are the mortgagor (borrower) and mortgagee (lender).

Deed of trust: A security instrument that serves the same purpose as a mortgage but gives the power of sale to a trustee, so that it can be foreclosed nonjudicially; the borrower is called the grantor (or trustor) and the lender is the beneficiary.

Judicial foreclosure: A court-supervised foreclosure, beginning with a lawsuit filed by a mortgagee (or beneficiary) to foreclose on property after the borrower has defaulted.

Nonjudicial foreclosure: Foreclosure under a power of sale clause in the security instrument, carried out without court proceedings.

Power of sale clause: A clause in a security instrument that allows the lender to foreclose nonjudicially in the event of default.

Reinstatement: The right of a defaulting borrower to prevent foreclosure by curing the default and paying costs.

Redemption: The right of a defaulting borrower to prevent foreclosure by paying off the entire loan balance plus costs.

Equitable right of redemption: A period prior to a sheriff's sale in which a mortgagor can stop the foreclosure and redeem the property by paying off the loan balance plus costs.

Statutory right of redemption: A period following the sheriff's sale in which a mortgagor can redeem the property by paying off the loan balance plus costs.

Sheriff's sale: A public auction of property after a judicial foreclosure.

Deficiency judgment: A court judgment requiring the debtor to pay to the lender the difference between the amount of the debt and the proceeds of the foreclosure sale.

Trustee's sale: A nonjudicial foreclosure sale conducted by a trustee under the power of sale clause in a deed of trust.

Loan workout: When the lender adjusts the payment schedule or modifies the loan terms to help the borrower avoid foreclosure.

Deed in lieu of foreclosure: When a borrower deeds the property to the lender to satisfy the debt.

Short sale: When a borrower obtains the lender's consent to sell the home for less than the full amount owed; the lender receives the sale proceeds and releases the borrower from the debt.

Subordination clause: A provision in a security instrument that permits a later security instrument to have a higher lien priority than the instrument in which the clause appears.

Prepayment provision: A clause allowing a lender to charge borrowers for prepaying principal on a loan, to compensate for lost interest.

Partial release clause: A clause allowing one or more parcels under a blanket lien to be released from the lien while other parcels remain subject to it.

Acceleration clause: A provision in a security instrument allowing the lender to declare the entire debt due if the borrower breaches one or more provisions.

Alienation clause: A clause in a security instrument giving the lender the right to accelerate the loan if the borrower sells the property or transfers a significant interest in it without the lender's approval. Also called a due-on-sale clause.

Assumption: When a buyer takes on responsibility for repaying an existing loan and becomes liable to the lender; the seller remains secondarily liable to the lender.

Certificate of reduction: A certificate from a lender that either acknowledges a transfer of ownership and waives the due-on-sale clause, or states the balance and status of the loan. Sometimes called an estoppel letter.

Junior mortgage: A mortgage that has lower lien priority than another mortgage against the same property (the senior mortgage).

Purchase money mortgage: Any loan used to purchase the property that secures the loan; or (more narrowly) a loan given to a buyer by a seller in a seller-financed transaction.

Home equity loan: A mortgage loan that uses a home that the borrower already owns as the collateral.

Refinance mortgage: A mortgage loan used to pay off an existing mortgage on the same property.

Budget mortgage: A mortgage where the monthly payments include a share of the property taxes and insurance, in addition to principal and interest.

Biweekly mortgage: A loan that requires a payment every two weeks instead of once a month; by making the equivalent of 13 payments per year, the borrower pays the loan off early and saves a considerable amount in interest.

Package mortgage: A mortgage secured by items of personal property as well as real property.

Blanket mortgage: A mortgage that encumbers more than one parcel of property.

Construction loan: A loan used to finance the construction of a building; it remains in place only until construction is completed, and then it is replaced with a take-out loan.

Reverse mortgage: An arrangement in which a homeowner mortgages a home (usually owned free and clear) in exchange for a lump sum, a line of credit, or monthly payments from the lender. Also called a reverse equity mortgage, reverse annuity mortgage, or home equity conversion mortgage.

Chapter Quiz

1. The purpose of a promissory note is to:
    a. give the lender the right to foreclose on the borrower's property in the event of default
    b. allow the lender to foreclose nonjudicially instead of judicially
    c. establish the borrower's legal obligation to repay the loan
    d. prevent the lender from accelerating the loan in the event of default

2. The equitable right of redemption:
    a. usually lasts until the sheriff's sale is held
    b. enables the mortgagor to redeem the property after the sheriff's sale
    c. allows the trustee to cure the default and reinstate the loan
    d. doesn't apply in a judicial foreclosure

3. If the proceeds of a foreclosure sale are not enough to pay off all the liens against the property:
    a. each lienholder receives a proportionate share of the proceeds
    b. the lien with the highest priority is paid off first, and the junior lienholders are paid only if there is money left over
    c. the sale is declared void, and the property is auctioned again
    d. the foreclosure sale purchaser must pay off the remaining liens

4. To redeem property after a sheriff's sale, the borrower is generally required to pay:
    a. only the amounts that were delinquent before the loan was accelerated, plus the costs of the sale
    b. the original principal amount of the loan, plus costs
    c. the amount paid for the property at the sheriff's sale, plus interest accrued from the time of the sale
    d. whatever the sheriff's sale purchaser asks for the property, as long as it is not more than the appraised value

5. As a general rule, the key difference between a mortgage and a deed of trust is that:
    a. the mortgage contains a power of sale clause
    b. the mortgage contains an acceleration clause
    c. the deed of trust contains an acceleration clause
    d. the deed of trust contains a power of sale clause

6. In a state where both mortgages and deeds of trust are used, a lender who wants to be able to foreclose quickly and inexpensively probably should choose a:
    a. mortgage
    b. deed of trust
    c. bridge loan
    d. package mortgage

7. A buyer can assume a seller's existing loan without the lender's permission only if the mortgage or deed of trust does not contain:

   a. a prepayment clause
   b. a subordination clause
   c. an acceleration clause
   d. an alienation clause

8. In a certificate of reduction:

   a. the buyer assumes legal responsibility for repayment of the seller's loan
   b. the lender acknowledges the transfer and waives the right to exercise the due-on-sale clause
   c. the seller agrees to pay a prepayment penalty
   d. the seller accepts secondary liability for repayment of the loan assumed by the buyer

9. Which of the following types of loans could call for the lender to make monthly payments to the borrower?

   a. Purchase money mortgage
   b. Wraparound mortgage
   c. Reverse mortgage
   d. Participation mortgage

10. A refinance loan:

   a. enables the borrower to pay off an existing mortgage
   b. is a modification of the existing mortgage, not a new loan
   c. must be arranged with the same lender as the existing mortgage
   d. All of the above

Answer Key

1. c. A promissory note is written evidence of a borrower's legal obligation to repay a loan.

2. a. The equitable right of redemption will usually last until the sheriff's sale has been held.

3. b. If foreclosure sale proceeds are inadequate to pay all lienholders in full, the lienholder with the highest priority is paid first, followed by each junior lienholder in order of priority until the money runs out. Some junior lienholders (or even all of them) may receive nothing.

4. c. To redeem the property during the statutory redemption period, the debtor usually must pay the amount that was paid for the property at the sheriff's sale, plus any interest accrued since the time of the sale.

5. d. A deed of trust, unlike most mortgages, contains a power of sale clause that allows the trustee to foreclose nonjudicially.

6. b. Given a choice between using a mortgage or a deed of trust, lenders typically prefer a deed of trust, since it can be foreclosed nonjudicially. Nonjudicial foreclosure is generally faster and less expensive than going to court. (Some states require judicial foreclosure, however.)

7. d. If a mortgage contains an alienation clause, the entire loan balance must be paid off if the property is sold without the lender's approval, preventing the possibility of assumption without permission.

8. b. A certificate of reduction is issued by a lender that wishes to acknowledge a transfer and waive the due-on-sale clause (alienation clause).

9. c. With a reverse mortgage, a lender may make monthly payments to a homeowner, typically an older homeowner who needs an income stream.

10. a. Refinancing is a loan taken out to pay off an existing loan on the same property. It is a new loan, and does not need to be with the same lender.

Chapter 6

Basic Features
of a Residential Loan

Amortization

Repayment Period
- Monthly payment
- Total interest
- Repayment period and interest rate

Loan-to-Value Ratio

Mortgage Insurance or Loan Guaranty

Secondary Financing

Fixed or Adjustable Interest Rate
- How ARMs work
- ARM features
- Explaining ARMs

Loan Features and Financing Options

Introduction

The size of loan a home buyer can get depends on the buyer's income, net worth, and credit history, and on the value of the property in question. It also depends on the features of the loan and the way it's structured. How long does the buyer have to repay the loan? How much of a downpayment does the lender require? Is the interest rate fixed or adjustable? Lenders offer different financing options at different times, depending on the current condition of the mortgage finance market and the cost of housing. Lenders structure their loans to limit the risk of foreclosure loss while still enabling buyers to purchase homes.

To understand the financing options available to home buyers in your area at a given time, you first need to understand the basic features of a mortgage loan. Variations in these features distinguish one loan program from another and determine which type of loan is right for a particular buyer. The basic features of a mortgage loan include:

- how the loan is amortized,
- the length of the repayment period,
- the loan-to-value ratio,
- whether there is mortgage insurance or a guaranty,
- whether there is secondary financing, and
- whether the interest rate is fixed or adjustable.

Amortization

Loan amortization refers to how principal and interest are paid to the lender over the course of the repayment period. A loan is **amortized** if the borrower is required to make regular installment payments that include some of the principal as well as interest on the principal. The regular payments are usually made in monthly installments.

Most home purchase loans made by institutional lenders are **fully amortized**. With a fully amortized loan, the regular monthly payments are enough to pay off all of the principal and interest by the end of the loan term. Each payment includes both a principal portion and an interest portion. When a payment is made, the principal portion is applied to the debt, paying back some of the amount originally borrowed. The remainder of the payment, the interest portion,

Fully amortized loan: level payments (including principal and interest) pay off loan by end of term

140

is retained by the lender as earnings or profit. With each payment, the amount of the debt is reduced and the interest due with the next payment is calculated based on the lower principal balance. The total monthly payment remains the same throughout the term of the loan, but every month the interest portion of the payment is smaller and the principal portion is correspondingly larger. The final payment pays off the loan completely; the principal balance is zero and no further interest is owed.

In the early years of a fully amortized loan, the principal portion of the payment is quite small, so it takes several years for the borrower's equity in the property to increase significantly through debt reduction. But toward the end of the loan term, the borrower's equity increases more rapidly.

> **Example:** A fully amortized, 30-year $100,000 loan at 6% interest calls for monthly payments of $599.55. Only $99.55 of the first payment is applied to the principal (see Figure 6.1). But by the twentieth year of the loan term, $327.89 of the $599.55 payment is applied to the principal.

There are two alternatives to a fully amortized loan: a partially amortized loan or an interest-only loan. Like a fully amortized loan, a **partially amortized** loan requires regular payments of both principal and interest. However, the regular payments are not enough to completely pay off the debt by the end of the loan term. The regular payments have repaid only part of the principal, and the remaining

Partially amortized loan: balloon payment required at end of term

Fig. 6.1 How an amortized loan's payments are applied to principal and interest

Example: $100,000 loan, 6%, 30-year term, monthly payments
(Figures approximate)

Payment Number	Principal Balance	Total Payment	Interest Portion	Principal Portion	Ending Balance
1	$100,000.00	$599.55	$500.00	$99.55	$99,900.45
2	$99,900.45	$599.55	$499.50	$100.05	$99,800.40
3	$99,800.40	$599.55	$499.00	$100.55	$99,699.85
4	$99,699.85	$599.55	$498.50	$101.05	$99,598.80
5	$99,598.80	$599.55	$497.99	$101.56	$99,497.24

balance must now be paid off. This final principal payment is called a **balloon payment**, because it is much larger than the regular payments made during the loan term.

> **Example:** A partially amortized $100,000 loan at 6% interest might require monthly payments of $599.55 for 15 years. At the end of that period, the remaining principal balance will be about $71,000. The borrower will have to make a balloon payment of $71,000 to pay off the loan.

In most cases, the borrower comes up with the funds for the balloon payment by refinancing. (Refinancing means using the funds from a new mortgage loan to pay off an existing mortgage.)

With an **interest-only** loan, the regular payments the borrower is required to make during the loan term cover the interest accruing on the loan, without paying down the principal.

> **Example:** With a $100,000 interest-only loan at 6% interest, the borrower must pay the lender $500 in interest each month during the loan term. At the end of the term, the borrower will have to pay the lender the entire $100,000 originally borrowed.

Interest-only loan requires no principal payments during the loan term, or for a specified period at the beginning of the term

Alternatively, an interest-only loan may allow the borrower to make interest-only payments for a specified period at the beginning of the loan term; at the end of this period, the borrower must begin making amortized payments that will pay off all principal and interest by the end of the term. This type of interest-only loan (sometimes called an "interest-first mortgage") was popular prior to the most recent financial crisis, especially in areas where housing prices were high; more stringent qualifying standards make them a less common option now.

Repayment Period

A loan's **repayment period** is the number of years the borrower has to repay the loan. The repayment period is often called the **loan term**.

Until the 1930s, the repayment period for a home purchase loan was ordinarily only five years, and the payments were interest-only. At the end of the five-year period, if the lender didn't renew the loan, a balloon payment of the full principal amount was required. When the Federal Housing Administration was established to help home buyers during the Depression, it made loans with a 30-year term available. With this longer repayment period, the loans could be fully amortized while keeping the monthly payments at an afford- able level. Lenders realized that this dramatically decreased the risk of default, and 30 years soon became the standard repayment period for all home purchase loans.

30-year loan term:
• Standard
• Affordable payments

While 30-year loans are still regarded as standard and are still the most common, lenders also offer 15-year and 20-year loans. In some cases, a term as short as 10 years or as long as 40 years will be allowed.

The length of the repayment period affects two important aspects of a mortgage loan:

1. the amount of the monthly payment, and
2. the total amount of interest paid over the life of the loan.

To see the impact that the repayment period has on the monthly payment and the total interest paid, let's compare a 30-year loan with a 15-year loan.

Monthly Payment Amount

A longer repayment period reduces the amount of the monthly payment, so a 30-year loan is more affordable than a 15-year loan.

> **Example:** The monthly payment on a $100,000 30-year loan at 7% interest is $665.30. The monthly payment on the same loan amortized over a 15-year period is $898.83.

The higher monthly payment required for a 15-year loan means that the borrower will build equity in the home much faster. But the higher payment also makes it much more difficult to qualify for a 15-year loan than for the same size loan with a 30-year term. A buyer who wants a 15-year loan might decide to make a larger downpayment and borrow less money to make the monthly payment amount more affordable. Or the buyer might decide to buy a much less expensive home than he could afford with a 30-year loan.

Shorter loan term means higher payment amount:
• Equity builds faster
• But many buyers can't qualify for a loan as large as they could with a 30-year term

Total Interest

Probably the biggest advantage of a shorter repayment period is that it substantially decreases the amount of interest paid over the life of the loan. With a 15-year mortgage, a borrower will end up paying

Shorter term means less total interest paid over loan term

less than half as much interest over the life of the loan as required by a 30-year mortgage.

> **Example:** Let's look at the $100,000 loan at 7% interest again. By the end of a 30-year loan term, the borrower will pay a total of $239,508. But by the end of a 15-year term, the borrower will pay only $161,789. After deducting the original $100,000 principal amount, you can see that the 30-year loan will require $139,508 in interest, while the 15-year loan will require only $61,789 in interest.

Repayment Period and Interest Rate

Shorter term typically means a lower interest rate

To simplify our comparison of a 15-year loan and a 30-year loan, we applied the same interest rate (7%) to both loans. In fact, however, a lender is likely to charge a lower interest rate on a 15-year loan than it charges on a comparable 30-year loan. Since the 15-year loan ties up the lender's capital for a shorter period, the lender's risk is reduced. So, for example, the interest rate on a 15-year loan might be half a percentage point lower than the rate on a 30-year loan.

Thus, the 30-year mortgage has affordable payments, but requires the borrower to pay much more interest over the life of the loan. On the other hand, the 15-year loan has higher monthly payments, but allows the borrower to pay far less interest over the life of the loan. Figure 6.2 compares $100,000, $150,000, and $200,000 mortgages at 6.5% interest for 15-year terms and 7% for 30-year terms.

15-year loan term
  Advantages:
    1. Lower interest rate
    2. Total interest much less
    3. Free and clear ownership in half the time
  Disadvantages:
    1. Higher monthly payments

As you can see, for a relatively small additional monthly payment, a 15-year loan offers substantial savings over its 30-year counterpart. A 15-year loan also provides the borrower with free and clear ownership of the home in half the time.

On the other hand, the higher monthly payments make the 15-year loan more difficult to afford in the short run. A larger downpayment would make the payments more affordable, but that's not an option for many buyers, so a 15-year loan would sharply reduce their buying power.

20-year loan is a compromise between a 15-year loan and a 30-year loan

20-year loans. A 20-year loan represents a compromise between the standard 30-year loan and the 15-year loan. Although the monthly payments for a 20-year loan are higher than the payments for a 30-year loan, they aren't as high as the payments for a 15-year loan. And yet the 20-year loan still provides significant interest savings over the life of the loan.

Fig. 6.2 Comparison of 15-year and 30-year loans (monthly payment amount and total payments)

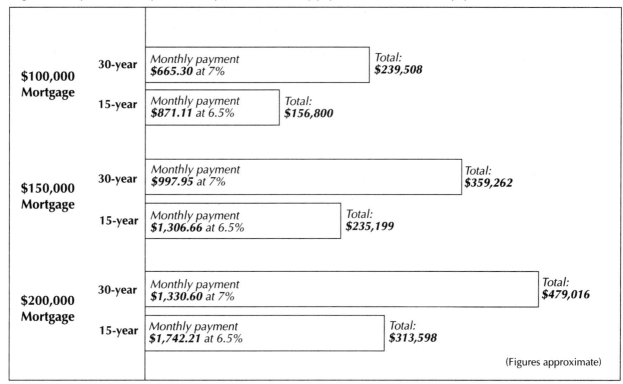

Example: For purposes of comparison, suppose that a $200,000 loan at 7% interest is amortized over 15, 20, and 30 years (not even taking into account that 15-year and 20-year loans are offered at lower interest rates than 30-year loans).

The monthly payment for the 30-year loan would be $1,330.60, and the borrower would have to pay about $479,016 over the life of the loan. The monthly payment for the 15-year loan would be $1,797.66 (35% more than the 30-year payment), but the total payments would be only $323,579 (32% less than the total payments on the 30-year loan). The monthly payment for the 20-year loan would be $1,550.60 (only 17% more than the 30-year payment), and the total payments would be $372,144 (still 22% less than the total payments on the 30-year loan).

40-year loans. A 40-year loan may be an option in areas where housing costs are very high and a standard 30-year loan is unlikely to be adequate to purchase a desirable house. Payments are lower for a 40-year loan than for a 30-year loan. However, most 40-year borrowers aren't looking for lower payments; instead, they want to use the same-sized payment to buy a more expensive home.

The main disadvantage of the 40-year loan is that the amortization schedule unfolds even more slowly than with a 30-year loan. The monthly payments will remain mostly interest for a much longer time period, and the borrower will build up equity much more slowly. The total interest paid over the life of the loan will be much higher, as well.

Loan-to-Value Ratio

A loan-to-value ratio (LTV) expresses the relationship between the loan amount and the value of the home being purchased. If a buyer is purchasing a $100,000 home with an $80,000 loan and a $20,000 downpayment, the loan-to-value ratio is 80%. If the loan amount were $90,000 and the downpayment were $10,000, the loan-to-value ratio would be 90%. The higher the LTV, the larger the loan amount and the smaller the downpayment.

A loan with a low LTV is generally less risky than one with a high LTV. The borrower's investment in her home is greater, so she'll try harder to avoid defaulting on the loan and losing the home. And if the borrower does default, the outstanding loan balance is lower, so it's more likely that the lender will be able to recoup the entire amount in a foreclosure sale.

Lenders use LTV limits to establish maximum loan amounts. For example, under the terms of a particular loan program, the maximum loan-to-value ratio might be 95% of the sales price or appraised value of the property, whichever is less. For a $100,000 home financed with a loan from that program, the maximum loan amount would be $95,000. The borrower would be required to make a downpayment of at least 5%, or $5,000.

As you can see, a loan program's maximum LTV determines not only the maximum loan amount for a transaction financed through that program, but also the minimum downpayment required. Thus, the maximum LTV is a key factor in determining how expensive a home a buyer can afford through a particular program.

> **Example:** The Allens have only $5,000 saved for a downpayment. They're hoping to buy a $100,000 house. If a particular loan program has a maximum LTV of 90%, the Allens won't be able to finance their purchase through that program unless they're able to come up with additional cash. Depending on the program's rules, they might be able to do that with gift funds

The higher the loan-to-value ratio, the smaller the downpayment

Lenders use loan-to-value ratios to establish maximum loan amounts

(see Chapter 8) or secondary financing (discussed later in this chapter). Otherwise, they'll have to finance the purchase through a different loan program that has a higher LTV limit.

To protect themselves against foreclosure loss, residential lenders traditionally had low LTV limits. For example, many lenders had a maximum LTV of 80%, requiring borrowers to make a 20% downpayment—a very substantial investment in the property. At one time, high-LTV home loans were available only through special programs such as the FHA and VA loan programs. Nowadays high-LTV loans, conventional as well as FHA and VA, are generally available. This helps make homeownership possible for more people, since coming up with even a modest downpayment is a challenge for many first-time buyers.

High-LTV loans help people buy homes when they don't have much money for a downpayment

There are various ways that lenders can compensate for the extra risk involved in making high-LTV loans. For instance, they can apply stricter qualifying standards or charge a higher interest rate. Probably the most effective way to minimize the risk of loss is with mortgage insurance or a loan guaranty. In fact, some form of mortgage insurance or guaranty is a requirement in almost all high-LTV home loan programs.

Mortgage Insurance or Loan Guaranty

Many home purchase loans are covered by a mortgage insurance policy or a loan guaranty. The purpose of the insurance or guaranty is to protect the lender from foreclosure loss. The coverage may be required by the lender or else offered as a feature of a particular loan program. (For example, the VA home loan program provides lenders with a guaranty on loans made to eligible veterans.) In either case, the insurance or guaranty serves as an incentive for lenders to make loans on terms that they would otherwise consider too risky. This may include not only high-LTV loans, as discussed above, but also loans to borrowers who represent extra risk (for example, a borrower with a high debt-to-income ratio or a mediocre credit score).

Mortgage insurance or loan guaranty often required for loan with high LTV or other increased risk factors

Mortgage Insurance

Mortgage insurance works basically like other types of insurance: in exchange for premiums, the insurer provides coverage for certain types of losses specified in the policy. Mortgage insurance premiums are ordinarily paid by the borrower. The policy protects the lender against losses that might result from the borrower's default on the mortgage and any subsequent foreclosure.

In the event that there is a default and foreclosure, the insurer will **indemnify** the lender. This means that if the proceeds of the foreclosure sale aren't enough to pay off the entire remaining amount that the borrower owes the lender, plus the lender's other expenses, the insurer will make up the shortfall. Depending on the policy, covered losses may include unpaid principal, interest, property taxes, hazard insurance, attorney's fees, and the cost of preserving the property during the period of foreclosure and resale, as well as the cost of the foreclosure sale itself.

Because the mortgage insurer assumes most of the risk of loan default, the insurer also underwrites the loan. In other words, the borrower must meet the qualifying standards of the mortgage insurer as well as the standards of the lender.

We'll discuss mortgage insurance in more detail in Chapter 10 (private mortgage insurance policies for conventional loans) and Chapter 11 (the mutual mortgage insurance coverage offered through the FHA-insured loan program).

Loan Guaranty

Loan guaranty: third party agrees to take on secondary responsibility for borrower's obligation

With a loan guaranty, a third party (called the **guarantor**) agrees to take on secondary legal responsibility for a borrower's obligation to a lender. If the borrower defaults on the loan, the guarantor will reimburse the lender for resulting losses. Thus, although a loan guaranty is not technically a form of insurance, from a mortgage lender's point of view it serves the same purpose as mortgage insurance.

The guarantor for a mortgage loan might be a private party, a nonprofit organization, or a governmental agency. The guarantor's motive for providing the guaranty is usually to help the borrower, rather than to turn a profit. The guaranty encourages the lender to make a loan on special terms favorable to the borrower, making it easier for the borrower to purchase a home. For example, the VA-guaranteed loan program is intended to promote homeownership among veterans.

Like a mortgage insurer, a guarantor may be involved in underwriting the loan. This is true for the VA loan program, which we'll cover in Chapter 12.

Secondary Financing

Sometimes a home buyer obtains two mortgage loans at once: a primary loan for most of the purchase price, and a second loan to pay part of the downpayment or closing costs required for the first loan. This second loan is called **secondary financing**. Secondary financing may come from an institutional lender, from the seller, or from a private third party. When an institutional lender is the source of the secondary financing, it may be the same lender that is making the first mortgage loan, or it may be a different lender.

Secondary financing: loan to pay part of downpayment or closing costs

A lender making a primary loan will usually place restrictions on the type of secondary financing arrangement that the borrower may enter into. For example, the primary lender will make sure that the payments required for the second loan don't exceed the borrower's ability to pay. When qualifying ratios are applied to the borrower's stable monthly income, the payments for both the first loan and the second loan will be taken into account. Also, in most cases the primary lender will still require the borrower to make at least a minimum downpayment out of her own funds, even if the secondary lender would be willing to supply the entire downpayment needed for the first loan.

Buyer must qualify for combined payments from both loans

The basic point of these and other restrictions on secondary financing is to minimize the risk of default on the second loan, since both loans are going to be secured by the same property. A second mortgage with a high risk of default would impair the primary lender's security interest and make default on the first mortgage more likely.

The specific restrictions that a primary lender imposes depend in part on whether the primary loan is conventional, FHA-insured, or VA-guaranteed. We'll discuss the secondary financing rules for each of the major loan programs in Chapters 10, 11, and 12.

Fixed or Adjustable Interest Rate

The final basic loan feature that we're going to cover in this chapter is the interest rate. A loan's interest rate can be either fixed or adjustable (variable).

With a **fixed-rate loan**, the interest rate charged on the loan remains constant throughout the entire loan term. If a borrower obtains a 30-year mortgage loan with a 6% fixed interest rate, the interest rate

Fixed-rate mortgage: interest rate remains the same throughout loan term

remains 6% for the whole 30-year period, no matter what happens to market interest rates during that time. If market rates increase to 10%, or if they drop to 4%, the interest rate charged on the loan will still be 6%.

The fixed-rate mortgage is regarded as the standard. It has been the cornerstone of residential financing since the Depression in the 1930s. In fact, through the end of the 1970s virtually all home purchase loans had fixed interest rates.

During the 1980s, however, market interest rates rose dramatically and also became more volatile—in other words, they changed more frequently. When mortgage interest rates are high, many potential home buyers can no longer afford financing. (Mortgage rates as high as 18% were not unheard of in the early 1980s.) And when rates are volatile, lenders are less willing to tie up their funds for a long period, such as 30 years, at a fixed rate.

For instance, suppose the current market rate for home mortgages is 6%, but economists are predicting much higher interest rates within the next year or so. A lender might hesitate to make a fixed-rate loan at 6% interest when it looks as though market rates might soon be up to 9%.

ARM: lender adjusts loan's interest rate from time to time to reflect changes in cost of money

To address both of these issues—affordability and volatility—the **adjustable-rate mortgage (ARM)** was introduced. An ARM allows the lender to periodically adjust the loan's interest rate to reflect changes in the cost of money. This allows the lender to share some of the risk of interest rate fluctuations with the borrower. If market rates climb, the borrower's interest rate and payment amount go up; if market rates decline, the borrower's rate and payment amount go down. Because ARMs shift some of the interest rate risk to the borrower, lenders have generally charged lower interest rates on ARMs than on fixed-rate loans—sometimes dramatically lower. For instance, under certain market conditions, a borrower who could get a fixed-rate loan at 6% might be able to get an ARM with an initial rate of 4.25%.

In the 1980s, when interest rates were at record highs, ARMs became a popular way to afford the financing needed to buy a home. When market rates are low, ARMs are less popular. But even when fixed-rate loans aren't very expensive, some buyers find ARMs attractive. For example, buyers who plan to own the property they're buying for only a few years might use an ARM with a low initial rate to buy "more house" than they otherwise could.

How ARMs Work

Next, let's look at how ARMs work and what their special features are. They're considerably more complicated than fixed-rate loans.

An ARM borrower's interest rate is determined initially by the cost of money (market interest rates) at the time the loan is made. Once the interest rate on the loan has been set, it is tied to one of several widely recognized indexes. Future interest rate adjustments are based on the upward and downward movements of that index. An **index** is a published statistical report that serves as a reliable indicator of changes in the cost of money.

ARM's interest rate tied to index that indicates changes in cost of money

When an ARM loan is made, the lender selects the index it prefers, and thereafter the loan's interest rate will be adjusted (increased or decreased) to reflect increases and decreases in the rates reported by that index. A change in the loan's interest rate will also result in an increase or decrease in the amount of the monthly payment the borrower is required to make.

ARM Features

To provide for interest rate and payment adjustments, adjustable-rate mortgages have a number of special features. Depending on the loan, an ARM may have all or only some of the following elements:

- a note rate,
- an index,
- a margin,
- a rate adjustment period,
- a mortgage payment adjustment period,
- a lookback period,
- an interest rate cap,
- a mortgage payment cap,
- a negative amortization cap, and
- a conversion option.

Note Rate. An ARM's initial interest rate is called the note rate because it is the rate stated in the promissory note. The note rate may also be referred to as the contract rate.

To attract borrowers, lenders sometimes offer ARMs with a discounted initial rate: an especially low interest rate for the first year. This is referred to as a "teaser rate." The teaser rate offered to a borrower is often the rate indicated by the index when the loan is made, without the lender's margin added (the margin is explained below).

Index. As we said above, an index is a statistical report that is used as an indicator of changes in the cost of money. There are several regularly published indexes that lenders use in connection with ARMs. Examples include the Treasury securities indexes, the 11th District cost of funds index, and the LIBOR index.

Some indexes are more responsive to changes in the cost of money than others. Lenders tend to prefer the more responsive indexes. A borrower benefits from a more responsive index when interest rates are decreasing, but may prefer a more stable index if rates are increasing.

Margin. An ARM's margin is the difference between the index rate and the interest rate that the lender charges the borrower. Since the index is a reflection of the lender's cost of money, it's necessary to add a margin to the index to cover the lender's administrative expenses and provide a profit. In fact, between lenders who use the same index, it's the size of the margin that makes the difference in the interest rates they charge. Margins vary from 2% to 3%. The index plus the margin equals the interest rate on the loan.

> Index
> + Margin
> ---
> Interest Rate

Example:

3.25%	Current index value
+ 2.00%	Margin
5.25%	ARM interest rate

It is the index rate that fluctuates during the loan term and causes the borrower's interest rate to increase and decrease; the lender's margin remains constant.

Rate Adjustment Period. The interest rate on an ARM isn't adjusted every time the index rate changes. Instead, the ARM has a rate adjustment period that determines when the lender may adjust the interest rate on the loan. It could provide for a rate adjustment every six months, once a year, or every three years, for example. A rate adjustment period of one year is the most common, and ARMs with one-year rate adjustment periods are referred to as one-year ARMs.

ARM's interest rate adjusted only at specified intervals

At the end of each rate adjustment period, the lender checks the index rate. If the index has increased or decreased, the lender makes a corresponding change in the loan's interest rate and notifies the borrower in writing of the change.

Some ARMs have a two-tiered rate adjustment structure. These loans are often called **hybrid ARMs**, because they're like a combination of an ARM and a fixed-rate loan. They provide for a longer initial period before the first rate adjustment, with more frequent adjustments after that.

> **Example:** The borrowers are financing their home with a 30-year ARM that has an initial rate adjustment period of three years, with annual rate adjustments from then on. The interest rate charged on their loan won't change during the first three years, but it will change each year after that.

The loan in the example would be called a 3/1 ARM. There are also 5/1 ARMs, 7/1 ARMs, and 10/1 ARMs. In each case, the first number is the number of years in the initial rate adjustment period, and the second number means that subsequent rate adjustments will occur once a year. Some borrowers who choose a hybrid ARM plan to sell or refinance their home before the end of the initial adjustment period.

Mortgage Payment Adjustment Period. An ARM's mortgage payment adjustment period determines when the lender changes the amount of the borrower's monthly principal and interest payment to reflect a change in the interest rate charged on the loan. For most ARMs, the mortgage payment adjustment period is the same as the rate adjustment period. As soon as the interest rate is adjusted, the lender also adjusts the mortgage payment.

With some ARMs, however, the payment adjustment period doesn't coincide with the rate adjustment period. Instead, the lender adjusts the interest rate more frequently than the mortgage payment. For example, the loan agreement might call for interest rate adjustments every six months, but changes in the amount of the mortgage payment only every two years. This arrangement can have undesirable consequences for the borrower. (See the discussion of negative amortization later in this section.)

Lookback Period. As we've just explained, how often the lender changes an ARM borrower's interest rate and payment amount depends on the loan's rate and payment adjustment period(s). You may also hear reference to an ARM's "lookback period." A typical lookback period is 45 days. That means that the loan's rate and payment adjustments will actually be determined by where the index stood

Hybrid ARMs have an initial fixed-rate period

Payment amount not necessarily adjusted every time interest rate is adjusted

45 days before the end of the adjustment period (not on the date the adjustment period ends).

> **Example:** A one-year ARM has a 45-day lookback period. At the end of the one-year rate adjustment period, on July 2, the index that the ARM is tied to has risen 0.75%. But 45 days earlier, on May 18, the index had risen only 0.50%. Therefore the lender can raise the interest rate on the borrower's loan only by 0.50%, not 0.75%.

Interest Rate Cap. Not long after adjustable-rate mortgages were introduced, some ARM borrowers encountered a problem that came to be known as **payment shock**. Payment shock occurs when market interest rates rise very rapidly. As market rates go up, so do ARM indexes, and that results in sharp increases in the interest rates lenders charge ARM borrowers. Of course, a higher interest rate also translates into higher monthly payments. In some cases, the payments can increase so dramatically that the borrowers can no longer afford them. Borrowers who fall victim to payment shock often have to sell their homes or face foreclosure.

To protect borrowers from payment shock (and protect themselves from default), many lenders include interest rate caps in their ARMs. An **interest rate cap** limits how much the interest rate on the loan can increase, regardless of what the index does. By limiting interest rate increases, the rate cap prevents the monthly payment from increasing too much.

Some ARMs have two kinds of rate caps. One limits the amount that the interest rate can change in any single adjustment period. The other type of cap limits the amount that the interest rate can increase over the entire loan term. For example, a one-year ARM might have a 2% annual rate cap and a 5% life-of-the-loan cap. When the lender adjusts the loan's interest rate each year, the annual rate cap prevents the lender from increasing the rate more than 2% at one time. And because of the life-of-the-loan cap, the borrower knows from the outset that no matter how much the index increases over the course of the loan term, the interest rate charged on the loan can never be more than 5% higher than the note rate.

For most ARMs, the annual interest rate cap applies to rate reductions as well as rate increases.

> **Example:** A loan agreement provides that the loan's interest rate can't increase or decrease more than 2% per year. If the index

Payment shock: sharp increase in payment due to rate increase

Interest rate cap limits how much rate can increase

rate rises 3% in one year, the lender can raise the loan's interest rate by only 2%; and if the index drops 3% in one year, the lender will reduce the loan's rate by only 2%.

In contrast, a life-of-the-loan cap typically limits only rate increases, not decreases.

Mortgage Payment Cap. A second way of limiting payment increases is with a mortgage payment cap. A **payment cap** directly limits how much the lender can raise the monthly mortgage payment. Typically, payment caps limit mortgage payment increases to 7.5% annually. (A 7.5% payment increase is considered to be approximately equivalent to an increase in the interest rate of one percentage point.) Note that payment caps apply only to increases in the principal and interest portion of the loan payment; there is no limit to how much the payment can increase because of higher property taxes or hazard insurance premiums.

Payment cap directly limits how much mortgage payment can increase

Some ARMs have only an interest rate cap and no mortgage payment cap. Some have both an interest rate cap and a payment cap, and still others have only a payment cap. Any of these arrangements will protect the borrower from payment shock if interest rates skyrocket. However, if a loan has a payment cap and no rate cap, the borrower may encounter the problem of negative amortization (see below).

While protections against payment shock are important, keep in mind that steadily rising interest rates and sharp payment increases are the worst case scenario for an ARM. Over the course of a 30-year loan term, the borrower's interest rate and payment will probably decrease from time to time, offsetting at least some increases.

Over time, interest rate increases may be offset by rate decreases

Negative Amortization. When an adjustable-rate mortgage has certain features, changes in the loan's interest rate may result in negative amortization. Before we define negative amortization, let's look at an example.

> **Example:** The Walkers borrowed $190,000 to buy their home. Their mortgage is a one-year ARM with a 7.5% annual payment cap but no interest rate cap. Their initial interest rate was 4.5%, and their monthly payment during the first year has been $962.70. At the end of the first year, the index that the Walkers' ARM is tied to has risen 2.75%. So the lender adjusts the loan's interest rate up by 2.75% (from 4.5% to 7.25%). Without a payment cap, this rate increase would increase the monthly payment by $325, to $1,287.70. Out of that payment amount, approximately $1,129.40 would be interest.

However, the payment cap limits the Walkers' payment increase to no more than 7.5% of the payment amount per year. In this case, that is $72.20:

$962.70	Year 1 payment
× 7.5%	Payment cap percentage
$72.20	Maximum payment increase for Year 2

As a result, the monthly payment during the second year of the Walkers' loan term can be no more than $1,034.90:

$962.70	Year 1 payment
+ 72.20	7.5% of the Year 1 payment
$1,034.90	Maximum Year 2 payment

In this situation, the payment cap has prevented the payment from increasing enough to cover all of the interest charged on the loan during the second year. Even if the Walkers' entire $1,034.90 monthly payment is applied only to interest (without paying down the principal balance at all), the interest accruing on the loan during the second year won't be fully covered. The shortfall will be about $94.50 per month, or $1,134 for the year.

Negative amortization: unpaid interest added to principal balance, increasing the amount owed

The lender will handle the situation in the example by adding the unpaid interest to the loan's principal balance. When unpaid interest is added to the loan balance, it is called **negative amortization**. Ordinarily, a loan's principal balance declines steadily, although gradually. But negative amortization causes the principal balance to go up instead of down. The borrower may owe the lender more than she originally borrowed.

In the example, negative amortization occurred because there was a payment cap and no interest rate cap. Negative amortization can also occur when an ARM's interest rate adjustment period and mortgage payment adjustment period do not coincide. Suppose a borrower has an ARM with a six-month rate adjustment period and a three-year payment adjustment period. Over a three-year period, the loan's interest rate might increase five times while the payment amount stayed the same (see Figure 6.3). The borrower would be paying too little interest during that period, which would result in negative amortization.

ARM features that can lead to negative amortization:
- Payment cap but no rate cap; or
- Payments adjusted less often than interest rate

Most adjustable-rate loans are now structured to prevent negative amortization from occurring. But when negative amortization is a possibility, the loan may have a **negative amortization cap**: a limit

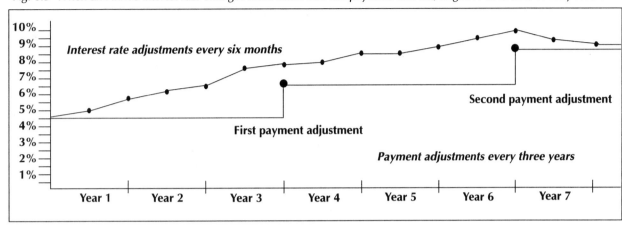

Fig. 6.3 When an ARM's interest rate changes more often than the payment amount, negative amortization may result

on the amount of unpaid interest that can be added to the principal balance. For example, a negative amortization cap might limit the total amount the borrower could owe to 115% of the original loan amount. When that point was reached, the loan would be recast and the monthly payment would be set to fully repay the loan over the remainder of the term.

Prior to the financial crisis that began in 2007, some ARMs were set up to allow negative amortization. Known as **option ARMs**, these loans allowed the borrower to choose one of several payment options every month. The various payment options included a traditional payment of principal and interest, based on a 15- or 30-year amortization period; interest-only payments; and a minimum (or limited) payment, which was even less than the interest-only payment. The last option resulted in negative amortization. The purpose of option ARMs was to allow sophisticated borrowers with growing but variable incomes to manage their cash flow. However, many borrowers simply relied on the negative amortization option every month, leading to many defaults after the loans were recast. Most lenders have stopped offering option ARMs.

Conversion Option. Some borrowers feel uncomfortable continuing to bear the risk of rate and payment increases that an ARM involves. Many ARMs allow the borrower to convert the loan to a fixed-rate mortgage at designated times during the loan term.

A conversion option ordinarily involves a limited time to convert, and the borrower is usually required to pay a conversion fee. For example, a borrower with a convertible ARM might have the option

Conversion option: opportunity to switch from adjustable to fixed interest rate of converting from an adjustable interest rate to a fixed rate between the first and fifth year of the loan term for a small conversion fee. If the borrower chooses to convert the loan, the fixed rate will be the current market rate.

Explaining ARMs

Clearly, adjustable-rate mortgages are a lot more complicated than fixed-rate mortgages. It's not surprising that many buyers have trouble understanding ARMs. To address that problem, the Truth in Lending Act requires lenders to make special disclosures to ARM loan applicants (see Chapter 14).

When you're working with buyers who are considering an ARM, it can be helpful to go over the lender's required disclosures with them. The list of questions shown in Figure 6.4 and an ARM comparison worksheet such as the one in Figure 6.5 may also be useful.

Loan Features and Financing Options

As a real estate agent, in addition to helping home buyers evaluate their financing options, you may occasionally be called upon to help design a financing option to fit a special situation. The loan features that we've covered in this chapter—amortization, repayment period, loan-to-value ratio, a fixed or adjustable interest rate, and (in some cases) mortgage insurance or secondary financing—are the basic elements used to design financing. In combination with one another, they determine whether a particular loan will enable a particular buyer to buy a particular property. They determine how much money the buyer can borrow (the loan amount), how much money the buyer will need to close the loan (the downpayment), and how affordable the loan will be (the monthly payment amount). Those are the key issues that will come up again and again throughout the rest of the book.

Fig. 6.4 ARM questions

Adjustable-Rate Mortgages

Buyers considering an ARM need to know the answers to these questions.

1. What will my initial interest rate be?

It usually isn't necessary to break the rate down into index and margin. The buyer is concerned only with the total. The initial rate (note rate or contract rate) will be based on the cost of money when the loan is made.

2. How often will my interest rate change?

The adjustment period will be stated in the loan agreement. Depending on the lender's preference, adjustments may occur every six months, annually, every three years, or every five years. Six-month and one-year intervals are most common.

3. How often will my payment change?

Again, in order to give an accurate answer, you have to be familiar with the policies of the particular lender. Most lenders prefer simultaneous rate and payment changes.

4. Is there any limit to how much my interest rate can be increased?

Most ARMs have interest rate caps. An annual cap is usually 1% or 2%; a life-of-the-loan cap is usually 5% or 6%.

5. Is there any limit to how much my payment can be increased at any one time?

Some ARMs have payment caps, but most keep payment increases under control with interest rate caps. When there is a payment cap, payment increases are usually limited to 7.5% of the payment amount per year.

6. Will my ARM involve negative amortization?

Most new ARMs don't allow negative amortization, and buyers generally should avoid ARMs that do. If negative amortization is a possibility, the loan should have a negative amortization cap.

7. Can my ARM be converted to a fixed-rate loan?

Many ARMs contain a conversion option that permits the borrower to convert to a fixed interest rate at certain points in the loan term, for a fee. The fixed rate will usually be the market interest rate at the time of conversion.

Fig. 6.5   ARM comparison worksheet

ARM Comparison Worksheet

	Loan 1	Loan 2	Loan 3
Lender	_____	_____	_____
Loan amount	$ _____	$ _____	$ _____
Discount fee	$ _____	$ _____	$ _____
Origination fee	$ _____	$ _____	$ _____
Index	_____	_____	_____
Current index rate	_____ %	_____ %	_____ %
Margin	_____ %	_____ %	_____ %
Note rate	_____ %	_____ %	_____ %
Initial payment	$ _____	$ _____	$ _____
Rate adjustment period	_____	_____	_____
Payment adjustment period	_____	_____	_____
Interest rate cap			
• periodic	_____ %	_____ %	_____ %
• life of loan	_____ %	_____ %	_____ %
Payment cap			
• periodic	_____ %	_____ %	_____ %
• life of loan	_____ %	_____ %	_____ %
Negative amortization			
• possible?	_____	_____	_____
• cap	_____ %	_____ %	_____ %
Conversion option			
• conversion fee	$ _____	$ _____	$ _____
• restrictions	_____	_____	_____

Outline: Basic Features of a Residential Loan

I. Amortization
   A. An amortized loan involves regular payments of both principal and interest.
      1. Most home purchase loans are fully amortized.
      2. Alternatives to fully amortized loans are partially amortized loans and interest-only loans.

II. Repayment Period
   A. The repayment period or loan term is how long the borrower has to pay off the loan.
      1. A 30-year loan term is regarded as standard, but other terms such as 15, 20, and 40 years are available.
      2. A 30-year loan has a lower monthly payment than a 15-year loan, but a 15-year loan will require payment of much less interest over the life of the loan.
      3. A 15-year loan is likely to have a lower interest rate than a 30-year loan.

III. Loan-to-Value Ratio
   A. The loan-to-value ratio reflects the relationship between the loan amount and the value of the home being purchased.
   B. A loan with a lower LTV is less risky than one with a higher LTV.

IV. Mortgage Insurance or Loan Guaranty
   A. Mortgage insurance or a loan guaranty may be used to protect the lender from loss in the event of default.
   B. Mortgage insurance
      1. In exchange for mortgage insurance premiums, an insurer will indemnify a lender for any shortfall resulting from a foreclosure sale.
      2. Mortgage insurance is used in conventional and FHA loans.
   C. Loan guaranty
      1. In a loan guaranty (used in VA loans), a guarantor takes on secondary responsibility for a borrower's obligation.
      2. If the borrower defaults, the guarantor will reimburse the lender for any resulting losses.

V. Secondary Financing
   A. A buyer may obtain, in addition to a primary loan, a secondary loan to cover part of the downpayment and closing costs.

    B.   Restrictions are placed on secondary financing, such as making sure that the borrower can afford payments on both loans.

VI. Fixed or Adjustable Interest Rate

    A.   A loan's interest rate can be fixed for the entire loan term, or adjustable.

    B.   Fixed-rate loans are regarded as the standard, and were used almost exclusively until high interest rates in the 1980s encouraged use of ARMs.

    C.   An adjustable-rate mortgage (or ARM) allows a lender to adjust the loan's interest rate periodically to reflect changes in the cost of borrowing money.

    D.   Adjustable-rate mortgage features

       1. Note rate: the initial rate stated in the promissory note is an ARM's note rate.

       2. Index: a statistical report indicating changes in the cost of money, which the lender will use in order to adjust the ARM's interest rate.

       3. Margin: the difference between an ARM's interest rate and the index rate, reflecting the lender's profit margin and administrative costs.

       4. Rate adjustment period: the period that determines how often a lender will adjust the interest rate on an ARM.

       5. Payment adjustment period: the period that determines how often a lender will adjust the payment amount on an ARM.

       6. Interest rate cap: a limit on how high the interest rate for an ARM can go; either limiting how high the rate can go in one adjustment or imposing a maximum rate for the entire loan.

       7. Payment cap: a limit on how high the monthly payment for an ARM can go.

       8. Negative amortization: when monthly payments on an ARM don't cover all of the monthly interest, thus adding to the principal balance instead of subtracting from it (which might occur if an ARM has a payment cap but no interest rate cap).

       9. Conversion option: a feature allowing an ARM borrower to convert to a fixed-rate loan during certain years of the loan term.

Key Terms

Amortization: Gradually paying off a loan through installment payments that include both principal and interest.

Fully amortized loan: A loan with monthly payments that completely pay off the principal and interest by the end of the loan term.

Partially amortized loan: A loan with monthly payments that include both principal and interest, but don't pay off the entire principal amount by the end of the loan term; as a result, a balloon payment is necessary.

Interest-only loan: A loan that allows the borrower to pay only the interest due (with no principal) during the loan term, or during a specified period at the beginning of the term.

Repayment period: The number of years a borrower is given to repay a loan. Also called the loan term.

Loan-to-value ratio (LTV): The relationship between the loan amount and either the sales price or the appraised value of the property (whichever is less), expressed as a percentage.

Mortgage insurance: Insurance protecting a mortgage lender against losses resulting from default and foreclosure.

Loan guaranty: An arrangement in which a third party guarantor accepts secondary liability for a loan and will reimburse the lender for losses resulting from the borrower's default.

Secondary financing: Money borrowed to pay part of the required downpayment or closing costs for a first loan; this loan is secured by the same property as the first loan.

Fixed-rate loan: A mortgage loan in which the lender charges an unchanging interest rate throughout the loan term.

Adjustable-rate mortgage: A loan in which the interest rate is periodically increased or decreased to reflect changes in the cost of money; commonly called an ARM.

Note rate: The interest rate specified in a loan's promissory note; also called the coupon rate or contract rate.

Index: A published statistical report that indicates changes in the cost of money (market interest rates), used as the basis for the interest rate adjustments in an ARM.

Margin: The difference between an ARM's index rate and the interest rate charged on the loan.

Rate adjustment period: The minimum interval between adjustments of an ARM's interest rate.

Payment adjustment period: The minimum interval between adjustments of an ARM's monthly payment amount.

Interest rate cap: A provision in an ARM that limits the amount that the interest rate may be increased (or in some cases, decreased).

Mortgage payment cap: A provision in an ARM that limits the amount the monthly payment may be increased.

Negative amortization: When deferred interest on an adjustable-rate loan is added to the principal balance.

Conversion option: A provision in an adjustable-rate mortgage allowing the borrower to convert the interest rate to a fixed rate during certain years of the loan term.

Hybrid ARM: An adjustable-rate mortgage with an initial fixed-rate period; for example, a 3/1 hybrid ARM has a fixed interest rate for the first three years and is subject to annual rate adjustments after that.

Option ARM: An adjustable-rate mortgage that allows the borrower to choose from among several payment options each month. Most lenders have discontinued the use of option ARMs.

Chapter Quiz

1. Unpaid interest added to the loan balance is referred to as:
   a. payment shock
   b. a conversion option
   c. negative amortization
   d. positive amortization

2. A limit placed on the amount an ARM interest rate can increase in any given year is:
   a. an index cap
   b. a margin cap
   c. a negative amortization cap
   d. an interest rate cap

3. All of the following are disadvantages of a 15-year mortgage, except:
   a. the interest rate is higher
   b. the monthly payments are higher
   c. it may mean buying a smaller house than desired
   d. a larger downpayment may be needed

4. An ARM with a conversion option:
   a. has graduated payments
   b. may be converted to a fixed-rate loan
   c. may be converted to a GEM
   d. has a negative amortization feature

5. A loan involves monthly payments of both interest and principal, but the borrower must still make a balloon payment at the end of the loan term. This is a/an:
   a. fully amortized loan
   b. partially amortized loan
   c. interest-only loan
   d. adjustable-rate loan

6. Which loan repayment period would involve paying the least amount of total interest over the life of the loan?
   a. 15 years
   b. 20 years
   c. 30 years
   d. 40 years

7. Which loan-to-value ratio would represent the greatest risk to a lender?
   a. 80%
   b. 90%
   c. 95%
   d. 97%

8. Which of the following will protect a lender against the risk of loss in the event of a borrower's default?

   a. Negative amortization
   b. Mortgage insurance
   c. Secondary financing
   d. A high loan-to-value ratio

9. When would secondary financing be used?

   a. The borrower wishes to purchase more than one property
   b. The borrower is using a VA loan
   c. The borrower has inadequate cash to make the downpayment and closing costs on the primary loan
   d. The borrower plans to finance the purchase of personal property as well as real property

10. An adjustable-rate mortgage is structured so that its interest rate remains the same for the first five years, and then changes once every year for the remaining loan term. Five years and then one year would be the:

   a. payment adjustment period
   b. rate adjustment period
   c. monthly payment cap
   d. interest rate cap

Answer Key

1. c. If monthly payments for an ARM are insufficient to meet the interest charged in that particular month, the unpaid interest is added to the principal balance. This is known as negative amortization.

2. d. An interest rate cap prevents an ARM's interest rate from increasing above a particular limit, either in a given period or for the life of the loan.

3. a. The interest rate of a 15-year mortgage is typically lower, to reflect the lower risk to the lender.

4. b. An ARM with a conversion option may be converted to a fixed-rate loan during certain years of the loan term.

5. b. A partially amortized loan involves monthly payments of both principal and interest, but does not pay off the entire loan balance over the loan term, requiring a balloon payment at the end of the loan term.

6. a. Although it requires the highest monthly payments, a 15-year loan will require the lowest amount of total interest paid over the life of the loan.

7. d. The higher the loan-to-value ratio, the greater the risk to the lender. This is because a buyer who has made a larger downpayment will work harder to avoid default and, if default occurs, the lender is more likely to recover the entire loan amount in a foreclosure sale.

8. b. Mortgage insurance is used to protect a lender against the risk of loss in the event of a borrower's default, as it will reimburse a lender for some or all of a shortfall resulting from a foreclosure sale.

9. c. Secondary financing involves the use of a second loan to cover some of the downpayment and closing costs associated with a first loan secured by the same property.

10. b. The rate adjustment period of an ARM dictates how frequently the interest rate may be increased or decreased.

Chapter 7
The Financing Process

Shopping for a Loan
- Assessing the buyers' circumstances
- Choosing a lender
- Loan costs
- Evaluating financing options

Applying for a Loan
- Loan application form
- Required disclosures
- Locking in the interest rate

Application Processing
- Underwriting decision

Closing a Loan Transaction
- Closing agent
- Steps in the closing process

Introduction

Getting a mortgage loan can be a straightforward, painless experience, or it can turn into a complicated, time-consuming hassle that ends in disappointment. In most cases, of course, the process of getting a loan falls somewhere between those two extremes. How smoothly it goes depends on many factors, including the buyers' financial situation, how expensive a home they want, and the lender they choose. Helping buyers get through the process as easily as possible, given their particular circumstances, is part of a real estate agent's job.

The financing process can be broken down into these stages, and we'll look at each of them in turn:

1. shopping for a loan,
2. applying for a loan,
3. application processing, and
4. closing.

Shopping for a Loan

Home buyers should comparison shop for financing

There are many financing options available to home buyers, and buyers are encouraged to comparison shop in order to find the best type of loan on the best possible terms. But understanding the advantages and disadvantages of different financing options can be complex and overwhelming.

For home buyers, shopping for a mortgage loan involves:

- assessing their own wants, needs, and finances;
- choosing a lender;
- comparing rates and fees; and
- evaluating financing options.

Although we'll be treating these as separate topics, keep in mind that they aren't really separate steps that take place in a certain order; instead, they overlap and influence one another. As a real estate agent, you can help buyers with all of these tasks, but they also need the input of a financing expert: a mortgage lender.

Assessing the Buyers' Circumstances

It's generally a good idea for buyers to start mortgage shopping even before they begin house hunting. They need to learn how large a loan they can qualify for in order to determine what kind of home they can afford. It's much better for buyers if they have a realistic idea of their price range before they start house hunting in earnest.

Before shopping for a house, buyers should learn their maximum loan amount

> **Example:** After talking about buying a home for a long time, the Morrisons have started driving through the neighborhood they like, keeping an eye out for "For Sale" signs. One day they find a house they love. It costs more than they planned to spend, but it's exactly what they want. They make a full-price offer, which the seller accepts.
>
> The Morrisons apply for a loan and start making arrangements to move into their new home. Then, to their surprise and embarrassment, their loan application is rejected. The sale, which was contingent on financing, terminates. The seller is inconvenienced and annoyed, and the Morrisons are so disappointed that they're reluctant to resume house hunting.

Because of the importance of financing to a transaction, in many markets home sellers won't even consider a buyer's offer until a lender has verified that the buyer will qualify for sufficient financing to purchase the property.

Preapproval. Home buyers can learn in advance how large a mortgage loan they'll qualify for by getting **preapproved** for financing. To get preapproved, buyers apply to a lender or a mortgage broker. (For simplicity's sake, we'll just use the term "lender" in most of this discussion. Depending on the transaction, the person working with the prospective borrowers might be either a loan officer employed by the lender, or an independent mortgage broker. See Chapter 4.)

Preapproval: formal process that can only be done by a lender

The buyers complete a loan application and provide the required documentation of their income, assets, debts, and credit history, just as if they were applying for a loan after finding a house. The lender may treat an application for preapproval like any loan application, sending it to the underwriting department for a full evaluation. (Some lenders call that getting "pre-underwritten" rather than preapproved.) Alternatively, the application might just be submitted to an automated underwriting system for a preliminary evaluation at this stage. Either way, additional underwriting will be necessary after the buyers have found the house they want and the appraisal and title report are available.

If the buyers are creditworthy, the lender sets a maximum loan amount based on their income and net worth. The lender gives the buyers a **preapproval letter**, which states that they're qualified to borrow up to a specified amount and pay up to a specified price. Although this

Preapproval letter states that lender will loan buyers up to a specified amount isn't a guarantee that the lender will make the loan once a property is found, it gives the buyers reliable information about the price range they can afford.

A preapproval letter can be an extremely valuable tool in negotiations with a seller. It provides assurance to the seller that the buyers' financing contingency shouldn't be a problem; the buyers are in fact able to buy at the price they're offering. (A financing contingency is a provision in a purchase agreement that allows the buyers to withdraw from the contract without penalty if they can't obtain the specified financing.) Preapproval is especially important in an active real estate market, when lots of buyers are competing for desirable homes.

Preapproval also helps streamline the closing process. The lender has already evaluated the buyers, so the parties can focus on inspections, the appraisal, and the title report. However, it's important for the parties to understand that the preapproval is subject to modification or cancellation if new information comes to light or circumstances change. Because the buyers' financial situation, loan program rules, or market conditions may change, most preapproval letters are valid for only a limited period of time, such as 30 days. If the buyers want to extend the preapproval beyond the initial time frame, some of the information it was based on will have to be verified again.

Note that while a mortgage broker can provide a preapproval letter stating that the buyers' financial information meets generally accepted underwriting standards that most lenders use, it's better for the buyers to have a preapproval letter issued directly by the lender that will ultimately fund the loan.

Prequalification. Sometimes buyers get **prequalified** (as opposed to preapproved) before applying for a loan. Prequalification is an informal process that can be performed by a loan officer, a mortgage broker, or a real estate agent, or using an online mortgage calculator. Buyers provide basic information about their income, assets, debts, and credit history, and then receive an estimate of an affordable price range for them based on this unverified data.

It's a fairly straightforward process to estimate the price range of homes that buyers should be able to afford. The maximum monthly mortgage payment the buyers qualify for, together with how much money they have for a downpayment and closing costs, determines their maximum loan amount—the largest mortgage a lender will give

Advantages of preapproval:
- Tool in negotiations
- Streamlines the closing process

them. The maximum loan amount plus their downpayment sets the upper limit of their price range.

Prequalifying buyers for financing was once a routine procedure for real estate agents, but now that preapproval by a lender is common, agents are no longer called upon to prequalify buyers very often, if at all. Formal preapproval is advisable as soon as the buyers feel ready to apply for it. Of course, in order to get preapproved for a loan, the buyers will need to choose a lender, which is our next topic.

Choosing a Lender

To choose a mortgage lender wisely, buyers first need to identify promising prospects and then use the right criteria to evaluate them.

Identifying Prospects. There are two main ways to decide which lenders to talk to: research and referrals.

Research. For buyers who are willing to do some research, advertisements and articles in the business or real estate section of a local newspaper can provide leads. The real estate section often includes a handy "Mortgage Comparison Chart" to help consumers see at a glance the various lenders and mortgage products available to them.

Research tools for finding lenders:
- Newspaper articles and ads
- Internet

An online search can be a particularly good source of information about both local and online lenders. Many websites allow buyers to quickly compare the interest rates and fees of several different lenders.

Whether in print or online, lenders' ads—like any ads—should be viewed with a critical eye. However, they can be a reasonable starting point if followed up with emails or phone calls to loan originators. As we mentioned, loan originators are either the lender's employees (also known as loan officers) or independent contractors (known as mortgage brokers) who meet with loan applicants, discuss their financing needs, and help them submit their mortgage applications.

Referrals. Referrals are also a reasonable way to find a good lender, especially since many buyers don't have the time or inclination to do the kind of research suggested above. In addition to asking family members, friends, and co-workers who recently bought homes to recommend a lender, many buyers ask their real estate agent for referrals. In fact, many rely entirely on the agent's advice. An experienced agent has typically worked with quite a few lenders and knows

Lender referrals may come from family, friends, co-workers, real estate agents that some are more knowledgeable and dependable than others. A less experienced agent should ask her broker or others in the office for the names of lenders to refer clients and customers to. As we'll discuss in Chapter 14, real estate agents should never accept referral fees or any other form of compensation in exchange for making these referrals.

Mortgage brokers. A mortgage broker specializes in bringing buyers and lenders together (see Chapter 4). While consulting a mortgage broker might seem to solve the problem of choosing a lender, buyers have to rely on the same kind of research and referrals described above to find a good mortgage broker.

If buyers work with a mortgage broker rather than directly with a lender, the broker performs most or all of the same tasks that loan officers employed by lenders do. However, mortgage brokers usually work with multiple lenders, so they may be able to present buyers with a wider variety of loan options. Typically, a mortgage broker presents the options that the buyers are qualified to pursue. It's up to the buyers to decide which option is the best one for them.

Buyer's own bank. When shopping for a mortgage, home buyers shouldn't overlook the financial institution where they do their banking. There may be special financing offers for established customers, and some people prefer, for the sake of convenience, to have one institution handle all of their financial transactions.

Interviewing Prospective Lenders. Whether buyers find prospective lenders through research or through referrals, mortgage financing experts generally recommend talking to at least three or four lenders before making a choice. Buyers should call or email each lender's office and arrange to talk to a loan originator, asking each a similar set of questions in order to compare their products and costs.

Buyers are encouraged to talk to three or four lenders, if possible

Unfortunately, some buyers don't talk to three or four lenders because they feel too busy, or because they find the jargon too complex or confusing. Inexperienced buyers may find talking to a loan originator intimidating. Even for more experienced buyers, shopping for a mortgage loan is still a relatively infrequent experience, making it hard to develop expertise or negotiating skill in this arena. Some buyers may be embarrassed about their financial situation, or worried that they're asking stupid questions and taking up too much of the loan originator's time. Some buyers who are perfectly competent in everyday life can become strangely passive in this context, accepting everything the loan originator says about their financing options as factual and not open to question or negotiation. Other buyers may feel obligated to go ahead and apply for a loan with the first lender they contact, just to keep the loan process moving.

Of course, good mortgage professionals won't let any of that happen. They're aware that many buyers feel intimidated, and they know how to put buyers at ease. They don't take advantage of the situation and push buyers into submitting an application before they're ready. Other loan originators, however, may be more focused on getting business than advising consumers to shop around. As a result, federal and state regulators have developed a number of consumer publications and regulations that encourage home buyers to seek both the best lender and the best mortgage they can. We'll discuss these consumer protection regulations more in Chapter 14, but for now it's enough to know that the government advises home buyers to get three or four written estimates from different lenders (with loan quotes for the same day) before committing to a formal loan application with just one lender.

Criteria for Choosing a Lender. Some buyers and even some real estate agents believe that one lender is much the same as another, and that the only real distinction between them is the interest rates and fees they charge. It's true that interest rates and fees are a very important consideration when choosing a lender, and in the next section we'll discuss how to compare the rates and fees that different lenders are offering. But rates and fees shouldn't be the only consideration when choosing a lender.

Buyers should also be concerned with a lender's expertise, efficiency, stability, and honesty. A lender might offer a low interest rate, but provide inaccurate or misleading information and slow, sloppy service. Loan originators who aren't really knowledgeable may not be aware of some financing options that would be well suited to certain buyers. Mistakes in loan processing can delay the closing of a real estate transaction, or even derail it altogether. And if a closing cost estimate is carelessly or deceptively prepared, the buyers may be surprised by unexpected fees at closing.

> Look for expertise, efficiency, and honesty, not just low interest rates and fees

In the absence of a referral, it may be difficult to judge the competence and trustworthiness of a lender and its representatives. Asking the loan originator for references from recent customers may be worthwhile. Researching customer satisfaction websites may also be beneficial. To a certain extent, however, buyers have to rely on their own impressions and instincts when they meet with a loan originator. Greater public awareness of predatory lending practices (see Chapter 14) may lead buyers to be more assertive and cautious when they're choosing a lender. Also, in response to the mortgage foreclosure and financial crisis, the Real Estate Settlement Procedures Act (RESPA), the Truth in Lending Act (TILA), and other lending regulations were strengthened, making it more likely that home buyers will receive accurate information about loan terms and costs throughout the financing process.

Loan Costs

For most buyers, the primary consideration in choosing a lender is how much their loan is going to cost. The interest rate is the major cost of borrowing money, but it's by no means the only one. Mortgage lenders also impose a variety of other charges that can make a big difference in the cost of a loan.

Loan fees:
• Origination fee
• Discount points

Types of Loan Fees. Most significant among these other charges are origination fees and discount points, which are often grouped together and referred to as "loan fees" or "points." The term "point" is short for "percentage point." One point is one percentage point (one percent) of the loan amount. For example, for a $100,000 loan, one point would be $1,000; six points would be $6,000.

One point =
1% of loan amount

Origination fee covers lender's administrative costs

Origination fee. An origination fee may also be called an administrative charge, a transaction fee, a service fee, or simply a loan fee. An origination fee is charged in almost every mortgage loan transaction, unless the loan is expressly designated as a "no fee" loan (discussed later in this section). Origination fees pay for the costs that a lender incurs in making loans, such as staff salaries, commissions, facilities costs, and other overhead expenses. A typical origination fee might be around 1% of the loan amount. Like other charges related to a home buyer's loan, it is ordinarily paid by the buyer rather than the seller.

Example: A home buyer is borrowing $325,000, and the lender is charging an origination fee of one point (one percentage point). That means the buyer must pay the lender a $3,250 origination fee ($325,000 × 1% = $3,250).

Discount points. In many transactions, in addition to the origination fee, the lender charges discount points, also known as a loan discount, a discount fee, or simply as points. The term "points" may cause confusion. Some lenders use "points" to mean only discount points, but others use it to mean the discount points and the origination fee combined.

Example: When Lender A says it's charging four points on a loan, that means four discount points. It doesn't include the origination fee that will be charged on top of the discount points.

When Lender B says it's charging four points on a loan, that refers to the discount points and the origination fee combined. For instance, Lender B would refer to three discount points plus a 1% origination fee as four points. Lender B would also call two discount points plus a 2% origination fee four points.

Either usage is considered correct. So when loan fees are discussed, it's important to make sure everyone involved is using "points" in the same way.

Discount points are designed to increase the lender's upfront yield, or profit, on the loan. By charging discount points, the lender not only gets the interest on the loan throughout the loan term, but also collects a sum of money in the beginning, right when the loan is funded. As a result, the lender is willing to make the loan at a lower interest rate than it would have without the points. In effect, the lender is paid a lump sum now so that the borrower can avoid paying more interest later. Depending on how long the borrower stays in the home (and keeps making payments on the loan), the discount points paid to reduce the interest rate may or may not save the buyer money in the long run.

Discount fee increases lender's upfront yield

Although discount points aren't charged in all transactions, they are quite common. The number of points charged is usually related to how the lender's quoted interest rate compares to market interest rates; typically, lenders who offer below-market interest rates charge more points. One lender might quote an interest rate of 5.25% plus two points, while another lender quotes 5% interest with four points.

Lenders with lower interest rates typically charge more points

Also, a given lender might offer different rates with different discounts (for example, 5% interest with four points, or 5.5% interest with no points). The choice is between paying more cash up front or more interest over the life of the loan.

The calculation of how many points it will take to reduce the interest rate is affected by a number of factors and varies with market conditions. As a result, it's difficult to come up with a set formula that tells borrowers how many points a lender might require them to pay to discount the quoted loan rate by one percentage point. In recent years the number of points required for a one percentage point reduction in the interest rate has ranged from four to six points.

Relationship between number of points and increase in yield varies with market conditions

To determine how much a loan discount will cost, multiply the loan amount by the number of discount points the lender requires.

Example: $250,000 sales price; $225,000 loan amount

$225,000	Loan amount
× ___4%	Discount of four points
$9,000	Cost of loan discount

Discount points may be paid by buyer or seller

Either the buyer or the seller can pay the discount points. In a buyer's market, a seller may agree to pay points: this makes her home more attractive to buyers by making financing more affordable. When buyers or sellers pay points to reduce the loan's interest rate, this arrangement is called a **buydown**, as the points are used to "buy down" the interest rate, making the buyer's monthly loan payments smaller and easier to qualify for. (Buydowns are discussed in more detail in Chapter 10.)

When the buyer pays the points, the lump sum must be paid to the lender in cash at closing. In contrast, when the seller pays the points, the proceeds the seller receives at closing are reduced by the cost of the points.

Example: The loan is for $510,000. The lender is charging four points, and the seller has agreed to pay the points on the buyer's behalf.

When the loan is funded, the lender retains 4% of the loan amount ($20,400) for the points. The remainder of the loan amount, $489,600, is delivered to the closing agent to finance the purchase. The buyer signs a promissory note and mortgage agreeing to repay the entire $510,000 at the stipulated rate of interest. Thus, the lender is advancing only $489,600 but will eventually be repaid $510,000.

At closing, the closing agent transfers the loan funds ($489,600) to the seller, so the seller's net proceeds from the sale are reduced by the cost of the points. In effect, the seller paid the lender $20,400 so the buyer could get a loan at the lower quoted interest rate.

Other fees. In addition to interest, a loan origination fee, and discount points, mortgage lenders usually charge a variety of other fees. For example, a buyer might be required to pay the lender an application fee, a document preparation fee, or an underwriting fee.

Lenders charge a variety of minor fees in addition to main loan fees

In addition to these miscellaneous lender fees, borrowers will also incur loan charges that relate to the loan but are paid to third parties instead of the lender. For instance, the appraisal fee and the credit report fee are paid to the appraiser and the credit reporting agency, not to the lender.

The fees that lenders charge vary considerably from one lender to another. Although many of the fees tend to be for comparatively small amounts, they do add up. Buyers can ask the loan originator if one or more of the fees can be reduced or waived altogether. Mortgages are consumer products just like a car or household furnishings, and borrowers are encouraged to discuss price reductions whenever possible. Some lenders may be quite willing to negotiate with buyers, and not just about miscellaneous fees, but also about the interest rate and points. Other lenders may not be as open to this type of negotiation, but there's no harm in asking.

Mortgage broker's fee. Buyers who are working with a mortgage broker are ordinarily charged a mortgage broker's fee or commission. Buyers should ask about the compensation arrangement before signing a contract with the broker.

Brokers usually charge one or two percent of the loan amount as their fee. However, as a general rule, the mortgage broker's compensation shouldn't make a loan obtained through a mortgage broker more expensive than one obtained directly from a lender. This is because mortgage brokers deal with wholesale lenders (see Chapter 4) who offer their loans to brokers at wholesale prices. The wholesale price plus the broker's fee generally equals what the borrower would've had to pay if she'd gone directly to a lender.

Mortgage broker's compensation doesn't necessarily make loan more expensive for buyer

Comparing Loan Costs. Because different lenders charge different origination fees, loan discounts, and other fees, it can be difficult to accurately compare the cost of two or more loans. For example, if one lender is quoting a 5.75% interest rate with four points, and another lender is quoting a 6% rate with two points, which loan is less expensive? The first loan (5.75% with four points) happens to be slightly less expensive, but it isn't easy to tell that just by looking at the lenders' quotes. Different types of loan products add further complications: which would be less expensive, a fixed-rate or an adjustable-rate mortgage?

Truth in Lending Act requires loan costs to be disclosed to borrowers

A law that's intended to help loan applicants with this type of problem is the **Truth in Lending Act** (TILA), one of the federal consumer protection laws covered in Chapter 14. Under TILA, lenders must make certain disclosures to consumer loan applicants to help them understand exactly how much they're paying for credit. This information enables loan applicants to compare loan costs and shop around for the best terms.

Annual percentage rate (APR): relationship of finance charge to amount financed

The most important disclosure required by TILA is the **annual percentage rate** (APR). The APR expresses the relationship of the **finance charge** to the amount financed, in the form of an annual percentage. In addition to interest, all of the following would be included in the finance charge: the origination fee; any discount points paid by the buyer; a mortgage broker's fee, finder's fee, or service fee; and mortgage guaranty or insurance fees. (Title insurance costs, credit report charges, the appraisal fee, and points paid by the seller would not be included in the finance charge.)

Because interest is rarely the only fee that a mortgage lender charges, the APR of a mortgage loan is almost always higher than the quoted interest rate. For example, a loan with an interest rate of 5% might have an APR of 5.32%, because the APR takes into account the origination fee and the mortgage insurance as well as the interest.

Compare APRs, not just interest rates

To help determine which of two or more loans is the least expensive, it's important to compare the APRs quoted by the lenders. A buyer who compares only the quoted interest rates can easily be misled. A lender might quote a very low interest rate, but charge an unusually large origination fee or several discount points. In that case, the total cost of the loan may in fact be much greater than the cost of a loan from a competitor who is quoting a higher interest rate. The APRs of the two loans will reveal this difference in cost.

Lenders must give loan applicants an estimate of all closing costs, including loan-related charges. Even before applying for a loan, it's possible to get an estimate of a loan's APR by calling the lender. Loan estimates and other disclosures are covered in Chapter 14.

No-fee/Low-fee Loans. Some lenders offer no-fee or low-fee loans. As the names suggest, the lender doesn't charge the usual loan fees a home buyer is typically expected to pay, such as an origination fee, discount points, or other lender fees. The interest on the loan is the only (or nearly only) finance charge. As a result, the APR is the same or close to the same as the interest rate.

A no-fee or low-fee loan can be very helpful for buyers who don't have much cash for closing. However, the interest rate on a no-fee or low-fee loan is likely to be significantly higher than the rate on a comparable loan with typical fees. As a result, the two loans might have very similar APRs. The choice for the borrower is between paying fees up front or paying additional interest over the long term.

No-fee loan reduces amount of money needed for closing

The same is true with financed closing costs, another option for cash-strapped buyers. The lender charges loan fees, but the fees and certain other closing costs are added to the loan amount and paid over time (as part of the mortgage payments) rather than at closing. Of course, interest is charged on the financed costs as well as the loan principal.

Evaluating Financing Options

When it comes time for buyers to evaluate their financing options and choose the loan they want, loan costs—interest rates, origination fees, discount points, and other lender charges—will naturally be a key consideration. But buyers should also consider how each of the different financing options is structured, and how each would affect their overall financial situation in the short term and the long term. For instance, would they have enough cash left over for furniture or necessary remodeling? Would they be required to dip into their retirement or college savings to pay the closing costs? All of these issues are important considerations when choosing a loan.

Buyers should ask themselves the following questions in connection with any mortgage loan they consider:

- How much money would we have left in savings after the transaction closes?
- How much spending money would we have left over each month after paying the mortgage payment?
- At what pace do we anticipate that our income will grow?
- How long do we plan to stay in the home we're buying?
- How rapidly would our equity build, based on reasonable market projections?
- How soon would the mortgage be paid off?
- Are we more concerned with the short-term cost of financing or the long-term cost?
- What alternative investment opportunities are available for money we don't put into the house?

The answers to these questions can affect a buyer's financing decision in a variety of ways. For example, some buyers are planning to live in the house they're purchasing for only a few years. These buyers might be good candidates for a loan with an adjustable interest rate. They can take advantage of a low initial rate with fewer worries about how high the rate may be ten years from now. However, this type of buyer must also consider whether market conditions will allow them to sell their house after only a few years without losing money.

Generally speaking, when buyers don't expect to own the house they're buying for very long, it doesn't make sense to pay a lot of discount points to get a lower interest rate. Only a fairly long period of ownership will enable the buyers to recoup the money paid up front with interest savings over the long run.

Buyers who hope to retire early or reduce their workload may be most concerned with building equity and paying off their mortgage as soon as possible. They might prefer a loan with a 15-year or 20-year term, rather than the standard 30-year term, even though it means they will qualify for a smaller loan amount and have to buy a less expensive home than they otherwise could.

Many first-time buyers with limited buying power want to purchase the largest, most expensive home they can possibly afford. They are interested in any and all financing arrangements that can boost their

Length of time buyers expect to own their new house may affect financing choices

182

price range: a downpayment assistance program, an adjustable interest rate, a high loan-to-value ratio, a 40-year loan term, secondary financing, and so on.

On the other hand, some buyers don't want to borrow as much money for a house as lenders would allow them to. They may want to invest their money differently, or they may simply prefer to avoid the financial stress that the maximum monthly mortgage payment would represent for them.

In short, buyers must evaluate every financing option in light of their own circumstances, goals, and preferences, along with relevant trends and developments in the housing market. Through qualifying standards, a lender takes certain aspects of the buyers' situation into account before agreeing to make a loan. But only the buyers themselves can decide which financing alternative is most comfortable for them and fits in best with their own financial plans.

Home Buyer Counseling Programs. Borrowing money to buy a house is such a complicated decision that it overwhelms many buyers, especially first-time buyers. In addition to asking real estate agents and loan officers for information and guidance, first-time buyers may benefit from participating in home buyer counseling before they decide what financing option will be best for them.

The Department of Housing and Urban Development (HUD) administers a Housing Counseling Assistance Program open to anyone who is house hunting and applying for a mortgage (as well as renters and current homeowners). The counseling, provided by HUD-approved nonprofit associations and state and local government agencies around the country, is intended to educate participants about the responsibilities of home ownership (or tenancy): making mortgage or rent payments, maintaining the home, avoiding foreclosure or eviction, and so on.

Applying for a Loan

After shopping for a loan and choosing a lender, the next step is to apply for the loan. To apply for a mortgage loan (or to obtain preapproval), the buyers talk with a loan originator. This discussion may be a face-to-face meeting between the buyers and the loan originator, or the discussion may take place over the phone, by fax, or online. We'll refer to these communications between a loan originator and the buyers as the "loan interview."

Prequalifying During the Interview. In the loan interview, the buyers and the loan originator will discuss the financing options the buyers have been considering and the loan programs and products that the lender offers. The loan originator will help the buyers decide which program best suits their needs.

While talking with the buyers, the loan originator may enter some key information about their finances into an automated underwriting system or other software. The system can provide a preliminary evaluation of what kind of loan the buyers are likely to qualify for and can be used to try out financing alternatives: How large a loan could the buyers qualify for if they made a $20,000 downpayment? What if they put only $10,000 down? What if they chose an adjustable-rate mortgage instead of a fixed-rate loan?

However, even if the system indicates at this stage that the buyers would qualify for the loan they want, that doesn't mean they've been preapproved for the loan. Preapproval doesn't take place until the buyers' background information has been documented and verified.

Deposit. When the buyers apply for the loan, they may be required to make a deposit to cover certain expenses that must be paid up front. Depending on the lender, these may include an application fee, a credit report fee, and other preliminary charges.

Contract and Closing Date. If the buyers have already found the home they want to buy and have entered into a purchase agreement with the sellers, the loan originator will ask for a copy of the agreement. In examining the agreement, the loan originator will pay particular attention to the terms of any financing contingency clause and the agreed-upon closing date. The agreement may set a closing date that's too soon to be realistic; the financing, inspections, or other arrangements may not be completed in time. If the loan originator feels the closing date should be changed, she will consult with the real estate agent, who will explain the problem to the parties. When everyone has agreed on a more suitable date, the agent will have the buyers and sellers sign an amendment to the purchase agreement.

In loan interview, buyers discuss financing options with loan originator and fill out application form

Some lenders require buyers to make a deposit to cover initial costs when application is submitted

Loan originator reviews purchase agreement for financing terms and closing date

The Loan Application Form

Lenders want their loans to be repaid without collection problems, and they try to make loans only to borrowers who can be expected to repay on time, as agreed. The purpose of the loan application is to gather the information the lender needs to determine whether the applicants will be reliable borrowers. It focuses on employment stability, income, credit scores, and net worth. The real estate agent working with the buyers should make sure they know in advance what information will be needed for the loan application, to avoid unnecessary delays in the process.

Virtually all residential lenders use the Uniform Residential Loan Application form shown in Figure 7.1. We'll go through the form to give you an overview of the information it requires. Note that the form shown here will be replaced with a form with a different format in the summer of 2019.

Uniform Residential Loan Application form is used by nearly all mortgage lenders

Type and Terms of Loan. The application begins with questions about the loan being applied for: the type of loan, loan amount, loan term, interest rate, whether the rate will be fixed or adjustable, and whether the loan will involve any special amortization arrangement.

Property Information and Purpose of Loan. The next section of the application asks for the address and legal description of the property and when the house was built. (If the applicants are applying for preapproval and haven't found a house yet, this part of the form is left blank for now.) It also asks the purpose of the loan (purchase, construction, or refinance; primary residence, secondary residence, or investment property); the manner in which the buyers will take title (for example, as tenants in common); and the source of the downpayment, settlement charges (closing costs), and any secondary financing. This information will be used to order an appraisal of the property and to determine the maximum loan amount.

Borrower Information. As a general rule, lenders require everyone who will have an ownership interest in the property being purchased to be jointly obligated to repay the loan. This means they must apply for the loan together. If there is a cosigner helping the buyer(s) qualify for financing, that person is also treated as one of the loan applicants. (See the discussion of co-borrowers and cosigners in Chapter 8.)

Fig. 7.1 Uniform Residential Loan Application form

Uniform Residential Loan Application

This application is designed to be completed by the applicant(s) with the Lender's assistance. Applicants should complete this form as "Borrower" or "Co-Borrower," as applicable. Co-Borrower information must also be provided (and the appropriate box checked) when ☐ the income or assets of a person other than the Borrower (including the Borrower's spouse) will be used as a basis for loan qualification or ☐ the income or assets of the Borrower's spouse or other person who has community property rights pursuant to state law will not be used as a basis for loan qualification, but his or her liabilities must be considered because the spouse or other person has community property rights pursuant to applicable law and Borrower resides in a community property state, the security property is located in a community property state, or the Borrower is relying on other property located in a community property state as a basis for repayment of the loan.

If this is an application for joint credit, Borrower and Co-Borrower each agree that we intend to apply for joint credit (sign below):

_____   _____
Borrower   Co-Borrower

I. TYPE OF MORTGAGE AND TERMS OF LOAN

Mortgage Applied for:	☐ VA ☐ FHA	☐ Conventional ☐ USDA/Rural Housing Service	☐ Other (explain):	Agency Case Number	Lender Case Number

Amount	Interest Rate	No. of Months	Amortization Type:	
$	%		☐ Fixed Rate ☐ GPM	☐ Other (explain): ☐ ARM (type):

II. PROPERTY INFORMATION AND PURPOSE OF LOAN

Subject Property Address (street, city, state & ZIP)	No. of Units

Legal Description of Subject Property (attach description if necessary)	Year Built

Purpose of Loan	☐ Purchase ☐ Refinance	☐ Construction ☐ Construction-Permanent	☐ Other (explain):	Property will be: ☐ Primary Residence ☐ Secondary Residence ☐ Investment

Complete this line if construction or construction-permanent loan.

Year Lot Acquired	Original Cost	Amount Existing Liens	(a) Present Value of Lot	(b) Cost of Improvements	Total (a + b)
	$	$	$	$	$

Complete this line if this is a refinance loan.

Year Acquired	Original Cost	Amount Existing Liens	Purpose of Refinance	Describe Improvements ☐ made ☐ to be made
	$	$		Cost: $

Title will be held in what Name(s)	Manner in which Title will be held	Estate will be held in: ☐ Fee Simple ☐ Leasehold (show expiration date)

Source of Down Payment, Settlement Charges, and/or Subordinate Financing (explain)

III. BORROWER INFORMATION

Borrower	Co-Borrower

Borrower's Name (include Jr. or Sr. if applicable)	Co-Borrower's Name (include Jr. or Sr. if applicable)

Social Security Number	Home Phone (incl. area code)	DOB (mm/dd/yyyy)	Yrs. School	Social Security Number	Home Phone (incl. area code)	DOB (mm/dd/yyyy)	Yrs. School

☐ Married ☐ Separated	☐ Unmarried (include single, divorced, widowed)	Dependents (not listed by Co-Borrower) no. ages	☐ Married ☐ Separated	☐ Unmarried (include single, divorced, widowed)	Dependents (not listed by Borrower) no. ages

Present Address (street, city, state, ZIP) ☐ Own ☐ Rent ___No. Yrs.	Present Address (street, city, state, ZIP) ☐ Own ☐ Rent ___No. Yrs.

Mailing Address, if different from Present Address	Mailing Address, if different from Present Address

If residing at present address for less than two years, complete the following:

Former Address (street, city, state, ZIP) ☐ Own ☐ Rent ___No. Yrs.	Former Address (street, city, state, ZIP) ☐ Own ☐ Rent ___No. Yrs.

IV. EMPLOYMENT INFORMATION

Borrower	Co-Borrower

Name & Address of Employer	☐ Self Employed	Yrs. on this job	Name & Address of Employer	☐ Self Employed	Yrs. on this job
		Yrs. employed in this line of work/profession			Yrs. employed in this line of work/profession

Position/Title/Type of Business	Business Phone (incl. area code)	Position/Title/Type of Business	Business Phone (incl. area code)

If employed in current position for less than two years or if currently employed in more than one position, complete the following:

Freddie Mac Form 65 6/09	Page 1 of 5	Fannie Mae Form 1003 6/09

Borrower				IV. EMPLOYMENT INFORMATION (cont'd)		Co-Borrower	
Name & Address of Employer	☐ Self Employed	Dates (from – to)		Name & Address of Employer	☐ Self Employed	Dates (from – to)	
		Monthly Income $				Monthly Income $	
Position/Title/Type of Business		Business Phone (incl. area code)		Position/Title/Type of Business		Business Phone (incl. area code)	
Name & Address of Employer	☐ Self Employed	Dates (from – to)		Name & Address of Employer	☐ Self Employed	Dates (from – to)	
		Monthly Income $				Monthly Income $	
Position/Title/Type of Business		Business Phone (incl. area code)		Position/Title/Type of Business		Business Phone (incl. area code)	

V. MONTHLY INCOME AND COMBINED HOUSING EXPENSE INFORMATION

Gross Monthly Income	Borrower	Co-Borrower	Total	Combined Monthly Housing Expense	Present	Proposed
Base Empl. Income*	$	$	$	Rent	$	
Overtime				First Mortgage (P&I)		$
Bonuses				Other Financing (P&I)		
Commissions				Hazard Insurance		
Dividends/Interest				Real Estate Taxes		
Net Rental Income				Mortgage Insurance		
Other (before completing, see the notice in "describe other income," below)				Homeowner Assn. Dues		
				Other:		
Total	$	$	$	Total	$	$

    *   **Self Employed Borrower(s) may be required to provide additional documentation such as tax returns and financial statements.**

Describe Other Income   *Notice:* **Alimony, child support, or separate maintenance income need not be revealed if the Borrower (B) or Co-Borrower (C) does not choose to have it considered for repaying this loan.**

B/C		Monthly Amount
		$

VI. ASSETS AND LIABILITIES

This Statement and any applicable supporting schedules may be completed jointly by both married and unmarried Co-Borrowers if their assets and liabilities are sufficiently joined so that the Statement can be meaningfully and fairly presented on a combined basis; otherwise, separate Statements and Schedules are required. If the Co-Borrower section was completed about a non-applicant spouse or other person, this Statement and supporting schedules must be completed about that spouse or other person also.

Completed ☐ Jointly ☐ Not Jointly

ASSETS Description	Cash or Market Value	Liabilities and Pledged Assets. List the creditor's name, address, and account number for all outstanding debts, including automobile loans, revolving charge accounts, real estate loans, alimony, child support, stock pledges, etc. Use continuation sheet, if necessary. Indicate by (*) those liabilities, which will be satisfied upon sale of real estate owned or upon refinancing of the subject property.		
Cash deposit toward purchase held by:	$			
List checking and savings accounts below		**LIABILITIES**	**Monthly Payment & Months Left to Pay**	**Unpaid Balance**
Name and address of Bank, S&L, or Credit Union		Name and address of Company	$ Payment/Months	$
Acct. no.	$	Acct. no.		
Name and address of Bank, S&L, or Credit Union		Name and address of Company	$ Payment/Months	$
Acct. no.	$	Acct. no.		
Name and address of Bank, S&L, or Credit Union		Name and address of Company	$ Payment/Months	$
Acct. no.	$	Acct. no.		

VI. ASSETS AND LIABILITIES (cont'd)

Name and address of Bank, S&L, or Credit Union		Name and address of Company	$ Payment/Months	$
Acct. no.	$	Acct. no.		
Stocks & Bonds (Company name/ number & description)	$	Name and address of Company	$ Payment/Months	$
		Acct. no.		
Life insurance net cash value	$	Name and address of Company	$ Payment/Months	$
Face amount: $				
Subtotal Liquid Assets	$			
Real estate owned (enter market value from schedule of real estate owned)	$			
Vested interest in retirement fund	$			
Net worth of business(es) owned (attach financial statement)	$	Acct. no.		
Automobiles owned (make and year)	$	Alimony/Child Support/Separate Maintenance Payments Owed to:	$	
Other Assets (itemize)	$	Job-Related Expense (child care, union dues, etc.)	$	
		Total Monthly Payments	$	
Total Assets a.	$	Net Worth (a minus b) ►	$	**Total Liabilities b.** $

Schedule of Real Estate Owned (If additional properties are owned, use continuation sheet.)

Property Address (enter S if sold, PS if pending sale or R if rental being held for income) ▼	Type of Property	Present Market Value	Amount of Mortgages & Liens	Gross Rental Income	Mortgage Payments	Insurance, Maintenance, Taxes & Misc.	Net Rental Income
		$	$	$	$	$	$
Totals		$	$	$	$	$	$

List any additional names under which credit has previously been received and indicate appropriate creditor name(s) and account number(s):

Alternate Name	Creditor Name	Account Number

VII. DETAILS OF TRANSACTION		VIII. DECLARATIONS				
a. Purchase price	$	If you answer "Yes" to any questions a through i, please use continuation sheet for explanation.	**Borrower**		**Co-Borrower**	
			Yes	No	Yes	No
b. Alterations, improvements, repairs		a. Are there any outstanding judgments against you?	☐	☐	☐	☐
c. Land (if acquired separately)		b. Have you been declared bankrupt within the past 7 years?	☐	☐	☐	☐
d. Refinance (incl. debts to be paid off)		c. Have you had property foreclosed upon or given title or deed in lieu thereof in the last 7 years?	☐	☐	☐	☐
e. Estimated prepaid items		d. Are you a party to a lawsuit?	☐	☐	☐	☐
f. Estimated closing costs		e. Have you directly or indirectly been obligated on any loan which resulted in foreclosure, transfer of title in lieu of foreclosure, or judgment?	☐	☐	☐	☐
g. PMI, MIP, Funding Fee		(This would include such loans as home mortgage loans, SBA loans, home improvement loans, educational loans, manufactured (mobile) home loans, any mortgage, financial obligation, bond, or loan guarantee. If "Yes," provide details, including date, name, and address of Lender, FHA or VA case number, if any, and reasons for the action.)				
h. Discount (if Borrower will pay)						
i. Total costs (add items a through h)						

Freddie Mac Form 65   6/09

Page 3 of 5

Fannie Mae Form 1003   6/09

VII. DETAILS OF TRANSACTION		VIII. DECLARATIONS				

			Borrower		Co-Borrower	
		If you answer "Yes" to any question a through I, please use continuation sheet for explanation.	Yes	No	Yes	No
j.	Subordinate financing	f. Are you presently delinquent or in default on any Federal debt or any other loan, mortgage, financial obligation, bond, or loan guarantee?	☐	☐	☐	☐
k.	Borrower's closing costs paid by Seller	g. Are you obligated to pay alimony, child support, or separate maintenance?	☐	☐	☐	☐
l.	Other Credits (explain)	h. Is any part of the down payment borrowed?	☐	☐	☐	☐
		i. Are you a co-maker or endorser on a note?	☐	☐	☐	☐
m.	Loan amount (exclude PMI, MIP, Funding Fee financed)	---				
		j. Are you a U.S. citizen?	☐	☐	☐	☐
n.	PMI, MIP, Funding Fee financed	k. Are you a permanent resident alien?	☐	☐	☐	☐
o.	Loan amount (add m & n)	l. Do you intend to occupy the property as your primary residence? If "Yes," complete question m below.	☐	☐	☐	☐
p.	Cash from/to Borrower (subtract j, k, l & o from i)	m. Have you had an ownership interest in a property in the last three years?	☐	☐	☐	☐
		(1) What type of property did you own—principal residence (PR), second home (SH), or investment property (IP)?	_____		_____	
		(2) How did you hold title to the home— by yourself (S), jointly with your spouse or jointly with another person (O)?	_____		_____	

IX. ACKNOWLEDGEMENT AND AGREEMENT

Each of the undersigned specifically represents to Lender and to Lender's actual or potential agents, brokers, processors, attorneys, insurers, servicers, successors and assigns and agrees and acknowledges that: (1) the information provided in this application is true and correct as of the date set forth opposite my signature and that any intentional or negligent misrepresentation of this information contained in this application may result in civil liability, including monetary damages, to any person who may suffer any loss due to reliance upon any misrepresentation that I have made on this application, and/or in criminal penalties including, but not limited to, fine or imprisonment or both under the provisions of Title 18, United States Code, Sec. 1001, et seq.; (2) the loan requested pursuant to this application (the "Loan") will be secured by a mortgage or deed of trust on the property described in this application; (3) the property will not be used for any illegal or prohibited purpose or use; (4) all statements made in this application are made for the purpose of obtaining a residential mortgage loan; (5) the property will be occupied as indicated in this application; (6) the Lender, its servicers, successors or assigns may retain the original and/or an electronic record of this application, whether or not the Loan is approved; (7) the Lender and its agents, brokers, insurers, servicers, successors, and assigns may continuously rely on the information contained in the application, and I am obligated to amend and/or supplement the information provided in this application if any of the material facts that I have represented herein should change prior to closing of the Loan; (8) in the event that my payments on the Loan become delinquent, the Lender, its servicers, successors or assigns may, in addition to any other rights and remedies that it may have relating to such delinquency, report my name and account information to one or more consumer reporting agencies; (9) ownership of the Loan and/or administration of the Loan account may be transferred with such notice as may be required by law; (10) neither Lender nor its agents, brokers, insurers, servicers, successors or assigns has made any representation or warranty, express or implied, to me regarding the property or the condition or value of the property; and (11) my transmission of this application as an "electronic record" containing my "electronic signature," as those terms are defined in applicable federal and/or state laws (excluding audio and video recordings), or my facsimile transmission of this application containing a facsimile of my signature, shall be as effective, enforceable and valid as if a paper version of this application were delivered containing my original written signature.

Acknowledgement. Each of the undersigned hereby acknowledges that any owner of the Loan, its servicers, successors and assigns, may verify or reverify any information contained in this application or obtain any information or data relating to the Loan, for any legitimate business purpose through any source, including a source named in this application or a consumer reporting agency.

Borrower's Signature X	Date	Co-Borrower's Signature X	Date

X. INFORMATION FOR GOVERNMENT MONITORING PURPOSES

The following information is requested by the Federal Government for certain types of loans related to a dwelling in order to monitor the lender's compliance with equal credit opportunity, fair housing and home mortgage disclosure laws. You are not required to furnish this information, but are encouraged to do so. The law provides that a lender may not discriminate either on the basis of this information, or on whether you choose to furnish it. If you furnish the information, please provide both ethnicity and race. For race, you may check more than one designation. If you do not furnish ethnicity, race, or sex, under Federal regulations, this lender is required to note the information on the basis of visual observation and surname if you have made this application in person. If you do not wish to furnish the information, please check the box below. (Lender must review the above material to assure that the disclosures satisfy all requirements to which the lender is subject under applicable state law for the particular type of loan applied for.)

BORROWER ☐ I do not wish to furnish this information		CO-BORROWER ☐ I do not wish to furnish this information	
Ethnicity: ☐ Hispanic or Latino ☐ Not Hispanic or Latino		Ethnicity: ☐ Hispanic or Latino ☐ Not Hispanic or Latino	
Race: ☐ American Indian or Alaska Native ☐ Native Hawaiian or Other Pacific Islander	☐ Asian ☐ Black or African American ☐ White	Race: ☐ American Indian or Alaska Native ☐ Native Hawaiian or Other Pacific Islander	☐ Asian ☐ Black or African American ☐ White
Sex: ☐ Female ☐ Male		Sex: ☐ Female ☐ Male	

To be Completed by Loan Originator:
This information was provided:
☐ In a face-to-face interview
☐ In a telephone interview
☐ By the applicant and submitted by fax or mail
☐ By the applicant and submitted via e-mail or the Internet

Loan Originator's Signature X		Date
Loan Originator's Name (print or type)	Loan Originator Identifier	Loan Originator's Phone Number (including area code)
Loan Origination Company's Name	Loan Origination Company Identifier	Loan Origination Company's Address

Freddie Mac Form 65   6/09   Page 4 of 5   Fannie Mae Form 1003   6/09

CONTINUATION SHEET/RESIDENTIAL LOAN APPLICATION		
Use this continuation sheet if you need more space to complete the Residential Loan Application. Mark **B** f or Borrower or **C** for Co-Borrower.	Borrower:	Agency Case Number:
	Co-Borrower:	Lender Case Number:

I/We fully understand that it is a Federal crime punishable by fine or imprisonment, or both, to knowingly make any false statements concerning any of the above facts as applicable under the provisions of Title 18, United States Code, Section 1001, et seq.

Borrower's Signature	Date	Co-Borrower's Signature	Date
X		X	

Freddie Mac Form 65   6/09

Fannie Mae Form 1003   6/09

The application form requests the following information about each applicant: name, social security number, phone number, date of birth, years of schooling, marital status, and address. The lender also wants to know how many dependents the applicants must support, since children and other dependents may add considerably to their financial obligations. If the applicants have lived at their present address for less than two years, information about previous residences must also be provided.

Although it's legal for a lender to ask about a loan applicant's marital status and dependents, it's illegal for the lender to use that information in a discriminatory fashion. (See the discussion of the Equal Credit Opportunity Act in Chapter 14.)

Employment Information. Each applicant must fill in the name and address of her employer, the number of years employed at this job, and the number of years employed in this line of work. The position, title, type of business, and business phone number must also be included. If an applicant has been at her current job for less than two years, the same information should be given for previous employers.

Lender uses application form to gather information about the applicant's employment stability, income, and net worth

Income and Monthly Housing Expense Information. This section requests information about primary employment income, overtime, bonuses, commissions, dividends and interest, net rental income, and income from any other sources. Each applicant must list his current monthly housing expense—either the rent or the house payment (including principal and interest, hazard insurance, property taxes, mortgage insurance, and homeowners association dues).

Assets and Liabilities. In the next section of the form, each loan applicant lists all of his assets and liabilities. Assets include the good faith deposit given to the seller (if a purchase agreement has been signed), money in checking and savings accounts, stocks and bonds, life insurance policies, retirement funds, automobiles, other personal property, and real estate already owned. (For real estate, a separate schedule in the application form must also be filled out.) If the applicants own a business, they must list its net worth and attach a financial statement to the application form.

Assets may include:
- Good faith deposit
- Money in bank
- Investments
- Life insurance policy
- Retirement account
- Automobile
- Personal property
- Real property

Liabilities may include:
- Student loan
- Car loan
- Real estate loan
- Other installment loan
- Charge accounts
- Credit cards
- Alimony or child support owed
- Job-related expenses

The applicants' liabilities may include student loans, car loans, real estate loans, and other installment debts; revolving credit (charge accounts and credit cards); alimony and/or child support payments; and job-related expenses such as child care or union dues. The applicants should also be prepared to list debts that have recently been paid off.

Details of Transaction. The next section asks for information on the real estate transaction itself. (Again, if the applicants are applying for preapproval and haven't found a house yet, this section will be left blank for the time being.) The applicants are to fill in the purchase price, the cost of alterations or improvements, the cost of the land (if the land is acquired separately), estimated prepaid expenses, and estimated closing costs. There are also blanks for the mortgage insurance or funding fee, discount fee, any secondary financing, any closing costs to be paid by the seller, and the loan amount. The lender will use these figures to calculate the cash the applicants will need to close the transaction.

Declarations. The loan applicants must answer several questions regarding outstanding judgments, bankruptcies, property foreclosures, lawsuits, loan defaults, and alimony or child support payments. Then the application asks whether any part of the downpayment is borrowed and whether each applicant is a co-maker or endorser on any promissory notes. Next, each applicant is asked whether she is a U.S. citizen or a permanent resident alien. Finally, the form asks if the applicants intend to occupy the property as a primary residence. If so, they are required to indicate whether they have owned any other property during the previous three years, what type of property it was (a principal residence, a second home, or an investment property), and how title was held. Applicants who haven't owned a home in the previous three years may be treated as first-time buyers for the purposes of certain loan programs.

Acknowledgment and Agreement. By signing and dating the application form, the applicants are agreeing to several provisions regarding the application and the loan.

Among other things, the applicants affirm that all information provided in the application is true and correct. They agree to inform the lender if any of the information changes before closing.

The applicants also acknowledge that any intentional or negligent misrepresentation may result in civil or criminal liability. This acknowledgement has greater significance in light of the most recent mortgage crisis, which prompted Congress to pass the Fraud Enforcement and Recovery Act, toughening existing federal antifraud provisions. The law takes particular aim at mortgage fraud issues, such as loan professionals misleading secondary market investors, or borrowers lying on their loan application in order to secure a loan that they wouldn't have qualified for otherwise.

Applicant agrees to correct or update information on the application if necessary

Information for Government Monitoring. One of the last sections of the application form sets forth optional questions regarding the applicants' ethnicity, race, and sex. If the applicants answer these questions, the federal government will use the information to evaluate the lender's compliance with fair lending laws.

Loan Originator's Information. The loan originator must indicate the method used to take the application (face to face, by phone, online, etc.) and provide his name, ID, phone number, employer's name, company ID, and company address.

Continuation Sheet. The last page of the loan application form is a continuation sheet, in case the applicants need more room to answer any of the questions on the previous pages. Note that the applicants must sign and date the continuation sheet in addition to the "Acknowledgment and Agreement" section on the previous page.

Application Checklist. Real estate agents can help buyers prepare for the application process by going over a checklist of required information and documentation with them. See the sample checklist in Figure 7.2.

Agent should let buyer know information needed for loan application

Required Disclosures

In residential mortgage transactions, federal law requires lenders and mortgage brokers to make certain disclosures. Most of the disclosures are made on a single loan estimate form. This form provides information about the loan's financing costs, including the annual percentage rate, the total interest as a percentage of the loan amount, and estimates of all the loan-related charges and other costs the buyers will be expected to pay at closing. The form also states whether the lender intends to service the loan or transfer servicing to someone else. In addition, lenders and mortgage brokers are required to give loan applicants a special information booklet, to help borrowers understand the home buying and settlement process better.

Lenders are required to provide these disclosures within three business days of receiving a written loan application, unless the loan application is declined before that. Most lenders give the disclosures to loan applicants at the time of application. If the disclosed information changes significantly over the course of the transaction, new disclosures must be made before closing. (These federal disclosure requirements are discussed more fully in Chapter 14.)

Lender must provide loan estimate within 3 days after application

Fig. 7.2 Checklist of application information and documentation

Loan Application Checklist

Purchase agreement (if the applicant has already entered into one)

Social security number for each applicant

Residence history:

✓ Addresses where the applicant has lived during the past few years

✓ Name and address of the applicant's current landlord

Employment history:

✓ Names and addresses of the employers the applicant has worked for in the last two years; positions held; whether employment was full- or part-time; and the wage or salary at time of departure

✓ If the applicant was recently in school or the military, a copy of the diploma or discharge papers

Income information:

✓ W-2 forms for the previous two years and payroll stubs for the previous 30 days (showing current and year-to-date earnings)

✓ If commissions are a significant part of the applicant's income, tax returns for the past two years

✓ If the applicant is self-employed, business and personal tax returns for the past two years, plus a year-to-date income and expense statement

✓ If the applicant is a major stockholder in a corporation (owns 25% or more of the stock), three years of corporate tax returns

✓ Amount and sources of income, including wages and secondary sources (such as a pension, social security, or child support)

✓ Documentation for all sources of income; child support/alimony requires a copy of the divorce decree

List of assets:

✓ Names, addresses, and account numbers for all bank accounts

✓ Bank statements for the past three months

✓ Investment statements for the past three months

✓ Value of household goods and other personal property

✓ Make, model, year, and market value of automobiles

✓ Cash and face value of insurance policies

✓ Address, description, and value of any real estate owned; any lease agreements

✓ Gift letter, if a gift is the source of part of the funds for closing (see Chapter 8)

✓ If the applicant's present home is to be sold, the net amount from the sale after deducting all selling expenses

✓ If the applicant is being relocated by an employer who is paying some of the closing costs, a letter from the employer stating which costs will be paid by the company

List of liabilities:

✓ For each debt, the name, address, and phone number of the creditor, and the balance, monthly payment, and account number

✓ Copy of divorce decree, for child support or alimony obligation

Current or estimated property taxes for the home being purchased

Certificate of Eligibility for VA loans

Locking In the Interest Rate

One other issue that should be addressed during the loan application process is whether the buyers want to have the interest rate on the loan they're applying for **locked in**, or guaranteed, for a certain period. If the rate isn't locked in, it will float, which means that it will move up or down with market interest rates until shortly before the transaction closes. Naturally, a change in the interest rate will also cause a change in the monthly payment for the loan.

> **Example:** When Jim Dawson applies for a loan, the loan officer says the interest rate will be 5.25%, and that's the figure filled in on the loan application form. Dawson doesn't ask to have the rate locked in, however.
>
> Market interest rates are going up, and by the time Dawson's loan closes six weeks later, the rate on his loan has risen to 5.5%. Dawson is faced with the prospect of paying a higher interest rate and making a larger monthly mortgage payment than he anticipated. With the new interest rate, his monthly payment amount has increased from $2,761 to $2,839.

A situation like the one in the example could be a serious problem, especially for buyers who barely qualified for their loan in the first place. A sharp increase in the interest rate might increase the monthly payment so much that they no longer qualify. They could reduce the monthly payment back to an affordable level by putting more money down (to reduce the loan amount) or by paying discount points (to reduce the interest rate). However, many buyers would be unable or unwilling to take either of those steps. If market interest rates are likely to rise, locking in the loan's rate can be extremely important.

Lock-in Period. When a loan officer quotes an interest rate, the buyers should ask whether the rate can be locked in, and if so, starting when and for how long. Some lenders automatically lock in the rate but others don't. The rate lock-in period may begin on the date the application is submitted or on the date the loan is approved.

Common lock-in periods are between 30 and 60 days, and the lock-in period should always extend beyond the expected loan processing time. The best arrangement is for the lock-in period to be extended automatically if the closing is delayed.

Lock-in Fee. Locking in an interest rate sometimes requires a lock-in fee, which is usually a percentage of the loan amount. The fee is typically applied to the buyers' closing costs if the transaction closes.

Written Agreement. As you can see, the details of interest rate lock-ins can have a significant impact on the total costs for a loan. Just like other details of the mortgage application process, it's a matter of contract between the lender and the buyers. A spoken commitment from the loan originator is not enough to protect the buyers' interests, and the consequences of a misunderstanding could be significant.

Application Processing

Verification forms and other documentation are used to check information on application

Once a loan application has been filled out, the next step is to verify the information provided by the buyers. Verification forms are sent out to the buyers' employers, banks or other financial institutions, and previous mortgage lender, if any. Credit reports and credit scores are obtained from the major credit reporting agencies (see Chapter 8). If the buyers have already entered into a contract for the purchase of a particular property, the lender orders a title report from a title insurance company and sends an appraiser to appraise the property.

Loan package sent to underwriting department

When the completed verification forms, reports, and other documentation have been received, a loan processor puts together a loan package and sends it to the underwriting department.

The Underwriting Decision

Underwriting a mortgage loan involves examining the prospective buyers' financial situation and evaluating the property that they want to buy. In most cases the process is carried out with the help of an automated underwriting system (see Chapter 8). The underwriter examines the loan application, verification forms, credit reports, and other documentation and applies the appropriate qualifying standards to the buyers. This may occur either before or after the buyers find a house they want to purchase. (See the discussion of preapproval earlier in this chapter.)

If the underwriter decides that the buyers meet the lender's standards, the lender typically gives the buyers a **commitment letter**, approving the loan on specific terms and subject to conditions stated in the letter. For example, if the lender is going to require a certain type of property inspection, the commitment letter will state that final approval of the loan will require submission of an inspection report acceptable to the lender.

As the name suggests, the commitment letter commits the lender to making the loan if all the conditions are fulfilled. However, depending on when (at what stage in the process) the commitment letter is prepared, it may list many conditions, including major ones such as an acceptable appraisal report and title report. The letter will also state that loan approval may be canceled if there are significant adverse changes in the buyers' financial situation before closing.

What's the difference between a commitment letter and the preapproval letter we discussed earlier? That can vary depending on the lender. For example, some lenders provide a preapproval letter as soon as the buyers' application has passed through automated underwriting, but issue a commitment letter only after the application has been fully evaluated by an underwriter. Also, a preapproval letter is usually intended for use in negotiations with sellers, so it often lists only the main features of the loan (for example, "30-year fixed-rate conventional financing"), rather than specific loan terms. In fact, most lenders are willing to give buyers multiple preapproval letters showing different loan amounts and prices; that way, the buyers can demonstrate that they're qualified to purchase a particular house without revealing to the seller the maximum amount they could pay. Also, a commitment letter (unlike a preapproval letter) may be issued after the buyers have entered into a purchase agreement with a seller.

When all of the conditions for loan approval have been fulfilled and the loan transaction is "clear to close," the lender will give the buyers a final approval letter, confirming the exact terms on which the loan will be made. The final approval letter will specify a date on which the lender's commitment to make the loan will expire.

If the buyers' loan application is rejected (which could happen at any stage during the loan process), the lender is required by federal law to provide the buyers with a written statement explaining why. Loan applicants are entitled to receive this statement within 30 days after submitting their completed application. Depending on the reasons for the rejection, the buyers might want to apply to a different lender, apply for a smaller loan or a different type of loan, or decide to wait until they can pay off some of their debts, improve their credit score, or save additional money for a larger downpayment.

When an application is rejected, some of the fees the applicants paid up front may be refunded, but others won't be. For example, the application fee and credit report fee are not refundable.

> Commitment letter states what conditions must be fulfilled

> Final approval states exact terms on which loan will be made

Closing the Loan

The last stage of the financing process is coordinated with the closing of the real estate transaction as a whole. We'll look at some aspects of closing that concern the buyer's financing.

The Closing Agent

Real estate closing procedures vary from one part of the country to another. In many areas, closings are handled through escrow. **Escrow** is an arrangement in which a third party holds money and documents on behalf of the buyer and seller until their transaction is ready to close. When all of the conditions set forth in the purchase agreement have been fulfilled, the third party—known as an **escrow agent** or **closing agent**—disburses the purchase price to the seller and delivers the deed to the buyer.

Escrow: third party holds money and documents for buyer and seller

Depending on local practices, the closing agent may be an independent escrow agent, an employee of the buyer's lender or the title company, a lawyer, or a real estate broker.

In other parts of the country, the parties to a transaction meet to exchange funds and documents, which may be known as a **roundtable closing** or "passing papers." Funds are not held in escrow prior to the meeting. The meeting is coordinated by a third party, who might be a real estate broker, a lawyer, or a title company employee; this person may also be referred to as the closing agent.

Steps in the Closing Process

The closing agent is usually responsible for handling all of the details that must be taken care of before the transaction can close. Some of these details involve requirements imposed by the lender.

Lender's closing concerns:
- Clearing liens from title
- Establishing condition of title
- Inspections and repairs
- Buyer's funds for closing
- Document preparation and recording

Clearing and Insuring Title. Since the property being purchased is going to serve as collateral for the new loan, the lender wants to make sure that the title is free of encumbrances that could interfere with the lender's security interest. Except for property tax liens and special assessment liens, any liens that would have higher priority than the new mortgage or deed of trust must be removed. These older liens are the seller's responsibility, and the closing agent will usually arrange for them to be paid off out of the seller's proceeds at closing. The appropriate lien releases will be recorded along with the other documents (the new deed, the new mortgage or deed of trust, and so on).

The lender's security interest will also be protected by an extended coverage title insurance policy, usually paid for by the buyer. Under the terms of the policy, if it turns out that there are liens against the property that weren't listed as exceptions from coverage, the title insurance company will reimburse the lender for resulting losses.

Inspections and Corrective Action. Another way for a lender to protect the value of its collateral is by requiring certain inspections to be carried out. For example, a pest control inspection, a soil percolation test, or a flood hazard inspection might be considered necessary, depending on the type of property and the area it's located in. Inspection reports will be submitted to the lender for review, and the lender may decide that specific repairs must be made or other corrective action must be taken. The repairs or corrective action may or may not have to be completed before closing.

Loan Documents and Buyer's Funds. Once the buyer's loan has been approved, the lender forwards the loan documents (promissory note, mortgage or deed of trust, and—if necessary—updated disclosure statements) to the closing agent. At this point, the buyer can complete his part of the transaction by depositing funds for the downpayment and closing costs into escrow and signing the loan documents. The signed documents are then returned to the lender.

Impound Account. In most transactions, the buyer is required to make a deposit into an impound account at closing. An impound account, also called a reserve account or escrow account, is a trust account set up by the lender to ensure that the buyer's real estate taxes and insurance premiums are paid on time. The buyer will pay the lender a portion of these expenses each month along with the principal and interest payment on the loan. The lender will deposit the tax and insurance payments into the impound account, and when taxes or insurance premiums become due, pay them out of the impound account. At closing, the lender usually has the buyer make an initial deposit into the impound account, to serve as a cushion for future expenses. Federal law caps the amount buyers can be required to deposit at no more than two months' worth of escrow payments.

Impound account ensures that taxes and insurance premiums are paid on time

Interim Interest. In the course of this chapter we've already mentioned most of the fees and charges connected with the loan that the buyer will pay as closing costs. They may include an origination fee, discount points, a mortgage broker's commission, and a document preparation fee. One charge the buyer will encounter at closing that we haven't explained yet is interim interest, also called prepaid interest.

Interim interest arises in part because of a custom concerning the due date of the buyer's initial loan payment. As a general rule, a buyer's first monthly mortgage payment is not due on the first day of the month immediately following closing, but rather on the first day of the next month after that.

> **Example:** Closing takes place on January 23. The buyer is not required to make a mortgage payment on February 1. Instead, the first payment on the loan is due on March 1.

This practice gives the buyer a chance to recover from the financial strain of closing. However, even though the first loan payment isn't due for an extra month, interest begins accruing on the loan starting with the day of closing.

Interest on a mortgage loan is paid in arrears. In other words, the interest that accrues during a given month is paid at the end of that month. So, to return to the example above, the March 1 payment will cover the interest that accrues during February. However, that first payment won't cover the interest that accrued between January 23 (the closing date) and January 31. The lender requires the interest for those nine days to be paid in advance, when the transaction closes. This advance payment of interest is called interim or prepaid interest and is one of the buyer's closing costs.

Funding the Loan. When the loan documents have been executed and all of the lender's conditions have been satisfied, including final verification of the buyer's employment status and other financial information, the lender releases the buyer's loan funds to the closing agent. This is referred to as funding the loan.

Closing Disclosure Form. Once precise figures for all of the closing costs have been determined, closing disclosure statements are prepared for the buyer and the seller in compliance with the **Real Estate Settlement Procedures Act** (see Chapter 14) and the Truth in Lend-

---

Interim interest covers period from closing date to end of month in which closing occurs

Buyer's first payment is due on the first day of the second month following the month in which closing occurs

Mortgage interest is paid in arrears

ing Act. RESPA requires the closing agent to provide an itemized list of each party's settlement charges and credits on a closing disclosure form. These charges and credits will be taken into account in closing the transaction and disbursing the funds. The closing disclosure must be given to the buyer at least three business days before closing.

Final Steps. The closing agent arranges for the deed, mortgage or deed of trust, lien releases, and other documents to be recorded, and disburses the appropriate funds to the seller, the real estate agent, and other parties entitled to payment. The title company issues the buyer's and lender's title insurance policies, the lender sends copies of the loan documents to the buyer, and the buyer provides a copy of the hazard insurance policy to the lender. The transaction has closed.

Closing disclosure form includes a detailed listing of each party's credits and debits at closing

Outline: The Financing Process

I. Shopping for a Loan
  A. Loan consumers should engage in comparison shopping for a loan, which involves assessing their own needs and finances as well as comparing rates and fees.
  B. Preapproval
    1. To get preapproved, buyer submits a loan application to the lender before finding a home to buy.
    2. Lender evaluates buyer's income, net worth, and credit history and prepares a preapproval letter stating a maximum loan amount.
    3. Benefits of preapproval: can make a buyer's offer more appealing to a seller, and streamlines the closing process.
  C. Choosing a lender
    1. A buyer should research lenders by comparing interest rates and fees.
    2. A buyer also may rely on referrals to find a reputable and competent lender.
    3. Buyers should be concerned with a lender's expertise and efficiency as well as its interest rates and fees.
  D. Loan costs
    1. Loan fees: usually described in terms of "points," where a point is one percentage point of the loan amount.
    2. Origination fee: a one-time service fee charged by the lender to cover administrative expenses associated with issuing the loan.
    3. Discount points: an additional charge imposed by a lender to increase the lender's upfront yield on the loan.
    4. A lender usually charges a lower interest rate in exchange for a buyer paying discount points up front.
    5. A seller may pay discount points on a buyer's behalf in order to "buy down" the buyer's interest rate.
    6. Other fees: a lender may charge additional fees for application, underwriting, or document preparation.
    7. Mortgage broker's fee: may be a separate charge or part of the points quoted for the loan; the amount should be disclosed in the loan estimate and closing disclosure forms.
  E. Comparing loan costs
    1. The Truth in Lending Act (TILA) is a federal consumer protection act requiring certain disclosures to help borrowers understand the true cost of credit.

      2.   TILA requires disclosure of the annual percentage rate (APR), which is the relationship of the finance charge to the loan amount, expressed as an annual percentage.

  F. Evaluating financing options

      1.   Buyers need to weigh considerations other than the loan costs, such as financial priorities, how long they will live in the house, and other investment opportunities.

      2.   Buyers may use a home buyer counseling program for assistance in deciding which financing option is most appropriate.

II. Applying for a Loan

  A. Loan interview and application

      1.   Buyers will provide financial information to the loan originator, which will be the basis for the loan approval or preapproval. Buyers may also need to pay certain expenses, such as a loan application fee.

      2.   The information provided to the originator includes information regarding employment, income, current monthly housing expense, assets and liabilities.

  B. Required disclosures

      1.   Lender must give loan applicant a loan estimate form, which discloses the annual percentage rate, estimated loan-related charges and other closing costs, and other information about the transaction.

      2.   Also must give applicant a booklet that explains the closing process.

  C. Locking in the interest rate

      1.   Buyers may lock in the interest rate on the application date, to avoid the risk of interest rates going up between the application date and the closing date.

      2.   A lender may charge a lock-in fee.

III. Application Processing

  A. Underwriting decision

      1.   An underwriter will evaluate the loan application and decide whether to approve it, reject it, or approve it subject to conditions.

      2.   A conditional commitment may require additional documentation, such as proof of sale of the buyers' current home.

      3.   When all conditions for loan approval are met, the lender will issue a final commitment letter.

IV. Closing the Loan

  A. Closing agent

      1.   A closing agent or escrow agent is a third party that holds money and documents on behalf of the buyer and seller until the transaction is ready to close.

B. Steps in closing process

1. Clearing and insuring title: the lender will want to ensure that the property is free of encumbrances that could interfere with its security interest.

2. Inspections: a lender may require certain inspections of the property to be performed, to make sure that the property will continue to be adequate collateral.

3. Impound account: the buyer will make an initial deposit into the impound account; a portion of each monthly loan payment will be deposited into the account as well. Property taxes and insurance will be paid out of this account.

4. Intcrim interest: because mortgage interest is paid in arrears, but no payment is due in the month following closing, a buyer will need to pay the partial first month's interest up front.

5. Closing disclosure form: when the transaction is ready to close, the closing agent uses a closing disclosure form to itemize all charges and credits for each party.

Key Terms

Preapproval: Formal loan approval from a lender stating a maximum loan amount that the lender is willing to issue, based on the borrower's income and assets.

Mortgage broker: An intermediary who brings lenders and borrowers together and negotiates loan agreements between them.

Loan fee: Any one-time fee that a lender charges at closing for a loan or an assumption, including origination fees and discount points.

Origination fee: A fee charged by a lender upon making a new loan, intended to cover the administrative cost of processing the loan.

Discount points: A fee a lender may charge at closing to increase its upfront profit on the loan.

Buydown: When a seller or third party pays the lender a lump sum at closing to lower the interest rate charged to the buyer.

Truth in Lending Act: A federal law that requires lenders to make disclosures concerning loan costs to consumer loan applicants.

Annual percentage rate: Under the Truth in Lending Act, the relationship between a loan's finance charge and the amount financed, expressed as an annual percentage.

Real Estate Settlement Procedures Act: A federal law that requires lenders to disclose certain information about closing costs to loan applicants; also known as RESPA.

Lock-in: When a lender guarantees a loan applicant a particular interest rate for a specific period of time.

Commitment letter: Approval of a loan after full evaluation by an underwriter (although the borrower generally must still fulfill certain conditions).

Escrow agent: A third party who holds things of value (such as money and documents) on behalf of parties to a transaction until specified conditions are fulfilled.

Impound account: A bank account maintained by a lender for the payment of property taxes and insurance premiums on the security property; the lender requires the borrower to make regular deposits into the account, and then pays the expenses out of the account. Also called a reserve account or escrow account.

Interim interest: Interest on a new loan that must be paid at the time of closing; it covers the interest due for the first month of the loan term.

Chapter Quiz

1. The best way to compare the cost of loans is by using the:
    a. lender's yield
    b. annual interest rate
    c. combination of the origination fee and the loan discount
    d. annual percentage rate

2. A lender will want to know a loan applicant's:
    a. current rent or house payment
    b. employment history for the past ten years
    c. tax bracket for the past three years
    d. All of the above

3. The Masons are buying a house. The sales price is $654,000, and they're borrowing $556,000. They've agreed to pay a loan discount fee of two points, which amounts to:
    a. $13,080
    b. $11,120
    c. $6,540
    d. $5,560

4. The fee that pays for the lender's overhead is the:
    a. loan discount
    b. APR
    c. origination fee
    d. interest rate

5. When a lender guarantees a particular interest rate for a certain period of time, it is called a/an:
    a. discount fee
    b. lock-in
    c. float
    d. annualized percentage rate

6. The portion of a borrower's monthly payment that goes toward property taxes and insurance will be held in a/an:
    a. trust fund
    b. recovery account
    c. impound account
    d. balloon payment

7. The exact charges payable by or to each of the parties in a residential real estate transaction are listed on the:
    a. closing disclosure
    b. RESPA report
    c. preapproval letter
    d. Uniform Residential Loan Application

8. Which of the following costs are reflected in a loan's APR?
   a. Interest, points paid by borrower, loan origination fee, mortgage insurance
   b. Interest, appraisal fee, loan origination fee, points paid by either party
   c. Appraisal fee, credit report fee, loan origination fee
   d. Points paid by borrower, origination fee, appraisal fee, credit report fee

9. The purpose of discount points is to:
   a. cover the administrative costs associated with issuing and servicing the loan
   b. increase the lender's upfront yield
   c. pay for costs associated with preparing the loan estimate form
   d. increase the loan's interest rate in exchange for no loan fees

10. Formal approval by a lender, in the form of a letter stating the maximum loan amount the lender is willing to authorize, is:
    a. preapproval
    b. prequalification
    c. predetermination
    d. preauthorization

Answer Key

1. **d.** To compare loan costs, applicants should compare the various loans' annual percentage rates.

2. **a.** A lender will want to know a loan applicant's current housing expenses. The lender will not be concerned with the applicant's tax bracket, and generally will want to see employment information for only the previous two years.

3. **b.** The Masons' loan amount is $556,000 and two points (two percent of the loan amount) on a $556,000 loan is $11,120 ($556,000 × .02 = $11,120).

4. **c.** An origination fee pays for the lender's administrative costs.

5. **b.** With a lock-in, a lender guarantees a borrower's interest rate even if rates go up between the application date and the closing date.

6. **c.** An impound account is used to hold the portion of a borrower's monthly payments that are applied to property taxes and hazard insurance until those bills come due.

7. **a.** The charges and credits that will be paid by or to each party during the settlement process must be itemized on a form called the closing disclosure.

8. **a.** Interest, borrower-paid points, the origination fee, and mortgage insurance are all considered part of the finance charge.

9. **b.** Discount points increase the lender's upfront yield, or profit. A lender charges a lower interest rate in exchange for the payment of discount points.

10. **a.** Preapproval is a formal approval process performed by a lender, which results in the lender agreeing to loan the buyer up to a specified amount when he finds a home he wishes to buy.

Chapter 8
Qualifying the Buyer

The Underwriting Process
- Qualifying standards
- Automated underwriting

Evaluating Creditworthiness

Credit Reputation
- Credit reports
- Length of credit history
- Payment record
- Major derogatory incidents
- Credit scores
- Obtaining credit information
- Explaining credit problems

Income Analysis
- Characteristics of income
- Stable monthly income
- Calculating stable monthly income
- Income ratios

Net Worth
- Funds for closing
- Assets
- Liabilities
- Gift funds
- Delayed financing

Other Factors in Underwriting

Subprime Lending

Risk-based Loan Pricing

Introduction

Before agreeing to make a real estate loan, a lender will evaluate both the buyer and the property to determine whether they **qualify** for the loan—that is, whether they meet the lender's minimum standards. This evaluation process is called **loan underwriting**; the person who performs the evaluation is called a loan underwriter or credit underwriter.

The primary purpose of the evaluation is to determine the degree of risk that the loan would represent for the lender. This determination hinges on the answers to two fundamental questions:

Loan underwriter evaluates:
1. Loan applicant's overall financial situation
2. Value of property

1. Does the buyer's overall financial situation indicate that he can reasonably be expected to make the proposed monthly loan payments on time?
2. Is there sufficient value in the property pledged as collateral to ensure recovery of the loan amount in the event of default?

The underwriter tries to make sure the buyer is someone who can afford the loan and who is unlikely to default. But since default always remains a possibility, the underwriter also tries to make sure that the property is worth enough so that the proceeds of a foreclosure sale would cover the loan amount.

Our discussion of underwriting is divided into two main parts: qualifying the buyer, covered in this chapter, and qualifying the property, covered in the next one. This chapter explains the factors that are taken into account in evaluating a home buyer's financial situation. The next chapter explains how a home is appraised and how the appraised value is used to set the loan amount. First, however, let's begin with some general information about the underwriting process.

The Underwriting Process

Underwriting a mortgage loan involves these basic tasks: reviewing the loan application; obtaining additional information about the applicant from other sources; applying the lender's qualifying standards; verifying information provided by the applicant; evaluating the property appraisal; and making a recommendation in favor of or against loan approval. How these tasks are carried out varies from one lender to another, of course. And the underwriting process changes over time, as new practices become established in the lending industry. In particular, the use of computer programs in underwriting has caused major changes, as we'll discuss shortly.

Qualifying Standards

The minimum standards used in underwriting—called **underwriting standards** or qualifying standards—draw a boundary line between acceptable risks and unacceptable risks. Loans that meet the standards are considered acceptable risks; loans that don't are considered unacceptable risks. Who sets those standards? In other words, who decides which loans are worth the risk of making them?

In theory, residential lenders have always been free to set their own qualifying standards. They could take virtually any risks they wanted, as long as they didn't violate the federal and state regulations governing financial institutions. However, provisions in the Dodd-Frank Act now require all underwriters of residential mortgage loans to conduct a good faith "ability to repay" determination for each applicant. Essentially this means that the borrower's income must be verified and that certain other steps must be taken by the lender to ensure, at a basic level, that the borrower will be able to make the payments.

Most residential lenders also use the qualifying standards set by the government-sponsored enterprises (Fannie Mae and Freddie Mac), by the FHA, or by the VA. If a conventional loan is going to be sold to Fannie Mae or Freddie Mac, their standards must be met. If the loan is going to be insured by the FHA or guaranteed by the VA, the FHA or VA standards must be met.

Underwriting standards:
- Most lenders use Fannie Mae/Freddie Mac standards for conventional loans
- FHA and VA standards must be used for FHA and VA loans

Each of these sets of qualifying standards (Fannie Mae, Freddie Mac, FHA, and VA) is different. The specific rules for the various loan programs are covered in Chapter 10, Conventional Financing; Chapter 11, FHA-Insured Loans; and Chapter 12, VA-Guaranteed Loans. But all of the different rules are based on the underlying principles and concepts that we'll be discussing in this chapter.

Automated Underwriting

Within the limits set by the qualifying standards they apply, underwriters often have to draw on their own experience and judgment in deciding whether to recommend that a particular loan be approved or denied. The qualifying standards guide them in evaluating various aspects of the loan application, but weighing the positive factors against the negative isn't always a simple matter. Underwriting has been described as an art, not a science.

However, **automated underwriting** (AU) has moved the underwriting process at least somewhat closer to the scientific end of the spectrum. An **automated underwriting system** (AUS) is a computer program designed to perform a preliminary analysis of loan applications and make a recommendation for or against approval. Introduced in the 1990s, these systems are now in widespread use. AU systems don't completely replace traditional underwriting (now referred to as **manual underwriting**). Instead, the two types of underwriting are used in conjunction with one another.

AU and the Secondary Market. Some large lenders have their own proprietary automated underwriting systems, but the predominant systems are the ones developed by Fannie Mae (Desktop Underwriter®) and Freddie Mac (Loan Product Advisor®). Both Desktop Underwriter and Loan Product Advisor can be used to underwrite conventional, FHA, or VA loans, applying the appropriate qualifying standards for each loan program.

The primary purpose of Desktop Underwriter and Loan Product Advisor is to make loan purchase decisions for Fannie Mae and Freddie Mac. (See Chapter 3 for a discussion of how lenders sell their loans to the secondary market entities.) However, a lender who plans to sell a loan to either GSE isn't required to use automated underwriting. Both Fannie Mae and Freddie Mac are still willing to purchase loans that have been underwritten manually, in the traditional way. Nonetheless, both entities favor automated underwriting and encourage lenders to use their AU systems.

Also, a lender may choose to use Desktop Underwriter or Loan Product Advisor to underwrite loans that it plans to keep in portfolio. Even though these loans don't have to meet Fannie Mae or Freddie Mac standards, the AU analysis can still be very useful to the lender's underwriters.

AU Programming. The programming of the secondary market entities' AU systems is based on the performance of millions of mortgage loans. The term "loan performance" simply refers to whether the loan payments are made as agreed. Statistical analysis of the performance

Automated underwriting system: a computer program designed to analyze loan applications and recommend approval or rejection

Loan performance: whether loan payments are made as agreed

of millions of loans provides strong evidence of precisely which factors in a loan application make default more likely or less likely.

For instance, it's generally understood that a home buyer who has funds left over (cash reserves) after making the downpayment and paying the closing costs is less likely to default than one who doesn't have anything left over. Accordingly, lenders prefer (and sometimes require) that borrowers have a specified amount in reserve after closing—for example, enough money to cover at least two months' mortgage payments, in case of emergency. What computerized statistical analysis of loan performance adds to this traditional, common-sense underwriting idea is greater precision. Exactly how much less likely to default is a borrower who has two months of reserves than one who has no reserves? What about a borrower with enough reserves for three months of payments, or six months? This type of information, along with computer analysis of all of the other factors that affect default risk, can be programmed into an automated underwriting system. The system will then be able to predict with considerable accuracy how likely it is that a particular loan applicant will default on the loan she is seeking.

This computer analysis of loan performance by the secondary market entities is ongoing, and they use the latest information to adjust their automated underwriting systems and their qualifying standards. Because Fannie Mae and Freddie Mac are so influential in residential lending, these adjustments have a nationwide impact on underwriting.

How AU Works. The first step in submitting a loan application for automated underwriting is entering the information from the application form into the AU system. (This may be done by the loan officer, by an underwriter, or by someone else in the lender's underwriting department.) The system then obtains the applicant's credit information directly from the major credit agencies. After analyzing all of this data using statistical models and the appropriate qualifying rules, the AUS provides a report for an underwriter to review.

The recommendations in an automated underwriting report fall into three main categories:

AU recommendation categories:
- Risk
- Documentation
- Appraisal

- a risk classification,
- a recommended level of documentation, and
- a recommendation concerning the property appraisal or inspection.

Risk classification. The risk classification determines the level of underwriting scrutiny the loan application should receive. If the information submitted to the automated underwriting system meets all of the applicable qualifying standards, the AUS will give the application a risk classification of "Approve" or "Accept." (The exact terminology depends on the system.) Another possible risk classification is "Approve/Ineligible" or "Out of Scope," which means that the loan meets credit risk standards but doesn't meet mortgage eligibility criteria in some other way. (For example, a loan term longer than 30 years or a loan amount that exceeds the conforming loan limit might result in an Ineligible classification.)

An application that doesn't appear to meet all of the qualifying standards will receive a risk classification of "Refer," "Caution," or "Refer with Caution." This doesn't necessarily mean that the loan should be denied, or that it can't be sold to Fannie Mae or Freddie Mac; instead, further review of the application is needed.

This further review will take the form of manual underwriting. In other words, the underwriter will now examine the loan application in the traditional way, to see if it can be approved even though it didn't receive a "passing grade" from the automated underwriting system. The AU report provides the underwriter with guidance, listing the main factors that led to the Refer or Caution classification and pointing out where additional information might make a difference. The underwriter looks for favorable information about the loan applicant's situation that the AUS has not already taken into account.

Note that some lenders have a policy of rejecting Refer or Caution loans without underwriting them manually. These lenders don't consider this extra step—and the extra cost—to be worth their while. Other lenders are willing to manually underwrite Refer or Caution loans, in the expectation that the extra cost will be covered by profits from the additional loans that are ultimately approved. This policy difference is one reason why a loan applicant who's been rejected by one lender may be accepted by another.

Fannie Mae or Freddie Mac may be willing to purchase a loan even though it was given a Refer or Caution classification by the AUS. In some cases, instead of being treated as a prime loan, it will be considered an A-minus loan, and the borrower will have to pay additional fees and/or a higher interest rate.

Documentation. The AU report will also indicate the level of documentation the underwriter should obtain in order to verify the information provided by the applicant. The stronger the application, the lower the documentation requirement may be.

There used to be three basic documentation levels: standard, streamlined ("low-doc"), and minimal ("no-doc"). However, one consequence of the 2007–2008 financial crisis (see Chapter 4) was a return to requiring more documentation. "No-doc" loans, requiring virtually no documentation or verification of information provided by the applicant, are much less common today.

As the name suggests, standard documentation is the full verification process used in traditional underwriting. An automated underwriting system generally requires standard documentation for loans that have been given a risk classification of "Refer" or "Caution" (and therefore must be manually underwritten).

Loans given an "Approve" or "Accept" classification are usually eligible for streamlined documentation. For example, if an applicant has a perfect credit reputation and is making a very large down-payment, a phone call to her employer might be sufficient verification of her employment. A verification of employment form signed by the employer isn't required. (Documentation requirements will be discussed in more detail later in the chapter.)

Appraisal or inspection. The third type of recommendation made in an AU report concerns the appraisal or inspection of the property. For example, the report might tell the underwriter that a full appraisal is appropriate, that an exterior-only inspection would be sufficient, or, in limited instances, that no inspection is necessary. This recommendation is based on the overall strength of the application and on information about the property that was submitted to the automated underwriting system. (Note, however, that an interior inspection is always required for some types of loans, such as FHA and VA loans, regardless of the property or the strength of the application.)

Advantages of AU. Automated underwriting has a number of advantages over traditional underwriting, with benefits for both lenders and borrowers. First, it can streamline the underwriting process for many mortgage loans, requiring significantly less paperwork and enabling lenders to make approval decisions more quickly.

Second, AU makes the underwriting process more objective and consistent, since it generally reduces reliance on the underwriter's experience and subjective judgment. This helps ensure fair, unbiased lending decisions.

Third, AU improves the accuracy of underwriting, because it can weigh all of the risk factors more precisely. Lenders (and the secondary market entities) can have greater confidence in a loan approval decision reached with the help of AU. This allows them to accept more loan applications and extend financing to more home buyers, while still managing risk.

In spite of these advantages, automated underwriting by no means eliminates the need for human underwriters. Both Fannie Mae and Freddie Mac emphasize that an AU system is only a tool. The final decision to approve or deny a loan is made by the lender, not the computer.

Evaluating Creditworthiness

Now that you have some background information about the underwriting process, we'll look more closely at the factors that are taken into account when qualifying a buyer. As we said at the beginning of the chapter, a lender's fundamental question concerning a buyer is: "Does the buyer's overall financial situation indicate that she can reasonably be expected to make the proposed monthly loan payments on time?" If the answer is yes, the buyer is considered **creditworthy**.

To decide whether a buyer is creditworthy, the underwriter—with or without the aid of an automated underwriting system—must consider dozens of factors in the buyer's financial situation. These can be grouped into three main categories:

- credit reputation,
- income, and
- net worth (assets).

You can think of a good credit reputation, stable income, and adequate net worth as the basic components of creditworthiness. We'll be discussing each of these as separate topics, but you should keep in mind that underwriters don't look at any aspect of a loan application in isolation from the rest of it. Strength in one area may or may not be enough to offset weakness in another. The recommendation to approve or deny the loan is based on the buyer's financial situation as a whole.

In much of our discussion we'll refer to the loan applicant (the buyer) as an individual, but keep in mind that it's very common for two or more buyers to apply for a loan together. For example, when a married couple buys a home, the spouses usually apply for financing together and are jointly obligated to repay the loan. Buyers who aren't married to one another may apply for a loan together in the same way.

Buyers applying for joint credit may be referred to as co-borrowers, or as the borrower and co-borrower. For the most part, lenders underwrite an application for joint credit in essentially the same way as an individual's application, evaluating the credit reputation of each applicant, and their combined income and net worth. (See the section on co-borrowers and cosigners later in this chapter.)

Credit Reputation

A good credit reputation is the first major component of creditworthiness. Many residential lending experts say it's the most important.

To evaluate a loan applicant's credit reputation, lenders rely on credit reports obtained from credit reporting agencies. If a report reveals significant derogatory information, the loan application could be turned down for that reason alone. Or the loan could be approved on less favorable terms (at a higher interest rate, for instance). (See the discussion of risk-based pricing at the end of this chapter.)

Credit Reports

A personal credit report presents information about an individual's loans, credit purchases, and debt repayment for the previous **seven years**. It typically covers revolving credit accounts (credit cards and charge accounts), installment debts (such as car loans and student loans), and mortgages. Other bills, such as utility bills, usually aren't listed unless they were turned over to a collection agency.

Personal credit report: individual's debts and repayment record

The credit reporting agencies (also called credit repositories or credit bureaus) are private companies, not government agencies. There are three major credit agencies in the U.S.: Equifax, Experian, and TransUnion. Keeping track of credit information about millions of people is complicated, and the reports that these companies issue on a particular individual don't necessarily match perfectly. To underwrite a mortgage loan application, a lender may obtain reports from all three agencies, or else use a "tri-merge" report that combines the information provided by the three agencies.

The credit information that's important to an underwriter includes:

- the length of the credit history,
- the payment record,

- derogatory credit incidents, and
- credit scores.

Length of Credit History

The term "credit history" is generally used as a synonym for "credit reputation." In this broad sense, it refers to an individual's overall record of borrowing and debt repayment—how well she has handled credit. But "credit history" is also used in a narrower sense, to mean the length or duration of the applicant's experience with credit—how many years she has been borrowing money and paying it back.

As a general rule, a mortgage loan applicant should have at least a one-year history of credit use with three or more active accounts (loans or credit cards). Although this requirement doesn't present a problem for most applicants, it is an obstacle for some. Young adults who are potential home buyers may not have had a chance to establish a credit history yet. A low-income head of household applying for an affordable housing program might never have been offered credit. And some people deliberately steer clear of credit, preferring to stay out of debt and manage their budgets strictly on a cash basis. While staying out of debt is a sensible course, it can backfire when it's time to borrow money to buy a home. If an applicant doesn't have an established credit history, a key set of data is missing, and it's harder for the lender to evaluate the risk of default.

In recent years, with the encouragement of Fannie Mae and Freddie Mac, lenders have become more willing to work with loan applicants who don't have an established credit history. To take the place of or supplement a traditional credit report, the applicant may provide records showing reliable, timely payment of rent, utility bills, insurance premiums, medical bills, school tuition, child care costs, and other regular non-credit payments. Typically, at least four different items such as these must be provided to piece together an adequate picture of the borrower's credit history.

Payment Record

For each account that appears on a credit report, there's a payment record showing whether the payments have been made on time. Late payments are shown as 30 days, 60 days, or 90 or more days overdue.

If a loan applicant is chronically late in making payments, the underwriter will interpret that as a sign that the applicant tends to be financially overextended or fails to take debt repayment seriously (or both). Late payments on a previous mortgage are particularly damaging. However, a spotless payment record generally isn't required, and late payments that occurred more than two years ago won't usually affect the underwriter's decision.

Major Derogatory Incidents

Serious credit problems that may show up on an individual's credit report include charge-offs, debt collection accounts, repossessions, foreclosures, and bankruptcy. (Until 2015, civil judgments, medical debts, and tax liens could also appear on a person's credit report, but those are no longer included.)

Negative information on credit report:
- Charge-offs
- Collections
- Repossessions
- Foreclosures
- Bankruptcies

- **Charge-offs.** When there has been no payment on an account for six months, the chances that it will ever be collected are low. The tax code allows the creditor to write off or "charge off" such a debt, treating it as a loss for income tax purposes.

  However, the charge-off doesn't relieve the debtor of legal responsibility for repaying the debt. The creditor may continue to try to collect the debt after it has been charged off. If the debtor pays off the debt—or the creditor is willing to settle for partial payment—the charge-off can still appear on the debtor's credit report unless the creditor agrees to have it removed.

- **Collections.** After several attempts to get a debtor to pay a bill, a frustrated creditor may turn the bill over to a collection agency. Once this happens, the debt will show up on the debtor's credit report, even if the original bill did not.

- **Repossessions.** If someone purchases an item on credit and fails to make the payments, the creditor may be able to repossess the item.

- **Foreclosures.** As you might expect, mortgage lenders regard a real estate foreclosure on a loan applicant's credit report as a matter of special concern. Giving a lender a deed in lieu of foreclosure is also considered a derogatory incident.

- **Bankruptcies.** Not surprisingly, lenders also consider a bankruptcy on an applicant's credit report to be a very bad sign.

Under the federal Fair Credit Reporting Act, all of these incidents may remain on a credit report for no more than seven years, with the exception of bankruptcies, which may remain for ten years.

An underwriter won't necessarily be concerned about an incident that occurred more than two years before the loan application, unless it was a foreclosure or a bankruptcy. These are taken very seriously; even after years have passed, a foreclosure or a bankruptcy will lead to an especially careful review of the application and may result in denial of the loan or less favorable terms.

Credit Scores

Most underwriters now use credit scores to help evaluate a loan applicant's credit history. A credit reporting agency calculates an individual's credit score using the information that appears in his credit report and a quantitative model developed by a national credit scoring company. Credit scoring models, which are based on statistical analysis of large numbers of mortgages, are designed to predict the likelihood of successful repayment or default on a mortgage. In general, someone with poor credit scores is much more likely to default than someone with good credit scores.

The most widely used type of credit score in residential lending is the FICO® score. (FICO is an acronym for Fair Isaac and Company, which developed the predominant credit scoring model.) FICO scores range from around 300 to 850. A relatively high FICO score (for example, over 750) is a positive sign. You may hear comparable credit scoring models referred to by other names; for example, Equifax calls the credit scores it bases on the FICO model Beacon scores.

Just as the three agencies' credit reports for a particular loan applicant won't always match perfectly, the applicant's credit score will typically vary a bit from one agency to another. Underwriting rules generally direct the underwriter to select the lower of two scores or the middle of three to use in the underwriting process. If there is more than one applicant, the underwriter compares their selected scores and uses the lowest.

Level of Review. An underwriter uses the applicant's credit scores to decide what level of review to apply to the applicant's credit history. For example, if the applicant has good credit scores, the underwriter might perform a basic review, simply confirming that the information in the credit report is complete and accurate without investigating further. Aside from a foreclosure or a bankruptcy, the underwriter probably won't question the applicant about derogatory information in the report, because it's already been taken into account in calculat-

Credit scores:
- Predict likelihood of default
- Determine appropriate level of review

ing the credit scores. On the other hand, if the applicant has mediocre or poor credit scores, the underwriter will perform a more complete review, looking into the circumstances that led to the credit problems.

Maintaining Good Credit Scores. Almost any information that appears on a person's credit report may affect the credit score he receives from the agency that prepared that report. Credit activity within the previous two years has the greatest impact, however.

While most people would expect chronically late payments and collection problems to hurt someone's credit scores, some of the other factors that can lower scores might come as a surprise. For example, with a credit card, maintaining a balance near the credit limit ("maxing out" the card) will have a negative impact on the cardholder's credit scores, even if he always makes his payments on time.

Applying for too much credit can also have a negative effect. Each time a person applies for credit (a store charge card, a car loan, and so on), the creditor makes a "credit inquiry" that becomes part of the applicant's credit history. Occasional inquiries are fine, but too many within the past year can lower the applicant's credit scores. From a lender's point of view, a lot of inquiries may indicate that the applicant is in danger of becoming overextended.

Special rules apply to credit inquiries for mortgages and car loans. Someone who wants to buy a home or a car often applies to several lenders, intending to compare financing offers and accept the best one. This will result in multiple credit inquiries, even though the consumer is looking for only one loan. To allow for that type of comparison shopping, when a credit score is calculated, mortgage and car loan credit inquiries in the previous 30 days are ignored. Also, multiple inquiries for a mortgage or a car loan within any 45-day period (a typical shopping period) are counted as a single inquiry.

Obtaining Credit Information

It's a good idea for prospective home buyers to obtain their credit reports and find out their credit scores well before they apply for a mortgage. (Obtaining a copy of your own credit report does not count as a credit inquiry.) A credit report may contain incorrect information, and the Fair Credit Reporting Act requires credit reporting agencies to investigate complaints and make corrections. This process can take a month or more.

Also, even if the negative information that appears on a buyer's credit reports is correct, reviewing the reports in advance will help prepare the buyer to explain her credit problems to potential lenders.

Explaining Credit Problems

In some cases, negative credit reports and poor credit scores may not prevent a home buyer from obtaining a loan. Credit problems can often be explained. If the underwriter is convinced that the past problems don't reflect the loan applicant's overall attitude toward credit and that the circumstances leading to the problems were temporary and are unlikely to recur, the loan application may well be approved.

Most people try to meet their credit obligations on time; when they don't, there's usually a good reason. Loss of a job, divorce, hospitalization, prolonged illness, or a death in the family can create extraordinary financial pressures and adversely affect bill paying habits. If a loan applicant has poor credit scores, it may be possible to show that the credit problems occurred during a specific period of time for an understandable reason, and that the applicant has handled credit well both before and since that period. The applicant should put this explanation in writing and provide supporting documentation from a third party (such as hospital records).

Letter explaining negative credit report:
- State reason for problem
- Problem occurred during specific period
- Problem no longer exists
- Good credit before and since
- Provide documentation from third party
- Don't blame creditors

When explaining credit problems to a lender, it's a mistake to blame the problems on misunderstandings or on the creditors. Underwriters hear too many explanations from loan applicants who refuse to accept responsibility for their own acts, insisting instead that the blame lies elsewhere. The reaction to these explanations is very predictable: skepticism, disbelief, and rejection. Underwriters reason that an applicant's reluctance to take responsibility for past credit problems is an indication of what can be expected from her in the future.

If a loan applicant's credit report is laced with problems over a period of years, there's little hope for approval of a prime loan, and even a subprime loan could be difficult to obtain. Perpetual credit problems are more likely to reflect an attitude than a circumstance, and it's reasonable to assume the pattern will continue in the future.

Most credit problems can be resolved with time, however. When buyers tell you they have had some credit problems in the past, it would be a mistake to leap to the conclusion that they can't qualify for a loan. Refer them to a lender and get an expert's opinion.

Income Analysis

Of course, a loan applicant's credit reputation is only one element of her creditworthiness. The underwriter must analyze the buyer's income as well. Even if the buyer has excellent credit, the lender won't approve her loan unless she has sufficient income to make the mortgage payments each month.

Characteristics of Income

From an underwriter's point of view, income has three dimensions: quantity, quality, and durability.

Quantity. A key consideration in underwriting is whether the loan applicant's monthly income is enough to cover the proposed monthly mortgage payment in addition to all of his other expenses. So the underwriter wants to know how much income the applicant has. Not all income is equal in an underwriter's eyes, however. Only income that meets the tests of quality and durability is taken into account in deciding whether the applicant has enough income to qualify for the loan.

Income analysis:
- Quantity
- Quality
- Durability

Quality (Dependability). To evaluate the quality of a loan applicant's income, the underwriter looks at the sources from which it is derived. The income sources should be reasonably dependable, such as an established employer, a government agency, or an interest-yielding investment account.

> **Example:** Jeanne Ellington is applying for a mortgage. She works for a medium-sized company that manufactures machine parts. The company has been in business for 35 years and hasn't been subject to downsizing or periodic layoffs in recent memory. Because Ellington's employer is well-established and stable, the underwriter sees it as a very dependable source of income. Thus, Ellington's salary will be considered high-quality income.

The less dependable the source (a brand new company or a high-risk investment, for example), the lower the quality of the income.

> **Example:** Suppose instead that Jeanne Ellington works for a small graphic design company that was started less than a year ago. The underwriter might decide that the company isn't a very dependable source of income, and therefore conclude that Ellington's salary is relatively low-quality income. That will count

as a weakness in her loan application, although by itself it won't lead to denial of the loan.

Durability (Probability of Continuance). Income is considered durable if it can be expected to continue in the future—preferably for at least the **next three years**. Wages from permanent employment (as opposed to a temporary job), permanent disability benefits, and interest on established investments are all examples of durable income.

Stable Monthly Income

Income that meets the tests of quality and durability is generally referred to as the loan applicant's **stable monthly income**. Typically, stable monthly income is made up of earnings from one primary income source, such as a full-time job, plus earnings from acceptable secondary sources. Secondary income can take many forms, such as bonuses, commissions, social security payments, military disability and retirement income, interest on savings or other investments, and so on.

The following types of income generally meet the tests of quality and durability, so that lenders are willing to count them as part of the loan applicant's stable monthly income.

Employment Income. Permanent employment is the major income source for most home buyers. The underwriter will consider not only the loan applicant's current job and wage or salary level, but also her recent employment history. Not surprisingly, a history of steady employment is viewed favorably. Ideally, a loan applicant will have been employed by the same employer or in the same field continuously for **at least two years**.

If the applicant has held his current position for two years or more, the underwriter usually won't consider it necessary to look at the applicant's previous employment. Otherwise, the underwriter may want to check into the applicant's two previous jobs.

Frequent changes in employment don't necessarily count against the applicant. While persistent job-hopping might indicate a problem, changing jobs for career advancement is usually a good sign. The key issue for the underwriter is whether the job changes have hurt the loan applicant's ability to pay her financial obligations.

Positive employment history:
- Consistency, usually 2 years in same job or field
- Job changes have been for advancement
- Special training or education

On the whole, job continuity isn't as important as continuity of earnings. As long as the applicant has consistently been able to find work that brings in a certain level of income, it may not matter that he hasn't stayed in the same line of work. But if the loan application reveals a period longer than 60 days with no employment income, the applicant may be asked to explain it.

Note that in some cases loan approval may be warranted even without an established two-year work history. For example, the applicant may have recently graduated from college or a vocational school. Training or education that has prepared the applicant for a specific kind of work can strengthen the loan application. Also, even in the absence of special training, an unimpressive employment history could be counterbalanced by other factors in the loan application.

Commissions, overtime, and bonuses. These forms of employment income are considered durable if they can be shown to have been a consistent part of the loan applicant's overall earnings pattern, usually for at least two years. (Some lenders count bonuses as stable income only if the applicant has received them for three years or more.)

In addition to regular wages from a job, stable monthly income may include:

- Bonuses
- Commissions
- Overtime
- Seasonal work
- Self-employment income
- Retirement income
- Investment income
- Rental income
- Alimony or child support
- Public assistance

The underwriter will calculate the average amount of overtime, bonus, or commission income, but will also consider the trend: Have these earnings been steady, or have they been increasing or decreasing? If they're decreasing, the underwriter may count less than the average amount as stable income.

Seasonal work. Seasonal or periodic earnings—wages from agricultural work or a construction job, for instance—may be treated as stable income if there is an established earnings pattern.

> **Example:** Harold Jensen has worked as a deckhand on a fishing boat every summer for the past three years, and he intends to continue doing that. Although his summer income alone isn't enough to qualify him for a mortgage loan, an underwriter would be willing to treat it as stable income and add it to his earnings from the rest of the year.

Self-employment income. When a loan applicant owns a business, the income received from that business is self-employment income. (It isn't necessary to be the sole owner of the business; lenders generally treat income from a business as self-employment income if the applicant has an ownership interest of 25% or more.) Consistent income from freelance or consulting work is also considered to be self-employment income.

To lenders, self-employment adds an extra element of risk to a loan, because the borrower's income is often unpredictable, and small businesses often fail. So a loan applicant should expect some extra scrutiny if self-employment is his main source of income. If the applicant hasn't been self-employed for very long, the underwriter may hesitate to approve the loan. Lenders are wary of new businesses and generally want to see that a self-employed applicant has operated her business profitably for at least two years, though less time may be acceptable if the applicant had considerable previous experience in the same field. The underwriter will consider the trend of the applicant's earnings, her training and experience, and the nature of the business.

For some self-employed loan applicants, a lender may be willing to avoid the issue of self-employment income altogether and focus instead on the applicant's assets and credit reputation. As a general rule, this is only an option for applicants who have a substantial net worth and excellent credit.

Verifying employment income. As we discussed earlier, the information provided in the loan application must be verified—that is, confirmed and documented. Generally, a lender will require either a standard or streamlined level of documentation, depending on the strength of the application. For applications submitted to an automated underwriting system, the AU report tells the underwriter what level of documentation is needed; in manual underwriting, the underwriter usually follows the documentation rules for the loan program in question.

The standard method of verifying a loan applicant's employment income is to send a "Request for Verification of Employment" form (see Figure 8.1) directly to the applicant's employer. The employer fills out the form and sends it directly back to the lender. To eliminate the possibility that the applicant might tamper with the verification form, the applicant isn't allowed to return the form to the lender. Note that the form asks the employer about the probability of continued employment.

For many mortgage loans, lenders now use a streamlined method of employment verification. The loan applicant can provide the lender with W-2 forms for the previous two years and payroll stubs or vouchers for the previous 30-day period. The pay stubs must identify the

Fig. 8.1 Request for Verification of Employment form

⚎ FannieMae

Request for Verification of Employment

Privacy Act Notice: This information is to be used by the agency collecting it or its assignees in determining whether you qualify as a prospective mortgagor under its program. It will not be disclosed outside the agency except as required and permitted by law. You do not have to provide this information, but if you do not your application for approval as a prospective mortgagor or borrower may be delayed or rejected. The information requested in this form is authorized by Title 38, USC, Chapter 37 (if VA); by 12 USC, Section 1701 et. seq. (if HUD/FHA); by 42 USC, Section 1452b (if HUD/CPD); and Title 42 USC, 1471 et. seq., or 7 USC, 1921 et. seq. (if USDA/FmHA).

Instructions: Lender — Complete items 1 through 7. Have applicant complete item 8. Forward directly to employer named in item 1.
Employer — Please complete either Part II or Part III as applicable. Complete Part IV and return directly to lender named in item 2.
The form is to be transmitted directly to the lender and is not to be transmitted through the applicant or any other party.

Part I — Request

1. To (Name and address of employer)	2. From (Name and address of lender)

I certify that this verification has been sent directly to the employer and has not passed through the hands of the applicant or any other interested party.

3. Signature of Lender	4. Title	5. Date	6. Lender's Number (Optional)

I have applied for a mortgage loan and stated that I am now or was formerly employed by you. My signature below authorizes verification of this information.

7. Name and Address of Applicant (include employee or badge number)	8. Signature of Applicant

Part II — Verification of Present Employment

9. Applicant's Date of Employment	10. Present Position	11. Probability of Continued Employment

12A. Current Gross Base Pay (Enter Amount and Check Period)
☐ Annual   ☐ Hourly
☐ Monthly   ☐ Other (Specify)
$ _____   ☐ Weekly

12B. Gross Earnings

Type	Year To Date	Past Year 19___	Past Year 19___
Base Pay	Thru _____ 19__ $	$	$
Overtime	$	$	$
Commissions	$	$	$
Bonus	$	$	$
Total	$	$	$

13. For Military Personnel Only

Pay Grade

Type	Monthly Amount
Base Pay	$
Rations	$
Flight or Hazard	$
Clothing	$
Quarters	$
Pro Pay	$
Overseas or Combat	$
Variable Housing Allowance	$

14. If Overtime or Bonus is Applicable, Is Its Continuance Likely?
Overtime ☐ Yes ☐ No
Bonus ☐ Yes ☐ No

15. If paid hourly — average hours per week

16. Date of applicant's next pay increase

17. Projected amount of next pay increase

18. Date of applicant's last pay increase

19. Amount of last pay increase

20. Remarks (If employee was off work for any length of time, please indicate time period and reason)

Part III — Verification of Previous Employment

21. Date Hired	23. Salary/Wage at Termination Per (Year) (Month) (Week)
22. Date Terminated	Base _____ Overtime _____ Commissions _____ Bonus _____

24. Reason for Leaving	25. Position Held

Part IV — Authorized Signature
- Federal statutes provide severe penalties for any fraud, intentional misrepresentation, or criminal connivance or conspiracy purposed to influence the issuance of any guaranty or insurance by the VA Secretary, the U.S.D.A., FmHA/FHA Commissioner, or the HUD/CPD Assistant Secretary.

26. Signature of Employer	27. Title (Please print or type)	28. Date
29. Print or type name signed in Item 26	30. Phone No.	

Fannie Mae
Form 1005   July 96

Employment verification:
- Verification form sent to employer, or
- W-2 forms for 2 years plus pay stubs for 30 days, with phone call to employer

applicant, the employer, and the applicant's gross earnings for both the current pay period and the year to date. The lender may then confirm the employment and earnings information with a phone call to the employer.

When commissions, overtime, bonuses, or seasonal earnings are a significant part of the applicant's employment income, the lender typically requires copies of the applicant's federal income tax returns for the previous two years to verify these earnings. (The lender may want to obtain these directly from the IRS, rather than from the applicant. This requires the applicant's written permission.) The lender will ask the employer if overtime or bonus income is likely to continue, and whether the applicant has business expenses that will be deducted from commissions.

Self-employed applicant needs financial records and income tax returns for 2 years

Self-employed loan applicants should be prepared to provide business and personal income tax returns for the two years prior to the loan application. (If the business is well-established and the applicant won't be using any funds from the business to close the loan, the requirement for business tax returns may be waived.) If the business is a sole proprietorship, the underwriter may also want to see a balance sheet covering the previous one or two fiscal years and a year-to-date profit and loss statement. This additional documentation is especially likely to be requested if the stability or durability of the applicant's self-employment income is in doubt.

Retirement Income. Pension and social security payments received by retired persons are usually dependable and durable, so they can be included in stable monthly income.

The federal Equal Credit Opportunity Act (see Chapter 14) prohibits age discrimination in lending. Nonetheless, it is not illegal for an underwriter to consider an elderly loan applicant's life expectancy when deciding whether or not to approve a loan.

Investment Income. Dividends or interest on investments may be counted as part of stable monthly income. The underwriter will calculate an average of the investment income for the previous two years. Of course, if the loan applicant is going to cash in an investment to raise the funds needed for closing, then the underwriter will not regard that investment as a durable source of income.

Rental Income. If a loan applicant already owns or is purchasing an investment property, rental income from that property generally can be counted as stable monthly income. The lender will decide the amount of monthly rental income to include in the applicant's stable monthly income based on documentation such as recent tax returns, any existing lease agreements, and/or an appraiser's estimate of the property's current market rental value. In some cases the lender will count only a specific percentage (for example, 75%) of the anticipated gross rental income, to provide a cushion in case of vacancies or unexpected operating expenses.

On the other hand, rents generated by non-investment property—the loan applicant's own principal residence or a second home—usually won't count as stable monthly income. For example, if the applicant is buying a second home for herself and plans to use it for short-term vacation rentals during part of the year, there's a good chance the lender will refuse to take that rental income into account. (However, if the property is a two- to four-unit residential building and the applicant will live in one of the units, rents from the other units will be included in her stable monthly income.)

If a loan applicant has negative rental income—if the operating expenses add up to more than the rent that the property generates—that will be treated as a monthly obligation when the underwriter calculates the applicant's income ratios (discussed shortly).

Separate Maintenance, Alimony, and Child Support. These types of income are considered part of stable monthly income only if it appears that the payments will be made reliably. That determination depends on whether the payments are required by a court decree, how long the loan applicant has been receiving the payments, the overall financial health of the person making the payments, and the applicant's ability to legally compel payment if necessary.

A copy of the court decree usually must be submitted to the lender. And unless the payments are made through the court, proof of receipt of payments is also required. Some lenders accept the loan applicant's bank statements (showing that the checks have been deposited) as proof of receipt; others require photocopies of the deposited checks.

The underwriter will examine the record of payment. If some payments in the preceding 6 to 12 months were missed or were significantly late, the underwriter will probably exclude the alimony, maintenance, or child support from the loan applicant's stable monthly income.

The obligation to pay child support ordinarily ends when the child turns 18. As a result, whether an underwriter will include child support payments in a loan applicant's stable monthly income

Alimony & child support:
- Copy of court decree
- Proof of receipt
- Payments must be reliable
- Child support no longer counts when child reaches mid-teens

depends on the age of the applicant's child. The closer a child gets to age 18, the less durable child support becomes. If the child is over 15, it is unlikely that the underwriter will count the child support payments as stable monthly income.

In some situations, a loan applicant who receives (or is entitled to receive) alimony, maintenance, or child support might prefer not to list that income on the application. That might be the case, for example, if an ex-spouse is hostile or uncooperative. The Equal Credit Opportunity Act, which prohibits discrimination based on marital status in the underwriting process, prevents lenders from asking borrowers if they're divorced and from requiring them to disclose alimony or child support. Of course, if a particular source of income isn't listed on the loan application, the lender won't count it as part of the applicant's stable monthly income.

Public Assistance. The Equal Credit Opportunity Act prohibits lenders from discriminating against loan applicants because all or part of their income is derived from a public assistance program (such as Temporary Aid for Needy Families or food stamps). Public assistance payments will be counted as part of a loan applicant's stable monthly income only if they meet the test of durability. If the applicant's eligibility for the assistance program will terminate in the near future, the underwriter will not take the payments into account.

Unacceptable Types of Income. The following are some types of income that underwriters usually exclude from a loan applicant's stable monthly income.

Temporary employment. Income from any job (full- or part-time) that the employer classifies as temporary ordinarily does not count as stable monthly income. That's true even if there's no definite termination date.

> **Example:** A recent flood damaged a large section of an industrial complex. The property manager has hired several full-time workers to help clean up the debris and repair the damage. These jobs have no termination date, but they're temporary in nature. As a result, the workers' wages wouldn't be considered stable monthly income.

In some cases, however, when a loan applicant has supported himself through a particular type of temporary work for years, that income can be presented to the lender as income earned through self-employment.

This will require a significant level of documentation to prove, similar to demonstrating self-employment income from one's own business.

Unemployment compensation. Unemployment compensation is rarely treated as stable monthly income because eligibility usually lasts only for a specified number of weeks (for example, 26 weeks). However, in some cases a worker receives unemployment compensation during a certain period each year because of the seasonal nature of her work. For example, a farm worker or resort employee who can't find other work during the off-season might collect some unemployment benefits every year. If a loan applicant's tax returns for the preceding two years establish that unemployment benefits have been a regular part of her income, and this pattern appears likely to continue, an underwriter may be willing to count the benefits as stable monthly income.

Income from unobligated family members. An underwriter will ordinarily consider only the earnings of the heads of the household—the loan applicants—when calculating stable monthly income. Contributions from other family members who are going to occupy the home, such as teenage children or an elderly parent, are usually voluntary rather than contractual. Since these other family members have no legal obligation to the lender or the borrower and may move out at any time, their contributions could stop without notice. As a result, they aren't regarded as durable.

However, if a primary borrower's family member is listed on the application as a co-borrower, that family member's income may be considered in the qualifying process. (See the discussion of cosigners later in this chapter.)

Calculating Stable Monthly Income

After deciding which portion of the loan applicant's income meets the tests of quality and durability, the underwriter returns to the question of quantity. The income from all the acceptable sources is added up to determine the applicant's stable monthly income.

Many types of income are paid to the recipient once a month, but others are paid weekly, every two weeks, quarterly, or annually. Since what matters for the purposes of underwriting is stable *monthly* income, all payments are converted to monthly figures.

To convert hourly wages to monthly earnings, multiply the hourly wage by the number of hours the loan applicant works per week, then multiply by 52 (weeks in a year) and divide by 12 (months in a year).

> Income that usually doesn't count as stable monthly income:
> - Wages from temporary job
> - Unemployment compensation
> - Contributions from unobligated family members

Example:

Hourly wage: $14.50

Hours per week: 40

Weekly income: $14.50 × 40 = $580

Annual income: $580 × 52 = $30,160

Monthly income: $30,160 ÷ 12 = $2,513

There's a shortcut. You can reach the same result by multiplying the hourly wage by 173.33 (as long as the buyer is being paid for a 40-hour week).

Example:

Hourly wage: $14.50

Hours per week: 40

Monthly income: $14.50 × 173.33 = $2,513

Notice that being paid every two weeks (26 payments per year) is not the same as being paid twice a month (24 payments per year). If the buyer is paid every two weeks, multiply the payment amount by 26 to get the annual total, then divide by 12 to get the monthly figure.

Nontaxable Income. To calculate a loan applicant's stable monthly income, an underwriter uses gross income figures—the full amount earned or received, without subtracting the taxes that have been withheld or that the applicant will have to pay. Qualifying standards have been set with the understanding that the applicant is required to pay taxes on most, if not all, of his stable monthly income, and only what's left over—the after-tax income—is actually available for personal use.

However, certain types of income, such as child support, disability payments, and some public assistance, are generally exempt from taxation. Since the recipient doesn't have to pay taxes on this income, 100% of it can be used for personal expenses, like paying the mortgage and other bills. An underwriter may take this into account when calculating a loan applicant's stable monthly income, by "grossing up" any nontaxable income. For instance, in the calculations, the underwriter might add 15 – 25% to the amount of child support a loan applicant actually receives, to approximate the equivalent amount of gross taxable income the child support payments represent.

Example: Each month, Cheryl Bowie earns $3,600 and receives $390 in child support from her ex-husband. When she applies for a mortgage, the underwriter grosses up the child support figure because Bowie won't have to pay income taxes on that part of her income. The underwriter estimates how much gross income the child support represents by adding 25% to it.

$390 + 25% = $487.50 (grossed up monthly child support)

$3,600.00	Employment income
+ 487.50	Child support
$4,087.50	Stable monthly income

Income Ratios

Once the underwriter has calculated the applicant's stable monthly income, the next step is to measure the adequacy of that income: Is it enough so that the applicant can afford the proposed monthly mortgage payment? To measure adequacy, underwriters use **income ratios**. The rationale behind the ratios is that if a borrower's expenses exceed a certain percentage of her monthly income, the borrower may have a difficult time making the payments on the loan.

There are basically two types of income ratios:

- A **debt to income ratio** (total obligations to income ratio) measures the proposed monthly mortgage payment plus any other regular debt payments against the pre-tax monthly income.
- A **housing expense to income ratio** measures the monthly mortgage payment alone against the pre-tax monthly income.

To measure adequacy of stable monthly income, underwriter uses income ratios:
- Debt to income ratio
- Housing expense to income ratio

For the purpose of income ratio calculations, the monthly mortgage payment includes principal, interest, property taxes, hazard insurance, and—if applicable—special assessments, mortgage insurance, and homeowners association dues. This aggregate payment is often abbreviated PITI, for principal, interest, taxes, insurance. (Several years ago Fannie Mae and Freddie Mac began calling this payment PITIA, to include association dues, but many in the industry still refer to it as PITI.) Each ratio is expressed as a percentage.

Example: Alice Cochrane's salary is $3,200 a month and her husband Eric's salary is $2,800, so their combined stable monthly income is $6,000. The mortgage they're applying for would require monthly PITI payments of $1,800. To calculate their housing expense to income ratio, divide the PITI payment by their monthly income:

$$\$1,800 \div \$6,000 = .30, \text{ or } 30\%$$

Their proposed housing expense represents 30% of their stable monthly income, so their housing expense to income ratio is 30%.

The Cochranes' other debt payments (credit cards, car loan, etc.) amount to $480 per month. To calculate their debt to income ratio, add the proposed housing expense and the other debt payments together, then divide by their monthly income:

$$\$1,800 + \$480 = \$2,280 \div \$6,000 = .38, \text{ or } 38\%$$

Their total monthly debt payments represent 38% of their stable monthly income, so their debt to income ratio is 38%.

Whether the income ratios in the example would be considered too high would depend on the lender and the type of loan the Cochranes were applying for. The specific income ratio limits used in each of the various financing programs—conventional, FHA, and VA—will be discussed in later chapters.

It's worth noting that in most loan programs, maximum income ratios are treated as guidelines rather than hard-and-fast limits. A loan may be approved in spite of a debt to income ratio or housing expense ratio that exceeds the recommended limit, as long as there are sufficient compensating factors—other strengths in the application that compensate for the weakness in income.

Lenders are generally more concerned about the debt to income ratio than the housing expense to income ratio. The ratio that takes into account all of the monthly debt payments (including the housing expense) is a better predictor of default than the ratio that takes into account only the housing expense.

Co-borrowers and Cosigners. As we said earlier, when two people apply for a loan together, they may be referred to as co-borrowers, or as borrower and co-borrower. The income and assets of both applicants, along with their debts and their credit reputations, are taken into account in the underwriting. If the application is approved, they will have joint and several liability for the loan, which means that a court could order either of them to pay the entire loan balance, not just half.

Co-borrowers generally hold title and occupy the property together; that's usually the case when a married or unmarried couple buys a home, for example. In some cases, though, one of the borrowers occupies the property and the co-borrower is a non-occupant (usually a parent or other family member). The non-occupant co-borrower may be a co-owner of the property, or may have no ownership interest.

A non-occupant co-borrower who will not have an ownership interest in the property is referred to as a **cosigner**, rather than a co-borrower. A cosigner signs a promissory note along with the primary borrower, but does not sign the mortgage or deed of trust, since she doesn't have an ownership interest in the property. A cosigner may also be called a guarantor, surety, or endorser.

Cosigner helps borrower qualify by sharing responsibility for loan

By sharing responsibility for repayment, a cosigner helps the primary borrower qualify for the loan. The most common cosigners are parents, who use their established income and financial status to help a child who otherwise would be unable to purchase a house. The lender is willing to make the loan because the borrower's parents will have to repay it if the borrower fails to do so.

Like any other loan applicant, a cosigner must have income, assets, and a credit reputation that are acceptable to the lender. Marginal cosigners shouldn't be used; they may do more harm than good to the application.

To analyze a loan application involving a cosigner, the underwriter combines the cosigner's stable monthly income with the primary borrower's, combines their monthly debt payments, and then calculates income ratios using these combined figures (along with the proposed housing expense). In addition, the underwriter calculates income ratios for the primary borrower alone, to make sure that they aren't too far over the standard limits. The primary borrower shouldn't be relying too heavily on the cosigner's income in order to qualify for the loan.

Exercise No. 1

Roy Cutter has recently been honorably discharged from the U.S. Air Force, where he received training as an airplane mechanic. After discharge, Roy and his wife Judy moved to a new city. Three months ago, Roy accepted a full-time job as an apprentice mechanic for an airline; two weeks later, Judy found a job with a local hospital as a vocational nurse. Roy's hourly wage is $26; Judy earns $685 a week.

1. What is the Cutters' stable monthly income?

2. Are there any special circumstances that might result in loan approval even though the Cutters have only been with their employers for a short time?

Net Worth

Net worth: assets minus liabilities
- Indicates ability to manage financial affairs
- Applicant must have enough liquid assets to close transaction

The third component of creditworthiness is net worth. An individual's net worth is determined by subtracting personal liabilities from total personal assets.

Someone who has built up a significant net worth from earnings, savings, and other investments clearly has the ability to manage financial affairs. Thus, lenders use net worth as a gauge of how well a loan applicant handles money.

Getting an idea of the applicant's financial management skills isn't the only reason for investigating his net worth, however. The underwriter also needs to make sure the applicant has sufficient liquid assets to close the purchase transaction.

Funds for Closing

Liquid assets: cash and other assets that can be easily converted into cash

Liquid assets include cash and any other assets that can be quickly converted to cash, such as stock. A loan applicant must have enough liquid assets to cover the cash downpayment, the closing costs, and other expenses incidental to the purchase of the property.

In addition, as we mentioned earlier in the chapter, the applicant may be required to have **reserves** left over after making the downpayment and paying the closing costs. Generally, these reserves must be enough cash or other liquid assets to cover a specified number of mortgage payments. This provides some assurance that the applicant could handle financial emergencies, such as unexpected bills or a temporary interruption of income, without defaulting on the mortgage.

Whether a loan applicant is required to have reserves—and if so, how many months of reserves—depends on the lender and the loan program. When reserves are required, the most common requirement is two or three months' worth of mortgage payments in reserve. Affordable housing programs (loan programs targeted at low-income and first-time buyers) often require only one month's payment in reserve. In any case, if the loan applicant will have more than the required amount in reserve after closing, that strengthens the application.

Assets

Almost any asset that a loan applicant has will help the application. Real estate, automobiles, furniture, jewelry, stocks, bonds, or cash value in a life insurance policy can all be listed on the application form, and the underwriter will take whatever steps are necessary to verify the information provided. Liquid assets tend to be more helpful than non-liquid ones, and the asset that underwriters usually regard most favorably is the most liquid one of all: money in the bank.

Bank Accounts. When standard documentation procedures are followed, a "Request for Verification of Deposit" form (Figure 8.2) is used to verify the loan applicant's funds. The verification form is sent directly to the bank holding the account, and returned to the underwriter without passing through the applicant's hands.

Verification of funds in bank accounts:
- Verification of deposit form sent to bank, or
- Bank statements for 2 or 3 months

In contrast, when streamlined documentation is allowed, the underwriter relies on bank statements to check how much money a loan applicant has in her bank account(s). The applicant is simply asked to submit original bank statements for the previous two or three months to show that there is sufficient cash for closing.

In reviewing either the applicant's bank statements or the completed Verification of Deposit form, the underwriter has these questions in mind:

1. Does the verified information conform to the statements in the loan application?
2. Does the applicant have enough money in the bank to meet the expenses of the purchase?
3. Has the bank account been opened only recently (within the last three months)?
4. Is the present balance notably higher than the average balance?
5. If the applicant claims that this account was the source of the good faith deposit (the earnest money), is the average balance high enough to confirm that?

Fig. 8.2 Request for Verification of Deposit form

FannieMae

Request for Verification of Deposit

Privacy Act Notice: This information is to be used by the agency collecting it or its assignees in determining whether you qualify as a prospective mortgagor under its program. It will not be disclosed outside the agency except as required and permitted by law. You do not have to provide this information, but if you do not your application for approval as a prospective mortgagor or borrower may be delayed or rejected. The information requested in this form is authorized by Title 38, USC, Chapter 37 (If VA); by 12 USC, Section 1701 et.seq. (If HUD/FHA); by 42 USC, Section 1452b (if HUD/CPD); and Title 42 USC, 1471 et.seq. or 7 USC, 1921 et.seq. (If USDA/FmHA).

Instructions: Lender — Complete Items 1 through 8. Have applicant(s) complete Item 9. Forward directly to depository named in Item 1.
Depository — Please complete Items 10 through 18 and return DIRECTLY to lender named in Item 2.
The form is to be transmitted directly to the lender and is not to be transmitted through the applicant(s) or any other party.

Part I — Request

1. To (Name and address of depository)	2. From (Name and address of lender)

I certify that this verification has been sent directly to the bank or depository and has not passed through the hands of the applicant or any other party.

3. Signature of lender	4. Title	5. Date	6. Lender's No. (Optional)

7. Information To Be Verified

Type of Account	Account in Name of	Account Number	Balance
			$
			$
			$

To Depository: I/We have applied for a mortgage loan and stated in my financial statement that the balance on deposit with you is as shown above. You are authorized to verify this information and to supply the lender identified above with the information requested in Items 10 through 13. Your response is solely a matter of courtesy for which no responsibility is attached to your institution or any of your officers.

8. Name and Address of Applicant(s)	9. Signature of Applicant(s)

To Be Completed by Depository

Part II — Verification of Depository

10. Deposit Accounts of Applicant(s)

Type of Account	Account Number	Current Balance	Average Balance For Previous Two Months	Date Opened
		$	$	
		$	$	
		$	$	

11. Loans Outstanding To Applicant(s)

Loan Number	Date of Loan	Original Amount	Current Balance	Installments (Monthly/Quarterly)		Secured By	Number of Late Payments
		$	$	$	per		
		$	$	$	per		
		$	$	$	per		

12. Please include any additional information which may be of assistance in determination of credit worthiness. (Please include information on loans paid-in-full in Item 11 above.)

13. If the name(s) on the account(s) differ from those listed in Item 7, please supply the name(s) on the account(s) as reflected by your records.

Part III — Authorized Signature - Federal statutes provide severe penalties for any fraud, intentional misrepresentation, or criminal connivance or conspiracy purposed to influence the issuance of any guaranty or insurance by the VA Secretary, the U.S.D.A., FmHA/FHA Commissioner, or the HUD/CPD Assistant Secretary.

14. Signature of Depository Representative	15. Title (Please print or type)	16. Date
17. Please print or type name signed in item 14	18. Phone No.	

Fannie Mae
Form 1006   July 96

Recently opened accounts or higher-than-normal balances must be explained, because these strongly suggest that the applicant has resorted to borrowed funds for the downpayment and closing costs. As a general rule, a home buyer is not allowed to borrow from relatives, friends, or other sources to come up with either the funds needed for closing or the reserves. Borrowing the money would defeat the purpose of the lender's requirements: the buyer would have an additional debt instead of an investment in the property.

There are exceptions to this rule, however. A buyer may be allowed to use funds from a loan secured by an asset such as a car, stock, a certificate of deposit, a life insurance policy, or real estate other than the home being purchased. Of course, the payments on such a secured loan would be counted as part of the buyer's total obligations when the debt to income ratio is calculated.

Also, affordable housing programs often have more flexible policies than standard programs. The buyer may be allowed to borrow part of the funds needed for closing from a relative or certain other sources. (See Chapter 10 for more information.)

Note, too, that a buyer may obtain the money needed for closing from a relative or another source if the buyer won't be required to repay it—in other words, if the money is a gift rather than a loan. We'll discuss gift funds later in this chapter.

Real Estate for Sale. If a loan applicant is selling another property to raise cash to buy the subject property, the net equity in the property that is for sale can be counted as an asset available to be applied to the downpayment, closing costs, and required reserves. The **net equity** is the difference between the market value of the property and the sum of the liens against the property plus the selling expenses:

Net Equity = Market Value – (Liens + Selling Expenses)

In other words, the loan applicant's net equity is the amount of money that he can expect to receive from the sale of the property.

Market value
– Liens and selling expenses
Net equity in real estate
to be sold

> **Example:** The Yamamotos put their home up for sale a month ago, and now they've found the home they want to buy. They've signed a purchase agreement for the new home that's contingent on the sale of the old home and also on their ability to obtain financing. When they apply for a loan to finance the purchase of their new home, the underwriter will count their net equity in the old home as a liquid asset.

$578,000	Market value of old home
− 426,000	First mortgage (to be paid off)
− 20,000	Home improvement loan (to be paid off)
$132,000	Gross equity
− 58,000	Estimated cost of selling old home
$74,000	Net equity in old home
+ 26,000	In savings account
$100,000	Available for purchase of new home

The underwriter's calculation of net equity may begin with the appraised value or the listing price of the old home or, if the loan applicant has already found a buyer for the old home, with the price that buyer has agreed to pay. Selling costs vary from one area of the country to another, but 10% of the listing or sales price is often used as a rough estimate.

If equity is the exclusive source or one of the main sources of money for the purchase of the new home, the lender will not actually fund the loan until it has been given proof that the old home has been sold and the borrower has received the sale proceeds. A copy of the final settlement statement or closing disclosure from the sale of the old home is usually required. (Of course, the purchase of the new home may be ready to close before the buyer has succeeded in selling the old home. In that case, the buyer may want to apply for a swing loan to obtain the cash needed for closing. The swing loan will be secured by the buyer's equity in the old home, and it will be paid off out of the proceeds from the eventual sale of the old home.)

Other Real Estate. Often a loan applicant owns real estate that she is not planning to sell. Whether the real estate is income producing (e.g., rental property) or not (e.g., vacant land), it is an asset and should be considered in connection with the loan application.

Bear in mind, though, that it's the equity, not the value of the property, that contributes to net worth. Only the equity can be converted into cash in the event of need. When a loan applicant owns real estate with little or no equity in it, its impact as a liability cancels out its value as an asset.

Liabilities

All of the loan applicant's personal liabilities are subtracted from the total value of his assets to calculate net worth. The balances owing on credit cards, charge accounts, student loans, car loans, and other installment debts are subtracted; so are any other debts, such as income taxes that are currently payable. If the applicant owns real estate, the remaining balance on the mortgage will be subtracted, along with the amount of any other liens against the property.

Liabilities include:
- Credit card & charge account balances
- Installment debts
- Taxes owed
- Liens against real estate owned

Gift Funds

If a loan applicant lacks some of the funds needed to close a transaction, her relatives may be willing to make up the deficit. The underwriter will usually accept this arrangement, as long as the money is a gift to the applicant rather than a loan.

The rules concerning gift funds vary from one loan program to another and from one lender to another. In most cases, the rules limit how much of the downpayment and closing costs may be covered by gift funds; the loan applicant has to come up with the rest out of his own money, as a minimum investment. (A buyer who has made a significant investment of her own funds is less likely to default. See Chapter 6.) The rules typically also restrict who can provide gift funds. For example, one program might permit gift funds only from close relatives, while another program might also accept gift funds from the applicant's employer or a nonprofit organization.

Whatever the source, the gift should be acknowledged by means of a **gift letter** signed by the donor. The letter should clearly state that the money is a gift and does not have to be repaid. Most lenders have forms for gift letters, and some require that their form be used.

Gift funds:
- Gift letter states funds do not have to be repaid
- Funds are deposited in applicant's account or escrow account

Both the existence and the source of the gift funds must be documented and verified, along with the identity of the donor. The lender wants to be sure that the funds are truly a gift, and don't represent additional debt for the borrower. Most loan programs have specific documentation requirements, which vary slightly depending on the way the gift funds are transferred. Some lenders require the funds to be deposited into the borrower's account well before closing, but many programs allow the donor to transmit the gift funds directly to the escrow agent at any point before closing.

Delayed Financing

A common trend in very competitive housing markets is the use of **delayed financing**. Buyers in those markets often end up in a "bidding war" with other buyers who want the same house. Making an all-cash offer may give them an edge over other buyers, or it can even be a stated or unstated requirement for having their offer considered at all. (Sellers prefer cash offers over offers that are contingent on financing, because a cash transaction is faster and closing is more certain.) In some cases, buyers win a bidding war with an all-cash offer, pay cash for the house, and then get a mortgage loan immediately after closing. In other words, financing is delayed until after the purchase transaction closes.

Delayed financing: buyer pays cash, obtains financing after closing

Of course, the buyers must actually have the cash available to close the transaction, so delayed financing is usually an option only for buyers who are at least moderately well-to-do. In some cases the buyers accumulate the necessary cash by temporarily liquidating other investments (like retirement funds or a stock portfolio). After the mortgage financing is in place, they can use the loan funds to replenish most of those investments.

Exercise No. 2

Mr. Able wants to buy a home. The downpayment would be $51,000, and his closing costs are estimated at $10,200; he would also be required to have reserves of $7,845 (two months' mortgage payments) left over after closing.

Able has been working at a large, established company for three years. He is paid $4,200 every two weeks. He is selling his current home for $487,500; the mortgage on the property has a principal balance of $399,750, and the estimated selling expenses are $43,500. Able has checking and savings accounts with a local bank and plans to draw on those accounts to close the transaction (refer to the filled-in Verification of Deposit form in Figure 8.3).

1. What is Able's stable monthly income?

2. What is Able's net equity in the home that he is selling?

3. Will Able have any problems closing the transaction? Explain.

Fig. 8.3 Verification of Deposit for Exercise No. 2

FannieMae

Request for Verification of Deposit

Privacy Act Notice: This information is to be used by the agency collecting it or its assignees in determining whether you qualify as a prospective mortgagor under its program. It will not be disclosed outside the agency except as required and permitted by law. You do not have to provide this information, but if you do not your application for approval as a prospective mortgagor or borrower may be delayed or rejected. The information requested in this form is authorized by Title 38, USC, Chapter 37 (If VA); by 12 USC, Section 1701 et.seq. (If HUD/FHA); by 42 USC, Section 1452b (if HUD/CPD); and Title 42 USC, 1471 et.seq. or 7 USC, 1921 et.seq. (If USDA/FmHA).

Instructions: Lender — Complete Items 1 through 8. Have applicant(s) complete Item 9. Forward directly to depository named in Item 1.
Depository — Please complete Items 10 through 18 and return DIRECTLY to lender named in Item 2.
The form is to be transmitted directly to the lender and is not to be transmitted through the applicant(s) or any other party.

Part I — Request

1. To (Name and address of depository)	2. From (Name and address of lender)
Seaside Savings 1919 Second Avenue Anytown, USA	Coastal Mortgage 332 Juniper Street Anytown, USA

I certify that this verification has been sent directly to the bank or depository and has not passed through the hands of the applicant or any other party.

3. Signature of lender	4. Title	5. Date	6. Lender's No. (Optional)
Warren Carter	Loan Officer	April 19	

7. Information To Be Verified

Type of Account	Account in Name of	Account Number	Balance
Checking	Carl B. Able	11616-6	$ 1,446.00
Savings	Carl B. Able	61161-1	$ 9,300.00
			$

To Depository: I/We have applied for a mortgage loan and stated in my financial statement that the balance on deposit with you is as shown above. You are authorized to verify this information and to supply the lender identified above with the information requested in Items 10 through 13. Your response is solely a matter of courtesy for which no responsibility is attached to your institution or any of your officers.

8. Name and Address of Applicant(s)	9. Signature of Applicant(s)
Carl B. Able 1800 Mill Street Anytown, USA	*Carl B Able*

To Be Completed by Depository

Part II — Verification of Depository

10. Deposit Accounts of Applicant(s)

Type of Account	Account Number	Current Balance	Average Balance For Previous Two Months	Date Opened
Checking	11616-6	$ 600.00	$ 645.00	2/20
Savings	61161-1	$ 10,800.00	$ 1,950.00	2/20
		$	$	

11. Loans Outstanding To Applicant(s)

Loan Number	Date of Loan	Original Amount	Current Balance	Installments (Monthly/Quarterly)		Secured By	Number of Late Payments
		$	$	$	per		
		$	$	$	per		
		$	$	$	per		

12. Please include any additional information which may be of assistance in determination of credit worthiness. (Please include information on loans paid-in-full in Item 11 above.)   none

13. If the name(s) on the account(s) differ from those listed in Item 7, please supply the name(s) on the account(s) as reflected by your records.

Part III — Authorized Signature - Federal statutes provide severe penalties for any fraud, intentional misrepresentation, or criminal connivance or conspiracy purposed to influence the issuance of any guaranty or insurance by the VA Secretary, the U.S.D.A., FmHA/FHA Commissioner, or the HUD/CPD Assistant Secretary.

14. Signature of Depository Representative	15. Title (Please print or type)	16. Date
Julia G. Hedges	Assistant Vice President	April 23
17. Please print or type name signed in item 14 Julia G. Hedges	18. Phone No. 809-9696	

Fannie Mae
Form 1006   July 96

4. Do you see any problems with his verification of deposit? If so, explain what they are.

5. List some possible solutions to Able's problems.

Other Factors in Underwriting

In addition to the main components of creditworthiness we've discussed, certain other aspects of a proposed loan affect whether or not it will be approved. These include:

- the loan type,
- the repayment period,
- owner-occupancy, and
- the property type.

These factors may either add risk, making approval of the loan less likely, or compensate for risk, making approval more likely. In a case where income, net worth, or credit reputation is somewhat marginal, one of these other factors can make a difference, for better or worse.

Loan Type

Loan type refers to whether the proposed loan is a fixed-rate mortgage, an adjustable-rate mortgage, or some other type, such as a balloon mortgage. Borrowers tend to default more often on ARMs and other loans that involve changes in the payment amount than they do on fixed-rate mortgages. So an application for an ARM generally receives closer scrutiny, and this could tip the balance toward denial of the loan.

Repayment Period

The length of a proposed loan's repayment period affects the qualifying process because of its impact on the size of the monthly mortgage payments. A 15-year loan requires much bigger monthly

CHAPTER 8: QUALIFYING THE BUYER

payments than a 30-year loan for the same amount (see Chapter 6), and therefore is considerably more difficult to qualify for. But the shorter repayment period also has a positive aspect. A 15-year loan presents less risk for the lender (or a secondary market purchaser) than a 30-year loan, since the loan funds are committed for a shorter period. As a result, the fact that a buyer is applying for a 15-year loan often counts as a compensating factor in the qualifying process.

Owner-Occupancy

Most home buyers intend to occupy the property they're buying. If a loan applicant won't be occupying the home he wants to purchase, the loan is referred to as an investor loan. Investor loans have a much higher default rate than owner-occupant loans, so an applicant's investor status is treated as an additional risk factor in the qualifying process. Because of the additional risk, investor loans are subject to tougher LTV requirements, additional fees, and/or higher interest rates.

Property Type

The type of home to be purchased can have an impact on the process of qualifying the buyer. Manufactured homes, condominium units, and some other types of residential property tend not to appreciate as much or as reliably as site-built single-family homes. If the home that the loan applicant wants to buy isn't a regular single-family home, that may be treated as an additional risk factor. That's true even when the appraisal shows that the home meets the lender's standards for the type of property in question. Fannie Mae and Freddie Mac will not even purchase investor loans secured by certain types of property with an increased risk of default.

Subprime Lending

Our discussion of qualifying the buyer has been focused on so-called "prime" lending: loans that meet the normal underwriting standards of the secondary market entities. But the mortgage market has another important segment: subprime lending. It was the boom and bust of subprime loans that precipitated the mortgage market and financial crisis in 2007–2008, one of the most significant developments in the history of the U.S. lending industry (see Chapter 4).

What is Subprime Lending?

The term "subprime lending" does not have a precise definition, but it generally refers to making loans to borrowers who pose greater risks than those who meet standard underwriting guidelines. Without subprime lending, these potential buyers might not be able to purchase the home they want—or, in some cases, any home at all.

Subprime lenders can often be distinguished from prime lenders by their advertisements: subprime ads are aimed at potential home buyers who would have trouble getting a standard loan, and they often place special emphasis on flexibility and personalized service. According to HUD, subprime lenders are more likely than prime lenders to have words such as "acceptance" or "consumer" in their names. Some subprime lenders have rebranded themselves as "nonprime" lenders, to avoid the negative connotations of "subprime." Refinancing and home equity loans (often for the purpose of debt consolidation) make up a large part of the subprime market, but there are many subprime home purchase loans as well.

Subprime Borrowers

Many of the home buyers who get subprime mortgages have blemished credit histories and mediocre credit scores. Depending on how poor the credit history is, these loans may be categorized as B, C, or D loans. (Prime, or standard, financing is often referred to as A credit.)

However, subprime lenders also deal with other categories of buyers: buyers who have good credit, but present some other risk factor. For example, subprime financing may be necessary for buyers who:

- can't (or would rather not have to) meet the income and asset documentation requirements of prime lenders;
- have more debt than prime lenders consider acceptable; or
- want to make a smaller downpayment than prime lenders would allow.

These buyers generally fall into the "A-minus" credit category. (Their credit is good—thus the "A" status—but the additional element of risk knocks the rating down to A-minus.) When Fannie Mae and Freddie Mac began buying some A-minus loans (see Chapter 3), it blurred the line between prime and subprime lending, leading some to argue that A-minus loans shouldn't be considered subprime

Subprime lending: making loans to borrowers who pose greater risks

loans at all. Nevertheless, an A-minus borrower will still pay higher fees or a higher interest rate than she would with a truly prime loan.

Subprime Rates and Fees

Subprime lenders can take on riskier borrowers and make riskier loans because they apply more flexible underwriting standards. In exchange, they typically charge much higher interest rates and fees than prime lenders charge.

Subprime lenders charge higher interest rates and loan fees

> **Example:** The Gundersons want to buy a home. Because of some recent credit problems, they can't qualify for a prime loan. Their subprime lender classifies them as B-risk borrowers and charges them 9% interest for their loan, although the market rate for prime loans (A loans) is only 6%. If the Gundersons had an even worse credit history and were classified as C-risk borrowers, the lender would charge them 10.5% interest. And if they were D-risk borrowers, they'd have to pay 12%.

Subprime lenders justify their higher rates and fees by pointing to their higher servicing costs and greater default rate. Subprime loans require more aggressive servicing because of higher delinquency rates. (Charging more for riskier loans is called risk-based pricing, and it's a key aspect of subprime lending. We'll discuss it in more detail in the next section.)

In addition to having high interest rates and fees, subprime loans are more likely than prime loans to have features such as prepayment penalties, balloon payments, and negative amortization (see Chapter 6). These features have helped subprime lenders counterbalance some of the extra risk involved in their loans, but they can also be burdensome for borrowers.

Subprime Lending and the Secondary Market

The subprime segment of the mortgage market is estimated to have increased from about $35 billion in 1994 to $332 billion in 2003, and then to $1.3 trillion at its peak in early 2007. This growth was fueled by the increasing number of Wall Street investors who bought subprime loans and used them as the basis for issuing private label mortgage-backed securities. (Today, private-label securities have only a small fraction of the share of the MBS market that they held prior to the financial crisis.)

Subprime loans were purchased by investors and packaged into mortgage-backed securities

Traditionally, Fannie Mae and Freddie Mac participated very little in the subprime market. In fact, their underwriting standards were at one time thought to define prime mortgage lending. However, HUD encouraged Fannie Mae and Freddie Mac to enter the subprime market to help meet their affordable housing goals (see Chapter 3), and in the years 2006 and 2007, both GSEs started buying more subprime loans. This drew protests from those already involved in the subprime market. However, for the most part, the GSEs only purchased the very top layer of the subprime market, A-minus loans, leaving other investors with the riskier subprime loans.

End of the Boom. The GSEs' expansion into A-minus territory was one of several ways in which the line between prime and subprime mortgage lending began to blur. As enthusiasm grew for purchasing subprime loans and repackaging them as mortgage-backed securities, underwriting standards for all loans—including prime loans—became increasingly lax, and default rates soared. The ripple effect from this wave of foreclosures, and the resulting losses, led to the failure of not only many subprime lenders but some major investment banks as well. Lenders who were known for making prime loans also suffered during the financial crisis, because they too had participated in the race to make more (and riskier) mortgage loans.

Today, many subprime lenders are gone and most other lenders have lost their appetite for risky loans. Subprime lending is now a much smaller segment of the market than in previous years.

Risk-based Loan Pricing

To end the chapter, we'll take a brief look at risk-based loan pricing. **Risk-based pricing** refers to charging different interest rates and loan fees depending how much risk a loan involves. Borrowers who have mediocre credit reputations are charged higher rates and fees than borrowers with good ones. Only applicants with very bad credit reputations are denied loans altogether.

Risk-based pricing: charging risky borrowers more for their loans

Risk-based pricing has long been the standard practice in subprime lending, but prime lenders traditionally used **average cost pricing**. That is, prime lenders charged the same interest rate and fees to all qualified borrowers, even if some of those borrowers barely squeaked over the approval threshold.

However, prime lenders now also use a form of risk-based pricing. When Fannie Mae and Freddie Mac purchase loans from lenders, they charge fees known as loan-level price adjustments (LLPAs). Higher LLPAs are charged for riskier loans, and lenders usually pass this cost on to the borrower in the form of a higher interest rate on the loan. (See Chapter 10.) Automated underwriting is one of the main reasons for this change. It's comparatively easy for an AUS to draw distinctions between strong and weak borrowers and price their loans accordingly.

Risk-based pricing means that more people are able to obtain loans, albeit more expensive ones. Some claim that risk-based pricing is fairer than average cost pricing, since the best credit risks don't have to subsidize those who aren't quite as good.

On the other hand, with risk-based pricing, some buyers who don't qualify for the best rates may be priced out of the market. Risk-based pricing can also make loan shopping more confusing, since lenders can't advertise one interest rate (or annual percentage rate) for all borrowers.

Whatever the advantages and disadvantages of risk-based pricing, it has taken hold in the prime market. This is a significant change for the residential mortgage industry.

Lenders who use risk-based pricing to extend credit to consumers must provide a written risk-based pricing notice to those borrowers who receive higher-priced loans because of their credit standing. In addition, if the borrower's credit score is used in setting the material terms of the loan pricing, the lender must include a notice stating that the borrower has 60 days to request a free credit report.

Outline: Qualifying the Buyer

I. The Underwriting Process
   A. Underwriting is the process of evaluating a proposed loan to assess whether the buyer and the property meet the lender's minimum standards.
   B. Qualifying standards
      1. Underwriting standards establish what a lender considers to be acceptable and unacceptable risks.
      2. Because most loans will be sold on the secondary market, most lenders use underwriting standards established by Fannie Mae, Freddie Mac, the FHA, or the VA.
   C. Automated underwriting
      1. Most underwriting is now done using software that makes a preliminary analysis of information provided on the loan application.
      2. Automated underwriting is based on the performance of millions of existing mortgage loans, which provides evidence of the factors that make default more or less likely.
      3. An automated underwriting decision will take the form of a risk classification. An application classified as "Accept" can be approved, while one classified as "Refer" won't necessarily be denied but will require further scrutiny by an underwriter.
      4. The automated underwriting report will also state whether a "low-doc" loan is possible, and whether a drive-by inspection or no inspection is possible instead of a full appraisal.

II. Evaluating Creditworthiness
   A. Creditworthiness can be divided into three basic categories: credit reputation, income, and net worth.
   B. Strength in one area can offset weakness in another aspect of creditworthiness.

III. Credit Reputation
   A. Credit report
      1. A credit report will contain information about an individual's loans, credit purchases, and repayments for the previous seven years.
      2. There are three credit reporting agencies, each of which can issue a separate credit report on an applicant.
   B. Credit history
      1. Credit history refers to how long an individual has been borrowing money and paying it back.
      2. Applicants should have at least a one-year credit history, but lending options are available for applicants who don't.

C. Major derogatory incidents that will be listed on a credit report include charge-offs, collections, repossessions, foreclosures, and bankruptcies.

D. Credit scores

  1. Credit scores predict the likelihood that an individual will default on a loan, given her previous credit history.

  2. The most widely used credit scores are FICO® scores.

IV. Income Analysis

A. Characteristics of income

  1. Income has three dimensions: quantity, quality (how dependable the source of income is), and durability (the likelihood the income will continue in the future).

  2. Income that meets tests for quality and durability is considered stable monthly income.

B. Stable monthly income

  1. If an applicant has held the same employment position for two years or more, it won't be necessary to investigate previous work history.

  2. Continuity of earnings is more important than job continuity, and education or training that will enhance earning power can substitute for a two-year work history.

  3. Commissions, overtime, bonuses, and seasonal work can be considered durable income if they have been earned consistently for two years or more.

  4. Self-employment income adds an extra level of risk; lenders will expect to see that the business has been operated profitably for at least two years.

  5. A lender may send a Request for Verification of Employment to the applicant's employer, or the applicant may be able to provide W-2 forms and payroll stubs.

  6. Sources of retirement income (such as pensions and social security) are considered dependable, so they are counted as stable monthly income.

  7. Dividends or interest from investment income may be counted as stable monthly income if they are earned reliably.

  8. Rental income from investment property will generally be considered stable monthly income.

  9. Alimony, maintenance, and child support will be included as stable monthly income if it appears payments have been made reliably.

  10. Unacceptable income includes income from unemployment benefits and income from temporary employment or unobligated family members.

C. Calculating stable monthly income

1. All income payments paid on a weekly or biweekly basis must be converted to monthly income.

2. Qualifying standards assume that income will be taxed, so if some income is nontaxable (such as child support), it may be "grossed up."

D. Income ratios

1. Debt to income ratio: the relationship between the total obligations (the proposed monthly mortgage payment plus all other regular debt payments) and the pre-tax monthly income.

2. Housing expense to income ratio: the relationship between the proposed monthly mortgage payment and the pre-tax monthly income.

3. The income of a cosigner, who will accept joint liability for the debt but will not be occupying the property, may be added to the applicant's income to increase the likelihood a loan will be approved.

V. Net Worth

A. Funds for closing

1. An applicant must have adequate liquid assets to cover the downpayment, closing costs, and other associated expenses.

2. The applicant may also be required to have two or three months' reserves left over after making the downpayment, to cover unexpected expenses without risk of default.

B. Assets

1. An underwriter will send a Request for Verification of Deposit to the applicant's bank to verify funds.

2. An underwriter will be suspicious of recently opened accounts or higher-than-normal balances, which may indicate funds for the downpayment were borrowed.

3. If the borrower is selling property to generate cash to buy new property, the lender will be concerned with the equity in the property (market value minus liens and selling expenses) rather than the property's market value alone.

4. If a buyer is unable to sell an old home in time to use the funds toward the new home, the buyer may use a temporary swing loan.

C. Gift funds

1. An underwriter will usually permit gift funds from friends or relatives, so long as it is specified that the money is a gift and not a loan.

2. The donor must sign a gift letter stating that the funds given do not need to be repaid.

VI. Other Factors in Underwriting
  A. Loan type: an ARM is riskier than a fixed-rate loan, and may require closer scrutiny.
  B. Loan term: a 15-year loan is less risky to a lender than a 30-year loan.
  C. Owner-occupancy: if a borrower doesn't plan to live in the property being purchased, it is considered an investor loan and a higher risk.
  D. Property type: loans for certain property types that don't appreciate as fast, such as condos and mobile homes, might be considered riskier.

VII. Subprime Lending
  A. Subprime lenders make loans with higher degrees of risk, either to borrowers with poor credit histories or to borrowers with good credit histories who have other risk factors.
  B. Subprime lenders apply more flexible underwriting standards and charge higher interest rates and fees.
  C. The boom and bust in subprime lending played an important role in the 2007–2008 mortgage market and financial crisis.

VIII. Risk-based Pricing
  A. Subprime lenders use risk-based pricing: they charge borrowers with mediocre credit histories higher rates and fees than they charge borrowers with better credit histories.
  B. Prime lenders have traditionally charged all borrowers who met their standards the same rates, and turned away loan applicants who didn't meet their standards.
  C. Now prime lenders are also using risk-based pricing, blurring the line between prime and subprime lending.
  D. Creditors who extend credit with risk-based pricing must provide a written risk-based pricing notice to those consumers receiving less favorable terms because of their credit standing.

Key Terms

Underwriting: The process of evaluating the financial status of a loan applicant and the value of the property he hopes to buy, to determine the risk of default and risk of loss in the event of foreclosure.

Underwriter: The employee of an institutional lender who evaluates loan applications, deciding which loans to approve.

Qualifying standards: The rules (concerning income, net worth, credit history, loan-to-value ratios) that an underwriter applies in deciding whether or not to approve a loan application; also called underwriting standards.

Automated underwriting (AU): Underwriting using software that makes a preliminary analysis of a loan application and makes a recommendation for approval or additional scrutiny.

Stable monthly income: Gross monthly income (from primary and secondary sources) that meets the lender's tests of quality and durability.

Income ratio: A test applied in qualifying a buyer for a loan, to determine whether or not he has sufficient income; the buyer's proposed housing expense and other monthly obligations should not exceed a specified percentage of his stable monthly income.

Debt to income ratio: An income ratio calculated by dividing total monthly obligations (including the proposed housing expense and other debt payments) by the pre-tax monthly income.

Housing expense to income ratio: An income ratio calculated by dividing only the proposed monthly housing expense (without other obligations) by the pre-tax monthly income.

Co-borrower: A person who applies for a loan with someone else and will share liability for repayment of the loan. (A non-occupant co-borrower who does not have an ownership interest in the property is called a cosigner.)

Cosigner: A co-borrower who agrees to share liability with a borrower in order to help the borrower qualify for the loan, but who will not occupy the property or have an ownership interest.

Net worth: An individual's personal financial assets, minus total personal liabilities.

Asset: Anything of value an individual owns.

Net equity: The market value of a property, minus any liens against the property and all anticipated selling expenses.

Gift funds: Money given to a buyer who would otherwise not have enough cash to close the transaction.

Gift letter: A document in which a donor of gift funds states that money given is not a loan and does not have to be repaid; required by a lender when the borrower intends to use gift funds as part of the downpayment or closing costs.

Credit report: A report prepared by a credit reporting agency outlining the credit history of an individual, showing amounts of debt and record of repayment.

Credit score: A figure used in underwriting to evaluate a loan applicant's credit history, calculated by a credit reporting agency.

Reserves: Cash or other liquid assets that a borrower will have left over after closing (after making the downpayment and paying the closing costs) and could use to pay the mortgage in the event of a financial emergency.

Chapter Quiz

1. To evaluate the quality of a loan applicant's income, an underwriter considers whether the income:
    a. is derived from a dependable source
    b. is taxable
    c. can be expected to continue for a sustained period
    d. can be treated as a liquid asset

2. As a general rule, a loan applicant should have been continuously employed in the same field for at least:
    a. one year
    b. two years
    c. three years
    d. five years

3. The loan applicant receives child support from her ex-husband. Their child is now 16 years old. Will the child support payments be counted as part of the applicant's stable monthly income?
    a. Yes
    b. Only if the ex-husband has made the payments reliably
    c. Only if the applicant can provide proof of receipt
    d. No

4. The Hendersons have applied for a mortgage loan. Which of these is the underwriter most likely to treat as part of their stable monthly income?
    a. Wages the Hendersons' teenage daughter earns at a part-time job
    b. Unemployment compensation the husband is collecting
    c. Overtime the wife has been earning at her permanent job
    d. Money the husband has earned through occasional freelance work

5. After determining the quantity of the loan applicant's stable monthly income, the underwriter measures the adequacy of the income using:
    a. the consumer price index
    b. income ratios
    c. gross multipliers
    d. federal income tax tables

6. One reason an underwriter looks at a loan applicant's net worth is to see how well the applicant manages her financial affairs. Another reason is to:
    a. determine if the applicant has enough liquid assets to cover the costs of purchase and the required reserves
    b. find out if the new mortgage will have first lien position
    c. verify the accuracy of the applicant's credit rating
    d. prevent the applicant from resorting to gift funds for part of the closing costs

7. The Stanleys are selling their old home, and they plan to use the sale proceeds as a downpayment in buying a new home. In adding up the Stanleys' liquid assets, an underwriter would be willing to include:
   a. the sales price of the old home
   b. the net equity of the old home
   c. the gross equity of the old home
   d. None of the above

8. Bronowski doesn't have enough money for closing, so his parents are going to give him $2,500. The underwriter will:
   a. reject the loan application
   b. deduct the amount of the gift from the maximum loan amount
   c. require the parents to sign the promissory note
   d. require the parents to sign a gift letter

9. A personal credit report generally includes information about an individual's debts and payment history for the preceding:
   a. fifteen years
   b. twelve years
   c. seven years
   d. five years

10. The Olsens have a proposed monthly housing expense of $1,800, a monthly student loan payment of $180, and a monthly credit card payment of $100. Their stable monthly income is $6,500. What is their debt to income ratio?
    a. 28%
    b. 32%
    c. 4%
    d. 312.5%

Answer Key

1. a. The quality of an applicant's income reflects the dependability of the source of the income.

2. b. An underwriter will prefer to see that an applicant has been employed in the same field for at least two years.

3. d. Child support usually is treated as stable monthly income, if the payments have been regularly received. But when the child is 16 or older, the payments aren't going to continue for three more years, so the child support won't be counted as stable monthly income.

4. c. Overtime, commissions, or bonuses regularly earned for several years as part of a permanent job can be considered stable monthly income.

5. b. Income ratios are used to determine whether the applicant's income is adequate to support the proposed monthly mortgage payment.

6. a. Investigating an applicant's net worth is important because the applicant must not only be able to make the downpayment and closing costs, but may also be required to have reserves left over.

7. b. The loan applicants' net equity in the house they're selling (the property's market value, minus the amount of all liens and anticipated selling expenses) is considered to be a liquid asset.

8. d. If a loan applicant's parents are giving him funds for the downpayment or closing costs, the parents must provide a gift letter stating that the funds do not need to be repaid.

9. c. The information on a credit report generally covers the previous seven years.

10. b. To calculate the debt to income ratio, add the proposed housing expense and all other monthly debt payments together, then divide the total by the pre-tax stable monthly income. The total monthly payments the Olsens will make add up to $2,080, which divided by $6,500 is 32%.

Chapter 9
Qualifying the Property

The Lender's Perception of Value
- Appraisals and loan-to-value ratios

Appraisal Standards

The Appraisal Process

Appraisal Methods
- Sales comparison method
- Replacement cost method
- Income method
- Final value estimate

Dealing with Low Appraisals
- Preventing low appraisals
- Request for reconsideration of value

Introduction

After qualifying the buyer, the underwriter's second major task is to qualify the property. Qualifying a property involves an analysis of its features to determine whether it has sufficient value to serve as collateral for the proposed loan.

As we've explained, a lender's willingness to make a loan depends on the likelihood that the borrower can repay the loan as promised. But regardless of the borrower's financial status, it is the property that serves as security for the debt. Only if the property constitutes adequate security can the underwriter approve the loan.

The Lender's Perception of Value

An underwriter's evaluation of a property is based on an appraisal prepared by a qualified appraiser. An **appraisal** is an *estimate* of the value of a piece of real estate. For a loan transaction, an **appraiser** is asked to analyze the property thoroughly and to issue an objective estimate of its **market value**. Here is the most widely accepted definition of market value, one used by Fannie Mae and Freddie Mac:

> The most probable price which a property should bring in a competitive and open market under all conditions requisite to a fair sale, the buyer and seller each acting prudently and knowledgeably, and assuming the price is not affected by undue stimulus.

Notice that according to this definition, market value is the *most probable* price (not "the highest price") that the property *should* bring (not "will bring"). Appraisal is a matter of estimation and likelihood, not certainty.

An appraiser's estimate of market value will not necessarily coincide with the price agreed on by the buyer and seller. A purchase agreement often reflects emotional or subjective considerations that matter to the buyer and seller, but that aren't pertinent to the property's market value. It's the true market value that the lender cares about.

Example: Jim thinks his home is worth $375,000 and lists the property for that amount. Sally is very willing to pay that price, because she loves the home's quirky characteristics. They enter into a purchase agreement. However, when Sally applies for financing, the appraiser estimates that the market value of Jim's

Fig. 9.1 Principles of value

1. **Highest and Best Use:** The use which, at the time of appraisal, is most likely to produce the greatest net return from the property over a given period of time.

2. **Change:** Property values are in a constant state of flux, increasing and decreasing in response to social, economic, and governmental forces.

3. **Anticipation:** Value is created by the expectation of benefits to be received in the future.

4. **Supply and Demand:** Value varies directly with demand and inversely with supply.

5. **Substitution:** The maximum value of property is set by how much it would cost to obtain another property that is equally desirable, assuming there would not be a long delay or significant incidental expenses involved in obtaining the substitute.

6. **Conformity:** The maximum value of property is realized when there is a reasonable degree of social and economic homogeneity in the neighborhood.

7. **Contribution:** The value of real property is greatest when the improvements produce the highest return commensurate with their cost (the investment).

property is only $350,000. Sally's lender will agree to a loan based on the $350,000 appraised value, not the $375,000 sales price. The lender isn't interested in what Jim and Sally think the property is worth, only in the property's market value.

To estimate market value, appraisers take into account the fundamental appraisal concepts known as the "principles of value." Figure 9.1 summarizes some of these principles.

Appraisals and Loan-to-Value Ratios

A lender uses a property's appraised value to help determine how much money it can safely loan using that property as security. The **loan-to-value ratio (LTV)** expresses the relationship between the loan amount and the property's value. For example, if a lender makes an $80,000 loan secured by a home appraised at $100,000, the loan-to-value ratio is 80%; the loan amount is 80% of the property's

Lender uses appraised value to help determine how much money to loan with property as security

value, and the buyer makes a 20% downpayment. A $75,000 loan on the same property would have a 75% LTV and a 25% downpayment. The lower the LTV, the smaller the loan amount and the bigger the downpayment.

LTVs and Risk. The loan-to-value ratio indicates the degree of risk involved in the loan—both the risk of default and the risk of loss in the event of default. Borrowers are less likely to default on loans with low LTVs. A borrower who makes a large downpayment has a substantial investment in the property, and will therefore try harder to avoid foreclosure. And when foreclosure is necessary, the lender is more likely to recover the entire debt if the LTV is relatively low. Foreclosure sale proceeds are often less than the full market value of the property, but if the original loan amount was only 75% of the value (for example), it's much more likely that the sale's proceeds will cover the outstanding loan balance.

The higher the LTV, the greater the lender's risk. So lenders use loan-to-value ratios to set maximum loan amounts. For example, if a lender's maximum loan-to-value ratio for a particular type of loan is 90%, and the property has been appraised at $100,000, then $90,000 is the maximum loan amount.

Loans with higher LTVs usually have higher interest rates. The higher rate helps offset the lender's increased risk.

As with other underwriting standards, the LTV rules that lenders apply depend on whether the loan is conventional, FHA-insured, or VA-guaranteed. These different loan types will be discussed in more detail in Chapters 10, 11, and 12.

Loan Based on Sales Price or Appraised Value. Lenders use the sales price or the appraised value, whichever is less, to determine the maximum loan amount. This is a universal policy.

> **Example:** Let's return to our previous example. Jim and Sally have agreed on a $375,000 sales price. However, Sally's lender will base the loan amount on the property's appraised value of $350,000, since that's less than the sales price.
>
> | $350,000 | Appraised value |
> |---|---|
> | × 80% | Maximum loan-to-value ratio |
> | $280,000 | Maximum loan amount |

In the example, the maximum loan amount is based on the lower of the two figures, the appraised value. If the lender applied the LTV to the higher of the two figures (the sales price), the loan amount would

Margin notes:

Loan-to-value ratio (LTV) affects:
- Risk of default
- Risk of loss if foreclosure required

Lower LTV = Lower risk

Lenders use LTVs to set maximum loan amounts

Loan-to-value ratio based on:
- sales price or
- appraised value,
- whichever is less

be too high for the lender's risk tolerance. Eighty percent of the sales price would equal a loan that is almost 86% of the appraised value ($375,000 × 80% = $300,000; $300,000 ÷ $350,000 = 85.71%). In the event of default, this lender would be very likely to lose money in a foreclosure sale.

Appraisal Standards

Because of the relationship between loan-to-value ratio and risk, an accurate appraisal is an essential element of the loan underwriting process. If the appraiser overvalues the property, the loan amount will be larger than it should be, and the lender's risk of loss in the event of foreclosure may be much greater.

The appraisal industry tends to come under scrutiny when mortgage foreclosures reach a crisis level. The industry was closely examined during the 1980s, after a substantial increase in foreclosure losses during the savings and loan crisis (see Chapter 4). Many analysts concluded that unreliable appraisals were a significant part of the problem. Congress responded by passing the Financial Institutions Reform, Recovery, and Enforcement Act (FIRREA) in 1989.

FIRREA required states to implement licensing and certification standards for appraisers. The law did not mandate that all appraisers be licensed or certified, but only appraisals prepared by licensed or certified appraisers can be used in "federally related" loan transactions. The majority of residential real estate loans are federally related, since the category includes loans made by any financial institution that is regulated or insured by the federal government.

Appraisals used for most home mortgage loans must be prepared by licensed or certified appraiser and in compliance with USPAP

FIRREA also required appraisals for federally related loans to be prepared in accordance with the Uniform Standards of Professional Appraisal Practice (USPAP). USPAP is a set of guidelines adopted by the Appraisal Foundation, a nonprofit professional organization established to improve the quality of appraisals.

Although FIRREA has an exemption for residential loans for $250,000 or less, the exemption is irrelevant in many cases. Loans sold to Fannie Mae or Freddie Mac, FHA-insured loans, and VA-guaranteed loans all must comply with FIRREA, regardless of the loan amount.

Despite the FIRREA reforms, inflated appraisals were a major factor in the mortgage foreclosure crisis about 20 years later (see Chapter 4). This led to new laws and rules intended to reduce the number of faulty appraisals. For example, in 2009 the FHA stopped adding state-licensed appraisers to its roster of approved appraisers; new appraisers on the FHA roster must be state-certified. Federal and state laws were passed to help ensure the appraiser's independence from the influence of lenders and real estate agents. This included the federal Dodd-Frank Act, which (among other things) made it illegal to attempt to influence an appraiser, and also required lenders to compensate appraisers at reasonable rates.

The Appraisal Process

It isn't necessary for real estate agents to be able to appraise real estate, at least not with the sophistication of a professional appraiser. It is helpful, however, to know something about the mechanics of the appraisal process and the reasoning that underlies many of the appraiser's conclusions. If an agent understands how appraisers estimate market value, it's easier to arrange sales that will hold together.

Real estate appraisers generally follow these steps when completing an appraisal:

1. **Define the problem.** This includes identifying the property to be appraised (referred to as the **subject property**), determining the purpose of the appraisal, and specifying the "as of" date. Since property values are constantly changing, an appraisal is only valid "as of" a particular date. For a standard residential appraisal, the "as of" date is the date the appraisal is performed. But property can also be appraised as of a specified date in the past (estimating the past value of property involved in a lawsuit, for example) or even a specified date in the future (estimating the future value of property that is going to be developed, for example).

2. **Determine the scope of work.** This refers to figuring out what's involved in solving the problem. The scope of work includes both the type and quantity of information needed, as well the type of analysis that will be used to carry out the appraisal assignment. Determining the scope of work also includes planning the tasks involved in performing the assignment; for example, a complex assignment might make it necessary to consult outside experts.

3. **Collect and verify data.** Appraisal data can be divided into two categories: general data and specific data. General data refers to information concerning factors outside

the property itself that have a bearing on the property's value. In a residential appraisal, this includes information about the region's economy and information about the neighborhood where the home is located. Specific data refers to information concerning the property itself—the site, the house, and other improvements on the site. (See the list of Neighborhood Considerations and Property Features in Figure 9.2.) All of the data collected must be verified in some way, such as by inspection and in-person measurements or by cross-checking information with county records.

4. **Analyze data.** In analyzing the data, the appraiser must judge the relevance of each piece of information collected. For instance, the appraiser will consider what the data regarding market trends indicates about the subject property's value.

5. **Determine site value.** Site valuation is an estimate of the value of a property, excluding the value of any existing or proposed improvements. For vacant land, site valuation is the same as appraising the property. For improved property (such as property with a house on it), site valuation involves appraising the property as if vacant. A separate site valuation may be necessary depending on the method of appraisal that will be used (for example, the cost approach to value; see below).

6. **Apply the appropriate methods of appraisal.** The three methods of appraisal are explained in the next section of this chapter. Each method that the appraiser applies results in a **value indicator**, a figure that the appraiser treats as an indication of the subject property's value.

7. **Reconcile the results to arrive at a final value estimate.** After taking into account the purpose of the appraisal, the type of property, and the reliability of the data gathered, the appraiser weighs the value indicators and decides on a final estimate of the subject property's market value.

8. **Issue the appraisal report.** The appraiser's last step is to prepare an appraisal report, presenting the value estimate and summarizing the underlying data for the client. When property is appraised to determine its value as collateral for a loan, the appraiser's client is the lender.

Steps in the appraisal process:
- Define the problem
- Determine scope of work
- Collect and verify data
- Analyze data
- Determine site value
- Apply appraisal methods
- Reconciliation
- Issue appraisal report

A residential appraiser usually gathers data about the subject property through an in-person inspection, walking through the rooms in the home and taking notes about the overall condition and particular features, good and bad. An inspection of the subject property inside and out is always required for FHA and VA loans and (under the Dodd-Frank Act) for higher-risk conventional loans secured by a principal residence. For other types of loans, though, a lender might order an **exterior-only inspection**, often called a "drive-by appraisal."

To complete this type of assignment, the appraiser first collects information about the subject property from online sources (such as the website of the multiple listing service), then pays a brief visit to the property to get an idea of its general condition. The appraiser simply looks at the exterior of the house, without going inside; in fact, she might not even get out of her car. Under the Uniform Standards of Professional Appraisal Practice, appraisers must acquire adequate information about the subject property to make an informed estimate of value. If that's not possible from an exterior-only inspection, the appraiser will tell the lender that an interior inspection is needed. Also, an exterior-only appraisal is generally appropriate only if the property is typical for the area.

As mentioned in Chapter 8, when a lender submits a buyer's loan application to Fannie Mae or Freddie Mac's automated underwriting system, the report generated by the AUS may authorize an exterior-only inspection. In a limited number of situations, the report may even say that the transaction is eligible for a **property inspection waiver**; if so, the lender isn't required to order an appraisal at all.

Appraisal Methods

Three methods of appraisal:
• Sales comparison
• Replacement cost
• Income

There are basically three ways to appraise real estate:

1. the sales comparison method,
2. the replacement cost method, and
3. the income method.

All three methods, or only one or two, may be applied in valuing a particular property, depending on the purpose of the appraisal and the type of property in question. As described above, each method yields a value indicator. The appraiser will base the final estimate of value on these value indicators.

Sales Comparison Method

Of the three appraisal methods, the sales comparison method (also known as the market data method) is the one preferred by appraisers, especially for residential property. This technique involves comparing the subject property with similar properties in the same neighborhood that have sold recently. These similar properties are called **comparable sales** or **comparables**. Appraisers know that competitive forces influence prices. Under ordinary circumstances, an informed buyer will not pay more for a particular property than he would have to pay for an equally desirable substitute property, and an informed owner will not sell property for less than it's worth. Thus, recent sales prices of comparables give a good indication of their market values and can be used to estimate the probable market value of the subject property.

Sales Comparison Appraisal vs. CMA. To help sellers set listing prices, many real estate agents use a **competitive market analysis** (CMA), also called a comparative market analysis or broker price opinion. The CMA is essentially a less formal version of the sales comparison method of appraisal, but it should not be referred to or treated as an appraisal. (In fact, federal law prohibits lenders from using a CMA as the primary basis for determining the value of a property that the buyers are purchasing as their principal residence.) A real estate agent performing a CMA may make use of certain data that an appraiser would not rely on. For example, in addition to using actual sales as comparables, the real estate agent might use properties that are listed for sale but have not sold yet. In an appraisal, although the appraiser may analyze current listings as supporting data (especially in a rapidly changing market), the main comparables must be actual sales.

Sales prices are excellent indicators of market value, because they represent actual agreements between buyers and sellers in a competitive marketplace. Listing prices, on the other hand, are less accurate indicators of market value. A home's listing price may be considerably higher than the price it eventually sells for.

Even so, current listings provide useful information about market conditions for a CMA. The seller's home will be competing with

Sales comparison method: sales prices of comparables are used to estimate market value of subject property

CMA: informal version of sales comparison appraisal

CMA may use current and expired listings; appraisal is based on actual sales

those other listings. Some CMAs also compare the subject property to homes that failed to sell before their listings expired; these homes apparently were priced too high.

Identifying Legitimate Comparable Sales. Sales make better comparables than listings, and some sales make better comparables than other sales. When evaluating a sale to see if it qualifies as a legitimate comparable, the appraiser is concerned with five issues:

Choosing comparables:
• Date of sale
• Location
• Physical characteristics
• Terms of sale
• Conditions of sale

- the date of the sale,
- the location of the property,
- the physical characteristics of the property,
- the terms of sale, and
- the conditions of the sale.

Date of comparable sale. The sale should be recent, within the past six months if possible. During times of rapid market change, however, sales within the last two or three months may be required. Recent sales give a more accurate indication of what's happening in the marketplace today, so appraisers will want to find the most recent sales possible.

At least three comps needed for sales comparison approach

An appraiser ordinarily needs at least three comparables to apply the sales comparison method. If the market has been inactive and there are not enough legitimate comparable sales from the past six months, the appraiser can go back farther. Comparable sales that sold more than six months ago should only be used if truly necessary; the appraiser should include an explanation of why that comparable had to be used.

Comps generally should not be more than six months old

If the comparable sales are more than a few months old, it is often necessary to make adjustments for inflationary or deflationary trends or other forces that have affected prices in the area.

> **Example:** A comparable residential property sold six months ago for $477,000. In general, local property values have fallen by 4% over the past six months. The comparable property, then, should be worth approximately 4% less than it was six months ago.
>
> | $477,000 | Value six months ago |
> |---|---|
> | × 96% | Deflation factor |
> | $457,920 | Approximate present value |

Fig. 9.2 Sales comparison considerations

Key Considerations in a Sales Comparison Appraisal

There are many things to consider during a residential appraisal. Here's a list of some of the elements that matter most to appraisers in choosing comparables and valuing homes.

Neighborhood Considerations

Percentage of home ownership. Is there a high degree of owner-occupancy or do rental properties predominate? Owner-occupied neighborhoods are generally better maintained and less susceptible to deterioration.

Foreclosures/Vacant homes and lots. An unusual number of vacant homes or lots suggests a low level of interest in the area, which has a negative effect on property values. On the other hand, construction activity in a neighborhood signals current interest in the area.

Conformity. The homes in a neighborhood should be reasonably similar to one another in style, age, size, and quality. Strictly enforced zoning and private restrictions promote conformity and protect property values.

Changing land use. Is the neighborhood in the midst of a transition from residential use to some other type of use? If so, the properties are probably losing their value as residences (even though the change promises higher values overall because of the potential for more productive use of the land in the future).

Contour of the land. Mildly rolling topography is preferred to terrain that is either monotonously flat or excessively hilly.

Streets. Wide, gently curving streets are more appealing than narrow or straight streets. Streets should be hard surfaced and well maintained.

Utilities. Are adequate utility services (electricity, gas, water, sewer, phone, and internet) available in the neighborhood?

Nuisances. Nuisances in or near a neighborhood (odors, eyesores, industrial noises or pollutants, or exposure to unusual winds, smog, or fog) hurt property values.

Prestige. Is the neighborhood considered prestigious in comparison to others in the community? If so, that will increase property values.

Proximity. How far is it to traffic arterials and to important points such as downtown, employment centers, and shopping centers?

Schools. What schools serve the neighborhood? Are they highly regarded? Are they nearby? The quality of a school or school district can make a major difference to property values in a residential neighborhood.

Public services. Are there adequate public services for the neighborhood, such as police and fire protection and public transportation?

Government influences. Does zoning in and around the neighborhood promote residential use and insulate the property owner from nuisances? How do the property tax rates compare with those of other neighborhoods nearby?

(continued)

Property Features

Site. The appraiser will note the lot's size, shape, and topography, and how much street frontage it has. Rectangular lots are more useful than lots with irregular shapes; unusually steep lots may have problems with soil instability. Drainage and landscaping are important, and a view can add substantially to value. An easement or encroachment will be taken into account, as well as zoning and private restrictions.

Design and appeal. Is the home's overall appeal good, average, or poor? There are dozens of house styles: ranch (rambler), colonial, Victorian, etc. The appraiser will try to find comparables in the same general style as the subject property. Comparisons between one- and two-story houses generally are not valid, but a one-story house can be compared to a split-level with certain adjustments.

Construction quality. Is the quality of materials and workmanship good, average, or poor?

Age/condition. When the subject property and comparables are in similar condition, a difference in age of up to five years is generally inconsequential. Is the property's overall condition good, average, or poor?

Size of house (square footage). The appraiser is concerned with the gross living area (GLA), which is the improved living area, excluding the garage, basement, and porches.

Basement. A functional basement, especially a finished basement, contributes to value. (In many cases, however, the amount a finished basement contributes to value is not enough to recover the cost of the finish work.)

Interior layout. Is the floor plan functional and convenient? It should not be necessary to pass through a public room (such as the living room) to reach other rooms, or to pass through one of the bedrooms to reach another.

Number of rooms. The appraiser will add up the total number of rooms in the house, excluding bathrooms and (usually) basement rooms. Usually the appraiser will try to find comparables with the same number of rooms as the subject.

Number of bedrooms. Differences in the number of bedrooms have a major impact on value. For instance, if all else is equal, a two-bedroom comparable is worth considerably less than a three-bedroom subject.

Number of bathrooms. A full bath is a lavatory (wash basin), toilet, and both a bathtub and a shower; a ¾ bath is a lavatory, toilet, and either a shower or a tub; a ½ bath is a lavatory and toilet only. The number of bathrooms can have a noticeable effect on value.

Air conditioning. The presence or absence of an air conditioning system is important in warm climates.

Energy efficiency. An energy-efficient home is more valuable than a comparable one that is not. Energy-efficient features include: double-paned windows; clock-controlled thermostats; insulated ducts and pipes in unheated areas; adequate insulation for floors, walls, and attic; and weather stripping for doors and windows.

Garage/carport. An enclosed garage is generally better than a carport. How many cars can it accommodate? Is there work or storage space in addition to parking space? Is it possible to enter the home directly from the garage or carport, protected from the weather?

Location of comparable sale. Whenever possible, comparables should be selected from the neighborhood where the subject property is located. In the absence of any legitimate comparables in the neighborhood, the appraiser can look elsewhere, but the properties selected should at least come from comparable neighborhoods.

If a comparable selected from an inferior neighborhood is structurally identical to the subject property, it is probably less valuable; conversely, a structurally identical comparable in a superior neighborhood is probably more valuable than the subject property. Location contributes a great deal to the value of real estate. A high-quality property's value suffers in a low-quality neighborhood. On the other hand, the value of a relatively weak property is enhanced by a stable and desirable neighborhood.

Physical characteristics. To qualify as a comparable, a property should have physical characteristics (construction quality, design, amenities, etc.) that are similar to those of the subject property. When a comparable has a feature that the subject property lacks—or lacks a feature that the subject property has—the appraiser will adjust the comparable's price.

> Comp's price adjusted to indicate value of subject:
> - Down if subject lacks feature
> - Up if subject has extra feature

> **Example:** One of the comparables the appraiser is using is quite similar to the subject property overall, but there are several significant differences. The subject property has a two-car garage, while the comparable has only a one-car garage. Based on experience, the appraiser estimates that space for a second car adds approximately $5,400 to the value of a home in this area. The comparable actually sold for $523,500. The appraiser will add $5,400 to that price, to reflect the fact that the subject property has more garage space than the comparable.
>
> On the other hand, the comparable has a fireplace and the subject property does not. The appraiser estimates a fireplace adds approximately $1,800 to the value of a home. She will subtract $1,800 from the comparable's price, to reflect the fact that the subject property has no fireplace.
>
> After adjusting the comparable's price up or down for each difference in this way, the appraiser can use the resulting figure as an indication of the value of the subject property.

Terms of sale. The terms of sale can affect the price a buyer will pay for a property. Attractive financing concessions (such as seller-

Special financing can make buyer willing to pay more, so appraiser takes terms of sale into account when evaluating a comparable

paid discount points or seller financing with an especially low interest rate) can make a buyer willing to pay a higher price than he would otherwise be willing to pay. These kinds of special terms become more common in a slow market. Sellers may also offer help with closing costs or even a free vacation to attract buyers.

An appraiser has to take into account the influence the terms of sale may have had on the price paid for a comparable property. If the seller offered the property on very favorable terms, there's an excellent chance that the sales price does not represent the true market value of the comparable.

Under the Uniform Standards of Professional Appraisal Practice, an appraiser giving an estimate of market value must state whether it is the most probable price in terms of cash, in terms of financial arrangements equivalent to cash, or in other precisely defined terms.

If the estimate is based on financing with special conditions or incentives, those terms must be clearly set forth, and the appraiser must estimate their effect on the property's value. Market data supporting the value estimate (that is, the selling prices of comparables) must be explained in the same way.

Conditions of sale. Finally, a comparable sale can be relied on as an indication of what the subject property is worth only if it occurred under normal conditions and the buyer and seller were typically motivated. This means the sale must meet these four criteria:

Conditions of sale:
- Arm's length transaction
- No unusual pressure to act
- Both parties fully informed
- Property on open market for reasonable time

- the sale was between unrelated parties (an "arm's length transaction");
- both parties were acting free of unusual pressure;
- both parties were informed of the property's attributes and deficiencies, and were acting in their own best interests; and
- the property was offered for sale on the open market for a reasonable length of time.

A property sold by one family member to another would not qualify as a comparable. Likewise, foreclosures and short sales normally can't serve as comparables, because the sales are essentially forced and the sellers are under unusual pressure. However, in some markets particularly hard hit by foreclosures, those may be the only types of comparables available. If foreclosed homes make up a significant portion of a local market, average buyers are likely to consider buying one, so their prices may represent usable values under the principle of substitution (see Figure 9.1). The appraiser will have to use experience and knowledge of the local market to judge which comparables are the most appropriate.

When appraising a property that is owned by a financial institution because of a mortgage default (referred to as an REO, for "real estate owned"), the appraiser should use only other REOs as comparables. REOs typically have lower market values than comparable properties owned by more typical homeowners or investors. There are various reasons for this. For one thing, REOs are usually vacant, which means an increased risk of vandalism or other deterioration. Further, there are often delays in the closing process, caused by institutional bureaucracy. Lengthy delays can jeopardize the buyer's financing and will certainly mean a later possession date. If an appraiser who is valuing an REO is forced to use a non-REO as a comparable, she will usually have to adjust the price of the comparable property downward.

Adjustments. An appraiser can rarely find three ideal comparables exactly like the subject property, in the same neighborhood, that all sold under the same terms within the previous month. So, as you've seen, the appraiser has to make adjustments, taking into account differences in time, location, physical characteristics, and terms of sale, in order to arrive at an adjusted selling price for each comparable.

Reconciliation. The appraiser bases his estimate of the subject property's value on the adjusted selling prices of the comparables. The appraiser reviews all the data regarding each comparable, then uses her judgment and experience to select a value within the range of the adjusted selling prices of the comparables. This process is referred to as **reconciliation**.

Reconciliation: the process of analyzing the adjusted selling prices of the comparables to arrive at a value indicator

Choosing an appropriate value for the subject property is not a mechanical process. The appraiser should never simply average the adjusted selling prices of the comparables. Instead, the appraiser considers the relative reliability of each comparable, and gives more weight to the ones that are the most reliable.

It stands to reason that the more adjustments an appraiser has to make, the less reliable the resulting estimate of value will be. In fact, if the necessary adjustments add up to a significant percentage of a comparable's sales price (for example, 25% of the price), then that property isn't sufficiently similar to the subject to make a good comparable.

Let's look at a simplified example of how reconciliation works.

Example: The appraiser found three comparables for the subject property:

Comparable	Adjusted Selling Price	Adjustments as Percentage of Sales Price
A	$365,000	9%
B	$342,700	18%
C	$359,000	6%

Comparables A and C had relatively modest adjustments to their prices. Comparable B had significant adjustments. Giving the least weight to Comparable B, the appraiser concludes that the subject property's fair market value is $361,000.

Market Conditions. For most residential loan transactions, appraisers are required to report their results using the Uniform Residential Appraisal Report form (see Figure 9.3). Among many other things, the form requires the appraiser to analyze supply and demand in the local housing market and note whether that market is growing or shrinking. The form also provides space to describe any other relevant market conditions. The appraiser may also be required to complete an addendum that summarizes the number and frequency of foreclosures in the market and reports the impact those foreclosures have on value—an important factor during an economic downturn.

Replacement Cost Method

The replacement cost method of appraisal (also called the cost method) is based on the premise that the value of a house or other building is limited by the cost of building a new one just like it. (This is a version of the principle of substitution: a buyer won't pay more for a property than it would cost to obtain an equally desirable substitute.) To use the cost method, appraisers must keep abreast of construction costs in their area. Here are the steps involved in the cost method:

Replacement cost method: a property's value won't exceed the cost of replacing it

Step 1: Estimate the cost of replacing the building(s) and any other improvements on the property.

Step 2: Estimate and deduct any accrued depreciation.

Step 3: Add the value of the lot to the depreciated value of the improvements.

Estimating Replacement Cost. A building's **replacement cost** is how much it would cost to construct a new building with equivalent utility—in other words, one that would have essentially the same features and could be used in essentially the same way. Replacement cost is not the same thing as **reproduction cost**, which is how much it would cost to construct an exact duplicate or replica of the building, at current prices. For older, better-quality structures, the reproduction cost is considerably higher than the replacement cost, and thus doesn't accurately indicate the property's market value. For an ordinary appraisal, the appraiser is concerned with replacement cost, not reproduction cost.

There are a number of ways to estimate replacement cost. The simplest is the comparative-unit method, also known as the square foot method. By analyzing the average cost per square foot of construction for recently built improvements comparable to the subject property's, the appraiser can estimate the square foot cost of replacing the improvements of the subject property.

Comparative-unit method: using square foot cost of recently built comps to estimate cost of replacing subject property

To calculate the cost of replacing the building on the subject property, the appraiser multiplies the estimated cost per square foot by the number of square feet in the building. The number of square feet in a house is determined by measuring the dimensions of each floor of the structure, including the outer wall surfaces. The square footage refers only to the improved living area; the garage, basement, and porches are excluded.

> **Example:** The subject property is a ranch-style house with a wooden exterior, containing 1,800 square feet. Based on an analysis of the construction costs of three recently built homes of comparable size and quality, the appraiser estimates that it would cost $126.37 per square foot to replace the home.
>
> | | |
> |---:|:---|
> | 1,800 | Square feet |
> | × $126.37 | Cost per square foot |
> | $227,466 | Estimated cost of replacing improvements |

Of course, a comparable structure (or "benchmark" building) is unlikely to be exactly the same as the subject property. Variations in design, shape, and grade of construction will affect the square foot cost—moderately or substantially. The appraiser will make appropriate adjustments to take these differences into account.

When there aren't any recently built comparable homes available, the appraiser relies on current cost manuals to estimate the basic construction costs.

Estimating Depreciation. When the home being appraised is one that has been lived in, the presumption is that it is not as valuable as a comparable new home; it has depreciated in value. So, after estimating replacement cost, the appraiser's next step is to estimate the depreciation. This is the most difficult part of the replacement cost method of appraisal.

Depreciation is a loss in value due to wear and tear or other causes. Value can be lost as a result of:

Depreciation: loss in value from any cause
- Physical deterioration
- Functional obsolescence
- External obsolescence

- physical deterioration,
- functional obsolescence, or
- external obsolescence.

Physical deterioration refers to physical wear and tear or other damage that reduces the value of the property.

Functional obsolescence, also called functional depreciation, is a loss in value due to inadequacies such as poor design or outmoded features. Not enough bathrooms in relation to the number of bedrooms is an example of functional obsolescence frequently found in older homes.

External obsolescence (also called external inadequacy, external depreciation, or economic obsolescence) is a loss in value due to factors outside the property, such as a deteriorating neighborhood, declining market values, zoning changes, or poor access to schools, shopping, or employment centers.

Depreciation is considered curable if the cost of correcting it could be recovered in the sales price when the property is sold. Depreciation is incurable if it is impossible to correct, or if it would cost so much to correct that it would not make sense to do so. Physical deterioration and functional obsolescence may be either curable or incurable. (Curable physical deterioration may be referred to as **deferred maintenance**.) External obsolescence, on the other hand, is almost always incurable, because it's caused by factors beyond the property owner's control.

After estimating how much the depreciation in each of the three categories is reducing the subject property's value, the appraiser deducts the depreciation from the estimated replacement cost of the improvements.

Example:

$227,466	Estimated replacement cost
8,510	Physical deterioration (roof in need of repair; garage door should be replaced)
7,050	Functional obsolescence (living room too small; family room too far from kitchen)
− 3,000	External obsolescence (odors from nearby factory)
$208,906	Depreciated value of improvements

Because estimating depreciation is difficult, the older the property, the less reliable the replacement cost method is. In many cases, an appraiser will decide not to use the cost method in an appraisal of an older home. The cost method also isn't used for appraising a unit in a condominium.

Deferred maintenance and underwriting. An appraisal is submitted to the underwriter in one of two ways: "as is" or "subject to." An "as is" appraisal reports deferred maintenance (curable physical deterioration, such as broken windows, worn-out roof, drainage problems, damaged siding, etc.), but the final value estimate represents the market value of the property in its current condition. In a "subject to" appraisal, the final value estimate represents what the market value of the property would be if the deferred maintenance were corrected.

Appraisal may be "as is," or "subject to" repairs

In some cases the underwriter will make correction of the deferred maintenance a condition of loan approval. These "lender-required repairs" must be completed before the loan can be funded.

Adding Land Value. The last step in the replacement cost method is to add the value of the land to the depreciated value of the improvements, to arrive at an estimate of value for the property as a whole.

Example:

$208,906	Depreciated value of the improvements
+ 59,000	Land value
$267,906	Depreciated value of the property

The value of the land is estimated by the sales comparison method. Prices recently paid for vacant lots similar to the subject property's lot are compared and used as indications of what the subject property's lot is worth.

Income Method

The income method of appraisal is based on the idea that there is a relationship between the income that a property generates and its value to a potential investor (a potential buyer). To arrive at an estimate of the subject property's value, its annual net income is divided by a capitalization rate that represents the return an investor would expect from the property.

Residences generally aren't regarded as income-producing properties, so formal income analysis techniques don't apply when a home is being appraised. If a residential appraiser uses the income method at all, she will use a simplified version called the **gross income multiplier method** (also known as the gross rent multiplier method).

In the gross income multiplier method, the appraiser looks at the relationship between a rental property's gross income and the price paid for the property.

> **Example:**
> Sales price: $246,000
> Monthly rent: $2,000
> Conclusion: Monthly rent is equal to 0.81% of the sales price; the sales price is approximately 123 times the monthly rent.

Monthly rents may run about one percent of selling prices in one market, and more or less in another. (A market exists where specific rental properties compete with each other for tenants.) For competitive reasons, rents charged for similar properties tend to be similar within the same market. As a result, if one rental property has a monthly income that is one percent of its sales price, comparable properties will have similar income-to-price ratios.

A monthly multiplier is calculated by dividing the sales price by the monthly rental income. An annual multiplier is calculated by dividing the sales price by the annual rental income.

Gross income multiplier method: used to estimate value of rental home

Example:

Sales Price		Monthly Rent		Monthly Multiplier
$346,000	÷	$2,000	=	173

Sales Price		Annual Income		Annual Multiplier
$346,000	÷	$24,000	=	14.42

After locating a sufficient number of comparable residential rental properties, the appraiser determines their monthly or annual gross income multipliers (either is acceptable—it's a matter of the appraiser's preference) by dividing the rents into their respective selling prices.

Example:

Comp.	Sales Price	Monthly Rent	Monthly Multiplier
1	$337,500	$1,950	173.08
2	$345,000	$1,975	174.68
3	$350,000	$2,025	172.84
4	$353,500	$2,100	168.33

The appraiser uses the multipliers of the comparables to determine an appropriate multiplier for the subject property, taking into account the similarities and differences between the properties. Then the appraiser multiplies the rent that the subject property is generating by the chosen gross income multiplier for a rough estimate of its value as an income-producing property.

Note that the number of comparables necessary to develop an appropriate multiplier for the subject property varies, depending on the size and type of the local market. In some cases, as few as three or four comparables will be sufficient (as in our example); in other markets, the appraiser may need more.

The principal weakness of the gross income multiplier method is that it's based on gross income figures and does not take into account vacancies or operating expenses. If two rental homes have the same rental income, the gross income multiplier method would indicate they are worth the same amount; but if one is older and has higher maintenance costs, the net return to the owner would be less, and so would its actual value. Unless the appraiser knows the comparables are truly similar (having similar vacancy rates and operating expenses), the appraiser must take into account the imprecise nature of the value indicated by this method.

If possible, the appraiser should use the subject property's **economic rent** or **market rent** (the rent the property could command in the marketplace if it were available for lease today) as opposed to the **contract rent** (the rent the owner is actually receiving).

> **Example:** The owner leased the home two years ago for $1,850 a month and the lease contract has another year to go. Market rents have risen sharply over the past two years, so that the property could now command a much higher rent—probably about $2,175 a month. If the appraiser were to use the $1,850 contract rent in the gross income multiplier method, it would distort the estimate of value.

Final Value Estimate

If the appraiser has applied all three appraisal methods (sales comparison, replacement cost, and income), he must analyze and compare the three results in order to draw a conclusion about the property's value. That process of interpretation is known as **reconciliation** or **correlation**. (This is essentially the same process used to arrive at the value indicator for the sales comparison approach.)

Appraiser weighs results to arrive at final value estimate

The appraiser's experience and judgment play a critical role in the reconciliation process. The final estimate of value is not simply the average of the results yielded by the three approaches. The appraiser must weigh each result carefully, considering all the factors that affect its reliability for the type of property in question. From that analysis, the appraiser decides on a figure that represents his expert opinion of the subject property's market value.

Sales comparison method most reliable for residential property

For single-family homes not used as rental properties, appraisers frequently base the final value estimate on the result of the sales comparison method alone. The income method can't be applied (since there's no income) and the cost approach is complicated and less accurate than the sales method, at least in markets where there are numerous comparables to choose from.

Once the appraiser arrives at a final estimate of value, she presents it to the client in an appraisal report. Typically—particularly for single-family residential real estate—the appraiser will use the Uniform Residential Appraisal Report, shown in Figure 9.3. Reviewing this form will give you a clearer idea of what the appraiser must do before she can issue a responsible estimate of value.

Dealing with Low Appraisals

Understanding the appraisal process helps real estate agents eliminate or at least minimize a common selling problem, the low appraisal. No one gets through an entire real estate career without facing the low appraisal problem at least a few times, and in rapidly rising or even falling markets, the likelihood of a low appraisal increases.

A **low appraisal** is an estimate of value that is below (perhaps way below) the price the buyer and seller agreed on. A sale is written, the parties are pleased, and then a week or so later the agent gets the bad news. A lower than expected appraisal puts the sale in serious jeopardy.

Low appraisal: value estimate below the price agreed on

If the transaction is contingent on financing, the buyer does not have to complete the sale if the appraisal comes in low. Buyers are understandably reluctant to pay more for a property than a professional appraiser says it is worth. And even when a buyer would like to go ahead with the purchase in spite of the low appraisal, he may not be able to afford to. Remember that the buyer's loan amount is based on the sales price or the appraised value, whichever is less; if the purchase price remains unchanged, the low appraisal means a smaller loan—and a bigger downpayment. The downpayment will have to increase by the amount of the shortfall.

Example:

1. Buyer is prepared to make a 10% downpayment and obtain a 90% loan.
2. Sales price is $300,000.
3. Appraisal is issued at $291,000.
4. Maximum loan amount is 90% of $291,000.

$291,000	Appraised value
× 90%	Loan-to-value ratio
$261,900	Maximum loan amount

Because of the low appraisal ($9,000 less than the sales price), the loan amount is limited to $261,900. The buyer expected to make a $30,000 downpayment ($300,000 sales price × 90% = $270,000 loan). But the buyer would now have to make a $38,100 downpayment ($300,000 – $261,900 loan = $38,100) to pay the $300,000 price.

Fig. 9.3 Uniform Residential Appraisal Report form

Uniform Residential Appraisal Report   File

The purpose of this summary appraisal report is to provide the lender/client with an accurate, and adequately supported, opinion of the market value of the subject property.

SUBJECT

Property Address		City		State	Zip Code
Borrower		Owner of Public Record		County	

Legal Description

Assessor's Parcel #		Tax Year	R.E. Taxes $

Neighborhood Name	Map Reference	Census Tract

Occupant ☐ Owner ☐ Tenant ☐ Vacant   Special Assessments $ ☐ PUD HOA $ ☐ per year ☐ per month

Property Rights Appraised ☐ Fee Simple ☐ Leasehold ☐ Other (describe)

Assignment Type ☐ Purchase Transaction ☐ Refinance Transaction ☐ Other (describe)

Lender/Client   Address

Is the subject property currently offered for sale or has it been offered for sale in the twelve months prior to the effective date of this appraisal? ☐ Yes ☐ No

Report data source(s) used, offering price(s), and date(s).

CONTRACT

I ☐ did ☐ did not analyze the contract for sale for the subject purchase transaction. Explain the results of the analysis of the contract for sale or why the analysis was not performed.

Contract Price $ Date of Contract   Is the property seller the owner of public record? ☐ Yes ☐ No Data Source(s)

Is there any financial assistance (loan charges, sale concessions, gift or downpayment assistance, etc.) to be paid by any party on behalf of the borrower? ☐ Yes ☐ No

If Yes, report the total dollar amount and describe the items to be paid.

NEIGHBORHOOD

Note: Race and the racial composition of the neighborhood are not appraisal factors.

Neighborhood Characteristics			One-Unit Housing Trends				One-Unit Housing		Present Land Use %	
Location ☐ Urban	☐ Suburban	☐ Rural	Property Values ☐ Increasing	☐ Stable	☐ Declining		PRICE	AGE	One-Unit	%
Built-Up ☐ Over 75%	☐ 25–75%	☐ Under 25%	Demand/Supply ☐ Shortage	☐ In Balance	☐ Over Supply		$ (000)	(yrs)	2-4 Unit	%
Growth ☐ Rapid	☐ Stable	☐ Slow	Marketing Time ☐ Under 3 mths	☐ 3–6 mths	☐ Over 6 mths		Low		Multi-Family	%
Neighborhood Boundaries							High		Commercial	%
							Pred.		Other	%

Neighborhood Description

Market Conditions (including support for the above conclusions)

SITE

Dimensions	Area	Shape	View

Specific Zoning Classification	Zoning Description

Zoning Compliance ☐ Legal ☐ Legal Nonconforming (Grandfathered Use) ☐ No Zoning ☐ Illegal (describe)

Is the highest and best use of the subject property as improved (or as proposed per plans and specifications) the present use? ☐ Yes ☐ No If No, describe

Utilities	Public	Other (describe)		Public	Other (describe)	Off-site Improvements—Type	Public	Private
Electricity	☐	☐	Water	☐	☐	Street	☐	☐
Gas	☐	☐	Sanitary Sewer	☐	☐	Alley	☐	☐

FEMA Special Flood Hazard Area ☐ Yes ☐ No FEMA Flood Zone   FEMA Map #   FEMA Map Date

Are the utilities and off-site improvements typical for the market area? ☐ Yes ☐ No If No, describe

Are there any adverse site conditions or external factors (easements, encroachments, environmental conditions, land uses, etc.)? ☐ Yes ☐ No If Yes, describe

IMPROVEMENTS

General Description		Foundation		Exterior Description	materials/condition	Interior	materials/condition
Units ☐ One ☐ One with Accessory Unit		☐ Concrete Slab ☐ Crawl Space		Foundation Walls		Floors	
# of Stories		☐ Full Basement ☐ Partial Basement		Exterior Walls		Walls	
Type ☐ Det. ☐ Att. ☐ S-Det./End Unit		Basement Area sq. ft.		Roof Surface		Trim/Finish	
☐ Existing ☐ Proposed ☐ Under Const.		Basement Finish %		Gutters & Downspouts		Bath Floor	
Design (Style)		☐ Outside Entry/Exit ☐ Sump Pump		Window Type		Bath Wainscot	
Year Built		Evidence of ☐ Infestation		Storm Sash/Insulated		Car Storage ☐ None	
Effective Age (Yrs)		☐ Dampness ☐ Settlement		Screens		☐ Driveway # of Cars	
Attic ☐ None		Heating ☐ FWA ☐ HWBB ☐ Radiant		Amenities ☐ Woodstove(s) #		Driveway Surface	
☐ Drop Stair ☐ Stairs		☐ Other Fuel		☐ Fireplace(s) # ☐ Fence		☐ Garage # of Cars	
☐ Floor ☐ Scuttle		Cooling ☐ Central Air Conditioning		☐ Patio/Deck ☐ Porch		☐ Carport # of Cars	
☐ Finished ☐ Heated		☐ Individual ☐ Other		☐ Pool ☐ Other		☐ Att. ☐ Det. ☐ Built-in	

Appliances ☐ Refrigerator ☐ Range/Oven ☐ Dishwasher ☐ Disposal ☐ Microwave ☐ Washer/Dryer ☐ Other (describe)

Finished area **above** grade contains: Rooms   Bedrooms   Bath(s)   Square Feet of Gross Living Area Above Grade

Additional features (special energy efficient items, etc.)

Describe the condition of the property (including needed repairs, deterioration, renovations, remodeling, etc.).

Are there any physical deficiencies or adverse conditions that affect the livability, soundness, or structural integrity of the property? ☐ Yes ☐ No If Yes, describe

Does the property generally conform to the neighborhood (functional utility, style, condition, use, construction, etc.)? ☐ Yes ☐ No If No, describe

Freddie Mac Form 70 March 2005	Page 1 of 6	Fannie Mae Form 1004 March 2005

Uniform Residential Appraisal Report   File

There are _____ comparable properties currently offered for sale in the subject neighborhood ranging in price from $ _____ to $ _____ .

There are _____ comparable sales in the subject neighborhood within the past twelve months ranging in sale price from $ _____ to $ _____ .

FEATURE	SUBJECT	COMPARABLE SALE # 1		COMPARABLE SALE # 2		COMPARABLE SALE # 3	
Address							
Proximity to Subject							
Sale Price	$		$		$		$
Sale Price/Gross Liv. Area	$ sq. ft.	$ sq. ft.		$ sq. ft.		$ sq. ft.	
Data Source(s)							
Verification Source(s)							
VALUE ADJUSTMENTS	DESCRIPTION	DESCRIPTION	+(-) $ Adjustment	DESCRIPTION	+(-) $ Adjustment	DESCRIPTION	+(-) $ Adjustment
Sale or Financing Concessions							
Date of Sale/Time							
Location							
Leasehold/Fee Simple							
Site							
View							
Design (Style)							
Quality of Construction							
Actual Age							
Condition							
Above Grade	Total	Bdrms.	Baths	Total	Bdrms.	Baths	Total	Bdrms.	Baths	Total	Bdrms.	Baths
Room Count							
Gross Living Area	sq. ft.	sq. ft.		sq. ft.		sq. ft.	
Basement & Finished Rooms Below Grade							
Functional Utility							
Heating/Cooling							
Energy Efficient Items							
Garage/Carport							
Porch/Patio/Deck							
Net Adjustment (Total)		☐ + ☐ -	$	☐ + ☐ -	$	☐ + ☐ -	$
Adjusted Sale Price of Comparables		Net Adj. % Gross Adj. %	$	Net Adj. % Gross Adj. %	$	Net Adj. % Gross Adj. %	$

I ☐ did ☐ did not research the sale or transfer history of the subject property and comparable sales. If not, explain

My research ☐ did ☐ did not reveal any prior sales or transfers of the subject property for the three years prior to the effective date of this appraisal.

Data source(s)

My research ☐ did ☐ did not reveal any prior sales or transfers of the comparable sales for the year prior to the date of sale of the comparable sale.

Data source(s)

Report the results of the research and analysis of the prior sale or transfer history of the subject property and comparable sales (report additional prior sales on page 3).

ITEM	SUBJECT	COMPARABLE SALE # 1	COMPARABLE SALE # 2	COMPARABLE SALE # 3
Date of Prior Sale/Transfer				
Price of Prior Sale/Transfer				
Data Source(s)				
Effective Date of Data Source(s)				

Analysis of prior sale or transfer history of the subject property and comparable sales

Summary of Sales Comparison Approach

Indicated Value by Sales Comparison Approach $

Indicated Value by: Sales Comparison Approach $ _____   Cost Approach (if developed) $ _____   Income Approach (if developed) $ _____

This appraisal is made ☐ "as is", ☐ subject to completion per plans and specifications on the basis of a hypothetical condition that the improvements have been completed, ☐ subject to the following repairs or alterations on the basis of a hypothetical condition that the repairs or alterations have been completed, or ☐ subject to the following required inspection based on the extraordinary assumption that the condition or deficiency does not require alteration or repair:

Based on a complete visual inspection of the interior and exterior areas of the subject property, defined scope of work, statement of assumptions and limiting conditions, and appraiser's certification, my (our) opinion of the market value, as defined, of the real property that is the subject of this report is $ _____ , as of _____ , which is the date of inspection and the effective date of this appraisal.

Freddie Mac Form 70 March 2005   Page 2 of 6   Fannie Mae Form 1004 March 2005

Uniform Residential Appraisal Report

File #

COST APPROACH TO VALUE (not required by Fannie Mae)

Provide adequate information for the lender/client to replicate the below cost figures and calculations.

Support for the opinion of site value (summary of comparable land sales or other methods for estimating site value)

ESTIMATED ☐ REPRODUCTION OR ☐ REPLACEMENT COST NEW	OPINION OF SITE VALUE .... = $		
Source of cost data	Dwelling	Sq. Ft. @ $	.... =$
Quality rating from cost service Effective date of cost data		Sq. Ft. @ $	.... =$
Comments on Cost Approach (gross living area calculations, depreciation, etc.)			
	Garage/Carport	Sq. Ft. @ $	.... =$
	Total Estimate of Cost-New		.... = $
	Less Physical	Functional	External
	Depreciation		=$( )
	Depreciated Cost of Improvements..		=$
	"As-is" Value of Site Improvements..		=$
Estimated Remaining Economic Life (HUD and VA only) Years	Indicated Value By Cost Approach		=$

INCOME APPROACH TO VALUE (not required by Fannie Mae)

Estimated Monthly Market Rent $ X Gross Rent Multiplier   = $ Indicated Value by Income Approach

Summary of Income Approach (including support for market rent and GRM)

PROJECT INFORMATION FOR PUDs (if applicable)

Is the developer/builder in control of the Homeowners' Association (HOA)? ☐ Yes ☐ No   Unit type(s) ☐ Detached ☐ Attached

Provide the following information for PUDs ONLY if the developer/builder is in control of the HOA and the subject property is an attached dwelling unit.

Legal name of project

Total number of phases   Total number of units   Total number of units sold

Total number of units rented   Total number of units for sale   Data source(s)

Was the project created by the conversion of an existing building(s) into a PUD? ☐ Yes ☐ No If Yes, date of conversion

Does the project contain any multi-dwelling units? ☐ Yes ☐ No Data source(s)

Are the units, common elements, and recreation facilities complete? ☐ Yes ☐ No If No, describe the status of completion.

Are the common elements leased to or by the Homeowners' Association? ☐ Yes ☐ No If Yes, describe the rental terms and options.

Describe common elements and recreational facilities

Uniform Residential Appraisal Report

File #

This report form is designed to report an appraisal of a one-unit property or a one-unit property with an accessory unit; including a unit in a planned unit development (PUD). This report form is not designed to report an appraisal of a manufactured home or a unit in a condominium or cooperative project.

This appraisal report is subject to the following scope of work, intended use, intended user, definition of market value, statement of assumptions and limiting conditions, and certifications. Modifications, additions, or deletions to the intended use, intended user, definition of market value, or assumptions and limiting conditions are not permitted. The appraiser may expand the scope of work to include any additional research or analysis necessary based on the complexity of this appraisal assignment. Modifications or deletions to the certifications are also not permitted. However, additional certifications that do not constitute material alterations to this appraisal report, such as those required by law or those related to the appraiser's continuing education or membership in an appraisal organization, are permitted.

SCOPE OF WORK: The scope of work for this appraisal is defined by the complexity of this appraisal assignment and the reporting requirements of this appraisal report form, including the following definition of market value, statement of assumptions and limiting conditions, and certifications. The appraiser must, at a minimum: (1) perform a complete visual inspection of the interior and exterior areas of the subject property, (2) inspect the neighborhood, (3) inspect each of the comparable sales from at least the street, (4) research, verify, and analyze data from reliable public and/or private sources, and (5) report his or her analysis, opinions, and conclusions in this appraisal report.

INTENDED USE: The intended use of this appraisal report is for the lender/client to evaluate the property that is the subject of this appraisal for a mortgage finance transaction.

INTENDED USER: The intended user of this appraisal report is the lender/client.

DEFINITION OF MARKET VALUE: The most probable price which a property should bring in a competitive and open market under all conditions requisite to a fair sale, the buyer and seller, each acting prudently, knowledgeably and assuming the price is not affected by undue stimulus. Implicit in this definition is the consummation of a sale as of a specified date and the passing of title from seller to buyer under conditions whereby: (1) buyer and seller are typically motivated; (2) both parties are well informed or well advised, and each acting in what he or she considers his or her own best interest; (3) a reasonable time is allowed for exposure in the open market; (4) payment is made in terms of cash in U. S. dollars or in terms of financial arrangements comparable thereto; and (5) the price represents the normal consideration for the property sold unaffected by special or creative financing or sales concessions* granted by anyone associated with the sale.

*Adjustments to the comparables must be made for special or creative financing or sales concessions. No adjustments are necessary for those costs which are normally paid by sellers as a result of tradition or law in a market area; these costs are readily identifiable since the seller pays these costs in virtually all sales transactions. Special or creative financing adjustments can be made to the comparable property by comparisons to financing terms offered by a third party institutional lender that is not already involved in the property or transaction. Any adjustment should not be calculated on a mechanical dollar for dollar cost of the financing or concession but the dollar amount of any adjustment should approximate the market's reaction to the financing or concessions based on the appraiser's judgment.

STATEMENT OF ASSUMPTIONS AND LIMITING CONDITIONS: The appraiser's certification in this report is subject to the following assumptions and limiting conditions:

1. The appraiser will not be responsible for matters of a legal nature that affect either the property being appraised or the title to it, except for information that he or she became aware of during the research involved in performing this appraisal. The appraiser assumes that the title is good and marketable and will not render any opinions about the title.

2. The appraiser has provided a sketch in this appraisal report to show the approximate dimensions of the improvements. The sketch is included only to assist the reader in visualizing the property and understanding the appraiser's determination of its size.

3. The appraiser has examined the available flood maps that are provided by the Federal Emergency Management Agency (or other data sources) and has noted in this appraisal report whether any portion of the subject site is located in an identified Special Flood Hazard Area. Because the appraiser is not a surveyor, he or she makes no guarantees, express or implied, regarding this determination.

4. The appraiser will not give testimony or appear in court because he or she made an appraisal of the property in question, unless specific arrangements to do so have been made beforehand, or as otherwise required by law.

5. The appraiser has noted in this appraisal report any adverse conditions (such as needed repairs, deterioration, the presence of hazardous wastes, toxic substances, etc.) observed during the inspection of the subject property or that he or she became aware of during the research involved in performing this appraisal. Unless otherwise stated in this appraisal report, the appraiser has no knowledge of any hidden or unapparent physical deficiencies or adverse conditions of the property (such as, but not limited to, needed repairs, deterioration, the presence of hazardous wastes, toxic substances, adverse environmental conditions, etc.) that would make the property less valuable, and has assumed that there are no such conditions and makes no guarantees or warranties, express or implied. The appraiser will not be responsible for any such conditions that do exist or for any engineering or testing that might be required to discover whether such conditions exist. Because the appraiser is not an expert in the field of environmental hazards, this appraisal report must not be considered as an environmental assessment of the property.

6. The appraiser has based his or her appraisal report and valuation conclusion for an appraisal that is subject to satisfactory completion, repairs, or alterations on the assumption that the completion, repairs, or alterations of the subject property will be performed in a professional manner.

Freddie Mac Form 70   March 2005   Page 4 of 6   Fannie Mae Form 1004   March 2005

Uniform Residential Appraisal Report   File

APPRAISER'S CERTIFICATION: The Appraiser certifies and agrees that:

1. I have, at a minimum, developed and reported this appraisal in accordance with the scope of work requirements stated in this appraisal report.

2. I performed a complete visual inspection of the interior and exterior areas of the subject property. I reported the condition of the improvements in factual, specific terms. I identified and reported the physical deficiencies that could affect the livability, soundness, or structural integrity of the property.

3. I performed this appraisal in accordance with the requirements of the Uniform Standards of Professional Appraisal Practice that were adopted and promulgated by the Appraisal Standards Board of The Appraisal Foundation and that were in place at the time this appraisal report was prepared.

4. I developed my opinion of the market value of the real property that is the subject of this report based on the sales comparison approach to value. I have adequate comparable market data to develop a reliable sales comparison approach for this appraisal assignment. I further certify that I considered the cost and income approaches to value but did not develop them, unless otherwise indicated in this report.

5. I researched, verified, analyzed, and reported on any current agreement for sale for the subject property, any offering for sale of the subject property in the twelve months prior to the effective date of this appraisal, and the prior sales of the subject property for a minimum of three years prior to the effective date of this appraisal, unless otherwise indicated in this report.

6. I researched, verified, analyzed, and reported on the prior sales of the comparable sales for a minimum of one year prior to the date of sale of the comparable sale, unless otherwise indicated in this report.

7. I selected and used comparable sales that are locationally, physically, and functionally the most similar to the subject property.

8. I have not used comparable sales that were the result of combining a land sale with the contract purchase price of a home that has been built or will be built on the land.

9. I have reported adjustments to the comparable sales that reflect the market's reaction to the differences between the subject property and the comparable sales.

10. I verified, from a disinterested source, all information in this report that was provided by parties who have a financial interest in the sale or financing of the subject property.

11. I have knowledge and experience in appraising this type of property in this market area.

12. I am aware of, and have access to, the necessary and appropriate public and private data sources, such as multiple listing services, tax assessment records, public land records and other such data sources for the area in which the property is located.

13. I obtained the information, estimates, and opinions furnished by other parties and expressed in this appraisal report from reliable sources that I believe to be true and correct.

14. I have taken into consideration the factors that have an impact on value with respect to the subject neighborhood, subject property, and the proximity of the subject property to adverse influences in the development of my opinion of market value. I have noted in this appraisal report any adverse conditions (such as, but not limited to, needed repairs, deterioration, the presence of hazardous wastes, toxic substances, adverse environmental conditions, etc.) observed during the inspection of the subject property or that I became aware of during the research involved in performing this appraisal. I have considered these adverse conditions in my analysis of the property value, and have reported on the effect of the conditions on the value and marketability of the subject property.

15. I have not knowingly withheld any significant information from this appraisal report and, to the best of my knowledge, all statements and information in this appraisal report are true and correct.

16. I stated in this appraisal report my own personal, unbiased, and professional analysis, opinions, and conclusions, which are subject only to the assumptions and limiting conditions in this appraisal report.

17. I have no present or prospective interest in the property that is the subject of this report, and I have no present or prospective personal interest or bias with respect to the participants in the transaction. I did not base, either partially or completely, my analysis and/or opinion of market value in this appraisal report on the race, color, religion, sex, age, marital status, handicap, familial status, or national origin of either the prospective owners or occupants of the subject property or of the present owners or occupants of the properties in the vicinity of the subject property or on any other basis prohibited by law.

18. My employment and/or compensation for performing this appraisal or any future or anticipated appraisals was not conditioned on any agreement or understanding, written or otherwise, that I would report (or present analysis supporting) a predetermined specific value, a predetermined minimum value, a range or direction in value, a value that favors the cause of any party, or the attainment of a specific result or occurrence of a specific subsequent event (such as approval of a pending mortgage loan application).

19. I personally prepared all conclusions and opinions about the real estate that were set forth in this appraisal report. If I relied on significant real property appraisal assistance from any individual or individuals in the performance of this appraisal or the preparation of this appraisal report, I have named such individual(s) and disclosed the specific tasks performed in this appraisal report. I certify that any individual so named is qualified to perform the tasks. I have not authorized anyone to make a change to any item in this appraisal report; therefore, any change made to this appraisal is unauthorized and I will take no responsibility for it.

20. I identified the lender/client in this appraisal report who is the individual, organization, or agent for the organization that ordered and will receive this appraisal report.

Freddie Mac Form 70 March 2005   Page 5 of 6   Fannie Mae Form 1004 March 2005

Uniform Residential Appraisal Report   File

21. The lender/client may disclose or distribute this appraisal report to: the borrower; another lender at the request of the borrower; the mortgagee or its successors and assigns; mortgage insurers; government sponsored enterprises; other secondary market participants; data collection or reporting services; professional appraisal organizations; any department, agency, or instrumentality of the United States; and any state, the District of Columbia, or other jurisdictions; without having to obtain the appraiser's or supervisory appraiser's (if applicable) consent. Such consent must be obtained before this appraisal report may be disclosed or distributed to any other party (including, but not limited to, the public through advertising, public relations, news, sales, or other media).

22. I am aware that any disclosure or distribution of this appraisal report by me or the lender/client may be subject to certain laws and regulations. Further, I am also subject to the provisions of the Uniform Standards of Professional Appraisal Practice that pertain to disclosure or distribution by me.

23. The borrower, another lender at the request of the borrower, the mortgagee or its successors and assigns, mortgage insurers, government sponsored enterprises, and other secondary market participants may rely on this appraisal report as part of any mortgage finance transaction that involves any one or more of these parties.

24. If this appraisal report was transmitted as an "electronic record" containing my "electronic signature," as those terms are defined in applicable federal and/or state laws (excluding audio and video recordings), or a facsimile transmission of this appraisal report containing a copy or representation of my signature, the appraisal report shall be as effective, enforceable and valid as if a paper version of this appraisal report were delivered containing my original hand written signature.

25. Any intentional or negligent misrepresentation(s) contained in this appraisal report may result in civil liability and/or criminal penalties including, but not limited to, fine or imprisonment or both under the provisions of Title 18, United States Code, Section 1001, et seq., or similar state laws.

SUPERVISORY APPRAISER'S CERTIFICATION: The Supervisory Appraiser certifies and agrees that:

1. I directly supervised the appraiser for this appraisal assignment, have read the appraisal report, and agree with the appraiser's analysis, opinions, statements, conclusions, and the appraiser's certification.

2. I accept full responsibility for the contents of this appraisal report including, but not limited to, the appraiser's analysis, opinions, statements, conclusions, and the appraiser's certification.

3. The appraiser identified in this appraisal report is either a sub-contractor or an employee of the supervisory appraiser (or the appraisal firm), is qualified to perform this appraisal, and is acceptable to perform this appraisal under the applicable state law.

4. This appraisal report complies with the Uniform Standards of Professional Appraisal Practice that were adopted and promulgated by the Appraisal Standards Board of The Appraisal Foundation and that were in place at the time this appraisal report was prepared.

5. If this appraisal report was transmitted as an "electronic record" containing my "electronic signature," as those terms are defined in applicable federal and/or state laws (excluding audio and video recordings), or a facsimile transmission of this appraisal report containing a copy or representation of my signature, the appraisal report shall be as effective, enforceable and valid as if a paper version of this appraisal report were delivered containing my original hand written signature.

APPRAISER

Signature_____
Name _____
Company Name _____
Company Address_____
_____
Telephone Number _____
Email Address_____
Date of Signature and Report _____
Effective Date of Appraisal _____
State Certification #_____
or State License #_____
or Other (describe) _____ State # _____
State _____
Expiration Date of Certification or License _____

ADDRESS OF PROPERTY APPRAISED

_____
_____
APPRAISED VALUE OF SUBJECT PROPERTY $ _____
LENDER/CLIENT
Name _____
Company Name _____
Company Address_____
_____
Email Address_____

SUPERVISORY APPRAISER (ONLY IF REQUIRED)

Signature_____
Name _____
Company Name _____
Company Address_____
_____
Telephone Number _____
Email Address_____
Date of Signature _____
State Certification # _____
or State License # _____
State _____
Expiration Date of Certification or License _____

SUBJECT PROPERTY

☐ Did not inspect subject property
☐ Did inspect exterior of subject property from street
    Date of Inspection _____
☐ Did inspect interior and exterior of subject property
    Date of Inspection _____

COMPARABLE SALES

☐ Did not inspect exterior of comparable sales from street
☐ Did inspect exterior of comparable sales from street
    Date of Inspection _____

Freddie Mac Form 70 March 2005   Page 6 of 6   Fannie Mae Form 1004 March 2005

Possible solutions after low appraisal:
- Buyer pays over value
- Seller lowers price to appraised value
- Compromise price
- Request for reconsideration of value

The simplest solution to the problem of a low appraisal is for the seller to lower the sales price to the appraised value. But don't be surprised if your seller resists a price reduction. Once a seller has become accustomed to a certain sales price, she will be reluctant to give it up.

Another possibility is a compromise price somewhere in between the appraised value and the original selling price. But this solution is likely to run up against both the seller's reluctance to lower the price and the buyer's reluctance (or inability) to pay more than the appraised value.

Because of these problems, when there's a significant gap between the sales price and the appraised value, the most likely result is termination of the sale. (According to some estimates, a low appraisal results in termination in two out of three cases.) But it's the real estate agent's job to help the parties avoid this outcome whenever possible.

In some cases the agent should ask the lender to reconsider the appraised value, in the hope that it will be increased to a figure more acceptable to the buyer and seller. This can work if it's handled properly. The correct way to request a reconsideration of value will be explained later in this chapter.

Of course, the best way to eliminate the problems that low appraisals create is to prevent them in the first place.

Preventing Low Appraisals

Prevent low appraisal by helping seller price property correctly
- Perform careful CMA
- Price personal property separately

A real estate agent can prevent most low appraisals by helping sellers price properties realistically. A seller should not be given an unrealistic estimate of the property's worth. Even if a buyer can be persuaded to make an offer at the inflated price, the appraisal will come back low (reflecting the property's true market value) and the real struggle to keep the transaction together will begin.

CMA. The best way for an agent to help a seller price a home is to perform a competitive market analysis (CMA). As mentioned earlier in the chapter, a competitive market analysis is an informal version of a sales comparison appraisal. The agent suggests an appropriate price for the seller's home based on a careful evaluation of comparable homes that were recently sold or listed.

Sales comparison information can be obtained from various sources, mainly multiple listing services. Acquaint yourself with the most comprehensive and accessible sources of information in your area.

Personal Property. One pitfall to avoid when writing a sale concerns the seller's personal property (such as furniture) that the buyer would like to buy along with the home. Real estate agents sometimes include this personal property in the real property transaction: the sale is written so that the price covers both the real property (the land, the house, and other attachments) and the personal property. This is a mistake and it can lead to a low appraisal.

Underwriting guidelines require residential appraisers to exclude the value of personal property from the estimate of value for the real property. When the sales price includes personal property and the appraised value does not, the appraised value may be much lower than the sales price.

The sale of personal property to a home buyer should be written up as a separate transaction, using the proper procedures for transferring title to personal property. (Those procedures vary from state to state, so check local requirements.)

On the other hand, an appraiser will include the value of fixtures (such as built-in appliances) in the estimate of value because fixtures are part of the real property. If you're not certain whether a particular item is likely to be treated as personal property or as a fixture in the appraisal, check with local sources. The distinction between personal property and fixtures sometimes depends on local custom.

Request for Reconsideration of Value

Regardless of how objective an appraiser might try to be, subjective considerations and conclusions are a part of every appraisal. In the end, the appraiser's finding is only an opinion of the property's value. If you are affected by a low appraisal and believe the appraiser has made a mistake, you can appeal his estimate and hopefully, with the proper documentation, get the appraised value increased—possibly to the figure the buyer and seller originally agreed on. (Be aware, though, that barring a genuine mistake, the appraiser isn't likely to change his estimate.)

The sooner you find out about a low appraisal, the better. After the property has been appraised, ask the loan officer or the underwriter to call you with the results of the appraisal as soon as possible. Don't try to get the results directly from the appraiser; the appraiser has a fiduciary relationship with the lender and can't disclose information about the appraisal to others without the lender's permission.

If the appraisal comes in low, ask the loan officer or the underwriter for:

1. the value indicated by the sales comparison method, and
2. the addresses of the three comparables the appraiser used.

When appraisal comes in low:
- Ask lender for information
- Evaluate appraisal
- Update CMA
- Consider local independent reappraisal
- Submit request for reconsideration only if lender likely to grant it

Evaluate the appraiser's three comparables and update your competitive market analysis. Then decide if a reappraisal is likely to lead to a higher estimate of value. If so, it might be worthwhile to get a new appraisal by an independent appraiser at the buyer's or seller's expense; local independent appraisers may produce more accurate results than bank appraisers who are often national and high-volume. Presenting the lender with this independent appraisal may be persuasive.

More commonly when there's a low appraisal, one of the real estate agents in the transaction submits a **request for reconsideration of value** to the lender. If you decide to do this, you will have to support your request with at least three comparable sales that indicate a higher value estimate is in order. If you're going to convince the lender that your comparables are more reliable than the appraiser's, yours must be at least as similar to the subject property as the appraiser's are.

If you believe the lender is likely to grant a request for reconsideration, prepare the request and a cover letter as outlined below.

Preparing the Request. Some lenders have their own form for requests for reconsideration of value. If so, you should use their form (you may even be required to). Otherwise, you can use your firm's form. The form should present your information in the same format that's used in the "Sales Comparison Analysis" section of the Uniform Residential Appraisal Report form, as in the example shown in Figure 9.4.

Write a cover letter making your request and attach your sales comparison analysis to it. The cover letter should be simple and very polite; do not criticize the appraiser.

Sometimes appraisers don't use the best information available, and when they don't, their findings may be successfully challenged. If your request for reconsideration of value contains well-researched, properly documented information and is presented in a professional manner, your chances of success will improve. Make your request carelessly and the reverse is true.

Fig. 9.4 Data sheet supporting request for reconsideration of value

	Sales Comparison Analysis **412 Acme Drive**			
Item	**Subject Property**	**Comparable 1**	**Comparable 2**	**Comparable 3**
Address	412 Acme Drive	131 Skip Road	221 Sutter Street	168 Bow Road
Sales price	$235,000	$238,000	$234,500	$229,500
Data source	sales contract	present owner	MLS	selling broker
Date of sale		8/29	9/14	10/17
Location	high quality suburb	same	same	same
Site/view	corner lot	inside lot	corner lot	inside lot
Design	rambler	same	same	same
Appeal	excellent	same	same	same
Construction	good	same	same	same
Age	7 years	6 years	8 years	8 years
Condition	good	same	same	same
No. of rooms	8	7	7	6
No. of bedrooms	4	4	3	3
Living area	2,400 sq. ft.	2,500 sq. ft.	2,350 sq. ft.	2,150 sq. ft.
Garage/carport	2-car attached garage	same	same	same
Patio	15' × 21' patio	15' × 26' patio	18' × 16' patio	15' × 17' patio
Additional features	2 fireplaces, range, oven, D/W, disposal, central air	2 fireplaces, range, oven, D/W central air	1 fireplace, range, oven, D/W central air	1 fireplace, range, oven, D/W, disposal, central air
Comments	Subject is more energy-efficient than Comps 2 and 3, and is at least equal in this respect to Comp 1.			

Outline: Qualifying the Property

I. Lender's Perception of Value

   A. An underwriter evaluates the property based on an appraisal: a professional appraiser's estimate of the property's value.

   B. A residential appraiser focuses on market value: the most probable price a property should bring in a competitive and open market where the parties act knowledgeably and without undue stimulus.

   C. The lender focuses on the loan-to-value ratio: the relationship between the loan amount and the property's value.

      1. A higher LTV creates greater risk for the lender, because:

         a. a buyer who makes a smaller downpayment is more likely to default; and

         b. it's less likely that the proceeds of a foreclosure sale would be enough to fully pay off the loan's remaining principal balance.

      2. The LTV is based on either the sales price or the appraised value, whichever is lower.

      3. Although many lenders are willing to make high-LTV loans, they often compensate for the greater risk by applying stricter qualifying standards or charging a higher interest rate.

II. Appraisal Standards

   A. To prevent unreliable appraisals, the federal government requires states to license and certify appraisers who perform appraisals for "federally related" loan transactions.

   B. Inflated appraisals played a role in the mortgage and foreclosure crisis; as a result, appraisal standards were strengthened at both the federal and state level.

III. Appraisal Process

   A. There are eight steps in the appraisal process:

      1. defining the problem,

      2. determining the scope of work,

      3. collecting and verifying data,

      4. analyzing data,

      5. determining the site value,

      6. applying the appropriate methods of appraisal,

      7. reconciling the results to arrive at a final value estimate, and

      8. issuing the appraisal report.

   B. In some situations, an appraiser may perform a "drive-by appraisal" instead of a full inspection of the property. In other situations, a property inspection waiver may be authorized.

IV. Appraisal Methods
    A. Sales comparison method
        1. Appraisers using the sales comparison method rely on the sales prices of comparable properties to estimate the value of the subject property.
        2. The sales comparison method uses the same principles as a competitive market analysis, although a CMA can use data from current listings and expired listings.
        3. To determine whether a recently sold property is comparable to the subject property, an appraiser considers: the date of the sale, the location of the property, the physical characteristics of the property, the terms of sale, and the conditions of the sale.
        4. The sale should have occurred within the previous six months, although the appraiser may have to adjust the sales price for changes in value if the property was sold more than a few months ago in a volatile market. Older sales may be used in slow markets.
        5. Comparable properties should be located in the same neighborhood and have similar size, design, and quality as the subject property.
        6. Comparable properties must have sold under normal conditions: the buyer and seller are unrelated parties, acting free of unusual pressure, and are fully informed; and the property was on the open market for a reasonable period of time.
        7. If there are differences between the subject property and a comparable, the appraiser should adjust the sales price of the comparable to reflect what it would have sold for if it were more similar to the subject property.
    B. Replacement cost method
        1. There are three steps in the replacement cost method: estimating the cost of replacing the improvements, deducting any depreciation, and adding the value of the land.
        2. The appraiser usually relies on the replacement cost (the cost of constructing a new building with equivalent utility) rather than the reproduction cost (the cost of building an exact replica using the same materials and techniques).
        3. The easiest way to estimate the construction cost is the square foot method, where the appraiser multiplies the estimated cost per square foot by the square footage of the building.
        4. There are three types of depreciation that must be estimated: physical deterioration, functional obsolescence, and external obsolescence.
        5. Depreciation may be considered curable or incurable, depending on whether correcting the problem adds more value than the cost of the repair.

6. An appraisal may be "as is," valuing the property in its current condition, or "subject to," valuing the property as if all physical deterioration were cured.

C. Income method

1. Value under the income method is calculated by dividing the property's annual net income by the rate of return an investor would expect from the property.

2. For residential rental properties, an appraiser will use a simplified version of the income method called the gross income multiplier method.

3. The appraiser finds the value by multiplying the property's rent by a multiplier indicated by the relationship between other properties' rents and values.

4. The appraiser should use the property's economic rent (the rent the owner would receive if the property were currently available) rather than contract rent (the rent the owner currently receives).

D. Final value estimate

1. The appraiser will reconcile the values indicated by the various appraisal methods to arrive at a final estimate of value.

2. The result is not an average of the figures; the appraiser may give more weight to certain methods based on the type of property.

V. Dealing with Low Appraisals

A. A low appraisal can terminate a transaction, since the lender will adjust its loan amount based on the property's appraised value, requiring the borrower to come up with a larger downpayment.

B. A real estate agent can play a role in preventing a low appraisal by:

1. helping the seller set a reasonable listing price, based on the agent's CMA; and

2. making sure that the listing price and sales price include only the value of the real property being sold, without the value of any personal property.

C. In the event of a low appraisal, an agent may submit a request for reconsideration of value to the lender.

1. The agent provides alternative comparables that indicate the subject property is worth more than the appraiser estimated.

2. A request for reconsideration should be submitted only if the lender is likely to grant it.

Key Terms

Appraisal: An expert's estimate of the value of a piece of real estate as of a particular date, based on a documented analysis of the property's features.

Appraiser: One who estimates the value of property, especially an expert qualified to do so by training and experience.

Market value: The most probable price a property should sell for if it is sold under normal conditions and the buyer and seller are typically motivated; also called objective value.

Loan-to-value ratio (LTV): The relationship between the loan amount and either the sales price or the appraised value of the property (whichever is less), expressed as a percentage.

Sales comparison method: A method of appraisal in which the sales prices of comparable properties are used to estimate the value of the subject property.

Subject property: In an appraisal, the property being appraised.

Comparables: In the sales comparison approach, properties similar to the subject property that have recently been sold; the appraiser uses the sales prices of the comparables as an indication of the value of the subject property.

Competitive market analysis (CMA): A real estate agent's estimate of the value of a listed home, based on the sales prices or listing prices of comparable homes; also called a comparative market analysis or broker price opinion.

Normal conditions of sale: A sale in which the buyer and the seller are unrelated to one another and both are fully informed of the property's attributes and deficiencies, neither is acting under unusual pressure, and the property has been offered on the open market for a reasonable period of time.

Replacement cost method: A method of appraisal in which an estimate of the subject property's value is arrived at by estimating the cost of replacing the improvements, then deducting estimated depreciation, and then adding the estimated market value of the land.

Replacement cost: The current cost of constructing a building with the same utility as the subject property, using modern materials and construction methods.

Reproduction cost: The current cost of constructing a replica of the subject property, using the same materials and methods as originally used but at current prices.

Depreciation: Loss in value due to physical deterioration or other causes.

Physical deterioration: Depreciation resulting from physical wear and tear.

Functional obsolescence: Depreciation resulting from functional inadequacies, such as poor or outmoded design.

External obsolescence: Depreciation resulting from factors outside the property owner's control.

Income method: A method of appraisal in which an estimate of the subject property's value is based on the net income it produces.

Gross income multiplier method: A method of appraisal used for residential rental property, in which an estimate of the subject property's value is based on the relationship between the sales prices and the rental incomes of comparable properties.

Economic rent: The rent a property could command in the marketplace if it were available for lease today.

Contract rent: The rent an owner is actually receiving from a property.

Reconciliation: The final step in an appraisal, when the appraiser assembles and interprets the data in order to arrive at a final value estimate.

Low appraisal: When the appraiser's estimated value is less than the agreed-upon sales price, which may affect financing and terminate the transaction.

Request for reconsideration of value: A letter asking a lender to reconsider an appraiser's low value estimate, based on alternative comparables that indicate the subject property is worth more than the appraiser concluded.

Chapter Quiz

1. A lender asks a residential appraiser to:
   a. estimate the book value of the home
   b. determine the assessed value of the home
   c. determine the subjective value of the home
   d. estimate the market value of the home

2. From the lender's point of view, a low-risk loan would be one that has:
   a. no downpayment
   b. a high loan-to-value ratio
   c. a low loan-to-value ratio
   d. a 100% loan-to-value ratio

3. For residential property, the most important method of appraisal is the:
   a. sales comparison method
   b. replacement cost method
   c. income method
   d. gross income multiplier method

4. A sales comparison appraisal is mainly based on:
   a. listing prices
   b. expired listings
   c. sales prices
   d. assessed values

5. A comparable sale should not:
   a. have occurred within the past six months
   b. be in the same neighborhood as the subject property
   c. be similar in style and condition to the subject property
   d. involve related parties

6. The most difficult step in the replacement cost method of appraisal is:
   a. finding benchmark buildings
   b. measuring square footage
   c. estimating depreciation
   d. calculating the gross income multiplier

7. If a home sold for $175,000 and rents for $1,150 per month, then its monthly gross income multiplier is:
   a. .079
   b. 12.68
   c. 66.0
   d. 152.17

8. A real estate agent is helping the Martins set a listing price for their home. The Martins have some furniture they would like to sell along with the home. The agent should advise the Martins:
   a. to include the value of the furniture in the price of the home
   b. to price the furniture separately from the home
   c. not to sell the furniture to the person who buys the home
   d. to treat the furniture as fixtures

9. In the event of a low appraisal, the listing agent should:
   a. always submit a request for a reconsideration of value
   b. submit a request for reconsideration only if the appraiser has made a significant mathematical error
   c. submit a request for reconsideration only if the loan officer recommends it
   d. evaluate the appraisal, update the CMA, and submit a request for reconsideration only if there is a good possibility that it will be granted

10. A property's value is diminished by its proximity to a paper mill. This would be considered:
   a. deferred maintenance
   b. functional obsolescence
   c. external obsolescence
   d. curable depreciation

Answer Key

1. d. An appraiser performing an appraisal for a residential lender is typically concerned with the property's market value.

2. c. A loan with a low loan-to-value ratio (for example, 80% or lower) is considered a low-risk loan. A larger downpayment reduces the risk of default, and it also increases the likelihood that the full loan amount can be recovered in a foreclosure sale.

3. a. The sales comparison method is the most relevant method for residential appraisals.

4. c. The sales comparison method uses the sales prices of recently sold comparable properties as the basis for estimating the subject property's value. The appraiser may analyze listings as supporting data, but the main comparables must be actual sales. (Listing prices may be used along with sales prices in a real estate agent's competitive market analysis, however.)

5. d. A sale that was not an arm's length transaction should not be used as a comparable. The appraiser may use comparables that need adjustments for the date of sale, the location of the property, or the financing terms.

6. c. The most difficult part of the replacement cost method is estimating depreciation.

7. d. To calculate the monthly gross income multiplier, divide the property's value by its monthly rent. In this case, the monthly multiplier is 152.17 ($175,000 ÷ $1,150 = 152.17).

8. b. Furniture and other personal property should be priced separately from the real estate. Including personal property can inflate the sales price and lead to a low appraisal.

9. d. When the appraised value is lower than the price the parties agreed to, the agent should review the appraisal and see if other comparables can be found that indicate a higher value for the subject property. If that is the case, the agent should request a reconsideration of value.

10. c. Loss of value caused by factors outside of the property, such as a nearby nuisance like a paper mill, would be external obsolescence. External obsolescence is almost always incurable.

Chapter 10
Conventional Financing

Conforming and Nonconforming Loans

Conventional Loan Characteristics

- Property types and owner-occupancy rules
- Loan amounts
- Repayment periods
- Amortization
- Loan-to-value ratios
- Loan fees and interest rates
- Private mortgage insurance
- Secondary financing

Qualifying Standards

- Evaluating risk factors
- Credit reputation
- Income analysis
- Available funds

Buydown Plans

- Types of buydown plans
- Buydowns and qualifying rules
- Limits on buydowns and other contributions

Conventional Low-Downpayment Programs

- Features and requirements
- Affordable housing programs
- Lender contributions

Introduction

Loans made by institutional lenders (such as banks, savings and loans, and mortgage companies) can be divided into two main categories: conventional loans and government-sponsored loans.

A **conventional loan** is any institutional loan that isn't insured or guaranteed by a government agency. For example, a loan that's made by a bank and insured by a private mortgage insurance company is a conventional loan. A loan that's made by a bank and insured by the FHA (Federal Housing Administration) or guaranteed by the VA (Department of Veterans Affairs) is not a conventional loan, because it is backed by a government agency.

The two main government-sponsored loan programs are covered in Chapters 11 and 12. In this chapter, we'll examine conventional loans.

Conventional loan: not insured or guaranteed by government

Conforming and Nonconforming Loans

Fannie Mae and Freddie Mac (the government-sponsored enterprises, or GSEs—see Chapter 3) are the major secondary market entities that purchase conventional loans, and most conventional loans are made in compliance with their underwriting guidelines. The guidelines of the two entities are similar in many respects, although they aren't identical. Loans that comply with (conform to) their guidelines are called **conforming loans**.

Conforming loan complies with Fannie Mae's and/or Freddie Mac's guidelines

Lenders making conventional loans aren't required to follow the guidelines of the GSEs; they're free to apply their own underwriting standards instead. But if a loan isn't made in compliance with Fannie Mae's or Freddie Mac's guidelines, it's **nonconforming** and can't be sold to either GSE, except by special arrangement.

Nonconforming loan:
- **Doesn't comply with GSE guidelines**
- **Fannie Mae and Freddie Mac won't buy it**

Conventional Loan Characteristics

Lenders like to have the option of selling their loans on the secondary market; when they make conforming loans, they know that they'll be able to sell them to Fannie Mae or Freddie Mac at good prices. As a result, the two entities' underwriting guidelines are widely followed by the mortgage industry. For that reason, our discussion of conventional loans generally focuses on those guidelines, particularly the rules governing owner-occupancy, loan amounts, loan-to-value ratios, mortgage insurance, and secondary financing. It's important to keep in mind, however, that not all conventional loans conform to the guidelines or have the characteristics we describe here.

Property Types and Owner-Occupancy Rules

Fannie Mae and Freddie Mac buy loans secured by residential properties, including detached site-built houses, townhouses, condominium units, cooperative units, and manufactured homes.

The borrowers may intend to occupy the security property either as their principal residence or as a second home. Generally, a principal residence may have up to four dwelling units, but a second home should have no more than one dwelling unit.

Fannie Mae and Freddie Mac are also willing to buy **investor loans** secured by property with up to four dwelling units. A loan is considered an investor loan if the borrower doesn't intend to occupy the property; in most cases, the borrower plans to rent it out to tenants instead. Investor loans are underwritten using different (and generally stricter) standards than loans for owner-occupied homes. We'll mainly be discussing owner-occupied homes, not investment properties.

Conventional loan may be secured by:
- Principal residence
- Second home
- Investment property

Loan Amounts

In order for a loan to be eligible for purchase by Fannie Mae or Freddie Mac, the loan amount must not exceed the applicable conforming loan limit. Conforming loan limits for dwellings with one, two, three, or four units are set by the Federal Housing Finance Agency (the agency that oversees the GSEs) based on median housing prices nationwide. The limits may be adjusted annually to reflect changes in median prices.

Conforming loan limits may be adjusted annually

In most parts of the country, the 2018 conforming loan limit for single-family homes and other one-unit dwellings is $453,100. In **high-cost areas**—areas where housing is more expensive—a higher limit based on the area median home price, up to a maximum of $679,650, applies (see Figure 10.1). There are higher limits for Alaska, Hawaii, Guam, and the Virgin Islands, where homes are exceptionally expensive.

Conventional loans that exceed the conforming loan limits are also available in many areas, although they're usually ineligible for sale to Fannie Mae and Freddie Mac. For these larger loans, known as **jumbo loans**, lenders generally apply stricter underwriting standards.

Jumbo loan: loan amount exceeds conforming loan limit

Fig. 10.1 Fannie Mae and Freddie Mac's conforming loan limits

2018 Conforming Loan Limits for single-family homes and other one-unit dwellings		
General Loan Limit	Limit in High-Cost Areas	Limits in Alaska, Guam, Hawaii, and the Virgin Islands
$453,100	Based on area median home price, up to $679,650	$679,650 generally, and up to $1,019,475 in high-cost areas in these locations

For example, the maximum loan-to-value ratio for a jumbo loan may be lower, and the buyers may be required to have higher credit scores and more money in reserve than they would for a conforming loan. Under some market conditions jumbo loans are more expensive than conforming loans, with higher interest rates or loan fees, but that's not always the case.

Repayment Periods

Repayment periods for conventional loans can range from ten years to forty years, but Fannie Mae and Freddie Mac generally won't buy a loan if the term is longer than thirty years. Fifteen-year loans have become increasingly popular, although thirty years is still considered the standard term (see Chapter 6).

Amortization

Most conventional loans are fully amortized, meaning the payments are large enough to pay off the loan completely by the end of the term. Fannie Mae and Freddie Mac generally do not purchase partially amortized or interest-only loans.

Loan-to-Value Ratios

Traditionally, the standard conventional loan-to-value ratio was 80%. A mortgage loan for 80% of the property's sales price or appraised value is generally regarded as a very safe investment. First, the 20% downpayment gives the borrower a substantial incentive to avoid default; second, if foreclosure does become necessary, the lender is likely to recover the full amount owed.

At one time, very few lenders were willing to make conventional loans with LTVs over 80%. That started changing in the 1980s. Due to a number of factors, including a growing private mortgage industry, more lenders became comfortable making conventional loans with higher LTVs, and eventually those loans were widely available. By the late 1990s they had become more common than 80% loans. Lenders routinely made conventional loans with LTVs up to 95%, requiring only a 5% downpayment.

Conventional loans with even higher loan-to-value ratios—97% or above—became widespread in the early 2000s. Some lenders even made 100% conventional loans, allowing the borrowers to put no money down.

Unfortunately, high LTV-loans played a significant role in the nationwide mortgage foreclosure crisis. In 2007 and 2008, when home values began dropping around the country, many borrowers who had started out with very little equity suddenly had none. As values continued to decline, these borrowers soon had negative equity—in other words, they owed their lenders more than their homes were worth. When these borrowers could no longer afford to pay their mortgages and defaulted, their lenders incurred serious losses. As a result of the foreclosure crisis, conventional loans with LTVs over 95% are less common now. They are available, though, often through special programs. (See the discussion of low-downpayment programs later in the chapter.) Loans with 95% LTVs have regained popularity, but they're harder to qualify for than they were before the crisis.

Applicants for conventional loans with higher LTVs are generally required to meet stricter qualifying standards than they would have to if they were making a larger downpayment. (For example, in a particular case, a credit score of 680 might be high enough to qualify for a loan with a 90% LTV, but too low for a 95% loan.) Also, loans with higher LTVs are more expensive for the borrower, with higher loan fees and/or a higher interest rate, as we'll discuss in the next section of the chapter.

High-LTV loans:
• Stricter underwriting
• More expensive

When there will be one or more junior mortgages against the property, the lender will be concerned with the **combined loan-to-value ratio** (CLTV), which is the ratio of all loans to the value of the property. (You may also see that figure called the total loan-to-value ratio, or TLTV.) For more about this, see the discussion of secondary financing later in the chapter.

Combined LTV ratio: the ratio of all loans to the value of the property

Exercise No. 1

Rita Maynard would like to buy the Chandlers' house, which she would use as her primary residence. The sales price is $318,750, and the appraisal came in at $321,000.

1. Maynard wants to make a $25,500 downpayment and obtain a conventional loan for the rest of the price. What would Maynard's loan-to-value ratio be?

2. If Maynard decreased her downpayment amount to $19,125, what would the loan-to-value ratio be?

Loan Fees and Interest Rates

Like residential borrowers in general, conventional borrowers are usually expected to pay an origination fee, and they may also agree to pay discount points (see Chapter 7). In addition, if their loan is going to be sold to Fannie Mae or Freddie Mac, the cost of the financing will probably also reflect one or more risk-based price adjustments. We'll refer to these as **loan-level price adjustments** (LLPAs), which is Fannie Mae's term. (Freddie Mac calls them "credit fees in price.") The riskier the loan, the more Fannie or Freddie will charge in LLPAs. Lenders pass this cost on to the borrower, although not usually as a fee collected at closing. Instead, most lenders recoup the LLPAs by increasing the interest rate on the borrower's loan.

There's one LLPA that applies to nearly all conventional loans that the GSEs buy. The amount varies based on credit score and loan-to-value ratio. Borrowers with comparatively low credit scores and high-LTV loans are charged the most. Borrowers who have better credit scores and/or lower LTVs (larger downpayments) are charged less. For instance, for a borrower with a 680 credit score and a 95% LTV, this LLPA might be 1.25% of the loan amount. For a borrower with a 760 credit score and an 80% LTV, it might be only 0.5% of the loan amount.

The GSEs also charge additional LLPAs for certain types of loans that involve more risk, such as investor loans, loans with secondary financing, adjustable-rate mortgages, and loans secured by certain types of properties, such as condominiums and duplexes.

> **Example:** Sanjay Desai is financing his house with an adjustable-rate conventional loan that will be sold to Freddie Mac. Two LLPAs apply to his loan: 1.0% of the loan amount based on his credit score and the loan-to-value ratio, plus another 0.25% because it's an ARM. Instead of having Desai pay these as a separate fee, the lender increases the interest rate on his loan to cover them.

Lenders don't simply add the LLPA percentages directly to the loan's interest rate. In the example, the buyer's interest rate won't be 1.25% higher than it would have been without the LLPAs; the actual impact on the interest rate will be much less than that. It will depend on market conditions and the method that the lender uses to annualize the LLPAs, among other factors. Whatever the exact impact, it is already reflected in the interest rate the lender quotes to the buyer. The essential thing to understand is that the interest rate charged on a conventional loan is likely to vary depending on risk factors such as credit score, loan-to-value ratio, type of loan, type of property, and so on.

Private Mortgage Insurance

Another financing cost that many borrowers face is **private mortgage insurance** (PMI). Private mortgage insurance is called "private" because it's obtained from private insurance companies, not through the FHA's mortgage insurance program. Like FHA mortgage insurance, PMI is designed to protect lenders from the greater risk of high-LTV loans; the insurance makes up for the reduced borrower equity. Both Fannie Mae and Freddie Mac require PMI on conventional loans if the loan-to-value ratio is greater than 80%.

PMI:
- Protects lender
- Premium(s) paid by borrower

How PMI Works. When insuring a loan, a private mortgage insurance company actually assumes only a portion of the risk of default. Instead of covering the entire loan amount, the insurance just covers the upper portion of the loan. The amount of coverage varies depending on the loan term and loan-to-value ratio, but coverage of 25% to 30% is typical.

PMI typically covers 25% to 30% of the loan amount

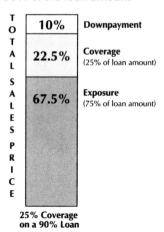

Example: 25% coverage

$200,000	Sales price
× 90%	LTV
$180,000	90% loan
× 25%	Amount of coverage
$45,000	Amount of policy

In the event of default and foreclosure, the lender, at the insurer's option, will either sell the property and make a claim for reimbursement of actual losses (if any) up to the policy's coverage amount, or else relinquish the property to the insurer and make a claim for actual losses up to the coverage amount.

As explained in Chapter 6, private mortgage insurance companies have their own underwriting standards. A company will insure only loans that meet its standards, since it's the company that will bear most of the risk of default and foreclosure loss. Like the underwriting standards of Fannie Mae and Freddie Mac, the standards set by the largest private mortgage insurance companies have been influential throughout the mortgage industry.

PMI Premiums. In return for insuring a loan, a mortgage insurance company charges insurance premiums, which are ordinarily paid by the borrower. Depending on the company, there are a variety of possible payment plans.

PMI premiums:
- Annual premium,
- Initial premium at closing, plus renewal premiums, or
- Financed one-time premium

Many insurers charge a flat annual premium that reflects the risk of the loan (based on factors such as the loan term, the loan-to-value ratio, and the borrower's credit reputation). For example, for someone with good credit and a loan with a 95% loan-to-value ratio, the annual premium might be 0.67% of the loan amount. The same borrower with a 90% LTV might pay an annual premium of 0.52%. The lender will usually require the borrower to pay one-twelfth of the annual premium each month, as part of the monthly payment on the mortgage.

Example: $200,000 sales price; 90% loan

$180,000	Loan amount
× 0.52%	For 25% coverage
$936	Annual premium
÷ 12	Months in a year
$78	Monthly payment

Alternatively, the borrower may pay more of the total cost upfront. With this kind of plan, the insurance company charges a large initial premium (paid at closing), plus smaller annual renewal premiums thereafter. These smaller annual renewal premiums are based on either the original loan amount or the declining loan balance. One-twelfth of the annual premium is charged to the borrower each month.

The final PMI payment plan we will mention is a single life-of-the-loan premium. This can be paid at closing or financed over the loan term. To finance the single premium, the lender adds the premium to the loan amount before calculating the monthly payment. An advantage of this plan is that the borrower doesn't have to come up with cash at closing for the PMI.

With some payment plans, the borrower may be entitled to a refund of part of the initial premium or financed premium if the borrower pays the loan off early or the lender cancels the mortgage insurance. Premiums are lower for plans that don't provide for refunds, however.

Cancellation/Termination of PMI. As a loan is paid off by the borrower, the loan-to-value ratio decreases (as long as the market value of the property serving as collateral isn't decreasing). With a lower LTV, the risk of default and foreclosure loss is reduced, and eventually the private mortgage insurance has fulfilled its purpose.

Under the federal **Homeowners Protection Act**, loan servicers must cancel the PMI on a borrower's loan under certain conditions. The law requires the PMI to be canceled once the loan has been paid down to 80% of the property's original value, if the borrower formally requests the cancellation. Automatic termination of the PMI, without a request from the borrower, is required once the loan balance reaches 78% of the property's original value.

By law, PMI must be terminated automatically when loan balance reaches 78% of original property value

If the PMI has not already been canceled or terminated under the rules described above, the loan servicer must terminate the PMI by the first day of the month following the midpoint of the loan's amortization period, as long as the borrower is current on the mortgage payments. For example, on a fully amortized 30-year mortgage, the midpoint is 15 years into the term; the servicer must terminate PMI on the first day of the month following the loan's 15-year anniversary.

The Homeowners Protection Act applies only to loans on single-family dwellings (including condominium and cooperative units, townhouses, and manufactured homes) occupied as the borrower's principal residence.

Secondary Financing

Lenders generally allow secondary financing, whatever the source, in conjunction with a conventional loan. However, most lenders impose some restrictions when secondary financing is used. Secondary financing increases the risk of default on the primary loan, and the primary lender wants to minimize that additional risk as much as possible.

Primary lender sets rules for secondary financing

Restrictions on Secondary Financing. Here are some of the rules that a lender might apply in a transaction that involves secondary financing:

1. **The borrower must be able to qualify for the payments on both the first and second mortgages.** For qualifying purposes, the primary lender will generally include the payments on the second loan in the borrower's housing expense.

2. **The borrower must make a minimum downpayment.** As mentioned earlier, in transactions involving a junior loan, lenders consider the combined loan-to-value ratio or CLTV. The primary lender usually sets a maximum CLTV for the transaction, to ensure that the borrower makes at least a small downpayment out of his own funds. For example, the primary lender often limits the total of the first and second mortgages (the CLTV) to 95%, so the borrower must make a minimum downpayment of 5%. Or the primary lender's maximum CLTV might be 90%, requiring the borrower to put at least 10% down.

3. **Scheduled payments must be due on a regular basis.** With a few exceptions, the primary lender is likely to require the second loan to have regularly scheduled payments. In some cases, quarterly, semi-annual, or annual payments might be acceptable, but usually the primary lender will insist that the second loan have monthly payments. The secondary loan payments can be designed to fully or partially amortize the debt, or to cover only the interest. If the loan is partially amortized or interest-only, a balloon payment will be due at the end of the loan term.

4. **The second mortgage can't require a balloon payment sooner than five years after closing.** If the second loan isn't fully amortized, the primary lender is likely to set a minimum term for it (often five years). This prevents the second lender from requiring a large balloon payment from the borrower early in the term of the primary loan, when the risk of default is greatest.

5. **If the first mortgage has variable payments, the second mortgage must have fixed payments.** In other words, the primary lender may require the second mortgage to be a fixed-rate loan if the first mortgage is an adjustable-rate loan, or if the first mortgage is subject to a temporary

buydown. (Buydowns are discussed later in this chapter.) Conversely, if the first mortgage is a fixed-rate loan without a buydown, the primary lender will usually allow the second mortgage to be an ARM.

6. **No negative amortization.** The primary lender may specify that the regular payments on the second mortgage must at least equal the interest due on the second mortgage.

7. **No prepayment penalty.** The primary lender often won't allow the second mortgage to have a prepayment penalty.

Again, these are just examples of secondary financing rules. If you're working with a buyer who plans to use secondary financing, ask the buyer's primary lender what rules will apply.

Piggyback Loans. As you may recall from Chapter 4, secondary financing is sometimes called a piggyback loan: the second loan "rides piggyback" on a first loan. More specifically, this term usually refers to a secondary financing arrangement that enables the borrower to avoid certain costs or requirements by limiting the size of the primary loan. (Also, in some cases the same lender is providing both of the loans, which is a departure from traditional secondary financing.)

In the early 2000s, piggybacking was commonly used to avoid paying private mortgage insurance or to avoid jumbo loan treatment. Buyers without much cash for a downpayment could still keep the loan-to-value ratio of their primary financing at 80% or less, so that they weren't required to pay for mortgage insurance. And buyers of very expensive properties could combine a conforming primary loan with a piggyback loan, instead of using a single jumbo loan with a higher interest rate and fees. Some piggyback arrangements allowed buyers to make only a very small downpayment, or none at all.

Following the mortgage crisis, piggyback financing all but disappeared. Although some piggyback loan options are available again, they are more expensive now and require a larger downpayment.

Exercise No. 2

A buyer is seeking conventional fixed-rate financing in order to purchase a home. The sales price is $289,500 and the property has been appraised at $291,500. The buyer is planning to make a 5% cash downpayment and finance the balance with two loans: an 80% conventional first mortgage at 7% interest for 30 years and a 15%

second mortgage from the seller at 6.5% interest. Payments on the second mortgage would be based on a 30-year amortization schedule, with a balloon payment of $40,650 due five years after closing.

The first loan has a 1.5% loan origination fee. Also, the primary lender is planning to sell the loan to Fannie Mae, who will charge loan-level price adjustments based on the secondary financing, the loan-to-value ratio, and the buyer's credit score. However, the lender took those LLPAs into account in setting the buyer's interest rate at 7%; so the origination fee is the only loan fee the buyer will pay at closing.

The first loan would require a monthly principal and interest payment of $1,540.84. The second loan would require a monthly principal and interest payment of $274.48. In addition, one-twelfth of the annual property taxes of $3,190 and one-twelfth of the annual hazard insurance premium of $720 would be included in the buyer's total monthly mortgage payment.

1. What would the loan amounts for the first and second loans be?

2. How much would the buyer pay at closing for the downpayment and loan origination fee?

3. What would the buyer's total monthly payment for both loans come to, including principal, interest, taxes, and insurance (PITI)?

Qualifying Standards

Chapter 8 explained the general process of qualifying buyers for home purchase loans. Now we'll discuss the qualifying standards that apply to conventional loans. As explained earlier, the qualifying standards most lenders use for conventional loans are based on guidelines established by Fannie Mae and Freddie Mac.

Evaluating Risk Factors

As discussed in Chapter 8, Fannie Mae and Freddie Mac each have their own automated underwriting system (AUS), and they both encourage lenders to use automated underwriting whenever possible. Manual underwriting is still necessary in various situations (for example, if the applicant doesn't have an established credit history). It may also be used after an application has received a "Refer" or "Caution" risk classification from the AUS. The underwriter might be able to justify loan approval based on information that wasn't available to the automated system (for instance, the applicant's documented explanation of extenuating circumstances surrounding earlier credit problems).

To a considerable extent, the same qualifying standards are applied in manual and automated underwriting. But an AUS is programmed to apply more flexible standards in many situations. The AUS is allowed greater leeway because a computer program can weigh risk factors more precisely than human underwriters can.

Whether the underwriting is automated or manual, it's intended to provide the lender with a clear understanding of how much risk the proposed loan would involve. Fannie Mae and Freddie Mac use differing terminology to explain how lenders should weigh the risk factors in a loan application, but they're describing much the same process. Both require an evaluation of the applicant's overall financial situation, with positive factors offsetting negative ones and vice versa.

Fannie Mae prescribes a "comprehensive risk assessment" approach. The applicant's credit reputation (as reflected in her credit scores) and cash investment (measured by the loan-to-value ratio) are generally treated as primary risk factors. Other aspects of the application, such as the debt to income ratio and cash reserves, are considered contributory risk factors. All of these factors must be weighed together in deciding whether to approve or reject the loan application.

Freddie Mac instructs lenders to separately evaluate each of the main components of creditworthiness—credit reputation, capacity to repay (income and liquid assets), and collateral (the value of the property)—and also evaluate the "overall layering of risk." Strength in one component of the application may compensate for weakness in another. But if the combined risk factors in the application amount to excessive layering of risk, the loan should be denied.

Credit Reputation

Credit reputation is probably the most important factor in determining whether an applicant qualifies for a loan. Fannie Mae and Freddie Mac require underwriters to use credit scores in evaluating a loan applicant's credit reputation if usable scores are available. (If not, the application will have to be underwritten manually, and nontraditional credit analysis may be necessary. See Chapter 8.)

Credit scores are a central factor in conventional underwriting

The credit scores (FICO® scores) that the three main credit bureaus provide for a particular loan applicant often vary somewhat from one another. In that case, one score is selected to use in underwriting. Underwriters typically use the lower of two scores, or the middle of three. For example, if a loan applicant's credit scores are 690, 705, and 710, then 705 will be used for underwriting purposes. The selected score may be referred to as the **indicator score**, the representative score, or the underwriting score, depending on the context.

One credit score selected to use in underwriting

An excellent credit score (for example, 740 or higher) can offset weaknesses in certain other aspects of the loan application, such as marginal income ratios, low reserves, or a small downpayment. A poor credit score, on the other hand, can be determinative. For example, Fannie Mae won't buy any loans made to borrowers with credit scores below 620, and for many types of loans the minimum score is 680. Freddie Mac has similar rules. Credit scores also affect the cost of a conventional loan; as discussed earlier, higher loan-level price adjustments apply to borrowers with lower credit scores, which usually translates into a higher interest rate on their loans.

When two people apply for a conventional loan together (as in the case of a married couple), the lender will obtain credit scores for both applicants and select one score for each of them using the "lower of two, middle of three" rule explained above. One applicant's high credit score may help offset the other applicant's lower score. However, the lower score is considered the indicator score for the application, and for certain purposes that's the only score that matters. For example, if the indicator score is below the minimum required for the type of loan in question, Fannie Mae or Freddie Mac won't buy the loan, even if the other applicant has a high score. And if the loan is eligible for purchase, the indicator score will be used to determine the loan-level price adjustment that's based on credit score and loan-to-value ratio.

Income Analysis

Stable monthly income is income that meets the lender's tests of quality and durability (see Chapter 8). Fannie Mae and Freddie Mac consider income durable if it is expected to continue for at least three years after the loan is made.

Once the underwriter (or the automated underwriting system) determines how much stable monthly income the loan applicant has, the next step is to decide if the amount of stable monthly income is adequate to support the proposed monthly mortgage payment. This is where income ratios come into play.

Debt to Income Ratio. If a lender submits an application for a conventional single-family purchase loan to Freddie Mac's automated underwriting system, the AUS can consider the applicant's income adequate if his total monthly obligations do not exceed 45% of his stable monthly income. Fannie Mae's AUS could even accept a debt to income ratio of up to 50%. With either GSE's system, though, the maximum debt to income ratio allowed for a given applicant varies based on all other factors taken into consideration by the AUS. So a ratio as high as 45% or 50% isn't necessarily acceptable in any given case.

For manually underwritten loans, the applicant's total monthly obligations generally must not exceed 36% without documentation of specific compensating factors, which we'll discuss shortly. If there are sufficient compensating factors, a debt to income ratio as high as 45% may be acceptable for a manually underwritten loan.

Whether the loan is underwritten using an AUS or manually, the **total monthly obligations** include the proposed housing expense plus the applicant's other recurring obligations. The **housing expense** includes PITI: principal, interest, property taxes, hazard insurance, and—if applicable—special assessments, mortgage insurance, and homeowners association dues.

A loan applicant's **recurring obligations** include installment debts, revolving debts, and other obligations. **Installment debts** have a fixed beginning and ending date. A car loan is a good example. The monthly payments are a fixed amount and continue for a fixed number of months. An installment debt will be included when calculating the loan applicant's debt to income ratio if more than ten months of payments remain to be made. (A debt that will be paid off in ten months or less may also be included if the required payments are very large.)

Maximum debt to income ratio for AUS loan: 45% or 50%

Maximum debt to income ratio for manually underwritten loan: 36%, or 45% with compensating factors

Total obligations include:
- Housing expense
- Installment debts
- Revolving debts
- Other obligations

Revolving debts involve an open-ended line of credit, with minimum monthly payments. The most obvious examples are Visa, MasterCard, and department store charge accounts. For each account, the required minimum payment should be included in the debt to income ratio calculation.

Another category of recurring obligations includes alimony, child support, and similar ongoing financial obligations. As with installment debts, these obligations are included in the debt to income ratio if more than ten months of payments remain to be made.

Debts paid by others. In some cases, a loan applicant can have a debt excluded from the calculation of her debt-to-income ratio. This is allowed when the payment on a certain revolving or installment debt has been made reliably for at least the past twelve months by another party who has no interest in the real estate transaction. For example, if Selia's mother has been regularly making the monthly payment on her student loan for the past two years, Selia's lender can probably exclude that debt from the calculation of her debt-to-income ratio.

Housing Expense to Income Ratio. For manually underwritten loans, Freddie Mac's guidelines also require underwriters to separately consider the loan applicant's housing expense to income ratio. The proposed housing expense (PITI) generally should not exceed **28%** of the loan applicant's stable monthly income.

If second income ratio is applied, housing expense to income ratio should not exceed 28%

Fannie Mae no longer sets a maximum housing expense to income ratio. If a loan is going to be sold to Fannie Mae, the monthly housing expense is considered only as a component of the debt to income ratio.

Applying Income Ratios. Income ratios can be used as a starting point to estimate the maximum monthly mortgage payment that a particular buyer can qualify for; that's how real estate agents used to prequalify buyers. The maximum payment determines the maximum loan amount, which is a key element in setting a realistic price range for house hunting. Since real estate agents typically don't prequalify buyers anymore (see Chapter 7), it's very likely you'll never have to do this type of calculation in the real world. Even so, an example based on the prequalifying method will help you understand the impact of rules concerning maximum income ratios on buying power. Although automated underwriting is used for most conventional loans now, the example below applies rules for manual underwriting, to demonstrate the basic process more clearly. (We'll also discuss how automated underwriting may reach a different result than manual underwriting.)

The first step in estimating a buyer's maximum monthly payment for a conventional loan is to multiply the buyer's stable monthly income by 36%. For a manually underwritten loan, the buyer's total monthly payments on all long-term obligations (including the proposed mortgage) generally should not exceed this amount. Take this figure and subtract the buyer's total monthly payments on long-term obligations other than the mortgage; the result is the largest mortgage payment allowed under the 36% guideline. Next, multiply the stable monthly income by the 28% housing expense to income ratio. This answer is the largest mortgage payment allowed under the 28% guideline. If an underwriter applies both ratios (rather than just the debt to income ratio, as Fannie Mae allows), the smaller of the two results is the maximum allowable payment.

> **Example:** Marianne Smith's stable monthly income is $4,200. She has four monthly obligations that the underwriter will count: a $310 car payment, a $65 personal loan payment, a $40 department store charge account payment, and a $45 MasterCard payment, which add up to $460 per month. What's the largest mortgage payment she can qualify for?

Total debt to income ratio:

$4,200	Stable monthly income
× 36%	Income ratio
$1,512	Maximum total obligations
− 460	Obligations other than housing expense
$1,052	Maximum mortgage payment under the 36% debt to income ratio

Housing expense to income ratio:

$4,200	Stable monthly income
× 28%	Income ratio
$1,176	Maximum mortgage payment under the 28% housing expense ratio

> Since it's the lower resulting figure that counts when both income ratios are applied, this indicates that Smith could probably qualify for a $1,052 mortgage payment.

Of course, if Smith could pay off some of her debts and reduce her total obligations, she could qualify for a larger mortgage payment. But even without taking that step, she may qualify for a larger payment if there are factors in her application to compensate for a higher debt to income ratio. (See the list of potential compensating factors in the next subsection of the chapter.) To estimate the maximum possible payment in that case, multiply Smith's stable monthly income by 45% instead of 36%, then subtract her total monthly obligations.

Example:

$4,200	Stable monthly income
× 45%	Income ratio
$1,890	Maximum total obligations
− 460	Total monthly obligations
$1,430	Maximum mortgage payment with a 45% debt to income ratio

Thus, with strong enough compensating factors, Smith could potentially qualify for a payment as high as $1,430 under the 45% ratio. With that payment amount, though, her housing expense to income ratio would be 34% ($1,430 ÷ $4,200 = .34), well above the 28% benchmark. If an underwriter were applying both ratios instead of just the debt to income ratio, that would have to be taken into account. But Freddie Mac allows underwriters more flexibility regarding the housing expense to income ratio than the debt to income ratio; there's no hard limit on the housing expense ratio like the 45% limit on the other ratio. So an underwriter could accept the 34% housing expense ratio, if that was prudent in light of all other aspects of Smith's loan application.

As you can see, compensating factors could make a big difference in how large a payment Smith can qualify for. If they are strong enough, she could qualify for a payment as high as $1,430, compared to the $1,052 payment she can qualify for without them.

Now let's consider what impact automated underwriting could have on Marianne Smith's maximum mortgage payment. Remember that an AUS evaluates all of a buyer's risks holistically; income ratios for the proposed loan are just one element in the overall picture. However, Freddie Mac's AUS can't accept a debt to income ratio over 45%, the same top limit that applies in manual underwriting. Also, for the AUS to approve a ratio that high, the application will need to include the same types of compensating factors that could allow a manual underwriter to approve a ratio as high as 45%. An AUS doesn't apply precisely the same rules and may weigh various factors differently, but the underlying considerations are essentially the same. As mentioned earlier, though, automated underwriting systems are designed with considerable flexibility built in, and they may be more likely to approve a higher payment than an underwriter applying the manual underwriting rules.

Since Fannie Mae's AUS can accept a 50% debt to income ratio, Marianne Smith could even be approved for a monthly payment up to $1,640 if the lender planned to sell her loan to Fannie Mae ($4,200 × .50 = $2,100 – $460 = $1,640). That's considerably more than the $1,430 payment allowed when 45% is the top limit, and more than half again as much as the $1,052 payment based on the 36% ratio. To give you a very rough idea of the tremendous difference these different payment levels could make in Smith's buying power, if the interest rate on the loan were 5%, the $1,052 payment corresponds to a maximum loan amount of about $196,000; with the $1,430 payment it would be about $266,400; and with the $1,640 payment it would be about $305,500. (Those figures assume a fixed interest rate and a 30-year repayment period.)

However, because our example doesn't provide information about the rest of Smith's situation, it's by no means certain she could actually qualify for either of those larger payment amounts. She won't qualify for a payment over $1,052 at all unless her application has at least one of the compensating factors discussed next. To qualify for a much higher payment, she'll probably need more than one. Otherwise, her maximum payment may be closer to $1,052 than $1,430, whether the application is underwritten manually or with an AUS.

Compensating Factors. As you've seen, the 36% and 28% income ratios are benchmarks for manual underwriters, not strict limits. Both GSEs will buy a manually underwritten loan even though the borrower's income ratios exceed those benchmarks, if there are compensating factors that justify making the loan in spite of the high ratios.

For example, Freddie Mac lists the following as potential compensating factors:

- an excellent credit reputation;
- a large downpayment;
- substantial liquid assets;
- education, job training, or employment history that indicates strong potential for increased earnings;
- short-term income that doesn't count as stable monthly income (because it won't last for three years);
- rent from a relative who will share the home being purchased;
- a demonstrated ability to carry a higher housing expense or a higher debt level than most people can manage; or
- significant energy-efficient features in the home.

Compensating factors:
- Excellent credit
- Large downpayment
- Liquid assets
- Potential for increased earnings
- Short-term income
- Rental income from family
- Ability to carry higher expenses
- Energy-efficient home

The stronger the compensating factors, the higher the income ratios are allowed to be, up to the 45% or 50% limit. Whenever a manually underwritten loan exceeds standard income ratio guidelines based on one or more of these factors, a written justification for the loan approval must be retained in the mortgage file. (That step isn't necessary if the application is approved by an automated underwriting system.)

Factors that Increase Risk. Of course, instead of compensating factors, some loan applications present factors that represent increased risk for the lender. In that situation, income ratios over the standard 36% and/or 28% benchmarks are more likely to be unacceptable. For example, an underwriter (or an AUS) might be less inclined to accept a high debt to income ratio if the loan is an adjustable-rate mortgage or has a high loan-to-value ratio.

Income Analysis for ARMs. The monthly payments for an ARM may increase significantly, sometimes in the first few years of the loan term, and that increases the risk that the borrower will default on the loan. (See the discussion of payment shock in Chapter 6.) Fannie Mae and Freddie Mac generally accept ARMs underwritten using the same income ratios that apply to fixed-rate loans. However, in many cases the lender won't use the loan's actual initial interest rate to qualify an ARM applicant. Instead, a higher "qualifying rate" will be used to calculate the applicant's proposed housing expense. Fannie Mae and Freddie Mac often require lenders to use the note rate plus 2% as the qualifying rate.

To make sure they'll be able to handle payment increases, ARM applicants are commonly qualified using a higher rate than the initial rate

> **Example:** The Conrads have applied for a $210,000 ARM from a lender that's offering an initial interest rate of 5.5% for the first year of the loan term.
>
> To qualify the Conrads, the lender calculates their income ratios using a proposed housing expense based on 7.5% interest (the note rate plus 2%) rather than the 5.5% they'll actually have to pay during the first year if the loan is approved. This means the Conrads will qualify only if their income is sufficient to handle a $1,468 principal and interest payment, as opposed to the $1,192 principal and interest payment they would actually be making during the first year.

That rule doesn't apply to hybrid ARMs that have an initial fixed-rate period longer than five years. For that type of hybrid, the lender will typically qualify the applicant using the note rate, just as if it were a fixed-rate loan.

Available Funds

Lenders must determine whether the applicant has enough money available for the downpayment and closing costs, and also whether there will be any money left over in reserve after closing.

Reserves. The more liquid assets borrowers have in reserve after closing, the more likely it is that they can weather financial emergencies without defaulting on their mortgage. Conventional loan applicants generally should have the equivalent of at least two months of mortgage payments in reserve after making the downpayment and paying all closing costs. Typically, less than that in reserve will weaken an application, while more will strengthen it. And for certain types of loans (such as investor loans), the borrower may be required to have a full six months of reserves on hand at closing.

Conventional borrower should have two months of mortgage payments in reserve

Reserves must be cash or liquid assets that could easily be converted to cash if necessary (for instance, the cash value of a life insurance policy, or the vested portion of a retirement account).

Gift Funds. In regard to the resources that a borrower has available for closing, Fannie Mae and Freddie Mac have some rules concerning the use of gift funds. The donor must be:

- the borrower's relative, fiancé, or domestic partner;
- the borrower's employer;
- a municipality or public agency; or
- a nonprofit religious or community organization.

Gift funds: donor must be a relative, employer, city, or nonprofit organization

Also, for certain loans, the borrower may be required to make a downpayment of at least 5% of the sales price out of her own resources.

> **Example:** Grace Wessel has agreed to buy a house for $425,000. Wessel hopes to qualify for a 90% loan; the loan amount would be $382,500 and the downpayment would be $42,500.
>
> Wessel's mother is willing to give her $30,000 to close the transaction. But the lender requires a 5% downpayment from the borrower's own funds. So Wessel must come up with $21,250 (5% of the sales price) out of her own resources, which means she can only use $21,250 in gift funds for the downpayment. Wessel may use the additional $8,750 gift from her mother for closing costs, however.
>
> If Wessel were trying to obtain a 95% loan, she could not use any gift funds for the downpayment, but she could use them for closing costs.

Gift funds may also count towards a borrower's reserves. However, if a particular loan program imposes a specific reserve requirement, the borrower cannot meet this requirement solely by using gift funds. The borrower must also have some of her own funds left in reserve after closing.

Exercise No. 3

Mike and Barbara Tanaka have recently married and want to buy a home. Mike makes $62,000 a year as a lead engineer for a small electronics company. Barbara makes $4,750 a month as an administrator at a local community college. They have two car payments, one at $317 a month (21 payments left) and the other at $375 a month (13 payments left). They have a personal loan with a remaining balance of $3,400, which requires monthly payments of $250. The Tanakas make three credit card payments every month, with the following minimum payments: $55 a month to a department store, $42 a month to Visa, and $54 a month to MasterCard. Barbara's credit is good; Mike has a few collections on his credit report due to an extended illness and the year of unemployment that resulted. He can provide documentation to explain the credit blemishes, but the mortgage application will have to be manually underwritten.

1. Suppose the Tanakas would like a fixed-rate conventional loan. Applying the standard income ratios, how large a mortgage payment would the Tanakas qualify for?

2. List two or three compensating factors that might allow the Tanakas to qualify for a somewhat larger payment, if these factors were present in their financial situation.

3. Even if there aren't any compensating factors in the Tanakas' financial situation that would lead the lender to accept income ratios higher than the standard limits, what can the Tanakas do to qualify for a larger payment?

Buydown Plans

One of the easiest ways to make a loan more affordable is a **buydown**. In a buydown arrangement, a property seller or a third party pays the lender a lump sum at closing to lower the interest rate on the buyer's loan. The lump sum payment increases the lender's upfront yield on the loan, and in return the lender charges a lower interest rate, which lowers the amount of the borrower's monthly payment. When the buydown is permanent, the lender will evaluate the borrower on the basis of a reduced payment, making it easier to qualify for the loan.

This is the equivalent of paying the lender discount points, but it's called a buydown when the seller or a third party pays the points on the buyer's behalf. Also, a buydown can be arranged even when the lender was quoting a specified interest rate without discount points.

> **Example:** Seaside Savings is offering fixed-rate 30-year loans at the market interest rate, 11%. To help buyers afford financing to purchase her home, Irene Glover is willing to pay for a 2% buydown, which would reduce the quoted interest rate to 9%.

Buydowns are generally used when interest rates are high, as in the example.

A buydown can be permanent or temporary. With a **permanent buydown**, the borrower pays the lower interest rate (and a lower payment) for the entire loan term. With a **temporary buydown**, the interest rate and monthly payment are reduced only during the first years of the loan term.

Permanent Buydowns. If a borrower's interest rate is bought down permanently (for the entire loan term), the buydown reduces the note rate—the interest rate stated in the promissory note.

> **Example:** Bowen needs to borrow $150,000 to buy Sanderson's property. The lender quoted a 12% interest rate for a 30-year fixed-rate loan, and Bowen can't quite afford the loan at that rate. Sanderson offers to buy down Bowen's interest rate to 11%. The lender agrees to make the loan to the buyer at this lower rate if Sanderson pays the lender $9,000.
>
> With this arrangement in place, the promissory note that Bowen signs sets the interest rate at 11%. She will pay 11% interest for the life of the loan. At closing, the lender will withhold $9,000 from the loan funds, reducing Sanderson's proceeds from the sale.

Buydown:
- Seller or third party pays lump sum to lender at closing
- Increases lender's upfront yield
- Lowers buyer's payment
- May make it easier to qualify

By reducing the interest rate from 12% to 11%, the buydown will lower Bowen's mortgage payment by $115 per month, enabling her to qualify for the loan.

$1,543	Payment at quoted 12% rate
− 1,428	Payment at 11% after buydown
$115	Monthly savings due to buydown

The fee the lender charges for a permanent buydown is calculated in terms of points (percentage points) of the loan amount. The number of points required to increase the lender's yield by 1% (and decrease the borrower's interest rate by 1%) varies from one area to another, but as we noted in Chapter 7, lenders in recent years have generally required the payment of four to six points to buy a 1% reduction in the interest rate. To know the exact cost of a permanent buydown, you should ask the lender.

Example: In the example above, the lender charged the seller six points for a 1% buydown.

$150,000	Loan amount
× 6%	Six points
$9,000	Cost of 1% buydown

Temporary Buydowns. A temporary buydown reduces the buyer's monthly payments in the early months or years of the loan term. Temporary buydowns appeal to buyers who feel they can grow into a larger payment, but need time to get established.

There are two types of temporary buydown plans: level payment plans and graduated payment plans.

Temporary buydowns:
- Level payment
- Graduated payment

Level payments. A level payment plan calls for an interest reduction that stays the same throughout the buydown period.

Example: The lender agrees to make a 30-year loan of $185,000 at 13% interest. The property seller buys down the borrower's interest rate to 11% for three years by paying the lender $10,224 at closing.

As shown in Figure 10.2, during the first three years of the loan term the buydown lowers the monthly payment by $284, from $2,046 to $1,762. At the beginning of the fourth year, the payment amount goes up to the unsubsidized level, $2,046, and stays at that level for the remaining 27 years of the loan term.

Graduated payments. A graduated payment buydown plan calls for the largest payment reduction in the first year, with progressively smaller reductions in each subsequent year of the buydown period.

Fig. 10.2 Three-year temporary buydown with level payments

Year	Note Rate	Buydown	Effective Rate	Payment at 13%	Actual Payment	Monthly Subsidy	Annual Subsidy
1	13%	2%	11%	$2,046	$1,762	$284	$3,408
2	13%	2%	11%	$2,046	$1,762	$284	$3,408
3	13%	2%	11%	$2,046	$1,762	$284	$3,408
4	13%	- 0 -	13%	$2,046	$2,046	- 0 -	- 0 -
						Total Buydown: $10,224	

Example: The lender agrees to make a 30-year loan of $185,000 at 13% interest. By paying the lender $10,188 at closing, the seller buys down the borrower's interest rate by 3% the first year, 2% the second year, and 1% the third year. Figure 10.3 shows how the monthly payment will change.

The graduated payment buydown in the example (with the interest rate bought down 3% the first year, 2% the second year, and 1% the third year) is called a 3-2-1 buydown. Probably the most common form of graduated payment buydown is the 2-1 buydown. In a 2-1 buydown, the interest rate is bought down 2% the first year and 1% the second year; the buyer starts paying the note rate in the third year.

Computing the cost of a temporary buydown. As with a permanent buydown, to get the exact cost of a temporary buydown, it's best to ask a lender for a quote. But the cost of a temporary buydown can be computed fairly accurately with a financial calculator.

1. Calculate the principal and interest payment without the buydown, at the full rate of interest the lender is charging.
2. Calculate the payment with the bought-down interest rate.
3. Subtract the bought-down payment from the actual payment and multiply by 12 for the annual buydown amount.

Estimating cost of temporary buydown:
- Calculate difference between unsubsidized and subsidized payments
- Multiply by 12 for annual cost
- Add up annual costs for total cost

Fig. 10.3 Three-year temporary buydown with graduated payments

Year	Note Rate	Buydown	Effective Rate	Payment at 13%	Actual Payment	Monthly Subsidy	Annual Subsidy
1	13%	3%	10%	$2,046	$1,624	$422	$5,064
2	13%	2%	11%	$2,046	$1,762	$284	$3,408
3	13%	1%	12%	$2,046	$1,903	$143	$1,716
4	13%	- 0 -	13%	$2,046	$2,046	- 0 -	- 0 -
						Total Buydown: $10,188	

4. For a level payment buydown, multiply the annual buydown amount by the number of years in the buydown plan.

Example: $203,000 loan with a three-year level payment buydown. The note rate is 11.25%. The bought-down rate is 9.25%.

1. Calculate the monthly principal and interest payment without the buydown: $1,971.66.

2. Calculate the payment with the buydown: $1,670.03.

3. Subtract the bought-down payment from the actual payment and multiply by 12 (months).

$1,971.66	Actual payment
− 1,670.03	Bought-down payment
$301.63	Monthly buydown amount
× 12	Months
$3,619.56	Annual buydown amount

4. Multiply the annual buydown amount by the number of years in the buydown plan.

$3,619.56	Annual buydown amount
× 3	Years in buydown plan
$10,858.68	Total (lump sum required by lender)

A graduated payment buydown is calculated in the same way, except that the amount of each year's buydown has to be calculated separately and then all the annual figures are added together. The sum is the total cost of the graduated payment buydown.

Buydowns and Qualifying Rules. As we said earlier, by lowering the monthly payment, a buydown can make it easier for the buyer to qualify for a loan. With a permanent buydown, the lender uses the bought-down interest rate to calculate the payment, and then determines if the buyer can qualify for that reduced payment. If the seller permanently buys down the loan's interest rate from 12% to 10%, the buyer only has to qualify for a payment at 10% interest.

It isn't that simple with a temporary buydown. Since the buydown is only going to last a few years, the buyer will eventually have to afford the larger payment based on the full note rate. So in many cases, instead of qualifying the buyer at the bought-down rate, the lender uses a higher rate to qualify the buyer.

Fannie Mae and Freddie Mac do not allow a buyer with a temporary buydown to be qualified using the bought-down rate. For

With permanent buydown, lender qualifies buyer at bought-down interest rate

With temporary buydown, lender typically uses note rate instead of bought-down rate to qualify buyer

Fig. 10.4 Limits on contributions from sellers or other interested parties

Contribution Limits for Owner-Occupied Homes	
Loan-to-Value Ratio	*Maximum Contribution*
Over 90%	3%
75.01% to 90%	6%
75% or less	9%

fixed-rate loans, the buyer generally must be qualified based on the note rate. For adjustable-rate loans, each GSE has more complicated rules that vary depending on the terms of the loan.

Many lenders follow other policies of their own in regard to temporary buydowns. When you're handling a transaction in which the parties would like to arrange a temporary buydown, ask the lender what interest rate and what income ratios will be used for qualifying.

Limits on Buydowns and Other Contributions. Fannie Mae and Freddie Mac both limit the amount of the rate reduction for buydowns. For example, Fannie and Freddie limit temporary buydowns to a maximum 3% rate reduction.

Limits also apply to most other contributions the buyer accepts from the seller, or from another interested party, such as the builder or a real estate agent involved in the transaction. These limits are based on a percentage of the property's sales price or appraised value, whichever is less, as shown in Figure 10.4. For example, if the seller agreed to pay closing costs that would ordinarily be paid by the buyer, these limits would apply.

If the seller's contributions exceed these guidelines, the excess contribution must be deducted from the sales price before determining the maximum loan amount.

If seller's contributions exceed limits, excess deducted from sales price in loan amount calculations

Example:

$300,000 sales price; $302,000 appraised value; 90% loan
Maximum contribution: $18,000 (6% of the sales price)

For this transaction, any contribution in excess of $18,000 would be deducted from the sales price, which would result in a lower loan amount. For instance, if the seller were to contribute $19,000, the extra $1,000 would be subtracted from the sales price, and the maximum loan amount would be only $269,100 instead of $270,000.

$300,000   Sales price
−   1,000   Excess contribution
$299,000
×   90%   LTV
$269,100   Loan amount

These limits on contributions from interested parties generally don't apply to contributions from someone who isn't participating in the transaction—for example, the buyer's employer, or a family member.

Exercise No. 4

The housing market is very slow, and Dan Johnson agrees to purchase Morris Callahan's home for $350,000, contingent on obtaining the necessary financing. But Johnson can afford to put only 10% down, and it turns out that he can't quite qualify for the monthly payment on a 90%, 30-year conventional loan at the market interest rate, 8.75%. Callahan offers to permanently buy the interest rate down to 7.75% so that Johnson can qualify for the loan and go through with the purchase.

1. In this market, lenders estimate that it takes about six points to increase the yield on a loan by 1%. Approximately how much would a permanent buydown cost Callahan?

2. With the buydown, Johnson's monthly principal and interest payment would be $2,256.70, compared to $2,478.11 without the buydown. How much could the buydown save Johnson over the life of the loan?

Conventional Low-Downpayment Programs

For many potential home buyers, especially first-time buyers, coming up with enough cash is the biggest challenge in buying a home. They have a steady, reliable income, but they don't have the savings to cover the downpayment and closing costs required for a standard conventional loan. Even the 5% downpayment required for a 95% loan may be beyond their means. Buyers in this situation may want to consider special programs that have reduced cash requirements and allow them to draw on alternative sources for the cash they need.

Features and Requirements

The details of conventional low-downpayment programs vary, but many of them allow a 97% loan-to-value ratio. In some cases, the 3% downpayment must come entirely from the borrower's own funds. In other cases, the downpayment may come partly from an alternative source, but the borrower is still required to make a small minimum contribution (such as 1%) from his own funds. And in some programs, the entire downpayment may come from an alternative source. Alternative sources may also be allowed to contribute to the borrower's closing costs.

Depending on the program, the allowable alternative sources of funds may include the borrower's relative, an employer, a public agency, a nonprofit organization, or a private foundation. More than one source can be tapped to get the necessary amount together. The money can take the form of gifts, grants, or unsecured loans.

Some of these programs don't require the borrower to have any reserves after closing. Others require one or two months' mortgage payments in reserve, but in some cases the reserves may be provided by an alternative source instead of the borrower.

Because Fannie Mae and Freddie Mac both require private mortgage insurance on loans with an LTV above 80%, PMI is usually required. Some low-downpayment programs waive PMI, but this generally occurs only when some other entity assumes first-loss position, such as a program that holds and services the loans for some time before selling them to Fannie or Freddie. (These programs are relatively rare.)

Affordable Housing Programs

Although some conventional low-downpayment programs are open to any prospective home buyer, others are specifically targeted at low- and moderate-income buyers. As a general rule, a buyer can qualify for one of these targeted programs if his stable monthly income does

Affordable housing programs:
- Easier to qualify
- Cash requirements reduced
- Eligibility based on income, property location, or job

not exceed the median income in the metropolitan area in question. (Increased income limits apply in high-cost areas.) To make it easier for low- and moderate-income buyers to qualify, these programs may allow higher income ratios than the usual maximums.

To encourage neighborhood revitalization, some affordable housing programs waive their income limits for buyers who are purchasing homes in low-income or rundown neighborhoods. Thus, a buyer whose income is well above the area median could still qualify for a low-downpayment program targeted at low-income buyers if she's buying a home in a neighborhood that meets the program's standards.

Other conventional low-downpayment programs are offered to specific groups such as teachers, police officers, and firefighters. These programs are intended to enable the borrowers to purchase homes in the urban areas they serve, instead of being priced out of their community.

Lender Contributions

Fannie Mae and Freddie Mac do not allow a lender to contribute any amount whatsoever toward the borrower's downpayment. However, the lender may make a contribution to help cover the borrower's closing costs, within certain limits. Generally, a lender's contribution may not:

- exceed the borrower's total closing costs;
- be used to fund any portion of the downpayment;
- be subject to any repayment requirement or financial obligation apart from the mortgage;
- result in differential pricing in the rate, points, or fees; or
- be passed to the lender from a third party.

Outline: Conventional Financing

I. Conforming and Nonconforming Loans

    A. Conforming loans: loans that comply with Fannie Mae and Freddie Mac underwriting guidelines.

    B. Nonconforming loans can't be sold to either GSE.

II. Conventional Loan Characteristics

    A. Property types and owner-occupancy

        1. Fannie Mae and Freddie Mac purchase residential loans secured by site-built homes, manufactured homes, townhouses, condos, or co-ops.

        2. The loan may be for a principal residence (with up to four units) or a second home (with no more than one unit).

        3. Fannie Mae and Freddie Mac also buy investor loans for properties that will be rented out to tenants; these are underwritten differently.

    B. Loan amounts

        1. Conforming loan limits are set annually, with higher limits in high-cost areas and special limits in Alaska, Guam, Hawaii, and the Virgin Islands.

        2. Jumbo loans exceed the conforming loan limits; they typically have higher interest rates and stricter qualifying standards.

    C. Repayment periods can range from ten to forty years, though the GSEs won't buy loans with terms over thirty years.

    D. Most conventional loans are fully amortized.

    E. Loan-to-value ratios

        1. The traditional loan-to-value ratio (LTV) for conventional loans is 80%, but loans with LTVs up to 97% are available.

        2. Private mortgage insurance is required on loans with LTVs over 80%.

        3. Lenders charge higher interest rates and fees for high-LTV loans and apply stricter qualifying standards.

    F. Loan fees and interest rates

        1. Fannie Mae and Freddie Mac charge lenders risked-based fees called loan-level price adjustments (LLPAs).

        2. Lenders usually increase borrower's interest rate to cover the LLPAs.

        3. Additional LLPAs are charged on riskier loans (such as investor loans or ARMs).

    G. Private mortgage insurance (PMI)

        1. PMI is issued by private companies instead of a government agency; it protects lenders from the greater risk of high-LTV loans.

2. PMI typically covers 25% to 30% of the loan amount.

3. PMI premiums are paid by the borrower, as a flat annual premium, an initial premium plus renewal premiums, or a one-time premium paid at closing or financed over the loan term.

4. PMI must be cancelled at the borrower's request when the loan is paid down to 80% of the property's original value, or automatically when the LTV reaches 78% of the original value.

H. Secondary financing

1. Lenders typically allow secondary financing, regardless of the source, but impose a number of restrictions to reduce the risk of default.

2. Examples of rules concerning secondary financing:

   a. Borrower must have enough income to qualify for the combined payments of the first and second mortgages.

   b. Borrower must make a minimum downpayment (often 5%).

   c. Payments must be regularly scheduled.

   d. Second mortgage can't require a balloon payment until at least five years after closing.

   e. If the first mortgage has variable payments, the second mortgage must have fixed payments.

   f. Second mortgage is not allowed to have negative amortization.

   g. Prepayment penalty on second mortgage may also be prohibited.

3. Piggyback loans: Using secondary financing to avoid private mortgage insurance or the costs and requirements associated with jumbo loans.

III. Qualifying Standards

A. Evaluating risk factors

1. Fannie Mae and Freddie Mac encourage lenders to use automated underwriting, but manual underwriting is still necessary in some cases.

2. AUS generally applies the same standards used in manual underwriting, but sometimes allows greater flexibility.

B. Credit reputation

1. Applicant's credit scores are obtained from the main credit agencies.

   a. One score is selected to use in underwriting (known as the underwriting score, representative score, or indicator score).

   b. Usually it's the lower of two scores, or the middle of three.

2. Good credit score can offset weaknesses in other areas, but a low score may prevent loan approval.

3. When two people apply for loan, a score is selected for each of them; lower score used to determine if loan can be sold to one of the GSEs.

   a. Minimum score for conventional loans in general: 620.

   b. Minimum score for many types of conventional loans: 680.

C. Income analysis

1. Debt to income ratio generally should not exceed 36% for manually underwritten loans, but can be up to 45% with compensating factors. For an AUS loan, 45% or 50% is the top limit.

2. Total monthly obligations include housing expense (PITI) and other recurring obligations: installment debts with more than ten payments remaining, revolving debts, and other debts, such as child support.

3. Housing expense to income ratio: for manually underwritten loans, proposed housing expense (PITI) generally should not exceed 28%.

4. The limits aren't strict maximums; higher ratios may be allowed with compensating factors; the stronger the compensating factors, the higher the income ratios can be, up to the 45% or 50% limit.

5. For ARM applicants, a special qualifying rate (often the note rate plus 2%) may be used to calculate the housing expense and income ratios, instead of the initial rate the borrower will actually pay.

   a. If the ARM is a hybrid with a fixed-rate period longer than five years, the note rate will be used as the qualifying rate.

D. Available funds

1. Gift funds can be used for most of downpayment and closing costs, but borrowers may be required to pay at least 5% of the sales price out of their own resources.

2. For some loans, the borrower may be required to have reserves left over after paying the downpayment and closing costs.

   a. A lender might require borrowers to have two months of mortgage payments in reserve, or even more for a higher-risk loan

   b. Reserves can be an important compensating factor even when not required.

IV. Buydown Plans

A. Buydown lowers interest rate permanently or temporarily.

1. A temporary buydown may have level or graduated payments.

2. Fannie Mae and Freddie Mac limit how much a seller or other interested party can contribute for buyer.

3. A permanent buydown helps the borrower qualify for the loan, because the bought-down rate is used to calculate the housing expense and income ratios.

4. With a temporary buydown, though, the borrower is usually qualified using the note rate or some other rate that is higher than the bought-down interest rate.

V. Conventional Low-Downpayment Programs

    A. These programs typically allow a 97% LTV, and may allow part or all of the downpayment to come from alternative sources instead of the borrower.

    B. Affordable housing programs with eligibility based on income, property location, or job; PMI is typically required.

    C. Lenders can contribute to the borrower's closing costs, within limits, but are generally not allowed to contribute any part of the downpayment.

Key Terms

Conventional loan: An institutional loan that is not insured or guaranteed by a government agency.

Conforming loan: A loan made in accordance with the underwriting criteria of the government-sponsored enterprises (GSEs), Fannie Mae and Freddie Mac, and which therefore can be sold to those entities.

Nonconforming loan: A loan that does not meet the underwriting guidelines set by Fannie Mae and Freddie Mac, and therefore can't be sold to those entities except by special arrangement.

Investor loan: A loan financing the purchase of property that will be rented to tenants rather than owner-occupied.

Jumbo loan: A loan that exceeds the conforming loan limits set annually by the Federal Housing Finance Agency based on national median housing prices.

Loan-to-value ratio (LTV): The relationship between the loan amount and either the sales price or the appraised value of the property (whichever is less), expressed as a percentage.

Loan-level price adjustments (LLPAs): Fees that the GSEs charge the lender when they purchase a conventional loan, based on risk factors such as the borrower's credit score, the loan-to-value ratio, the type of loan, or the type of property. The lender usually passes this cost on to the borrower through a higher interest rate on the loan.

Private mortgage insurance (PMI): Insurance used to diminish the risk of high-LTV conventional loans; provided by a private insurance company (instead of a government agency).

Homeowners Protection Act: A federal law that requires lenders to eliminate private mortgage insurance premiums when the loan-to-value ratio has been paid down and the insurance is no longer needed.

Secondary financing: Money borrowed to pay part of the required downpayment or closing costs for a first loan, when the second loan is secured by the same property that secures the first loan.

Piggyback loan: Secondary financing that is used to avoid the payment of private mortgage insurance by keeping the primary loan's loan-to-value ratio at 80% or less, or used to avoid the higher costs or other requirements for a jumbo loan.

Debt to income ratio: A figure used in loan underwriting to measure the adequacy of a loan applicant's income; it indicates what percentage of her stable monthly income would be required to cover the proposed housing expense and her other recurring obligations.

Housing expense to income ratio: A figure that indicates what percentage of the applicant's stable monthly income would be required to cover the proposed housing expense alone, without other recurring obligations.

Recurring obligations: Financial obligations that a borrower must meet each month in addition to the housing expense, including installment debts, revolving debts, and other obligations. (The recurring obligations plus the housing expense are called the total monthly obligations.)

Buydown: When the seller or a third party pays the lender a lump sum at closing to lower the interest rate charged on the buyer's loan.

Permanent buydown: A buydown that lowers the loan's interest rate for the entire loan term.

Temporary buydown: A buydown that lowers the loan's interest rate for only the first few years of the term; the monthly payments during the buydown period may be level or graduated.

Affordable housing program: A loan program that features easier qualifying standards and lower downpayment requirements, with eligibility limited to buyers who have low or moderate incomes or are purchasing property in a targeted neighborhood.

Chapter Quiz

1. A buydown plan:
   a. helps lower the buyer's initial monthly mortgage payments
   b. may help the buyer qualify for the loan
   c. involves someone other than the borrower paying a lump sum to the lender up front to reduce the interest rate on the loan
   d. All of the above

2. Secondary financing is sometimes used to avoid:
   a. manual underwriting
   b. jumbo loan treatment
   c. most or all documentation requirements
   d. credit scoring

3. Private mortgage insurance is ordinarily required only if the loan-to-value ratio is:
   a. 75% or higher
   b. 90% or higher
   c. over 95%
   d. over 80%

4. Fannie Mae and Freddie Mac will not purchase a conventional loan secured by a:
   a. four-unit residential building, when the borrower will occupy one unit as her principal residence
   b. duplex, when the borrower will rent both units to tenants
   c. manufactured home
   d. None of the above; any of these loans could be purchased by one of the GSEs

5. The Turinos are applying for a conventional loan with a 75% LTV. The maximum allowable debt to income ratio is most likely to be:
   a. 25%
   b. 30%
   c. 33%
   d. 45%

6. Herrera is applying for a conventional loan and her application is being manually underwritten. Her debt to income ratio is 39%. The application will probably be approved only if:
   a. the loan-to-value ratio exceeds 90%
   b. she is making a downpayment of at least 5% out of her own resources
   c. the application presents one or more compensating factors
   d. the lender intends to keep the loan in portfolio instead of selling it on the secondary market

7. Shaw is applying for a conventional loan with an 85% LTV. He has some issues with his documentation, so his loan must be underwritten manually. His credit score is 680 and his stable monthly income is $5,900. His monthly debt payments total $500. In the absence of any compensating factors, what is the maximum monthly mortgage payment he will qualify for?

   a. $1,350
   b. $1,624
   c. $1,652
   d. $2,124

8. A 2-1 buydown plan calls for:

   a. the interest rate to be bought down by 1% for two years
   b. the seller and the broker to buy down the interest rate by 1%
   c. the interest rate to be bought down by 2% the first year and 1% the second year
   d. the interest rate to be bought down by 1% the first year and 2% the second year

9. As a general rule, a conventional lender will take an installment debt into consideration when calculating income ratios:

   a. only if it has more than twelve payments remaining
   b. only if it has more than ten payments remaining
   c. no matter how many payments remain to be made
   d. only if the borrower has a poor credit history

10. For secondary financing used in conjunction with a conventional loan, the primary lender is likely to apply all of the following rules, except:

   a. The second loan may not have a balloon payment due within the first five years of the primary loan's term
   b. The payments on the second loan must be due on a regular schedule
   c. The borrower must have enough stable monthly income to qualify for the combined loan payments
   d. The second loan must provide for a prepayment penalty

Answer Key

1. d.   In a buydown, a seller or third party pays a lump sum to the lender to reduce the loan's interest rate and lower the borrower's payment amount, either permanently or temporarily. A permanent buydown makes it easier for the borrower to qualify for the loan.

2. b.   A buyer can sometimes use secondary financing to keep the primary loan amount within Fannie Mae and Freddie Mac's conforming loan limits, avoiding jumbo loan status and the extra costs and requirements that may entail. This type of secondary financing is often referred to as a piggyback loan.

3. d.   Private mortgage insurance is usually required for loans with an LTV over 80%.

4. d.   Fannie Mae and Freddie Mac can purchase conventional loans secured by a principal residence with up to four units; a single-unit second home; or a residential investor property with up to four units all rented to tenants. It may be a single-family house or other site-built building, a manufactured home, a condominium unit, a cooperative unit, or a townhouse.

5. d.   Automated underwriting is used for most conventional loans, and Freddie Mac's AUS can accept a debt to income ratio no higher than 45%. That's also the maximum debt to income ratio for a manually underwritten loan with compensating factors, such as the Turinos' large downpayment. They won't necessarily qualify for the proposed loan if their debt to income ratio is as high as 45%, but they might.

6. c.   Even when the lender intends to sell the loan to Fannie Mae or Freddie Mac, a conventional loan may be approved in spite of a high debt to income ratio if the application presents one or more compensating factors that offset the extra risk. (A 25% downpayment would certainly be considered a compensating factor, but there are a variety of others, such as an excellent credit reputation. A high loan-to-value ratio would be an additional layer of risk, not a compensating factor.)

7. b.   To calculate the maximum monthly mortgage payment, multiply the stable monthly income by the standard debt to income ratio ($5,900 × .36 = $2,124) and then subtract the monthly debt payments ($2,124 − $500 = $1,624). The payment calculated with the 28% housing expense to income ratio would be $1,652 ($5,900 × .28 = $1,652), but the maximum payment is the lower of the two figures—in this case, $1,624.

8. c.   The 2-1 buydown plan is a temporary buydown where the interest rate is reduced 2% in the first year and 1% in the second year.

9. b.   An installment debt will ordinarily be considered when calculating income ratios only if more than ten months of payments remain to be made. (There's an exception to that rule if the monthly payment amount is very large.)

10. d.   In most cases the primary lender will not allow the second loan to have a prepayment penalty, rather than requiring it to have one. The other rules listed are commonly applied.

Case Study: Conventional Financing

Rick and Teresa Cortina are hoping to buy their first home, and they're going to get pre-approved for financing (by a lender) before they start house shopping in earnest. To give you some insight into the underwriting process, let's consider how much money the Cortinas might be qualified to borrow and how that translates into a suitable price range for their search. Based on the financial information shown below, answer the questions that follow. There are worksheets at the end of the case study that you can use for the calculations.

Current housing expense

The Cortinas have lived in the same rental house for five years; for the past two years, their rent has been $3,450 per month.

Employment

Teresa has been a paralegal at Tarman & Andrews, a law firm, for two and a half years. Rick has been a sales manager at Acme Tire, Inc. for four years.

Income

Rick earns a monthly salary of $2,400, plus commissions. His commissions have averaged $2,985 per month for the past two years. Teresa earns $30.50 per hour for a full-time (40-hour) work week.

Taxes (monthly figures)

Rick's taxes:
- Federal income taxes: $570
- State income taxes: $218
- Social Security/Medicare: $306

Teresa's taxes:
- Federal income taxes: $563
- State income taxes: $212
- Social Security/Medicare: $327

Credit scores from the three major agencies

Rick: 677, 685, 687
Teresa: 746, 750, 752

Assets

- Savings account: $87,000
- Miscellaneous (cars, jewelry, etc.): $63,000

Liabilities (monthly payments)

- Car loan: $417 (30 payments remaining)
- Car loan: $323 (17 payments remaining)
- Installment contract: $183 (15 payments remaining)
- Credit cards: $165 (minimum payments)
- Student loan: $98 (8 payments remaining)
- Student loan: $155 (12 payments remaining)

Interest rates and fees (30-year conventional loans)

In the area where the Cortinas live, lenders are typically charging borrowers with credit histories like theirs the following rates and fees. Assume that the applicable loan-level price adjustment(s) are reflected in these interest rates; they won't be charged separately.

Fixed-rate loans

LTV 90% or less: 5.5% interest
LTV over 90%: 6.0% interest

ARMs

LTV 90% or less: 4.5% interest
LTV over 90%: currently unavailable in the Cortinas' area

Discount points

In the current market, if discount points are paid on either a fixed-rate loan or an ARM, each point reduces the interest rate by one-quarter of one percent (0.25%).

1. Use the "lower of two, middle of three" rule to select a credit score for each of the Cortinas. Which of those two scores will be the indicator score (representative score) for their application?

2. What's their stable monthly income? (Round the answer down to the next dollar.)

3. When the Cortinas apply for preapproval, what's the maximum monthly principal and interest payment they could expect to qualify for in each of the following cases?

   a) They're preapproved for Loan A, a fixed-rate conventional loan with an 80% LTV.

   b) They're preapproved for Loan B, a conventional ARM with a 90% LTV.

   c) They're preapproved for Loan C, a fixed-rate conventional loan with a 95% LTV.

   For each of these loans, first use the 36% debt to income ratio and the 28% housing expense to income ratio to calculate the largest housing expense (the PITI payment) they can qualify for if those two standard ratios are applied. Then, to calculate the maximum principal and interest payment, assume that 15% of their total mortgage payment will go toward property taxes and hazard insurance. If mortgage insurance is required, assume that an additional 10% of their total mortgage payment will be used for that. (These percentages provide only a rough approximation for the purposes of this exercise.)

   Next, just for the sake of comparison, calculate the Cortinas' maximum housing expense by applying a 45% debt to income ratio to their stable monthly income. (Assume that 25% of their total payment will go toward property taxes, hazard insurance, and mortgage insurance.) Also, calculate what their housing expense to income ratio would be with that payment amount. Briefly describe under what circumstances, if any, the Cortinas might qualify for a monthly housing expense that large. (Consider the difference between income ratios applied in manual underwriting and automated underwriting, and also whether compensating factors would make a difference.) Also describe some circumstances that would make it more likely that the Cortinas' maximum payment would be determined by the 36% and 28% income ratios instead.

4. With the maximum principal and interest payment you calculated for Question 3 using the 36% and 28% ratios, the Cortinas could qualify for the maximum loan amounts shown below.

   For each loan, state the interest rate that would be charged, taking any discount points into account. (Refer back to the rates listed at the beginning of the case study; each point reduces the listed rate by 0.25%.)

   Then use the loan-to-value ratio to calculate an estimated house price: the sales price they could afford to pay with the maximum loan amount plus the corresponding minimum downpayment. For example, a $180,000 loan with a 90% LTV and a 10% downpayment would make it possible to buy a $200,000 house: $180,000 ÷ .90 = $200,000.

   a) Loan A: fixed rate, 80% LTV; no discount points will be paid. Maximum loan amount: $397,968

b) Loan B: ARM, 90% LTV; no discount points will be paid. **Maximum loan amount: $410,284**

c) Loan C: fixed rate, 95% LTV; three discount points will be paid. **Maximum loan amount: $376,465**

5. Now calculate how much cash would be needed at closing for each of the transactions in Question 4. Add together the downpayment, origination fee, and any discount points. Use 3% of the sales price as an estimate of the rest of the closing costs; add that to the other amounts. Also add two months of mortgage payments (PITI) as reserves. For each transaction, do the Cortinas have enough cash to qualify?

a) Loan A, the 80% fixed-rate loan, with no discount points. Origination fee: 1.50%

b) Loan B, the 90% ARM, with no discount points. Origination fee: 1.50%

c) Loan C, the 95% fixed-rate loan, with three discount points. Origination fee: 2.00%

6. The Cortinas would rather not get an ARM; they don't want to be faced with interest rate and payment increases down the road. They also don't like the idea of a 95% fixed-rate loan; they'd rather make a larger investment in the property and spend less on loan costs. And the $397,968 fixed-rate loan with an 80% LTV requires too much cash at closing. So the Cortinas are looking for alternatives to the three loans we've been considering.

a) Suppose the Cortinas decide they want to get preapproved for a 90% fixed-rate loan. They'll pay one discount point, so the interest rate will be 0.25% below the ordinary fixed interest rate. How would that loan compare to Loan B in Question 5, the 90% ARM? You can just consider this question in general terms; it's not necessary to do specific calculations.

b) What if the Cortinas apply for an 80% fixed-rate loan (like Loan A in Question 5) but decide to buy a house that costs much less than $497,460? For example, suppose they wanted to buy a house for $400,000. Could they qualify for an 80% fixed-rate loan to make that purchase? (You'll be able to answer this question just by calculating the downpayment and 3% of the sales price for an estimate of closing costs. Calculations involving the monthly payment amount or the loan fees won't be necessary.)

7. Finally, suppose that the Cortinas have found a house they really want to buy. It's priced at $505,000. The sellers just put the property on the market, so they aren't willing to sell it for less than the listing price or negotiate about points or other financing concessions. If the Cortinas apply for a 90% fixed-rate loan at 5.25% interest with one discount point and a 1.5% origination fee, their PITI payment would be $3,137.21 and they'd need about $83,287 in cash (including two months of reserves).

a) What are the Cortinas' income ratios with this PITI payment?

b) Is it possible that the Cortinas could qualify for this loan in spite of those income ratios? Explain why or why not.

c) Are there any aspects of the Cortinas' financial situation that a lender would regard as compensating factors? Refer back to the information about the Cortinas given at the beginning of the case study.

d) On the other hand, are there any risk factors in the Cortinas' situation that might make a lender more reluctant to approve a conventional loan with a debt to income ratio over 36%?

e) Suppose the lender won't approve this loan for the Cortinas because their debt to income ratio and housing expense to income ratio are so high. What are some steps they could take that would reduce those ratios?

Income Qualifying—Conventional Loans
Loan A: Fixed Interest Rate, 80% Loan-to-Value Ratio

Stable Monthly Income

Base salary

Wage earner 1 _____

Wage earner 2 _____

Overtime _____

Commissions _____

Bonuses _____

Other + _____

Total _____

Recurring Obligations

Car loans _____

Credit cards _____

Student loans _____

Other debts _____

Child support _____

Alimony _____

Other + _____

Total _____

Debt to Income Ratio

_____ Stable monthly income

_____ x .36 Maximum ratio (36%)

_____ Maximum obligations

− _____ Recurring obligations

_____ Maximum mortgage payment (PITI) under debt to income ratio

Housing Expense to Income Ratio

_____ Stable monthly income

_____ x .28 Maximum ratio (28%)

_____ Maximum mortgage payment (PITI) under housing expense ratio

Maximum Mortgage Payment (PITI) _____

_____ Maximum PITI payment

_____ ÷ 1.15 15% for taxes and hazard insurance

_____ Maximum principal and interest payment

Interest rate _____

Maximum Loan Amount _____

_____ Maximum loan amount

_____ ÷ .80 Loan-to-value ratio (80%)

_____ Sales price

Sales Price _____

Income Qualifying—Conventional Loans
Loan B: Adjustable Interest Rate, 90% Loan-to-Value Ratio

Stable Monthly Income

Base salary

    Wage earner 1 _____

    Wage earner 2 _____

Overtime _____

Commissions _____

Bonuses _____

Other   + _____

Total _____

Recurring Obligations

Car loans _____

Credit cards _____

Student loans _____

Other debts _____

Child support _____

Alimony _____

Other   + _____

Total _____

Debt to Income Ratio

_____   Stable monthly income

_____ x .36   Maximum ratio (36%)

_____   Maximum obligations

– _____   Recurring obligations

_____   Maximum mortgage payment (PITI) under debt to income ratio

Housing Expense to Income Ratio

_____   Stable monthly income

_____ x .28   Maximum ratio (28%)

_____   Maximum mortgage payment (PITI) under housing expense ratio

Maximum Mortgage Payment (PITI) _____

_____   Maximum PITI payment

_____ ÷ 1.25   25% for taxes, hazard insurance, and PMI

_____   Maximum principal and interest payment

Interest rate _____

Maximum Loan Amount _____

_____   Maximum loan amount

_____ ÷ .90   Loan-to-value ratio (90%)

_____   Sales price

Sales Price _____

Income Qualifying—Conventional Loans
Loan C: Fixed Interest Rate, 95% Loan-to-Value Ratio

Stable Monthly Income

Base salary

    Wage earner 1 _____

    Wage earner 2 _____

Overtime _____

Commissions _____

Bonuses _____

Other   + _____

Total _____

Recurring Obligations

Car loans _____

Credit cards _____

Student loans _____

Other debts _____

Child support _____

Alimony _____

Other   + _____

Total _____

Debt to Income Ratio

_____   Stable monthly income

_____ x .36   Maximum ratio (36%)

_____   Maximum obligations

_____ −   Recurring obligations

_____   Maximum mortgage payment (PITI) under debt to income ratio

Housing Expense to Income Ratio

_____   Stable monthly income

_____ x .28   Maximum ratio (28%)

_____   Maximum mortgage payment (PITI) under housing expense ratio

Maximum Mortgage Payment (PITI) _____

_____   Maximum PITI payment

_____ ÷ 1.25   25% for taxes, hazard insurance, and PMI

_____   Maximum principal and interest payment

Interest rate _____

Maximum Loan Amount _____

_____   Maximum loan amount

_____ ÷ .95   Loan-to-value ratio (95%)

_____   Sales price

Sales Price _____

Chapter 11

FHA-Insured Loans

Overview of FHA Loans

- FHA mortgage insurance
- Role of FHA loans
- FHA loan programs

Rules for FHA-Insured Transactions

- Owner-occupancy requirement
- Local maximum loan amounts
- Maximum loan-to-value ratios
- Minimum cash investment
- Closing costs and loan charges
- Interested party contributions
- Secondary financing
- Property flipping prevention rules
- Assumption

FHA Insurance Premiums

- Upfront premium
- Annual premiums

FHA Underwriting Standards

- Credit reputation
- Income analysis
- Assets for closing

FHA Rehabilitation Loans and Reverse Mortgages

Introduction

In Chapter 10 we discussed conventional loans: institutional loans that are not insured or guaranteed by a government agency. Now we'll look at institutional loans that have government backing.

The federal government has two major home financing programs: the FHA-insured loan program and the VA-guaranteed loan program. These programs were established to encourage residential lending and make housing more affordable, and they are available to eligible home buyers throughout the United States. This chapter covers the FHA program; we'll discuss VA-guaranteed loans in Chapter 12.

There are other federal home financing programs, such as the Rural Housing Service loan program, but those are much more limited in scope than the FHA and VA programs. Also, many state, county, and city governments offer financing programs for their own residents. These local options are sometimes called "bond programs." Although we're only going to cover the two main federal programs here, you may want to take the time to find out whether there are other government-sponsored financing programs available to home buyers in your area.

An Overview of FHA Loans

The **Federal Housing Administration (FHA)** was created by Congress in 1934, during the Great Depression, with the passage of the National Housing Act. The purpose of the act, and of the FHA, was to generate new jobs through increased construction activity, to exert a stabilizing influence on the mortgage market, and to promote the financing, repair, improvement, and sale of residential real estate nationwide.

FHA:
• Insures loans
• Does not make loans itself

Today the FHA is part of the **Department of Housing and Urban Development (HUD)**. The FHA's primary function is to insure mortgage loans; lenders who make loans through its programs are compensated for losses that result from borrower default. The FHA does not build homes or make loans.

FHA Mortgage Insurance

The FHA's insurance program, the Mutual Mortgage Insurance Plan, is funded with premiums paid by FHA borrowers. Under the plan, lenders who have been approved by the FHA to make insured loans either submit applications from prospective borrowers to the local FHA office for approval or, if authorized by the FHA to do so, perform the underwriting functions themselves. (Note that prospective borrowers always apply to an FHA-approved lender, not to the FHA itself.)

Lenders who are authorized to underwrite their own FHA loan applications are called **direct endorsement lenders**. Direct endorsement lenders are responsible for the entire loan origination process, from application processing through loan approval. After a direct endorsement lender has approved a loan, it may be required to submit an application for mortgage insurance to the FHA, or it may be authorized to close the transaction without any prior review by the FHA.

Direct endorsement lenders: lenders authorized to handle entire origination process for FHA loans

As the insurer, the FHA is liable to the lender for the full amount of any losses resulting from default. After the FHA has compensated the lender, however, the borrower must reimburse the federal government for the amount paid. This liability is considered a delinquent federal debt, which means that the government can collect it out of any federal income tax refund owed to the borrower, or garnish any pay the borrower receives from the federal government. Unless the borrower enters into an agreement to repay the debt, he won't be eligible for another FHA-insured loan (or for a VA-guaranteed loan).

If FHA borrower defaults:
- FHA reimburses lender for full amount of loss
- Borrower required to repay FHA

In exchange for insuring loans, the FHA requires lenders to follow certain procedures and dictates many of the terms and conditions on which the loans are made. Lenders must comply with FHA regulations, which have the force and effect of law. If the FHA pays a lender's claim after a borrower defaults, and it's later determined that the loan didn't actually meet FHA standards, the lender can be required to reimburse the government. The lender may also lose its authorization to make FHA loans and could face prosecution for fraud.

The Role of FHA Loans

FHA-insured loans are designed to help people with low or moderate incomes buy homes. The program doesn't have income restrictions, so eligibility isn't limited to borrowers whose incomes are under a certain limit. But it does have restrictions on loan amounts, and the maximum loan amounts are, in many areas, only enough to finance comparatively modest homes. In addition, the FHA has always

FHA-insured loans are designed for low- and moderate-income buyers had low downpayment requirements, lenient underwriting standards, and other policies that help first-time buyers and others who might otherwise have difficulty affording a home.

For much of the twentieth century, FHA loans were the main financing option for home buyers who didn't have a lot of savings or a substantial income. But in the first years of this century, during the subprime boom, buyers lost interest in FHA loans. Conventional underwriting standards were loosened, and buyers with very little cash for closing could get conventional loans. At the same time, home prices increased so dramatically in some parts of the country that FHA loans were no longer useful there; the maximum loan amount wasn't enough to finance the purchase of even a modest home.

These developments led to a sharp reduction in the use of FHA programs. For example, FHA loans financed about 10% of home purchases in the U.S. in fiscal year 2001, but less than 3% in 2006.

However, after the subprime boom turned into the subprime crisis, low-downpayment conventional loans became much harder to get. Also, FHA maximum loan amounts for high-cost areas were increased. As a result, buyers with tight budgets and limited funds for a downpayment once again began turning to FHA-insured loans.

FHA Loan Programs

FHA financing includes several specific loan programs that address different needs. These programs are commonly referred to by their section numbers, which are taken from the numbered provisions in the National Housing Act. Here are the FHA programs that are of the most interest to the average home buyer or owner:

Most FHA loans are 203(b) loans

- **Section 203(b): Standard FHA Loans.** The 203(b) program is the basic FHA mortgage insurance program; it accounts for a substantial majority of all FHA-insured loans. A loan made through the 203(b) program can be used to purchase or refinance a residential property with up to four dwelling units. The property must be the borrower's principal residence. The 203(b) program is our primary focus in this chapter.
- **Section 203(k): Rehabilitation Loans.** The 203(k) program insures loans that are used to purchase (or refinance) and then

rehabilitate "fixer-uppers." We'll discuss 203(k) loans in more detail later in the chapter.

FHA loan programs:
- 203(b): standard FHA loans
- 203(k): rehab loans
- 234(c): condos
- 251: ARMs
- 255: reverse mortgages

- **Section 234(c): Condominium Units.** The 234(c) program covers the purchase or refinancing of individual condominium units. It works in tandem with other programs, such as 203(b).

  Only units in FHA-approved condominium projects are eligible for FHA financing. Developers can apply for approval when a project is built or converted, but approval can also be obtained later on. The project must meet a variety of FHA guidelines. For example, at least 50% of the units must be owner-occupied, and the project must have adequate insurance coverage and funds in reserve. (The owner-occupancy requirement shrinks to 35% if additional conditions are met.)

- **Section 251: ARMs.** Section 251 provides mortgage insurance for adjustable-rate loans. It's administered in conjunction with either the 203(b) or the 203(k) program, so an FHA ARM may be used to purchase, refinance, or rehabilitate a principal residence with up to four units. The loan must have a 30-year term; the FHA won't insure ARMs with shorter terms. Annual and life-of-the-loan interest rate caps are required.

  As a general rule, the applicant for an FHA ARM is qualified using the loan's initial interest rate. There's an exception if it's a one-year ARM with a loan-to-value ratio of 95% or above; in that case, the applicant must be qualified using the initial rate plus 1%—in other words, the maximum possible second-year interest rate. Also note that temporary buydowns are not allowed with FHA ARMs.

- **Section 255: Reverse Mortgages (HECMs).** Section 255 provides FHA insurance for home equity conversion mortgages (HECMs), also known as reverse mortgages (see Chapter 5). We'll take a closer look at the HECM program later in the chapter.

Again, for the most part we'll be discussing the rules for standard FHA purchase loans made through the 203(b) program. Many of those rules also apply to the other programs, which are largely based on 203(b).

Rules for FHA-Insured Transactions

When a home purchase is financed with an FHA-insured loan, the transaction must comply with the FHA's rules concerning owner-occupancy, loan amount, borrower's cash investment, interested party contributions, secondary financing, property flipping, and assumption.

Owner-Occupancy Requirement

General rule: FHA borrower must intend to occupy home as principal residence

FHA borrowers must intend to occupy the property they're buying, generally as their principal residence. If the property has more than one dwelling unit, the borrower must intend to use one of the units as her principal residence.

A person can have only one principal residence at a time, so this requirement means that a borrower can ordinarily have only one FHA loan outstanding at a time. There are limited exceptions for situations involving relocation, divorce, or an increase in family size.

Secondary Residences. A secondary residence is a home the borrower occupies less than 50% of the time. An FHA loan can be used to buy a secondary residence only if denial of the loan would cause undue hardship. The secondary residence must be needed for employment-related reasons; it can't be a vacation home. And the borrower must show that there is no suitable rental housing available in the area.

Investor Loans. Although it did so at one time, the FHA generally does not insure investor loans—loans that allow the borrower to buy the property merely as an investment, not as a home. The FHA may make an exception for an investor who wants to purchase a property that HUD owns as a result of foreclosure.

Local Maximum Loan Amounts

Local maximum loan amount:
- Based on local median housing costs
- May change annually

As we said earlier, the FHA limits the size of loans that it will insure. FHA maximum loan amounts are based on local median house prices, so they vary from one area to another. Each area has local maximums for one-, two-, three-, and four-unit residences. The maximums are higher in areas where home prices are above average. All of these local limits are subject to annual adjustments, to reflect changes in housing costs.

Fig. 11.1 Example illustrating the FHA's rules for local maximum loan amounts

Location	Median House Price	2018 Maximum FHA Loan for Single-family Homes
Lowood	$172,000	$294,515 (basic maximum)
Anytown	$255,000	$294,515 (basic maximum)
Midville	$314,700	$361,905 (115% of median price)
Highline	$529,300	$608,695 (115% of median price)
Goldenvale	$812,600	$679,650 (ceiling for high-cost areas)

In 2018, the FHA's basic maximum loan amount for a one-unit property is $294,515. This maximum applies anywhere in the country that doesn't qualify as a high-cost area.

In a high-cost area, the maximum loan amount is generally 115% of the area median house price. Regardless of local prices, however, the maximum loan amount in any area can't exceed an upper limit that the FHA refers to as "the ceiling." (By analogy, the basic maximum mentioned above is sometimes called "the floor.")

In 2018, the FHA ceiling for one-unit properties in high-cost areas is $679,650. (A higher ceiling applies in parts of Alaska, Hawaii, Guam, and the Virgin Islands.)

Figure 11.1 shows how the rules for local maximum loan amounts would apply to hypothetical places with various median housing costs.

HUD usually sets maximum loan amounts on a county-by-county basis. As a result, if a county includes a large city where housing is expensive, the entire county is treated as a high-cost area, even if housing in its rural sections is relatively inexpensive. Sometimes an extensive metropolitan area will be treated as a single high-cost area, even if it overlaps county lines.

Check with a local lender for the current FHA maximum loan amount in your community. Remember that the limit may be adjusted annually to reflect changes in the cost of housing. To get the maximum loan amount for a particular area increased, lenders or other interested parties can submit a request to HUD with recent sales price data supporting an increase.

Maximum Loan-to-Value Ratios

The maximum loan amount for a particular transaction is determined not just by the FHA loan limit for the local area, but also by the FHA's rules concerning loan-to-value ratios.

The maximum loan-to-value ratio for an FHA loan depends on the borrower's credit score. If the borrower's credit score is 580 or above, the maximum LTV is 96.5%. If his score is 500 to 579, the maximum LTV is 90%. (Someone with a score below 500 isn't eligible for an FHA loan; see the discussion of credit scores later in the chapter.) Those are the general rules; a lower maximum LTV will apply in certain types of transactions—for example, in some sales between family members.

Maximum LTV for FHA loan:
- 96.5% if credit score is 580 or higher
- 90% if credit score is 500 to 579

Minimum Cash Investment

The difference between the maximum loan amount for the transaction and the property's appraised value or sales price (whichever is less) is called the borrower's **minimum cash investment**—that's the FHA's term for the downpayment required on their loans. In a transaction with maximum FHA financing (a 96.5% loan), the borrower must make a downpayment of at least 3.5%.

The borrower cannot use secondary financing from the seller or a lender for the minimum cash investment, but may be allowed to use funds provided by a family member or certain other sources. We'll discuss these rules later in this chapter.

Exercise No. 1

Jerry Fletcher has agreed to pay $627,200 for a single-family home that he will occupy as his principal residence. It has been appraised at $627,800. Fletcher would like to finance the transaction with an FHA loan. He lives in a high-cost county where the area median house price is $540,000, and his credit score is 615.

1. What is the maximum FHA loan amount for a one-unit property in Fletcher's area? (Refer to the chart in Figure 11.1.)

2. What is the maximum FHA loan amount for Fletcher's transaction?

3. If Fletcher gets the maximum allowable FHA loan for this purchase, how much will the required minimum cash investment be?

Closing Costs and Loan Charges

FHA borrowers are permitted to pay whatever closing costs are considered "customary and reasonable" in their area. A lender may not charge an FHA borrower more for a service than it actually cost the lender.

The loan charges (points and other lender fees) for an FHA loan generally may not exceed a limit set in the Truth in Lending Act. For most FHA loans, the limit is 3% of the loan amount. Note that prepayment penalties are prohibited; an FHA loan may be paid off at any time without penalty.

FHA borrowers may pay customary and reasonable closing costs

Loan charges are subject to TILA limit

No prepayment penalties on FHA loans

Interested Party Contributions

As you know, sometimes a seller pays for a buydown, or pays all or part of the buyer's closing costs, or makes some other type of financial contribution to help the buyer afford the property. In Chapter 10 we explained that there are limits on these types of contributions in transactions financed with conventional loans. Similar limits apply in FHA transactions, to prevent the parties from using contributions to defeat the maximum LTV and minimum cash investment rules.

The FHA limits interested party contributions to 6% of the sales price. It's an interested party contribution if the seller or another interested party (such as a real estate agent or a developer) pays for:

- the origination fee,
- any discount points,

Seller or other interested party can contribute up to 6% of sales price toward buyer's loan fees and other closing costs

- a temporary or permanent buydown,
- the buyer's mortgage interest,
- the upfront premium for the FHA mortgage insurance, or
- other closing costs customarily paid by the buyer.

Interested party contributions that exceed the 6% limit are treated as "inducements to purchase." So are interested party contributions that exceed the borrower's actual loan fees and closing costs for the transaction. For instance, the FHA considers it to be an inducement to purchase if the seller or another interested party:

If interested party contributions exceed 6% of sales price, excess is inducement to purchase

- gives the buyer a decorating or repair allowance;
- pays for the buyer's moving expenses;
- pays the real estate agent's commission on the sale of the buyer's current home; or
- gives the buyer items of personal property other than those that are customarily included in the sale of a home.

Inducements to purchase are subtracted from sales price before maximum LTV is applied

The total value of any inducements to purchase is subtracted from the property's sales price before the maximum loan-to-value ratio is applied. This reduces the loan amount available to the FHA borrower.

Secondary Financing with FHA Loans

As you'll recall, secondary financing refers to a loan secured by a second mortgage against the same property that is being purchased with a first mortgage. The rules concerning secondary financing in conjunction with an FHA loan depend on whether the secondary financing is being used for the minimum cash investment, or simply as a supplement to make up the permitted maximum loan amount.

Secondary financing from the seller or a lender can't be used for FHA minimum cash investment

Secondary Financing and the Minimum Cash Investment. An FHA borrower generally is not allowed to use secondary financing from the seller, another interested party, or an institutional lender to pay the required minimum cash investment. However, secondary financing may be used to cover the minimum cash investment if the loan is provided by a member of the borrower's family (a child, parent, grandparent, or other close relation of the borrower or of the borrower's spouse).

Secondary financing from a family member or government agency may be used for minimum cash investment

When a family member provides this kind of secondary financing, the total financing (the FHA base loan plus the second loan) can't exceed the property's value or sales price, whichever is less. If the secondary financing calls for regular installment payments, the combined payments for the FHA loan and the secondary financing can't exceed the borrower's ability to pay. (In other words, the borrower is qualified based on the total of both payments.) The secondary financing can't require a balloon payment within ten years after closing or impose a prepayment penalty.

Alternatively, a government agency may provide an FHA borrower with secondary financing to cover the minimum cash investment. Again, various restrictions apply.

Secondary Financing and the Loan Amount. FHA borrowers are permitted to use secondary financing to make up part of the maximum loan amount (as opposed to the minimum cash investment). This type of secondary financing can come from anyone; it doesn't have to be a family member or a government agency.

When secondary financing is used for part of the loan amount, the following conditions usually must be met:

FHA rules for secondary financing from seller or lender:
- Not for minimum cash investment
- Combined loans can't exceed maximum LTV
- Borrower must qualify for combined payment
- Balloon payment allowed only after 10 years
- No prepayment penalty

1. The combined loan amount (the first and second loans together) may not exceed the local FHA loan limit or the maximum loan-to-value ratio for the transaction.

2. The combined payments for the first mortgage and the second mortgage may not exceed the borrower's ability to pay.

3. If the second loan has periodic installment payments, the payments must be collected on a monthly basis. Each payment must be substantially the same amount as the others.

4. The second loan can't have a balloon payment due sooner than ten years after closing.

5. The second loan may not include a prepayment penalty (although the borrower may be required to give the second lender 30 days' notice before prepaying).

Since the borrower will still have to come up with the same cash investment, why would anyone choose this arrangement? When market interest rates are high, a seller might be willing to offer a second mortgage at a lower rate than the FHA first mortgage (see Chapter 13). That would make the total payments on the two loans less than the payment on an FHA-insured mortgage for the full loan amount. In a marginal case, this might benefit a buyer whose income would otherwise be insufficient to qualify for an FHA loan.

Property Flipping Prevention Rules

Property flipping refers to reselling a property for a substantial profit shortly after purchasing it. This is considered a predatory practice when an appraiser, a lender, a mortgage broker, and/or a real estate agent collude to resell a home to an unsophisticated buyer at an inflated price. (See Chapter 14.) The FHA has rules designed to prevent FHA loans from being used to take advantage of buyers in this way. Here's a summary of the rules:

FHA's property flipping rules:
• Seller must own property for at least 90 days before resale
• Second appraisal required if home resold within 180 days for double the price the seller paid

1. An FHA loan can't be used to finance a purchase unless more than 90 days have elapsed since the seller bought the property. (The days are counted from the closing date of the previous transaction to the date of the purchase agreement for the current transaction.)

2. If the seller bought the home within the previous 91 to 180 days and the resale price is 100% or more above what the seller paid, the FHA requires the lender to obtain a second appraisal from a different appraiser. If the second appraiser's value estimate is more than 5% lower than the first appraiser's estimate, the lower value must be used. The borrower can't be charged for the second appraisal.

There are several exemptions from these rules. For example, they don't apply if the home is being sold by an employer or a relocation company that acquired it when the previous owner relocated for employment reasons. Also exempt are sales of inherited property, sales of newly built homes, sales of homes in federal disaster areas, sales by various government agencies, and certain other types of transactions.

Assumption of FHA Loans

Lender evaluates new buyer's creditworthiness before allowing assumption of FHA loan

FHA loans contain due-on-sale clauses, and various limitations on assumption apply. Generally, the buyer must intend to occupy the property as his primary residence. Also, the lender must evaluate the creditworthiness of the buyer before agreeing to the assumption. This evaluation is very similar to the process of qualifying a buyer for a new FHA loan, except that a minimum cash investment is not required. If the buyer assuming the loan is creditworthy, the lender is required to release the original borrower from liability.

Exercise No. 2

Alison Lee is buying a house with an FHA loan; her credit score is 720. The property's appraised value is the same as the sales price, $170,000. In addition to the minimum cash investment, Lee will pay closing costs and prepaid expenses totaling $12,700.

1. Suppose the seller contributes $12,000 to help Lee cover the costs of the transaction. How will that affect Lee's FHA loan amount?

2. Suppose instead that Lee's parents are willing to loan her $15,000 for her purchase. If their loan would be secured by a second mortgage on the house Lee is buying, how would that affect Lee's FHA loan? Would she still have to make the minimum cash investment out of her own funds?

3. It's July 1. Lee and the seller signed their purchase agreement on June 20. Now the lender has discovered that the seller has only owned the property since April 12. How will this information affect Lee's FHA loan?

FHA Insurance Premiums

Mortgage insurance is required on every FHA loan, regardless of the loan-to-value ratio. The premiums for FHA mortgage insurance are referred to as **MMI** (mutual mortgage insurance) or **MIP** (mortgage

FHA insurance premiums:
- Upfront (one-time) MIP
- Annual premiums

Upfront MIP
- Paid in cash, or financed
- Percentage of base loan amount

insurance premiums). For most programs, an FHA borrower must pay both an upfront premium and annual premiums, as described below.

Upfront MIP

The upfront mortgage insurance premium (UFMIP) is also called the one-time mortgage insurance premium (OTMIP). For almost all purchase loans, the UFMIP is currently 1.75% of the loan amount.

Example: John Rubino is buying a house with a $350,280 FHA loan. His upfront premium will be $6,129.90.

$350,280	Loan amount
× .0175	Premium percentage
$6,129.90	UFMIP

Paying the UFMIP. As the name suggests, the upfront premium may be paid up front—in other words, at closing, before the loan term begins—by either the borrower or the seller. Or, despite the name, the upfront premium can be financed over the loan term instead. In that case, the amount of the premium is added to the base loan amount. (The base loan amount is simply the loan amount excluding the upfront premium.)

Example: Rubino has chosen to finance his upfront MIP instead of paying it in cash at closing.

$350,280.00	Base loan amount
+ 6,129.90	UFMIP
$356,409.90	Total amount financed

However, the total amount financed (or the base loan amount, if the upfront premium is paid in cash) is rounded down to the next dollar. So if the base loan and the UFMIP add up to $356,409.90, the total amount financed will be rounded down to $356,409.

When the upfront premium is financed, the borrower's monthly payment amount is increased so that the total amount financed, plus interest on the total, will be paid off by the end of the loan term.

Financed UFMIP and loan amount. When the local loan amount limits and maximum LTV rules are applied to a transaction, the financed upfront premium is not considered part of the loan amount. The borrower can borrow the maximum loan amount allowed plus the full amount of the UFMIP.

Base loan
+ Financed UFMIP
Total amount financed

The loan-to-value ratio for an FHA loan is calculated by dividing the base loan amount (not including any financed UFMIP) by the sales price or appraised value, whichever is less.

Annual Premiums

In addition to the upfront premium, most FHA borrowers are required to pay annual premiums (also called periodic premiums). One-twelfth of each year's premium is added to the borrower's monthly payment.

The annual premium ranges from 0.45% to 1.05% of the loan balance (not including any financed UFMIP), depending on the original loan amount, the loan term, and the loan-to-value ratio. (Higher premiums are charged for larger loan amounts, longer loan terms, and higher LTVs.)

Duration of Annual MIP. How long an FHA borrower is required to pay the annual premium depends in part on when the loan was made, because the FHA's cancellation rules have changed more than once. For loans closed since June 2013, if the original LTV was 90% or less, the annual MIP will be canceled after 11 years (the insurance policy itself remains in effect, though). If the original LTV was over 90%, the annual MIP must be paid for the life of the loan.

Exercise No. 3

Diane Skillin is buying a house for $374,000, and she's applying for a 30-year FHA loan. The house is in an area where the maximum FHA loan amount for a single-family home is $362,900. The appraised value of the property is $373,000. Skillin's credit score is 700.

1. Assuming that Skillin is going to get the largest FHA loan she can, calculate her upfront premium amount for this transaction. Also, for how many years will Skillin be required to pay an annual premium on her loan?

2. If Skillin finances the upfront premium, what will the total amount financed be? Does it matter that the total amount financed exceeds the maximum FHA loan amount for the area where the property is located?

FHA Underwriting Standards

As with any institutional mortgage loan, the underwriting for an FHA-insured loan involves analysis of the applicant's credit reputation, income, and net worth (see Chapter 8). But the FHA's underwriting standards are less strict than the Fannie Mae/Freddie Mac standards for conventional loans, which were described in Chapter 10. The FHA standards make it easier for low- and moderate-income home buyers to qualify for a mortgage.

FHA underwriting standards are less strict than conventional standards

Credit Reputation

The evaluation of an FHA loan applicant's credit reputation is based on his credit report and credit scores, unless the applicant has no established credit history (see below). Mediocre credit scores won't necessarily rule out loan approval, but the FHA does set a lower limit: an applicant whose credit score is below 500 isn't eligible for an FHA loan. (That's not a very high hurdle to clear, however; in comparison, Fannie Mae's lower limit is 620.) Also, as we mentioned earlier, borrowers with a credit score between 500 and 579 are not eligible for maximum FHA financing; for them, the maximum loan-to-value ratio is 90% instead of 96.5%.

Minimum credit score for FHA loan: 500

If the three main credit reporting agencies provide different scores for an applicant, the underwriter must select one score (known as the "decision credit score") to use. The FHA has essentially the same rules as Fannie Mae and Freddie Mac for making this selection: the middle of three scores is used, or the lower of two. When two or more people are applying for an FHA loan together, one score is selected

Decision credit score:
• Middle of three scores
• Lower of two scores

for each applicant, and the lowest of those scores will be used as the decision credit score.

Although most prospective borrowers have an established credit history, some do not. For example, low-income first-time buyers may never have used credit before; the same may be true of younger buyers or recent immigrants to the United States. As part of its efforts to help underserved borrowers, the FHA has issued detailed rules for "nontraditional credit analysis." These rules allow a lender to manually underwrite an FHA loan application even when a standard credit report and credit scores aren't available. For example, the underwriter may ask the applicant to provide documentation showing how reliably he has paid rent, utility bills, or other obligations over the past 12 months.

Nontraditional credit analysis allowed for applicant with no credit report or credit scores

Income Analysis

The income analysis for an FHA loan is based on the applicant's monthly **effective income**, which is basically the same thing as stable monthly income (see Chapter 8). The FHA defines effective income as the applicant's gross income from all sources that are reasonably likely to continue for the first three years of the loan term.

Effective income: gross income that's reasonably likely to continue for three years

The underwriter applies two income ratios to determine the adequacy of the applicant's effective income: a debt to income ratio and a housing expense to income ratio. (The FHA's official term for the debt to income ratio is "total fixed payment to effective income ratio.") As a general rule, an FHA borrower's debt to income ratio should not exceed 43%. In addition, the housing expense to income ratio should not exceed 31%. The limits are increased to 45% and 33% if the house that the applicant wants to buy qualifies as an energy-efficient home (EEH).

FHA income ratios:
- 43% debt to income ratio
- 31% housing expense to income ratio
- 45% and 33% if EEH

The applicant's proposed housing expense (which is used in both income ratios) includes principal and interest (based on the total amount financed), property taxes, hazard insurance, one-twelfth of the annual premium for the FHA mortgage insurance, and any dues owed to a homeowners association.

To calculate the debt to income ratio, the proposed housing expense is added to the applicant's other monthly obligations, sometimes referred to as recurring liabilities or recurring charges. This includes the monthly payment on any installment debt with ten or more payments remaining. (Debts with fewer than ten remaining payments

Recurring charges:
- Installment debts with 10 or more payments remaining
- Revolving credit accounts
- Alimony or child support

will also be considered if the monthly payments for all such debts add up to more than 5% of the applicant's gross monthly income.) For revolving credit (credit cards and charge accounts), the minimum monthly payment is included. Alimony and child support payments are also counted.

Example: Helen Crowder wants to buy a home using FHA financing. In the area where she lives, the maximum FHA loan amount is $294,515 and lenders are generally charging about 5.5% interest for 30-year fixed-rate FHA loans. She'd like to get preapproved for the maximum loan amount in her area. The monthly payment (including principal, interest, taxes, hazard insurance, and mortgage insurance) for a loan that size would be approximately $1,923.

Crowder's monthly salary is $4,680. Her ex-husband reliably sends her a child support payment each month for their four-year-old daughter. The child support is tax-exempt, so the lender "grosses up" the payment, and concludes that it's the equivalent of $1,200 in taxable income. Thus, Crowder's effective income is $5,880.

Aside from her housing expense, Crowder has to make the following payments every month:

$253	Car payment (11 payments remaining)
205	Student loan (63 payments remaining)
65	Furniture store payment (15 payments remaining)
29	Minimum MasterCard payment
55	Minimum Visa payment
+ 60	Minimum payment on department store credit card
$667	Total recurring charges

To calculate Crowder's debt to income ratio, first add the proposed housing expense to her recurring charges to determine her total obligations. Then divide that figure by her effective income.

$1,923	Proposed housing expense
+ 667	Recurring charges
$2,590	Total obligations

$2,590	Total obligations
÷ 5,880	Effective income
0.4404	Debt to income ratio (44%)

With the $1,923 proposed monthly payment, Crowder's housing expense to income ratio would be approximately 33%:

$1,923	Proposed housing expense
÷ 5,880	Effective income
0.3270	Housing expense to income ratio (33%)

So with the maximum loan amount and a $1,923 monthly payment, both of Crowder's income ratios would slightly exceed the FHA's usual limits (43% and 31%).

The applicant in the example ordinarily would not qualify for the proposed loan. However, she will qualify for the loan if the house she decides to buy is an energy-efficient home. In that case, as we said, a lender could accept income ratios of 45% and 33%.

The FHA will also permit higher ratios if the applicant's credit score is 580 or above and there are compensating factors that reduce the risk of default. This can make a big difference; with certain combinations of compensating factors, a debt to income ratio as high as 50% and a housing expense to income ratio up to 40% may be acceptable.

Here are the compensating factors that the FHA allows lenders to consider:

Possible compensating factors for FHA loan, if credit score is 580 or above:
- No discretionary debt
- Three months of reserves
- Minimal increase in housing expense
- Residual income
- Significant extra income

- No discretionary debt: The only installment debt with an outstanding balance is the applicant's current housing expense, and the balance on any revolving credit accounts has been paid in full each month for the past six months.
- Reserves: The applicant will have at least three months' mortgage payments in reserve after closing.
- Minimal increase in housing expense: The proposed monthly mortgage payment exceeds the applicant's current housing expense by no more than $100 or 5%, whichever is less, and the applicant has had no more than one late monthly mortgage or rent payment in the previous 12 months.
- Residual income: After paying monthly obligations, the applicant will have at least the amount of residual income that would be required for a VA loan (see Chapter 12).
- Significant additional income: The applicant receives income that was not counted as effective income (for example, because it will not continue for at least three years), but which directly affects his ability to pay the mortgage.

Compensating factors don't help if credit score is under 580

Remember that compensating factors don't increase the allowable income ratios for loan applicants with nontraditional credit (no credit score) or a decision credit score under 580. For those applicants the maximum income ratios are 43% and 31% (45% and 33% if the home is energy-efficient) even if some of the compensating factors listed above are present.

Temporary buydowns are allowed in connection with fixed-rate FHA loans, but the buyer must qualify at the note rate. So, for example, even if a buydown brings the buyer's interest rate down from 8% to 6% in the first year, the buyer would still be required to qualify for the loan at 8%.

Exercise No. 4

The Herrons are applying for an FHA loan. Maggie Herron works for the Northshore Boat Company as a bookkeeper, earning $2,300 a month. Her husband, Bob, earns $510 a week as a customer service representative for Garner Industries. They have two personal loans from a local bank. The first loan has a monthly payment of $114 and a balance of $1,254. The second loan calls for monthly payments of $135, with $2,655 still owing. Their Visa card requires a minimum payment of $47; the balance is $9,400.

1. What is the Herrons' effective income?

2. What's the maximum housing expense the Herrons could qualify for under the FHA's rules? Assume that they aren't buying an energy-efficient home, and that there aren't any compensating factors that would allow increased income ratios.

3. How does the answer to Question 2 compare to the maximum housing expense the Herrons could qualify for if they were applying for a manually underwritten conventional loan? (See the Income Analysis section in Chapter 10.)

Assets for Closing

At closing, an FHA borrower will need to have enough cash to cover the:

- minimum cash investment;
- prepaid expenses (tax and insurance impounds and interim interest on the loan);
- loan fees (the origination fee and any discount points that the borrower has agreed to pay);
- upfront MIP, if it isn't being financed; and
- other closing costs and repair costs that aren't being financed.

If the borrower has agreed to pay a sales price higher than the property's appraised value, then she has to come up with the difference in cash, in addition to the minimum cash investment and the costs listed above. Ordinarily, no reserves are required for an FHA loan (although as you saw, reserves may be used as a compensating factor if the borrower's income ratios exceed the FHA limits). However, if the application is manually underwritten (for example, because the applicant doesn't have an established credit history), then a one-month reserve requirement applies.

The borrower may use gift funds for part or even all of the cash required for closing, except that they can't be used as reserves. The donor must be the borrower's employer or labor union, a family member, a close friend with a clearly defined interest in the borrower, a charitable organization, or a government agency. The funds must be deposited in the borrower's bank account or with the closing agent, and a gift letter will be required (see Chapter 8).

> **Cash required for closing:**
> - Minimum cash investment
> - Prepaid expenses
> - Loan fees
> - Upfront MIP
> - Closing costs
> - Repair costs
> - Difference between sales price and appraised value

> Reserves not required unless loan is manually underwritten

> **Sources of cash for closing:**
> - Borrower's own funds
> - Gift funds
> - Secondary financing
> - Loan secured by collateral other than home

FHA borrowers may use other sources of cash besides gift funds. As we discussed earlier, a borrower may use secondary financing (a second loan secured by the property being purchased with the FHA loan) to obtain funds needed for closing. Remember, though, that secondary financing can't be used for the minimum cash investment unless the source is a family member or a government agency.

Also, the borrower may be permitted to borrow the cash needed for closing if the loan is secured by collateral other than the home being purchased with the FHA mortgage. For example, the collateral might be a vacation property, or financial assets such as stocks and bonds. This loan must be from an independent third party, not from the seller, the lender making the FHA loan, or a real estate agent involved in the transaction.

FHA Rehabilitation Loans and Reverse Mortgages

We'll end this chapter with a closer look at two specific FHA programs: the Section 203(k) program, which insures rehabilitation loans, and the Section 255 program, for reverse mortgages.

FHA Rehabilitation Loans

203(k) loan: used to purchase or refinance and rehabilitate residential property

The 203(k) program insures mortgages used to buy (or refinance) and rehabilitate residential property with up to four units. A portion of the loan proceeds is used to purchase the property or refinance an existing mortgage, and the remaining funds are deposited into an escrow account, to be released as the rehabilitation work progresses. The borrower usually must intend to occupy the rehabilitated property as her principal residence.

A home financed under this program must be at least a year old, and the FHA imposes structural and energy-efficiency standards on all rehabilitation work. A wide range of repairs and improvements qualify as rehabilitation, from major structural changes and additions to cosmetic upgrades such as new kitchen cabinets. Luxury or temporary improvements are not eligible for the program, however.

Borrower may be required to use 203(k) consultant

For standard 203(k) financing, the borrower is required to work with an FHA-approved 203(k) consultant. (Among other things, the consultant evaluates the project, prepares an independent cost estimate, and inspects the property periodically to monitor progress.) That requirement doesn't apply to limited 203(k) financing, which provides up to $35,000 for minor remodeling and nonstructural repairs.

The appraisal for a 203(k) loan generally includes estimates of both the property's "as is value" and its "after improved value": how much it will probably be worth once the rehabilitation work has been completed. To calculate the maximum loan amount, the lender applies the appropriate loan-to-value ratio to the as is value plus the rehabilitation costs, or to 110% of the after improved value, whichever is less. The loan amount also can't exceed the local FHA limit.

FHA Home Equity Conversion Mortgages (HECMs)

A reverse mortgage offers an older homeowner a way to convert equity into income (see Chapter 5). The FHA calls its reverse mortgages "home equity conversion mortgages," or **HECMs**. It was the FHA that first popularized reverse mortgages.

Home equity conversion mortgage = reverse mortgage

A HECM borrower receives the loan proceeds from the lender as a single lump sum payment, monthly payments, a line of credit, or a combination of these. Repayment is not required as long as the property remains the owner's principal residence.

To be eligible for an FHA HECM, a homeowner must be at least 62 years old. The property may be a dwelling with up to four units, a unit in an FHA-approved condominium, or a manufactured home. It must be owned free and clear, or have only a small balance remaining on the mortgage.

HECM applicant must:
- Be at least 62 years old
- Own property free and clear, or with small balance only

The FHA requires potential HECM borrowers to consult an FHA-approved HECM counselor to help decide if this type of mortgage would suit their needs. The lender's evaluation of the applicant's financial situation must include a credit analysis, a residual income analysis, documentation of income and assets, and consideration of compensating factors.

A HECM can have a fixed or adjustable interest rate. The loan amount can't exceed the FHA's ceiling for high-cost areas ($679,650 in 2018), and it will also depend on the value of the home, the current interest rate, and the age of the borrower. (If there's more than one borrower, the age of the youngest is the one that counts.) Generally speaking, the older the borrower, the larger the loan amount can be.

The lender recovers the amount borrowed, plus interest, when the property is sold. If the sale proceeds exceed the amount owed, the excess goes to the borrower (the seller) or his heirs. If the proceeds don't cover the amount owed, the FHA will make up the difference to the lender.

FHA HECM can be used to purchase a new principal residence

HECM for Purchase. Although the original idea behind reverse mortgages was to help older homeowners stay in homes they already owned, a HECM can also be used to purchase a new principal residence. The lender will provide the loan proceeds in a lump sum, to be applied to the purchase price like an ordinary mortgage loan. But since this is a reverse mortgage, the borrowers won't have to make monthly payments to the lender. Instead, the loan will be repaid when the home is sold.

Outline: FHA-Insured Loans

I. FHA Mortgage Insurance
  A. The Federal Housing Administration (FHA) is part of the Department of Housing and Urban Development (HUD). The purpose of the FHA is to promote the financing, improvement, and sale of residential real estate.
  B. The primary function of the FHA is insuring mortgage loans. It does not build homes or provide mortgage loans.
    1. A borrower applies to an FHA-approved lender who either underwrites the loan application directly or submits it to the FHA for approval.
    2. The borrower is liable to the federal government for any compensation the FHA must pay the lender as a result of the borrower's default.
  C. FHA loans are designed to help people with low or moderate incomes buy homes.
  D. FHA Loan Programs
    1. Section 203(b) is the standard FHA loan program. It provides insurance for loans used to purchase or refinance one- to four-unit properties.
    2. Section 203(k) insures rehabilitation loans.
    3. Section 234(c) insures loans used to purchase or refinance individual condominium units.
    4. Section 251 insures adjustable-rate mortgages.
      a. The loan term must be 30 years.
      b. Temporary buydowns are not allowed.
    5. Section 255 insures home equity conversion mortgages (HECMs), commonly called reverse mortgages.
II. Rules for FHA-Insured Transactions
  A. A home purchased with an FHA loan generally must be the borrower's principal residence.
  B. The FHA's local maximum loan amounts are based on median housing costs in the area and may be adjusted annually.
  C. Maximum loan-to-value ratio
    1. The LTV of an FHA loan generally can't exceed 96.5% of the appraised value or sales price, whichever is less.
    2. If the borrower's credit score is under 580, the LTV can't exceed 90%.

3. The borrower's minimum cash investment (required downpayment) is the difference between the sales price or appraised value, whichever is less, and the maximum loan amount.

D. Closing costs and loan charges

1. FHA borrowers may pay customary and reasonable closing costs.

2. Points and fees for an FHA loan are subject to a limit set in the Truth in Lending Act.

3. FHA loans may not have a prepayment penalty.

E. The FHA restricts contributions from the seller or other interested parties, to prevent circumvention of the LTV rules.

1. Interested party contributions include buydowns and payments toward the buyer's loan fees, UFMIP, or other closing costs.

   a. These contributions are limited to 6% of the sales price.

   b. Contributions in excess of 6% are inducements to purchase. So are contributions that exceed the actual loan fees and closing costs.

2. Inducements to purchase are deducted from the property's sales price before the LTV is applied, lowering the allowable maximum loan amount.

F. Secondary financing

1. Secondary financing may be used with an FHA loan if the borrower qualifies for the combined loan payment.

2. As a general rule, secondary financing cannot be used for the borrower's minimum cash investment; the combined LTV can't exceed the maximum LTV for the transaction.

3. Exception: Secondary financing provided by a family member or a government agency may be used to cover the minimum cash investment, if the total financing doesn't exceed the property's value or sales price, whichever is less.

G. Property flipping prevention rules

1. An FHA loan can't be used to finance a purchase unless more than 90 days have elapsed since the seller bought the home.

2. If the seller bought the home within the previous 91 to 180 days and the resale price is 100% or more above what the seller paid, the lender must obtain a second appraisal.

      H. Assumption

          1. An FHA loan can be assumed only by a creditworthy buyer who intends to occupy the property as a principal residence.

          2. If the assumption is approved, the lender must release the original borrower from liability.

III. FHA Insurance Premiums

      A. The mortgage insurance premiums (MIP) for most FHA programs include an upfront premium (UFMIP) and annual premiums.

      B. The UFMIP is 1.75% of the base loan amount.

          1. It may be paid in cash at closing by the buyer or the seller, or it may be financed.

          2. The maximum LTV rules apply to the base loan amount, not including the financed UFMIP.

      C. The annual MIP is a percentage of the loan balance.

          1. The percentage varies depending on the loan term, base loan amount, and LTV.

          2. If the original LTV is 90% or less, the annual MIP will be canceled after 11 years. Otherwise it must be paid throughout the loan term.

IV. FHA Underwriting Standards

      A. FHA underwriting standards are less strict than the Fannie Mae and Freddie Mac standards for conventional loans.

      B. The lender must consider the applicant's credit report and credit scores if those are available.

          1. The applicant's decision credit score is the middle score of three, or the lower of two.

          2. If that score is between 500 and 579, the maximum LTV is 90% (instead of 96.5%).

          3. If that score is under 500, the applicant isn't eligible for an FHA loan.

          4. Nontraditional credit analysis is allowed when necessary; the loan must be underwritten manually.

      C. The applicant's monthly effective income is measured with both a debt to income ratio and a housing expense to income ratio.

          1. Effective income is the total amount of income from all sources that is reasonably likely to continue for the first three years of the loan term.

2. An FHA borrower generally should have a debt to income ratio no higher than 43% and a housing expense to income ratio no higher than 31%.

   a. The allowable ratios are increased to 45% and 33% if it's an energy-efficient home.

3. Higher income ratios are allowed if the borrower's credit score is 580 or above and there are compensating factors.

   a. Possible compensating factors: no discretionary debt, three months of reserves, residual income, a minimal increase in housing expense, or significant extra income.

V. Assets Required for Closing

A. An FHA borrower must have enough cash to cover the minimum cash investment, prepaid expenses, origination fee, discount points, upfront MIP (if it isn't being financed), and any other closing costs or repair costs that are not being financed or paid for by the seller.

B. Reserves are generally not required. But if the loan is manually underwritten, the borrower must have one month's mortgage payment in reserve.

C. Allowable sources for the cash required for closing, besides the borrower's own funds:

1. Gift funds (can't be used for reserves).

2. Secondary financing (can't be used for the minimum cash investment unless the source is a family member or a government agency).

3. A loan from an independent third party secured by collateral other than the home being purchased.

VI. FHA Rehabilitation Loans and Reverse Mortgages

A. Section 203(k) insures mortgages used to purchase (or refinance) and then rehabilitate a home.

1. After the purchase or refinancing, the remaining loan proceeds are put into an escrow account and released as the rehab work progresses.

2. Rehabilitation work must meet HUD standards. The work can't include temporary or luxury improvements.

3. The borrower is usually required to use a 203(k) consultant.

B. Section 255 insures home equity conversion mortgages (HECMs), also known as reverse mortgages.

1. Allows older homeowners to convert equity into a lump sum payment, monthly payments, or a line of credit.

2. Repayment is not required as long as the property remains the owner's principal residence.

3. The loan amount depends on the home's appraised value, the current interest rate, and the age of the borrower. It can't exceed the local FHA loan limit.

4. The lender recovers the amount borrowed, plus interest, when the property is sold. The FHA will make up any shortfall in the sale proceeds.

Key Terms

HUD: The Department of Housing and Urban Development, a cabinet-level department of the federal government.

Federal Housing Administration (FHA): An agency within the Department of Housing and Urban Development that provides mortgage insurance to encourage lenders to make more affordable home loans.

FHA-insured loan: A loan made by an institutional lender with mortgage insurance provided by the Federal Housing Administration, protecting the lender against losses due to borrower default.

MMI: The Mutual Mortgage Insurance program, the formal name of the FHA insurance program.

Direct endorsement lender: A lender authorized to underwrite its own FHA loan applications, rather than having to submit them to the FHA for approval.

Minimum cash investment: The required downpayment for an FHA loan; the difference between the sales price or appraised value, whichever is less, and the maximum loan amount for the transaction.

Effective income: In FHA underwriting, the loan applicant's gross monthly income from all sources that are reasonably likely to continue for at least three years; the FHA's term for stable monthly income.

MIP: The mortgage insurance premiums charged for FHA insurance coverage, which generally include an initial premium (the upfront or one-time MIP) plus annual premiums.

Chapter Quiz

1. The FHA:
   a. makes loans
   b. insures loans
   c. buys and sells loans
   d. All of the above

2. Bill Zelinski is buying a duplex. He can finance the transaction with an FHA loan if he intends to:
   a. occupy one of the units as his principal residence
   b. occupy one of the units as a secondary residence
   c. rent out both of the units
   d. Any of the above

3. The appraised value of a single-family home is $365,000, and it's selling for $364,000. The local maximum FHA loan amount is $362,790. The maximum FHA loan amount available for this transaction is:
   a. $350,092
   b. $351,260
   c. $352,225
   d. $362,790

4. FHA local maximum loan amounts are based on local:
   a. median income
   b. debt to income ratios
   c. median housing costs
   d. mortgage insurance costs

5. All of the following statements about FHA loans are true except:
   a. any discount points must be paid by the borrower, not by the seller
   b. the borrower is allowed to pay customary and reasonable closing costs
   c. mortgage insurance is required on all loans
   d. the government does not set a maximum interest rate

6. The Howells are buying a house worth $320,000 with a 30-year FHA 203(b) loan. The local maximum FHA loan amount is $307,900. If the Howells qualify for maximum FHA financing and decide to finance the upfront MIP:
   a. the maximum loan amount will be reduced by the amount of the MIP
   b. the total amount financed, including the MIP, cannot exceed $307,900
   c. the total amount financed will be $307,900 minus the MIP
   d. the total amount financed will be $307,900 plus the MIP

7. Continuing with the previous question, if the Howells obtain a 30-year loan for $307,900, they will be required to pay an annual premium for:
   a. the first 11 years of the loan term
   b. the first 15 years of the loan term
   c. the entire loan term
   d. None of the above; an annual premium is not required if the MIP is financed

8. Secondary financing may be used to cover the borrower's minimum cash investment:
   a. if the borrower's credit score is above 620
   b. if the second loan comes from the seller or an institutional lender
   c. if the second loan comes from a close family member
   d. under no circumstances

9. The Munnimans bought their house in 2002 with an FHA loan. Now they're selling it. The FHA loan can be assumed:
   a. by a creditworthy investor
   b. by a creditworthy buyer who will occupy the property as her principal residence
   c. as long as the sellers aren't planning to get another FHA loan to buy their next house
   d. None of the above; FHA loans are no longer assumable

10. Which of the following statements about qualifying for an FHA-insured loan is correct?
    a. The borrower's gross income generally may not exceed the FHA's nationwide cap
    b. The minimum credit score for an FHA loan is 580
    c. The underwriter may adjust a low credit score if there are compensating factors that reduce the risk of default
    d. Most FHA borrowers are not required to have cash reserves

Answer Key

1. b.   The FHA insures mortgage loans made by FHA-approved lenders in accordance with FHA rules.

2. a.   An FHA loan generally must be used to finance an owner-occupied principal residence.

3. b.   Multiply the property's sales price or appraised value, whichever is less, by 96.5% (the maximum LTV ratio). $364,000 × 96.5% = $351,260. Since this doesn't exceed the local FHA loan limit ($362,790), $351,260 is the maximum loan amount for the transaction. Note that to be eligible for maximum financing (a 96.5% LTV), the borrower must have a credit score of 580 or higher.

4. c.   FHA local maximum loan amounts are based on local median housing costs.

5. a.   Discount points may be paid by the borrower or by another party, such as the seller.

6. d.   The Howells can borrow the maximum allowable loan amount (based on the local FHA loan limit and the LTV rules), plus the amount of the upfront MIP.

7. c.   If the original loan-to-value ratio is over 90%, the annual premium must be paid during the entire loan term. The Howells are borrowing $307,900 to buy a house valued at $320,000, which means their LTV is 96.2% ($307,900 ÷ $320,000 = .962). So they'll have to keep paying the annual premium until they've paid off the loan.

8. c.   Secondary financing may be used for the borrower's required minimum cash investment if the second loan comes from a family member or a government agency. It cannot come from the seller, another interested party, or an institutional lender.

9. b.   FHA loans may be assumed, but only by a creditworthy buyer who intends to occupy the home as her principal residence.

10. d.   FHA borrowers generally aren't required to have any cash reserves. (There's an exception if the loan is manually underwritten; in that case, the borrower must have at least one month's mortgage payment in reserve.) There's no upper limit on the borrower's income, and the minimum credit score is 500, not 580. Compensating factors may increase the allowable income ratios, but they don't affect the applicant's credit score.

Case Study: FHA-Insured Loans

After considering conventional loans, Rick and Teresa Cortina want to know whether an FHA-insured loan might work for them. They live in an area where the maximum FHA loan amount for single-family homes is $294,515. Refer back to the case study at the end of Chapter 10 for the information about the Cortinas' financial situation that you'll need to answer the questions below. There's a worksheet at the end of this case study that you can use for the calculations.

Interest rates and fees (30-year FHA loans)

In the Cortinas' area, lenders are typically charging the following interest rates and fees for 30-year FHA loans (regardless of the loan-to-value ratio):

- Fixed-rate FHA loans: 5.5% interest
- FHA ARMs: 4.5% interest
- 1% origination fee for either type of loan
- Discount points: each point paid reduces the interest rate by 0.25%

1. The Cortinas' effective income is $10,671 and their recurring charges add up to $1,243. (Those are the same figures as the stable monthly income and recurring obligations that you calculated for conventional loans in the Chapter 10 case study.) Apply the FHA's standard income ratios to find the maximum housing expense the Cortinas can expect to qualify for. Assume that their application presents no compensating factors that would allow them to have higher-than-standard income ratios.

2. Suppose the Cortinas want to get preapproved to borrow as much as FHA rules concerning maximum loan amounts would allow in the area where they live. What's the largest base loan amount an FHA borrower can get in the Cortinas' area? If the Cortinas are planning to finance the upfront MIP, what would the total amount financed be? Round the total amount financed down to the next dollar.

3. Now determine whether the Cortinas could qualify for the total amount financed (from Question 2) if they choose a fixed-rate FHA loan and don't pay discount points. The principal and interest payment would be $1,701.49. To calculate the PITI payment, add 15% to the principal and interest payment to cover estimated property taxes and hazard insurance. Also add the monthly share of the FHA annual mortgage insurance premium, which will be 0.85% of the base loan amount during the first year.

4. Suppose the Cortinas are borrowing the maximum FHA loan amount (and the upfront premium) calculated for Question 2. Apply the FHA's maximum loan-to-value ratio. How much would the Cortinas' minimum cash investment be? What home price could they afford with the FHA financing plus the minimum cash investment?

5. For the transaction in Question 4, how much cash would the Cortinas be required to have at closing? They'll need enough for the minimum cash investment and the origination fee, plus other closing costs. Use 3% of the sales price as an estimate of the other closing costs, including the prepaid expenses (impound account deposits). It isn't necessary to include cash reserves, since those generally aren't required in FHA transactions.

6. What if the Cortinas want to buy a house that costs more than the sales price you arrived at in Question 4? Could they use FHA financing for that purchase?

7. For the Cortinas, would there be any advantage to getting an FHA loan instead of a conventional loan? (Compare the results of your FHA calculations to your answers to the questions in the case study for conventional loans at the end of Chapter 10.)

Income Qualifying—FHA-Insured Loans

Effective Income

Base salary

    Wage earner 1 _____

    Wage earner 2 _____

Overtime _____

Commissions _____

Bonuses _____

Other   + _____

Total _____

Recurring Charges

Car loans _____

Credit cards _____

Student loans _____

Other debts _____

Child support _____

Alimony _____

Other   + _____

Total _____

Debt to Income Ratio

_____

_____ x .43   Effective income

    Maximum ratio (43%)

_____   Maximum fixed payments

– _____   Recurring charges

_____   Maximum mortgage payment (PITI) under debt to income ratio

Housing Expense to Income Ratio

_____   Effective income

_____ x .31   Maximum ratio (31%)

_____   Maximum mortgage payment (PITI) under housing expense ratio

Maximum Mortgage Payment (PITI) _____

Maximum Loan Amount _____

_____   Loan amount

x   .0175   1.75% of base loan

_____   Upfront MIP

+ _____   Loan amount

_____   Total amount financed

_____   1/12 of taxes, insurance

_____   1/12 of annual MIP

+ _____   P&I payment

_____   PITI payment for loan with financed UFMIP

Total Amount Financed _____

_____   Maximum loan amount

÷ .965   Loan-to-value ratio (96.5%)

_____   Sales price

– _____   Loan amount

_____   Minimum cash investment

Sales Price _____

Chapter 12

VA-Guaranteed Loans

Characteristics of VA Loans

- Overview
- Funding fees
- Loan fees and other closing costs
- Sales concessions

Eligibility for VA Loans

- Service requirements
- Eligibility of spouse

VA Guaranty

- Guaranty amount
- Restoration of guaranty entitlement
- Entitlement and co-ownership

VA Loan Amounts

- 25% rule
- Making a downpayment
- Secondary financing

Underwriting Guidelines

- Credit reputation
- Income
  - Income ratio analysis
  - Residual income analysis
  - Compensating factors

Introduction

The VA home loan program was established after World War II to help military veterans finance the purchase of their homes with affordable loans. For eligible borrowers, VA financing offers several advantages over conventional financing and has few disadvantages. This chapter begins with an overview of the characteristics of VA loans, then covers eligibility requirements, the VA guaranty, and the underwriting standards used to qualify VA loan applicants.

Characteristics of VA Loans

VA-guaranteed loans are made by institutional lenders, just like conventional loans and FHA-insured loans. However, when a VA-guaranteed loan is approved by the lender, a portion of the loan amount is guaranteed by the Department of Veterans Affairs (the VA). The loan guaranty serves the same purpose as mortgage insurance: it protects the lender against a large loss if the borrower defaults and the foreclosure sale proceeds fail to cover the full amount owed.

VA guaranty protects lender against losses from default

The term "VA-guaranteed loan" causes some confusion. You may occasionally encounter buyers who believe that, as eligible veterans or current members of the armed forces, they are guaranteed to receive a VA home loan, no matter what their financial circumstances are. But an eligible applicant has to qualify for a VA loan, just as for any other kind of mortgage loan; there are specific underwriting standards the applicant has to meet for the loan to be approved. The VA guaranty refers only to the lender's protection against loss.

Here are the key characteristics of VA-guaranteed loans:

- A VA loan can be used to finance the purchase of a single-family home, a multifamily residential property with up to four units, or a unit in a VA-approved condominium, or for home construction, rehabilitation, or refinancing.
- The VA doesn't guarantee investor loans, so the borrower must intend to occupy the home (or one of the units, if it's a multifamily property). It ordinarily must be the principal residence.
- VA borrowers generally need less cash than they would with conventional or FHA financing. The main reason is that the VA doesn't require borrowers to make a downpayment; the loan-to-value ratio can be 100%. VA borrowers also aren't required to have cash reserves.

- The VA does not set a maximum loan amount. (However, as we'll discuss later, lenders generally follow some rules of their own concerning VA loan amounts.)
- There are no maximum income limits; VA loans aren't restricted to low- or middle-income buyers.
- VA underwriting standards are less stringent than conventional underwriting standards, so it's generally easier to qualify for a VA loan.
- A VA loan can be a fixed-rate loan or a hybrid ARM. (If it's a hybrid, the initial fixed-rate period must be at least three years.)
- VA loans typically have a 30-year term, although shorter terms are permitted.
- Mortgage insurance isn't required on a VA loan, but the borrower is charged a funding fee (discussed below).
- VA loans can't have prepayment penalties.
- A VA loan may be assumed by any buyer who meets the VA's underwriting standards—the buyer doesn't have to be a veteran or service member. The interest rate on the loan won't be increased, and the original borrower will be released from liability when the assumption is approved.
- Forbearance is extended to VA borrowers who are experiencing temporary financial difficulties resulting from problems such as unemployment, disability, large medical bills, or the death of a spouse. In addition, the VA gives lenders discretion to modify the terms of VA loans to make them more affordable to distressed borrowers. VA representatives can help borrowers and lenders negotiate repayment plans for delinquent loans.

Characteristics of VA loans:
- Used to buy or build residence with up to four units
- Borrower must occupy property
- No downpayment and no reserves required
- VA doesn't set maximum loan amount
- No maximum income limits
- Less stringent qualifying standards
- Fixed-rate loan or hybrid ARM
- Funding fee instead of mortgage insurance
- No prepayment penalty
- Can be assumed by creditworthy buyer, veteran or non-veteran
- Forbearance for borrower in financial difficulties

Funding Fees

Unlike FHA loans and other high-LTV loans, VA loans don't involve mortgage insurance, so VA borrowers don't have to pay mortgage insurance premiums. However, they do have to pay a **funding fee**, which the VA uses to help fund the guaranteed loan program. The funding fee for a transaction may be paid at closing or financed along with the loan amount.

For a veteran of the regular military obtaining a no-downpayment loan, the funding fee is 2.15% of the loan amount. If the borrower is making a downpayment of 5% or more, the funding fee is reduced to 1.5%. With a downpayment of 10% or more, it's 1.25%.

Funding fee: 2.15% of loan amount, unless veteran makes downpayment of 5% or more

Funding fees are slightly higher for members of the Reserves or the National Guard. The fees are also higher for borrowers who have had a VA-guaranteed loan before.

Veterans with service-related disabilities are generally exempt from the funding fee requirement.

Loan Fees and Other Closing Costs

The VA places restrictions on the types of lender fees and other closing costs that VA borrowers can be charged. A borrower can be charged only fees and costs that are included on the VA's list of allowable charges. The amount of the charges must be reasonable and customary.

VA borrower can pay only reasonable and customary costs allowed by VA

A standard origination fee is not permitted on a VA loan. Instead, to defray the cost of making the loan, the lender can charge the borrower a flat fee of no more than 1% of the amount financed. The borrower may also pay reasonable discount points.

Lender may charge 1% flat fee plus discount points

In addition, the borrower can be required to pay many of the standard charges that the lender (or closing agent) pays to third parties, such as an appraisal fee, title insurance costs, and recording fees. But certain third-party charges, such as an escrow fee or a mortgage broker's fee, can't be paid by the borrower. And the lender can't tack on miscellaneous charges of its own, such as a document preparation fee, a processing fee, or an interest rate lock-in fee. Those types of costs are supposed to be covered by the lender's 1% flat fee.

Also, VA borrowers aren't permitted to pay a real estate agent's commission. That means a buyer's agent must be compensated by the seller. (This is true even in a "for sale by owner" transaction, where there's no listing agent and therefore no commission split to compensate the buyer's agent.)

Sales Concessions

In a transaction financed with a VA loan, sales concessions cannot total more than 4% of the property's appraised value. Examples of payments from a seller that are subject to this 4% limit include:

- payment of the buyer's funding fee;
- prepayment of the buyer's property taxes and insurance;
- a temporary or permanent buydown; or
- gifts of household items, such as furniture or appliances.

However, the 4% limit doesn't apply to payment of the buyer's closing costs, or to payment of discount points that are in line with the market.

Eligibility for VA Loans

Eligibility for VA-guaranteed loans is based on length of active duty service in the U.S. armed forces. The minimum requirement varies depending on when the service occurred. For veterans whose service began in the 1980s (a few years after the Vietnam War ended) or later, the requirement is:

Eligibility for VA loan:
1. *Minimum active duty service requirement*
2. *Other than dishonorable discharge*
3. *Surviving spouse may be eligible*

- **24 months** of continuous active duty, or
- the full period for which the veteran was called to active duty, so long as that was at least **90 days**, any part of which occurred during wartime, or at least **181 days** of continuous active duty during peacetime.

A service member who applies for a VA loan while still on active duty is eligible after at least 90 days of active duty service, any part of which occurred during wartime, or after at least 181 days of continuous active duty during peacetime.

Wartime periods include World War II, the Korean conflict, the Vietnam War, and the Persian Gulf War; intervening periods are peacetime. VA regulations specify beginning and ending dates for each period. For the purposes of the VA loan program, the Gulf War period began on August 2, 1990 and continues through the present.

Someone who has served in the Reserves or the National Guard for at least six years is eligible for a VA loan even without meeting the minimum active duty service requirement.

Veterans who were discharged because of a service-connected disability are eligible for a VA loan no matter how brief their period of service was—even if it was just a single day.

Veterans who received a dishonorable discharge are not eligible for a VA loan. Veterans whose discharge was neither honorable nor dishonorable may be eligible, however.

The VA, not the lender, determines whether a veteran or service member is eligible for a VA loan. If so, the VA will issue a **Certificate of Eligibility**. The certificate can be obtained online or by mail.

Eligibility of a Spouse. If a married service member was killed in action, died while on active duty, or died of service-related injuries, the surviving spouse may be eligible for a VA loan. The spouse of a service member who is a prisoner of war or listed as missing in action may also be eligible. Spouses should check with the VA for more details.

The VA Guaranty

VA loans are guaranteed by the U.S. government, which significantly reduces the lender's risk of loss in case the borrower defaults. It's because of the government guaranty that lenders are willing to make no-downpayment loans through the program. VA regulations determine the guaranty amount available for a transaction and how a veteran's guaranty entitlement can be restored after use.

Guaranty Amount

Like private mortgage insurance, the VA guaranty covers only a portion of the loan amount. The amount of coverage is referred to as the **guaranty amount**.

As shown in Figure 12.1, the guaranty amount available in a particular transaction depends on the loan amount. It also depends on the maximum guaranty amount that applies in the county where the home being purchased is located. The county maximum is tied to the Federal Housing Finance Agency's annual conforming loan limit (see Chapter 10). It takes the local median housing price into account, so high-cost counties have higher maximum guaranty amounts than other areas. (See the footnote in Figure 12.1.)

The following example illustrates how the guaranty amount is calculated for different transactions.

VA guaranty amount:
- Covers only part of loan amount
- Varies based on loan amount
- Also limited by county maximum

> **Example:** Alan Cho is using a VA loan to buy a house in a high-cost county where the maximum VA guaranty is $129,375. He plans to borrow $390,000, the property's appraised value. When the loan amount is over $144,000 but not over $453,100, the guaranty amount is 25% of the loan amount (see Figure 12.1). That means the guaranty amount for Cho's loan is $97,500 ($390,000 × .25 = $97,500).

Fig. 12.1 The VA guaranty amount for a transaction depends on the loan amount

Loan Amount	Guaranty Amount
Up to $45,000	50% of loan amount
$45,001 – $56,250	$22,500
$56,251 – $144,000	40% of loan amount, up to a maximum of $36,000
$144,001 – $453,100	25% of loan amount
Over $453,100	25% of loan amount or county maximum (whichever is less)*

* In 2018, the maximum guaranty for a loan over $453,100 ranges from $113,275 in most counties up to a ceiling of $169,912.50 in the most expensive counties. (Higher limits may apply in Alaska, Hawaii, Guam, and the Virgin Islands.)

Marlene Crosby is using a VA loan to buy a more expensive house in the same county. She wants to borrow $530,000, the appraised value. For a loan amount over $453,100, the guaranty amount is 25% of the loan amount, up to the county maximum. In this case, 25% of the loan amount is $132,500 ($530,000 × .25 = $132,500). Since that's over the county maximum, the guaranty on Crosby's loan will be $129,375, the county maximum.

As you'll see later in the chapter, the guaranty amount that applies to a transaction affects how large a VA loan a lender is willing to make. For instance, there's a good chance the lender in the example would consider the $129,375 maximum guaranty inadequate for a $530,000 loan, and therefore would require Crosby to make a downpayment.

Restoration of Guaranty Entitlement

The guaranty amount available to a particular veteran or service member is referred to as that person's **entitlement**. Guaranty entitlement doesn't expire. It's available until it is used to buy a home.

A veteran who has never used the VA home loan benefit has full guaranty entitlement. When the vet finances a home purchase with a VA loan, the entitlement is reduced by the amount of the guaranty on that loan. After paying off that loan, the vet can apply to the VA to have full guaranty entitlement **restored**. (Restoration of entitlement is sometimes referred to as reinstatement.)

Entitlement: guaranty amount available to particular veteran

Full entitlement can be restored when veteran pays off loan

Example: Kevin Arnold just sold his home and paid off his VA loan. He applies to the VA and his full guaranty entitlement is restored. He can use it to buy a new home with another VA loan.

A borrower's entitlement can also be restored after paying off the VA loan without selling the property. The vet can then use the entitlement to get a new VA loan secured by the same property. That's what happens when a borrower uses a VA loan to refinance an existing VA loan.

VA rules also allow for a one-time restoration of entitlement to a borrower who paid off a VA loan without selling the property and now wants another VA loan to buy an additional property. In other words, the borrower can keep the first home and use the restored entitlement to obtain a second VA loan to buy a new home. (The newly purchased property would have to become the borrower's residence, because of the VA's owner-occupancy requirement.) This is permitted only once, however; after that, if the borrower wants to obtain another VA loan to buy a new home, the entitlement won't be restored unless the borrower sells all of the property previously financed with VA loans.

Substitution of Entitlement. We mentioned earlier that a VA loan can be assumed by any creditworthy buyer; the buyer doesn't have to be a veteran or member of the armed services. However, the original borrower's guaranty entitlement will be restored only if the buyer who assumes the loan is an eligible veteran or service member. The buyer's entitlement must be equal to (or greater than) the assumed loan's guaranty amount, and the buyer must agree to substitute his entitlement for the original borrower's. The substitution of entitlement must be requested from the VA.

Full entitlement restored after assumption only if buyer is also veteran and agrees to substitution of entitlement

Remaining Entitlement. As we explained, a VA borrower's full entitlement won't be restored until the loan is paid off or there is an assumption with a substitution of entitlement.

However, even without a restoration of full entitlement, the borrower may still have **remaining entitlement** (also called partial entitlement) that could be used to get another VA loan. This might be the case if it wasn't necessary to use the maximum guaranty available when the earlier loan was made, or perhaps the maximum guaranty has been increased since the loan was made. VA borrowers who want to know whether they have any remaining entitlement should contact the VA.

Entitlement and Co-Ownership

Suppose a married couple is buying a home with a $400,000 VA loan; one spouse is a veteran with full VA entitlement and the other is a non-veteran. The guaranty on their loan will be $100,000 (25% of $400,000), just as if an unmarried veteran were buying the property alone.

Now suppose instead that both of the spouses are eligible veterans with full guaranty entitlement. They can't combine their entitlements to increase the guaranty amount for their loan beyond the maximum allowed. For example, if the couple is borrowing $400,000, the guaranty is still only $100,000. Either of them can use their entitlement for the loan, or they can each contribute part of their entitlement. It generally works the same way for two eligible veterans who aren't married to each other, if they're both using their entitlement. (The rules are too complicated to discuss in more detail here.)

If a veteran and a non-veteran who aren't married to one another use a VA loan to buy a home together, the guaranty is based only on the veteran's portion of the loan. The guaranty doesn't cover the non-veteran's portion. For example, suppose two brothers are purchasing a home together. Only one of them served in the military and is eligible for a VA loan. If they're borrowing $400,000, the amount of the guaranty will be $50,000—the guaranty amount for a $200,000 loan.

> Co-ownership:
> - Even if buyers are both eligible veterans, maximum guaranty is not increased
> - If veteran buys home with non-veteran other than spouse, guaranty applies only to vet's half of the loan

Exercise No. 1

As a U.S. Navy Reservist, John Woods served 12 months on active duty, the full period he was called up for. Woods now wants to buy his first home, and he's applying for a $325,000 VA-guaranteed loan.

1. Is Woods eligible for a VA loan? Why or why not? Based on the 2018 rules concerning guaranty amounts, what would the amount of his entitlement be?

2. If Woods gets a $325,000 loan, how much of it will be covered by the VA guaranty?

VA Loan Amounts

VA doesn't set maximum loan amount, but loan amount can't exceed appraised value

Although the VA doesn't set a maximum loan amount, a VA loan generally may not exceed the appraised value of the property. (There's an exception if the borrower is financing the funding fee or the cost of certain energy-efficient improvements; then the loan amount may exceed the appraised value by those amounts.)

A VA-approved appraiser must perform the appraisal, and a **Notice of Value** (NOV) will be issued, stating the appraised value. (An NOV is sometimes called a Certificate of Reasonable Value, or CRV.) If the sales price is greater than the appraised value, the difference must be made up with a cash downpayment out of the borrower's own funds.

The 25% Rule

Lenders generally require guaranty to equal 25% of loan amount
• With no downpayment, maximum loan amount is usually four times the guaranty amount

The only other limit on the loan amount comes from the lender and the secondary market, not the VA. Most lenders require the veteran's guaranty entitlement to equal at least 25% of the loan amount. In other words, they won't make a no-downpayment loan that's more than four times the guaranty amount. A loan that exceeded that limit would be more difficult to sell on the secondary market.

So in most parts of the country, where the maximum guaranty is currently $113,275, the largest no-downpayment loan that most lenders will make is $453,100 ($113,275 × 4 = $453,100). And in the most expensive high-cost counties, where the maximum guaranty is $169,912.50, the largest no-downpayment loan would usually be $679,650 ($169,912.50 × 4 = $679,650).

Making a Downpayment

If guaranty is less than 25% of loan amount, lender requires downpayment

If a borrower wants a VA loan that exceeds this limit, most lenders will require the borrower to make a downpayment. Lenders usually require the downpayment plus the guaranty amount to equal 25% of the sales price. This provides essentially the same level of protection against default as the lender would have if the borrower were buying a less expensive loan with a no-downpayment loan.

Example: Robert Mendez wants to buy a home that has been valued at $480,000. He has full entitlement, and the maximum VA guaranty for his area is $113,275. His lender won't loan him more than $453,100 unless he makes a downpayment.

$480,000   Sales price
×   25%   Desired ratio of guaranty + downpayment to price
$120,000   25% of sales price
− 113,275   Maximum guaranty
   $6,725   Downpayment required by lender

$480,000   Sales price
−   6,725   Downpayment
$473,275   Loan amount

> Guaranty + downpayment should equal 25% of sales price

Secondary Financing

If a VA borrower doesn't have enough cash for a downpayment required by the lender, part or all of the downpayment can be financed if the following conditions are met:

1. the total financing doesn't exceed the appraised value of the property;
2. the borrower has enough income to qualify based on the payments required for both loans; and
3. the second loan doesn't restrict the borrower's ability to sell the property more than the VA loan does (in other words, the second loan must be assumable by a creditworthy buyer).

> For a lender-required downpayment, veteran may use secondary financing
> • Combined loans may not exceed appraised value
> • Buyer must qualify for combined payment
> • Second loan must be assumable

Here's an important limitation, however: secondary financing can't be used to cover the downpayment that's required by the VA when the sales price exceeds the appraised value. It can be used for a downpayment required by the lender because of the 25% rule, though.

> Secondary financing can't be used for downpayment required by VA

Exercise No. 2

In each of the following cases, assume that it's 2018, the prospective borrower is an eligible veteran with full entitlement, the house isn't located in a high-cost county, and the lender follows the 25%

rule explained above. Refer back to Figure 12.1 to determine the guaranty amounts.

1. Jeffrey Bates wants to buy a home with an appraised value of $259,000. What is the largest VA-guaranteed loan that the lender is likely to offer him? How large a downpayment would he have to make for that loan? How much would the guaranty amount be?

2. Helen Moreau is going to finance the purchase of a condominium unit with a VA loan. The sales price is $465,000, and the appraised value is $466,500. What is the largest loan that the lender is likely to offer her? How large a downpayment would she be required to make for that loan? How much would the guaranty amount be?

Underwriting Guidelines

When deciding whether to approve a VA-guaranteed loan, the lender must use VA underwriting guidelines to analyze the credit-worthiness of the applicant or applicants. (Remember that when two or more people apply for a loan together, the underwriter evaluates the credit reputation of each applicant and their combined stable monthly income, assets, and liabilities.) Most of the VA's guidelines are very similar to the general qualifying principles discussed in Chapter 8, but some of them represent a departure from the rules used in other loan programs.

Credit Reputation

The underwriter evaluates the applicant's credit report, or else performs a nontraditional credit analysis (using rent and utility payments, for example) if the applicant doesn't have an established credit history. An application that would otherwise be acceptable can be rejected based on a poor credit reputation alone. However, in contrast to Fannie Mae, Freddie Mac, and the FHA, the VA hasn't set a specific minimum credit score for its home loan program.

Income

A VA loan applicant's income is analyzed using two different methods: the income ratio method and the residual income method. The applicant must qualify under both methods.

Two methods of income analysis for VA loans:
- Income ratio
- Residual income

Income Ratio Analysis. Instead of both a housing expense to income ratio and a debt to income ratio, the VA uses only a debt to income ratio. As usual, the calculation takes into account the proposed housing expense (the PITI payment), payments on installment debts and revolving credit accounts, and other monthly obligations such as child support payments to an ex-spouse. As a general rule, unless there are compensating factors, a VA loan applicant's debt to income ratio can't exceed 41%.

Debt to income ratio generally can't exceed 41% without compensating factors

> **Example:** Robin Young is eligible for a VA loan. She and her husband, Mike Appleton, have a combined income of $6,000 per month. Aside from their housing expense, their monthly obligations add up to $1,030.
>
> | | |
> |---|---|
> | $6,000 | Monthly income |
> | × 41% | Maximum debt to income ratio |
> | $2,460 | Maximum total payments |
> | − 1,030 | Monthly recurring obligations |
> | $1,430 | Maximum housing expense (PITI) |
>
> Young and Appleton could qualify for a $1,430 monthly housing expense under the VA's debt to income ratio rule.

A debt or obligation must be included in the income ratio calculation if there are ten or more payments remaining. Even one with fewer payments remaining must be included if the payments are large enough to severely affect the borrower's finances for even a short period.

Note that the VA requires lenders to include one kind of monthly obligation that generally isn't considered in underwriting other types of loans: job-related expenses. If the applicant's job-related expenses (such as child care costs, union dues, or unusual commuting expenses) add up to a significant monthly amount, that will be treated as a recurring obligation in the income ratio calculation.

Residual Income Analysis. The second method used to analyze a VA loan applicant's income is residual income analysis, also called cash flow analysis. This method uses a **monthly shelter expense**, which is the proposed housing expense (the monthly PITI payment) plus the estimated cost of property maintenance and utilities. (The estimate is based on the square footage of the home being purchased.)

An applicant's **residual income** is monthly gross income minus:

- payroll taxes (the amount withheld by the employer for income taxes, Social Security, and Medicare),
- the monthly shelter expense, and
- the other recurring obligations.

Residual income: gross monthly income minus payroll taxes, monthly shelter expense, and recurring obligations

Fig. 12.2 Minimum residual income requirements for VA loan applicants

Table of Residual Incomes by Region For loan amounts of $79,999 and below				
Family Size	**Northeast**	**Midwest**	**South**	**West**
1	$390	$382	$382	$425
2	$654	$641	$641	$713
3	$788	$772	$772	$859
4	$888	$868	$868	$967
5	$921	$902	$902	$1,004
Over 5: Add $75 for each additional member up to a family of 7.				

Table of Residual Incomes by Region For loan amounts of $80,000 and above				
Family Size	**Northeast**	**Midwest**	**South**	**West**
1	$450	$441	$441	$491
2	$755	$738	$738	$823
3	$909	$889	$889	$990
4	$1,025	$1,003	$1,003	$1,117
5	$1,062	$1,039	$1,039	$1,158
Over 5: Add $80 for each additional member up to a family of 7.				

How much residual income is required depends on the region of the country where the loan applicant lives, family size, and the size of the proposed loan. The minimum requirements are shown in Figure 12.2.

> **Example:** Continuing with the previous example, suppose Young and Appleton have two children and live in the VA's Midwest region. They're planning to buy a 1,500-square-foot house for $220,000. To meet the VA's guidelines, they should have at least $1,003 in residual income (see Figure 12.2).
>
> The taxes withheld from the couple's monthly pay add up to $1,810. The monthly shelter expense for the proposed loan would be $1,640 (that's a $1,430 PITI payment plus $210 for estimated maintenance and utility costs). Here's how their residual income will be calculated:

$6,000	Gross monthly income
− 1,810	Payroll taxes withheld
$4,190	Net monthly income
1,030	Recurring obligations
− 1,640	Monthly shelter expense
$1,520	Residual income

Young and Appleton's residual income is well above the $1,003 minimum requirement. With the $1,430 PITI payment their debt to income ratio is 41%, so the lender is likely to approve this VA loan. In fact, because the couple's residual income exceeds the required minimum by so much, they probably could have qualified for a larger loan (see below).

Compensating Factors. The VA emphasizes that the 41% income ratio and the figures on the residual income chart are only guidelines, and failure to meet them shouldn't automatically result in rejection of the loan application if there are compensating factors.

VA underwriting standards are guidelines, not hard and fast rules

The VA lists the following as examples of compensating factors which could help an application that is weak in certain respects:

Compensating factors may allow loan approval in spite of marginal income or other weakness

- an excellent long-term credit history,
- conservative use of consumer credit,
- minimal consumer debt,
- long-term employment,
- significant liquid assets,
- a sizable downpayment,
- little or no increase in the shelter expense,
- military benefits,
- satisfactory previous experience with home ownership,

- high residual income,
- a low debt to income ratio,
- tax credits for child care,
- tax benefits of home ownership, and
- (for refinancing) significant equity in the property.

The VA points out that a particular compensating factor helps only if it's relevant to the particular weakness in the loan application. For example, if the applicant's residual income is somewhat below the VA's minimum, significant liquid assets are a relevant compensating factor, because the family could draw on the liquid assets to supplement their income. On the other hand, long-term employment isn't relevant. The fact that the applicant has an exceptionally stable employment history strengthens the application in a general sense, but it doesn't specifically address the issue of marginal residual income—whether the applicant's family will have enough money to live on after paying all the bills. Without any compensating factors that are relevant to marginal residual income, the underwriter would probably reject the application, despite the applicant's good employment history.

If a VA loan is approved even though the applicant's debt to income ratio is over 41%, the lender is generally required to submit a statement to the VA listing the relevant compensating factors that justify loan approval. However, if the applicant's residual income is at least 20% over the required minimum, the lender can approve the loan (in spite of the high income ratio) without any other compensating factors, and without submitting a statement of justification to the VA.

Overall, the VA's qualifying rules are considerably less stringent than the Fannie Mae/Freddie Mac rules. A borrower who would be considered marginal for a conventional loan might easily qualify for a VA loan. Eligible veterans should always keep VA financing in mind.

If residual income exceeds minimum by 20% or more, loan can be approved even though vet's income ratio is over 41%, without any other compensating factors

Exercise No. 3

Vince Martin, a former marine, is eligible for a VA loan, and he hasn't used any of his entitlement yet. He and his wife, Cheryl, have three children, and they live in the VA's Western region.

The Martins have found a house they'd like to buy. They apply for a VA loan, and the NOV establishes the appraised value of the property as $207,500. The Martins' gross monthly income is $5,200. The withheld taxes come to $1,325 per month. Their recurring obligations (not counting their housing expense) add up to $807 per month.

The Martins aren't planning to make a downpayment. At the market interest rate, the monthly PITI payment for this loan would be about $1,475. Maintenance and utilities are estimated at $168, so the monthly shelter expense (for the residual income analysis) is $1,643.

1. What would the Martins' debt to income ratio be?

2. Could the Martins qualify for this VA loan? Why or why not?

Outline: VA-Guaranteed Loans

I. Characteristics of VA Loans

    A. VA loans are made by institutional lenders, but a portion of the loan amount is guaranteed by the Department of Veterans Affairs.

        1. Loan guaranty functions like mortgage insurance, protecting the lender against a loss in the event of buyer default.

    B. Overview of VA loan characteristics:

        1. Loan can be used for the purchase, construction, or rehabilitation of a residence with up to four units, or for refinancing.

        2. The home (or one of the units) must be the borrower's principal residence. Investor loans are not allowed.

        3. No downpayment required, unless the loan amount is more than the appraised value.

        4. No reserves required.

        5. No maximum loan amount.

        6. No maximum income limits.

        7. Less stringent qualifying standards.

        8. Can be a fixed-rate loan, or a hybrid ARM with a fixed-rate period of at least three years.

        9. Loan term is typically 30 years.

      10. Borrower pays a funding fee instead of mortgage insurance premiums.

      11. No prepayment penalty allowed.

      12. Can be assumed by a creditworthy buyer, who may be a veteran or a non-veteran.

      13. Forbearance is extended to borrowers in temporary financial difficulties.

    C. Funding fee is a percentage of the loan amount.

        1. Varies depending on the amount of the downpayment (if any) and other factors.

        2. May be paid in cash or financed.

    D. VA borrowers can't be charged closing costs that aren't on the VA's list of allowable charges.

        1. For example, borrowers can't pay the escrow fee, mortgage broker's fee, or real estate commission.

        2. Instead of an ordinary origination fee and miscellaneous processing fees, the lender charges a 1% flat fee; may also charge discount points.

    E. Limit on sales concessions (such as a buydown) is 4% of the property's appraised value.

II. Eligibility for VA Loans

   A. Eligibility depends on length of active duty service in the U.S. armed forces.

   B. Minimum service requirement: 24 months of continuous active duty or the full period the veteran was called up for, whichever is less.

      1. Full period must be at least 90 days during wartime or 181 continuous days during peacetime.

      2. Minimum service requirement doesn't apply to veterans with service-related disabilities.

   C. Eligible veteran is issued a Certificate of Eligibility.

   D. Spouse may be eligible for a VA loan if the veteran or service member is deceased, a prisoner of war, or missing in action.

III. VA Guaranty

   A. Amount of coverage is referred to as "guaranty amount."

   B. Guaranty available for a particular loan depends on the size of loan and the maximum guaranty for the county. High-cost counties have a higher maximum.

   C. After the loan is fully repaid, the veteran can request restoration of entitlement, which can then be used for a new VA loan to buy another home.

   D. After an assumption, the original borrower's entitlement is restored only if the buyer is an eligible veteran who agrees to a substitution of entitlement.

   E. If spouses are both veterans, they cannot combine their entitlements to increase the guaranty amount for a single VA loan.

   F. If a veteran buys a home with a non-veteran, the guaranty only applies to the veteran's portion of the loan.

IV. VA Loan Amounts

   A. No maximum VA loan amount, but the loan may not exceed the property's appraised value.

      1. Exception: Loan amount can exceed value by the amount of the financed funding fee or the cost of energy-efficient improvements.

      2. VA-approved appraiser appraises the property; Notice of Value (NOV) is issued.

   B. Most lenders require the guaranty to equal at least 25% of the loan amount.

      1. They won't make a no-downpayment loan for more than four times the guaranty amount.

      2. If the sales price is more than four times the guaranty, the lender requires a downpayment.

      3. Downpayment plus guaranty amount should equal 25% of the sales price.

    C. Borrower can finance part or all of a lender-required downpayment if:

        1. total financing doesn't exceed appraised value;

        2. buyer's income is enough to qualify based on the payments for both loans; and

        3. second loan is assumable by a creditworthy buyer.

V. Underwriting Guidelines

    A. No minimum credit score for VA loans, but an application can be rejected based on poor credit alone.

    B. Applicant must qualify under both methods of income analysis: income ratio and residual income.

        1. Debt to income ratio generally must be 41% or less.

        2. Residual income must satisfy VA's minimum requirement, which varies with the region of the country, family size, and loan size.

            a. To calculate residual income, start with gross monthly income, then subtract payroll taxes, monthly shelter expense, and recurring obligations.

            b. Monthly shelter expense is PITI payment plus estimate of maintenance and utility costs.

        3. Both methods of income analysis are only guidelines.

            a. Even though borrower doesn't meet the standards exactly, loan can still be approved if there are relevant compensating factors.

            b. If the debt to income ratio exceeds 41% but the residual income is at least 20% over the required minimum, the lender may approve the loan without any other compensating factors.

Key Terms

VA: The U.S. Department of Veterans Affairs.

VA-guaranteed loan: A home loan made to an eligible veteran or service member by an institutional lender and guaranteed by the Department of Veterans Affairs, protecting the lender against losses resulting from default.

Guaranty amount: The portion of a VA loan guaranteed by the Department of Veterans Affairs; the maximum amount that the VA will pay the lender for a loss resulting from the borrower's default.

Funding fee: A charge paid by a VA borrower that the lender submits to the VA, used to fund the VA-guaranteed loan program.

Certificate of Eligibility: A document issued by the VA, indicating a veteran or service member's eligibility for a VA-guaranteed loan.

Guaranty entitlement: The guaranty amount available to a particular veteran or service member; part or all of the entitlement is applied when a VA loan is used to buy a home, but full entitlement may be restored after the loan is paid off.

Substitution of entitlement: When a VA borrower sells the home to another eligible veteran or service member who assumes the loan; the buyer's guaranty entitlement is substituted for the seller's, so that the seller's entitlement is restored.

Notice of Value (NOV): A document showing the estimate of a property's current market value from a VA-approved appraisal. Previously referred to as a Certificate of Reasonable Value.

Residual income: The amount of income that an applicant for a VA loan has left over after payroll taxes, the monthly shelter expense, and other recurring obligations have been deducted from gross monthly income.

Monthly shelter expense: A VA loan applicant's proposed monthly housing expense plus estimated monthly maintenance and utility costs.

Chapter Quiz

1. Because VA loans are guaranteed by the VA:
   a. veterans are not obligated to repay their loans
   b. lenders are willing to make no-downpayment VA loans
   c. VA loans cannot be assumed by non-veterans
   d. veterans are not required to meet qualifying standards

2. If a seller's VA loan is going to be assumed by the buyer, the seller's entitlement can be restored only if:
   a. the buyer is an eligible veteran or service member with entitlement
   b. the buyer agrees to a substitution of entitlement
   c. a request for a substitution of entitlement is submitted to the VA
   d. All of the above

3. Which of the following is *not* true of a VA loan?
   a. A small prepayment penalty is allowed
   b. Owner occupancy is required
   c. The loan amount can't exceed the appraised value of the property
   d. No mortgage insurance is required

4. If a veteran with full entitlement wanted to obtain a $325,000 loan, how much would the required downpayment be?
   a. No downpayment is required
   b. $3,250
   c. $2,479
   d. $1,112

5. A veteran may obtain a VA-guaranteed loan on a:
   a. single-family residence only
   b. residence with up to four units, as long as all units are rented out
   c. residence with up to four units, as long as the veteran occupies one unit
   d. residence with up to six units, as long as at least one unit is rented out

6. Martha Jones served in the army on active duty for 120 days in 1989. Jones is:
   a. eligible for full VA entitlement
   b. eligible for partial VA entitlement
   c. eligible for a VA loan only if she meets the underwriting standards
   d. not eligible for a VA loan

7. Ryan Spar is an air force veteran with full entitlement. He's buying a home for $132,000, financing the purchase with a VA loan. The VA guaranty for his loan will be:
   a. $24,800
   b. $32,800
   c. $36,000
   d. $5,500

8. The VA allows secondary financing to be used in conjunction with a VA-guaranteed loan only if the:
   a. total amount financed does not exceed the appraised value
   b. borrower's income is sufficient to qualify for the payments on both loans
   c. second loan allows assumption by a creditworthy buyer
   d. All of the above

9. An underwriter starts with the VA loan applicant's gross income and subtracts payroll taxes, the monthly shelter expense, and the applicant's other recurring obligations. She is calculating the applicant's:
   a. maximum guaranty amount
   b. projected maintenance and utility costs
   c. residual income
   d. remaining entitlement

10. Unless there are compensating factors, a VA loan applicant's debt to income ratio usually cannot exceed:
    a. 36%
    b. 33%
    c. 41%
    d. 53%

Answer Key

1. b.   The government's guaranty reduces the lender's risk of loss in case of default by the borrower. Because of this, lenders are willing to make VA loans without requiring the borrower to make a downpayment.

2. d.   When a VA loan is assumed, the original borrower's entitlement can be restored only if there is a substitution of entitlement. The buyer assuming the loan must be an eligible veteran or service member with adequate guaranty entitlement who agrees to the substitution of entitlement, and a request for a substitution of entitlement must be submitted to the VA.

3. a.   No prepayment penalties are allowed with VA loans.

4. a.   Currently, lenders in most areas will lend up to $453,100 without a downpayment. As long as the sales price doesn't exceed the appraised value of the property, the veteran won't need to make a downpayment.

5. c.   A VA loan can be used to buy a residential property with up to four units, if the borrower will occupy one of the units.

6. d.   For veterans whose service began in the 1980s, eligibility requires a minimum of 181 days of continuous active duty service during peacetime. The year Jones served (1989) is considered peacetime, since that was after the Vietnam War, but before the Gulf War period began in August 1990. Because Jones only served 120 days during peacetime, she isn't eligible for a VA loan, even if that was the full period for which she was called to active duty.

7. c.   For a loan amount between $56,251 and $144,000, the VA guaranty amount is 40% of the loan amount, up to a maximum of $36,000 (see Figure 12.1). Forty percent of $132,000 is $52,800, so the guaranty amount would be $36,000.

8. d.   A VA borrower may finance a downpayment if the total financing doesn't exceed the appraised value, the borrower's income is enough to qualify for the payments on both loans, and the second loan is assumable. However, this applies only to a downpayment that the lender requires because the guaranty is less than 25% of the sales price. Secondary financing can't be used for a downpayment that's required by VA rules because the sales price exceeds the appraised value.

9. c.   This is how a loan applicant's residual income is calculated.

10. c.   A VA loan applicant's debt to income ratio generally can't exceed 41% unless there are compensating factors, such as more residual income than the minimum required.

Case Study: VA-Guaranteed Loans

Once again, let's return to Rick and Teresa Cortina. This time we'll assume that they're thinking of buying their first home with a VA loan. (Rick was in the Army; his service included more than 24 months of continuous active duty, and he received an honorable discharge.) The Cortinas live in the VA's Southern region, and they have no children. The maximum VA guaranty amount in their area is $113,275.

Refer back to the case study at the end of Chapter 10 for the information you will need about the Cortinas' financial situation in order to answer the following questions. There's a worksheet at the end of this case study that you can use for the calculations.

Interest rates and fees

Lenders in the Cortinas' area are generally charging the following interest rates and fees for VA loans:

Fixed rate: 5.5% interest, 1% origination fee, no discount points
ARM: 4.625% interest, 1% origination fee, no discount points

1. Using the same figures for the Cortinas' monthly income and recurring charges that you used for the case studies in Chapters 10 and 11, apply the standard VA income ratio to determine their maximum mortgage payment (PITI) for a VA loan. Round that figure up to the next dollar for Question 2.

2. Calculate how much residual income the Cortinas would have if they had the monthly housing expense you arrived at in Question 1 and were considering a 1,450-square-foot home. (You'll need the Cortinas' payroll tax figures, which are listed at the beginning of the Chapter 10 case study.) The estimated maintenance and utility costs, which are included in the monthly shelter expense, will be 14 cents per square foot (the figure that the VA currently requires lenders to use for the estimate). Check the residual income chart in this chapter (Figure 12.2) and compare the Cortinas' residual income to the VA's required minimum. (Assume that they'll be borrowing over $80,000.) Do the Cortinas have enough residual income to qualify for this monthly housing expense?

3. Now consider whether the Cortinas can qualify for a larger VA loan payment than the one from Question 1. What's the largest PITI payment they could qualify for if they were allowed a 45% debt to income ratio? With that larger payment, what would their residual income be? Do the Cortinas have enough extra residual income so that the lender could approve a loan with that larger payment even if there were no other compensating factors in their financial situation?

4. If 15% of the larger PITI payment from Question 3 would go toward property taxes and hazard insurance, how much would the principal and interest portion of the payment be? With that principal and interest payment, the maximum VA loan that the Cortinas could qualify for (at 5.5% interest) is approximately $545,050. Using the 2018 limits shown in Figure 12.1, how much would the VA guaranty for this loan amount be? (Again, the Cortinas live in a county where the maximum guaranty is $113,275.)

5. The Cortinas still want to buy the home priced at $505,000 that they considered buying with a conventional loan (see Question 7 in the Chapter 10 case study). If they use a VA loan to buy that house instead of a conventional loan, will the lender require the Cortinas to make a downpayment? How much cash would the Cortinas need at closing? They would have to pay the funding fee (2.15% of the loan amount) and the origination fee (the lender's flat fee); assume that they'd also have to pay other closing costs adding up to about 3% of the sales price. No reserves are required.

6. Are the Cortinas likely to choose a VA loan over a conventional loan or an FHA loan? Why or why not?

Income Qualifying—VA-Guaranteed Loans

Taxes (per month)

Wage earner 1

_____ Federal income tax

_____ State income tax

_____ Social Security/Medicare

Wage earner 2

_____ Federal income tax

_____ State income tax

+ _____ Social Security/Medicare

_____ Total taxes withheld

Recurring Charges

Car loans _____

Credit cards _____

Student loans _____

Other debts _____

Job-related costs _____

Child support _____

Alimony _____

Other + _____

Total _____

Gross Monthly Income

Base salary

Wage earner 1 _____

Wage earner 2 _____

Overtime _____

Commissions _____

Bonuses _____

Other + _____

Total _____

Estimated Maintenance & Utilities

_____ Square feet of living area

x $0.14 Per square foot

_____ Maintenance and utilities

Debt to Income Ratio

_____ Gross monthly income

_____ x .41 Standard ratio (41%)

_____ Maximum obligations

− _____ Recurring obligations

_____ Maximum PITI payment
with standard 41% ratio

_____ Gross monthly income

_____ x .45 Higher ratio (45%)

_____ Maximum obligations

− _____ Recurring obligations

_____ Maximum PITI payment
with a 45% ratio

Income Qualifying—VA-Guaranteed Loans

Residual Income Analysis

Required minimum residual income _____

_____	Gross monthly income
_____	Taxes
_____	Recurring obligations
− _____	Monthly shelter expense (housing expense from 41% ratio, plus maintenance and utilities)
_____	**Residual Income**

_____	Gross monthly income
_____	Taxes
_____	Recurring obligations
− _____	Monthly shelter expense (housing expense from 45% ratio, plus maintenance and utilities)
_____	**Residual Income**

Income ratio over 41% acceptable with compensating factors.

If residual income exceeds the minimum by more than 20%, a ratio over 41% is acceptable even without any other compensating factors.

PITI Payment with 45% ratio _____

_____	Maximum PITI payment
_____ ÷ 1.15	15% for property taxes and hazard insurance
_____	Maximum principal and interest payment
	Interest rate _____

Sales Price _____

_____	Sales price
_____ × .25	Guaranty percentage for VA loan over $453,100
_____	25% of sales price
− _____	Maximum guaranty in county
_____	Downpayment required by lender
_____	Sales price
− _____	Downpayment
_____	Loan amount

Chapter 13
Seller Financing

How Seller Financing Works

When and Why Seller Financing is Used

Seller Seconds

- Supplementing a new loan
- Supplementing an assumption

Seller Financing as Primary Financing

- Unencumbered property
  - Protecting seller's security
  - Seller financing plus institutional second
  - Land contracts
- Encumbered property: wraparound financing

Alternatives to Seller Financing

- Buydowns
- Contributions to closing costs
- Equity exchanges
- Lease arrangements

Legal Responsibilities in Seller-Financed Transactions

- Disclosure statements
- Buyer's ability to repay
- Agent's liability

Introduction

Institutional lenders are not the only source of residential financing; home sellers are another important source. The variety of ways in which a seller can finance a buyer's purchase is the subject of this chapter.

We will begin with a basic explanation of how seller financing works and why it is used. Then we'll examine the forms seller financing can take, looking first at how it can function as secondary financing, and then at how it can function as primary financing. After that, we will briefly consider a few alternatives to seller financing—ways a seller can help the buyer without actually financing the purchase. In the last section of the chapter, we'll discuss the real estate agent's responsibilities in a seller-financed transaction.

How Seller Financing Works

Purchase money loan:
- Seller extends credit to buyer
- Buyer gives seller mortgage or deed of trust

Just like a bank or a savings and loan, a seller can use a promissory note accompanied by a mortgage or deed of trust to finance the buyer's purchase. The buyer takes title to the property and makes regular payments to the seller; the seller is the mortgagee or beneficiary, with the right to foreclose if the buyer defaults. This kind of transaction, where a mortgage or deed of trust is given by a buyer to a seller (instead of a third-party lender), is commonly called a **purchase money loan** or a **seller carryback loan**.

A purchase money loan differs from an institutional loan in that the seller is simply extending credit to the buyer, rather than actually supplying loan funds. The seller finances the purchase by allowing the buyer to pay the price in installments over time, instead of requiring payment in full at closing.

Land contract: alternative to purchase money loan in certain situations

For certain transactions, a seller has an alternative that institutional lenders do not have: the land contract. With a **land contract**, the buyer (vendee) takes possession of the property, but the seller (vendor) retains title until the contract price has been paid in full. Like a purchase money loan, a land contract represents an extension of credit from the seller to the buyer. We'll discuss land contracts in more detail later in this chapter.

In some transactions, seller financing is secondary financing: a "seller second" that supplements an institutional first mortgage. In other cases, the seller provides primary financing, serving as the buyer's main source or only source of financing for the purchase.

In a transaction that involves both institutional financing and seller financing, the seller probably will not be allowed to use a land contract. As a general rule, an institutional lender is not willing to make a loan to someone who will not initially have title to the security property (which is the case with the vendee in a land contract).

Aside from that consideration, a seller will usually decide which type of finance instrument to use based on the remedies each type allows in the event of default, which varies depending on state law (see Chapter 5). For example, in many states, sellers who want to be able to foreclose without going to court would choose a deed of trust. Foreclosure laws are generally the same for a purchase money mortgage or deed of trust as for any other mortgage or deed of trust, but there may be important exceptions. For instance, in some states a seller cannot obtain a deficiency judgment after foreclosure of a purchase money loan, even if it was a judicial foreclosure.

The finance instruments used in a seller-financed transaction should be prepared by a real estate lawyer, or at least reviewed by a lawyer before the parties sign them. If the seller uses a deed of trust, she will have to appoint a trustee when the loan documents are executed. Institutional lenders, title insurance companies, and lawyers often serve as trustees.

Terminology. The term "purchase money loan" can be confusing. Sometimes, instead of referring to a loan from a property seller to a buyer, it's used more broadly to mean any mortgage loan used to purchase the property that serves as the collateral for that loan (in contrast to a loan secured by property that the borrower already owns, such as a home equity loan or refinancing). In this book, however, we use the term "purchase loan," as opposed to "purchase money loan," for that broader meaning.

When and Why Seller Financing Is Used

What's the point of seller financing? It can help sell the property, especially when institutional loans are hard to get.

In a tight money market, sometimes the only way a seller can find a buyer is to finance part of the purchase price himself. When

Seller financing can be secondary financing or primary financing

417

Seller financing can:
- Attract buyers when interest rates are high
- Help buyers qualify for institutional loan
- Enable sellers to charge higher price
- Provide tax benefits to sellers

prevailing market interest rates are very high, many potential home buyers can't qualify for institutional financing. Others decide not to buy because they aren't willing to take on an expensive institutional loan. In this situation, a seller can attract buyers by offering financing at an interest rate significantly below the market rate. Even if the seller isn't in a position to finance the entire transaction, a seller second at a lower interest rate can offset the high rate charged on the institutional loan and enable the buyer to qualify. However, interest rates have been low by historical standards for decades, so the use of seller financing for this reason is rare now. If rates rise high enough, though, the practice may well become more common again.

Although seller financing is especially important when interest rates are high, it can also be used as a marketing tool at other times. In some cases, buyers are willing to pay more for a home if the seller offers financing. It may allow the buyers to avoid or reduce certain loan costs (such as an origination fee and discount points), enabling them to close with less cash. A seller could agree to a payment plan that might not be available from local lenders: graduated payments, biweekly payments, or a partially amortized or interest-only loan with a balloon payment. Or the seller might be willing to extend credit to buyers who can't qualify for a conventional loan even though market interest rates are low.

> **Example:** Grandma Perkins owns her house free and clear. She has decided to move to her sister's farm, so she wants to sell her house. The Jarrells, a young couple from Grandma's church, are interested in buying it. They couldn't qualify for conventional financing, but Grandma believes they are honest and reliable people who can be trusted to pay off a loan.
>
> She offers them the following deal: a sales price of $120,000, with $5,000 down and the balance in the form of a purchase money loan, secured by a deed of trust with Grandma as the beneficiary. Interest will accrue at the rate of 3% for the first year, and increase 0.5% per year until it reaches 6%, where it will stay for the balance of the 30-year loan term. Payments are to be interest-only for the first five years, with the principal then fully amortized over the balance of the term.

Seller should evaluate risks, but does not have to follow institutional lending rules

A typical home seller isn't bound by institutional lending policies regarding yields, loan-to-value ratios, or debt to income ratios. There are risks involved in setting those rules aside, and these risks should be carefully weighed. (The unusual financing arrangement in the example above could turn out badly for both parties. See the "Legal Responsibilities" section at the end of this chapter.) But some extra risk may be justified if the financing arrangement allows the sale to proceed or enables the seller to get a higher price for the home.

The flexibility of seller financing has a dark side, though. Because seller financing has traditionally been subject to comparatively little government oversight, predatory companies have used it to circumvent regulations that apply to standard mortgage lending.

> **Example:** Blackguard Homes buys foreclosed houses in economically disadvantaged urban neighborhoods and then resells them on contract to vulnerable buyers. The company doesn't care whether a buyer will actually be able to pay off the purchase price, since it will also profit if the buyer forfeits the house because the payments are unaffordable.

However, under the Dodd-Frank Act, land contracts and other forms of seller financing are now generally subject to the same rules that require strict scrutiny of a residential mortgage loan applicant's ability to repay a loan. This requirement (and which transactions are exempt from it) is explained at the end of the chapter.

In addition to making it easier to sell the home, seller financing can have tax benefits for the seller. Because the buyer is paying in installments over a period of years, the seller is not required to report the full profit from the sale on her federal income tax return in the year of the sale. Only the amount of profit actually received in a given year is considered taxable income for that year. Not only is the seller allowed to defer payment of part of the taxes, the profit from the sale may be taxed at a lower rate. (If it had been received in one lump sum, it could have pushed the seller into a higher tax bracket.)

Of course, seller financing is most useful when the seller has a cushion of significant home equity. It isn't an option for a seller who needs to be fully cashed out right away—for example, a seller who is planning to use all of his net equity from this home to buy a new one. But in many circumstances a downpayment is enough to satisfy the seller's need for cash at closing.

Now that you have a general understanding of how seller financing works and why it's used, we'll look more closely at the different forms it can take. First we'll focus on secondary financing from the seller, used in conjunction with an institutional loan. Then we'll discuss seller financing as primary financing.

Seller Seconds

Seller financing is often secondary financing. The buyer is paying most of the purchase price with an institutional loan—either by taking out a new loan, or by assuming the seller's existing loan. But instead of requiring the buyer to pay the difference between the loan amount and the purchase price in cash, the seller accepts a second mortgage for part of the remainder.

Seller second can supplement new institutional loan or assumption

In this section of the chapter, we will show how a seller second can help a buyer qualify for an institutional loan. We'll also discuss the factors that shape a seller second for a particular transaction—how much of the price the seller will finance, and on what terms. At the end of this section, we'll look at how a seller second can supplement an assumption.

Supplementing a New Loan

When it supplements a new institutional loan, a seller second has to meet certain standards applied by the lender. If the new loan is conventional, the lender will usually apply secondary financing rules similar to the ones discussed in Chapter 10, which are summarized in Figure 13.1. (There are also specific rules for secondary financing in conjunction with FHA and VA loans—see Chapters 11 and 12.)

Seller second supplementing new loan must comply with lender's rules

Fig. 13.1 Summary of common secondary financing rules

Secondary Financing with a Conventional First Loan

1. Total financing (the combined LTV) may not exceed 95%.

2. The second loan must have regularly scheduled payments.

3. The second loan can't require a balloon payment less than five years after closing.

4. If the first loan has variable payments, the second loan may be required to have fixed payments.

5. The second loan can't permit negative amortization.

6. The second loan can't have a prepayment penalty.

7. The buyer must qualify for both loan payments.

Although the secondary financing rules in Figure 13.1 impose significant limitations, many versions of a seller second (with different loan amounts, interest rates, and other features) could comply with them. The seller second in the following example is just one version that meets the case. In the example, the institutional loan combined with a seller second is compared to an institutional loan without seller financing. This comparison demonstrates how a seller second can help a buyer qualify for an institutional loan.

> **Example:** The Bukowskis are selling their home; its appraised value is $405,000. The Fulbrights have offered to buy the house for $400,000. Setting aside enough cash for closing costs and reserves, they have about $40,000 left over for a downpayment. Market interest rates are high; the Fulbrights will have to pay 9.5% interest for a fixed-rate mortgage.
>
> If the Fulbrights applied for a 30-year, 90% conventional loan from an institutional lender, they would have to qualify for a monthly payment of approximately $3,390. That includes principal, interest, taxes, and hazard insurance, and also private mortgage insurance, since the LTV is over 80%.
>
> However, the Fulbrights' stable monthly income is only $10,500, and their monthly debt payments (other than their housing expenses) add up to $850. There aren't any compensating factors in their financial situation that would lead the lender to accept an income ratio higher than the standard 36%. That means the highest monthly mortgage payment the Fulbrights are likely to qualify for is $2,930.

$10,500	Stable monthly income
× 36%	Maximum total obligations ratio
$3,780	
− 850	Monthly debt payments
$2,930	Maximum allowable monthly housing expense

Thus, the 90% conventional loan is out of the Fulbrights' reach at current market rates. But suppose the Bukowskis are willing to finance part of the purchase price in order to close the sale. They agree to finance $160,000 at 7% interest; there will be monthly interest-only payments, with a balloon payment of $160,000 (the entire principal amount) due in seven years. Now the Fulbrights will only need to borrow $200,000 from an institutional lender, instead of $360,000. Here's how the transaction would work:

Downpayment: $40,000

Conventional first mortgage:
$200,000, 30-year term, 9.5% fixed interest rate
$1,840 monthly payment (PITI, but no mortgage insurance)

Seller second mortgage:
$160,000, 7-year term (no amortization)
7% fixed interest rate
$1,064 monthly interest payment
$160,000 balloon payment due after 7 years
Total monthly payment for both loans: $2,904

The total monthly payment for both loans will be $2,904, which is $486 a month less than the payment on the $360,000 conventional loan. That's enough of a difference to enable the Fulbrights to qualify for this combination of an institutional loan and a seller second.

The $160,000, 7%, interest-only seller second in the example is by no means the only one that would comply with the rules for secondary financing in conjunction with a conventional loan. The sellers could have financed a larger share of the price, charged a different interest rate, partially amortized the loan, provided for interest rate adjustments, and so on. In combining a conventional loan with a seller second (a process sometimes called "loan structuring"), several different elements can be manipulated: the relative amounts of the two loans; the downpayment amount; and the amortization, term, payment schedule, and interest rate of the seller second. Taken altogether, there are dozens of combinations for financing a $400,000 single-family home with a conventional first mortgage and a seller second.

Of course, all combinations are not created equal. Only certain combinations will fit the financial circumstances of a particular buyer and a particular seller.

Buyer's Situation. As the previous example suggests, two factors in a prospective buyer's financial situation shape the design of a seller second. The first is how much money the buyer has for a downpayment (after setting aside enough cash for the closing costs and the required reserves). The second factor is the total monthly payment that the buyer can qualify for.

In evaluating a seller second, the buyer will naturally focus on these two factors. But many seller seconds have another feature that the buyer should consider carefully: the balloon payment.

Look at the example again. This interest-only seller second has a low monthly payment. However, after seven years the buyers will have to come up with $160,000 to pay off the sellers. If the buyers aren't planning to keep the house that long, the balloon payment

Loan structuring: combining a first mortgage with secondary financing

Buyer's evaluation of first loan + seller second:
- *Downpayment amount*
- *Combined monthly payment for both loans*
- *Balloon payment*

doesn't present much of a problem; they will pay it when they sell the property. Otherwise, the buyers will have to save up the amount of the balloon payment, or else refinance the property when the time comes.

> **Example:** Nearly seven years have passed, and it's almost time for the Fulbrights to make their $160,000 balloon payment to the Bukowskis. The house the Fulbrights bought is now worth about $484,000, and their equity in the property is about $134,000.
>
> The Fulbrights apply to an institutional lender for refinancing. Interest rates have fallen, and the Fulbrights' income has increased. The lender loans them $350,000 and accepts a new mortgage against the home. The Fulbrights use part of this refinance loan to make the balloon payment on the seller second, and they pay off their old conventional loan with the rest.

In many situations, it's easy to refinance, especially when the property has appreciated substantially. (In the example, the LTV for the refinance loan is only 72%.) And if interest rates have fallen, refinancing can result in lower mortgage payments. Under other circumstances, however, such as declining property values or increasing interest rates, refinancing may be difficult to obtain or may increase the mortgage payments. Also, refinancing usually costs at least a few thousand dollars (for loan fees, an appraisal, and so forth).

Seller financing arrangements that require a large balloon payment can work out fine, so a buyer should not necessarily avoid them. But the buyer should give careful thought to where the money for the balloon payment will come from.

Seller's Situation. When a seller evaluates possible secondary financing arrangements, she should consider cash flow and yield. How much cash is needed at closing? Will the monthly payment on the seller second be an adequate addition to her income? How soon does she need the balloon payment (if any)? Does the interest rate on the second loan represent a reasonable return?

Seller's evaluation of second:
- Cash at closing
- Monthly income
- Timing of payoff (balloon payment)
- Yield on investment
- Tax consequences
- Lien priority

The seller also has to consider the tax consequences of each possible arrangement, preferably with expert advice. Although seller financing often has tax benefits for the seller, some arrangements will backfire. For instance, a seller who offers financing at an exceptionally low interest rate may run up against the "imputed interest" rules in the federal tax code. Under those rules, if the stated interest rate on seller financing is below a specified minimum, the Internal Revenue Service will treat a portion of the principal received each year as if it were interest. In effect, the IRS treats the sale as if the seller had charged a lower price for the home, but a higher interest rate on the financing. This can have an impact on the seller's income taxes, since all of the interest on an installment sale is taxed, while only a portion (if any) of the principal payments is taxed. (For instance, if the seller took a loss on the sale, the principal wouldn't be taxed at all.)

Lien priority is another important consideration for a seller who offers secondary financing. Purchase money mortgages are subject to the same priority rules as institutional mortgages. In the event of foreclosure, the first mortgage must be paid in full from the sale proceeds before any proceeds are allocated to the second mortgage (see Chapter 5). The seller should keep this in mind when negotiating the amount of a seller second. Is the property worth enough so that the proceeds of a foreclosure sale would be likely to cover both the first and second mortgages? The seller should be especially careful when there is a possibility that property values will decline in the next few years.

Supplementing an Assumption

Assumption + seller second: when existing mortgage has low interest rate and no due-on-sale clause

In some cases, a seller second can supplement the buyer's assumption of an existing mortgage on the property. The buyer will make a monthly payment to the seller, and also take over responsibility for the monthly payment the seller has been making to the lender.

> **Example:** The current market interest rate for a fixed-rate loan is 9%. The Rainwaters' property has an existing mortgage with a $376,500 balance and a 6% interest rate. The mortgage has 240 payments of $2,697.36 remaining.
> Ray McCarthy is interested in buying the Rainwaters' property and assuming their mortgage, but he does not have the $109,500 in cash needed to meet the $486,000 sales price. McCarthy can make a $30,000 downpayment if the Rainwaters will take back a second deed of trust for the remaining $79,500. The Rainwaters agree to accept the second deed of trust at 8% interest (partially amortized, with a balloon payment due in ten years), and the sale closes. Each month, McCarthy sends $2,697.36 to the Rainwaters' lender for the first loan, and $583.34 to the Rainwaters themselves for the second loan.

Assumption is attractive to buyers whenever the interest rate on the seller's existing mortgage is significantly lower than market rates at the time of the sale. But an assumption is only possible if the existing mortgage does not include a due-on-sale clause, or if the lender agrees to the assumption (see Chapter 5).

Whether or not there is a due-on-sale clause, the lender's consent is always necessary if the seller wants to be released from liability on the existing mortgage. When the assumption is going to be supplemented by a seller second, the lender will scrutinize the second loan before releasing the seller from the first loan. The lender will generally apply the same standards to a seller second supplementing an assumption as it would to a seller second supplementing a new loan (see above). For example, the lender will make sure that the buyer can afford the payments on both loans before agreeing to the release—or, if there is a due-on-sale clause, before agreeing to the assumption at all.

Exercise No. 1

The Pengs listed their house for $715,000; it's been on the market for quite a while, and they'd like to get it sold soon. Mary Underwood and Joe Schirmer have offered to buy the property for $695,000, its appraised value. The current market interest rate for a fixed-rate mortgage is 8%. Underwood and Schirmer have a combined stable monthly income of $22,000, and their debt payments total $2,000 per month, not including the housing expense. They don't have enough cash to qualify for a 95% conventional loan, though.

Suppose that the Pengs accept the $695,000 offer and are willing to finance part of the purchase price—$55,000—at 6% interest. This seller second would be amortized over 30 years, so the monthly principal and interest payment would be only $329.75, but a balloon payment of the remaining principal balance would be due after five years. (The remaining principal balance after five years would be approximately $51,435.) Underwood and Schirmer would make a $35,000 downpayment and apply to an institutional lender for a conventional loan at 8% interest, with a monthly principal and interest payment of $4,439.28.

1. What percentage of the purchase price do the downpayment and the seller second represent? What would the loan-to-value ratio of the institutional loan be?

2. Calculate the loan amounts for the institutional loan and the seller second. What is the combined loan amount?

3. Does this loan arrangement comply with the typical rules for secondary financing in conjunction with a conventional loan that are listed in Figure 13.1?

4. In addition to the principal and interest for both loans, the monthly housing expense payment will include $560 for property taxes and $100 for hazard insurance, plus $440 for private mortgage insurance on the institutional loan. What would Underwood and Schirmer's debt to income ratio and housing expense to income ratio be? Based on the information about qualifying standards for conventional loans in Chapter 10, could they qualify for this conventional loan combined with the seller second? Explain why or why not.

Seller Financing as Primary Financing

Seller financing is most flexible when it is the buyer's only source or main source of financing. We'll look first at financing arrangements for unencumbered property, including land contracts, and then at wraparound financing, a technique used for property that is subject to an existing mortgage.

Unencumbered Property

When the seller has clear title to the property, free of any mortgages or other liens, seller financing is straightforward. The buyer and seller simply negotiate the sales price and the terms of their financing ar-

Seller financing is very flexible when property is not encumbered by an existing loan

rangement and have the appropriate documents drawn up. Of course, they still have to consider how much of a downpayment the buyer can make, how much cash the seller needs, and whether the buyer can afford the monthly payments—but they are not constrained by any institutional rules.

Even if the seller requires a substantial downpayment, the buyer is likely to need less cash for seller financing than for a comparable institutional loan. The buyer won't have to pay discount points or an origination fee, and in some cases other closing costs will be lower.

Protecting the Seller's Security. Lien priority does not present the same problem here that it does with a seller second. As long as the finance instruments are recorded at closing, the seller is ordinarily assured of first lien position. The seller's security interest will not be threatened by the foreclosure of most other liens. If a junior lienholder were to foreclose, the purchaser at the foreclosure sale would take title subject to the seller's lien.

However, the seller should still be concerned about protecting her security interest. Even a mortgage in first lien position has lower lien priority than the lien for general property taxes and any special assessment liens. (In some states, mortgage liens also have lower priority than homeowners association liens.) If the buyer fails to pay the taxes or assessments, the government can foreclose, and the seller may take a loss at the foreclosure sale. Also, if the buyer fails to keep the property insured, the seller's security interest could become worthless if the property is damaged or destroyed.

Of course, failure to pay the taxes or insure the property is a default under the terms of virtually all finance instruments (see Chapter 5). But the seller can help prevent this type of default by setting up an impound account for taxes and hazard insurance, just as many institutional lenders do (see Chapter 7). The seller may choose to have a loan servicer handle the buyer's payments, in exchange for a servicing fee. Many banks, savings and loans, and mortgage companies service loans on behalf of private parties; so do many certified public accountants. Each month, the servicer will deposit part of the buyer's payment into the impound account and pass the remainder on to the seller.

Seller can require impound account to protect security interest

Seller Financing Plus an Institutional Second. Sometimes a seller is willing to finance a good part of the purchase price, but also needs a substantial amount of cash at closing. For example, the seller may

Institutional second can supplement seller financing if seller needs cash

need the funds to make a downpayment on another property. If the buyer does not have enough cash, it may be possible to bridge the gap between the seller financing and the downpayment with a second mortgage from an institutional lender.

> **Example:** Linda Stanford has agreed to buy Charlotte Halvorsen's house for $480,000. Halvorsen is willing to accept a purchase money mortgage for $423,000 (at 7% interest, partially amortized with a balloon payment due in ten years), but she needs at least $57,000 at closing.
>
> Stanford can only afford a $33,000 downpayment, so she applies to an institutional lender for a $24,000 loan. The lender agrees to make the loan at 9% interest (fully amortized over a ten-year term), accepting second lien position for its mortgage. Stanford will pay $2,814 per month to Halvorsen and $304 per month to the institutional lender.

This is the mirror image of the financing arrangements we looked at earlier, where a seller second made up the difference between an institutional loan and the downpayment. Like an institutional lender, a seller offering primary financing should find out where the buyer is going to get the rest of the purchase price. If a second mortgage is involved, the seller should investigate the terms of the proposed second before agreeing to the transaction. Can the buyer afford the monthly payment on both loans? Does the second have any provisions that make default likely? For example, a second that requires a large balloon payment 18 months after closing is quite risky; the buyer could end up defaulting on the seller's loan as well as the second.

Land Contracts. A seller who is providing primary financing for the buyer might choose to use a land contract instead of a mortgage or deed of trust. Land contracts used to be particularly common in rural areas that had few banking options and where parties were likely to already know and trust each other. While they are no longer prevalent in rural areas, thanks to the rise of nationwide banks and uniform underwriting standards, they are still regularly used for seller financing in some parts of the country. They are known by several different names in different states; they may be called contracts for deed, bonds for deed, conditional sales contracts, installment sales contracts, installment land contracts, or real estate contracts.

Land contract: when seller is financing whole transaction, or for wraparound

Like a mortgage or deed of trust, a land contract is used to secure repayment of a debt. But while either a seller or a third-party lender can finance a buyer's purchase with a mortgage or deed of trust, only a seller can use a land contract. And a land contract works in quite a different way than those other instruments.

When the purchase of property is financed with either a mortgage or a deed of trust, the buyer takes title to the property immediately. Under a land contract, however, the seller (referred to as the **vendor**) retains legal title to the property until the buyer (the **vendee**) pays off the entire purchase price in installments. While paying off the contract—which may take many years—the vendee has the right to possess and enjoy the property, but is not the legal owner. (The vendee's interest in the property is sometimes called equitable title, in contrast to the vendor's legal title.) The vendor typically delivers the deed to the vendee only after the contract price has been paid in full.

In a land contract:
• Vendee has equitable title
• Vendor has legal title

A land contract should always be recorded. A mortgage or a deed of trust is recorded to protect the lender by establishing lien priority, but a land contract is recorded to protect the vendee. It gives public notice of the vendee's interest in the property and establishes the priority of his interest.

Unlike a mortgage or a deed of trust, a land contract is generally not accompanied by a promissory note. The contract states all of the terms of the sale and the financing arrangement between the vendor and vendee: the price, the interest rate, and the monthly payment amount; when the vendee can take possession; when the vendor will be required to deliver the deed to the vendee; and what action the vendor can take if the vendee breaches the contract by failing to pay as agreed.

Remedies for breach of contract. Land contracts sometimes provide that if the vendee defaults on the contract obligation, all of the vendee's rights in the property are terminated, all payments made may be retained by the vendor as liquidated damages, and the vendor may retake possession of the property immediately. This severe penalty for breach of a land contract is called **forfeiture**. Unfortunately for vendors and fortunately for vendees, courts do not always enforce land contracts exactly the way they are written.

Forfeiture:
• Vendee's rights terminated
• Payments are liquidated damages
• Vendor retakes possession

If the contract has been recorded, or if the vendee is in possession and refuses to leave, the vendor will usually have to take some legal action to clear title and/or remove the vendee from possession. As with a judicial foreclosure, the delay in reaching trial may be a matter of many months, depending on various factors, including court congestion in the county where the property is located. Once the case finally goes to trial, the judge may have a wide range of discretion in fashioning a remedy for the vendor. Depending on state law and on the circumstances of the case, a judge may:

- enforce the contract as written, allowing the seller to retain all payments received, terminating the vendee's rights, and ordering the vendee to vacate the property;
- give the vendee a certain amount of time (anywhere from one month to one year) to pay off the entire contract balance;
- allow the vendee to simply reinstate the contract by paying delinquent payments plus interest; or
- order a sheriff's sale of the property with any surplus to go to the vendee, as would occur with a mortgage foreclosure.

In some states, the vendee's rights depend on how far along in the contract term it is when the vendee defaults. If the vendee has been making payments to the vendor for a long time, forfeiture would be especially harsh. In that situation, the law might not allow a forfeiture.

Some states do not allow forfeiture as remedy in certain circumstances

Advantages and disadvantages. For the vendor, one advantage of a contract sale may be the sense of security that can come from remaining the legal owner and not giving the vendee a deed until the entire purchase price has been paid. As our discussion of the forfeiture remedy suggests, however, this feeling of security may be largely illusory.

When forfeiture is allowed, the vendor may reacquire the property—which may have appreciated in value—instead of having to sell it and give any surplus to the debtor (as would be required in a mortgage or deed of trust foreclosure). This can be a substantial advantage for the vendor.

The main disadvantage for the vendor under a land contract is the delay and expense involved in court proceedings, which are frequently necessary in the event of breach. In many states, this disadvantage is increased by the uncertainty concerning the result after the case gets to trial.

For the vendee, the slow court proceedings in the event of a breach can be an advantage, although the uncertainty is undesirable. A serious disadvantage for the vendee under a land contract is that the vendor remains the legal owner of the property. This can create a variety of problems for the vendee. For example, in some states, a court judgment entered against the vendor might cloud the vendee's interest in the property, since the vendor is still the legal owner. And it might be difficult or even impossible for the vendee to obtain bank financing for construction or improvements. As we're about to discuss, banks are very reluctant to lend to someone who does not have legal title.

Using a land contract. A seller who is financing the entire transaction is free to use a land contract if she prefers it to a mortgage or deed of trust. But if the buyer wants to combine primary financing from the seller with institutional secondary financing, it will be hard to find a lender to make the second loan if the seller is using a land contract.

> **Example:** In an earlier example, Linda Stanford agreed to buy Charlotte Halvorsen's house for $480,000. Halvorsen was willing to accept a purchase money mortgage for $423,000, but she needed at least $57,000 at closing. Stanford could only afford a $33,000 downpayment, so she applied to an institutional lender for a $24,000 second mortgage.
>
> Now suppose Halvorsen offers to sell Stanford the property on those same terms, but she wants to use a land contract instead of a purchase money mortgage. Stanford still needs to pay Halvorsen $57,000 at closing, and she still has only $33,000 in cash. When she applies to a lender for a $24,000 mortgage, the lender turns her down.
>
> The problem is that under the contract, Stanford will not have legal title to the property. For that reason, she cannot use the property as security for the loan.

In theory, there are two possible solutions to this dilemma. Halvorsen (the vendor, who still has title) could agree to let the property stand as security for a loan to Stanford, without assuming personal responsibility for repayment. If Stanford were to default on the institutional second, the lender could foreclose on the property, but could not sue Halvorsen for a deficiency judgment. This might be acceptable to the lender, but it would present an additional risk for the vendor.

The other solution would be for Stanford to mortgage her equitable interest in the property. In a foreclosure, the lender would merely acquire Stanford's contract rights; the lender could not force the sale of the property. To obtain title, the lender would still have to pay Halvorsen the remainder of the contract price. Very few lenders regard a vendee's equitable interest as an acceptable form of collateral.

Neither of these solutions is particularly serviceable. So as a practical matter, a land contract only works in three situations. It works when the seller is able to provide all the financing the buyer needs. It works when the seller is supplementing an assumption, as long as the mortgagee's consent is not required; then the seller can use a contract for the secondary financing. And a land contract can also work for wraparound financing, which is our next topic.

Encumbered Property: Wraparound Financing

Most sellers own property that is encumbered by some form of mortgage lien. And if a seller must pay off an existing mortgage at closing, he usually can't afford to offer primary financing to the buyer.

> **Example:** Hank Ellison is selling his home for $404,000. Ellison would prefer to sell the property on an installment basis, receiving payments over a long period. But there is a mortgage against the property that has a 6.25% interest rate and a $305,200 balance. With an installment sale, Ellison would not have enough money at closing to pay off that balance.

Ellison might be able to arrange for the buyer to assume the existing mortgage, then finance the rest of the purchase price himself with a seller second (as explained earlier in the chapter). But there is another alternative that might appeal to Ellison: wraparound financing.

With a wraparound, the property remains subject to the seller's existing mortgage after the sale. The amount of the seller financing is larger than the balance owed on the existing mortgage, so the seller financing "wraps around" the existing mortgage. The buyer does not take on responsibility for the existing mortgage, which is usually referred to as the **underlying loan**. The seller remains responsible for making the payments on the underlying loan. Each month, the buyer makes a payment to the seller on the wraparound loan, and the seller uses a portion of that payment to make the payment on the underlying loan.

Wraparound:
- Seller accepts mortgage for most of purchase price
- Property remains subject to underlying loan

> **Example:** Continuing with the example above, suppose Ellison sells his house to Janet Kingman for $404,000, accepting $40,000 down and financing the balance of the purchase price ($364,000) with a deed of trust at 8.5%.
>
> Kingman takes title to the property subject to the $305,200 underlying mortgage, but she does not assume that loan. Her monthly payment to Ellison is $2,800. Out of that amount, $2,230 goes to the underlying mortgagee and Ellison gets to keep $570. The underlying mortgage will be paid off in 20 years, and at that point Kingman will be required to make a balloon payment to Ellison for the remaining balance on the wraparound loan.

For a wraparound, the seller can use a mortgage, a deed of trust, or a land contract. When a deed of trust is used for a wrap, it is often referred to as an "all-inclusive trust deed."

Wraparound financing is attractive because it enables the buyer to finance the purchase at a below-market interest rate while still providing a market rate of return (or better) for the seller. To clarify this apparent contradiction, let's continue with the example given above.

> **Example:** Although Ellison has received a $364,000 deed of trust from Kingman, he has actually extended only $58,800 in credit to her:
>
> | | |
> |---|---|
> | $404,000 | Sales price |
> | 40,000 | Downpayment |
> | − 305,200 | Underlying mortgage balance |
> | $58,800 | Credit extended — net owed to seller |
>
> Yet Ellison will receive 8.5% interest on the entire $364,000 wraparound, while paying only 6.25% interest on the $305,200 underlying loan balance. This means that in the first year he will pay out $19,075 in interest on the underlying mortgage, but will receive $30,940 in interest on the wrap from the buyer. That gives him a net gain of $11,865. Since he extended only $58,800 in credit, he is earning $11,865 on $58,800, which represents a 20% annual return.
>
> If the market interest rate is currently 9.5%, the seller is receiving more than double the market rate, while the buyer is paying 1% below the market rate.

Wraparound financing is fairly rare, for several reasons. First, a wrap makes sense only when current interest rates are significantly higher than they were when the seller obtained the underlying loan. More importantly, a wrap won't work if the underlying loan has a due-on-sale clause, and most institutional loans do contain this clause. Occasionally a seller will try to get around a due-on-sale clause by using a wraparound land contract and failing to notify the lender of the transaction; this is called a "silent wrap." But even though a contract sale does not involve an immediate transfer of title, it still gives the lender the right to accelerate the underlying loan pursuant to the due-on-sale clause. So if the lender finds out about the secret transaction, both the seller and the buyer will be in jeopardy. A real estate agent should never get involved in a silent wrap.

Wraparound works only if underlying loan does not have due-on-sale clause

Alternatives to Seller Financing

Short of financing purchase, seller can help buyer with:
- Buydown
- Contribution to closing costs
- Equity exchange
- Lease/option
- Lease/purchase

As you have seen, with a mortgage, deed of trust, or land contract, the seller can play the role of a lender by extending credit to the buyer. But in these seller financing arrangements, the seller often has to wait several years to collect the full profit from the sale. Not every seller is in a position to do that. In this section of the chapter, we will discuss some ways that a seller can help a buyer purchase his property without financing the transaction.

Buydowns

One way for a seller to assist a buyer is a buydown. Buydowns were explained in detail in Chapter 10. To buy down the interest rate on the buyer's institutional loan, the seller does not actually have to pay the lender a lump sum at closing. Instead, the seller's proceeds from the sale are reduced by the amount of the buydown. From the seller's point of view, it's as if she had agreed to lower the sales price, but the buydown could have greater benefits for the buyer than a straight price reduction would have (see Chapter 10).

Contributions to Closing Costs

Occasionally, after coming up with the required downpayment and reserves for an institutional loan, the buyer doesn't have quite enough cash left over to pay for closing costs. The seller may be willing to make up the shortfall. Depending on the circumstances, this type of cash contribution from the seller may be more helpful than a price reduction for the same amount.

However, there are limits on how much a seller can contribute to the buyer's closing costs for a conventional loan. If the seller's contribution exceeds those limits, the loan amount will be reduced (see Chapter 10). Because of these rules, in some cases a large contribution from the seller doesn't really help the buyer.

Equity Exchanges

When a buyer can't come up with enough cash for a purchase, the seller may be willing to accept other assets and reduce the cash sales price. Maybe the buyer has equity in some vacant land, or in personal property such as a recreational vehicle or a boat. If the seller wants the property and the buyer is ready to part with it, they can work out an exchange.

Example: Ellen Jarvis has decided to sell a rental house she owns. She lists the house for $450,000.

Frank Tillman would like to buy the house. He has $44,000 for a downpayment, which would be enough if he could obtain an institutional loan for $406,000. But Tillman can't qualify for a loan that large.

However, Tillman has meticulously restored a vintage sports car and is planning to sell it. The appraised value of the car is $55,000. In the course of a conversation with Jarvis, Tillman discovers that she happens to be a sports car buff. He shows her the car he restored, and after long negotiations, Jarvis agrees to reduce the sales price on her house to $400,000 if Tillman will give her the car.

With the sales price reduced to $400,000, Tillman applies for an 80% conventional loan ($320,000). He easily qualifies for this smaller loan, and the transaction closes.

Lease Arrangements

In some cases, a prospective buyer is interested in leasing a home before actually buying it. The buyer may need additional time to acquire enough cash for a downpayment or closing costs—by saving, or by selling other property, for instance. Or perhaps the buyer is currently unable to qualify for a large enough loan, but has reason to believe that circumstances will change before long.

If the seller is willing, the property can be leased to the prospective buyer in one of two ways: with a lease/option (a lease agreement that includes an option to purchase) or with a lease/purchase contract (a purchase contract that allows the buyer to lease the property for an extended period before closing). Although the two arrangements are related, there are important differences between them.

Lease/Option. A lease/option is made up of a lease and an option to purchase. A seller leases her property to a prospective buyer for a specific term (often six months or one year), and grants the buyer an option to purchase the leased property at a specified price during the term of the lease. The seller is the landlord and optionor, and the prospective buyer is the tenant and optionee. The tenant/optionee is under no obligation to buy the property, but the landlord/optionor is not supposed to sell the property to anyone else during the option period.

Lease/option:
- Lease with option to buy
- Limited time period
- Option money
- Rent credit

435

A lease/option is by no means the equivalent of a sale. A seller considering this type of arrangement should be warned that in the majority of cases, the tenant/optionee decides not to buy. However, a carefully structured lease/option may keep a possible sale alive until the buyer is in a position to close.

Because the failure rate is high, a seller generally only grants a lease/option when it seems unlikely that other offers will be forthcoming in the near future, or when the arrangement allows the seller to ask a higher price for the property. Of course, a lease/option won't work for residential property unless the seller has somewhere else to live. But the lease provides the seller with some income from the property, which can be used to make mortgage payments on a new house until the old house is sold, or to cover payments on an existing mortgage on the old house.

Note that unlike wraparound financing, a lease/option can be used with a property where there is a due-on-sale clause on the seller's loan. The due-on-sale clause is not triggered until the option is exercised.

How a lease/option works. The prospective buyer pays the seller a sum of money in exchange for the option. This **option money** is the consideration that makes the option a binding contract. Once paid, the option money is not refundable, whether or not the optionee goes through with the purchase. Many lease/option agreements provide that the option money will be applied to the purchase price, much like the good faith deposit (earnest money) in an ordinary purchase agreement.

A lease/option may also provide that part of the rental payments will be applied to the purchase if the tenant/optionee decides to buy. This is called a **rent credit** provision.

Option money:
- Consideration for option
- Not refundable
- Often applied to purchase

Example: John Caldwell is selling a house for $315,000. Mark Bettelheim is interested in the property, but he will not be able to qualify for a loan until he receives a raise that he's expecting this year. The parties execute a lease/option, and Bettelheim pays Caldwell $6,000 as option money.

Under the terms of their agreement, Bettelheim will lease the house for six months, paying $2,200 per month in rent. Bettelheim has the right to purchase the property at the agreed price at any time until the lease expires. If Bettelheim exercises his option, the option money and $1,100 out of each rental payment will be applied to the sales price.

So if Bettelheim decides to buy at the end of six months, he will pay $302,400, the amount owed after deducting the option money and $6,600 in rental payments from the original price. If Bettelheim decides not to buy, Caldwell will keep the option money and all of the rent.

The rent charged in a lease/option is often considerably higher than the rent that would be charged for the property under an ordinary lease. This gives the optionee an incentive to exercise the option as soon as possible, and also provides additional compensation to the seller for the uncertainty and inconvenience of the option.

Lease/option rent:
- Often higher than market rent
- Partial rent credit applied to purchase

There are two ways a rent credit can be applied toward the purchase: the amount of the credit can be deducted from the sales price (as it was in the example above), or the credit can be treated as part of the downpayment. A buyer who is short of cash might prefer to treat the credit as part of the downpayment. However, most institutional lenders will only accept a rent credit as part of the downpayment to the extent that the credit represents an extra amount paid above the fair market rent for the property. For instance, if the fair market rent was $1,500 and the lease/option rent was $1,800, no more than $300 out of each month's rent could be applied to the downpayment.

Provisions of a lease/option agreement. A lease/option should include all the terms of the lease and, in addition, all the terms of the potential purchase contract. That way, a binding purchase contract will be formed immediately if the optionee exercises the option to purchase.

Lease/option includes:
- All terms of lease
- All terms of potential purchase contract

The lease/option agreement should state that if the tenant/optionee defaults in connection with the lease (by failing to pay the rent, for example), the option rights will be forfeited.

The agreement should also make it clear that the option money is not a security deposit. (In most states, a tenant's security deposit must be kept in a trust account and refunded at the end of the lease. The seller can require a security deposit in a lease/option arrangement, but the deposit must be separate from the option money.) The agreement should specify that the option money may be disbursed to the seller/optionor as soon as the tenant/optionee moves into the home.

The amount of option money is negotiable, but it should be at least enough to pay the real estate brokerage fee. In some cases, the broker arranges to collect part of her fee out of the option money, and the remainder if the optionee goes through with the purchase. Keep in mind that the more option money the prospective buyer pays, the more likely it is that the option will be exercised.

Before signing the lease/option, the seller—like any other land-lord—should review a copy of the prospective tenant's credit report, to make sure that he is a good credit risk.

Buyers should be wary of using lease/option agreements in markets where home values are poised to decline. If values go down, the buyer will be left with the choice of buying the property for more than its current value, or losing the previously paid option money.

Lease/Purchase Contract. A number of variations on the lease/option have been used by sellers attempting to improve the chances that a sale will eventually take place. One of these variations is the lease/purchase contract.

For a lease/purchase contract, instead of signing an option, the seller and the prospective buyer actually sign a purchase contract along with the lease. The buyer usually gives the seller a substantial good faith deposit, and the closing date is set quite far off—six months to a year away. In the meantime, the buyer leases the property.

The practical effect of a lease/purchase contract is very similar to that of a lease/option. If the tenant/buyer decides not to buy the property, he simply forfeits the deposit—which isn't very different from losing option money, in practical terms. But there is a significant psychological difference; the buyer tends to feel more committed with a lease/purchase contract. Deciding not to go through with the purchase means breaching a contract, as opposed to merely choosing not to exercise an option. Some real estate agents believe a lease/purchase contract is much more likely to result in a sale than a lease/option.

A lease/purchase contract should have many of the same provisions as a lease/option. There may be a rent credit provision, and the contract should clearly state that the good faith deposit is not a security deposit. Again, the seller should be sure the buyer has a satisfactory credit history before signing the contract.

One use of "rent-to-own" contracts, especially lease/purchase contracts, is to encourage the purchase of fixer-uppers. A tenant/buyer can start building equity in the home during the lease phase by repairing and improving the property. Some companies, in fact, specialize in this kind of transaction, purchasing dilapidated houses and then selling them through rent-to-own contracts. Unfortunately, as with land contracts, this has recently become the domain of preda-

Lease/purchase contract:
- Parties sign purchase agreement, not option
- Closing date far off
- Eventual sale more likely than with lease/option

tory companies that finance unqualified buyers using a method less transparent than a standard mortgage loan.

Legal Responsibilities in Seller-Financed Transactions

The old saying "Where there's a will, there's a way" could be used as a slogan for seller financing. Open-minded negotiation between the buyer and the seller (and the lender, when applicable) can close transactions that otherwise would not make it. A creative real estate agent can be the catalyst, showing the parties that they have many alternatives.

However, there are risks in any seller financing arrangement, even if it's straightforward and carefully planned. An extension of credit always involves the risk of default. In a badly planned transaction without adequate safeguards, default may be more likely than repayment, and may result in a devastating financial loss for the seller. The risks affect the buyer, too. Suppose a seller offers graduated payment financing with very low initial payments; if the buyer can't afford the payment increases when the time comes, he may lose the home and everything he's put into it.

A real estate agent negotiating a seller-financed transaction should always suggest—and in most cases should strongly recommend—that the parties get legal and tax advice from real estate lawyers and/or certified public accountants. (It's best to make this recommendation in writing.) An agent should never give legal or tax advice. And as we said at the beginning of the chapter, the finance instruments for a seller-financed transaction should be prepared or reviewed by a lawyer.

Real estate agent should encourage both parties to consult a lawyer or CPA

Disclosure Statements

When a real estate agent (or another third party) helps arrange seller financing, some states require the agent to make certain written disclosures to the parties. The agent is usually supposed to fill out a disclosure form and give a copy to both the seller and the buyer before they commit themselves to the transaction. As an example, a form that meets the requirements of California's seller financing disclosure law is shown in Figure 13.2. This particular form is an addendum to the purchase agreement; it details all of the terms of the financing, from the interest rate to the late payment charge, while also providing disclosures about the legal obligations of the parties and the agent.

Seller financing disclosure statement:
- *Discloses all financing terms*
- *Informs seller of buyer's financial situation*
- *Required in some states*

Fig. 13.2 Seller financing disclosure statement

CALIFORNIA ASSOCIATION OF REALTORS®

SELLER FINANCING ADDENDUM AND DISCLOSURE
(SEE IMPORTANT DISCLOSURE ON PAGE 4)
(California Civil Code §§2956-2967)
(C.A.R. Form SFA, Revised 11/13)

This is an addendum to the ☐ Residential Purchase Agreement, ☐ Counter Offer, or ☐ Other _____
_____, ("Agreement"), dated _____,
On property known as _____ ("Property"),
between _____ ("Buyer"),
and _____ ("Seller").
Seller agrees to extend credit to Buyer as follows:

1. **PRINCIPAL; INTEREST; PAYMENT; MATURITY TERMS:** ☐ Principal amount $ _____, interest at _____%
   per annum, payable at approximately $ _____ per ☐ month, ☐ year, or ☐ other _____,
   remaining principal balance due in _____ years.

2. **LOAN APPLICATION; CREDIT REPORT:** Within **5 (or ☐ _____) Days** After Acceptance: (a) Buyer shall provide Seller a completed
   loan application on a form acceptable to Seller (such as a FNMA/FHLMC Uniform Residential Loan Application for residential one to
   four unit properties); and (b) Buyer authorizes Seller and/or Agent to obtain, at Buyer's expense, a copy of Buyer's credit report. Buyer
   shall provide any supporting documentation reasonably requested by Seller. Seller, after first giving Buyer a Notice to Buyer to Perform,
   may cancel this Agreement in writing and authorize return of Buyer's deposit if Buyer fails to provide such documents within that time,
   or if Seller disapproves any above item within **5 (or ☐ _____) Days** After receipt of each item.

3. **CREDIT DOCUMENTS:** This extension of credit by Seller will be evidenced by: ☐ Note and deed of trust; ☐ All-inclusive
   note and deed of trust; ☐ Installment land sale contract; ☐ Lease/option (when parties intend transfer of equitable title);
   OR ☐ Other (specify) _____

THE FOLLOWING TERMS APPLY ONLY IF CHECKED. SELLER IS ADVISED TO READ ALL TERMS, EVEN THOSE NOT
CHECKED, TO UNDERSTAND WHAT IS OR IS NOT INCLUDED, AND, IF NOT INCLUDED, THE CONSEQUENCES THEREOF.

4. ☐ **LATE CHARGE:** If any payment is not made within _____ **Days** After it is due, a late charge of either $ _____,
   or _____% of the installment due, may be charged to Buyer. **NOTE:** On single family residences that Buyer intends to occupy,
   California Civil Code §2954.4(a) limits the late charge to no more than 6% of the total installment payment due and requires a
   grace period of no less than 10 days.

5. ☐ **BALLOON PAYMENT:** The extension of credit will provide for a balloon payment, in the amount of $ _____
   plus any accrued interest, which is due on _____ (date).

6. ☐ **PREPAYMENT:** If all or part of this extension of credit is paid early, Seller may charge a prepayment penalty as follows (if
   applicable): _____. Caution: California Civil Code
   §2954.9 contains limitations on prepayment penalties for residential one-to-four unit properties.

7. ☐ **DUE ON SALE:** If any interest in the Property is sold or otherwise transferred, Seller has the option to require immediate
   payment of the entire unpaid principal balance, plus any accrued interest.

8.* ☐ **REQUEST FOR COPY OF NOTICE OF DEFAULT:** A request for a copy of Notice of Default as defined in California Civil
   Code §2924b will be recorded. If Not, Seller is advised to consider recording a Request for Notice of Default.

9.* ☐ **REQUEST FOR NOTICE OF DELINQUENCY:** A request for Notice of Delinquency, as defined in California Civil Code §2924e,
   to be signed and paid for by Buyer, will be made to senior lienholders. **If not,** Seller is advised to consider making a Request
   for Notice of Delinquency. Seller is advised to check with senior lienholders to verify whether they will honor this request.

10.*☐ **TAX SERVICE:**
   A. If property taxes on the Property become delinquent, a tax service will be arranged to report to Seller. **If not,** Seller is
      advised to consider retaining a tax service, or to otherwise determine that property taxes are paid.
   B.☐ Buyer, ☐ Seller, shall be responsible for the initial and continued retention of, and payment for, such tax service.

11. ☐ **TITLE INSURANCE:** Title insurance coverage will be provided to **both** Seller and Buyer, insuring their respective interests
   in the Property. **If not,** Buyer and Seller are advised to consider securing such title insurance coverage.

12. ☐ **HAZARD INSURANCE:**
   A. The parties' escrow holder or insurance carrier will be directed to include a loss payee endorsement, adding Seller to the
      Property insurance policy. If not, Seller is advised to secure such an endorsement, or acquire a separate insurance
      policy.
   B. Property insurance **does not** include earthquake or flood insurance coverage, unless checked:
      ☐ Earthquake insurance will be obtained; ☐ Flood insurance will be obtained.

13. ☐ **PROCEEDS TO BUYER:** Buyer will receive cash proceeds at the close of the sale transaction. The amount received will be
   approximately $ _____, from _____ (indicate source of
   proceeds). Buyer represents that the purpose of such disbursement is as follows: _____.

14. ☐ **NEGATIVE AMORTIZATION; DEFERRED INTEREST:** Negative amortization results when Buyer's periodic payments
   are less than the amount of interest earned on the obligation. Deferred interest also results when the obligation does not
   require periodic payments for a period of time. In either case, interest is not payable as it accrues. This accrued interest
   will have to be paid by Buyer at a later time, and may result in Buyer owing more on the obligation than at its origination.
   The credit being extended to Buyer by Seller will provide for negative amortization or deferred interest as indicated below.
   (Check A, B, or C. CHECK ONE ONLY.)
   ☐ **A.** All negative amortization or deferred interest shall be added to the principal _____
      (e.g., annually, monthly, etc.), and thereafter shall bear interest at the rate specified in the credit documents (compound interest);
   OR ☐ **B.** All deferred interest shall be due and payable, along with principal, at maturity;
   OR ☐ **C.** Other _____

*(For Paragraphs 8-10) In order to receive timely and continued notification, Seller is advised to record appropriate notices and/or to
notify appropriate parties of any change in Seller's address.

Buyer's Initials (_____)(_____)   Seller's Initials (_____)(_____)

Reviewed by _____ Date _____

EQUAL HOUSING OPPORTUNITY

SFA REVISED 11/13 (PAGE 1 OF 3) Print Date

SELLER FINANCING ADDENDUM AND DISCLOSURE (SFA PAGE 1 OF 4)

Reprinted with permission, California Association of REALTORS®. Endorsement not implied.

Property Address: _____ Date: _____

15. ☐ **ALL-INCLUSIVE DEED OF TRUST; INSTALLMENT LAND SALE CONTRACT:** This transaction involves the use of an all-inclusive (or wraparound) deed of trust or an installment land sale contract. That deed of trust or contract shall provide as follows:
   A. In the event of an acceleration of any senior encumbrance, the party responsible for payment, or for legal defense is:
   ☐ Buyer ☐ Seller ; OR ☐ **Is not** specified in the credit or security documents.
   B. In the event of the prepayment of a senior encumbrance, the responsibilities and rights of Buyer and Seller regarding refinancing, prepayment penalties, and any prepayment discounts are: _____;
   OR ☐ **Are not** specified in the documents evidencing credit.
   C. Buyer will make periodic payments to _____ (Seller, collection agent, or any neutral third party), who will be responsible for disbursing payments to the payee(s) on the senior encumbrance(s) and to Seller. NOTE: The Parties are advised to designate a neutral third party for these purposes.

16. ☐ **TAX IDENTIFICATION NUMBERS:** Buyer and Seller shall each provide to each other their Social Security Numbers or Taxpayer Identification Numbers.

17. ☐ **OTHER CREDIT TERMS** _____

18. ☐ **RECORDING:** The documents evidencing credit (paragraph 3) will be recorded with the county recorder where the Property is located. If not, Buyer and Seller are advised that their respective interests in the Property may be jeopardized by intervening liens, judgments, encumbrances, or subsequent transfers.

19. ☐ **JUNIOR FINANCING:** There will be additional financing, secured by the Property, junior to this Seller financing. Explain: _____

20. SENIOR LOANS AND ENCUMBRANCES: The following information is provided on loans and/or encumbrances that will be senior to Seller financing. NOTE: The following are estimates, unless otherwise marked with an asterisk (*). If checked: ☐ A separate sheet with information on additional senior loans/encumbrances is attached

	1st	2nd
A. Original Balance	$	$
B. Current Balance	$	$
C. Periodic Payment (e.g. $100/month):	$	$ /
Including Impounds of:		$ /
D. Interest Rate (per annum)	%	%
E. Fixed or Variable Rate:		
If Variable Rate: Lifetime Cap (Ceiling)		
Indicator (Underlying Index)		
Margins		
F. Maturity Date		
G. Amount of Balloon Payment	$	$
H. Date Balloon Payment Due		
I. Potential for Negative Amortization? (Yes, No, or Unknown)		
J. Due on Sale? (Yes, No, or Unknown)		
K. Pre-payment penalty? (Yes, No, or Unknown)		
L. Are payments current? (Yes, No, or Unknown)		

21. BUYER'S CREDITWORTHINESS: (CHECK EITHER A OR B. Do not check both.) In addition to the loan application, credit report and other information requested under paragraph 2:
   A. ☐ No other disclosure concerning Buyer's creditworthiness has been made to Seller;
OR **B.** ☐ The following representations concerning Buyer's creditworthiness are made by Buyer(s) to Seller:

Borrower	Co-Borrower
1. Occupation _____	1. Occupation _____
2. Employer _____	2. Employer _____
3. Length of Employment _____	3. Length of Employment _____
4. Monthly Gross Income _____	4. Monthly Gross Income _____
5. Other_____	5. Other _____

22. ADDED, DELETED OR SUBSTITUTED BUYERS: The addition, deletion or substitution of any person or entity under this Agreement or to title prior to close of escrow shall require Seller's written consent. Seller may grant or withhold consent in Seller's sole discretion. Any additional or substituted person or entity shall, if requested by Seller, submit to Seller the same documentation as required for the original named Buyer. Seller and/or Brokers may obtain a credit report, at Buyer's expense, on any such person or entity.

Buyer's Initials (_____)(_____)   Seller's Initials (_____)(_____)

SFA REVISED 11/13 (PAGE 2 OF 4)   Reviewed by _____ Date _____

SELLER FINANCING ADDENDUM AND DISCLOSURE (SFA PAGE 2 OF 4)

Property Address: _____ Date: _____

23. CAUTION:

    A. If the Seller financing requires a balloon payment, Seller shall give Buyer written notice, according to the terms of Civil Code §2966, at least 90 and not more than 150 days before the balloon payment is due if the transaction is for the purchase of a dwelling for not more than four families.

    B. If **any** obligation secured by the Property calls for a balloon payment, Seller and Buyer are aware that refinancing of the balloon payment at maturity may be difficult or impossible, depending on conditions in the conventional mortgage marketplace at that time. There are no assurances that new financing or a loan extension will be available when the balloon prepayment, or any prepayment, is due.

    C. If **any** of the existing or proposed loans or extensions of credit would require refinancing as a result of a lack of full amortization, such refinancing might be difficult or impossible in the conventional mortgage marketplace.

    D. In the event of default by Buyer: (1) Seller may have to reinstate and/or make monthly payments on any and all senior encumbrances (including real property taxes) in order to protect Seller's secured interest; (2) Seller's rights are generally limited to foreclosure on the Property, pursuant to California Code of Civil Procedure §580b; and (3) the Property may lack sufficient equity to protect Seller's interests if the Property decreases in value.

If this three-page Addendum and Disclosure is used in a transaction for the purchase of a dwelling for not more than four families, it shall be prepared by an Arranger of Credit as defined in California Civil Code §2957(a). (The Arranger of Credit is usually the agent who obtained the offer.)

_____

Arranger of Credit - (Print Firm Name)   By _____ Date _____

Address _____ City _____ State _____ Zip _____

Phone _____ Fax _____

> BUYER AND SELLER ACKNOWLEDGE AND AGREE THAT BROKERS: (A) WILL NOT PROVIDE LEGAL OR TAX ADVICE; (B) WILL NOT PROVIDE OTHER ADVICE OR INFORMATION THAT EXCEEDS THE KNOWLEDGE, EDUCATION AND EXPERIENCE REQUIRED TO OBTAIN A REAL ESTATE LICENSE; OR (C) HAVE NOT AND WILL NOT VERIFY ANY INFORMATION PROVIDED BY EITHER BUYER OR SELLER. BUYER AND SELLER AGREE THAT THEY WILL SEEK LEGAL, TAX AND OTHER DESIRED ASSISTANCE FROM APPROPRIATE PROFESSIONALS. BUYER AND SELLER ACKNOWLEDGE THAT THE INFORMATION EACH HAS PROVIDED TO THE ARRANGER OF CREDIT FOR INCLUSION IN THIS DISCLOSURE FORM IS ACCURATE. BUYER AND SELLER FURTHER ACKNOWLEDGE THAT EACH HAS RECEIVED A COMPLETED COPY OF THIS DISCLOSURE FORM.

Buyer _____ Date _____
        (signature)

Address _____ City _____ State _____ Zip _____

Phone _____ Fax _____ E-mail _____

Buyer _____ Date _____
        (signature)

Address _____ City _____ State _____ Zip _____

Phone _____ Fax _____ E-mail _____

Seller _____ Date _____
        (signature)

Address _____ City _____ State _____ Zip _____

Phone _____ Fax _____ E-mail _____

Seller _____ Date _____
        (signature)

Address _____ City _____ State _____ Zip _____

Phone _____ Fax _____ E-mail _____

Published and Distributed by:
REAL ESTATE BUSINESS SERVICES, INC.
a subsidiary of the California Association of REALTORS®
525 South Virgil Avenue, Los Angeles, California 90020

Reviewed by _____ Date _____

SFA REVISED 11/13 (PAGE 3 OF 4)

SELLER FINANCING ADDENDUM AND DISCLOSURE (SFA PAGE 3 OF 4)

Property Address: _____ Date: _____

IMPORTANT SELLER FINANCING DISCLOSURE - PLEASE READ CAREFULLY

The Dodd-Frank Wall Street Reform and Consumer Protection Act (Dodd-Frank) has made significant and important changes affecting seller financing on residential properties. Effective January 10, 2014, sellers who finance the purchase of residential property containing 1-4 units may be considered "loan originators" required to comply with certain Truth In Lending Act ("TILA") requirements. Even under Dodd-Frank however, the following two exemptions exist:

1. The seller finances only **ONE** property in any 12 month period and:
   a. The seller is a natural person, a trust or an estate, and
   b. The seller did not construct the property, and
   c. The financing has a fixed rate or does not adjust for the first 5 years, and
   d. The financing does not result in negative amortization.

OR

2. The seller finances no more than **THREE** properties in any 12 month period and:
   a. The seller is a natural person or organization (corporation, LLC, partnership, trust, estate, association, etc.), and
   b. The seller did not construct the property, and
   c. The loan is fully amortized, i.e., no balloon payment, and
   d. The financing has a fixed rate or does not adjust for the first 5 years, and
   e. The borrow has the reasonable ability to repay the loan.

Sellers who finance the purchase of residential property containing 1-4 units meeting either of the two exemptions are not subject to the TILA requirements above may continue to, and are required by California Law to, use the Seller Financing Addendum.

Sellers who finance the purchase of residential property containing 1-4 units who do not meet either of the two tests above should still complete the Seller Finance Addendum and speak to a lawyer about other TILA disclosures that may be required.

Sellers who finance the purchase of residential property containing 5 or more units, vacant land, or commercial properties are not subject to the TILA disclosures nor are they required to use the Seller Financing Addendum.

A seller who originates a single extension of credit through a mortgage broker and additionally meets the definition of a "high-cost" mortgage under Dodd-Frank may be subject to the Truth in Lending Act's requirement to verify the borrower's ability to repay.

Buyer's Initials (_____)(_____)   Seller's Initials (_____)(_____)

SFA REVISED 11/13 (PAGE 4 OF 4)   Reviewed by _____ Date _____

SELLER FINANCING ADDENDUM AND DISCLOSURE (SFA PAGE 4 OF 4)

Even when state law doesn't require a disclosure statement, it's a good idea for a real estate agent handling a seller-financed transaction to provide one. A local real estate organization (such as a multiple listing association or a Board of Realtors®) may have a form available for this purpose that accurately reflects state law concerning the rights of the parties.

Buyer's Ability to Repay

In addition to setting out the terms of the seller financing arrangement, the form in Figure 13.2 has provisions concerning the buyer's creditworthiness (see paragraphs 2 and 22). In a seller-financed transaction, the seller should always thoroughly investigate the buyer's financial situation—income, net worth, and credit history. After obtaining (and verifying) this information, the seller doesn't have to apply the same standards to it that an institutional lender would. But the seller should at least have a clear picture of the buyer's circumstances.

Evaluating the buyer's ability to pay off a purchase money loan or land contract as agreed helps protect the seller from the inconvenience and financial losses that could result if the buyer defaults. It protects the buyer, too; if the monthly payments are unaffordable, there's a very good chance that the buyer will eventually lose the home.

As was mentioned in Chapter 8, to protect home buyers from predatory financing arrangements, the Dodd-Frank Act added a requirement known as the **ability to repay rule** to the Truth in Lending Act. In transactions involving residential property with up to four units, mortgage lenders and loan originators are required to make a reasonable, good faith determination that the buyer has the ability to repay the loan. The ability to repay rule applies not only to institutional mortgage loans, but also to seller financing, including both purchase money loans and land contracts.

However, the ability to repay rule does not apply to an individual seller who provides financing for no more than one home sale in a 12-month period and meets other conditions. (See paragraph 1 on page 4 of the form in Figure 13.2 for more information about this exemption.)

Under some circumstances a real estate agent involved in a seller-financed transaction could be responsible for evaluating the buyer's ability to repay the seller. That's because a third party who receives compensation for arranging financing on behalf of the parties to a residential real estate transaction may be considered a loan originator under federal or state law. However, a real estate agent providing brokerage services in an ordinary home sale (even a seller-financed sale) generally isn't a loan originator, since the agent usually isn't being compensated for arranging the financing.

Agents who offer services that might be regarded as loan origination activities need to know the law in this area. They should ask the real estate licensing agency in their state for information and also consider consulting an attorney.

Agent's Liability

Disclosure forms like the one in Figure 13.2 protect the parties by helping them understand the financing transaction. They can also protect the real estate agent, by documenting that certain information was provided to the parties. However, the agent should not regard a disclosure statement as a shield against liability. With or without disclosures, an agent who suggests or encourages a financing arrangement that is plainly imprudent could be held liable for breach of fiduciary duty if his principal later suffers a loss. This is especially true when an unsophisticated party relies on the real estate agent alone instead of consulting another professional (such as a lawyer or a CPA).

In a seller-financed transaction, a court could hold that a seller's agent also had fiduciary duties to the buyer. An inadvertent dual agency may arise if the buyer believes the agent is representing his interests in negotiating the financing arrangement with the seller. In that case, the agent could be held liable for breach of duties owed to the buyer/debtor as well as to the seller/creditor. And even without a finding of dual agency, a seller's agent who persuaded a buyer to enter into an extremely unwise transaction might be held liable for fraud.

Seller financing can be creative, but don't lose touch with reality. While seller financing can close a sale, what happens after closing matters too. The buyer must be able to pay as agreed, and the seller must be well protected in case of default. Make sure both parties get good professional advice and understand every aspect of their transaction.

Outline: Seller Financing

I. How Seller Financing Works

  A. A seller can use a promissory note and security instrument to finance the buyer's purchase; such a loan is known as a purchase money loan.

  B. A seller may also use a land contract, where the buyer takes possession of the property but the seller retains legal title until the price has been paid in full.

  C. Seller financing is usually secondary financing, where a "seller second" supplements an institutional first mortgage.

II. When and Why Seller Financing is Used

  A. If interest rates are high and buyers have difficulty qualifying for loans, the only way a seller may be able to sell the property is by financing part of the purchase price.

  B. Sellers may use seller financing as a marketing tool; buyers may pay more for a house if they can get favorable seller financing terms.

  C. Seller financing may have tax advantages: if payments are made over a period of years, the seller doesn't have to report the full profit from the sale in the first year.

III. Seller Seconds

  A. Often, seller financing is secondary financing, where the seller accepts a second mortgage (a "seller second") for the difference between the loan amount and the purchase price.

  B. Supplementing a new loan

    1. The seller second must meet lender requirements; for instance, for a conventional loan, the total financing may not exceed 95% of the sales price, and the second loan may not require a balloon payment within five years after closing.

    2. A buyer considering a seller second needs to consider how much he has for a downpayment, the total monthly payment he can qualify for, and how large the balloon payment for the seller second will be.

    3. A seller considering a seller second needs to think about whether cash flow and yield will be adequate, possible negative tax consequences (such as the imputed interest rule), and lien priority.

  C. Supplementing an assumption

    1. A seller second can supplement a buyer's assumption of an existing loan; the buyer will make a monthly payment to the seller as well as making the monthly payment the seller has been making to the lender.

2. If the loan has a due-on-sale clause, an assumption isn't possible unless the lender agrees to it.

3. Regardless of whether there is a due-on-sale clause, the lender's consent is necessary for the seller to be released from liability.

IV. Seller Financing as Primary Financing

A. Unencumbered property

1. Seller financing is straightforward if the seller owns the property free and clear.

2. While lien priority is not as much of a concern with primary seller financing, the seller must make sure that taxes and special assessment liens are paid so that the government doesn't foreclose.

3. An escrow account can be set up to handle the buyer's tax and hazard insurance payments.

4. If a seller is willing to provide substantial financing but needs cash at closing, a possibility is seller financing with an institutional second mortgage.

5. Land contracts

a. A seller providing primary financing might choose to use a land contract (also known as a conditional sales contract or installment sales contract) instead of a mortgage.

b. Under a land contract, the seller (or vendor) retains legal title to the property until the buyer (or vendee) pays off the entire purchase price in installments.

c. A land contract is not accompanied by a promissory note; the contract describes the terms of sale and the financing arrangements.

d. For some land contracts, if a vendee defaults on the contract obligation, the vendee's rights in the property are terminated and the vendor retains all payments made so far; this remedy is known as forfeiture.

e. Courts won't necessarily allow forfeiture, depending on how long the vendee has been making payments.

f. The expense and delay of court proceedings in the event of breach of a land contract is the main disadvantage.

g. Lenders are not likely to offer institutional secondary financing if the primary financing is through a land contract.

B. Encumbered property: Wraparound financing

1. With a wraparound, the property remains subject to the existing mortgage (or underlying loan), and the seller continues to make payments.

2. Each month, the buyer makes a payment to the seller, and the seller uses a portion of that payment to make the payment on the underlying loan.

3. A wraparound can use a mortgage, deed of trust (called an all-inclusive deed of trust), or land contract.

4. The underlying loan cannot have a due-on-sale clause. It is never a good idea to use a "silent wrap," where the lender isn't informed of the sale of the property.

5. Wraparound financing can be attractive since it allows the buyer to finance a purchase at a below-market rate on the total amount financed while the seller receives an above-market rate on the credit extended.

V. Alternatives to Seller Financing

A. Buydowns: The seller may assist a buyer with a buydown, by paying discount points to reduce the buyer's interest rate.

B. Contributions to closing costs: The seller may pay some of the buyer's closing costs, which can be more helpful than a price reduction for the same amount.

C. Equity exchanges: A seller may accept other assets from a buyer in addition to cash.

D. Lease arrangements: A seller may lease a property to a buyer for a time before the buyer purchases it, either through a lease/option or a lease/purchase.

1. A lease/option involves a lease for a specific term and then the option to purchase the property at a specified price during that term.

2. The rental payments may be applied toward the purchase price in a lease/option, either deducted from the sales price or treated as part of the downpayment.

3. In a lease/purchase, buyer and seller sign a purchase contract along with the lease, so that deciding not to purchase at lease's end means a breach of the contract.

VI. Legal Responsibilities in Seller-Financed Transactions

A. An agent should recommend that both parties get legal and tax advice, and have the documents reviewed by a lawyer, before proceeding with seller financing.

B. Disclosure statements: Some states require disclosures to both the buyer and the seller when a third party (such as a real estate agent) helps arrange seller financing.

C. Buyer's ability to repay: Residential lenders are required to make a good faith determination that the buyer has the ability to repay the loan.

    1. Ability to repay rule generally applies to seller financing as well as institutional financing, but a typical home seller is exempt from this requirement.

    2. Real estate agents providing brokerage services are also usually exempt, as long as they aren't compensated for arranging the financing.

D. Liability: An agent who encourages an unwise financial arrangement might be liable to either party, or both, for breach of fiduciary duties.

    1. An agent who arranges seller financing might create an inadvertent dual agency and owe fiduciary duties to the buyer as well as the seller.

    2. Even if the agent is not held to have fiduciary duties to the buyer, the agent could be liable to the buyer for fraud.

Key Terms

Seller financing: When a seller extends credit to a buyer to finance the purchase of the property, as opposed to having the buyer obtain a loan from a third party.

Institutional loan: A mortgage loan made by a bank or other regulated lending institution, or by a mortgage company, in contrast to seller financing or a loan made by an individual private lender.

Purchase money loan: A mortgage or deed of trust given by a buyer to a seller.

Secondary financing: Money borrowed to pay part of the required downpayment or closing costs for a first loan, when the second loan is secured by the same property that secures the first loan.

Seller second: Secondary financing from the seller, when a purchase money loan is used to supplement an institutional first mortgage.

Land contract: A contract for the sale of property in which the buyer (vendee) pays the seller (vendor) in installments, taking possession of the property immediately but not taking legal title until the purchase price has been paid in full. Also called a contract for deed, bond for deed, conditional sales contract, installment sales contract, installment land contract, or real estate contract.

Wraparound financing: A seller financing arrangement in which the seller uses part of the buyer's payments to make the payments on an existing loan (called the underlying loan); the buyer takes title subject to the underlying loan, but does not assume it.

Buydown: When the seller or a third party pays the lender a lump sum at closing to lower the interest rate charged to the buyer, either for the life of the loan or during the first years of the loan term.

Equity exchange: When a buyer gives a seller real or personal property in addition to or instead of cash for the purchase price.

Lease/option: A lease that includes the option to purchase the leased property during the term of the lease.

Lease/purchase: A variation on the lease/option, in which the parties sign a purchase contract (instead of an option) and the prospective buyer leases the property for a specified period before closing.

Chapter Quiz

1. A seller can finance a buyer's purchase with:
   a. an all-inclusive trust deed
   b. a purchase money mortgage
   c. a land contract
   d. Any of the above

2. Historically, the most common use for a seller second was to supplement a new institutional loan when:
   a. market interest rates were high
   b. the seller needed an exceptionally high yield on her investment
   c. the buyer had no cash for a downpayment at all
   d. negative amortization was a possibility

3. The Kramers are applying for a conventional loan that would be combined with a seller second. The monthly payment (PITI) on the institutional loan would be $1,838, and the payment on the seller financing would be $520; the Kramers' other debts add up to $490 per month. Applying a 36% maximum debt to income ratio, the lender will make the loan if the Kramers' stable monthly income is at least:
   a. $5,106
   b. $6,467
   c. $6,550
   d. $7,911

4. Which of the following statements regarding balloon payments is true?
   a. A large balloon payment usually results in default
   b. In some cases, the buyer raises the cash for the balloon payment by refinancing
   c. A real estate agent should never suggest a seller financing arrangement that involves a balloon payment
   d. A new conventional loan cannot be combined with a seller second that requires a balloon payment

5. Which of the following instruments generally couldn't be used for a seller second supplementing a new institutional loan?
   a. Deed of trust
   b. Mortgage
   c. Land contract
   d. None of these could be used

6. The buyer made a downpayment, assumed the seller's mortgage, and gave the seller a deed of trust for the balance of the purchase price. The buyer defaults and the mortgagee forecloses on the assumed loan. If the foreclosure sale proceeds are not sufficient to cover the outstanding balance on the assumed mortgage:
   a. the seller will not be paid
   b. the mortgagee will not be paid
   c. the seller will be paid before the mortgagee is paid
   d. the mortgagee and the seller will each receive a prorated share of the sale proceeds

7. With wraparound financing:
   a. the buyer assumes the underlying loan
   b. the balance owed on the underlying loan is larger than the wraparound loan amount
   c. the seller remains responsible for making the payments on the underlying loan
   d. the more credit the seller extends to the buyer, the higher the seller's yield

8. The chief advantage of wraparound financing is that:
   a. it complies with the secondary financing rules that institutional lenders apply
   b. the seller can get an exceptionally high yield on the credit extended
   c. the due-on-sale clause on the underlying loan is not triggered, as it would be by an assumption
   d. the seller retains title to the property until the buyer has paid the full price

9. A lease/purchase agreement differs from a lease/option in that:
   a. a good faith deposit is usually involved
   b. a prospective buyer often feels more committed to purchasing the property
   c. a closing date is set
   d. All of the above

10. In a lease/option arrangement, the rent charged:
    a. is usually refunded if the tenant exercises the option to buy
    b. cannot be applied toward the purchase price
    c. cannot exceed the fair market rent for the property
    d. is often higher than the fair market rent for the property

Answer Key

1. d. A seller may use an all-inclusive trust deed, a purchase money mortgage, or a land contract to finance a buyer's purchase.

2. a. A seller second is likely to be used when market interest rates are high. If interest rates are high, few buyers may be able to qualify for a loan large enough to afford the full purchase price, so a seller may offer secondary financing as an incentive.

3. d. To calculate the required stable monthly income, add all of the monthly debt payments ($1,838 + $520 + $490 = $2,848) and then divide that figure by the maximum debt to income ratio ($2,848 ÷ .36 = $7,911).

4. b. When a balloon payment comes due, a borrower may be able to refinance the mortgage rather than having to pay the full amount in cash.

5. c. A land contract generally cannot be used for a seller second that supplements an institutional loan.

6. a. If a lender forecloses on an assumed loan, and the foreclosure sale proceeds are not sufficient to cover the balance on the assumed loan, then the seller will not be paid any of the proceeds.

7. c. A seller who uses wraparound financing will remain responsible for making payments on the underlying loan.

8. b. With wraparound financing, a seller can get an above-market yield on the credit extended.

9. d. In a lease/purchase agreement, the prospective buyer usually provides a good faith deposit and the parties set a closing date. The prospective buyer tends to be more committed to the transaction, since backing out involves breaching a purchase contract (as opposed to simply not exercising an option to purchase).

10. d. The rent in a lease/option arrangement is usually higher than the market rate, since the tenant is receiving an additional benefit in having the possibility of purchase.

Case Study: Seller Financing

Let's return to the Cortinas once more. This time, suppose that neither Rick nor Teresa is eligible for a VA loan. They've decided against FHA financing because they want a more expensive house than the FHA maximum loan amount in their area would enable them to buy. Based on their maximum payment amount of $2,598.56 (see the Chapter 10 case study), they've been preapproved for a 90% fixed-rate conventional loan at 5.5% interest for up to $366,000, which will enable them to buy a house for about $406,650.

Although the Cortinas have seen several houses that would meet their needs, they haven't felt enthusiastic about any of them—until now. This afternoon they looked at a house they really want. Unfortunately, at $435,000, the property is beyond their price range.

The seller, Bonnie Wellman, was recently widowed and is about to retire. She plans to use part of the sale proceeds as a downpayment on a condominium, and to invest the rest to supplement her income. She'll have to pay off her mortgage, which has a due-on-sale clause; the current balance is about $94,000.

Wellman's home has been listed for almost four months; the market is very slow. Several people have looked at the property, but the only offer so far was for $415,000—$18,500 less than the appraised value, $433,500—and Wellman turned it down. She might accept $425,000 for the property, but at this point she's not willing to go any lower than that.

The Cortinas tell Wellman how much they like her house, and they explain that they can't qualify for a bank loan large enough to buy it. They ask if she would consider accepting a second deed of trust for part of the price. If so, they'd be willing to pay her full asking price, $435,000. Wellman says she's willing to discuss it. She estimates that she needs to take away at least $225,000 in cash from the closing. She would like to be paid at least 6% interest on any financing she provides, since that's about the rate of return she expects she could get on some other secure investment.

Answer the following questions to determine whether the Cortinas could qualify for a conventional loan supplemented by a seller second that would meet Wellman's needs.

Interest rates for fixed-rate 30-year conventional loans

> LTV 80% or less: 5.375% interest
> LTV 80.01% to 90%: 5.50% interest
> LTV over 90%: 5.75% interest

1. Assume that the Cortinas will get their primary financing from a lender with these secondary financing rules: the primary loan may not exceed 75% of the property's value, and the buyers must make at least a 10% downpayment. If the Cortinas buy Wellman's home for $435,000, what is the largest conventional loan they could supplement with a

seller second? If they get a conventional loan for that amount, what is the largest amount of financing Wellman could provide? How much would the total amount financed be?

2. Suppose that the Cortinas obtain a 30-year fixed-rate conventional loan for the maximum amount (determined in Question 1) at the market interest rate, and Wellman finances her maximum share at 6% interest. If both the conventional loan and the seller second are amortized over a 30-year term, the monthly principal and interest payment for the conventional loan would be $1,820.61, and the monthly principal and interest payment for the seller second would be $389.86. To find the monthly housing expense, add 15% to the combined principal and interest payment to cover property taxes and hazard insurance. (Since the loan-to-value ratio of the primary loan is 80% or less, the lender won't require mortgage insurance.) Could the Cortinas qualify for this combined housing expense?

3. The primary lender would require the Cortinas to pay a 1.5% origination fee, and other closing costs estimated at 3% of the sales price. The lender will also require them to have two months of combined PITI payments as reserves. And, of course, they'll have to make the downpayment. How much cash would they need at closing for this transaction? Will their $87,000 in savings be enough?

4. Not surprisingly, Wellman isn't willing to wait 30 years to collect her full profit from the sale; she would like it in five years. How could this be arranged, without preventing the Cortinas from qualifying for the institutional loan?

5. If her selling costs came to 10% of the sales price, how much cash would Wellman receive at closing in this transaction? Remember that she would have to pay off her mortgage.

Chapter 14

Fair Lending and Consumer Protection

Fair Lending Laws

- Equal Credit Opportunity Act
- Fair Housing Act
- Community Reinvestment Act
- Home Mortgage Disclosure Act

Consumer Protection Laws

- Truth in Lending Act
- Real Estate Settlement Procedures Act
- TILA/RESPA Integrated Disclosures

Predatory Lending

- Predatory lending practices
- Targeted victims
- Predatory lending laws

Introduction

In this chapter we'll discuss several federal laws that promote fairness, clarity, and honesty in residential mortgage lending. Some of these are fair lending laws that make it illegal for lenders to discriminate when they evaluate loan applications and make loan approval decisions. Others are consumer protection laws designed to help buyers understand the lending process and make informed borrowing decisions. In spite of these laws, unscrupulous lenders and mortgage brokers continue to manipulate vulnerable and unsophisticated borrowers into taking out expensive loans. We'll examine predatory lending at the end of this chapter.

Fair Lending Laws

Residential mortgage loan transactions are subject to federal anti-discrimination laws, including the Equal Credit Opportunity Act, the Fair Housing Act, the Community Reinvestment Act, and the Home Mortgage Disclosure Act.

Equal Credit Opportunity Act

Equal Credit Opportunity Act prohibits discrimination based on:
- Race
- Color
- Religion
- National origin
- Sex
- Marital status
- Age
- Public assistance

The Equal Credit Opportunity Act (ECOA), which became law in 1974, applies to both individuals and businesses seeking credit. However, our discussion of ECOA will be limited to consumer credit. **Consumer credit** is credit that is extended to an individual (not a corporation or other business) for personal, family, or household purposes. This includes residential mortgage loans.

ECOA prohibits discrimination against loan applicants based on race, color, religion, national origin, sex, marital status, or age (as long as an applicant is old enough to have contractual capacity under the laws of his state). In addition, the act prohibits discrimination against applicants who receive all or part of their income from a public assistance program, such as welfare. ECOA also prohibits discrimination against applicants who have exercised their rights under federal credit laws (for example, by requesting corrections to a credit report).

Lenders have to comply with ECOA when interviewing and communicating with loan applicants, and when analyzing the applicants' financial situation. The credit terms lenders offer applicants must also comply with ECOA.

Lenders must not discourage anyone from applying for a loan, and they must apply their credit guidelines to every loan applicant in the same manner, based on amount and stability of income, net worth, and credit reputation. Under ECOA, it's illegal for lenders to base lending decisions on assumptions about the creditworthiness of members of particular racial, ethnic, and religious groups; women or men; unmarried couples, divorced people, or single people; or elderly people or young adults.

Note that the law permits lenders to ask about a loan applicant's age, receipt of public assistance, or marital status, provided the information isn't used as a basis for discrimination. The applicant's age or receipt of public assistance may be considered in determining the applicant's creditworthiness. Unless the spouse is a co-borrower, inquiries about marital status are limited to asking whether an applicant is married, unmarried, or separated (divorced, widowed, and single people are all categorized as unmarried) and whether the applicant prefers to be addressed as Mr., Ms., Mrs., or Miss.

Applicants may be asked about the number and age of their dependents and about expenses related to the dependents. However, lenders can't ask whether loan applicants are planning to bear, adopt, or raise children (or more children in addition to the ones they already have), even if that could result in diminished income. It's also illegal for a lender to assume that applicants who belong to certain groups are more likely to bear or raise children.

Lenders aren't allowed to ask loan applicants about childbearing or adoption plans

Under ECOA, credit applicants must be informed within 30 days of submitting a completed application whether their application was accepted or rejected. If the application is rejected, the creditor must give the applicant a notice informing her of the specific reason for the denial, or her right to inquire further within 60 days.

ECOA is one of the federal laws that are enforced by the Consumer Financial Protection Bureau, or CFPB. (Some of the other laws covered in this chapter also fall within the CFPB's scope, including the Home Mortgage Disclosure Act, the Truth in Lending Act, and the Real Estate Settlement Procedures Act.)

Fair Housing Act

The federal Fair Housing Act, a 1968 law, includes provisions that address lending discrimination. The act applies to transactions involving residential properties with one to four dwelling units, and it prohibits discrimination based on race, color, national origin, religion, sex, disability, or familial status (a term that refers to families with minor children).

Under the Fair Housing Act, it is illegal for lenders to do any of the following for discriminatory reasons:

- refuse to provide information about mortgage loans,
- refuse to make a mortgage loan, or
- impose different terms or conditions on a loan.

The Fair Housing Act also prohibits **redlining**. Redlining is the refusal to make loans secured by property located in a certain neighborhood because the people who live in that neighborhood belong to a particular racial or ethnic group. At one time, lenders routinely refused to make loans in minority neighborhoods because it was assumed that property values in those areas were declining. (The term "redlining" originates from the practice of using red ink to mark off these neighborhoods on a community map; mortgages weren't available for properties inside the red lines.) Redlining can turn discriminatory assumptions into self-fulfilling prophecies. When it isn't possible to obtain purchase or renovation loans in a redlined neighborhood, it's difficult to sell, maintain, or improve homes there, and then property values actually will decline as a result. While redlining is not as widespread as it once was, the problem remains.

Note, however, that a lender may legally refuse to make a loan if, in fact, property values in the neighborhood are declining. But the refusal has to be based on objective economic criteria concerning the condition and value of the properties in the neighborhood, without regard to the neighborhood's racial or ethnic composition. It is illegal for lenders to automatically assume that certain neighborhoods have declining property values.

Community Reinvestment Act

In 1977, Congress decided to address their continuing concern about redlining and other forms of discrimination by passing a law that encourages certain lenders to serve low- and moderate-income people living in the communities where the lenders do business. Under the provisions of the Community Reinvestment Act (CRA), all depository institutions (commercial banks and savings institutions) must regularly report on the number of home and business loans they have provided to low- and moderate-income consumers living in their market neighborhoods. The law doesn't require lenders to modify their traditional underwriting standards to originate these loans; in fact lenders are encouraged to apply "safe and sound" lending practices. The main goal of the law is to illustrate to lenders that negative assumptions about certain neighborhoods (and the people living in those neighborhoods) are unfounded, and that lenders can serve these groups without incurring any additional risk.

Data reported under this law is considered during bank examinations, and is particularly important when a bank seeks to expand its operations. Regulators also consider input from community groups when determining whether a bank has met its CRA obligations.

As a result of the CRA, those who were underserved by lenders in the past are now better able to get home and business loans. Because the CRA has been so successful in increasing access to loans, there have been discussions about expanding the law to cover nondepository lenders, including independent mortgage companies.

Home Mortgage Disclosure Act

The Home Mortgage Disclosure Act (HMDA) was enacted in 1975. It provides a way for the government to monitor whether lenders are fulfilling their obligation to serve the full spectrum of housing needs in their communities. (For example, institutions covered by the Community Reinvestment Act would include their CRA data in their HMDA reports.) HMDA also facilitates enforcement of other laws that prohibit lending discrimination (including redlining) and predatory lending.

Home Mortgage Disclosure Act helps the government spot redlining and predatory lending

HMDA applies to a broad range of mortgage lenders doing business in metropolitan areas, including banks, thrifts, credit unions, and independent mortgage companies, depending on their size and level of mortgage activity. Lenders subject to HMDA requirements must submit an annual report to the government describing the residential mortgage loans—purchase loans, home improvement loans, and refinancing—that they originated or purchased from other lenders during the fiscal year.

If a lender's report reveals areas where few or no home loans have been made, regulators investigate whether the lender may have redlined those neighborhoods.

Consumer Protection Laws

Federal consumer protection laws that apply to mortgage loan transactions include the Truth in Lending Act and the Real Estate Settlement Procedures Act. Many states have enacted similar consumer protection laws on a state level as well.

Truth in Lending Act

The Truth in Lending Act (TILA) was passed in 1968. It's enforced by the Consumer Financial Protection Bureau (CFPB) and implemented through the CFPB's **Regulation Z**. As we'll discuss, the Truth in Lending Act regulates the advertising of consumer credit, requires lenders to disclose information to loan applicants, and provides borrowers with a right of rescission in certain types of mortgage loan transactions.

Truth in Lending Act is implemented by Regulation Z

Loans Covered by TILA. A loan is a consumer loan if it is used for personal, family, or household purposes. A consumer loan is covered by the Truth in Lending Act if it is to be repaid in more than four installments, or is subject to finance charges, and is either:

- for $55,800* or less, or
- secured by real property.

TILA applies to any mortgage loan used for personal, family, or household purposes

Thus, any mortgage loan is covered by TILA as long as the proceeds are used for personal, family, or household purposes (such as buying or remodeling a home, consolidating personal debt, or sending children to college).

Loans Exempt from TILA. The Truth in Lending Act applies only to loans made to natural persons, so loans made to corporations or organizations aren't covered. Loans for business, commercial, or agricultural purposes are also exempt. So are loans in excess of $55,800, unless the loan is secured by real property. (Mortgage loans

---

* This is the 2018 limit; the dollar figure may be increased annually for inflation.

for personal, family, or household purposes are covered regardless of the loan amount.) Most seller financing is exempt, because extending credit isn't in the seller's ordinary course of business.

Advertising Under TILA. TILA's advertising rules apply to anyone who advertises consumer credit, not just lenders. For example, a real estate broker advertising financing terms for a listed home must also comply with TILA and Regulation Z.

The purpose of TILA's advertising rules is to make sure consumers don't receive—and act on—misleading financing information. For example, the law prohibits lenders from using "bait and switch" tactics: advertising products that aren't really available as a way to draw in prospective borrowers. TILA also forbids lenders from advertising only their most attractive financing terms, a practice that disguises the true costs of the loan.

It is always legal under TILA to include the cash price or the APR in a consumer credit ad. An ad may also state the interest rate on the loan, as long as the APR is also included. However, if an ad mentions any "trigger terms" (the downpayment amount or percentage, the amount of any payment, the number of payments, the repayment period, or the amount of any finance charge), it must also disclose the APR, the downpayment, and the terms of repayment. This helps ensure that the consumer has enough information to understand the true cost of the loan product.

> **Example:** A newspaper ad says, "Buyer can assume seller's loan. Payments only $1,525 a month!" Because it mentions the payment amount, the ad will violate the Truth in Lending Act if it doesn't go on to reveal the APR, the downpayment, and the other terms of repayment.

In this example, the reference to the payment amount triggered the full disclosure requirement. However, general statements such as "low monthly payments," "easy terms," or "affordable interest rate" would not trigger the full disclosure requirement.

As you might expect, TILA has special requirements that apply to advertisements for ARM loans and other loans that involve variable terms. For these loans, the ad must contain language alerting consumers to the fact that the rates or other terms quoted are subject

Fig. 14.1 The wording of an actual flyer that violates TILA's advertising rules

GET THAT DREAM HOME...

...NOW!!!

$400,000 HOME LOAN FOR
$958/MONTH

PURCHASE/REFINANCE

1-800-555-4321

FREE $400 APPRAISAL

to change. It is also a violation of TILA to refer to a loan as "fixed" when in fact the interest rate can change over the life of the loan.

An example of a flyer that violates the Truth in Lending Act is shown in Figure 14.1.

Right of Rescission. TILA provides a right of rescission in connection with home equity loans and some refinancing, but not purchase or construction loans. When the security property is the borrower's principal residence, the borrower may rescind the loan agreement within three business days of: 1) signing the loan documents, 2) receiving a disclosure statement, or 3) receiving notice of the right of rescission, whichever happens latest. The notice of the right to rescind can't be part of other TILA disclosures or loan documents; it must be a separate document. If the borrower never receives the statement or the notice, the right of rescission does not expire for three years.

TILA's three-day right of rescission applies only to home equity loans and to some refinancing

Disclosures to Loan Applicants. As mentioned, the Truth in Lending Act also requires lenders to disclose information to loan applicants. These disclosure rules have been integrated with similar requirements in the Real Estate Settlement Procedures Act, so we'll discuss them after giving you an overview of RESPA.

Real Estate Settlement Procedures Act (RESPA)

The Real Estate Settlement Procedures Act (RESPA) is another federal law intended to ensure that residential mortgage borrowers receive accurate information about finance charges and other closing costs. In addition, RESPA aims to keep closing costs reasonable by eliminating kickbacks (referral fees) that unnecessarily increase the borrower's costs. RESPA's consumer protection provisions apply to **settlement service providers**, a term that covers all professionals involved in the settlement of a transaction (the closing process), including real estate agents. Like TILA, RESPA is enforced by the Consumer Financial Protection Bureau.

Transactions Covered by RESPA. RESPA applies to all "federally related" loan transactions. A loan is federally related if:

1. it will be secured by a mortgage or deed of trust against:
   - property on which there is (or on which the loan proceeds will be used to build) a dwelling with four or fewer units;
   - a condominium unit or a cooperative apartment;
   - a lot with (or on which the loan proceeds will be used to place) a mobile home; and
2. the lender is federally regulated, has federally insured accounts, is assisted by the federal government, makes loans in connection with a federal program, sells loans to Fannie Mae or Freddie Mac, or makes residential loans that total more than $1,000,000 per year.

In short, the act applies to almost all institutional lenders and to most residential loans.

Exemptions. RESPA doesn't apply to the following transactions:

- a loan used to purchase 25 acres or more;
- a loan primarily for a business, commercial, or agricultural purpose;
- a loan used to purchase vacant land, unless there will be a one- to four-unit dwelling built on it or a mobile home placed on it;
- temporary financing, such as a construction loan; or
- an assumption for which the lender's approval is neither required nor obtained.

RESPA also doesn't apply to seller-financed transactions, since those do not involve a federally related loan (see the definition above).

RESPA Requirements. In transactions covered by RESPA, these rules must be followed:

RESPA prohibits lenders and other settlement service providers from:
- Requiring excessive impound deposits
- Paying or receiving kickbacks or referral fees
- Collecting unearned fees
- Charging for preparation of impound account statement or disclosure forms required by law

1. If the lender or another settlement service provider requires the borrower to use a particular attorney, credit reporting agency, or real estate appraiser, that requirement must be disclosed to the borrower when the loan application or service agreement is signed.

2. If any settlement service provider refers a borrower to an affiliated provider, that joint business relationship must be fully disclosed, along with the fact that the referral is optional. Fee estimates for the services in question must also be given.

3. If the borrower is required to make deposits into an impound account to cover taxes, insurance, and other recurring expenses, the lender cannot require excessive deposits—more than those necessary to cover the expenses when they come due. (According to RESPA, it's excessive to require a deposit of more than two months' worth of payments for the recurring expenses.)

4. A lender or any other settlement service provider is not permitted to:
   - pay or receive a **kickback** or referral fee (a payment from one settlement service provider to another for referring customers);
   - pay or receive an **unearned fee** (a charge that one settlement service provider shares with another provider who hasn't actually performed any services in exchange for the payment); or
   - charge a document preparation fee for the preparation of an impound account statement or any of the required disclosure forms.

5. The property seller may not require the buyer to use a particular title company.

RESPA's prohibition on kickbacks (referral fees) and unearned fees, listed in number 4 above, is designed to help curb practices that generate extra compensation for settlement service providers at the expense of home buyers. Note that this RESPA rule does not apply to referral fees paid by one real estate agent or brokerage firm to another for referral of potential real estate clients. (Whether those referral fees are legal or not depends on the state's real estate license law.)

Integrated Disclosures under TILA and RESPA

In addition to the requirements we've just discussed, TILA and RESPA also require lenders to make extensive disclosures to mortgage loan applicants. Until 2015, the two laws' requirements were overlapping and inconsistent. For example, TILA rules applied to some construction loans and loans for vacant land that were exempt from RESPA. Also, TILA required disclosures to be made on a form called the Truth in Lending disclosure statement, while RESPA required much of the same information to be disclosed on a Good Faith Estimate form.

Congress addressed this problem in the Dodd-Frank Act by combining the disclosure rules under the two laws. A lender handling a loan application now must comply with a set of requirements known as the **TILA-RESPA Integrated Disclosure (TRID)** rule.

Coverage and Exemptions. The TRID rule applies to most consumer loans secured by real property, including home purchase, home equity, construction, and refinance loans. It does not apply to home equity lines of credit (HELOCs), reverse mortgages, or mortgages secured by a mobile home or any dwelling not attached to land. It also does not apply to loans made by a lender who makes five or fewer mortgage loans in a year.

Loans that are covered by TILA or RESPA but exempt from the TRID rule are still subject to the old disclosure requirements. For these loans, lenders must use the Truth in Lending, Good Faith Estimate, and HUD-1 settlement statement forms required under the original TILA and RESPA rules. They can't use the TRID disclosure forms in place of the old disclosure forms.

Information Booklet. The TRID rule requires lenders to give loan applicants an information booklet published by the CFPB. This booklet is intended to help consumers understand real estate transactions and the loan costs and settlement fees involved. The lender must provide the booklet to the loan applicant within three business days after receiving the loan application. The booklet requirement does not apply to loans for properties with more than four units, refinance loans, home equity loans, or reverse mortgages.

Disclosure Requirements. TRID's disclosure requirements vary depending on the type of loan; for example, there are special disclosures for adjustable-rate mortgages. The required disclosures must be made on one or both of the two main TRID disclosure forms, the loan estimate and the closing disclosure. (These forms will be discussed shortly.)

Among the key disclosures are the finance charge, the annual percentage rate, and the total interest percentage.

The **finance charge** is the cost of the loan as a dollar amount. It's the sum of all fees and charges that the borrower will pay in connection with the loan, which might include interest, an origination fee, borrower-paid discount points, mortgage insurance premiums, service charges, a finder's fee, and/or a mortgage broker's fee. It does not include the application fee or fees for transaction services such as an appraisal, credit reports, surveys and inspections, document preparation, and title insurance. The lender's finance charge calculation will generally be considered accurate enough if it is within $100 of the actual charge. The finance charge does not appear on the loan estimate form, but it must be listed on the closing disclosure form. The figure is used in calculating the annual percentage rate.

APR shows relationship of finance charge to amount financed

The **annual percentage rate** (APR), as we explained in Chapter 7, expresses the relationship of the finance charge to the amount financed, in the form of an annual percentage. The APR is a tool that makes it easier for prospective borrowers to accurately compare the cost of different loans. It must appear on both the loan estimate form and the closing disclosure form. The lender's APR calculation will generally be considered acceptable if it is accurate to within one-eighth of one percent.

The **total interest percentage** (TIP) expresses the total amount of interest that the borrower will pay over the loan term as a percentage of the loan amount. It includes only interest, with none of the other fees and costs that are included in the finance charge and reflected in the APR. The TIP gives the prospective borrower a clearer picture of how interest impacts the total amount paid over the life of the loan. The calculation of the TIP is based on the assumption that during the entire loan term the borrower will make all payments on time and will pay no more than the amount due each month (in other words, no prepayments). The TIP must appear on both disclosure forms.

ARM disclosures. As we said, some special disclosures are required for adjustable-rate mortgages. Because the total amount of interest that will be collected over the loan term can't be calculated with certainty (since it will fluctuate based on market changes), the disclosure requirements for the APR and related figures are different for an ARM than for a fixed-rate loan.

For ARMs secured by a principal residence, the lender must give the applicant a government booklet called the "Consumer Handbook on Adjustable-Rate Mortgages" (sometimes referred to as the CHARM booklet). In addition, the applicant must be given disclosures for each ARM program that she expresses interest in, including the index that would be used, how often the interest rate and payment amount can change, and whether there are caps on interest rate or payment increases.

For most mortgage loans, the disclosure requirements end when the transaction closes. But when an ARM is secured by the borrower's principal residence, there are some ongoing disclosure requirements even after closing. Whenever the loan's interest rate is about to be adjusted, the lender must send the borrower an adjustment notice that explains the effects of the rate adjustment on the payment amount, the loan balance, and other aspects of the loan. If the payment amount is going to change, the adjustment notice must be sent at least 25 days, but not more than 120 days, before the first new payment is due. (For rate adjustments that don't result in a change in the payment amount, an adjustment notice must be sent at least once each year.)

Disclosure Forms. The two essential disclosure documents prescribed by the TRID rule are the loan estimate, which is required in connection with the loan application, and the closing disclosure, which is required in connection with the closing of the transaction. The information that must be disclosed on these forms will vary depending on the type of loan, the payment schedule, the fees charged, and the terms of the transaction, and it may also be affected by state law.

Loan Estimate. Within three business days after receiving a loan application, a lender must give the applicant a **loan estimate** form. The disclosures in the loan estimate are intended to help applicants understand the features, risks, and cost of the mortgage loan that they're applying for. Applicants can use the information to compare credit costs and shop around for the best terms.

The loan estimate is also intended to ensure that the lender doesn't change the loan's costs or terms once it's too late for the applicant to change lenders. Accordingly, the lender is generally held to the amounts and other figures set forth in the original loan estimate, unless there is a change in circumstances that necessitates a change in the disclosed figures. (In that situation, a revised loan estimate must be provided, as we'll explain shortly.)

A lender can't require an applicant to pay any fees (such as an application fee, an appraisal fee, or an underwriting fee) until the loan estimate has been provided and the applicant has indicated an intent to proceed with the loan transaction. (One exception is the credit report fee, which may be collected beforehand.) The applicant's intent can be communicated orally, by email, or by signing an acknowledgement. Documentation of the applicant's expressed intent must be kept along with the lender's other loan records.

An example of a completed loan estimate form is shown in Figure 14.2. The information that the lender is required to disclose on the form includes:

- loan terms such as the interest rate, the payment amount, and any balloon payment or prepayment penalty;
- any scheduled interest rate increases or payment increases;
- estimated closing costs (loan costs and other costs);
- the total amount of cash the buyer needs to close the loan;
- if the loan has an adjustable interest rate, information about how and when the rate may change;
- the annual percentage rate;
- the total interest percentage;
- late payment fees;
- whether the loan will be assumable; and
- whether the lender will service the loan or transfer servicing.

Fig. 14.2 Loan estimate form

FICUS BANK

4321 Random Boulevard • Somecity, ST 12340

Save this Loan Estimate to compare with your Closing Disclosure.

Loan Estimate

DATE ISSUED	2/15/20XX
APPLICANTS	Michael Jones and Mary Stone
	123 Anywhere Street
	Anytown, ST 12345
PROPERTY	456 Somewhere Avenue
	Anytown, ST 12345
SALE PRICE	$240,000

LOAN TERM	30 years
PURPOSE	Purchase
PRODUCT	5 Year Interest Only, 5/3 Adjustable Rate
LOAN TYPE	☒ Conventional ☐ FHA ☐ VA ☐ _____
LOAN ID #	123456789
RATE LOCK	☐ NO ☒ YES, until 4/16/20XX at 5:00 p.m. EDT

*Before closing, your interest rate, points, and lender credits can change unless you lock the interest rate. All other estimated closing costs expire on **3/4/20XX** at 5:00 p.m. EDT*

Loan Terms

		Can this amount increase after closing?
Loan Amount	$211,000	**NO**
Interest Rate	4%	**YES** • Adjusts **every 3 years** starting in year 6 • Can go **as high as 12%** in year 15 • See **AIR Table on page 2** for details
Monthly Principal & Interest *See Projected Payments below for your Estimated Total Monthly Payment*	$703.33	**YES** • Adjusts **every 3 years** starting in year 6 • Can go **as high as $2,068** in year 15 • Includes **only interest** and **no principal** until year 6 • See **AP Table on page 2** for details
		Does the loan have these features?
Prepayment Penalty		**NO**
Balloon Payment		**NO**

Projected Payments

Payment Calculation	Years 1-5	Years 6-8	Years 9-11	Years 12-30
Principal & Interest	$703.33 ***only interest***	$1,028 min $1,359 max	$1,028 min $1,604 max	$1,028 min $2,068 max
Mortgage Insurance	+ 109	+ 109	+ 109	+ —
Estimated Escrow *Amount can increase over time*	+ 0	+ 0	+ 0	+ 0
Estimated Total Monthly Payment	**$812**	**$1,137–$1,468**	**$1,137–$1,713**	**$1,028–$2,068**

Estimated Taxes, Insurance & Assessments *Amount can increase over time*	$533 a month	This estimate includes **In escrow?** ☒ Property Taxes NO ☒ Homeowner's Insurance NO ☐ Other: *See Section G on page 2 for escrowed property costs. You must pay for other property costs separately.*

Costs at Closing

Estimated Closing Costs	$8,791	Includes $5,851 in Loan Costs + $2,940 in Other Costs – $0 in Lender Credits. *See page 2 for details.*
Estimated Cash to Close	$27,791	Includes Closing Costs. *See Calculating Cash to Close on page 2 for details.*

Visit **www.consumerfinance.gov/mortgage-estimate** for general information and tools.

LOAN ESTIMATE

PAGE 1 OF 3 • LOAN ID # 123456789

Source: Consumer Financial Protection Bureau

Closing Cost Details

Loan Costs

A. Origination Charges	$3,110
1 % of Loan Amount (Points)	$2,110
Application Fee	$500
Processing Fee	$500

B. Services You Cannot Shop For	$820
Appraisal Fee	$305
Credit Report Fee	$30
Flood Determination Fee	$35
Lender's Attorney Fee	$400
Tax Status Research Fee	$50

C. Services You Can Shop For	$1,921
Pest Inspection Fee	$125
Survey Fee	$150
Title – Courier Fee	$32
Title – Lender's Title Policy	$665
Title – Settlement Agent Fee	$325
Title – Title Search	$624

D. TOTAL LOAN COSTS (A + B + C)	$5,851

Other Costs

E. Taxes and Other Government Fees	$152
Recording Fees and Other Taxes	$152
Transfer Taxes	

F. Prepaids	$1,352
Homeowner's Insurance Premium (12 months)	$1,000
Mortgage Insurance Premium (months)	
Prepaid Interest ($23.44 per day for 15 days @ 4.00%)	$352
Property Taxes (months)	

G. Initial Escrow Payment at Closing		
Homeowner's Insurance	per month for	mo.
Mortgage Insurance	per month for	mo.
Property Taxes	per month for	mo.

H. Other	$1,436
Title – Owner's Title Policy (optional)	$1,436

I. TOTAL OTHER COSTS (E + F + G + H)	$2,940

J. TOTAL CLOSING COSTS	$8,791
D + I	$8,791
Lender Credits	

Calculating Cash to Close

Total Closing Costs (J)	$8,791
Closing Costs Financed (Paid from your Loan Amount)	$0
Down Payment/Funds from Borrower	$29,000
Deposit	– $10,000
Funds for Borrower	$0
Seller Credits	$0
Adjustments and Other Credits	$0
Estimated Cash to Close	$27,791

Adjustable Payment (AP) Table

Interest Only Payments?	YES for your first 60 payments
Optional Payments?	NO
Step Payments?	NO
Seasonal Payments?	NO
Monthly Principal and Interest Payments	
First Change/Amount	$1,028 – $1,359 at 61st payment
Subsequent Changes	Every three years
Maximum Payment	$2,068 starting at 169th payment

Adjustable Interest Rate (AIR) Table

Index + Margin	MTA + 4%
Initial Interest Rate	4%
Minimum/Maximum Interest Rate	3.25%/12%
Change Frequency	
First Change	Beginning of 61st month
Subsequent Changes	Every 36th month after first change
Limits on Interest Rate Changes	
First Change	2%
Subsequent Changes	2%

Additional Information About This Loan

LENDER	Ficus Bank	**MORTGAGE BROKER**	
NMLS/__ LICENSE ID		**NMLS/__ LICENSE ID**	
LOAN OFFICER	Joe Smith	**LOAN OFFICER**	
NMLS/__ LICENSE ID	12345	**NMLS/__ LICENSE ID**	
EMAIL	joesmith@ficusbank.com	**EMAIL**	
PHONE	123-456-7890	**PHONE**	

Comparisons

Use these measures to compare this loan with other loans.

In 5 Years	$54,944	Total you will have paid in principal, interest, mortgage insurance, and loan costs.
	$0	Principal you will have paid off.
Annual Percentage Rate (APR)	4.617%	Your costs over the loan term expressed as a rate. This is not your interest rate.
Total Interest Percentage (TIP)	81.18%	The total amount of interest that you will pay over the loan term as a percentage of your loan amount.

Other Considerations

Appraisal	We may order an appraisal to determine the property's value and charge you for this appraisal. We will promptly give you a copy of any appraisal, even if your loan does not close. You can pay for an additional appraisal for your own use at your own cost.
Assumption	If you sell or transfer this property to another person, we ☐ will allow, under certain conditions, this person to assume this loan on the original terms. ☒ will not allow assumption of this loan on the original terms.
Homeowner's Insurance	This loan requires homeowner's insurance on the property, which you may obtain from a company of your choice that we find acceptable.
Late Payment	If your payment is more than *15* days late, we will charge a late fee of *5% of the monthly principal and interest payment.*
Refinance	Refinancing this loan will depend on your future financial situation, the property value, and market conditions. You may not be able to refinance this loan.
Servicing	We intend ☐ to service your loan. If so, you will make your payments to us. ☒ to transfer servicing of your loan.

Confirm Receipt

By signing, you are only confirming that you have received this form. You do not have to accept this loan because you have signed or received this form.

_____   _____   _____   _____
Applicant Signature   Date   Co-Applicant Signature   Date

LOAN ESTIMATE

Space is provided at the bottom of the form for the date and the applicant's signature, which confirms receipt of the loan estimate. The applicant's signature does not obligate him to accept the loan.

Accuracy. The fees and costs stated in the loan estimate must be estimated in good faith using the best information available at the time. Generally, if the actual charge (as shown in the closing disclosure) is equal to or less than the estimated charge, the estimate is considered to have been made in good faith. If the actual charge exceeds the estimated charge, the estimate is not considered to have been in good faith, regardless of the reason for the discrepancy. In some cases the lender will be required to refund the difference to the borrower.

Exactly how accurate an estimated figure has to be depends on the "tolerance limitation" that applies to the particular charge in question. Some charges have a **zero tolerance limitation**, meaning that the borrower cannot be charged more than the amount originally disclosed on the loan estimate. Other charges are subject to a **10% cumulative tolerance limitation**. This means that increases from the amounts estimated are permitted as long as the cumulative total of all such charges shown on the closing disclosure does not exceed the cumulative total for those charges shown on the loan estimate by more than 10%. Finally, some charges do not have a specified tolerance limitation. The borrower can be charged more than the estimated amount for these items.

The rules concerning which charges for third-party services belong in which category are too complicated for this discussion. It's worth noting, however, that the lender's own charges, such as the origination fee and discount points, are always in the zero tolerance category.

Overpayments. For items subject to zero tolerance, any amount paid in excess of the estimated figure must be refunded to the borrower. Similarly, if the borrower has paid more than allowed for items subject to the 10% cumulative tolerance limitation, the lender must refund enough so that the cumulative total paid does not exceed the cumulative total estimated by more than 10%. These refunds must be received by the borrower within 60 days after closing.

Revision and redisclosure. A lender is generally bound by the first loan estimate provided to a loan applicant; it can't issue a revised estimate simply because a miscalculation or other error is discovered.

However, a revised loan estimate is permitted and appropriate in various situations—for example, when a change in circumstances affects the borrower's eligibility for the loan, or when the borrower requests a change in the loan terms.

Generally, the lender must issue the revised loan estimate within three business days after receiving the information establishing that a revision is needed. The borrower must receive the revised form at least four business days before becoming obligated on the loan. (In most cases that occurs when the borrower signs the loan agreement, typically on the closing date or within a few days before closing.)

Closing Disclosure. If the transaction proceeds to closing, the lender must provide the borrower (the buyer) with a closing disclosure at least three business days before the closing date. The property seller is also entitled to receive a closing disclosure and must receive it no later than the closing date. Closing disclosures are typically prepared by the closing agent, who may fill out one closing disclosure form for both parties or (more commonly) a separate form for each of them. (That way each one receives information only about their own side of the transaction.)

The closing disclosure reiterates much of the information in the loan estimate, with actual charges replacing estimates, and it also includes additional disclosures. An example of a closing disclosure form, with the information for both buyer and seller filled in, is shown in Figure 14.3.

The second and third pages of the closing disclosure contain the "Closing Cost Details" section, which sets out all of the financial details of the transaction in a settlement statement format. There are columns for costs paid by the borrower, by the seller, and by others.

On page 3 in the closing disclosure there are transaction summaries for the borrower and the seller. The borrower's summary shows amounts due from the borrower (including total closing costs) offset by payments the borrower has already made, along with other credits and adjustments. These figures are used to calculate how much cash the buyer needs in order to close the transaction. In the seller's summary, similar calculations are used to determine how much cash the seller will receive at closing.

Fig. 14.3 Closing disclosure form

Closing Disclosure

This form is a statement of final loan terms and closing costs. Compare this document with your Loan Estimate.

Closing Information

Date Issued	4/15/20XX
Closing Date	4/15/20XX
Disbursement Date	4/15/20XX
Settlement Agent	Epsilon Title Co.
File #	12-3456
Property	456 Somewhere Ave
	Anytown, ST 12345
Sale Price	$180,000

Transaction Information

Borrower	Michael Jones and Mary Stone
	123 Anywhere Street
	Anytown, ST 12345
Seller	Steve Cole and Amy Doe
	321 Somewhere Drive
	Anytown, ST 12345
Lender	Ficus Bank

Loan Information

Loan Term	30 years
Purpose	Purchase
Product	Fixed Rate
Loan Type	☒ Conventional ☐ FHA ☐ VA ☐ _____
Loan ID #	123456789
MIC #	000654321

Loan Terms

		Can this amount increase after closing?
Loan Amount	$162,000	**NO**
Interest Rate	3.875%	**NO**
Monthly Principal & Interest *See Projected Payments below for your Estimated Total Monthly Payment*	$761.78	**NO**
		Does the loan have these features?
Prepayment Penalty		**YES** • As high as **$3,240** if you pay off the loan during the first 2 years
Balloon Payment		**NO**

Projected Payments

Payment Calculation	Years 1-7		Years 8-30	
Principal & Interest		$761.78		$761.78
Mortgage Insurance	+	82.35	+	—
Estimated Escrow *Amount can increase over time*	+	206.13	+	206.13
Estimated Total Monthly Payment		**$1,050.26**		**$967.91**

		This estimate includes	In escrow?
Estimated Taxes, Insurance & Assessments *Amount can increase over time* *See page 4 for details*	**$356.13** a month	☒ Property Taxes ☒ Homeowner's Insurance ☒ Other: Homeowner's Association Dues *See Escrow Account on page 4 for details. You must pay for other property costs separately.*	YES YES NO

Costs at Closing

Closing Costs	$9,712.10	Includes $4,694.05 in Loan Costs + $5,018.05 in Other Costs – $0 in Lender Credits. *See page 2 for details.*
Cash to Close	$14,147.26	Includes Closing Costs. *See Calculating Cash to Close on page 3 for details.*

CLOSING DISCLOSURE

Source: Consumer Financial Protection Bureau

Closing Cost Details

Loan Costs		Borrower-Paid		Seller-Paid		Paid by Others
		At Closing	Before Closing	At Closing	Before Closing	
A. Origination Charges		**$1,802.00**				
01 0.25 % of Loan Amount (Points)		$405.00				
02 Application Fee		$300.00				
03 Underwriting Fee		$1,097.00				
04						
05						
06						
07						
08						
B. Services Borrower Did Not Shop For		**$236.55**				
01 Appraisal Fee	to John Smith Appraisers Inc.					$405.00
02 Credit Report Fee	to Information Inc.		$29.80			
03 Flood Determination Fee	to Info Co.	$20.00				
04 Flood Monitoring Fee	to Info Co.	$31.75				
05 Tax Monitoring Fee	to Info Co.	$75.00				
06 Tax Status Research Fee	to Info Co.	$80.00				
07						
08						
09						
10						
C. Services Borrower Did Shop For		**$2,655.50**				
01 Pest Inspection Fee	to Pests Co.	$120.50				
02 Survey Fee	to Surveys Co.	$85.00				
03 Title – Insurance Binder	to Epsilon Title Co.	$650.00				
04 Title – Lender's Title Insurance	to Epsilon Title Co.	$500.00				
05 Title – Settlement Agent Fee	to Epsilon Title Co.	$500.00				
06 Title – Title Search	to Epsilon Title Co.	$800.00				
07						
08						
D. TOTAL LOAN COSTS (Borrower-Paid)		**$4,694.05**				
Loan Costs Subtotals (A + B + C)		$4,664.25	$29.80			

Other Costs

		Borrower-Paid		Seller-Paid		Paid by Others
		At Closing	Before Closing	At Closing	Before Closing	
E. Taxes and Other Government Fees		**$85.00**				
01 Recording Fees	Deed: $40.00 Mortgage: $45.00	$85.00				
02 Transfer Tax	to Any State			$950.00		
F. Prepaids		**$2,120.80**				
01 Homeowner's Insurance Premium (12 mo.) to Insurance Co.		$1,209.96				
02 Mortgage Insurance Premium (mo.)						
03 Prepaid Interest ($17.44 per day from 4/15/13 to 5/1/13)		$279.04				
04 Property Taxes (6 mo.) to Any County USA		$631.80				
05						
G. Initial Escrow Payment at Closing		**$412.25**				
01 Homeowner's Insurance $100.83 per month for 2 mo.		$201.66				
02 Mortgage Insurance per month for mo.						
03 Property Taxes $105.30 per month for 2 mo.		$210.60				
04						
05						
06						
07						
08 Aggregate Adjustment		– 0.01				
H. Other		**$2,400.00**				
01 HOA Capital Contribution	to HOA Acre Inc.	$500.00				
02 HOA Processing Fee	to HOA Acre Inc.	$150.00				
03 Home Inspection Fee	to Engineers Inc.	$750.00			$750.00	
04 Home Warranty Fee	to XYZ Warranty Inc.			$450.00		
05 Real Estate Commission	to Alpha Real Estate Broker			$5,700.00		
06 Real Estate Commission	to Omega Real Estate Broker			$5,700.00		
07 Title – Owner's Title Insurance (optional) to Epsilon Title Co.		$1,000.00				
08						
I. TOTAL OTHER COSTS (Borrower-Paid)		**$5,018.05**				
Other Costs Subtotals (E + F + G + H)		$5,018.05				
J. TOTAL CLOSING COSTS (Borrower-Paid)		**$9,712.10**				
Closing Costs Subtotals (D + I)		$9,682.30	$29.80	$12,800.00	$750.00	$405.00
Lender Credits						

Calculating Cash to Close

Use this table to see what has changed from your Loan Estimate.

	Loan Estimate	Final	Did this change?
Total Closing Costs (J)	$8,054.00	$9,712.10	YES • See **Total Loan Costs (D)** and **Total Other Costs (I)**
Closing Costs Paid Before Closing	$0	− $29.80	YES • You paid these Closing Costs **before closing**
Closing Costs Financed (Paid from your Loan Amount)	$0	$0	NO
Down Payment/Funds from Borrower	$18,000.00	$18,000.00	NO
Deposit	− $10,000.00	− $10,000.00	NO
Funds for Borrower	$0	$0	NO
Seller Credits	$0	− $2,500.00	YES • See Seller Credits in **Section L**
Adjustments and Other Credits	$0	− $1,035.04	YES • See details in **Sections K and L**
Cash to Close	$16,054.00	$14,147.26	

Summaries of Transactions

Use this table to see a summary of your transaction.

BORROWER'S TRANSACTION

K. Due from Borrower at Closing	$189,762.30
01 Sale Price of Property	$180,000.00
02 Sale Price of Any Personal Property Included in Sale	
03 Closing Costs Paid at Closing (J)	$9,682.30
04	
Adjustments	
05	
06	
07	
Adjustments for Items Paid by Seller in Advance	
08 City/Town Taxes to	
09 County Taxes to	
10 Assessments to	
11 HOA Dues 4/15/13 to 4/30/13	$80.00
12	
13	
14	
15	

L. Paid Already by or on Behalf of Borrower at Closing	$175,615.04
01 Deposit	$10,000.00
02 Loan Amount	$162,000.00
03 Existing Loan(s) Assumed or Taken Subject to	
04	
05 Seller Credit	$2,500.00
Other Credits	
06 Rebate from Epsilon Title Co.	$750.00
07	
Adjustments	
08	
09	
10	
11	
Adjustments for Items Unpaid by Seller	
12 City/Town Taxes 1/1/13 to 4/14/13	$365.04
13 County Taxes to	
14 Assessments to	
15	
16	
17	

CALCULATION	
Total Due from Borrower at Closing (K)	$189,762.30
Total Paid Already by or on Behalf of Borrower at Closing (L)	− $175,615.04
Cash to Close ☒ From ☐ To Borrower	**$14,147.26**

SELLER'S TRANSACTION

M. Due to Seller at Closing	$180,080.00
01 Sale Price of Property	$180,000.00
02 Sale Price of Any Personal Property Included in Sale	
03	
04	
05	
06	
07	
08	
Adjustments for Items Paid by Seller in Advance	
09 City/Town Taxes to	
10 County Taxes to	
11 Assessments to	
12 HOA Dues 4/15/13 to 4/30/13	$80.00
13	
14	
15	
16	

N. Due from Seller at Closing	$115,665.04
01 Excess Deposit	
02 Closing Costs Paid at Closing (J)	$12,800.00
03 Existing Loan(s) Assumed or Taken Subject to	
04 Payoff of First Mortgage Loan	$100,000.00
05 Payoff of Second Mortgage Loan	
06	
07	
08 Seller Credit	$2,500.00
09	
10	
11	
12	
13	
Adjustments for Items Unpaid by Seller	
14 City/Town Taxes 1/1/13 to 4/14/13	$365.04
15 County Taxes to	
16 Assessments to	
17	
18	
19	

CALCULATION	
Total Due to Seller at Closing (M)	$180,080.00
Total Due from Seller at Closing (N)	− $115,665.04
Cash ☐ From ☒ To Seller	**$64,414.96**

Additional Information About This Loan

Loan Disclosures

Assumption

If you sell or transfer this property to another person, your lender

☐ will allow, under certain conditions, this person to assume this loan on the original terms.

☒ will not allow assumption of this loan on the original terms.

Demand Feature

Your loan

☐ has a demand feature, which permits your lender to require early repayment of the loan. You should review your note for details.

☒ does not have a demand feature.

Late Payment

If your payment is more than *15* days late, your lender will charge a late fee of *5% of the monthly principal and interest payment.*

Negative Amortization (Increase in Loan Amount)

Under your loan terms, you

☐ are scheduled to make monthly payments that do not pay all of the interest due that month. As a result, your loan amount will increase (negatively amortize), and your loan amount will likely become larger than your original loan amount. Increases in your loan amount lower the equity you have in this property.

☐ may have monthly payments that do not pay all of the interest due that month. If you do, your loan amount will increase (negatively amortize), and, as a result, your loan amount may become larger than your original loan amount. Increases in your loan amount lower the equity you have in this property.

☒ do not have a negative amortization feature.

Partial Payments

Your lender

☒ may accept payments that are less than the full amount due (partial payments) and apply them to your loan.

☐ may hold them in a separate account until you pay the rest of the payment, and then apply the full payment to your loan.

☐ does not accept any partial payments.

If this loan is sold, your new lender may have a different policy.

Security Interest

You are granting a security interest in

456 Somewhere Ave., Anytown, ST 12345

You may lose this property if you do not make your payments or satisfy other obligations for this loan.

Escrow Account

For now, your loan

☒ will have an escrow account (also called an "impound" or "trust" account) to pay the property costs listed below. Without an escrow account, you would pay them directly, possibly in one or two large payments a year. Your lender may be liable for penalties and interest for failing to make a payment.

Escrow		
Escrowed Property Costs over Year 1	$2,473.56	Estimated total amount over year 1 for your escrowed property costs: *Homeowner's Insurance Property Taxes*
Non-Escrowed Property Costs over Year 1	$1,800.00	Estimated total amount over year 1 for your non-escrowed property costs: *Homeowner's Association Dues* You may have other property costs.
Initial Escrow Payment	$412.25	A cushion for the escrow account you pay at closing. See Section G on page 2.
Monthly Escrow Payment	$206.13	The amount included in your total monthly payment.

☐ will not have an escrow account because ☐ you declined it ☐ your lender does not offer one. You must directly pay your property costs, such as taxes and homeowner's insurance. Contact your lender to ask if your loan can have an escrow account.

No Escrow		
Estimated Property Costs over Year 1		Estimated total amount over year 1. You must pay these costs directly, possibly in one or two large payments a year.
Escrow Waiver Fee		

In the future,

Your property costs may change and, as a result, your escrow payment may change. You may be able to cancel your escrow account, but if you do, you must pay your property costs directly. If you fail to pay your property taxes, your state or local government may (1) impose fines and penalties or (2) place a tax lien on this property. If you fail to pay any of your property costs, your lender may (1) add the amounts to your loan balance, (2) add an escrow account to your loan, or (3) require you to pay for property insurance that the lender buys on your behalf, which likely would cost more and provide fewer benefits than what you could buy on your own.

Loan Calculations

Total of Payments. Total you will have paid after you make all payments of principal, interest, mortgage insurance, and loan costs, as scheduled.	$285,803.36
Finance Charge. The dollar amount the loan will cost you.	$118,830.27
Amount Financed. The loan amount available after paying your upfront finance charge.	$162,000.00
Annual Percentage Rate (APR). Your costs over the loan term expressed as a rate. This is not your interest rate.	4.174%
Total Interest Percentage (TIP). The total amount of interest that you will pay over the loan term as a percentage of your loan amount.	69.46%

Questions? If you have questions about the loan terms or costs on this form, use the contact information below. To get more information or make a complaint, contact the Consumer Financial Protection Bureau at **www.consumerfinance.gov/mortgage-closing**

Other Disclosures

Appraisal
If the property was appraised for your loan, your lender is required to give you a copy at no additional cost at least 3 days before closing. If you have not yet received it, please contact your lender at the information listed below.

Contract Details
See your note and security instrument for information about
• what happens if you fail to make your payments,
• what is a default on the loan,
• situations in which your lender can require early repayment of the loan, and
• the rules for making payments before they are due.

Liability after Foreclosure
If your lender forecloses on this property and the foreclosure does not cover the amount of unpaid balance on this loan,
☒ state law may protect you from liability for the unpaid balance. If you refinance or take on any additional debt on this property, you may lose this protection and have to pay any debt remaining even after foreclosure. You may want to consult a lawyer for more information.
☐ state law does not protect you from liability for the unpaid balance.

Refinance
Refinancing this loan will depend on your future financial situation, the property value, and market conditions. You may not be able to refinance this loan.

Tax Deductions
If you borrow more than this property is worth, the interest on the loan amount above this property's fair market value is not deductible from your federal income taxes. You should consult a tax advisor for more information.

Contact Information

	Lender	Mortgage Broker	Real Estate Broker (B)	Real Estate Broker (S)	Settlement Agent
Name	Ficus Bank		Omega Real Estate Broker Inc.	Alpha Real Estate Broker Co.	Epsilon Title Co.
Address	4321 Random Blvd. Somecity, ST 12340		789 Local Lane Sometown, ST 12345	987 Suburb Ct. Someplace, ST 12340	123 Commerce Pl. Somecity, ST 12344
NMLS ID					
ST License ID			Z765416	Z61456	Z61616
Contact	Joe Smith		Samuel Green	Joseph Cain	Sarah Arnold
Contact NMLS ID	12345				
Contact ST License ID			P16415	P51461	PT1234
Email	joesmith@ ficusbank.com		sam@omegare.biz	joe@alphare.biz	sarah@ epsilontitle.com
Phone	123-456-7890		123-555-1717	321-555-7171	987-555-4321

Confirm Receipt

By signing, you are only confirming that you have received this form. You do not have to accept this loan because you have signed or received this form.

_____   _____   _____   _____
Applicant Signature   Date   Co-Applicant Signature   Date

CLOSING DISCLOSURE

PAGE 5 OF 5 • LOAN ID # 123456789

The table at the top of page 3 in the closing disclosure is where the estimated figures from the loan estimate form are compared with the amounts the borrower is actually being charged. Key disclosures, such as the loan's annual percentage rate, appear on page 5.

Revision and redisclosure. If the amounts listed in the closing disclosure change, the lender generally must provide the borrower with a revised closing disclosure form at or before closing. At the borrower's request, the lender must make the revised form available for inspection one business day before closing.

If the disclosure revisions are necessary as a result of an increased APR, the addition of a prepayment penalty, or a change in the loan product, the borrower must receive the revised disclosure at least three business days before closing.

After closing. If the lender issues a refund to the borrower to cure a tolerance limitation violation, the lender must provide a revised closing disclosure to document the refund. The lender must also provide a revised closing disclosure to correct any errors in the original disclosure form. In both cases, the revised closing disclosure must be provided to the borrower within 60 days after closing.

Predatory Lending

Over the years, as the subprime mortgage market expanded, policy makers and concerned citizens focused their attention on the problem of predatory lending. **Predatory lending** refers to practices that unscrupulous lenders and mortgage brokers use to take advantage of unsophisticated borrowers. Real estate agents, appraisers, and home improvement contractors sometimes participate in predatory lending schemes; in some cases, a buyer or seller may participate in deceiving the other party, too. It's widely believed that predatory lending practices played a major role in the mortgage foreclosure crisis (discussed in Chapter 4).

Predatory lending became a widespread problem that contributed to the mortgage foreclosure crisis

For a number of reasons, predatory lending is especially likely to occur in the subprime market. Also, predatory lending tends to be most common in refinancing and home equity lending.

We'll examine some of the tactics and loan terms predatory lenders use, describe the buyers and homeowners they tend to target, and consider the laws that have been implemented to address the problem.

Predatory Lending Practices

Some predatory lending practices involve tactics that are always abusive; others involve ordinary lending practices and loan terms that can be misused for a predatory purpose. The following list doesn't separate those two categories, but you should keep the distinction in mind.

Predatory Steering. Steering a buyer toward a more expensive loan (one with a higher interest rate and/or fees) when the buyer could qualify for a less expensive loan.

Fee Packing. Charging interest rates, points, or processing fees that far exceed the norm and are not justified by the cost of the services provided. This includes charges for unnecessary products that increase the cost of the borrower's loan.

Equity Stripping. A foreclosure rescue scam, based on assisting a homeowner facing foreclosure by purchasing the home, and selling or leasing it back to the homeowner on terms likely to result in default and/or lost equity.

Loan Flipping. Encouraging repeated refinancing even though there is no benefit to the borrower. (The predatory lender benefits from the loan fees.)

Property Flipping. Purchasing property at a discount (because the seller needs a quick sale) and then rapidly reselling it to an unsophisticated buyer for an inflated price. This isn't illegal in and of itself, but it is illegal when a real estate agent, appraiser, and/or lender commit fraud to make the buyer believe the property is worth substantially more than it's actually worth.

Disregarding Buyer's Ability to Repay. Making a loan based on unverified income information or only on the property's value, without considering the borrower's ability to afford the loan payments. (See Chapter 13 for more about this issue.)

Impound Waivers. Not requiring a borrower to make monthly deposits for property taxes and insurance into an impound account, even though the borrower is unlikely to be able to pay the taxes and insurance when they're due. Waiving the impound requirement encourages a home buyer or owner to borrow more because it reduces the monthly payment. Predatory brokers or lenders use this tactic when they are planning to sell the loan, because they won't be affected by any default and foreclosure.

Loan in Excess of Value. Loaning a home buyer or owner more than the actual value of the property. This usually involves a fraudulent appraisal. It may occur when a lender and an appraiser collude in a property flipping scheme, or when a mortgage broker and an appraiser collude to deceive a lender, victimizing both the lender and the borrower.

Negative Amortization Schemes. Deliberately making a loan with payments that don't cover the interest. The unpaid interest will be added to the outstanding principal balance and the loan will become very difficult to pay off. When adjustable-rate mortgages were a new type of loan, negative amortization was an unfortunate side effect of the way some ARMs were structured. Legitimate lenders now generally structure loans to avoid negative amortization, but predatory lenders might not.

Balloon Payment Abuses. Making a partially amortized or interest-only loan that has low monthly payments, without properly disclosing to the borrowers that a large balloon payment will be required after a short period. When the time comes, the borrowers will be told that their only alternative to foreclosure is an expensive refinancing loan from the same lender.

Fraud. Misrepresenting or concealing unfavorable loan terms or excessive fees, falsifying documents, or using other fraudulent means to induce a prospective borrower to enter into a loan agreement.

High-pressure Sales Tactics. Telling prospective borrowers that they must decide on a loan immediately, and that no other lender will loan them the money they need. This includes pressuring borrowers to accept higher-risk loans, such as balloon loans or loans with interest-only payment arrangements, by making borrowers think that the higher-risk loan is their only option for financing.

Advance Payments from Loan Proceeds. Requiring a series of the borrower's mortgage payments to be paid at closing, out of the loan proceeds.

Excessive or Unfair Prepayment Penalties. Imposing an unusually large penalty, failing to limit the penalty period to the first few years of the loan term, and/or charging the penalty even if the loan is prepaid because the borrower is refinancing with the same lender. Prepayment penalties can also be used to prevent refinancing by borrowers who were steered into an unfavorable loan.

Unfair Default Interest Rate. Increasing a loan's interest rate by an excessive amount when the borrower defaults, in a way that isn't justified by the additional risk involved in the situation.

Discretionary Acceleration Clause. Including an acceleration clause in the loan documents that allows the lender to accelerate the loan at any time, not just because the payments are delinquent or the property is being sold.

Single-premium Credit Life Insurance. A credit life insurance policy will pay off a mortgage if the borrower dies. Some borrowers choose to purchase credit life insurance with reasonable premiums that are paid in installments, but predatory lenders often require their victims to purchase a credit life policy with a single large premium due at closing.

Predatory Loan Servicing. In addition to predatory lenders and brokers, there are predatory loan servicers. They charge improper late fees, fail to credit payments the borrower has made, and sometimes even institute foreclosure proceedings against borrowers who are not in default.

Targeted Victims

Targeted victims of predatory lending tend to be uninformed and vulnerable

Why do borrowers take out loans containing the kind of burdensome terms described above? Predatory lenders and brokers deliberately target prospective borrowers who may have trouble understanding the transaction they're entering into, or who lack better alternatives. This group includes the elderly, and those with limited education, limited English, low income, significant debt, or poor or no credit history.

Predatory lending concerns overlap with fair lending issues, because racial and ethnic minority groups are disproportionately represented in the ranks of predatory lending victims.

Elderly people with lots of equity are frequently targeted by predatory lenders

Elderly people who are cognitively impaired and who have a lot of equity in their homes are the most frequent victims of predatory refinancing.

Here is some of the advice that experts offer borrowers to help them avoid being victimized by predatory lenders:

1. Don't let a real estate agent, a mortgage broker, or anyone else steer you to one particular lender. Shop around and compare costs.
2. Don't assume that you can't qualify for a loan on reasonable terms from a legitimate lender.
3. Don't let anyone persuade you to make false statements on a loan application.
4. Don't let anyone persuade you to borrow more money than you can afford to repay.
5. Don't let anyone convince you that you've committed yourself to a transaction before you actually have. For example, signing a loan estimate form does not obligate you to proceed with the loan.
6. Don't sign documents with blanks that haven't been filled in. If provisions don't apply in the current transaction, the blank lines should have "N/A" (for "not applicable") written in them, or should be plainly crossed out.
7. Don't sign documents without reading them first and asking questions about provisions you don't understand. Get the assistance of a translator or a housing counselor or other expert, if necessary. By calling the local bar association, low-income loan applicants may be able to find a free legal clinic where they can get legal advice.

Predatory Lending Laws

There are statutes and regulations designed to curb predatory lending at the federal level and also at the state level.

Federal Law. In 2008, with subprime defaults mounting, Congress and the Federal Reserve added provisions to TILA and Regulation Z aimed at protecting subprime borrowers. These rules, along with others added later to implement the Dodd-Frank Act, apply to mortgage loans that meet TILA's criteria for "higher-priced loans," a category that includes virtually all subprime loans.

The ability to repay rule discussed in Chapter 13 is primarily targeted at higher-priced loans. (All residential lenders must evaluate the buyer's financial ability to repay as agreed, but loans in the higher-priced category are subject to stricter scrutiny.) Lenders making higher-priced loans must document their ATR evaluation and be able to show that the loan was approved on reasonable grounds and in good faith.

Lenders making higher-priced mortgage loans also must:

TILA imposes rules on lenders making higher-priced (expensive) loans

- obtain a full written appraisal from a licensed or certified appraiser who has visited the subject property in person, including the interior of the home;
- disclose to the borrower that an appraisal will be performed on the property, and that the borrower will be charged for it and is entitled to a copy;
- provide a second appraisal for the home, free of charge, if it is a "flipped" home (a home that the seller purchased less than six months ago and is selling for a certain level of profit); and
- if it is a first-lien loan, maintain an escrow (impound) account and require the borrower to make deposits to cover payment of property taxes and insurance during at least the first five years of the loan term.

In addition, a higher-priced loan cannot include a prepayment penalty that lasts beyond the first two years of the loan term. Note that TILA imposes even stricter rules on loans that have an extremely high APR, which are referred to as "high-cost loans" in the law.

State Predatory Lending Laws. While TILA is the primary federal consumer protection law that addresses predatory lending, most states now have their own predatory lending laws. Of course, the coverage and provisions of these state laws vary. Some apply only to home equity and refinance loans; others also apply to purchase loans.

Homeowners facing foreclosure may, in their distress, fall prey to fraudulent schemes—paying high fees and ending up in no better position than they were in when they started. To address this problem, many states have passed distressed property laws that strictly regulate all activities related to loan modifications and impose penalties for predatory practices.

Outline: Fair Lending and Consumer Protection

I. Fair Lending Laws

   A. Equal Credit Opportunity Act

      1. Applies to all consumer credit, including residential mortgages.

      2. Prohibits discrimination against loan applicants based on race, color, religion, national origin, sex, marital status, age, or whether income comes from public assistance.

      3. Lenders may not base lending decisions on assumptions about the creditworthiness of racial, ethnic, or religious groups.

   B. Fair Housing Act

      1. Applies to transactions involving residential properties and prohibits discrimination based on race, color, national origin, religion, sex, disability, or familial status.

      2. Prohibits lenders from refusing to provide information about loans, refusing to make a loan, or imposing different terms or conditions on a loan for discriminatory reasons.

      3. Prohibits redlining: refusing to make loans secured by property in particular neighborhoods because persons of a particular racial or ethnic group live there.

      4. Lenders may refuse to make a loan in a neighborhood where property values are declining, but the decision must be based on objective economic criteria.

   C. Community Reinvestment Act

      1. Requires depository institutions to collect information on loans made to low- and moderate-income borrowers living in the communities where they do business.

      2. Lenders submit CRA data to the government as part of their annual examination process and required HMDA disclosures.

   D. Home Mortgage Disclosure Act

      1. Requires most lenders in metropolitan areas to make disclosures to the federal government regarding all loans they originate or purchase.

      2. Helps the government monitor whether lenders are engaging in redlining or other discriminatory lending practices, or in predatory practices.

II. Consumer Protection Laws

   A. Truth in Lending Act

      1. Requires disclosure of finance charges to loan applicants; it is enforced by the Consumer Financial Protection Bureau and implemented through Regulation Z.

2. Covers many consumer loans, including those secured by real property.

3. Applies only to loans made to natural persons (not corporations), and excludes loans made for business or agricultural purposes; seller financing is also exempt, since it doesn't originate with an institutional lender.

4. Bans "bait and switch" advertising and advertising loan terms that provide a false picture of the lender's product.

5. If certain loan terms are stated in an advertisement, then certain other information about the terms of repayment must also be included.

    a. APR and cash price can be stated without triggering this full disclosure requirement.

    b. Slightly different rules apply for advertising ARMs.

6. For home equity loans and some refinancing, borrowers have a right of rescission for three business days after signing the loan agreement, receiving the disclosure statement, or receiving the notice of the right to rescind.

B. Real Estate Settlement Procedures Act

1. Provides borrowers with information about closing costs and prohibits kickbacks that increase settlement costs.

2. Applies to federally related loan transactions; it doesn't apply to loans used to purchase 25 acres or more, loans for business or agricultural purposes, loans used to purchase vacant land, temporary financing, or assumptions where the lender's approval isn't required.

3. If the borrower will be required to use a particular attorney, credit reporting agency, or real estate appraiser, that must be disclosed in advance.

4. If a settlement service provider refers the borrower to an affiliate, the joint business relationship must be fully disclosed.

5. Lenders cannot require excessive deposits into impound accounts for taxes and insurance.

6. Lenders and other settlement service providers cannot pay or receive kickbacks or referral fees, pay or receive unearned fees, or charge a document preparation fee for an impound account statement or any of the disclosure statements required by law.

C. TILA/RESPA Integrated Disclosures (TRID)

1. TRID disclosure requirements apply to most home purchase, home equity, and refinance loans.

    a. Exempt transactions: HELOCs, reverse mortgages, loans secured by mobile homes, and loans made by creditors who make five or fewer mortgage loans per year.

      b.   Transactions exempt from the TRID requirements may still be subject to previous TILA and/or RESPA disclosure requirements, including use of the older disclosure forms.

  2. TRID requires extensive disclosures on two main disclosure forms, the loan estimate and the closing disclosure.

      a.   Key disclosures include the finance charge, the annual percentage rate, and the total interest percentage.

      b.   Additional disclosures are necessary for ARMs secured by the borrower's principal residence.

  3. Loan estimate

      a.   Within three business days after receiving a loan application, a lender must give the applicant a loan estimate form that can be used to compare the costs and terms of different loans. The estimates must be made in good faith.

      b.   The borrower may be charged more than estimated for certain items, up to a certain tolerance; other items are subject to a zero tolerance rule.

      c.   If a revised estimate is necessary, the borrower must receive it at least four business days before closing.

  4. Closing disclosure

      a.   At least three business days before closing, the lender must provide the borrower with a closing disclosure form. The property seller is also entitled to receive a closing disclosure on or before the closing date.

      b.   If there are changes to amounts shown on the closing disclosure, the lender must provide a revised copy to the borrower at or before closing. An additional waiting period of three business days is required if the revisions result from an increased APR, addition of a prepayment penalty, or a change in the loan product.

III. Predatory Lending

  A. Predatory lending refers to practices in the mortgage lending business that take advantage of uninformed and vulnerable borrowers for profit.

  B. Predatory practices include predatory steering, fee packing, equity stripping, loan flipping, property flipping, disregarding the buyer's ability to repay, impound waivers, issuing loans in excess of value, waiving impound accounts, negative amortization schemes, balloon payment abuses, fraud, high-pressure sales tactics, advance payments from loan proceeds, excessive prepayment penalties or default interest rates, discretionary acceleration clauses, single-premium credit life insurance, and predatory loan servicing.

C. Predatory lenders tend to target borrowers who aren't able to understand the transaction they're entering into and aren't aware of better alternatives.

D. TILA has provisions to curb predatory practices.

    1. These rules apply to loans in the higher-priced category: loans with high rates and fees that are secured by a principal residence.

    2. Among other things, the rules require documentation of the buyer's ability to repay, limit prepayment penalties, impose strict property appraisal standards, and require lenders to collect tax and insurance impounds.

E. Many states also have predatory lending laws that require disclosures and prohibit certain practices. Recently, some states have added laws protecting borrowers from predatory practices in the loan modification process.

Key Terms

Equal Credit Opportunity Act (ECOA): A federal law prohibiting discrimination by lenders against loan applicants on the basis of race, color, religion, national origin, sex, marital status, age, or whether income comes from public assistance.

Fair Housing Act: A federal law prohibiting discrimination in residential property transactions, including mortgage lending, on the basis of race, color, national origin, religion, sex, disability, or familial status.

Community Reinvestment Act (CRA): A federal law requiring banks and other depository institutions to serve low- and middle-income borrowers and to report these loans to the government.

Redlining: Refusing to make loans for the purchase or rehabilitation of property in a certain neighborhood because of its racial or ethnic composition.

Home Mortgage Disclosure Act (HMDA): A federal law requiring institutional lenders to report on residential loans they originated or purchased from other lenders; the law's intent is to detect redlining and other discriminatory lending practices.

Truth in Lending Act (TILA): A federal law that requires lenders to make disclosures to loan applicants concerning loan costs and regulates the advertising of credit terms.

RESPA: The Real Estate Settlement Procedures Act, a federal law that governs the closing process in residential mortgage transactions.

TILA-RESPA Integrated Disclosure (TRID) rule: A set of requirements regarding disclosures to loan applicants (buyers) and property sellers, coordinating the disclosure requirements of the two statutes.

Finance charge: The cost of the loan as a dollar amount; the sum of all fees and charges the borrower will pay in connection with the loan, including the interest, loan fees, discount points, service fees, mortgage insurance costs, and/or a mortgage broker's fee.

Annual percentage rate (APR): The relationship between a loan's finance charge and the amount financed, expressed as an annual percentage.

Total interest percentage: The total amount of interest that the borrower will pay over the loan term, expressed as a percentage of the loan amount.

Loan estimate: A disclosure statement that lenders must provide to loan applicants within three business days of receiving an application for a mortgage loan covered by the TRID rule.

Closing disclosure: A disclosure statement that must be provided to the borrower (the buyer) at least three business days before closing, and to the seller on or before closing, in a transaction covered by the TRID rule.

Tolerance limitations: The borrower can be charged more than stated in the loan estimate for certain items, subject to a 10% cumulative tolerance limit.

Zero tolerance: For certain charges there is a zero tolerance limitation, which means the borrower cannot be charged more than the amount originally disclosed in the loan estimate.

Predatory lending: Lending practices unscrupulous lenders or mortgage brokers use to take advantage of uninformed or vulnerable borrowers.

Chapter Quiz

1. Which of these is federal legislation that (among other things) prevents discrimination against loan applicants on the basis of race?
   a. RESPA
   b. Truth in Lending Act
   c. Equal Credit Opportunity Act
   d. Regulation Z

2. All of the charges payable by or to either of the parties in a residential real estate transaction are ordinarily disclosed on a form called the:
   a. closing disclosure
   b. financial statement
   c. loan estimate
   d. impound account statement

3. Under the Real Estate Settlement Procedures Act, lenders:
   a. may pay real estate agents a fee for referring loan applicants to them
   b. must make a disclosure when referring applicants to an affiliated service provider
   c. must require borrowers to use a particular title insurance company
   d. must disclose the APR of the loan they are offering to make

4. The TILA/RESPA Integrated Disclosure rule requires a lender to give a loan applicant a loan estimate:
   a. at the time of application
   b. within three business days of application
   c. within seven business days of application
   d. before closing

5. The purpose of the Home Mortgage Disclosure Act is to:
   a. require that lenders provide good faith estimates of all closing costs
   b. require that lenders disclose the finance charge and annual percentage rate
   c. require that lenders disclose information that may provide evidence of redlining
   d. prohibit discrimination against individuals whose income is derived from public assistance

6. Which of the following phrases in an advertisement would NOT trigger the requirement, under TILA, that the annual percentage rate and the repayment terms must be disclosed?
   a. "Low monthly payments of $1,200"
   b. "Great financing terms for borrowers with good credit"
   c. "Own with a downpayment of just $10,000"
   d. "Assume seller's 30-year loan"

7. Which of the following practices is prohibited under the Real Estate Settlement Procedures Act?
   a. Kickbacks
   b. Redlining
   c. Equity stripping
   d. Loan flipping

8. Which of the following predatory lending practices involves charging processing fees or points that are higher than normal and not justified by the services provided?
   a. Property flipping
   b. Predatory steering
   c. Impound waivers
   d. Fee packing

9. Which of the following groups is NOT typically targeted by predatory lenders?
   a. Borrowers who speak limited English
   b. Subprime borrowers
   c. Low-income borrowers
   d. Young couples

10. Which of the following loans would be covered by the TILA/RESPA Integrated Disclosure Rule?
   a. Unsecured loan for $75,000
   b. Loan secured by a farm property used to purchase farm equipment
   c. Loan made by a savings and loan and used to purchase a single-family home
   d. Second mortgage offered by a seller to cover part of the downpayment

Answer Key

1. c. The Equal Credit Opportunity Act prevents discrimination against loan applicants on the basis of race, color, religion, national origin, sex, marital status, age, or whether income is received from public assistance.

2. a. A closing disclosure is used to show all closing costs payable by or to a party in a real estate transaction. (The loan estimate form discloses only the buyer's closing costs, not the seller's.)

3. b. Under RESPA, lenders who make referrals to an affiliated settlement service provider must disclose the relationship and explain that the loan applicant is not required to use that provider.

4. b. Under the TRID rule, a lender must provide a loan estimate to an applicant within three business days after receiving the loan application.

5. c. The Home Mortgage Disclosure Act requires large lenders to disclose information about all loans that they purchase or originate so that patterns suggesting redlining or other prohibited lending practices may be observed.

6. b. If an advertisement doesn't state any specific loan terms but contains only general statements, it does not trigger TILA's requirement that the annual percentage rate and the repayment terms be included in the ad.

7. a. Referral fees paid or received by lenders and other settlement service providers are illegal kickbacks under the Real Estate Settlement Procedures Act.

8. d. Fee packing is a predatory practice involving points or processing fees that are much higher than usual and not justified by the services provided.

9. d. Predatory lenders target those who have trouble understanding loan terms or who have little choice in loan terms (such as subprime borrowers). Young couples on the whole do not fall into either group.

10. c. The TRID rule applies to most consumer loans secured by real property, including home purchase loans. It does not apply to seller financing, to loans that aren't secured by real property, or to loans for business or agricultural purposes.

Answer Key for Exercises

Chapter 8, Qualifying the Buyer

Chapter 8, Exercise No. 1

1.

$26	Roy's hourly wage
× 40	Hours in a work week
$1,040	Weekly income
× 52	Weeks in a year
$54,080	Annual income
÷ 12	Months in a year
$4,507	Roy's monthly income

Shortcut:

$26	Roy's hourly wage
× 173.33	(Result of 40 × 52 ÷ 12)
$4,507	Roy's monthly income

$685	Judy's weekly income
× 52	Weeks in a year
$35,620	Annual income
÷ 12	Months in a year
$2,968	Judy's monthly income
+ 4,507	Roy's monthly income
$7,475	Total stable monthly income

2. Yes, there are special circumstances in this case that may persuade the lender to approve the loan. Roy had special training in the Air Force, and Judy is a vocational nurse, which implies special training. They've been at their jobs for only a short time because they are new to the area. The lender will want to know whether Judy was employed as a nurse while Roy was in the Air Force.

Chapter 8, Exercise No. 2

1.

$4,200	Received every two weeks
× 26	Number of paychecks per year
$109,200	Annual income
÷ 12	Months in a year
$9,100	Able's stable monthly income

2.

$487,500	Sales price for old home
− 399,750	Mortgage to be paid off
$87,750	Gross equity
− 43,500	Estimated selling expenses
$44,250	Net equity in old home

3. Yes, Able will have problems closing the transaction. He doesn't even have enough cash and other liquid assets to cover the downpayment and closing costs, much less the required reserves.

$10,800	In savings account
600	In checking account
+ 44,250	Net equity in old home
$55,650	Liquid assets available

$51,000	Required downpayment
+ 10,200	Closing costs
$61,200	Needed at closing
+ 7,845	Required reserves
$69,045	Total liquid assets needed
− 55,650	Liquid assets available
$13,395	Shortfall

4. The savings account was opened quite recently, and the current balance in the account is significantly higher than its average balance. These facts would lead an underwriter to wonder where the money in the account came from: Did Able borrow it?

5. Able might be able to sell some personal property to raise more cash, or his relatives might be willing to give him some money with a gift letter. If he has a life insurance policy, he might consider tapping into its cash value. Or perhaps the seller would be willing to pay part of Able's closing costs.

Able will also have to explain where the money in his savings account came from. Maybe he recently sold his old car, or received a bonus at work, or closed an account at another bank and transferred the funds. (Of course, if the money was in fact borrowed, it won't count as money available to close the transaction, which will make Able's cash problem even worse.)

Chapter 10, Conventional Financing

Chapter 10, Exercise No. 1

1. Maynard's LTV would be 92%. To determine this, first divide the downpayment by the sales price to find out what percentage of the sales price the downpayment represents. (Remember that the LTV is based on the sales price or the appraised value, whichever is less. In this problem, the sales price, $318,750, is less than the appraised value, $321,000.)

$$\$25,500 \div \$318,750 = 8\%$$

Since the downpayment is 8% of the sales price, a loan for the remainder would be 92% of the sales price:

$$100\% - 8\% = 92\%$$

2. The new downpayment amount would be 6% of the sales price.

$$\$19,125 \div \$318,750 = 6\%$$

The new LTV would be 94%.

$$100\% - 6\% = 94\%$$

Chapter 10, Exercise No. 2

1.
$289,500	Sales price (less than appraised value)
× 80%	LTV for first mortgage
$231,600	First mortgage loan amount

$289,500	Sales price
× 15%	LTV for second mortgage
$43,425	Second mortgage loan amount

2.
$289,500	Sales price
× 5%	
$14,475	Downpayment

$231,600	Amount of first mortgage
× 1.5%	
$3,474	Loan origination fee

3. The total monthly payment for both loans would be $2,141.15.

$1,540.84	Principal and interest for first loan
274.48	Principal and interest for second loan
265.83	Share of property taxes ($3,190 ÷ 12)
+ 60.00	Share of insurance premium ($720 ÷ 12)
$2,141.15	Total monthly payment for both loans

Chapter 10, Exercise No. 3

1. For a conventional loan, the Tanakas could qualify for a $2,477 payment.

Stable monthly income: $9,917

$62,000	Mike's annual salary
÷ 12	Months in a year
$5,167	Mike's monthly income
+ 4,750	Barbara's monthly income
$9,917	Stable monthly income

Recurring obligations: $1,093

$317	Car payment
375	Car payment
250	Payment on personal loan
55	Store charge card payment
42	Visa payment
+ 54	MasterCard payment
$1,093	Total recurring obligations

Debt to income ratio calculation:

$9,917	Stable monthly income
× 36%	
$3,570	Maximum total obligations
− 1,093	Recurring obligations
$2,477	Maximum housing expense under debt to income ratio

Housing expense to income ratio calculation:

$9,917	Stable monthly income
× 28%	
$2,777	Maximum housing expense under housing expense ratio

The result of the debt to income ratio calculation will be the maximum housing expense for the Tanakas (since that's less than the result of the housing expense ratio calculation). Thus, using the standard ratios, the maximum mortgage payment they could qualify for would be $2,477.

2. Possible compensating factors that might help the Tanakas qualify for a larger payment include (for example) a large downpayment, substantial liquid assets, a strong potential for increased earnings, or a demonstrated ability to carry a higher housing expense than most people. Buying an energy-efficient home is another potential compensating factor. (An excellent credit reputation is another compensating factor, but that doesn't apply to the Tanakas because of Mike's earlier credit problems.)

3. If the Tanakas can afford to pay off their personal loan, or pay off one or more of their charge accounts, that would enable them to qualify for a larger mortgage payment.

Chapter 10, Exercise No. 4

1.
$350,000	Sales price
× 90%	LTV
$315,000	Loan amount
× 6%	Six points (= 1% interest)
$18,900	Approximate cost of buydown

2. The buydown could save Johnson as much as $79,708. (The savings would be less if he paid the loan off before the end of the 30-year term.)

$2,478.11	Monthly P&I payment at 8.75% (without buydown)
− 2,256.70	Monthly P&I payment at 7.75% (with buydown)
$221.41	Monthly savings
× 360	Months (30 years)
$79,708	Savings over 30 years

Chapter 11, FHA-Insured Loans

Chapter 11, Exercise No. 1

1. In 2018, the maximum FHA loan amount for a one-unit property in a high-cost area is 115% of the area median house price, up to a ceiling of $679,650. So the maximum loan amount for a one-unit property in Fletcher's area is 115% of $540,000, or $621,000 ($540,000 × 1.15 = $621,000).

2. To calculate the maximum FHA loan amount for Fletcher's transaction, multiply the sales price by 96.5%, the maximum loan-to-value ratio for an FHA borrower with a credit score of 580 or above. (You're using the sales price because it's less than the appraised value in this case.) $627,200 × .965 = $605,248. So Fletcher's maximum FHA loan amount is $605,248.

3. The required minimum cash investment for an FHA transaction is 3.5% of the sales price or appraised value, whichever is less. That means Fletcher's minimum cash investment is 3.5% of the $627,200 sales price, or $21,952 ($627,200 × .035 = $21,952). You would get the same result by subtracting the maximum loan amount (calculated for Question 2) from the sales price.

Chapter 11, Exercise No. 2

1. With a sales price and appraised value of $170,000, Lee's maximum loan amount would ordinarily be $164,050 (96.5% of the price or value), and she'd be required to make a minimum cash investment of $5,950 (3.5%).

$170,000	Sales price/appraised value
× .965	Maximum loan-to-value ratio (96.5%)
$164,050	Loan amount

$170,000	Sales price/appraised value
− 164,050	Maximum loan amount
$5,950	Minimum cash investment

To determine how the seller's contribution of $12,000 would affect the transaction, start by multiplying the sales price by 6%. That's the limit on interested party contributions in an FHA transaction.

$170,000	Sales price
× .06	Contribution limit (6%)
$10,200	Maximum contribution

The seller's $12,000 contribution exceeds the limit by $1,800 ($12,000 − $10,200 = $1,800). That excess amount will be treated as an inducement to purchase and subtracted from the sales price before the maximum loan amount is calculated.

$170,000	Sales price
− 1,800	Contribution in excess of 6% limit
$168,200	Adjusted sales price (less than appraised value)
× .965	Maximum loan-to-value ratio (96.5%)
$162,313	Maximum loan amount after seller's contribution

Lee's loan amount would be $1,737 less with the $12,000 contribution than without it ($164,050 − $162,313 = $1,737). Any amount that the seller contributes over $10,200—the maximum allowed in this case under the 6% limit—reduces the amount that Lee is able to borrow, increasing her required downpayment.

2. Secondary financing from a family member can be used for the minimum cash investment. However, the two loans combined can't exceed the sales price or the appraised value. So if the FHA loan amount is $164,050 (see Question 1), the amount of the family member's secondary financing can be no more than $5,950—in other words, no more than the minimum cash investment. (To help their daughter with her closing costs and prepaid expenses, Lee's parents could provide gift funds instead of secondary financing.)

3. Since the seller acquired the home within the 90-day period before the buyer signed the purchase agreement, this transaction can't be financed with an FHA loan unless one of the exemptions from the property flipping rules applies. For example, if the seller inherited the home, the transaction would be exempt, so Lee would be able to use an FHA loan to buy it.

Chapter 11, Exercise No. 3

1. To calculate the amount of Skillin's upfront premium, it's first necessary to determine her maximum loan amount. With a credit score of 700, she's eligible for maximum FHA financing (a loan-to-value ratio of 96.5%).

$373,000	Appraised value (less than sales price)
× .965	Maximum LTV
$359,945	Maximum loan amount
× .0175	1.75% upfront premium
$6,299.04	UFMIP amount

Since Skillin's LTV is over 90%, she'll be required to pay the annual premium for the entire loan term (until the loan is paid off).

2. If Skillin were to finance the upfront MIP, the total amount financed would be $366,244.

$359,945	Base loan
+ 6,299	UFMIP
$366,244	Total amount financed

It doesn't matter that the total amount financed exceeds the local maximum loan amount ($362,900), as long as the base loan is under the limit (which it is in this case).

Chapter 11, Exercise No. 4

1. The Herrons' effective income is $4,510.

$510	Bob's weekly income
× 52	Weeks in a year
$26,520	Bob's annual income
÷ 12	Months in a year
$2,210	Bob's monthly income
+ 2,300	Maggie's monthly income
$4,510	Effective income

2. With an FHA loan, the Herrons could qualify for a maximum housing expense of $1,398.

$114	Personal loan payment
135	Personal loan payment
+ 47	Visa payment
$296	Total recurring charges

$4,510	Effective income
× 43%	
$1,939	Maximum fixed payments
− 296	Recurring charges
$1,643	Maximum housing expense under FHA debt to income ratio

$4,510	Effective income
× 31%	
$1,398	Maximum housing expense under FHA housing expense to income ratio

The maximum housing expense would be $1,398, the result of the housing expense to income ratio calculation, since that's less than the result of the debt to income ratio calculation.

3. If the Herrons were applying for a conventional loan, the standard 36% debt to income ratio and a 28% housing expense ratio would be used in manual underwriting, since there are no compensating factors. With those ratios, the Herrons could only qualify for a mortgage payment of $1,263. That's $135 less than the FHA payment they could qualify for.

$4,510	Stable monthly income
× 36%	Conventional debt to income ratio
$1,624	Maximum total obligations
− 296	Recurring obligations
$1,328	Maximum housing expense under conventional debt to income ratio

$4,510 Stable monthly income
× 28% Conventional housing expense ratio
$1,263 Maximum housing expense under
conventional housing expense ratio

Chapter 12, VA-Guaranteed Loans

Chapter 12, Exercise No. 1

1. Yes, Woods is eligible for a VA-guaranteed loan. Since he served for the full period he was called to active duty, the applicable minimum service requirement would be 181 continuous days during peacetime, or only 90 days during wartime. (He wouldn't be eligible if he was dishonorably discharged, however.)

   It's clear that Woods hasn't used up any of his entitlement, because he's buying his first home. So his entitlement is the same as the 2018 maximum guaranty amount for the county where the property is located. That's $113,275 in most areas; but a higher maximum would apply in a high-cost county, and his entitlement would be correspondingly greater.

2. For a $325,000 loan, the VA guaranty will cover $81,250. The 2018 guaranty for loan amounts between $144,001 and $453,100 is 25% of the loan amount, up to a maximum of $113,275. $325,000 × .25 = $81,250. That's the guaranty amount for this transaction even if the house is in a high-cost county. (A county's maximum guaranty amount only comes into play for loans over $453,100.)

Chapter 12, Exercise No. 2

1. The lender would offer Bates a loan for as much as $259,000, the full price of the home, with no downpayment necessary. Since the guaranty is 25% of the loan amount for a loan between $144,001 and $453,100, the guaranty amount would be $64,750.

   $259,000 Loan amount
   × 25%
   $64,750 Guaranty for $259,000 loan

2. For a loan amount over $453,100, the guaranty is 25% or the county maximum, whichever is less. In this case, the county maximum would apply; since this is not a high-cost county, the maximum guaranty is $113,275. The lender would be willing to loan Moreau up to $462,025 and would require a $2,975 downpayment. The downpayment plus the guaranty amount would cover 25% of the cost of the home.

$465,000	Sales price
× 25%	Ratio of guaranty + downpayment to price
$116,250	25% of sales price
− 113,275	Guaranty
$2,975	Downpayment required by lender

Chapter 12, Exercise No. 3

1. With a $1,475 PITI payment, the Martins would have a 43.9% debt to income ratio.

$1,475	Housing expense
+ 807	Other recurring obligations
$2,282	Total obligations
÷ 5,200	Monthly income
0.439	Debt to income ratio (43.9%)

2. The Martins may be able to qualify for a VA loan with a $1,475 PITI payment, even though their debt to income ratio would be over 41%, because their residual income is considerably higher than the required minimum. If a VA loan applicant's residual income is at least 20% above the minimum, the lender can approve the loan in spite of a debt to income ratio over 41%, even if there are no other compensating factors, and without submitting a statement justifying the decision to the VA.

To apply this 20% rule, first calculate how much residual income the Martins would have with the proposed monthly shelter expense.

$5,200	Monthly gross income
1,325	Taxes withheld
807	Recurring obligations
− 1,643	Proposed monthly shelter expense
$1,425	Residual income

Next, check to see if the Martins' residual income exceeds the VA's minimum requirement by at least 20%. The minimum residual income for a family of five in the Western region is $1,158 if they're borrowing $80,000 or more (see Figure 12.2 in Chapter 12).

$1,158	Minimum residual income
× 20%	
$232	20% of the required minimum

Add $232 to $1,158 to find that the Martins need a residual income of $1,390 in order to be at least 20% over the minimum. Their residual income of $1,425 exceeds $1,390, so a lender could accept an income ratio over 41% without other compensating factors.

Chapter 13, Seller Financing

Chapter 13, Exercise No. 1

1. A $35,000 downpayment is 5% of the $695,000 purchase price.

$$\$35,000 \div \$695,000 = 0.05$$

The Pengs' $55,000 loan is about 8% of the price.

$$\$55,000 \div \$695,000 = 0.079$$

Together, the downpayment and the seller second would make up about 13% of the price, so Underwood and Schirmer would need an institutional loan with an 87% loan-to-value ratio.

2. To determine the amount of the institutional loan, subtract the seller second and the downpayment from the purchase price. The amount of the institutional loan would be $605,000. The combined loan amount would be $660,000.

$695,000	Purchase price
55,000	Seller second
− 35,000	Downpayment
$605,000	Loan amount for institutional loan
$605,000	Institutional loan
+ 55,000	Seller second
$660,000	Combined loan amount

3. Yes, this arrangement complies with the rules for secondary financing in conjunction with a conventional loan listed in Figure 13.1. The combined LTV for the first and second loans together does not exceed 95%; the second loan does not require a balloon payment in less than five years; and there is no possibility of negative amortization on the second.

$660,000 (combined loan amount) ÷ $695,000 (price) = 94.9% CLTV

4. Yes, the couple probably could qualify for this combination of a conventional loan and a seller second. The total monthly payment (PITI) will be about $5,869. With stable monthly income of $22,000 and debts totaling $2,000 without the housing expense, their debt to income ratio is about 36% and their housing expense to income ratio is about 27%. Even if the standard 36% and 28% ratios used in manual underwriting are applied, Underwood and Schirmer could qualify (without compensating factors).

$4,439.28	Principal and interest for institutional loan
329.75	Principal and interest for seller second
560.00	Property taxes
100.00	Hazard insurance
+ 440.00	PMI
$5,869.03	Proposed monthly housing expense

$5,869	Proposed housing expense
+ 2,000	Other monthly obligations
$7,869	Total monthly obligations
÷ 22,000	Stable monthly income
35.7%	Debt to income ratio

$5,869	Proposed housing expense
÷ 22,000	Stable monthly obligations
26.7%	Housing expense to income ratio

Case Study Answers

Case Study for Chapter 10, Conventional Financing

Question 1

Rick's middle score (685) will be the indicator score (also called the representative score) for the Cortinas' loan application. Here's how the indicator score would typically be selected when there's more than one applicant and each of them has three credit scores: First, for each applicant, select the middle score out of the three scores listed. (Rick's middle score is 685, and Teresa's is 750.) Then compare those selected scores; the lowest score is used as the indicator score for the application. Since 685 is lower than 750, the Cortinas' indicator score is 685. It will be used to determine whether the Cortinas clear the minimum credit score threshold (680 for many conventional loans, including the loans they're considering). It will also be used to determine the applicable percentage for the loan-level price adjustment that's based on credit score. (Note that even though it isn't the couple's indicator score, Teresa's 750 score might help strengthen the application in a more general sense.)

Question 2

The Cortinas' stable monthly income is $10,671 (rounded down to the nearest dollar).

$30.50	Teresa's hourly wage
× 173.33	Factor for translating hourly wage into monthly income
$5,286.57	Teresa's monthly income
2,400.00	Rick's monthly salary
+2,985.00	Rick's average monthly commissions
$10,671.57	Stable monthly income

Question 3

The first step in calculating the maximum principal and interest payment is to add up the Cortinas' monthly recurring obligations (aside from their housing expense).

$417	Car payment
323	Car payment
183	Installment contract payment
165	Credit card payments
+ 155	Student loan payment
$1,243	Recurring obligations

(The $98 student loan payment shouldn't be counted, since only eight payments remain to be made.)

Next, calculate the Cortinas' maximum housing expense using the 36% and 28% conventional income ratios.

$10,671   Stable monthly income
×   .36   Total debt to income ratio
$3,841.56   Maximum total obligations
−1,243.00   Recurring obligations
$2,598.56   Maximum housing expense under the 36% debt to income ratio

$10,671   Stable monthly income
×   .28   Housing expense to income ratio
$2,987.88   Maximum housing expense under the 28% housing expense ratio

With those ratios, their maximum housing expense would be $2,598.56, the result of the debt to income ratio calculation, since that's less than the result of the housing expense to income ratio calculation. The next step is to set aside 15% for taxes and insurance, plus another 10% for mortgage insurance if required, to determine their maximum principal and interest payment.

$2,598.56   Maximum housing expense
÷   1.15   15% for taxes and hazard insurance
$2,259.62   Maximum P&I payment if PMI isn't required (LTV 80% or less)

$2,598.56   Maximum housing expense
÷   1.25   15% for taxes and hazard insurance, plus 10% for mortgage insurance
$2,078.85   Maximum P&I payment if PMI is required (LTV over 80%)

So if they apply for Loan A, which has an 80% LTV, the Cortinas should qualify for a principal and interest payment of approximately $2,259.62. For either Loan B (90% LTV) or Loan C (95% LTV), the maximum principal and interest payment would be approximately $2,078.85. The Cortinas qualify for a larger maximum principal and interest payment with Loan A because it doesn't require private mortgage insurance. (PMI is required only when the loan-to-value ratio is above 80%.) Without PMI, a larger portion of the maximum housing expense can be devoted to principal and interest.

If they were allowed to have a 45% debt to income ratio, their maximum housing expense would be $3,558.95, as shown below. (That's $960 more than the maximum housing expense under the 36% ratio.) With that payment amount, their housing expense to income ratio would be 33%.

$10,671   Stable monthly income
×   .45   Total debt to income ratio
$4,801.95   Maximum total obligations
−1,243.00   Recurring obligations
$3,558.95   Maximum housing expense under a 45% debt to income ratio

$3,558.95   Maximum housing expense
÷ 10,671   Stable monthly income
0.33   33% housing expense to income ratio

Some buyers can qualify for a conventional loan with a debt to income ratio as high as 45%. That's the maximum debt to income ratio for a loan underwritten using Freddie Mac's automated underwriting system (and Fannie Mae's AUS can accept a 50% debt to income ratio). It's also the GSEs' maximum debt to income ratio for manually underwritten loans, if the underwriter documents adequate compensating factors. Although the 33% housing expense to income ratio is significantly higher than the standard 28% guideline, it won't necessarily be considered too high in the context of the application as a whole, with either automated or manual underwriting. (If the loan is going to be sold to Fannie Mae, the housing expense ratio isn't separately considered.)

The Cortinas' maximum monthly housing expense will probably be determined by the 36% and 28% ratios if their application is manually underwritten and there are no compensating factors to offset the extra risk of ratios over the standard limits. (Manual underwriting is used in a number of situations. For example, if an application is first submitted to an automated system and the AUS gives it a "Refer" or "Caution" rating instead of "Approve" or "Accept," the application generally must be manually underwritten.)

Question 4

a) The interest rate on an 80% fixed-rate loan with no discount points would be 5.50%. A $397,968 loan could buy a $497,460 house, with a downpayment of $99,492.

$397,968	Loan amount
÷ .80	80% LTV
$497,460	Sales price
− 397,968	Loan amount
$99,492	Downpayment

b) The interest rate on a 90% ARM with no discount points would be 4.5%. A $410,284 loan could buy a $455,871 house, with a downpayment of $45,587.

$410,284	Loan amount
÷ .90	90% LTV
$455,871	Sales price
− 410,284	Loan amount
$45,587	Downpayment

c) The interest rate on a 95% fixed-rate loan with three discount points would be 5.25%. (Three points would reduce the interest rate by 0.75%, from 6.00% to 5.25%. $0.25 \times 3 = 0.75$.) A $376,465 loan could buy a $396,279 house, with a downpayment of $19,814.

$376,465	Loan amount
÷ .95	95% LTV
$396,279	Sales price
− 376,465	Loan amount
$19,814	Downpayment

Question 5

For the 80% fixed-rate loan, the Cortinas would need about $125,600 in cash. For the 90% ARM, they'd need about $70,600. For the 95% fixed-rate loan, about $55,700.

a) 80% fixed-rate loan at 5.50% interest, with a 1.50% origination fee.

Sales price: $497,460   Loan amount: $397,968
Downpayment: $99,492   Monthly mortgage payment (PITI): $2,598.56

$397,968	Loan amount
× .015	Origination fee percentage (1.50%)
$5,969.52	Origination fee

$497,460	Sales price
× .03	Closing cost percentage (3.00%)
$14,923.80	Closing costs

$2,598.56	PITI payment
× 2	Months
$5,197.12	Reserves

$99,492	Downpayment
5,970	Total loan fees
+ 14,924	Closing costs
$120,386	Cash for closing
+ 5,197	Reserves
$125,583	Total cash requirement

b) 90% ARM at 4.5% interest, with no discount points and a 1.50% origination fee.

Sales price: $455,871   Loan amount: $410,284
Downpayment: $45,587   Monthly mortgage payment (PITI): $2,598.56

$410,284	Loan amount
× .015	Origination fee percentage (1.50%)
$6,154.26	Origination fee

$455,871	Sales price
× .03	Closing cost percentage (3.00%)
$13,676.13	Closing costs

$2,598.56	PITI payment
× 2	Months
$5,197.12	Reserves

$45,587	Downpayment
6,154	Total loan fees
+ 13,676	Closing costs
$65,417	Cash for closing
+ 5,197	Reserves
$70,614	Total cash requirement

c) 95% loan at 5.25% interest, with three discount points and a 2.00% origination fee.

Sales price: $396,279   Loan amount: $376,465
Downpayment: $19,814   Monthly mortgage payment (PITI): $2,598.56

$376,465	Loan amount
× .03	Three discount points (3.00%)
$11,293.95	Discount points

$376,465	Loan amount
× .02	Origination fee percentage (2.00%)
$7,529.30	Origination fee

$396,279	Sales price
× .03	Closing cost percentage (3.00%)
$11,888.37	Closing costs

$2,598.56	PITI payment
× 2	Months
$5,197.12	Reserves

$19,814	Downpayment
18,823	Total loan fees
+ 11,888	Closing costs
$50,525	Cash for closing
+ 5,197	Reserves
$55,722	Total cash requirement

The Cortinas have $87,000 in savings, so they have enough cash to buy a $455,871 house with Loan B, the 90% ARM that requires about $70,600 in cash, or to buy a $396,279 house with Loan C, the 95% fixed-rate loan that requires about $55,700 in cash.

They don't have nearly enough in savings to buy a $497,460 house with Loan A, the 80% fixed-rate loan, which would require $125,600 in cash.

Question 6

a) For a fixed-rate loan with one discount point, the Cortinas' interest rate would be 5.25%. That's considerably higher than the 4.5% rate they'd pay with the ARM. If the principal and interest payment is unchanged, the higher rate will result in a smaller loan amount. So they'd have to make a larger downpayment to make up the difference.

Let's see whether they could qualify for a fixed-rate loan to buy the same house (priced at $455,871) they could buy with the ARM. With the 5.25% fixed interest rate, the Cortinas could get a $376,464 loan, compared to $410,284 for the ARM. We'll assume that in addition to one discount point, they'll pay a 1.5% origination fee. There will also be closing costs and two months of reserves. Adding all that together, the Cortinas would need roughly $107,692 in cash to buy a $455,871 house, compared to $70,614 with the ARM for the larger loan amount. Since the Cortinas have only $87,000 in savings, that house would probably be out of reach with the fixed-rate loan.

So let's consider the other alternative, buying a less expensive home. With a 90% loan-to-value ratio and a fixed 5.25% interest rate, the same loan amount ($376,464) would translate into a sales price of about $418,293 ($376,464 ÷ .90 = $418,293). For that purchase, the Cortinas would need around $68,990 in cash, including the downpayment, closing costs, one discount point, a 1.5% origination fee, and two months of reserves. They probably could qualify for this 90% fixed-rate loan, if they're willing to lower their price range by about $40,000 ($455,871 – $418,293 = $37,578).

b) Even though the $400,000 sales price is almost $100,000 less than the $497,460 price the Cortinas were considering with Loan A, they don't have enough cash to qualify for an 80% loan. The loan amount would be $320,000, with an $80,000 downpayment. The downpayment plus $12,000 in closing costs ($400,000 × .03 = $12,000) exceeds their $87,000 in savings, and that's before even considering the effect of the origination fee and reserves, which would add almost $9,000 more to the amount of cash they'd need to qualify for this loan.

$400,000	Sales price
× .80	80% LTV
$320,000	Loan amount

$400,000	Sales price
– 320,000	Loan amount
$80,000	Downpayment

Notice that the $400,000 price tag the Cortinas can't qualify for with an 80% fixed-rate loan is very close to the $396,279 price they could qualify for with a 95% fixed-rate loan and high loan fees (Loan C—see Question 5c). They simply don't have enough savings to afford a 20% downpayment in this price range.

Question 7

a) With a $3,137.21 PITI payment, the Cortinas' income ratios are 41% and 28%.

$3,137.21	PITI
+1,243.00	Recurring obligations
$4,380.21	Total monthly obligations
÷ 10,671	Stable monthly income
0.41	Debt to income ratio (41%)

$3,137.21	PITI
÷ 10,671	Stable monthly income
0.294	Housing expense to income ratio (29%)

b) It is not out of the question that the Cortinas could qualify for a loan with a PITI payment this large, although it's by no means certain that they could.

Their 41% debt to income ratio is well above the 36% benchmark. Even so, a debt to income ratio that high may be acceptable for a conventional loan. An automated underwriting system can allow a debt to income ratio as high as 45% (Freddie Mac) or 50% (Fannie Mae), if that's an acceptable risk in light of the application as a whole. Even if the Cortinas' application is manually underwritten, Fannie Mae and Freddie Mac guidelines allow a debt to income ratio up to 45% if there are sufficient compensating factors to offset the extra risk.

Although the 29% housing expense to income ratio is higher than the standard 28% benchmark, that particular factor probably wouldn't prevent the Cortinas from qualifying for a payment this large. The housing expense ratio is generally regarded as less important than the debt to income ratio; in fact, if the loan is going to be sold to Fannie Mae, the housing expense ratio doesn't have to be separately considered. Also, in order for the Cortinas to have a chance at qualifying for the loan with a 41% debt to income ratio, there would have to be some solid compensating factors in their application, and those would probably outweigh a slightly high housing expense to income ratio.

c) The Cortinas have been paying $3,450 a month in rent, considerably more than the $3,137 housing expense they'd have if this loan were approved. Their rent is 32.3% of their monthly income, so they've demonstrated that they can devote more of their income to housing than most people. A lender might be willing to treat that as a compensating factor to help offset the high debt to income ratio. How much it would help would depend on the "overall layering of risk" presented by their whole application.

Other considerations that can be treated as compensating factors include an excellent credit reputation; a large downpayment; substantial liquid assets; education or employment history indicating strong potential for increased earnings; short-term income not counted as stable monthly income; rental income from a family member; or energy-efficient features in the house being purchased. None of these appears to apply in the Cortinas' case, with the possible exception of the last one. If the house they want has special energy-efficient features, they should bring that to the lender's attention.

d) The risk factor that will probably concern the lender most is the Cortinas' indicator credit score. While 685 isn't a terrible score, it's weak enough so that the lender might decide that a 41% debt to income ratio would be one layer of risk too many.

Another problem with the Cortinas' financial situation is that they have quite a lot of debt. The proposed housing expense is 29% of their income, yet their other obligations are enough to push their debt to income ratio up to 41%.

e) Depending on the financial circumstances of their families, the Cortinas might be able to use gift funds to make a larger downpayment, reducing the loan amount and the monthly payment without increasing their debts or expenses. There are other ways gift funds could be applied; for example, they could be used to pay additional discount points and reduce the loan's interest rate and monthly payment.

If the Cortinas paid off one or more of their debts (like the student loan with only 12 payments left), that could also help them qualify for the mortgage and buy this house. They should consult the lender before they do that, however, to make sure it would make a difference.

Case Study for Chapter 11, FHA-Insured Loans

Question 1

Applying the FHA's 43% and 31% income ratios, the maximum housing expense the Cortinas qualify for is $3,308.01 (the result of the housing expense to income ratio calculation, which is lower than the result of the debt to income ratio calculation).

$10,671	Effective income
× .43	FHA maximum debt to income ratio
$4,588.53	Maximum total obligations
− 1,243.00	Recurring charges
$3,345.53	Maximum housing expense under the debt to income ratio
$10,671	Effective income
× .31	FHA maximum housing expense to income ratio
$3,308.01	Maximum housing expense under the housing expense ratio

Question 2

FHA borrowers are permitted to borrow enough to cover the upfront MIP in addition to the local maximum loan amount. So the Cortinas could be preapproved to borrow the maximum base loan amount for their area ($294,515), plus the upfront MIP (1.75% of the base loan amount, or $5,154.01). The total amount financed would be $299,669.

$294,515	Maximum base loan amount
× .0175	Upfront MIP percentage (1.75%)
$5,154.01	Upfront MIP
$294,515.00	Loan amount
+ 5,154.01	Upfront MIP
$299,669.01	Total amount financed (rounded down to $299,669)

Question 3

The Cortinas should easily qualify for a $294,515 FHA loan with the upfront MIP financed ($299,669 total amount financed). A fixed-rate FHA loan at 5.50% interest would have PITI payments of approximately $2,165, considerably less than the Cortinas' $3,308 maximum FHA housing expense.

First calculate the estimated monthly share of the property taxes and hazard insurance.

$1,701.49	Principal and interest payment for loan at 5.5% interest
× .15	15% for taxes and hazard insurance
$255.22	Monthly share of property taxes and hazard insurance

Next, calculate the monthly share of the annual premium.

$294,515   Loan balance (base loan amount)
× .0085   Annual premium percentage (.85%)
$2,503.38   Annual premium
÷ 12   Months in a year
$208.62   Monthly share of annual premium

Now add those two figures to the principal and interest payment.

$255.22   Monthly share of property taxes and hazard insurance
208.62   Monthly share of annual premium
+ 1,701.49   P&I payment
$2,165.33   PITI payment for $294,515 FHA loan at 5.5% with financed UFMIP

Question 4

The loan-to-value ratio for an FHA loan can't exceed 96.5% of the appraised value or sales price, whichever is less. The minimum cash investment (3.5%) would be $10,682. With the maximum loan amount plus the minimum cash investment, the Cortinas could pay about $305,200 for a house (assuming that the appraised value isn't less than the price).

$294,515   Base loan amount
÷ .965   LTV percentage (96.5% of sales price or value)
$305,197   Sales price
− 294,515   Loan amount
$10,682   Minimum cash investment (3.5% of sales price or value)

Note that the financed upfront premium isn't involved in these calculations.

Question 5

For this transaction, the Cortinas would need approximately $22,800 at closing.

$294,515   Loan amount
× .01   Origination fee percentage (1.00%)
$2,945.15   Origination fee

$305,197   Sales price
× .03   Closing cost percentage (3.00%)
$9,155.91   Closing costs

$10,682   Minimum cash investment (from Question 4)
2,945   Origination fee
+ 9,156   Closing costs
$22,783   Total cash needed at closing

Question 6

Even though the Cortinas' $305,197 price is based on the maximum FHA loan amount in their area, they could use their FHA financing to buy a more expensive house if they wanted to. They'd simply have to make a larger downpayment than the required 3.5% minimum cash investment.

For example, if they wanted to buy a house for $350,000, they'd have to make a $55,485 downpayment. That's the minimum cash investment ($10,682) plus the difference between $350,000 and $305,197 ($44,803). That would bring their total cash requirement to about $67,600 ($44,803 + $22,783 = $67,586).

Question 7

For home buyers, an FHA loan has two chief advantages over a comparable conventional loan: they may qualify for a significantly larger monthly payment, and they'll probably need significantly less cash for closing.

In the Cortinas' case, they easily qualify for the maximum FHA loan amount allowed in their area, $294,515. Their PITI payment for that loan at 5.5% interest would be $2,165.33, much less than the $3,308 maximum payment the FHA's 43% and 31% maximum income ratios would allow them to qualify for even without compensating factors in their application. The amount of cash they need to bring to closing ($22,783) is also well within their means. In contrast, their $87,000 in savings was a limiting factor in their ability to qualify for some of the conventional loans we considered.

However, if you look at the sales prices that the Cortinas can contemplate with an FHA loan ($305,000 with the $10,682 minimum cash investment; $350,000 if they make a downpayment that takes up much more of their savings), you can see a common problem for potential FHA borrowers in some places. In areas where prices have rapidly appreciated, FHA loan limits may not have kept pace, and that can limit FHA borrowers to homes at the lower end of the local market. The Cortinas—who, like many first-time buyers, have a solid income but a lot of other debts and not a lot of cash—can't use an FHA loan if they want to purchase a house in the same price range ($400,000 to $500,000) they were considering with conventional loans. (Homes in that range might be within reach with FHA financing if the Cortinas were looking in a high-cost area, where the maximum FHA loan amount could be as high as $679,650.)

The Cortinas may well still prefer to use an FHA loan and purchase a less expensive home, though. The FHA loan will cost them less in loan fees, and it will also allow them to hold on to more of their savings and make smaller monthly payments (because of the lower loan amount). That frees up more of their income for them to enjoy—or to pay down some of their debts, which will be helpful for affording a more expensive home if they look to trade up in the future.

Case Study for Chapter 12, VA-Guaranteed Loans

Question 1

Under the VA's standard 41% debt to income ratio, the Cortinas could have a maximum housing expense of $3,132.11, which we'll round down to $3,132.

$10,671	Monthly income
× .41	Maximum debt to income ratio (41%)
$4,375.11	Maximum total obligations
− 1,243.00	Recurring obligations
$3,132.11	Maximum housing expense (PITI)

Question 2

With a $3,132 PITI payment, the Cortinas' residual income would be $3,897. To calculate that figure, start by adding up all of the taxes that are withheld from their paychecks. Then calculate the proposed monthly shelter expense. Finally, subtract the taxes, the recurring obligations, and the monthly shelter expense from monthly income.

$570	Federal income tax (Rick)
218	State income tax (Rick)
306	Social Security/Medicare (Rick)
563	Federal income tax (Teresa)
212	State income tax (Teresa)
+ 327	Social Security/Medicare (Teresa)
$2,196	Total taxes

1,450	Square feet of living area
× 0.14	Per square foot
$203	Estimated maintenance and utilities
+ 3,132	PITI payment
$3,335	Monthly shelter expense

$10,671	Monthly income
2,196	Taxes
1,243	Recurring obligations
− 3,335	Monthly shelter expense
$3,897	Residual income

The Cortinas' residual income is far more than the $738 minimum required for a two-person family in the Southern region borrowing $80,000 or more. As long as other aspects of their application (such as their credit reputation) meet VA standards, they can easily qualify for a $3,132 payment.

Question 3

If the lender is willing to accept a 45% ratio in their case, the Cortinas' maximum housing expense would be $3,559. Their residual income would be $3,470.

```
$10,671    Monthly income
×  .45    Debt to income ratio (45%)
$4,801.95   Maximum total obligations
−1,243.00   Recurring obligations
$3,558.95   Maximum housing expense (PITI)
```

```
$10,671    Monthly income
 2,196    Taxes
 1,243    Recurring obligations
− 3,762    Monthly shelter expense ($3,559 PITI + $203 estimated costs)
$3,470    Residual income
```

When a VA loan applicant's residual income exceeds the required minimum by more than 20%, the lender can approve the loan even if the debt to income ratio is over 41%, without other compensating factors. For the Cortinas, 20% of the minimum requirement ($738) is $147.60. Even with the $3,559 payment, their residual income would exceed the minimum requirement by far more than 20%.

```
$738    Minimum residual income
×  20%
$147.60    20% of required minimum
```

```
$3,470    Residual income (with $3,762 monthly shelter expense)
− 738    Minimum residual income
$2,732    Amount by which residual income exceeds required minimum
```

That means the lender could approve a VA loan with that larger payment for the Cortinas without having to submit a statement justifying the decision to the VA.

Question 4

With 15% of the payment going toward taxes and insurance, a $3,559 PITI payment translates into a maximum principal and interest payment of $3,095.

```
$3,559    Maximum housing expense
÷  1.15    15% for property taxes and hazard insurance
$3,094.78    Maximum principal and interest payment
```

For loans over $453,100, the guaranty amount is 25% of the loan amount or the county maximum, whichever is less. In this case, the county maximum ($113,275) is less than 25% of the loan amount ($136,263), so the guaranty amount is $113,275.

```
$545,050    Loan amount
×  .25    Guaranty percentage for VA loan between $144,001 and $453,100
$136,263    25% of loan amount (higher than maximum guaranty)
```

Question 5

In the Cortinas' area, lenders typically require a downpayment for loan amounts over $453,100, since the maximum guaranty, $113,275, would be less than 25% of a loan amount larger than that. So a downpayment would be required in this case.

However, the Cortinas' downpayment does not have to be the full amount of the difference between the $505,000 sales price and the $453,100 figure (which would be over $50,000).

$505,000	Sales price
× .25	Desired ratio of guaranty + downpayment to price
$126,250	25% of sales price
− 113,275	Maximum guaranty
$12,975	Downpayment required by lender

To find the loan amount for the transaction, subtract the downpayment from the sales price.

$505,000	Sales price
− 12,975	Downpayment
$492,025	Loan amount

Additional costs would be the 1% origination fee (the lender's flat fee), the 2.15% funding fee, and closing costs. The Cortinas would need around $43,625 in cash to close this loan, and their $87,000 in savings will easily cover that. The Cortinas could use a VA loan to buy the $505,000 home.

$492,025	Loan amount
× .01	Origination fee percentage (1%)
$4,920.25	Origination fee

$492,025	Loan amount
× .0215	Funding fee percentage (2.15%)
$10,578.54	Funding fee

$505,000	Sales price
× .03	Closing costs percentage (3%)
$15,150	Closing costs

12,975	Downpayment
4,920	Origination fee
10,579	Funding fee
+ 15,150	Closing costs
$43,624	Due at closing

Question 6

The Cortinas might well choose a VA loan over a conventional or FHA loan, so that they could buy a more expensive house with less cash. Buying a $505,000 house would mean taking on a much larger monthly payment, though, and they might not want to do that. However, a VA loan would also allow them to buy a house in the $350,000–$400,000 price range using a lot less of their savings than conventional or FHA financing would require.

Case Study for Chapter 13, Seller Financing

Question 1

The lender doesn't allow a conventional loan that's supplemented with secondary financing to exceed 75% of the sales price or appraised value, whichever is less (in this case, it's the appraised value, $433,500). As a result, the amount of the primary loan will be $325,125.

$433,500	Appraised value (less than $435,000 sales price)
× .75	Maximum LTV for primary loan (75%)
$325,125	Maximum conventional loan amount

This lender's secondary financing rules also require the Cortinas to make at least a 10% downpayment, so the loan-to-value ratio of Wellman's seller second can't exceed 15% of the appraised value. That means she can finance no more than $65,025. The total amount financed would be $390,150.

$433,500	Appraised value
× .15	Maximum LTV for secondary financing (15%)
$65,025	Maximum seller second
+ 325,125	Conventional loan amount
$390,150	Total amount financed

Question 2

The monthly housing expense for this combination of a conventional loan and a seller second would be $2,542.04. Since the Cortinas are preapproved for a $2,598.56 PITI payment, they shouldn't have a problem qualifying for this combined payment.

$1,820.61	Principal and interest for first loan
+ 389.86	Principal and interest for seller second
$2,210.47	Combined principal and interest payment
× 1.15	15% for taxes and hazard insurance
$2,542.04	Combined PITI payment (total monthly housing expense)

Question 3

The Cortinas would need about $62,777 to close, plus $5,084 in reserve, for a total cash requirement of approximately $67,861. Their $87,000 in savings is more than enough.

$435,000	Sales price
− 390,150	Total amount financed
$44,850	Downpayment

$325,125	Conventional loan amount
× .015	Origination fee percentage (1.50%)
$4,876.88	Origination fee

435,000	Sales price
× .03	Closing cost percentage (3.00%)
$13,050	Closing costs

$2,542.04	Combined loan payment
× 2	Months
$5,084.08	Reserves

$44,850	Downpayment
4,877	Origination fee
+ 13,050	Closing costs
$62,777	Cash for closing
+ 5,084	Reserves
$67,861	Total cash requirement

Question 4

The seller second can be amortized over 30 years (so that the monthly payment is only $389.86), but require a balloon payment of the entire unpaid principal balance after five years. At that point, the remaining balance would be approximately $60,800. The Cortinas should plan ahead regarding the balloon payment. If all goes well—in terms of their own financial situation, property values, and the economy in general—refinancing will be an option when the time comes. But that isn't guaranteed.

Question 5

Wellman would receive approximately $232,475 at closing.

$435,000	Sales price
× .10	Selling costs percentage (10%)
$43,500	Selling costs

$435,000	Sales price
43,500	Selling costs
94,000	Mortgage payoff
− 65,025	Credit extended to the buyers
$232,475	Cash to seller at closing

Income Qualifying—Conventional Loans
Loan A: Fixed Interest Rate, 80% Loan-to-Value Ratio

Stable Monthly Income

Base salary	
Wage earner 1	$2,400
Wage earner 2	$5,286
Overtime	
Commissions	$2,985
Bonuses	
Other	+
Total	$10,671

Recurring Obligations

Car loans	$740
Credit cards	$165
Student loans	$155
Other debts	$183
Child support	
Alimony	
Other	+
Total	$1,243

Debt to Income Ratio

$10,671	Stable monthly income
x .36	Maximum ratio (36%)
$3,841.56	Maximum obligations
– 1,243.00	Recurring obligations
$2,598.56	Maximum mortgage payment (PITI) under debt to income ratio

Housing Expense to Income Ratio

$10,671	Stable monthly income
x .28	Maximum ratio (28%)
$2,987.88	Maximum mortgage payment (PITI) under housing expense ratio

Maximum Mortgage Payment (PITI) $2,598.56

$2,598.56	Maximum PITI payment
÷ 1.15	15% for taxes and hazard insurance
$2,259.62	Maximum principal and interest payment
Interest rate	5.50%

Maximum Loan Amount $397,968

$397,968	Maximum loan amount
÷ .80	Loan-to-value ratio (80%)
$497,460	Sales price

Sales Price $497,460

Income Qualifying—Conventional Loans
Loan B: Adjustable Interest Rate, 90% Loan-to-Value Ratio

Stable Monthly Income

Base salary	
Wage earner 1	$2,400
Wage earner 2	$5,286
Overtime	
Commissions	$2,985
Bonuses	
Other	+
Total	$10,671

Recurring Obligations

Car loans	$740
Credit cards	$165
Student loans	$155
Other debts	$183
Child support	
Alimony	
Other	+
Total	$1,243

Debt to Income Ratio

$10,671	Stable monthly income
x .36	Maximum ratio (36%)
$3,841.56	Maximum obligations
– 1,243.00	Recurring obligations
$2,598.56	Maximum mortgage payment (PITI) under debt to income ratio

Housing Expense to Income Ratio

$10,671	Stable monthly income
x .28	Maximum ratio (28%)
$2,987.88	Maximum mortgage payment (PITI) under housing expense ratio

Maximum Mortgage Payment (PITI) $2,598.56

$2,598.56	Maximum PITI payment
÷ 1.25	25% for taxes, hazard insurance, and PMI
$2,078.85	Maximum principal and interest payment
Interest rate	4.50%

Maximum Loan Amount $410,284

$410,284	Maximum loan amount
÷ .90	Loan-to-value ratio (90%)
$455,871	Sales price

Sales Price $455,871

Income Qualifying—Conventional Loans
Loan C: Fixed Interest Rate, 95% Loan-to-Value Ratio

Stable Monthly Income

Base salary		
Wage earner 1	$2,400	
Wage earner 2	$5,286	
Overtime		
Commissions	$2,985	
Bonuses		
Other	+	
Total	$10,671	

Recurring Obligations

Car loans	$740
Credit cards	$165
Student loans	$155
Other debts	$183
Child support	
Alimony	
Other +	
Total	$1,243

Debt to Income Ratio

$10,671	Stable monthly income
x .36	Maximum ratio (36%)
$3,841.56	Maximum obligations
– 1,243.00	Recurring obligations
$2,598.56	Maximum mortgage payment (PITI) under debt to income ratio

Housing Expense to Income Ratio

$10,671	Stable monthly income
x .28	Maximum ratio (28%)
$2,987.88	Maximum mortgage payment (PITI) under housing expense ratio

Maximum Mortgage Payment (PITI) $2,598.56

$2,598.56	Maximum PITI payment
÷ 1.25	25% for taxes, hazard insurance, and PMI
$2,078.85	Maximum principal and interest payment
Interest rate	5.25% (with three points)

Maximum Loan Amount $376,465

$376,465	Maximum loan amount
÷ .95	Loan-to-value ratio (95%)
$396,279	Sales price

Sales Price $396,279

Income Qualifying—FHA-Insured Loans

Effective Income

Base salary	
Wage earner 1	$2,400
Wage earner 2	$5,286
Overtime	
Commissions	$2,985
Bonuses	
Other	+
Total	$10,671

Recurring Charges

Car loans	$740
Credit cards	$165
Student loans	$155
Other debts	$183
Child support	
Alimony	
Other	+
Total	$1,243

Debt to Income Ratio

$10,671	Effective income
x .43	Maximum ratio (43%)
$4,588.53	Maximum obligations
− 1,243.00	Recurring charges
$3,345.53	Maximum mortgage payment (PITI) under debt to income ratio

Housing Expense to Income Ratio

$10,671	Effective income
x .31	Maximum ratio (31%)
$3,308.01	Maximum mortgage payment (PITI) under housing expense ratio

Maximum Mortgage Payment (PITI) $3,308.01

Maximum Loan Amount $294,515

$294,515	Loan amount
x .0175	1.75% of base loan
$5,154	Upfront MIP
+ 294,515	Loan amount
$299,669	Total amount financed

$255.22	1/12 of taxes, insurance
208.62	1/12 of annual MIP
+ 1,701.49	P&I payment at 5.5%
$2,165.33	PITI payment for $271,050 loan with financed UFMIP

Total Amount Financed $299,669

$294,515	Maximum loan amount
÷ .965	Loan-to-value ratio (96.5%)
$305,197	Sales price
− $294,515	Loan amount
$10,682	Minimum cash investment

Sales Price $305,197

Income Qualifying—VA-Guaranteed Loans

Taxes (per month)

	Wage earner 1
$570	Federal income tax
$218	State income tax
$306	Social Security/Medicare
	Wage earner 2
$563	Federal income tax
$212	State income tax
+ $327	Social Security/Medicare
$2,196	Total taxes withheld

Recurring Charges

Car loans	$740
Credit cards	$165
Student loans	$155
Other debts	$183
Job-related costs	
Child support	
Alimony	
Other	+
Total	$1,243

Gross Monthly Income

Base salary	
Wage earner 1	$2,400
Wage earner 2	$5,286
Overtime	
Commissions	$2,985
Bonuses	
Other	+
Total	$10,671

Estimated Maintenance & Utilities

1,450	Square feet of living area
x $0.14	Per square foot
$203	Maintenance and utilities

Debt to Income Ratio

$10,671	Gross monthly income		$10,671	Gross monthly income
x .41	Standard ratio (41%)		x .45	Higher ratio (45%)
$4,375.11	Maximum obligations		$4,801.95	Maximum obligations
− 1,243.00	Recurring obligations		− 1,243.00	Recurring obligations
$3,132.11	Maximum PITI payment with standard 41% ratio		$3,558.95	Maximum PITI payment with a 45% ratio

Income Qualifying—VA-Guaranteed Loans

Residual Income Analysis

Required minimum residual income _____ $738 _____

$10,671	Gross monthly income
2,196	Taxes
1,243	Recurring obligations
− 3,335	Monthly shelter expense (housing expense from 41% ratio, plus maintenance and utilities)
$3,897	**Residual Income**

$10,671	Gross monthly income
2,196	Taxes
1,243	Recurring obligations
− 3,762	Monthly shelter expense (housing expense from 45% ratio, plus maintenance and utilities)
$3,470	**Residual Income**

Income ratio over 41% acceptable with compensating factors.

If residual income exceeds the minimum by more than 20%, a ratio over 41% is acceptable even without any other compensating factors.

PITI Payment with 45% ratio _____ $3,559 _____

$3,559	Maximum PITI payment
÷ 1.15	15% for property taxes and hazard insurance
$3,094.78	Maximum principal and interest payment

Interest rate _____ 5.5% _____

Sales Price _____ $505,000 _____

$505,000	Sales price
× .25	Guaranty percentage for VA loan over $453,100
$126,250	25% of sales price
− 113,275	Maximum guaranty in county
$12,975	Downpayment required by lender

$505,000	Sales price
− 12,975	Downpayment
$492,025	Loan amount

Glossary

The definitions given here explain how the listed terms are used in the field of real estate finance. Some of the terms have additional meanings, which can be found in a standard dictionary.

Acceleration—Declaring a loan's entire balance immediately due and payable, because the borrower has defaulted or (if the loan includes an alienation clause) sold the security property without the lender's approval. Also referred to as calling the loan.

Acceleration Clause—A provision in a security instrument that allows the lender to declare the entire debt due immediately if the borrower breaches one or more provisions of the agreement. Also called a call provision.

Acknowledgment—When a person who has signed a document formally declares to an authorized official (usually a notary public) that he signed voluntarily. The official can then attest that the signature is voluntary and genuine.

Acquisition Cost—The amount of money a buyer was required to expend in order to acquire title to a piece of property; in addition to the purchase price, this ordinarily includes a variety of closing costs, and may also include other expenses.

Adjustable-Rate Mortgage (ARM)—A loan with an interest rate that is periodically increased or decreased to reflect changes in the cost of money. *Compare:* Fixed-Rate Loan.

Age, Actual—The age of a structure from a chronological standpoint (as opposed to its effective age); how many years it has actually been in existence.

Age, Effective—The age of a structure indicated by its condition and remaining usefulness (as opposed to its actual age).

Alienation—The transfer of ownership or an interest in property from one person to another, by any means.

Alienation Clause—A provision in a security instrument that gives the lender the right to accelerate the loan if the borrower sells the property or transfers a significant interest in it without the lender's approval. Also called a due-on-sale clause.

All-Inclusive Trust Deed—A deed of trust used for wraparound financing.

Amortization—The gradual reduction of a debt through installment payments that include principal as well as interest.

Annual Percentage Rate (APR)—Under the Truth in Lending Act, a figure that expresses the relationship between a loan's finance charge and loan amount as an annual percentage.

Anti-Deficiency Rules—Laws that prohibit a secured lender from suing the borrower for a deficiency judgment after foreclosure, in certain circumstances.

Appraisal—An expert's estimate of the value of a piece of real estate as of a particular date, based on a documented analysis of the property's features. Also called a valuation.

Appraiser—One who estimates the value of property, especially an expert qualified to do so by training and experience.

Appreciation—An increase in the value of an asset over time, as a result of economic forces; the opposite of depreciation.

APR—*See:* Annual Percentage Rate.

ARM—*See:* Adjustable-Rate Mortgage.

Arm's Length Transaction—A sale in which the buyer and the seller are unrelated parties with no preexisting personal or business relationship.

Asset—Anything of value owned by a person or other entity.

Assets, Liquid—Cash or other assets that can be readily turned into cash (liquidated), such as stock.

Assign—To transfer rights (especially contract rights) or interests to another.

Assignee—One to whom rights or interests have been assigned.

Assignment—A transfer of contract rights from one person to another.

Assignor—One who has assigned her rights or interests to another.

Assumption—When a buyer takes on personal responsibility for repayment of the seller's existing mortgage loan, becoming liable to the lender. The seller remains secondarily liable unless released by the lender.

Assumption Fee—A fee charged by the lender when a buyer assumes a seller's loan.

Assumptor—One who assumes a mortgage or deed of trust, usually when buying the property that secures the debt.

Audit—An examination and verification of records, particularly the financial accounts of a business or other organization.

Automated Underwriting (AU)—*See:* Underwriting, Automated.

Average Cost Pricing—Charging all borrowers who are approved for a particular type of loan the same interest rate and fees, without regard to the borrowers' varying degrees of creditworthiness. *Compare:* Risk-Based Pricing.

Balance Sheet—*See:* Financial Statement.

Balloon Mortgage—A mortgage loan (partially amortized or interest-only) that requires the borrower to make a balloon payment.

Balloon Payment—1. The payment of the remaining principal balance due at the end of the term of a partially amortized or interest-only loan; so called because it is much larger than the regular payments made during the loan term. 2. Any loan payment that is larger than the regular payments.

Basis—A figure used in calculating a gain on the sale of real estate for federal income tax purposes. Also called cost basis.

Basis, Adjusted—A property owner's initial basis in the property, plus capital expenditures for improvements, and minus any allowable cost recovery (depreciation) deductions.

Basis, Initial—The amount of a property owner's original investment in the property; what it cost to acquire the property, which may include closing costs and certain other expenses, as well as the purchase price.

Beneficiary—1. A person on whose behalf a trust is established and administered. 2. A person who receives money or property through a will. 3. In a deed of trust transaction, the lender. *Compare:* Mortgagee.

Bill of Sale—A document used to transfer title to personal property from one person to another.

Biweekly Mortgage—A fixed-rate loan that requires a payment every two weeks instead of once a month, so that the borrower makes 26 half payments per year, the equivalent of 13 monthly payments.

Blanket Mortgage—A mortgage that encumbers more than one parcel of real property.

Bond—A certificate of indebtedness issued by a governmental body or a corporation; the bondholder typically receives a return in the form of periodic payments of interest until the principal is repaid in a lump sum.

Breach—Violation of an obligation, duty, or law; especially an unexcused failure to perform a contractual obligation.

Brokerage Fee—The commission or other compensation charged for a real estate broker's services.

Broker Price Opinion—*See:* Competitive Market Analysis.

Budget Mortgage—A mortgage with monthly payments that include a share of the property taxes and insurance, in addition to principal and interest. The tax and insurance portions are kept in an impound account maintained by the lender until payment is due.

Buydown—When the seller or a third party pays the lender a lump sum at closing to lower the interest rate charged to the buyer, either for the life of the loan (permanent buydown) or during the first years of the loan term (temporary buydown); essentially the same thing as paying discount points on the buyer's behalf.

Call Provision—*See:* Acceleration Clause.

Capital Expenditures—Money spent on property improvements and modifications that add to the property's value or prolong its life.

Capitalization—Estimating a property's value by dividing its annual net income by a percentage that represents the rate of return an investor would expect from the property (the capitalization rate).

Capitalization Method—*See:* Income Approach to Value.

Carryback Loan—*See:* Purchase Money Loan.

Certificate of Deposit (CD)—A savings arrangement in which a depositor agrees to leave money on deposit for a specified period, or pay a penalty for early withdrawal.

Certificate of Eligibility—A document issued by the Department of Veterans Affairs, indicating a veteran's eligibility for a VA-guaranteed loan.

Certificate of Reasonable Value (CRV)— *See:* Notice of Value.

Certificate of Reduction—A document signed by a lender when property is sold subject to an existing mortgage. It either acknowledges the transfer and waives the right to accelerate the loan pursuant to a due-on-sale clause, or else merely states the balance due and the status of the loan. Sometimes called an estoppel letter.

Certificate of Sale—The document that a purchaser of foreclosed property at a sheriff's sale is given instead of a deed; it is replaced with a sheriff's deed only after the statutory redemption period expires.

Charge-Off—When a creditor writes off a delinquent debt for tax purposes, because no payment has been received for six months or more and the debt will probably never be collected.

Closed Mortgage—A mortgage loan that cannot be paid off early.

Closing—The final stage in a real estate transaction, when the loan funds are disbursed, the seller is paid the purchase price, and the buyer receives the deed. Also called settlement.

Closing Costs—Expenses incurred in a transfer of real estate, aside from the purchase price; for example, the appraisal fee, title insurance premiums, brokerage fee, and transfer taxes. Also called settlement costs.

Closing Disclosure—A form required by TILA-RESPA Integrated Disclosure rules that shows the charges and credits that will apply to each party at closing.

CMA—*See:* Competitive Market Analysis.

Co-Borrower—A person who applies for a loan with someone else and will share liability for repayment of the loan. A non-occupant co-borrower who will not have an ownership interest in the property, but agrees to share liability in order to help the primary borrower qualify for the loan, is called a cosigner.

Collateral—Property (personal or real) accepted by a lender as security for a loan. If the borrower fails to repay the loan, the lender has the right to keep or sell the collateral.

Commercial Bank—A financial institution that holds deposits and makes loans, which emphasizes commercial lending but also makes many residential mortgage loans. *Compare:* Investment Bank.

Commission—The compensation paid to a real estate broker for services in connection with a real estate transaction; usually a percentage of the sales price.

Commitment—A lender's promise to make a loan, usually after the underwriter evaluates both the borrower as well as the property that will serve as security.

Co-Mortgagor—*See:* Co-Borrower.

Comparables—In a sales comparison appraisal, properties similar to the subject property that have recently been sold; the appraiser uses the sales prices of the comparables as an indication of the value of the subject property.

Competitive Market Analysis (CMA)—A real estate agent's estimate of the value of a listed home, based on the sales prices or listing prices of comparable homes. Also called a comparative market analysis or a broker price opinion.

Compound Interest—*See:* Interest, Compound.

Condition—A provision in an agreement that makes the parties' rights and obligations depend on the occurrence (or nonoccurrence) of a particular event. Also called a contingency clause.

Conforming Loan—A loan made in accordance with the underwriting criteria of the major secondary market entities, Fannie Mae and Freddie Mac, and which therefore can be sold to those entities without special negotiations. A loan that does not meet Fannie Mae or Freddie Mac standards is called a nonconforming loan.

Conforming Loan Limit—The maximum conventional loan amount that Fannie Mae and Freddie Mac will purchase.

Consideration—Something of value given to induce another to enter into a contract. An agreement is not a legally binding contract unless the parties exchange consideration.

Construction Loan—A loan to finance the construction of a building; when construction is completed, it is replaced by a take-out loan. Also called an interim loan.

Consumer Financial Protection Bureau (CFPB)—A federal financial oversight agency created in 2011. The CFPB administers the Home Mortgage Disclosure Act, Truth in Lending Act, and Real Estate Settlement Procedures Act, among other responsibilities.

Consumer Price Index—An index that tracks changes in the cost of goods and services for a typical consumer. Formerly called the cost of living index.

Contingency Clause—*See:* Condition.

Contract Rate—*See:* Note Rate.

Contract Rent—The rent a property owner is currently receiving for the property. *Compare:* Economic Rent.

Conventional Loan—An institutional loan that is not insured or guaranteed by a government agency.

Convertible ARM—An adjustable-rate mortgage that includes a conversion option.

Conversion Option—A provision in an adjustable-rate mortgage that gives the borrower the option of converting to a fixed interest rate at one or more specified points during the loan term.

Cosigner—*See:* Co-Borrower.

Cost, Replacement—In appraisal, the current cost of constructing a building with the same utility as the subject property, using modern materials and construction methods. *Compare:* Cost, Reproduction.

Cost, Reproduction—In appraisal, the cost of constructing a replica (an exact duplicate) of the subject property, using the same materials and construction methods that were originally used, but at current prices. *Compare:* Cost, Replacement.

Cost Approach to Value—One of the three main methods of appraisal (along with the income approach and the sales comparison approach), in which an estimate of the subject property's value is arrived at by estimating the cost of replacing the improvements, then deducting the estimated accrued depreciation and adding the estimated market value of the land. Also called the replacement cost method.

Cost Basis—*See:* Basis.

Cost Recovery Deductions—Tax deductions allowed to owners of income property and property used in a trade or business, for the cost of assets that will wear out and eventually have to be replaced. Also called depreciation deductions.

Coupon Rate—*See:* Note Rate.

Credit—A payment receivable by a party at closing; the opposite of a debit, which is a payment owed by that party at closing.

Creditor—One who is owed a debt.

Creditor, Secured—A creditor with a lien on a property that enables her to foreclose and collect the debt from the sale proceeds if the debtor does not pay.

Credit Report—A report prepared by a credit reporting agency that outlines the credit history of an individual or entity, listing current and past debts and records of repayment, and usually including a credit score.

Credit Score—A figure used in underwriting that encapsulates the likelihood that a loan applicant will default, calculated using a credit scoring model and the information from the applicant's credit history.

Credit Union—A type of financial institution that serves only the members of a particular group, such as a professional organization or a labor union. Credit unions make consumer loans, including residential mortgage loans.

CRV—*See:* Notice of Value.

Cure—To remedy a default, by paying money that is overdue or by fulfilling other obligations.

Debit— A payment owed by a party at closing; the opposite of a credit, which is a payment receivable by that party at closing.

Debtor—One who owes money to another.

Debt Investment—*See:* Investment, Debt.

Debt Relief—The forgiving of debt by a lender (usually refers to a mortgage lender reducing the debt so that foreclosure won't be necessary). The IRS treats debt relief as taxable income, but there are significant exceptions.

Debt Service—The amount of money required to make the periodic payments of principal and interest on an amortized debt such as a mortgage.

Debt Service Ratio—*See:* Debt to Income Ratio.

Debt to Income Ratio—A figure used in underwriting, calculated by dividing total monthly obligations (including the housing expense and other debts) by monthly income. *Compare:* Housing Expense to Income Ratio.

Deduction—An amount a taxpayer is allowed to subtract from his income before the tax on the income is calculated.

Deed in Lieu of Foreclosure—A deed given by a borrower to a lender, transferring title to the security property to the lender to satisfy the debt and avoid foreclosure.

Deed of Reconveyance—A document which acknowledges that a deed of trust has been paid in full, releasing the security property from the lien. *Compare:* Satisfaction of Mortgage.

Deed of Trust—A real property security instrument that is similar to a mortgage, but which gives a third party the power to foreclose and sell the property in the event of default. The parties are the grantor or trustor (the borrower), the beneficiary (the lender), and the trustee (the neutral third party).

Default—Failure to fulfill a contractual obligation, such as when a borrower fails to make payments, or a tenant fails to pay rent.

Deferred Interest—*See:* Interest, Deferred.

Deferred Maintenance—Curable depreciation resulting from physical wear and tear.

Deficiency Judgment—A court judgment against a debtor requiring the debtor to pay the creditor the shortfall between the amount of the debt and the proceeds of the foreclosure sale.

Delivery Fee—*See:* Loan-Level Price Adjustment.

Depreciation—A loss in value due to any cause.

Depreciation, Curable—Depreciation (resulting from deferred maintenance or functional obsolescence) that a prudent property owner would ordinarily correct, because the cost of correction could be recovered in the sales price when the property is sold.

Depreciation, Incurable—Depreciation that is either impossible to correct, or not economically feasible to correct, because the cost could not be recovered in the sales price when the property is sold.

Depreciation Deductions—*See:* Cost Recovery Deductions.

Direct Endorsement Lender—A lender authorized to underwrite its own FHA loan applications, rather than having to submit them to the FHA for approval.

Discount Fee—*See:* Discount Points.

Discount Points—A fee (often stated as a percentage of the loan amount) that a lender may charge at closing to increase its upfront yield on the loan in return for reducing the loan's interest rate. Also called a discount fee.

Discount Rate—The interest rate that a Federal Reserve Bank charges on short-term loans to member banks. *Compare:* Federal Funds Rate.

Disintermediation—When depositors withdraw their savings from financial institutions and put the money into other types of investments with higher yields.

Diversification—The practice of investing in a variety of different sectors of the economy, to make a portfolio safer.

Dividend—A share of a company's profits paid to a stockholder as a return on the investment.

Documentation Levels—The automated underwriting system will tell the underwriter what amount of documentation is needed to verify the borrower's income and assets: standard, streamlined ("low-doc"), or minimal ("no-doc"). No-doc loans, requiring virtually no documentation from the applicant, are rare.

Dodd-Frank Wall Street Reform and Consumer Protection Act—A sweeping federal statute that addresses several aspects of the U.S. financial system, passed in 2010 in response to the economic crisis.

Downpayment—The part of the purchase price of property that the buyer is not borrowing; the difference between the purchase price and the financing.

Due-on-Sale Clause—*See:* Alienation Clause.

Earnest Money—A deposit that a prospective buyer gives the seller when the purchase agreement is signed, as evidence of her good faith intention to complete the transaction. Also called a good faith deposit.

Economic Obsolescence—*See:* External Obsolescence.

Economic Rent—The rent a property could command in the current marketplace if it were available for lease today. Also called market rent. *Compare:* Contract Rent.

Effective Income—In FHA underwriting, the loan applicant's gross monthly income from all sources that can be expected to continue; the FHA equivalent of stable monthly income.

Elements of Comparison—In the sales comparison approach to appraisal, considerations taken into account in selecting comparables and comparing them to the subject property; they include the date of sale, location, physical characteristics, and terms of sale.

Encumber—To place a lien or other encumbrance against the title to a property.

Encumbrance—A nonpossessory interest in real property; a right or interest held by someone other than the property owner; it may be a lien, an easement, or a restrictive covenant.

Entitlement—*See:* VA Entitlement.

Equal Credit Opportunity Act (ECOA)—A federal law prohibiting discrimination by lenders against loan applicants on the basis of race, color, religion, national origin, sex, marital status, age, or whether income comes from public assistance.

Equitable Title—*See:* Title, Equitable.

Equity—1. The difference between a property's value and the liens against it; an owner's unencumbered interest in his property. 2. Fairness.

Equity Exchange—When a buyer gives a seller real or personal property in addition to or instead of cash for the purchase price.

Equity Stripping—A foreclosure rescue scam, based on assisting a homeowner facing foreclosure by purchasing the home, and selling or leasing it back to the homeowner on terms likely to result in default and/or lost equity.

Escalation Clause—A clause in a contract or mortgage that provides for payment or interest increases if specified events occur, such as a change in the property taxes or in the prime interest rate. Also called an escalator clause.

Escrow—A system in which the parties to a transaction can have a disinterested third party hold things of value (such as money or documents) until specified conditions have been fulfilled.

Escrow Agent—A third party who holds things of value on behalf of the parties to a transaction in an escrow arrangement. May be called a closing agent.

Estoppel Letter—*See:* Certificate of Reduction.

Exclusion of Gain on Sale of Home—Under the federal income tax code, a gain of up to $250,000 (or $500,000 for a married couple filing jointly) on the sale of a principal residence may be excluded from taxation.

Execution, Order of—A court order directing a public officer (such as the sheriff) to seize and sell property to satisfy a debt; also called a writ of execution.

Expenses, Operating—For income-producing property, the regular expenses such as insurance, maintenance, and money set aside for eventual replacement of worn-out building elements; does not include debt service.

External Obsolescence—Depreciation resulting from factors outside the property itself and outside the owner's control. Also called economic obsolescence.

Fair Housing Act—A federal law prohibiting discrimination in residential property transactions, including lending, on the basis of race, color, national origin, religion, sex, disability, or familial status.

Fannie Mae—The Federal National Mortgage Association (FNMA), a government-sponsored enterprise supervised by the Federal Housing Finance Agency; along with Freddie Mac, it makes up the bulk of the secondary market.

Farmers Home Administration (FmHA)—*See:* Rural Housing Service.

Federal Deficit—A shortfall in funds that occurs when the federal government spends more money than it collects in a particular year.

Federal Funds Rate—The interest rate that banks charge one another for overnight loans; a target for the rate is set by the Federal Reserve. *Compare:* Discount Rate.

Federal Home Loan Mortgage Corporation (FHLMC)—*See:* Freddie Mac.

Federal Housing Administration (FHA)—An agency within the Department of Housing and Urban Development that provides mortgage insurance to encourage lenders to make more affordable home loans.

Federal Housing Finance Agency (FHFA)—An independent federal agency that oversees Fannie Mae and Freddie Mac.

Federal National Mortgage Association (FNMA)—*See:* Fannie Mae.

Federal Open Market Committee—A board that makes decisions regarding the Federal Reserve's open market operations (its purchase and sale of government securities).

Federal Reserve Bank—An entity that performs a variety of functions for commercial banks in one of the 12 Federal Reserve Districts.

Federal Reserve Board—The seven-member Board of Governors that controls the Federal Reserve System and sets monetary policy.

Federal Reserve System—The system that regulates commercial banks and implements U.S. monetary policy. Often referred to as "the Fed."

Fee Packing—A predatory loan practice in which a lender charges points or processing fees that are higher than usual and not justified by the services provided.

FHA—*See:* Federal Housing Administration.

FHA-Insured Loan—A loan made by an institutional lender with mortgage insurance provided by the Federal Housing Administration, protecting the lender against losses due to borrower default.

FHLMC—*See:* Freddie Mac.

FICO Score—A credit score calculated using the credit scoring model developed by Fair Isaac and Company; the type of credit score most widely used in residential mortgage lending.

Finance Charge—Under the Truth in Lending Act, all charges associated with a loan that the lender requires the borrower to pay, including the interest, any discount points paid by the borrower, the origination fee, other loan fees, and mortgage insurance costs. See also: Annual Percentage Rate.

Financial Institutions Reform, Recovery and Enforcement Act (FIRREA)—A federal law enacted in 1989 in response to the savings and loan crisis; it reorganized the federal agencies that oversee financial institutions.

Financial Statement—A summary of facts showing the financial condition of an individual or a business, including a detailed list of assets and liabilities. Also called a balance sheet.

Financing Statement—A brief instrument that is recorded to establish and give public notice of a creditor's security interest in an item of personal property.

FIRREA—*See:* Financial Institutions Reform, Recovery and Enforcement Act.

First Lien Position—The position of lien priority held by a mortgage or deed of trust that has higher priority than any other mortgage or deed of trust against the property.

First Mortgage—The mortgage (or deed of trust) against a property that has first lien position; the one with higher lien priority than any other mortgage against that property.

Fiscal Policy—Actions taken by the federal government to raise revenue through taxation, spend tax revenues, and finance budget deficits. *Compare:* Monetary Policy.

Fixed-Rate Loan—A mortgage loan in which the lender charges an unchanging interest rate throughout the loan term. *Compare:* Adjustable-Rate Mortgage.

Fixture—An item that was originally personal property, but which has been attached to or closely associated with real property in such a way that it has legally become part of the real property.

Flip—*See:* Property Flipping.

FmHA—*See:* Rural Housing Service.

Foreclosure—When a lienholder forces property to be sold, so the unpaid debt secured by the lien can be satisfied from the sale proceeds.

Foreclosure, Judicial—A court-supervised foreclosure proceeding that begins when a mortgagee or other lienholder files a lawsuit against a property owner who has defaulted on the debt secured by the mortgage or lien.

Foreclosure, Nonjudicial—Foreclosure by a trustee pursuant to the power of sale clause in a deed of trust.

FNMA—*See:* Fannie Mae.

Freddie Mac—The Federal Home Loan Mortgage Corporation (FHLMC), a government-sponsored enterprise supervised by the Federal Housing Finance Agency; along with Fannie Mae, it makes up the bulk of the secondary market.

Fully Amortized Loan—A loan structured so that regular installment payments pay off all of the principal and interest owed by the end of the loan term. *Compare:* Interest-Only Loan; Partially Amortized Loan.

Functional Obsolescence—Depreciation of property resulting from functional inadequacies, such as those caused by poor or outmoded design.

Funding Fee—A charge paid by a VA borrower to the lender at closing.

Gain—The amount of money left over after subtracting the basis from the sales price of a property (such as real estate). It is the seller's profit. *Also see:* Exclusion of Gain on Sale of Home.

Garnishment—A legal process by which a creditor gains access to a debtor's funds or personal property held by a third party. For example, if a debtor's wages are garnished, the employer is required to turn over part of each paycheck to the creditor.

Gift Funds—Money given (usually by a family member) to a buyer who otherwise would not have enough cash to close the transaction.

Gift Letter—A document in which a donor of gift funds states that the money given is not a loan and does not have to be repaid; required by the lender when the borrower intends to use gift funds as part of the downpayment or closing costs.

Ginnie Mae—The Government National Mortgage Association (GNMA), a government agency within HUD; it helps to stabilize the secondary market by guaranteeing mortgage-backed securities on FHA and VA loans. It does not buy or sell loans or securities.

GNMA—*See:* Ginnie Mae.

Good Faith Deposit—*See:* Earnest Money.

Government-Sponsored Enterprise (GSE)—An entity that is privately owned and functions as a private corporation, but is created, chartered, and supervised by the government, such as Fannie Mae and Freddie Mac.

Grantor—1. In a deed of trust transaction, the borrower, also called the trustor. 2. One who deeds title to real property to another.

Gross Income—An individual's income before payroll taxes have been deducted.

Gross Income Multiplier—A figure used to estimate the value of residential rental property, determined by dividing the sales price by the rental income. Also called a gross rent multiplier.

Guarantor—*See:* Guaranty.

Guaranty—An arrangement in which one party (the guarantor) accepts liability to another party for the payment of a third party's obligations, if the third party fails to pay them. *See also:* Loan Guaranty; VA Guaranty Amount.

Hard Money Mortgage—A mortgage given to a lender in exchange for cash, as opposed to one given in exchange for credit.

Hazard Insurance—Insurance against damage to property caused by fire, flood, or other mishaps. Also called casualty insurance.

HECM—*See:* Reverse Equity Mortgage.

HOA—*See:* Homeowners Association.

HOEPA—*See:* Home Ownership and Equity Protection Act.

Holder in Due Course (HDC)—A third party purchaser of a promissory note who purchased the note for value and in good faith. A HDC is entitled to payment by the maker of the note, even if the maker has a defense that would defeat a claim by the original payee.

Home Buyer Counseling Programs—HUD-approved agencies around the country offer counseling to educate participants about the responsibilities of home ownership, including making mortgage or rent payments, maintaining the home, avoiding foreclosure or eviction, and so on.

Home Equity Conversion Mortgage—*See:* Reverse Equity Mortgage.

Home Equity Line of Credit (HELOC)—A line of credit secured by the borrower's home. In practice, a HELOC is similar to a credit card, with a credit limit and minimum monthly payments based on the amount borrowed.

Home Equity Loan—A loan obtained by the borrower using a home he already owns as collateral.

Home Mortgage Disclosure Act—A federal law requiring large institutional lenders to submit reports concerning the residential loans they've originated or purchased from other lenders; regulators use the reports to detect redlining.

Home Mortgage Interest Deduction—The federal income tax code allows a taxpayer to deduct interest paid on mortgage loans secured by her home or homes, up to certain limits.

Homeowners Association (HOA)—A nonprofit association made up of all of the homeowners in a subdivision, which is responsible for enforcing the restrictive covenants and managing other community affairs.

Homeowner's Insurance—Insurance that covers loss of or damage to a homeowner's personal property and real property, and also provides some liability protection.

Home Ownership and Equity Protection Act (HOEPA)—A federal law concerning high-cost home equity loans that requires certain disclosures and prohibits certain predatory lending practices.

Housing Expense to Income Ratio—A figure used in underwriting, calculated by dividing the monthly housing expense by monthly income. *Compare:* Debt to Income Ratio.

HUD—The Department of Housing and Urban Development, a cabinet-level department of the federal government that includes agencies such as the FHA and Ginnie Mae.

Hybrid ARM—An adjustable-rate mortgage with an initial fixed-rate period; for example, a 3/1 hybrid ARM has a fixed interest rate for the first three years and is subject to annual rate adjustments after that.

Hypothecation—Making property security for a loan by transferring title to the lender without surrendering possession. *Compare:* Pledge.

Impound Account—An escrow account maintained by a lender for paying property taxes and insurance premiums for the security property; the lender requires the borrower to make regular deposits, and pays the expenses out of the account when they come due. Also called a reserve account.

Improvements—Man-made additions to real property.

Income Approach to Value—A method of appraisal in which an estimate of the subject property's value is based on the net income it produces. Also called the income method or the capitalization method.

Income Property—Property that generates rent or other income for the owner, such as an apartment building.

Income Ratio—A figure used in underwriting to determine whether a loan applicant's income is adequate for the monthly payments on the proposed loan; a percentage calculated by dividing monthly housing expense or total monthly debt payments by monthly income.

Index—A published statistical report that indicates changes in the cost of money (market interest rates), used as the basis for interest rate adjustments in an ARM.

Inflation—A trend of general price increases throughout the economy.

Installment Land Contract—*See:* Land Contract.

Installment Note—*See:* Note, Installment.

Institutional Lender—A bank or other regulated lending institution; in some contexts, the term also includes mortgage companies.

Institutional Loan—A mortgage loan made by a bank or other regulated lending institution, or by a mortgage company, in contrast to seller financing or a loan made by an individual private lender.

Instrument—A legal document; especially one that transfers title, creates a lien, or establishes a right to payment.

Interest—A periodic charge a lender requires a borrower to pay for the temporary use of the borrowed funds, until the loan is repaid; usually expressed as an annual percentage of the principal balance. *Compare:* Principal.

Interest, Compound—Interest calculated as a percentage of both the principal and any accumulated interest that has not yet been paid. *Compare:* Interest, Simple.

Interest, Deferred—Interest that accumulates over the course of one or more payment periods but is not payable until some later time; a feature of some adjustable-rate loans.

Interest, Interim—*See:* Interest, Prepaid.

Interest, Prepaid—Interest on a new loan that must be paid at closing; it covers the interest that will accrue for the month in which the loan term begins. Also called interim interest.

Interest, Simple—Interest calculated as a percentage of the principal balance only. *Compare:* Interest, Compound.

Interest-Only Loan—A loan that requires only payments of the interest due (with no principal) during the loan term, or during a specified period at the beginning of the loan term. *Compare:* Fully Amortized Loan; Partially Amortized Loan.

Interest Rate Cap—A provision in an ARM that limits how much the interest rate may be increased (and in some cases, decreased) during a single rate adjustment period or over the life of the loan.

Interest Rate Risk—The risk that, after a loan is made for a specified term at a fixed interest rate, market interest rates will rise and the lender will miss the opportunity to invest the loaned funds at a higher rate.

Interest Rates, Market—The rates that are generally being paid on particular types of investments or charged for particular types of loans under current economic conditions.

Interim Loan—*See:* Construction Loan.

Intermediary—1. An individual or entity who originates and/or services loans on behalf of another. 2. Any type of go-between.

Investment—When a person (an investor) makes a sum of money (investment capital) available for use by another person or entity, in the expectation that it will generate a return (a profit) for the investor.

Investment, Debt—An investment in which temporary use of an investor's funds is exchanged for interest payments, under an agreement that requires repayment of the funds or allows withdrawal of the funds.

Investment, Liquid—An investment that can be quickly and easily converted into cash.

Investment, Ownership—An investment in which the investor's funds are used to purchase an asset or a property interest in an asset.

Investment, Return of—*See:* Return of Investment.

Investment, Return on—*See:* Return on Investment.

Investment Bank—A firm that handles corporate finances, arranges for the issuance of government and corporate bonds, and provides investment advice to clients. Also called a securities firm or stock brokerage. *Compare:* Commercial Bank.

Investor Loan—A loan for the purchase of residential property that will be rented to tenants rather than owner-occupied.

Judicial Foreclosure—*See:* Foreclosure, Judicial.

Jumbo Loan—A conventional loan with a loan amount that exceeds the conforming loan limit set by Fannie Mae and Freddie Mac.

Junior Lienholder—A secured creditor whose lien is lower in priority than another lien against the same property.

Junior Mortgage—A mortgage that has lower lien priority than another mortgage against the same property. Also called a second mortgage or secondary mortgage.

Land Contract—A contract for the sale of property in which the buyer (vendee) pays the seller (vendor) in installments, taking possession of the property immediately but not taking title until the purchase price has been paid in full. Also called a contract for deed, conditional sales contract, installment sales contract, or real estate contract.

Law of Supply and Demand—*See:* Supply and Demand, Law of.

Lease—A contract in which one party (the tenant) pays the other (the landlord) rent in exchange for the possession of real estate.

Lease/Option—A lease that includes an option to purchase the leased property during the term of the lease.

Lease/Purchase—A variation on the lease/option, in which the parties sign a purchase contract (instead of an option) and the prospective buyer leases the property for an extended period before closing.

Legal Title—*See:* Title, Legal.

Leverage—The effective use of borrowed money to finance an investment, such as a real estate purchase.

Liability—1. A debt or obligation. 2. Legal responsibility.

Liable—Legally responsible.

Lien—A nonpossessory interest in real property giving the lienholder the right to foreclose if the property owner does not pay a debt owed to the lienholder; a financial encumbrance on the owner's title.

Lienholder—A secured creditor who has a lien against a debtor's real property.

Lien Priority—The order in which liens will be paid off out of the proceeds of a foreclosure sale.

Liquid Investment—*See:* Investment, Liquid.

Listing—A contract between a real estate broker and a seller, in which the seller appoints the broker as his agent in order to put the property up for sale.

LLPA—*See:* Loan-Level Price Adjustment.

Loan Correspondent—An intermediary who originates or arranges loans on behalf of a wholesale lender or a large investor, and may also service the loans.

Loan Estimate—A form required by TILA and RESPA Integrated Disclosure rules that lists the borrower's loan costs and related information. The lender must provide this form to a loan applicant within three days of receiving his application.

Loan Fee—Any one-time fee that a lender charges a borrower at closing for making the loan (or for making it on certain terms), such as an origination fee, discount points, a loan-level price adjustment, or an assumption fee; usually a percentage of the loan amount.

Loan Guaranty—An arrangement in which a third party guarantor accepts secondary liability for a loan and will reimburse the lender for losses resulting from the borrower's default.

Loan-Level Price Adjustment (LLPA)—A one-time fee, charged upon the sale of a loan on the secondary market, that varies depending on the risks presented by the loan. Also called a delivery fee.

Loan Officer—A loan originator who works for a particular lender. *Compare:* Mortgage Broker.

Loan Origination—The process of making a new loan: processing the application, deciding whether to approve or reject it, and funding the loan if approved. *Compare:* Loan Servicing.

Loan Origination Fee—A fee charged by a lender upon making a new loan, intended to cover the administrative costs involved. Also called an origination fee or a loan fee.

Loan Originator—The person who helps prospective borrowers apply for a loan; either a loan officer (who works for a particular lender) or a mortgage broker (who arranges loans with more than one lender).

Loan Servicing—Administering a loan after it has been made; collecting the payments, keeping payment records, and handling defaults. *Compare:* Loan Origination.

Loan Term—*See:* Repayment Period.

Loan Workout—When a lender adjusts a loan's payment schedule or modifies the loan terms to help the borrower avoid foreclosure.

Loan-to-Value Ratio (LTV)—The relationship between the loan amount and either the sales price or the appraised value of the property (whichever is less), expressed as a percentage; the loan amount divided by the sales price or the appraised value.

Lock-In—When a lender guarantees a loan applicant a particular interest rate if the transaction closes within a specified period.

LTV—*See:* Loan-to-Value Ratio.

Low Appraisal—An appraisal with a value estimate lower than the agreed-upon sales price, which may affect financing and lead to the termination of the transaction.

Maker—In a promissory note, the party who promises to pay; the debtor or borrower. *Compare:* Payee.

Margin—The difference between an ARM's index rate and the interest rate charged on the loan.

Market Data Approach—*See:* Sales Comparison Approach.

Market Interest Rates—*See:* Interest Rates, Market.

Market Price—The price for which a property actually sold; the final sales price.

Market Value—The most probable price a property should sell for if it is sold under normal conditions and the buyer and seller are typically motivated; also called objective value.

MBS—*See:* Securities, Mortgage-Backed.

Minimum Cash Investment—The minimum downpayment required for an FHA-insured loan.

MIP—Mortgage insurance premium. Most often used to refer to the fee charged for FHA insurance coverage. The initial FHA premium is referred to as the UFMIP (upfront MIP) or the OTMIP (one-time MIP).

MMI—The Mutual Mortgage Insurance program, the formal name of the FHA insurance program. Also, FHA mortgage insurance premiums are sometimes called the MMI.

Monetary Policy—Actions taken by the Federal Reserve to control the money supply and the cost of borrowing money, to keep the economy running smoothly. *Compare:* Fiscal Policy.

Monthly Shelter Expense—A VA loan applicant's proposed monthly housing expense plus estimated monthly maintenance and utility costs.

Mortgage—1. An instrument creating a voluntary lien on a property to secure repayment of a debt; the two parties involved are the mortgagor (borrower) and the mortgagee (lender). 2. A mortgage loan.

Mortgage-Backed Securities—*See:* Securities, Mortgage-Backed.

Mortgage Banker—*See:* Mortgage Company.

Mortgage Broker—An intermediary who brings real estate lenders and borrowers together and negotiates loan agreements between them; a loan originator who doesn't work for a particular lender and who may help borrowers apply to a number of different lenders. *Compare:* Loan Officer.

Mortgage Company—A type of real estate lender that originates residential mortgage loans on behalf of large investors or for sale on the secondary market, and may also service the loans; not a depository institution. Also called a mortgage banking company or a mortgage banker.

Mortgagee—The one who is given a mortgage by the mortgagor; the lender.

Mortgage Insurance—Insurance coverage protecting a mortgage lender against losses resulting from default and foreclosure.

Mortgage Loan—A loan secured by a mortgage or a deed of trust against property owned by the borrower.

Mortgage Payment Cap—A provision in an ARM that limits the amount the monthly payment can be increased, either during a given period, or over the entire life of the loan.

Mortgaging Clause—A clause in a mortgage that describes the security interest given to the mortgagee.

Mortgagor—A property owner (usually a borrower) who gives a mortgage against the property to another (usually a lender) as security for payment of an obligation.

Mutual Fund—A company that invests its capital in a diversified portfolio of securities on behalf of its investors, who own shares in the fund.

Mutual Savings Bank—A savings bank originally organized as a mutual company, owned by and operated for the benefit of its depositors (as opposed to stockholders).

Negative Amortization—When deferred interest on an adjustable-rate loan is added to the principal balance, increasing the amount owed.

Negative Amortization Cap—In an ARM, a limit on the amount of deferred interest that can be added to the principal balance.

Negotiable Instrument—An instrument establishing a right to payment, which is freely transferable from one person to another. It can be a check, a promissory note, a bond, a draft, or stock.

Net Equity—The market value of a property, minus any liens against the property and all anticipated selling expenses.

Net Worth—A person's financial assets, minus her liabilities.

Nonconforming Loan—A loan that does not meet underwriting guidelines set by Fannie Mae or Freddie Mac and therefore can't be sold to those entities, except by special arrangement.

Nonjudicial Foreclosure—*See:* Foreclosure, Nonjudicial.

Note—*See:* Note, Promissory.

Note, Demand—A promissory note that is due whenever the holder of the note demands payment.

Note, Installment—A promissory note that calls for regular payments of principal and interest until the debt is paid off; used for an amortized loan.

Note, Joint—A promissory note signed by two or more persons with equal liability for payment.

Note, Promissory—A written, legally binding promise to repay a debt; may or may not be a negotiable instrument.

Note, Straight—A promissory note that calls for regular payments of interest only.

Note Rate—The interest rate specified in a loan's promissory note. Also called the coupon rate or contract rate.

Notice of Default—A notice sent by a lender (mortgagee or deed of trust beneficiary) to the borrower, informing the borrower that she has breached the terms of the loan agreement and warning that the lender is going to begin the foreclosure process.

Notice of Sale—A notice stating that foreclosure proceedings have been commenced against a property.

Notice of Value (NOV)—A document setting forth a property's current market value, based on a VA-approved appraisal. Formerly called a Certificate of Reasonable Value (CRV).

NOV—*See:* Notice of Value.

Obligatory Advances—Disbursements of construction loan funds that the lender is obliged to make (by prior agreement with the borrower) when the borrower has completed certain phases of construction.

Obsolescence—*See:* External Obsolescence; Functional Obsolescence.

Open End Loan—A loan that permits the borrower to reborrow the money he has repaid on the principal, usually up to the original loan amount, without executing a new loan agreement; similar to a line of credit.

Open Market Operations—The purchase and sale of government securities by the Federal Reserve to adjust the money supply; purchases increase and sales reduce the amount of money in circulation.

Option—A contract that gives one party the right to do something (such as purchase a property or renew a lease), without obligating her to do it.

Optionee—The person to whom an option is given.

Optionor—The person who gives an option to the optionee.

Option to Purchase—An option giving the optionee the right to buy property owned by the optionor at an agreed price during a specified period.

Origination—*See:* Loan Origination.

OTMIP—*See:* MIP.

Ownership Investment—*See:* Investment, Ownership.

Package Mortgage—A mortgage secured by items of personal property (such as appliances) in addition to the real property.

Partial Reconveyance—*See:* Partial Release Clause.

Partial Release Clause—A clause in a security instrument allowing one or more of the parcels of property under a blanket lien to be released from the lien while other parcels remain subject to it. Also called a partial reconveyance clause (in a deed of trust) or a partial satisfaction clause (in a mortgage).

Partial Satisfaction—*See:* Partial Release Clause.

Partially Amortized Loan—A loan with monthly payments that include both principal and interest, but aren't sufficient to fully pay off the loan balance by the end of the loan term. *Compare:* Fully Amortized Loan; Interest-Only Loan.

Participation Loan—A loan that gives the lender a share of the earnings generated by the property, usually in addition to interest payments on the principal; the lender may also participate by becoming a part owner of the property.

Payee—In a promissory note, the party who is entitled to be paid; the creditor or lender. *Compare:* Maker.

Payment Adjustment Period—The minimum interval between adjustments of the monthly payment amount on an ARM.

Permanent Buydown—*See:* Buydown.

Personal Property—Any property that is not real property; movable property not affixed to land. Also called chattels or personalty.

Piggyback Loan—Secondary financing used to avoid the payment of private mortgage insurance by keeping the primary loan's loan-to-value ratio at 80% or less, or used to avoid the higher interest rate a jumbo loan would require.

PITI Payment—A mortgage borrower's full monthly payment, including principal, interest, property taxes, and hazard or homeowner's insurance, and also, if applicable, mortgage insurance and homeowners association dues.

Pledge—When a debtor transfers possession of property to the creditor as security for repayment of the debt, such as when an item of personal property is pawned. *Compare:* Hypothecation.

PMI—*See:* Private Mortgage Insurance.

Point—One point is one percent of the loan amount.

Points—1. Discount points. 2. All of the loan fees paid to a lender at closing; for example, the origination fee as well as discount points.

Portfolio—The collection of investments and cash reserves that are held by an investor.

Portfolio Loan—A mortgage loan that the lender keeps in its own investment portfolio until the loan is repaid (as opposed to selling it on the secondary market).

Power of Sale—A provision in a deed of trust that gives the trustee the right to foreclose nonjudicially (sell the property without court supervision) in the event of default.

Preapproval—Formal loan approval (based on a full evaluation of a prospective buyer's creditworthiness, including verification of income and assets) given before the buyer has chosen property to purchase, establishing the maximum loan amount that the lender is willing to provide. *Compare:* Prequalification.

Predatory Lending—Lending practices that unscrupulous lenders and mortgage brokers use to take advantage of unsophisticated borrowers for their own profit.

Prepayment—Paying off part or all of a loan before payment is due.

Prepayment Penalty—A penalty some lenders charge a borrower who prepays a loan, to compensate for the lost interest that the lender would have received if the borrower had continued paying off the loan over its entire term; not allowed in most residential loans.

Prepayment Risk—The risk that a loan will be paid off sooner than expected, reducing the lender's anticipated yield.

Prequalification—An informal evaluation of a prospective buyer's financial situation to estimate the maximum amount the buyer can afford to spend on a home. In the past, this was performed by a real estate agent; buyers can now carry out this step themselves using an online calculator. *Compare*: Preapproval.

Primary Market—The market in which real estate loans are originated, where lenders make loans to borrowers. *Compare:* Secondary Market.

Principal—1. The original amount of a loan, or the remainder of that amount after part of it has been paid. *Compare:* Interest. 2. The person an agent is representing. 3. One of the parties to a transaction (such as a buyer or a seller), as opposed to those who are involved in the transaction as agents or employees (such as a real estate broker or an escrow agent).

Principal Residence Property—Real property that is the owner's main dwelling. Under the federal income tax laws, a taxpayer can only have one principal residence at a time.

Priority—*See:* Lien Priority.

Private Mortgage Insurance (PMI)—Mortgage insurance provided by a private insurance company instead of a government agency; required for conforming conventional loans with loan-to-value ratios over 80%.

Promissory Note—*See:* Note, Promissory.

Property Flipping—1. Reselling property at a substantial profit soon after buying it. 2. Buying property at a discount (because the seller needs a quick sale or is unaware of the property's true value) and then rapidly reselling it to an unsophisticated buyer for an inflated price.

Proration—The process of dividing or allocating something (especially a sum of money or an expense) proportionately, according to time, interest, or benefit.

Purchase Agreement—A contract in which a seller promises to convey title to real property to a buyer in exchange for the purchase price. Also called a purchase and sale agreement, earnest money agreement, deposit receipt, sales contract, purchase contract, or contract of sale.

Purchase Money Loan—1. Generally, any loan used to purchase the property that secures the loan. 2. More narrowly, a loan given to a buyer by a seller in a seller-financed transaction; also called a carryback loan.

Qualifying—*See:* Underwriting.

Qualifying Standards—The rules (concerning credit reputation, income, net worth, loan-to-value ratios, etc.) that are applied in the underwriting process to determine whether a loan should be approved. Also called underwriting standards.

Rate Adjustment Period—The minimum interval between adjustments of an ARM's interest rate.

Real Estate Contract—*See:* Land Contract.

Real Estate Cycles—Ups and downs in the level of activity in a real estate market, where a boom may be followed by a slump, or vice versa.

Real Estate Investment Trust (REIT)—A real estate investment business organized in compliance with IRS rules in order to qualify for certain tax advantages.

Real Estate Settlement Procedures Act (RESPA)—A federal law that requires lenders to disclose certain information about closing costs to loan applicants, and prohibits kickbacks (referral fees) between settlement service providers, such as title insurance companies and lenders.

Recapture—*See:* Return of Investment.

Reconciliation—The final step in an appraisal, when the appraiser assembles and interprets the data in order to arrive at a final value estimate. Also called correlation.

Reconveyance—*See:* Deed of Reconveyance.

Recording—Filing a signed mortgage, deed, or similar document with the county, making it part of the public record.

Redemption—The right of a defaulting borrower to avoid losing his property to foreclosure by paying the full amount of the debt, plus costs. This is called redeeming the property.

Redemption, Equitable Right of—In a judicial foreclosure, the mortgagor's (borrower's) right to redeem the property before the sheriff's sale takes place.

Redemption, Statutory Right of—In a judicial foreclosure, the mortgagor's (borrower's) right to redeem the property during a specified period following the sheriff's sale.

Redlining—When a lender refuses to make loans secured by property in a certain neighborhood because of the racial or ethnic composition of the neighborhood, in violation of fair lending laws.

Refinancing—Obtaining a new mortgage loan that will be used to pay off an existing mortgage on the same property.

Regulation Z—The regulation that implements the Truth in Lending Act.

Reinstatement—The right of a defaulting borrower to prevent foreclosure by curing the default (paying the delinquent amount, plus costs). The loan is reinstated and repayment resumes.

Release—1. To give up a legal right. 2. A document in which a legal right is given up.

Repayment Period—The number of years a borrower is given to repay a loan, usually with regularly scheduled installment payments. Also called the loan term.

Replacement Cost—*See:* Cost, Replacement.

Replacement Cost Method—*See:* Cost Approach to Value.

Request for Reconsideration of Value—A request that a real estate agent submits to a lender after a low appraisal, asking the lender to consider a higher value for the property based on evidence provided by different comparables than the ones the appraiser selected.

Reserve Account—*See:* Impound Account.

Reserve Requirements—The Federal Reserve requires commercial banks to hold a certain portion of their deposits on reserve for immediate withdrawal by depositors.

Reserves—1. Cash or other liquid assets that a borrower will have left over after closing (after making the downpayment and paying the closing costs) and could use to pay the mortgage in the event of a financial emergency. 2. Money set aside on a regular basis to pay for the replacement of structures and equipment that will eventually wear out.

Residual Income—The amount of income that an applicant for a VA loan has left over after taxes, recurring obligations, and the proposed monthly shelter expense have been deducted from her gross monthly income.

RESPA—*See:* Real Estate Settlement Procedures Act.

Retail Lending—Loan transactions in which the borrower applies directly to the lender, rather than to a loan correspondent or mortgage broker. *Compare:* Wholesale Lending.

Return of Investment—When an investment generates enough money for the investor to replace the amount she invested in it. Also called recapture.

Return on Investment—The profit an investment generates for an investor, over and above the amount of money she invested in it.

Reverse Equity Mortgage—An arrangement in which a homeowner mortgages her home to a lender in exchange for a monthly payment from the lender. Also called a home equity conversion mortgage (HECM).

RHS—*See:* Rural Housing Service.

Risk Analysis—*See:* Underwriting.

Risk Classification—A classification assigned to a loan application by an automated underwriting system, categorizing the application as one that meets all requirements ("Approve" or "Accept"), meets qualifying standards but doesn't meet other mortgage eligibility criteria ("Approve/Ineligible"), or does not appear to meet qualifying standards ("Refer" or "Caution") and therefore requires additional review by an underwriter.

Risk-Based Loan Pricing—Charging borrowers different interest rates and loan fees based on their creditworthiness. *Compare:* Average Cost Pricing.

Rural Housing Service—A federal agency within the Department of Agriculture that subsidizes or guarantees loans for the purchase, development, or rehabilitation of property located in rural areas.

Sale-Leaseback—A financing arrangement in which the owner of industrial or commercial property sells the property and leases it back from the buyer, instead of mortgaging the property in exchange for a loan.

Sales Comparison Approach to Value—A method of appraisal in which the sales prices of comparable properties are used to estimate the value of the subject property. Also called the sales comparison method or the market data approach.

Sales Concessions—Seller-provided financial assistance to the buyer (other than a reduction of the sales price), through interest rate buydowns or by paying some or all of the buyer's closing costs.

Satisfaction of Mortgage—A document which acknowledges that a mortgage has been paid in full, releasing the security property from the mortgage lien. *Compare:* Deed of Reconveyance.

Savings and Loan Association—*See:* Thrift Institution.

Savings Bank—*See:* Thrift Institution.

Seasoned Loan—A loan with an established record of timely payment by the borrower.

Second Mortgage—A mortgage that does not have first lien position. Also called a junior mortgage.

Secondary Financing—A loan used to reduce or eliminate the downpayment amount and/or to cover closing costs for a first loan, which is secured by the same property as the first loan.

Secondary Liability—Liability that arises only in the event that the person who has primary liability for a debt fails to pay it.

Secondary Market—The market in which investors (chiefly Fannie Mae and Freddie Mac) purchase real estate loans from lenders. *Compare:* Primary Market.

Secure and Fair Enforcement for Mortgage Licensing Act—Federal law aimed at preventing abusive practices during loan origination. Often called the SAFE Mortgage Licensing Act.

Securities—Investment instruments, such as stocks and bonds, that confer an interest or a right to payment, without allowing direct managerial control over the enterprise invested in.

Securities, Mortgage-Backed (MBS)—Investment instruments that have pools of mortgage loans as collateral, and which are primarily issued by Fannie Mae and Freddie Mac.

Securitization—When a secondary market entity creates mortgage-backed securities by buying a large number of mortgage loans, "pooling" them together, and pledging the pool as collateral for the securities.

Security Instrument—A document that creates a voluntary lien against real property, to secure repayment of a loan; either a mortgage or a deed of trust.

Security Interest—A secured creditor's interest in property owned by the debtor, which entitles the creditor to have the property seized and sold if the debtor does not pay as agreed.

Security Property—Property owned by a borrower that is serving as collateral (the lender's security) for a loan.

Seller Financing—When a seller extends credit to a buyer to finance the purchase of the property; as opposed to having the buyer obtain a loan from a third party, such as an institutional lender.

Seller Second—Secondary financing from the seller, when a purchase money loan is used to supplement an institutional first mortgage.

Servicing—*See:* Loan Servicing.

Servicing Fee—A fee paid by a secondary market entity or other investor to the entity that is servicing a mortgage loan.

Settlement—*See:* Closing.

Settlement Statement—A document that presents a final, detailed accounting for a real estate transaction, listing each party's debits and credits and the amount each will receive or be required to pay at closing. Also called a closing statement. *See also:* Closing disclosure.

Sheriff's Deed—The deed that is given to someone who purchases property at a foreclosure sale, after the statutory redemption period has expired.

Sheriff's Sale—A public auction of property after judicial foreclosure.

Short Sale—When a borrower obtains the lender's consent to sell the home for less than the full amount owed; the lender receives the sale proceeds and releases the borrower from the debt.

Stable Monthly Income—Gross monthly income (from primary and secondary sources) that meets the lender's tests of quality and durability.

Straight Note—*See:* Note, Straight.

Subject Property—In an appraisal, the property that is being appraised.

Subject To—When a borrower sells the security property without paying off the mortgage or deed of trust, and the purchaser takes title "subject to" the lien, but does not assume the loan.

Subordination—When a mortgagee or deed of trust beneficiary agrees to accept lower lien priority than she would otherwise have, allowing a lender with a lien recorded later to have higher priority.

Subordination Clause—A provision in a security instrument that permits a later security instrument to have higher lien priority than the one in which the clause appears.

Subprime Lending—Making riskier loans to borrowers who might otherwise be unable to qualify for a loan, often requiring higher interest rates and fees to make up for the increased risk of default.

Substitution, Principle of—A principle of appraisal holding that the maximum value of a property is set by how much it would cost to obtain another property that is equally desirable, assuming that there would not be a long delay or significant incidental expenses involved in obtaining the substitute.

Substitution of Entitlement—When a VA borrower sells the security property to another eligible veteran, who agrees to substitute his guaranty entitlement for the seller's, so that the seller's entitlement is restored.

Supply and Demand, Law of—A basic rule of economics holding that prices rise when supply decreases or demand increases, and that prices fall when supply increases or demand decreases.

Take-Out Loan—Long-term financing used to replace a construction loan (an interim loan) when construction has been completed. Also called a permanent loan.

Temporary Buydown—*See:* Buydown.

Term—A prescribed period of time; especially the length of time allotted to a borrower in which to pay off a loan.

Thrift Institution—A type of depository institution that has traditionally focused on providing financial services to individuals, with an emphasis on residential mortgage lending; it may be a savings and loan association or a savings bank.

Tight Money Market—A real estate market in which loan funds are scarce and lenders are charging high interest rates and loan fees.

TILA—*See:* Truth in Lending Act.

Title, Equitable—The interest of the vendee under a land contract, including the right to possession of the property and the right to acquire legal title by paying off the contract according to its terms. *Compare:* Legal Title.

Title, Legal—Title held as security, without the right to possess the property. *Compare:* Equitable Title.

Trust—A legal arrangement in which title to property is vested in one or more trustees who manage the property for the benefit of one or more beneficiaries, in accordance with instructions provided by the person who established the trust.

Trust Account—A bank account in which funds held in trust on behalf of another person are kept separate from the holder's own money.

Trust Deed—*See:* Deed of Trust.

Trustee—1. In a deed of trust transaction, a neutral third party appointed by the lender to handle nonjudicial foreclosure (if necessary) or reconveyance after the loan has been repaid. 2. The person appointed to administer a trust on behalf of the beneficiary.

Trustee's Deed—The deed given to the purchaser at a trustee's sale.

Trustee's Sale—A nonjudicial foreclosure sale conducted by a trustee under the power of sale clause in a deed of trust.

Trustor—In a deed of trust transaction, the borrower. Also called the grantor.

Truth in Lending Act (TILA)—A federal law that requires lenders to make disclosures concerning loan costs (including the finance charge and the annual percentage rate) to consumer loan applicants.

UCC—*See:* Uniform Commercial Code.

UFMIP—*See:* MIP.

Underlying Loan—*See:* Wraparound Financing.

Underwriter—The employee of an institutional lender who evaluates loan applications to determine which loans should be approved.

Underwriting—The process of evaluating the financial status of a loan applicant and the value of the property he hopes to buy, to determine the risk of default and the risk of loss in the event of default and foreclosure. Also called risk analysis or qualifying.

Underwriting, Automated (AU)—Underwriting using software that performs a preliminary analysis of a loan application and makes a recommendation for approval or additional scrutiny.

Underwriting Standards—*See:* Qualifying Standards.

Uniform Residential Appraisal Report—A form used by appraisers to report an estimate of value for residential property.

Uniform Commercial Code (UCC)—A body of law that has been adopted in slightly varying versions in all states, intended to standardize commercial law dealing with matters such as negotiable instruments and sales of personal property.

Uniform Standards of Professional Appraisal Practice—Guidelines for appraisers adopted by the Appraisal Foundation, a nonprofit organization of professional appraiser associations.

Usury—Charging an interest rate that exceeds legal limits.

VA—The U.S. Department of Veterans Affairs.

Vacancy Factor—In the income approach to appraisal, a percentage deducted from a property's potential gross income, estimating the income that's likely to be lost because of vacancies and tenants who don't pay.

VA Entitlement—The VA guaranty amount that a particular veteran is entitled to.

VA-Guaranteed Loan—A home loan to an eligible veteran made by an institutional lender and guaranteed by the Department of Veterans Affairs, protecting the lender against losses resulting from default.

VA Guaranty Amount—The portion of a VA loan guaranteed by the Department of Veterans Affairs; the maximum amount that the VA will pay the lender for a loss resulting from the borrower's default.

Valuation—*See:* Appraisal.

Vendee—The buyer in a transaction financed with a land contract.

Vendor—The seller in a transaction financed with a land contract.

Verification of Deposit—A form a lender sends to a financial institution for confirmation that a loan applicant has the funds on deposit that she claims to have.

Verification of Employment—A form a lender sends to a loan applicant's employer to confirm that the applicant is actually employed as claimed, and to verify the amount of the applicant's salary.

Wholesale Lending—Loans made by large lenders or investors through loan correspondents or mortgage brokers. *Compare:* Retail Lending.

Wraparound Financing—A seller financing arrangement in which the seller uses part of the buyer's payments to make the payments on an existing loan (called the underlying loan); the buyer takes title subject to the underlying loan, but does not assume it.

Writ of Execution—*See:* Execution, Order of.

Yield—The rate of return a lender or other investor receives on an investment, usually stated as an annual percentage of the amount loaned or invested.

Index

W

Y

Z